FINANCIAL ACCOUNTING

Visit the Tony Davies *Financial Accounting* Companion Website at

www.pearsoned.co.uk/daviestony

to find valuable **student** learning material including:

- Multiple-choice questions to test your understanding
- Additional case studies
- Additional chapter-end exercises
- An online glossary to explain key terms
- Flashcards to test your understanding of key terms
- Links to relevant sites on the World Wide Web
- Author biographies and interview

FINANCIAL ACCOUNTING

TONY DAVIES

and

IAN CRAWFORD

PEARSON

Harlow, England • London • New York • Boston • San Francisco • Toronto • Sydney
Auckland • Singapore • Hong Kong • Tokyo • Seoul • Taipei • New Delhi
Cape Town • São Paulo • Mexico City • Madrid • Amsterdam • Munich • Paris • Milan

Pearson Education Limited
Edinburgh Gate
Harlow
Essex CM20 2JE
England

and Associated Companies throughout the world

Visit us on the World Wide Web at:
www.pearson.com/uk

First published by Pearson Education Limited in 2012

ISBN: 978-0-273-72307-3

British Library Cataloguing-in-Publication Data
A catalogue record for this book is available from the British Library

Library of Congress Cataloging-in-Publication Data
A catalog record for this book is available from the Library of Congress

10 9 8 7 6 5 4 3 2 1
16 15 14 13 12

Typeset in 9.5/13 pt ITC Charter by 73
Printed and bound by Rotolito Lombarda, Italy

Brief contents

Detailed contents

Supporting resources

Visit www.pearsoned.co.uk/daviestony to find valuable online resources

Companion Website for students
- Multiple-choice questions to test your understanding
- Additional case studies
- Additional chapter-end exercises
- An online glossary to explain key terms
- Flashcards to test your understanding of key terms
- Links to relevant sites on the World Wide Web
- Author biographies and interview

For instructors
- Teaching notes for each chapter
- Debriefs to all case-studies in the book
- Additional case studies and debriefs
- Solutions to all chapter-end exercises
- Additional exercises and solutions
- PowerPoint presentations for each chapter, including all illustrations from the book

Also: The Companion Website provides the following features:
- Search tool to help locate specific items of content
- E-mail results and profile tools to send results of quizzes to instructors
- Online help and support to assist with website usage and troubleshooting

For more information please contact your local Pearson Education sales representative or visit **www.pearsoned.co.uk/daviestony**

Features

Case Studies

Press Extracts

Figures

This book is dedicated to Nina

Preface

Financial Accounting has two key aims. One aim is to provide undergraduates, postgraduates and others with a book about financial accounting in a practical business context that is clear and easy to understand. In *Financial Accounting* we have maintained a rigorous approach and full coverage of all the theoretical and technical aspects of accounting, together with their practical application. At the same time, we have tried to remove the fear and intimidation that sometimes accompanies this subject, by making it more user-friendly and a little more fun to study.

The other aim is to provide a comprehensive and flexible teaching and learning resource, with a wide range of study and assessment material supported by an 'easy to use' accessible website. There are links between each of the chapters, which follow a structure that has been designed to facilitate effective teaching and learning of financial accounting in a progressive way. Alternatively, each chapter may be used on a standalone basis; chapters may also be excluded if they relate to subjects that are not essential for a specific module. For example, double-entry bookkeeping covered in Chapter 2 is a topic that may or may not be a requirement of some modules that may be referred to as required.

Accounting is of critical importance in the support of all business activities. The formal study of accounting is exciting because it introduces a toolkit that enables a better understanding of the performance of businesses, and the decisions and problems they face. These issues are discussed daily by managers and in the media. This textbook provides you with the toolkit and shows you how to apply it in practice, utilising a comprehensive range of learning features, illustrative examples and assessment material to support and reinforce your study.

This textbook is aimed primarily at students who are not majoring in accounting, but who are undertaking an introductory-level module as part of their degree or diploma course in business management, economics or any other subject. *Financial Accounting* is a tightly written, clear and engaging text which distils the core principles of financial accounting for those students who may not have the luxury of devoting all their time to its study.

Content and structure

Each topic in *Financial Accounting* has been carefully researched to closely follow the typical current requirements of introductory undergraduate and MBA modules. The text assumes no prior knowledge of the subject, starting at square one and taking you step-by-step through the concepts and application of techniques, with clear explanations and numerous worked examples.

This textbook is primarily about financial accounting, which is broadly concerned with the recording and analysis of historical financial data, the presentation of financial information, and compliance with current legislation, and accounting rules and standards. Another branch of accounting, management accounting, uses financial and non-financial information and also provides information for the costing of products for the valuation of inventories, the pricing of products and services, and the planning, control and decision-making functions. It is mainly involved in the support of the management of an organisation in dealing with current problems and in the evaluation of the future outcomes of various different scenarios and decisions.

Financial Accounting includes coverage of some contemporary issues and topics of growing importance, for example:

- IFRS and IASs reporting requirements
- corporate governance
- sustainability reporting.

Chapter 1 begins with an introduction to the fundamentals of accounting and the next four chapters deal with the recording and classification of accounting transactions and the three key financial statements: income statement (profit and loss account); balance sheet; statement of cash flows (cash flow statement), and in particular those relating to limited companies. In most respects these also apply to other profit-making and not-for-profit organisations in both the private and public sectors.

Chapter 2 shows how commercial transactions are accounted for. It is about the system used to record accounting transactions and accounting data and provides the fundamental basis for the further analysis and reporting of financial information. It provides an introduction to double-entry bookkeeping. Bookkeeping is a process that records accounting data in a way that allows subsequent preparation of financial reports in appropriate formats which inform shareholders and others about the financial position and the financial performance of the business.

Chapter 3 begins with an introduction to the preparation of simple financial statements and then goes on to look in detail at the balance sheet.

Chapter 4 looks in detail at the income statement. It looks at how to recognise that a profit (or loss) has been made and how it is linked with the balance sheet and statement of cash flows.

Chapter 5 deals with the statement of cash flows, which shows from where an organisation has received cash during an accounting period and how cash was used.

In Chapter 6 we broaden the scope of our study of accounting to provide an introduction to corporate governance. This is a topic that has become increasingly important as the behaviour of directors and managers towards their shareholders and to society in general receives greater and greater attention and comes under closer and closer scrutiny by investors, the media, governments and the general public. The burden also lies with management to run businesses in strict compliance with statutory, regulatory and accounting requirements, so it is crucial that directors are aware of the rules and codes of practice in place to regulate the behaviour of directors of limited companies.

Chapter 7 is headed *Financial statements analysis*. The three financial statements provide information about business performance. Much more may be gleaned about the performance of the business through further analysis of the financial statements, using financial ratios and other techniques, for example trend analysis, industrial analysis and inter-company analysis.

Chapter 8 looks at the analysis and interpretation of the annual report and accounts of a business. It uses the report and accounts for the year ended 31 March 2011 of Johnson Matthey Plc to illustrate the type of financial and non-financial information provided by a major UK public company.

Chapter 9 deals primarily with long-term, external sources of business finance for investment in businesses. This relates to the various types of funding available to business, including the raising of funds from the owners of the business (the shareholders) and from lenders external to the business. This chapter includes evaluation of the costs of the alternative sources of capital, which may be used in the calculation of the overall cost of capital that may be used by companies as a basis for the discount rate to evaluate proposed investments in capital projects.

This text has been written primarily for non-specialist students, and so each chapter aims to help students understand the broader context and relevance of financial accounting in the business environment. Every chapter provides comprehensive examples and commentary on company activity, including at least one press extract. Companies featured include: Birmingham City FC; Persimmon; Thorntons; and EasyDate. In addition, two of the chapters feature extracts and analysis of the report and accounts 2011 of Johnson Matthey Plc.

Using this book

To support your study and reinforce the topics covered, we have included a comprehensive range of learning features and assessment material in each chapter, including:

- learning objectives
- introduction
- highlighted key terms
- fully worked examples
- integrated progress checks
- key points summary
- questions
- discussion points
- exercises.

Within each chapter we have also included numerous diagrams and charts that illustrate and reinforce important concepts and ideas. The Guided Tour of the Book that follows (on pages xx–xxii) summarises the purpose of these learning features and the chapter-end assessment material. To gain maximum benefit from this text and to help you succeed in your study and exams, you are encouraged to familiarise yourself with these elements now, before you start the first chapter.

Accounting is essentially a 'hands-on' subject; just reading about it is not enough. Believe us, from our own experience we know that repeated practice of examples and exercises is the only way to become proficient in its techniques. You may think that reading through this book or your lecture notes, highlighting the odd sentence and gliding through the worked examples, progress checks and chapter-end questions and exercises, will instil the knowledge and expertise required to pass your exams. This would be a big mistake. Active learning needs to be interactive: if you haven't followed a topic or an example, go back and work through it again; try to think of other examples to which particular topics may be applied. The only way to check that you have a comprehensive understanding of things is to attempt all the integrated progress checks and worked examples, and the chapter-end assessment material, and then to compare with the text and answers provided. Fully worked solutions are given for each worked example, and solutions to about 45% of the chapter-end exercises (those with their numbers in colour) are provided in Appendix 2. Additional self-assessment material is available on the book's accompanying website.

Case studies

The book includes three case studies that may be tackled either individually or as a team. The case studies are a little more weighty than the chapter-end exercises; in addition, they integrate many of the topics included in the chapters in each part of the text to which they relate, although not exclusively. Each case study therefore gives you an opportunity to apply the knowledge and techniques gained from each part of the book, and to develop these together with the analytical skills and judgement required to deal with real-life business problems. Additional cases are provided on the accompanying website.

We hope this textbook will enhance your interest, understanding and skills. Above all, relax, learn and enjoy!

Guided tour of the book

Learning objectives

Listed at the start of each chapter, these bullet points identify the core learning outcomes you should have acquired after completing each chapter.

Learning objectives

Completion of this chapter will enable you to:
- outline the uses and purpose of accounting and the practice of accountancy
- explain the development of the conceptual frameworks of accounting
- outline the contents of the UK Statement of Principles (SOP)
- explain the main UK accounting concepts and accounting and financial reporting standards
- appreciate the meaning of true and fair view
- consider the increasing importance of international accounting standards
- explain what is meant by financial accounting, management accounting and financial management
- illustrate the different types of business entity: sole traders, partnerships, private limited companies, public limited companies
- explain the nature and purpose of financial statements
- identify the wide range of users of financial information
- consider the issues of accountability and financial reporting.

Introduction

This section gives you a brief overview of the coverage and purpose of each chapter, and how it links to the previous chapter.

Introduction

This chapter begins by explaining what is sometimes referred to as the dual aspect rule. This rule recognises that for all transactions there is a two-sided effect within the entity. A manager in a non-accounting role may not be expected to carry out the recording of transactions in this way, but an appreciation of how accounting data has been recorded will be extremely helpful in the interpretation of financial information. We will go on to describe the processes that deal with the two sides of each transaction, the 'debits' and 'credits' of double-entry bookkeeping.

Don't worry if at first these topics seem a little difficult and confusing. They will become clearer as we follow through some transactions step-by-step into the accounts of a business and show how these accounts are kept in balance.

The chapter continues with an introduction to the way in which each of the accounts is held in what are termed the books of account and ledgers of the business. The balances on all the accounts in an entity are summarised in what is called a trial balance. The trial balance may be adjusted to allow for payments in advance, charges not yet received, and other adjusting entries. From this information we will show how to prepare a simple income statement, balance sheet and statement of cash flows.

This chapter refers to some of the accounting concepts introduced in Chapter 1. In that context we will look at the time period chosen by a business, to which the financial reporting relates – the accounting period.

Key terms

These are colour-highlighted the first time they are introduced, alerting you to the core concepts and techniques in each chapter. A full explanation is contained in the glossary of key terms section at the end of the book.

3. Profitability

A number of financial indicators and ratios may be considered to assess the profitability of the company, which may include:

- gross profit (or gross margin) to sales
- return on sales (ROS)
- return on capital employed (ROCE), or return on investment (ROI).

4. Efficiency

The efficiency of the company may be considered in terms of its:

- operating cycle – its receivables collection days, payables days and inventories days
- asset turnover
- vertical analysis of its income statement (which we will look at in Chapter 8).

In a vertical analysis of the income statement (which may also be applied to the balance sheet) each item is expressed as a percentage of the total sales. The vertical analysis provides evidence

Worked examples

The numerous worked examples in each chapter provide an application of the learning points and techniques included within each topic. By following and working through the step-by-step solutions, you have an opportunity to check your knowledge at frequent intervals.

Worked example 6.1

Directors of companies are concerned with the important issues of agency-related problems and their impact. What is the basis of discussions they may have to consider what actions they may implement to try and minimise the impact of such problems?

Their discussions may include the following:

- The agency problem emerges when directors or managers make decisions that are inconsistent with the objective of shareholder wealth maximisation.
- There are a number of alternative approaches a company can adopt to minimise the possible impact of such a problem, which may differ from company to company. In general, such approaches would range between:
  - the encouragement of goal congruence between shareholders and managers through the monitoring of managerial behaviour and the assessment of management decision outcomes and
  - the enforcement of goal congruence between shareholders and managers through the incorporation of formalised obligations and conditions of employment into management contracts.

Any such approach would invariably be associated with some form of remuneration package to include an incentive scheme to reward managers, such as performance-related pay, or executive share options.

Progress checks

Each topic within each chapter includes one or more of these short questions that enable you to check and apply your understanding of the preceding key topics before you progress to the next one in the chapter.

Progress check 3.4

Which of the following do you think may be classified as liabilities or shareholders' equity within a balance sheet, and under which headings should they appear?

- bank overdraft
- computer
- five-year bank loan
- amounts owed by customers
- accruals
- amounts owed to suppliers
- ordinary shares
- share premium

Press extracts

Included in every chapter, these topical extracts feature real company examples from the press, including commentary that highlights the practical application of accounting and finance in the business environment.

Anything you can do I can do better

Summary of key points

Following the final section in each chapter there is a comprehensive summary of the key points in terms of the learning outcomes listed at the start of each chapter. These allow you to check that you understand all the main points covered before moving on to the next chapter.

Summary of key points

- The main aims of a business performance review are to provide an understanding of the business and provide an interpretation of results.
- Care must be taken in reviewing business performance, primarily because of lack of consistency in definitions and changes in economic conditions.
- An important area of business performance review is the use of ratio analysis looking at profitability, efficiency, liquidity, investment and growth, and financial structure.
- Cash flow and cash ratios are becoming increasingly as important as profit and profitability ratios in the measurement of business performance.
- There is no best way of evaluating financial performance and there are advantages and disadvantages in using earnings per share or cash flow as the basis of measurement.
- Earnings before interest, tax, depreciation and amortisation (EBITDA) is sometimes used as an approximate measure of a cash flow performance.

Questions

These are short narrative-type questions that encourage you to review and check your understanding of all the key topics. There are typically 7 to 10 of these questions at the end of each chapter.

Assessment material

Questions

Q7.1 (i) Who is likely to carry out a business performance review?
(ii) Describe what may be required from such reviews giving some examples from different industries and differing perspectives.

Q7.2 (i) Outline how the business performance review process may be used to evaluate the position of a dot.com company like Amazon UK.
(ii) What are the limitations to the approach that you have outlined?

Q7.3 How is ratio analysis, in terms of profitability ratios, efficiency ratios, liquidity ratios, investment ratios and financial structure ratios used to support the business review process?

Q7.4 Why should we be so careful when we try to compare the income statement of a limited company with a similar business in the same industry?

Q7.5 (i) Why does profit continue to be the preferred basis for evaluation of the financial performance of a business?
(ii) In what ways can cash flow provide a better basis for performance evaluation, and how may cash flow be approximated?

Discussion points

This section typically includes 2 to 4 thought-provoking ideas and questions that encourage you to critically apply your understanding and/or further develop some of the topics introduced in each chapter, either individually or in team discussion.

Discussion points

D8.1 'The annual reports and accounts prepared by the majority of UK plcs serve to ensure that shareholders, and other stakeholders, are kept very well informed about the affairs of their businesses.' Discuss.

D8.2 'In the global competitive world in which we live, company directors should be able to exercise their full discretion as to the amount of information they disclose in their annual reports and accounts. If they are not allowed this discretion in disclosure, their companies may be driven out of business by their competitors, particularly foreign competitors who may not have the restriction of such extensive reporting requirements.' Discuss.

D8.3 'The main reason that companies increasingly include sustainability reports in their annual reports and accounts is to change the views of users and regulators about the activities in which their businesses are engaged, in order to pre-empt and avoid any negative or harmful reactions.' Discuss this statement by drawing on examples of the type of businesses to which this might apply.

(Hint: You may wish to research British Gas, as well as Johnson Matthey Plc, to provide material for this discussion.)

Exercises

These comprehensive examination-style questions are graded by their level of difficulty, and also indicate the time typically required to complete them. They are designed to assess your knowledge and application of the principles and techniques covered in each chapter. There are typically 6 to 8 exercises at the end of each chapter. Full solutions to the colour-highlighted exercise numbers are provided in Appendix 2 to allow you to self-assess your progress.

Exercises

Solutions are provided in Appendix 2 to all exercise numbers highlighted in colour.

Level I

E9.1   *Time allowed – 30 minutes*

A critically important factor required by a company to make financial decisions, for example the evaluation of investment proposals and the financing of new projects, is its cost of capital. One of the elements included in the calculation of a company's cost of capital is the cost of equity.

(i) Explain in simple terms what is meant by the 'cost of equity capital' for a company.

The relevant data for Normal plc and the market in general are given below.

Normal plc
Current price per share on the London Stock Exchange	£1.20
Current annual dividend per share	£0.10
Expected average annual growth rate of dividends	7%
β beta coefficient for Normal plc's shares	0.5

The market
Expected rate of return on risk-free securities	8%
Expected return on the market portfolio	12%

(ii) Calculate the cost of equity capital for Normal plc, using two alternative methods:
    (a) the Capital Asset Pricing Model (CAPM)
    (b) a dividend growth model of your choice.

E9.2   *Time allowed – 30 minutes*

Normal plc pays £20,000 a year interest on an irredeemable debenture, which has a nominal value of £200,000 and a market value of £160,000. The rate of corporation tax is 30%.

Glossary of key terms

At the end of the book a glossary of key terms in alphabetical order provides full definitions of all main terms that have been introduced. The numbers of the pages on which key term definitions appear are colour-highlighted in the index.

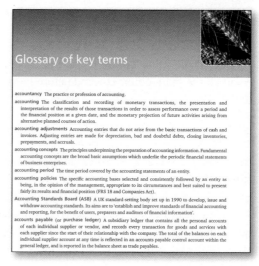

Glossary of key terms

accountancy The practice or profession of accounting.

accounting The classification and recording of monetary transactions, the presentation and interpretation of the results of those transactions in order to assess performance over a period and the financial position at a given date, and the monetary projection of future activities arising from alternative planned courses of action.

accounting adjustments Accounting entries that do not arise from the basic transactions of cash and invoices. Adjusting entries are made for depreciation, bad and doubtful debts, closing inventories, prepayments, and accruals.

accounting concepts The principles underpinning the preparation of accounting information. Fundamental accounting concepts are the broad basic assumptions which underlie the periodic financial statements of business enterprises.

accounting period The time period covered by the accounting statements of an entity.

accounting policies The specific accounting bases selected and consistently followed by an entity as being, in the opinion of the management, appropriate to its circumstances and best suited to present fairly its results and financial position (FRS 18 and Companies Act).

Accounting Standards Board (ASB) A UK standard-setting body set up in 1990 to develop, issue and withdraw accounting standards. Its aims are to 'establish and improve standards of financial accounting and reporting, for the benefit of users, preparers and auditors of financial information'.

accounts payable (or purchase ledger) A subsidiary ledger that contains all the personal accounts of each individual supplier or vendor, and records every transaction for goods and services with each supplier since the start of their relationship with the company. The total of the balances on each individual supplier account at any time is reflected in an accounts payable control account within the general ledger, and is reported in the balance sheet as trade payables.

Acknowledgements

Thank you to the lecturers who were involved in either the initial market research and/or in providing useful review comments and technical checks of the draft chapters during the development phase of this project.

Thank you to CIMA (the Chartered Institute of Management Accountants) for their permission to include material from their Management Accounting Official Terminology 2005 edition.

Thank you to Johnson Matthey Plc for their permission to use extracts of their Report and Accounts 2011 as an excellent example of the information provided to shareholders by a major UK plc. Thanks also to *The Times*, *The Guardian,* and the *Daily Telegraph, Financial Times, Business Week, Daily Mail, Birmingham Post,* and *Observer* for their permissions to use extracts from their publications.

Thank you to Katie Rowland for her support and encouragement in the writing of this book and the development of the website, and to Colin Reed, Tim Parker and Gemma Papageorgiou for their design and production wizardry.

Publisher's acknowledgements

We are grateful to the following for permission to reproduce copyright material:

Figures
Figure 8.2 from Johnson Matthey Plc year-end 31 March share price 2002 to 2011, Johnson Matthey Plc.

Text
Article on page 8 from 'Birmingham's place in Europe threatened by financial concerns', *The Guardian*, 15/04/2011 (James, S); Article on page 39 from 'Greek crisis deepens with S & P downgrade; worry about true scale of undisclosed military spending adds to concerns', *Daily Telegraph*, 17/12/2009 (Evans-Pritchard, A), copyright © Telegraph Media Group Limited; Article on page 98 from 'Persimmon returns to profit after revaluation', *Daily Telegraph*, 03/03/2010 (Midgely, D), copyright © Telegraph Media Group Limited; Article on page 99 from 'The value of 5,000 years of history? £51m', *Daily Telegraph*, 25/05/2010 (Butterworth, M), copyright © Telegraph Media Group Limited; Article on pages 141–2 from 'Anger grows at the Thorntons board as UK's famous chocolate brand goes stale', *The Observer*, 08/05/2011 (Clark, A); Article on page 229 from 'The small cases that will have a big influence on the way we work: Gary Slapper reflects on the deaths that have led to the change in corporate manslaughter law', *The Times*, 11/07/2009 (Slapper, G); Article on page 245 from 'Farewell then . . . floppy discs', *Daily Mail*, 28/04/2010 (Beanland, C); Article on page 255 from 'Late payments mean bigger write-offs for small business', *Daily Express*, 15/04/2010 (Gribben, R), copyright © Telegraph Media Group Limited; Article on page 313 from 'Cars and the road to growth', *The Times*, 25/11/2010 (Waller, M); Article on page 346 from 'Online dating site seeks to woo investors', *Daily Telegraph*, 18/05/2010 (Smith, P), copyright © Telegraph Media Group Limited;

Extract on pages 282–310 from 'Chairman's Statement' and various extracts from Johnson Matthey Annual Report and Accounts 2011; Extracts on pages 194–212 from Annual Report & Accounts 2011, Johnson Matthey, We are grateful to Johnson Matthey Plc for their kind permission to use these extracts from their Report and Accounts 2011 as an excellent example of information provided to shareholders by a major UK plc.

The Financial Times

Article on page 15 from 'Push for accounting convergence threatened by EU reform drive', *Financial Times*, 05/04/2010 (Saunderson, R).

Photos

The publisher would like to thank the following for their kind permission to reproduce their photographs:

v Photodisc. Bruce W. Heinemann; vii Photodisc. Bruce W. Heinemann; xiii Photodisc. Photolink; xvii Photodisc. Bruce W. Heinemann; xx Photodisc. Photolink; xxiii Photodisc. Bruce W. Heinemann; 1 Imagestate. John Foxx Collection; 37 Imagestate. John Foxx Collection; 69 Imagestate. John Foxx Collection; 111 Imagestate. John Foxx Collection; 151 MIXA Co., Ltd; 185 Photodisc. Cybermedia; 193 Siede Preis Photography. Photodisc; 239 MIXA Co., Ltd; 277 Photodisc. Trevor Clifford; 281 Photodisc. Don Farrall; 341 Imagestate. John Foxx Collection; 377 Photodisc. Cybermedia; 379 Photodisc. Bruce W. Heinemann; 381 Photodisc. Photolink; 383 Imagestate. John Foxx Collection; 411 Photodisc. Bruce W. Heinemann; 425 Photodisc. Photolink

In some instances we have been unable to trace the owners of copyright material, and we would appreciate any information that would enable us to do so.

1

The importance of financial accounting

Contents

Learning objectives

Completion of this chapter will enable you to:

- outline the uses and purpose of accounting and the practice of accountancy
- explain the development of the conceptual frameworks of accounting
- outline the contents of the UK Statement of Principles (SOP)
- explain the main UK accounting concepts and accounting and financial reporting standards
- appreciate the meaning of true and fair view
- consider the increasing importance of international accounting standards
- explain what is meant by financial accounting, management accounting and financial management
- illustrate the different types of business entity: sole traders, partnerships, private limited companies, public limited companies
- explain the nature and purpose of financial statements
- identify the wide range of users of financial information
- consider the issues of accountability and financial reporting.

Introduction

This chapter explains why accounting and finance are such key elements of business life. Both for aspiring accountants, and those of you who may not continue to study accounting and finance beyond the introductory level, the fundamental principles of accounting and the ways in which accounting is regulated to protect owners of businesses, and the public in general, are important topics. A broad appreciation will be useful not only in dealing with the subsequent text, but also in the context of the day-to-day management of a business.

This chapter will look at why accounting is needed and how it is used and by whom. Accounting and finance are wide subjects, which often mean many things to many people. They are broadly concerned with the organisation and management of financial resources. Accounting and accountancy are two terms which are sometimes used to mean the same thing, although they more correctly relate separately to the subject and the profession.

Accounting and accountancy are generally concerned with measuring and communicating the financial information provided from accounting systems, and the reporting of financial results to shareholders, lenders, creditors, employees and Government. The owners or shareholders of the wide range of business entities that use accounting may be assumed to have the primary objective of maximisation of shareholder wealth. Directors of the business manage the resources of the business to meet shareholders' objectives.

Accounting operates through basic principles and rules. This chapter will examine the development of conceptual frameworks of accounting, which in the UK are seen in the Statement of Principles (SOP). We will discuss the rules of accounting, which are embodied in what are termed accounting concepts and accounting standards.

Over the past few years there has been an increasing focus on trying to bring together the rules, or standards, of accounting that apply in each separate country, into one set of accounting standards. For example, with effect from January 2005 all the stock exchange listed companies within the European Union were required to comply with one such set of accounting standards relating to the way in which they report financial information. We will discuss how this may affect the topics we shall be covering in this book.

We will consider the processes used in accounting and look at an overview of the financial statements used in financial reporting, and the way in which financial reporting is used to keep shareholders informed. The timely and accurate disclosure of accounting information is a fundamental requirement in the preparation of appropriate statements of the financial performance and the financial position of a business. Directors and managers are responsible for running businesses and their accountability to shareholders is maintained through their regular reporting on the activities of the business.

A large number of accounting concepts and terms are used throughout this book, the definitions of which may be found in the glossary of key terms at the end of the book.

What is accounting, and what are its uses and purposes?

The original, basic purposes of **accounting** were to classify and record monetary transactions (see Chapter 2) and present the financial results of the activities of an entity, in other words the scorecard that shows how the business is doing. The accounting profession has evolved and accounting techniques have been developed for use in a much broader business context. To look at the current nature of accounting and the broad purposes of accounting systems we need to consider the three questions these days generally answered by accounting information:

■ how are we doing, and are we doing well or badly?   **a scorecard (like scoring a game of cricket, for example)**

■ which problems should be looked at?   **attention-directing**

■ which is the best alternative for doing a job?   **problem-solving**

Although accountants and the accounting profession have retained their fundamental roles they have grown into various branches of the profession, which have developed their own specialisms and responsibilities.

Accounting is a part of the information system within an organisation (see Chapter 2, which explains double-entry **bookkeeping**, and how data are identified, recorded and presented as information in the ways required by the users of financial information). Accounting also exists as a service function, which ensures that the financial information that is presented meets the needs of the users of financial information. To achieve this, accountants must not only ensure that information is accurate, reliable and timely but also that it is relevant for the purpose for which it is being provided, consistent for comparability, and easily understood (see Figure 1.1).

In order to be useful to the users of financial information, the accounting data from which it is prepared, together with its analysis and presentation, must be:

■ accurate – free from error of content or principle

■ reliable – representing the information that users believe it represents

■ timely – available in time to support decision-making

■ relevant – applicable to the purpose required, for example a decision regarding a future event or to support an explanation of what has already happened

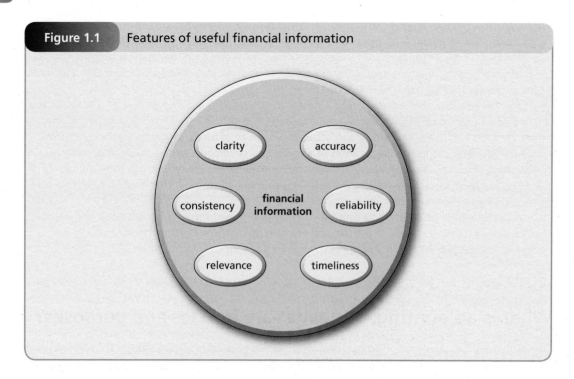

Figure 1.1 Features of useful financial information

- consistent – the same methods and standards of measurement of data and presentation of information to allow like-for-like comparison
- clear – capable of being understood by those for whom the information has been prepared.

In the next few sections we will see just how important these features are, and the ways they are included in the development of various **conceptual frameworks of accounting**, and the accounting policies selected by companies.

The conceptual frameworks of accounting

How can the credibility and usefulness of accounting and financial information be ensured? Accounting operates within a framework. This framework is constantly changing and evolving as new problems are encountered, as new practices and techniques are developed, and the objectives of users of financial information are modified and revised.

The search for a definitive conceptual framework, a theoretical accounting model, which may deal with any new accounting problem that may arise, has resulted in many conceptual frameworks having been developed in a number of countries worldwide. The basic assumption for these conceptual frameworks is that **financial statements** must be useful. The general structure of conceptual frameworks deals with the following six questions:

1. What is the purpose of financial statement reporting?
2. Who are the main users of accounting and financial information?
3. What type of financial statements will meet the needs of these users?
4. What type of information should be included in financial statements to satisfy these needs?
5. How should items included in financial statements be defined?
6. How should items included in financial statements be recorded and measured?

In 1989 the **International Accounting Standards Board (IASB)** issued a conceptual framework that largely reflected the conceptual framework of the Financial Accounting Standards Board of the USA issued in 1985. This was based on the ideas and proposals made by the accounting profession since the 1970s in both the USA and UK. In 1999 the **Accounting Standards Board (ASB)** in the UK published its own conceptual framework called the **Statement of Principles (SOP)** for financial reporting.

Progress check 1.1

What is meant by a conceptual framework of accounting?

The Statement of Principles (SOP)

The 1975 Corporate Report was the first UK attempt at a conceptual framework. This, together with the 1973 Trueblood Report published in the USA, provided the basis for the conceptual framework issued by the IASB in 1989, referred to in the previous section. It was followed by the publication of the SOP by the ASB in 1999. The SOP is a basic structure for determining objectives, in which there is a thread from the theory to the practical application of accounting standards to transactions that are reported in published accounts. The SOP is not an accounting standard and its use is not mandatory, but it is a statement of guidelines; it is, by virtue of the subject, constantly in need of revision.

The SOP identifies the main users of financial information as:

■ investors
■ lenders
■ employees
■ suppliers
■ customers
■ Government
■ the general public.

The SOP focuses on the interests of investors and assumes that each of the other users of financial information is interested in or concerned about the same issues as investors.

The SOP consists of eight chapters that deal with the following topics:

1. The objectives of financial statements, which are fundamentally to provide information that is useful for the users of that information.
2. Identification of the entities that are required to provide financial statement reporting by virtue of the demand for the information included in those statements.
3. The qualitative characteristics required to make financial information useful to users:
   – **materiality** (inclusion of information that is not material may distort the usefulness of other information)
   – relevance
   – reliability
   – comparability (enabling the identification and evaluation of differences and similarities)
   – comprehensibility.
4. The main elements included in the financial statements – the 'building blocks' of accounting such as assets and liabilities.

5. When transactions should be recognised in financial statements.
6. How assets and liabilities should be measured.
7. How financial statements should be presented for clear and effective communication.
8. The accounting by an entity in its financial statements for interests in other entities.

The UK SOP can be seen to be a very general outline of principles relating to the reporting of financial information. The SOP includes some of the basic concepts that provide the foundations for the preparation of financial statements. These accounting concepts will be considered in more detail in the next section.

Progress check 1.2

What are the aims of the UK Statement of Principles and how does it try to achieve these aims?

Accounting concepts

The accounting framework revolves around the practice of accounting and the accountancy profession, which is bounded by rules, or concepts (see Figure 1.2, in which the five most important

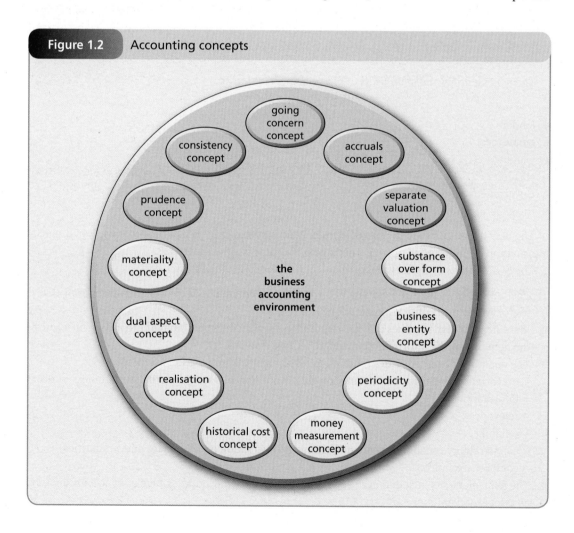

Figure 1.2 Accounting concepts

concepts are shown in a darker colour) of what data should be included within an accounting system and how that data should be recorded.

Accounting concepts are the principles underpinning the preparation of accounting information relating to the ethical rules, boundary rules and recording and measurement rules of accounting. Ethical rules, or principles, are to do with limiting the amount of judgement (or indeed creativity) that may be used in the reporting of financial information. Boundary rules are to do with which types of data, and the amounts of each, that should be held by organisations, and which elements of financial information should be reported. Recording and measurement rules of accounting relate to how the different types of data should be recorded and measured by the organisation.

Fundamental accounting concepts are the broad, basic assumptions, which underlie the periodic financial accounts of business enterprises. The five most important concepts, which are discussed in FRS 18, Accounting Policies, are as follows.

The prudence concept

Prudence means being careful or cautious. The **prudence concept** is an ethical concept that is based on the principle that revenue and profits are not anticipated, but are included in the income statement only when realised in the form of either cash or other assets, the ultimate cash realisation of which can be assessed with reasonable certainty. Provision must be made for all known liabilities and expenses, whether the amount of these is known with certainty or is a best estimate in the light of information available, and for losses arising from specific commitments, rather than just guesses. Therefore, companies should record all losses as soon as they are known, but should record profits only when they have actually been achieved in cash or other assets.

The consistency concept

The **consistency concept** is an ethical rule that is based on the principle that there is uniformity of accounting treatment of like items within each accounting period and from one period to the next. However, as we will see in Chapter 3, judgement may be exercised as to the application of accounting rules to the preparation of financial statements. For example, a company may choose from a variety of methods to calculate the **depreciation** of its machinery and equipment, or how to value its inventories. Until recently, once a particular approach had been adopted by a company for one accounting period then this approach should normally have been adopted in all future accounting periods, unless there were compelling reasons to change. The ASB now prefers the approaches adopted by companies to be revised by them, and the ASB encourages their change, if those changes result in showing a truer and fairer picture. If companies do change their approaches then they have to indicate this in their annual reports and accounts.

The going concern concept

The **going concern concept** is a boundary rule that assumes that the entity will continue in operational existence for the foreseeable future. This is important because it allows the original, historical costs of assets to continue to be used in the balance sheet on the basis of their being able to generate future income. If the entity was expected to cease functioning then such assets would be worth only what they would be expected to realise if they were sold off separately (their break-up values) and therefore usually considerably less.

Birmingham City's financial blues

Birmingham City face the threat of being denied their licence to play in Europe next season if they cannot convince the Premier League and the Football Association that their finances are not a major cause for concern.

The Premier League is set to hold discussions with the Birmingham board this month before deciding in conjunction with the FA whether they should be granted a Uefa licence and allowed to play in the Europa League, for which they qualified after winning the Carling Cup.

It is understood that a final decision on Birmingham's participation is not expected to be made until the middle of next month, when representatives from the governing bodies meet to determine which clubs meet the criteria for a licence. Uefa delegates its licensing scheme to national associations, meaning that Birmingham will need to satisfy the FA and the Premier League that they can meet their financial liabilities for the year ahead.

This time last year Portsmouth, FA Cup finalists, were told that they would not be allowed to compete in the Europa League after the FA and the Premier League decided against endorsing their application for a Uefa licence. Portsmouth, however, had failed to submit their application on time and were in administration with debts of £119m. Birmingham's situation is far different, although there are genuine concerns at the Premier League, who have additional reasons for wishing to ask questions of the St Andrew's board.

Under the disclosure rules brought in after the collapse of Portsmouth last year, clubs must submit 'independently audited accounts to the Premier League by 1 March each year with requirements to note any material qualifications or issues raised by auditors'. Clubs are also required to submit 'future financial information' to the Premier League by 31 March each year that 'will act as an improved early warning system should any club take undue financial risks which may have consequences for future financial stability'.

As the accounts for Birmingham City football club and their parent company, Birmingham International Holdings, included qualifications in their audit reports about both companies' ability to continue as a 'going concern', the Premier League wish to learn more information about Birmingham's financial position, the ownership structure at the club and recent share activity.

A spokesman for the Premier League said: 'Under our financial criteria all the clubs have to submit future financial information. There are a number of triggers that would result in us taking a closer look at a club's financial circumstances, such as an "emphasis of matter" (e.g. a doubt on the club's ability to continue as a going concern) on the accounts. This could result in measures being placed upon a club to ensure its sustainability going forward.'

Under the new rules, which were approved in 2009, the Premier League has a range of sanctions available to it for clubs that fall into financial difficulties, including a transfer embargo, a ban on player contracts being extended or improved, or the enforced sale of players. Carson Yeung, who yesterday bought 8.6% of the club to increase his stake in Birmingham International Holdings to 24.9%, provided written assurances to the Premier League last year in relation to the club's finances.

Birmingham's fiscal position has come under scrutiny at various points in the past 12 months, including soon after their Carling Cup final victory, when Birmingham International Holdings announced that Yeung was preparing to mortgage his private properties in a cash-raising exercise. The statement to the Hong Kong stock exchange added that without fresh funds the business may suffer 'significant curtailment of its operation'.

It is understood that the Premier League is also interested in whether Birmingham will be able to raise the £24.65m that was outlined in the club's most recent accounts, which were signed off in October.

Peter Pannu, Birmingham's acting chairman, maintains that the club remain on a sound financial footing.

Source: **Birmingham's place in Europe threatened by financial concerns,** by Stuart James © *The Guardian*, 15 April 2011

Even the most high-profile enterprises are not immune to the threat of failure to continue to trade. Carson Yeung, a Hong-Kong businessman, acquired 29.9% of the shares of Birmingham City Football Club in July 2007 through his company Grandtop International Holdings Limited. In August 2009 more shares were purchased giving the holding company more than 90% of the shares. Birmingham City plc (which owns the football club) was re-registered as a private company in November 2009 and the holding company renamed as Birmingham International Holdings the following month. The latest accounts to 30 June 2010, which were signed off in October 2010, show that the club has debts of over £29m, of which £23m is owed to one creditor (HSBC). The bank has a charge over the club's land and buildings, which includes the club's St Andrew's stadium. Birmingham City qualified to play in the 2011/12 season UEFA Europa League, but the Premier League rules state that if doubts should arise over a club's ability to remain a going concern then the licence necessary to enter European competition will not be granted unless documentary evidence is supplied to the Football Association which is accepted as indicative of the club's ability to remain a going concern until the end of the season. Birmingham City's financial position was not helped by their relegation from the Premier League at the end of the 2010/11 season.

The accruals concept

The **accruals concept** (or the matching concept) is a recording and measurement rule that is based on the principle that revenues and costs are recognised as they are earned or incurred, are matched with one another, and are dealt with in the income statement of the period to which they relate, irrespective of the period of receipt or payment. It would be misleading to report profit as the difference between cash received and cash paid during a period because some trading and commercial activities of the period would be excluded, since many transactions are based on credit.

Most of us are users of electricity. We may use it over a period of three months for heating, lighting and running our many home appliances, before receiving an invoice from the electricity supplier for the electricity we have used. The fact that we have not received an invoice until much later doesn't mean we have not incurred a cost for each month. The costs have been accrued over each of those months, and we will pay for them at a later date.

The separate valuation concept

The **separate valuation concept** is a recording and measurement rule that relates to the determination of the aggregate amount of any item. In order to determine the aggregate amount of an asset or a liability, each individual asset or liability that makes up the aggregate must be determined separately. This is important because material items may reflect different economic circumstances. There must be a review of each material item to comply with the appropriate accounting standards:

- IAS 16 (Property, Plant and Equipment)
- IAS 36 (Impairment of Assets)
- IAS 37 (Provisions, Contingent Liabilities and Contingent Assets).

(See the later section, which discusses UK and international accounting and financial reporting standards called **Financial Reporting Standards (FRSs)**, **International Financial Reporting Standards (IFRSs)**, and **International Accounting Standards (IASs)**.)

Note the example of the Millennium Dome 2000 project, which was developed in Greenwich, London, throughout 1999 and 2000 and cost around £800m. At the end of the year 2000 a valuation of the individual elements of the attraction resulted in a total of around £100m.

The further eight fundamental accounting concepts are as follows.

The substance over form concept

Where a conflict exists, the **substance over form concept**, which is an ethical rule, requires the structuring of reports to give precedence to the representation of financial or economic reality over strict adherence to the requirements of the legal reporting structure. This concept is dealt with in IAS 17, Leases. When a company acquires an asset using a finance lease, for example a machine, it must disclose the asset in its balance sheet even though not holding legal title to the asset, whilst also disclosing separately in its balance sheet the amount that the company still owes on the machine. The reason for showing the asset in the balance sheet is because it is being used to generate income for the business, in the same way as a purchased machine. The substance of this accounting transaction (treating a leased asset as though it had been purchased) takes precedence over the form of the transaction (the lease itself).

The business entity concept

The **business entity concept** is a boundary rule that ensures that financial accounting information relates only to the activities of the business entity and not to the other activities of its owners. An owner of a business may be interested in sailing and may buy a boat and pay a subscription as a member of the local yacht club. These activities are completely outside the activities of the business and such transactions must be kept completely separate from the accounts of the business.

The periodicity concept

The **periodicity concept** (or time interval concept) is a boundary rule. It is the requirement to produce financial statements at set time intervals. This requirement is embodied, in the case of UK companies, in the Companies Act 2006 (all future references to the Companies Act will relate to the Companies Act 2006 unless otherwise stated). Both annual and interim financial statements are required to be produced by **public limited companies (plcs)** each year.

Internal reporting of financial information to management may take place within a company on a monthly, weekly, daily, or even an hourly basis. But owners of a company, who may have no involvement in the running of the business or its internal reporting, require the external reporting of their company's accounts on a six-monthly and yearly basis. The owners of the company may then rely on the regularity with which the reporting of financial information takes place, which enables them to monitor company performance, and compare figures year on year.

The money measurement concept

The **money measurement concept** is a recording and measurement rule that enables information relating to transactions to be fairly compared by providing a commonly accepted unit of converting quantifiable amounts into recognisable measures. Most quantifiable data are capable of being converted, using a common denominator of money, into monetary terms. However, accounting deals only with those items capable of being translated into monetary terms, which imposes a limit on the scope of accounting to report such items. You may note, for example, that in a university's balance sheet there is no value included for its human resources, that is its lecturers, managers, and secretarial and support staff.

The historical cost concept

The **historical cost concept** is a recording and measurement rule that relates to the practice of valuing assets at their original acquisition cost. For example, you may have bought a mountain bike two years ago for which you were invoiced and paid £150, and may now be wondering what it is currently worth.

One of your friends may consider it to be worth £175 because they feel that the price of new mountain bikes has increased over the past two years. Another friend may consider it to be worth only £100 because you have used it for two years and its condition has deteriorated. Neither of your friends may be incorrect, but their views are subjective and they are different. The only measure of what your bike is worth on which your friends may agree is the price shown on your original invoice, its historical cost.

Although the historical cost basis of valuation may not be as realistic as using, for instance, a current valuation, it does provide a consistent basis for comparison and almost eliminates the need for any subjectivity.

The realisation concept

The **realisation concept** is a recording and measurement rule and is the principle that increases in value should only be recognised on realisation of assets by arm's-length sale to an independent purchaser. This means, for example, that sales revenue from the sale of a product or service is recognised in accounting statements only when it is realised. This does not mean when the cash has been paid over by the customer; it means when the sale takes place, that is when the product or service has been delivered, and ownership is transferred to the customer. Very often, salespersons incorrectly regard a 'sale' as the placing of an order by a customer because they are usually very optimistic and sometimes forget that orders can get cancelled. Accountants, being prudent individuals, ensure that sales are correctly recorded through the issuing of an invoice when services or goods have been delivered (and installed).

The dual aspect concept

The **dual aspect concept** is the recording and measurement rule that provides the basis for double-entry bookkeeping. It reflects the practical reality that every transaction always includes both the giving and receiving of value. For example, a company may pay out cash in return for a delivery into its warehouse of a consignment of products that it subsequently aims to sell. The company's reduction in its cash balance is reflected in the increase in its inventory of products.

The materiality concept

Information is material if its omission or misstatement could influence the economic decisions of users taken on the basis of the financial statements. Materiality depends on the size of the item or error judged, its significance, in the particular circumstances of its omission or misstatement. Thus, materiality provides a threshold or cut-off point rather than being a primary qualitative characteristic that information must have if it is to be useful. The **materiality concept** is the overriding recording and measurement rule, which allows a certain amount of judgement in the application of all the other accounting concepts. The level of materiality, or significance, will depend on the size of the organisation and the type of revenue or cost, or asset or liability being considered. For example, the cost of business stationery is usually charged as an expense regardless of whether or not all the items have been used; it would be pointless to try and attribute a value to such relatively low-cost unused items.

True and fair view

The term **true and fair view** was introduced in the Companies Act 1947, requiring that companies' reporting of their accounts should show a true and fair view. It was not defined in that Act and has not been defined since. Some writers have suggested that conceptually it is a dynamic concept but over the years it could be argued that it has failed, and various business scandals and collapses have occurred without users being alerted. The concept of true and fair was adopted by the European Community Council in its fourth directive, implemented by the UK in the Companies Act 1981, and subsequently in the implementation of the seventh directive in the Companies Act 1989 (sections 226 and 227). Conceptually the directives require additional information where individual provisions are insufficient.

In practice true and fair view relates to the extent to which the various principles, concepts and standards of accounting have been applied. It may therefore be somewhat subjective and subject to change as new accounting rules are developed, old standards replaced and new standards introduced. It may be interesting to research the issue of derivatives and decide whether the true and fair view concept was invoked by those companies that used or marketed these financial instruments, and specifically consider the various collapses or public statements regarding losses incurred over the past few years. Before derivatives, the issue which escaped disclosure in financial reporting under true and fair view was leasing.

UK accounting and financial reporting standards

A number of guidelines, or standards (some of which we have already discussed), have been developed by the accountancy profession to ensure truth, fairness and consistency in the preparation and presentation of financial information.

A number of bodies have been established to draft accounting policy, set accounting standards, and to monitor compliance with standards and the provisions of the Companies Act. The Financial Reporting Council (FRC), whose chairman is appointed by the Secretary of State for Business, Innovation and Skills and the Bank of England, develops accounting standards policy and gives guidance on issues of public concern. The ASB, which is composed of members of the accountancy profession, and on which the Government has an observer status, has responsibility for development, issue and withdrawal of accounting standards.

The accounting standards are called Financial Reporting Standards (FRSs). Up to 1990 the accounting standards were known as **Statements of Standard Accounting Practice (SSAPs)**, and were issued by the Accounting Standards Committee (ASC), the forerunner of the ASB. Although some SSAPs have now been withdrawn there are, in addition to the new FRSs, a large number of SSAPs that are still in force.

The ASB is supported by the Urgent Issues Task Force (UITF). Its main role is to assist the ASB in areas where an accounting standard or Companies Act provision exists, but where unsatisfactory or conflicting interpretations have developed or seem likely to develop. The UITF also deals with issues that need to be resolved more quickly than through the issuing of an accounting standard. A recent example of this was the guidance on the accounting aspects of a recent EU directive which makes producers of electrical equipment responsible for financing waste management costs of their products, such as the costs of collection, treatment and environmentally sound disposal. The Financial Reporting Review Panel (FRRP) reviews comments and complaints from users of financial information. It enquires into the annual accounts of companies where it appears that the requirements of the Companies Act, including the requirement that annual accounts shall show a true and fair view, might have been breached. The Stock Exchange rules covering financial disclosure of publicly quoted companies require such companies to comply with accounting standards and reasons for non-compliance must be disclosed.

Pressure groups, organisations and individuals may also have influence on the provisions of the Companies Act and FRSs (and SSAPs). These may include some Government departments (for example HM Revenue & Customs and the Office of Fair Trading) in addition to the Department for Business, Innovation and Skills (BIS) and employer organisations such as the Confederation of British Industry (CBI), and professional bodies like the Law Society, Institute of Directors, and Chartered Management Institute.

There are therefore many diverse influences on the form and content of company accounts. In addition to legislation, standards are continually being refined, updated and replaced and further enhanced by various codes of best practice. As a response to this the UK Generally Accepted Accounting Practice (UK GAAP), first published in 1989, includes all practices that are considered to be permissible or legitimate, either through support by statute, accounting standard or official pronouncement, or through consistency with the needs of users and of meeting the fundamental requirement to present a true and fair view, or even simply through authoritative support in the accounting literature. UK GAAP is therefore a dynamic concept, which changes in response to changing circumstances.

Within the scope of current legislation, best practice and accounting standards, each company needs to develop its own specific **accounting policies**. Accounting policies are the specific accounting bases selected and consistently followed by an entity as being, in the opinion of the management, appropriate to its circumstances and best suited to present fairly its results and financial position. Examples are the various alternative methods of valuing inventories of materials, or charging the cost of a machine over its useful life, that is, its depreciation.

The accounting standard that deals with how a company chooses, applies and reports on its accounting policies is called FRS 18, Accounting Policies, and was issued in 2000 to replace SSAP 2, Disclosure of Accounting Policies. FRS 18 clarified when profits should be recognised (the realisation concept), and the requirement of 'neutrality' in financial statements in neither overstating gains nor understating losses (the prudence concept). This standard also emphasised the increased importance of the going concern concept and the accruals concept. The aims of FRS 18 are:

- to ensure that companies choose accounting policies that are most suitable for their individual circumstances, and incorporate the key characteristics stated in Chapter 3 of the SOP
- to ensure that accounting policies are reviewed and replaced as necessary on a regular basis
- to ensure that companies report accounting policies, and any changes to them, in their annual reports and accounts so that users of that information are kept informed.

Whereas FRS 18 deals with the disclosure by companies of their accounting policies, FRS 3, Reporting Financial Transactions, deals with the reporting by companies of their financial performance. Financial performance relates primarily to the income statement, whereas financial position relates primarily to the balance sheet. FRS 3 aims to ensure that users of financial information get a good insight into the company's performance during the period to which the accounts relate. This is in order that decisions made about the company may be made on an informed basis. FRS 3 requires the following items to be included in company accounts to provide the required level of reporting on financial performance (all to be discussed in greater detail in Chapter 4 which is about the income statement, and Chapter 8, which looks at published reports and accounts):

- analysis of sales, cost of sales, operating expenses and profit before interest
- exceptional items
- extraordinary items
- statement of recognised gains and losses (a separate financial statement along with the balance sheet, income statement and statement of cash flows).

International accounting standards

The International Accounting Standards Committee (IASC), set up in 1973, which is supported by each of the major professional accounting bodies, fosters the harmonisation of accounting standards internationally. To this end each UK FRS (Financial Reporting Standard) includes a section explaining its relationship to any relevant international accounting standard.

There are wide variations in the accounting practices that have been developed in different countries. These reflect the purposes for which financial information is required by the different users of that information, in each of those countries. There is a different focus on the type of information and the relative importance of each of the users of financial information in each country. This is because each country may differ in terms of:

■ who finances the businesses – individual equity shareholders, institutional equity shareholders, debenture holders, banks, etc.
■ tax systems either aligned with or separate from accounting rules
■ the level of government control and regulation
■ the degree of transparency of information.

The increase in international trade and globalisation has led to a need for convergence, or harmonisation, of accounting rules and practices. The IASC was created in order to develop international accounting standards, but these have been slow in appearing because of the difficulties in bringing together differences in accounting procedures. Until 2000 these standards were called International Accounting Standards (IASs). The successor to the IASC, the IASB (International Accounting Standards Board), was set up in April 2001 to make financial statements more comparable on a worldwide basis. The IASB publishes its standards in a series of pronouncements called International Financial Reporting Standards (IFRSs). It has also adopted the body of standards issued by the IASC, which continue to be designated IASs.

The former chairman of the IASB, Sir David Tweedie, who retired in June 2011, said that 'the aim of the globalisation of accounting standards is to simplify accounting practices and to make it easier for investors to compare the financial statements of companies worldwide'. He also said that 'this will break down barriers to investment and trade and ultimately reduce the cost of capital and stimulate growth' (*Business Week*, 7 June 2004). On 1 January 2005 there was convergence in the mandatory application of the IFRSs by listed companies within each of the European Union member states. The impact of this should be negligible with regard to the topics covered in this book, since UK accounting standards have already moved close to international standards. The reason for this is that the UK SOP was drawn up using the 1989 IASB conceptual framework for guidance. A list of current IFRSs and IASs is shown in Appendix 1 at the end of this book.

At the time of writing this book, major disagreements between the EU and accountants worldwide over the influence of the EU on the process of developing International Accounting Standards are causing concern that the dream of the globalisation of accounting standards may not be possible (see the article below from the 5 April 2010 edition of the *Financial Times*).

Who controls the IASB?

FT

The European Union's new internal market commissioner has proposed reforms to the body that sets international accounting rules, infuriating accountants and potentially scotching fragile hopes of global convergence.

In an apparent power grab by Brussels, Michel Barnier has suggested future funding of the International Accounting Standards Board might depend on whether it bows to political pressure from the European Commission to make changes to its governance.

Mr Barnier's suggestion, made at a meeting of top accountants and regulators in London, stunned the accounting community by raising questions about IASB independence during crucial talks to establish an international set of accounting rules.

The Group of 20 most industrialised nations last September pledged support for a single set of accounting standards to improve capital flows and reduce cross-border arbitrage in response to the financial crisis. However, achieving consensus is proving increasingly difficult.

Crucially, many European policymakers believe prudential regulators should be more involved in IASB governance so that accounting can be used as a tool for financial stability.

But accountants and business leaders – particularly in the US and Japan – argue that accounts should not be the subject of regulatory intervention but should focus on providing an accurate snapshot of a company's value.

During an increasingly tense meeting on future funding for the IASB, Mr Barnier said that "the two issues of financing and governance can be linked".

"We want to see more issuers – more banks and more companies – and more prudential regulators represented on the governing board [of the IASB]", he said.

Mr Barnier went on to say that it was "premature" to expect the EU to increase its annual £4.3m ($6.5m) budget contribution for the IASB. Moreover, Brussels intended to reconsider its funding annually.

Senior accountants said Mr Barnier's salvo could bring Brussels into conflict with the US and Asia and derail the convergence process.

More than 110 countries, including most of Europe and Asia, use the International Financial Reporting Standards drawn up by the IASB. US companies continue to report under Generally Accepted Accounting Principles while regulators consider whether to endorse IFRS.

Source: **Push for accounting convergence threatened by EU reform drive,** by Rachel Sanderson © *Financial Times*, 5 April 2010

Progress check 1.4

What is the significance of the International Financial Reporting Standards (IFRSs) that have been issued by the IASB?

Worked example 1.1

Young Fred Osborne decided that he would like to start to train to become an accountant. Some time after he had graduated (and after an extended backpacking trip across a few continents) he registered with the Chartered Institute of Management Accountants (CIMA). At the same time Fred started employment as part of the graduate intake in the finance department of a large engineering group. The auditors came in soon after Fred started his job and he was intrigued and a little confused at their conversations with some of the senior accountants. They talked about accounting concepts and this standard and that standard, SSAPs, FRSs, and IFRSs, all of which meant very little to Fred. Fred asked his boss, the Chief Accountant Angela Jones, if she could give him a brief outline of the framework of accounting one evening after work over a drink.

Angela's outline might have been something like this:

- Accounting is supported by a number of rules, or concepts, that have evolved over many hundreds of years, and by accounting standards to enable consistency in reporting through the preparation of financial statements.
- Accounting concepts relate to the framework within which accounting operates, ethical considerations and the rules relating to measurement of data.
- A number of concepts relate to the boundaries of the framework: business entity; going concern; periodicity.
- A number of concepts relate to accounting principles or ethics: consistency; prudence; substance over form.
- A number of concepts relate to how data should be measured and recorded: accruals; separate valuation; money measurement; historical cost; realisation; materiality; dual aspect.
- Accounting standards are formulated by a body comprised of members of the accounting institutes (Accounting Standards Board – ASB) and are guidelines which businesses are recommended to follow in the preparation of their financial statements.
- The original standards were the Statements of Standard Accounting Practice (SSAPs) which have been and continue to be superseded by the Financial Reporting Standards (FRSs).
- The aim of the SSAPs/FRSs is to cover all the issues and problems that are likely to be encountered in the preparation of financial statements and they are the authority to ensure that 'financial statements of a **reporting entity** give a true and fair view of its state of affairs at the balance sheet date and of its profit or loss for the financial period ending on that date' (as quoted from the ASB foreword to *Accounting Standards*).
- SSAPs were promulgated by the Accounting Standards Committee (ASC) and FRSs are promulgated by the ASB.
- In recent years the International Accounting Standards Board (IASB), which is an independent standard-setting board based in the UK, has sought to develop a set of high-quality globally accepted financial reporting standards based upon clearly articulated accounting principles.
- From 2005 all listed companies in the EU have been required to prepare their financial statements in accordance with the standards of the IASB, which are called International Financial Reporting Standards (IFRSs).

There is considerable convergence between the international and UK standards and indeed the ASB develops and amends its standards in the light of IFRSs.

Financial accounting, management accounting and financial management

The provision of a great deal of information, as we shall see as we progress through this book, is mandatory; it is needed to comply with, for example, the requirements of Acts of Parliament, and HM Revenue & Customs. However, there is a cost of providing information that has all the features that have been described, which therefore renders it potentially useful information. The benefits from producing information, in addition to mandatory information, should therefore be considered and compared with the cost of producing that information to decide on which information is 'really' required.

Accountants may be employed by accounting firms, which provide a range of accounting-related services to individuals, companies, public services and other organisations. Alternatively, account-ants may be employed within companies, public services and other organisations. Accounting firms may specialise in **audit**, corporate taxation, personal taxation, VAT, or consultancy (see the right-hand column of Figure 1.3). Accountants within companies, public service organisations etc., may be employed in the main functions of **financial accounting, management accounting**, and **treasury management** (see the left-hand column of Fig. 1.3), and also in general management. Accounting skills may also be required in the areas of **financial management** and corporate finance. Within companies this may include responsibility for investments, and the management of cash and foreign currency risk. External to companies this may include advice relating to mergers and acquisitions, and Stock Exchange **flotations**.

Financial accounting

Financial accounting is primarily concerned with the first question answered by accounting informa-tion, the scorecard function. Taking a car-driving analogy, financial accounting makes greater use of the rear-view mirror than the windscreen; financial accounting is primarily concerned with historical information.

Financial accounting is the function responsible in general for the reporting of financial in-formation to the owners of a business, and specifically for preparation of the periodic external reporting of financial information, statutorily required, for shareholders. It also provides simi-lar information as required for Government and other interested third parties, such as potential

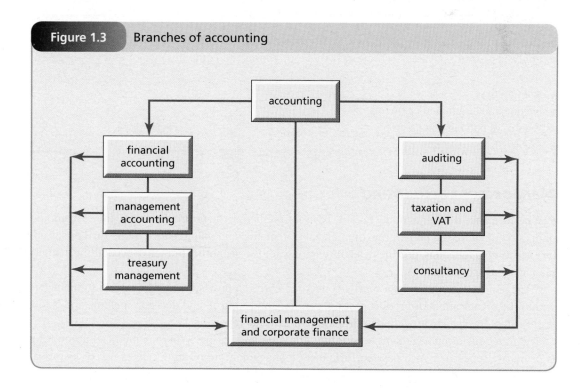

Figure 1.3   Branches of accounting

investors, employees, lenders, suppliers, customers and financial analysts. Financial accounting is concerned with the three key financial statements: the **balance sheet**; **income statement**; **statement of cash flows**. It assists in ensuring that financial statements are included in published reports and accounts in a way that provides ease of analysis and interpretation of company performance.

The role of financial accounting is therefore concerned with maintaining the scorecard for the entity. Financial accounting is concerned with the classification and recording of the monetary transactions of an entity in accordance with established concepts, principles, accounting standards and legal requirements and their presentation, by means of income statements, balance sheets and statements of cash flows, during and at the end of an **accounting period**.

Within most companies, the financial accounting role usually involves much more than the preparation of the three main financial statements. A great deal of analysis is required to support such statements and to prepare information both for internal management and in preparation for the annual audit by the company's external **auditors**. This includes sales analyses, bank reconciliations, and analyses of various types of expenditure.

A typical finance department has the following additional functions within the financial accounting role: control of **accounts payable** to suppliers (the **purchase ledger**); control of **accounts receivable** from customers (the **sales ledger**), and credit control; control of cash (and possible wider treasury functions) including cash payments, cash receipts, managers' expenses, petty cash and banking relationships. The financial accounting role also usually includes responsibility for payroll, whether processed internally or by an external agency. However, a number of companies elect to transfer the responsibility for payroll to the personnel, or human resources department, bringing with it the possibility of loss of **internal control**.

The breadth of functions involved in financial accounting can require the processing of high volumes of data relating to purchase invoices, supplier payments, sales invoices, receipts from customers, other cash transactions, petty cash, employee expense claims and payroll data. Control and monitoring of these functions therefore additionally requires a large number of reports generated by the accounting systems, for example:

- analysis of trade receivables (debtors): those who owe money to the company – by age of debt
- analysis of trade payables (creditors): those to whom the company owes money – by age of invoice
- sales analyses
- cheque and automated payments
- records of non-current assets
- invoice lists.

Management accounting

Past performance is never a totally reliable basis for predicting the future. However, the vast amount of data required for the preparation of financial statements, and maintenance of the further subsidiary accounting functions, provides a fertile database for use in another branch of accounting, namely management accounting.

Management accounting is primarily concerned with the provision of information to managers within the organisation for product costing, planning and control, and decision-making, and is to a lesser extent involved in providing information for external reporting.

The functions of management accounting are wide and varied. Whereas financial accounting is primarily concerned with past performance, management accounting makes use of historical data, but focuses almost entirely on the present and the future. Management accounting is involved with the scorecard role of accounting, but in addition is particularly concerned with the other two areas of accounting, namely problem-solving and attention-directing. These include cost analysis, decision-making, sales pricing, forecasting and budgeting, all of which will be discussed later in this book.

Financial management

Financial management has its roots in accounting, although it may also be regarded as a branch of applied economics. It is broadly defined as the management of all the processes associated with the efficient acquisition and deployment of both short- and long-term financial resources. Financial management assists an organisation's operations management to reach its financial objectives. This may include, for example, responsibility for corporate finance and treasury management, which is concerned with cash management, and the management of interest rate and foreign currency exchange rate risk.

The management of an organisation generally involves the three overlapping and interlinking roles of strategic management, risk management and operations management. Financial management supports these roles to enable management to achieve the financial objectives of the shareholders. Financial management assists in the reporting of financial results to the users of financial information, for example shareholders, lenders and employees.

The responsibility of the finance department for financial management includes the setting up and running of reporting and control systems, raising and managing funds, the management of relationships with financial institutions, and the use of information and analysis to advise management regarding planning, policy and capital investment. The overriding requirement of financial management is to ensure that the financial objectives of the company are in line with the interests of the shareholders; the underlying fundamental objective of a company is to maximise shareholder wealth.

Financial management, therefore, includes both accounting and treasury management. Treasury management includes the management and control of corporate funds, in line with company policy. This includes the management of banking relationships, borrowings and investment. Treasury management may also include the use of the various financial instruments, which may be used to hedge the risk to the business of changes in interest rates and foreign currency exchange rates, and advising on how company strategy may be developed to benefit from changes in the economic environment and the market in which the business operates. This book will identify the relevant areas within these subjects, which will be covered as deeply as considered necessary to provide a good introduction to financial management.

As management accounting has continued to develop its emphasis on decision-making and strategic management, and broaden the range of activities that it supports, it has now come to be regarded as an integral part of financial management.

Worked example 1.2

A friend of yours is thinking about pursuing a career in accounting and would like some views on the major differences between financial accounting, management accounting and financial management.

The following notes provide a summary that identifies the key differences.

Financial accounting: The financial accounting function deals with the recording of past and current transactions, usually with the aid of computerised accounting systems. Of the various reports prepared, the majority are for external users, and include the income statement, balance sheet, and the statement of cash flows. In a plc, such reports must be prepared at least every 6 months, and must comply with current legal and reporting requirements.

Management accounting: The management accounting function works alongside the financial accounting function, using a number of the day-to-day financial accounting reports from the accounting system. Management accounting is concerned largely with looking at current issues and problems and the future in terms of decision-making and forecasting, for example the consideration of 'what if' scenarios during the course of preparation of forecasts and budgets. Management accounting outputs are mainly for internal users, with much confidential reporting, for example to the directors of the company.

Financial management: Financial management may include responsibilities for corporate finance and the treasury function. This includes the management and control of corporate funds, within parameters specified by the board of directors. The role often includes the management of company borrowings, investment of surplus funds, the management of both interest rate and exchange rate risk, and giving advice on economic and market changes and the exploitation of opportunities. The financial management function is not necessarily staffed by accountants. Plcs report on the treasury activities of the company in their periodic reporting and financial review.

Some of the important functions in which management accounting and financial management may be involved include:

- forecasting revenues and costs
- planning activities
- managing costs
- identifying alternative sources and costs of funding
- managing cash
- negotiations with bankers
- evaluation of investments
- measurement and control of performance
- union negotiations
- negotiating with government
- costing compliance with social, environmental and sustainability requirements.

Progress check 1.5

What are the main differences between financial accounting, management accounting and financial management?

Accounting and accountancy

Accounting is sometimes referred to as a process of identifying, measuring and communicating economic information to permit informed judgements and decisions by users of the information, and also to provide information, which is potentially useful for making economic and social decisions. The term 'accounting' may be defined as:

- the classification and recording of monetary transactions
- the presentation and interpretation of the results of those transactions in order to assess performance over a period and the financial position at a given date
- the monetary projection of future activities arising from alternative planned courses of action.

Accounting processes are concerned with how data are measured and recorded and how the accounting function ensures the effective operation of accounting and financial systems. Accounting processes follow a system of recording and classification of data, followed by summarisation of financial information for subsequent interpretation and presentation. An accounting system is a series of tasks and records of an entity by which the transactions are processed as a means of maintaining financial records. Such systems identify, assemble, analyse, calculate, classify, record, summarise and report transactions.

Most companies prepare an accounting manual that provides the details and responsibilities for each of the accounting systems. The accounting manual is a collection of accounting instructions governing the responsibilities of persons, and the procedures, forms and records relating to preparation and use of accounting data.

There may be separate accounting manuals for the constituent parts of the accounting system, for example:

- financial accounting manual – general ledger and coding
- management accounting manual – budget and cost accounting
- financial management/treasury manual – bank reconciliations and foreign currency exposure management.

Accountancy is defined as the practice of accounting. A **qualified accountant** is a member of the accountancy profession, and in the UK is a member of one of the six professional accountancy bodies (see Figure 1.4). An accountant becomes qualified within each of these institutes through passing a large number of extremely technically demanding examinations and completion of a mandatory period of three years' practical training. The examination syllabus of each of the professional bodies tends to be very similar; each body provides additional emphasis on specific areas of accounting.

Chartered Management Accountants (qualified members of CIMA) receive their practical training in industrial and commercial environments, and in the public sector, for example the NHS. They are involved in practical accounting work and development of broader experience of strategic and operational management of the business. Certified Accountants (qualified members of ACCA) and Chartered Accountants (qualified members of ICAEW, ICAS, or ICAI) usually receive training while working in a practising accountant's office, which offers services to businesses and the general public, but may also receive training while employed in industrial and commercial organisations. Training focuses initially on auditing, and may then develop to include taxation and general business advice. Many accountants who receive training while specialising in central and local government usually, but not exclusively, are qualified members of CIPFA.

There are also a number of other accounting bodies like the Association of Accounting Technicians (AAT), Association of International Accountants, and Association of Authorised Public Accountants. The AAT, for example, provides bookkeeping and accounting training through examination and

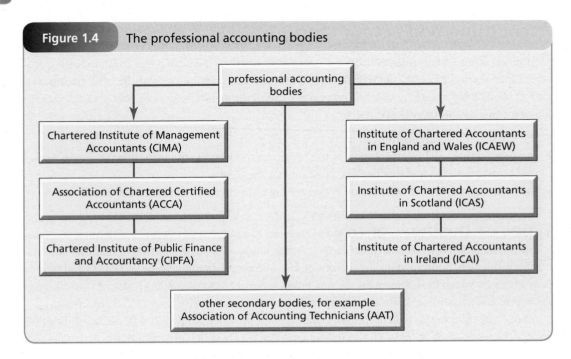

Figure 1.4 The professional accounting bodies

experience to a high level of competence, but short of that required to become a qualified account-ant. Treasury management is served by the Association of Corporate Treasurers (ACT). This quali-fication has tended to be a second qualification for accountants specialising in corporate funding, cash and working capital management, interest rate and foreign currency exchange rate risk man-agement. In the same way, the Institute of Taxation serves accountants who are tax specialists.

Progress check 1.6

What services does accounting offer and why do businesses need these services?

Worked example 1.3

Of which professional bodies are accountants likely to be members if they are employed as audi-tors, or if they are employed in the industrial and commercial sectors, or if they are employed in local government?

The following list of each of the types of professional accounting bodies links them with the sort of accounting they may become involved in.

Chartered Institute of Management Accountants (CIMA): management accounting and financial accounting roles with a focus on management accounting in the industrial and com-mercial sectors, and strategic and operational management

Institutes of Chartered Accountants (ICAEW, ICAS, ICAI): employment within a firm of ac-countants, carrying out auditing, investigations, taxation and general business advice – possible opportunities to move into an accounting role in industry

Chartered Institute of Public Finance and Accountancy (CIPFA): accounting role within central government or local government

Association of Chartered Certified Accountants (ACCA): employment either within a firm of accountants, carrying out auditing etc., or management accounting and financial accounting roles within commerce/industry

Association of Corporate Treasurers (ACT): commercial accounting roles with almost total emphasis on treasury issues: corporate finance; funding; cash management; working capital management; financial risk management

Types of business entity

Business entities are involved either in manufacturing (for example, food and automotive components) or in providing services (for example retailing, hospitals or television broadcasting). Such entities include profit-making and not-for-profit organisations, and charities. The main types of entity, and the environments in which they operate are represented in Figure 1.5. The four main types of profit-making organisations are explained in the sections that follow.

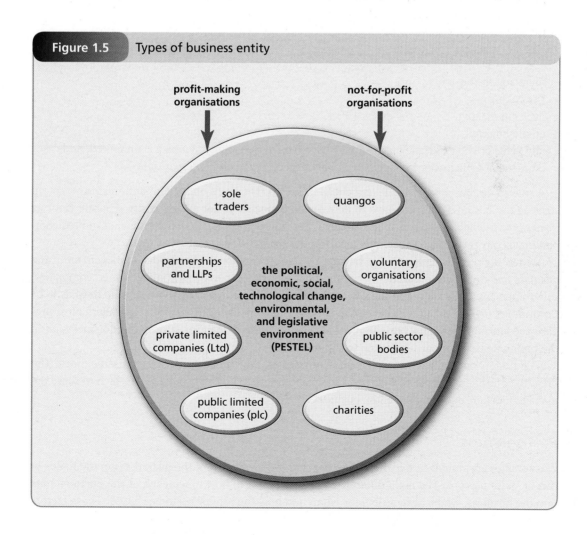

Figure 1.5   Types of business entity

The variety of business entities can be seen to range from quangos (quasi-autonomous non-government organisations) to partnerships to limited companies. Most of the topics covered in this book apply to any type of business organisation that has the primary aim of maximising the wealth of its owners: limited liability companies, both private (Ltd) companies and public (plc) limited companies, sole traders and partnerships.

> ### Progress check 1.7
>
> What are the different types of business entity? Can you think of some examples of each?

Sole traders

A sole trader entity is applicable for most types of small business. It is owned and financed by one individual, who receives all the profit made by the business, even though more than one person may work in the business.

The individual sole trader has complete flexibility regarding:

- the type of (legal) activities in which the business may be engaged
- when to start up or cease the business
- the way in which business is conducted.

The individual sole trader also has responsibility for:

- financing the business
- risk-taking
- decision-making
- employing staff
- any debts or loans that the business may have (the responsibility of which is unlimited, and cases of financial difficulty may result in personal property being used to repay debts).

A sole trader business is simple and cheap to set up. There are no legal or administrative set-up costs as the business does not have to be registered since it is not a legal entity separate from its owner. As we shall see, this is unlike the legal position of owners, or shareholders, of limited companies who are recognised as separate legal entities from the businesses they own.

Accounting records are needed to be kept by sole traders for the day-to-day management of the business and to provide an account of profit made during each tax year. Unlike limited companies, sole traders are not required to file a formal report and accounts each year with the **Registrar of Companies** (in some countries called the chamber of commerce). However, sole traders must prepare accounts on an annual basis to provide the appropriate financial information for inclusion in their annual tax return for submission to HM Revenue & Customs.

Sole traders normally remain quite small businesses, which may be seen as a disadvantage. The breadth of business skills is likely to be lacking since there are no co-owners with which to share the management and development of the business.

Partnerships

Partnerships are similar to sole traders except that the ownership of the business is in the hands of two or more persons. The main differences are in respect of how much each of the partners puts into the business, who is responsible for what, and how the profits are to be shared. These factors are normally set out in formal partnership agreements, and if the partnership agreement is not specific then the provisions of the Partnership Act 1890 apply. There is usually a written partnership agreement (but this is not absolutely necessary) and so there are initial legal costs of setting up the business.

A partnership is called a firm and is usually a small business, although there are some very large partnerships, for example firms of accountants like PricewaterhouseCoopers. Partnerships are formed by two or more persons and, apart from certain professions like accountants, architects and solicitors, the number of persons in a partnership is limited to 20.

A partnership:

- can carry out any legal activities agreed by all the partners
- is not a legal entity separate from its partners.

The partners in a firm:

- can all be involved in running the business
- all share the profits made by the firm
- are all jointly and severally liable for the debts of the firm
- all have unlimited liability for the debts of the firm (and cases of financial difficulty may result in personal property being used to repay debts)
- are each liable for the actions of the other partners.

Accounting records are needed to be kept by partnerships for the day-to-day management of the business and to provide an account of profit made during each tax year. Unlike limited companies, partnership firms are not required to file a formal report and accounts each year with the Registrar of Companies, but partners must submit annual returns for tax purposes to HM Revenue & Customs.

A new type of legal entity was established in 2001, the limited liability partnership (LLP). This is a variation on the traditional partnership, and has a separate legal identity from the partners, which therefore protects them from personal bankruptcy.

One of the main benefits of a partnership is that derived from its broader base of business skills than that of a sole trader. A partnership is also able to share risk-taking, decision-making and the general management of the firm.

Limited companies

A **limited company** is a legal entity separate from the owners of the business, which may enter into contracts, own property, and take or receive legal action. The owners limit their obligations to the amount of finance they have put into the company by way of the share of the company they have paid for. Normally, the maximum that may be claimed from shareholders is no more than they have paid for their shares, regardless of what happens to the company. Equally, there is no certainty that shareholders may recover their original investment if they wish to dispose of their shares or if the business is wound up, for whatever reason.

A company with unlimited liability does not give the owners, or members, of the company the protection of limited liability. If the business were to fail, the members would be liable, without limitation, for all the debts of the business.

The legal requirements relating to the registration and operation of limited companies is contained within the Companies Act 2006. Limited companies are required to be registered with the Registrar of Companies as either a private limited company (designated Ltd) or a public limited company (designated plc).

Private limited companies (Ltd)

Private limited companies are designated as Ltd. There are legal formalities involved in setting up a Ltd company which result in costs for the company. These formalities include the drafting of the company's Memorandum and Articles of Association (M and A) that describe what the company is and what it is allowed to do, registering the company and its director(s) with the Registrar of Companies, and registering the name of the company.

The shareholders provide the financing of the business in the form of share capital, of which there is no minimum requirement, and are therefore the owners of the business. The shareholders must appoint at least one director of the company, who may also be the company secretary, who carries out the day-to-day management of the business. A Ltd company may only carry out the activities included in its M and A.

Limited companies must regularly produce annual accounts for their shareholders and file a copy with the Registrar of Companies, and therefore the general public may have access to this information. A Ltd company's accounts must be audited by a suitably qualified accountant, unless it is exempt from this requirement, currently (with effect from 6 April 2008) by having annual sales of less than £6.5m and a balance sheet total of less than £3.26m. The exemption is not compulsory and having no audit may be a disadvantage: banks, financial institutions, customers and suppliers may rely on information from Companies House to assess creditworthiness and they are usually reassured by an independent audit. Limited companies must also provide copies of their annual accounts for Her Majesty's Revenue & Customs (HMRC) and also generally provide a separate computation of their profit on which corporation tax is payable. The accounting profit of a Ltd company is adjusted for:

- various expenses that may not be allowable in computing taxable profit
- tax allowances that may be deducted in computing taxable profit.

Limited companies tend to be family businesses and smaller businesses with the ownership split among a few shareholders, although there have been many examples of very large private limited companies. The shares of Ltd companies may be bought and sold but they may not be offered for sale to the general public. Since ownership is usually with family and friends there is rarely a ready market for the shares and so their sale usually requires a valuation of the business.

The Companies Act 2006 removed the requirement of a private limited company to hold an annual general meeting (AGM). However, if companies' Articles of Association require an AGM, then they must continue to be held unless the Articles are amended. Under the provisions of the Companies Act 2006, directors or 10% of the shareholders of a company may at any time request a general meeting to be held.

Public limited companies (plc)

Public limited companies are designated as plc. A plc usually starts its life as a Ltd company and then becomes a plc by applying for a listing of its shares on the Stock Exchange or the Alternative Investment Market, and making a public offer for sale of shares in the company. Plcs must have a minimum issued share capital of (currently) £50,000. The offer for sale, dealt with by a financial institution and the company's legal representatives, is very costly. The formalities also include the redrafting of the company's M and A, reflecting its status as a plc, registering the company and its director(s) with the Registrar of Companies, and registering the name of the plc.

The shareholders must appoint at least two directors of the company, who carry out the day-to-day management of the business, and a suitably qualified company secretary to ensure the plc's compliance with company law. A plc may only carry out the activities included in its M and A.

Plcs must regularly produce annual accounts, which they copy to their shareholders. They must also file a copy with the Registrar of Companies, and therefore the general public may have access to this information. The larger plcs usually provide printed glossy annual reports and accounts which they distribute to their shareholders and other interested parties. A plc's accounts must be audited by a suitably qualified accountant. Plcs must also provide copies of their annual accounts for HM Revenue & Customs and also generally provide a separate computation of their profit on which corporation tax is payable. The accounting profit of a plc is adjusted for:

- various expenses that may not be allowable in computing taxable profit
- tax allowances that may be deducted in computing taxable profit.

The shareholders provide the financing of the plc in the form of share capital and are therefore the owners of the business. The ownership of a plc can therefore be seen to be spread amongst many shareholders (individuals and institutions like insurance companies and pension funds), and the shares may be freely traded and bought and sold by the general public.

Worked example 1.4

Ike Andoowit is in the process of planning the setting up of a new residential training centre. Ike has discussed with a number of his friends the question of registering the business as a limited company, or being a sole trader. Most of Ike's friends have highlighted the advantages of limiting his liability to the original share capital that he would need to put into the company to finance the business. Ike feels a bit uneasy about the whole question and decides to obtain the advice of a professional accountant to find out:

(i) the main disadvantages of setting up a limited company as opposed to a sole trader
(ii) if Ike's friends are correct about the advantage of limiting one's liability
(iii) what other advantages there are to registering the business as a limited company.

The accountant may answer Ike's questions as follows:

Setting up as a sole trader is a lot simpler and easier than setting up a limited company. A limited company is bound by the provisions of the Companies Act 2006, and for example, may be required to have an independent annual audit. A limited company is required to be much more open about its affairs.

The financial structure of a limited company is more complicated than that of a sole trader. There are also additional costs involved in the setting up, and in the administrative functions of a limited company.

Running a business as a limited company requires registration of the business with the Registrar of Companies.

As Ike's friends have pointed out, the financial obligations of a shareholder in a limited company are generally restricted to the amount he or she has paid for his or her shares. In addition, the number of shareholders is potentially unlimited, which widens the scope for raising additional capital.

It should also be noted that:

- a limited company is restricted in its choice of business name
- if any director or 10% of the shareholders request it, a limited company is required to hold a general meeting at any time
- any additional finance provided for a company by a bank is likely to require a personal guarantee from one or more shareholders.

An introduction to financial statement reporting

Limited companies produce financial statements for each accounting period to provide adequate information about how the company has been doing. There are three main financial statements – balance sheet, income statement (or **profit and loss account**), and statement of cash flows. Companies are also obliged to provide similar financial statements at each year end to provide information for their shareholders, HMRC, and the Registrar of Companies. This information is frequently used by City analysts, investing institutions and the public in general.

After each year end companies prepare their **annual report and accounts** for their shareholders. Copies of the annual report and accounts are filed with the Registrar of Companies and copies are available to other interested parties such as financial institutions, major suppliers and other investors. In addition to the income statement and statement of cash flows for the year and the balance sheet as at the year end date, the annual report and accounts includes notes to the accounts, and much more financial and non-financial information such as company policies, financial indicators, corporate governance compliance, directors' remuneration, employee numbers, business analysis, and segmental analysis. The annual report also includes an operating and financial review of the business, a report of the auditors of the company, and the chairman's statement.

The auditors' report states compliance or otherwise with accounting standards and that the accounts are free from material misstatement, and that they give a true and fair view prepared on the assumption that the company is a going concern. The chairman's statement offers an opportunity for the chairman of the company to report in unquantified and unaudited terms on the performance of the company during the past financial period and on likely future developments. However, the auditors would object if there was anything in the chairman's statement that was inconsistent with the audited accounts.

Fred explained the subject of financial statements to Jack, bearing in mind that he is very much a non-financial person.

Limited companies are required to produce three main financial statements for each accounting period with information about company performance for:

- shareholders
- HMRC
- banks
- City analysts
- investing institutions
- the public in general.

The three key financial statements are the:

(a) balance sheet
(b) income statement (or profit and loss account)
(c) statement of cash flows.

(a) **Balance sheet:** a financial snapshot at a moment in time, or the financial position of the company comparable with pressing the 'pause' button on a DVD. The DVD in 'play' mode shows what is happening as time goes on second by second, but when you press 'pause' the DVD stops on a picture; the picture does not tell you what has happened over the period of time up to the pause (or what is going to happen after the pause). The balance sheet is the consequence of everything that has happened up to the balance sheet date. It does not explain how the company got to that position.

(b) **Income statement:** this is the DVD in 'play' mode. It is used to calculate whether or not the company has made a gain or deficit on its operations during the period, its financial performance, through producing and selling its goods or services. Net earnings or net profit is calculated from revenues derived throughout the period between two 'pauses', minus costs incurred in deriving those revenues.

(c) **Statement of cash flows:** this is the DVD again in 'play' mode, but net earnings is not the same as cash flow, since revenues and costs are not necessarily accounted for when cash transfers occur. Sales are accounted for when goods or services are delivered and accepted by the customer but cash may not be received until some time later. The income statement does not reflect non-trading events like an issue of shares or a loan that will increase cash but are not revenues or costs. The statement of cash flows summarises cash inflows and cash outflows and calculates the net change in the cash position for the company throughout the period between two 'pauses'.

Users of accounting and financial information

Financial information is important to a wide range of groups both internal and external to the organisation. Such information is required, for example, by individuals outside the organisation to make decisions about whether or not to invest in one company or another, or by potential suppliers who wish to assess the reliability and financial strength of the organisation. It is also required by managers within the organisation as an aid to decision-making. The main users of financial information are shown in Figure 1.6.

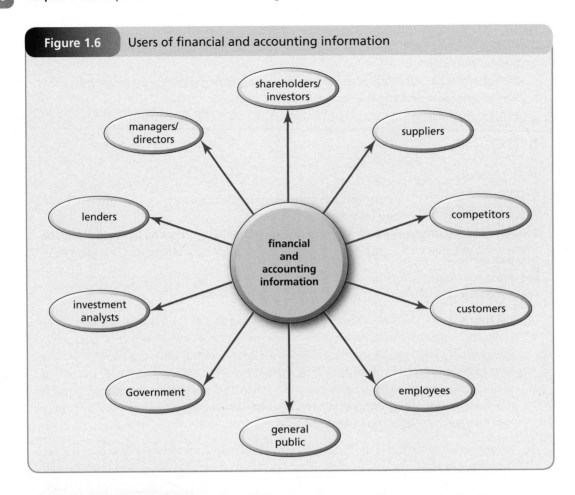

Figure 1.6   Users of financial and accounting information

Progress check 1.10

How many users of financial information can you think of and in what ways do you think they may use this information?

Worked example 1.6

Kevin Green, a trainee accountant, has recently joined the finance department of a newly formed public limited company. Kevin has been asked to work with the company's auditors who have been commissioned to prepare some alternative formats for the company's annual report.

As part of his preparation for this, Kevin's manager has asked him to prepare a draft report about who is likely to use the information contained in the annual report, and how they might use such information.

Kevin's preparatory notes for his report included the following:

- **Competitors** as part of their industry competitive analysis studies to look at market share, and financial strength
- **Customers** to determine the ability to provide a regular, reliable supply of goods and services, and to assess customer dependence

- **Employees** to assess the potential for providing continued employment and assess levels of remuneration
- **General public** to assess general employment opportunities, social, political and environmental issues, and to consider potential for investment
- **Government value added tax (VAT)** and corporate taxation, Government statistics, grants and financial assistance, monopolies and mergers
- **Investment analysts** investment potential for individuals and institutions with regard to past and future performance, strength of management, risk versus reward
- **Lenders** the capacity and the ability of the company to service debt and repay capital
- **Managers/directors** to a certain extent an aid to decision-making, but such relevant information should already have been available internally
- **Shareholders/investors** a tool of accountability to maintain a check on how effectively the directors/managers are running the business, and to assess the financial strength and future developments
- **Suppliers** to assess the long-term viability and whether the company is able to meet its obligations and pay suppliers on an ongoing basis.

Accountability and financial reporting

When we talk about companies we are generally referring to limited companies, as distinct from sole traders and partnerships (or firms – although this term is frequently wrongly used to refer to companies). As we have discussed, limited liability companies have an identity separate from their owners, the shareholders, and the liability of shareholders is limited to the amount of money they have invested in the company, that is their shares in the company. Ownership of a business is separated from its stewardship, or management, by the shareholders' assignment to a board of directors the responsibility for running the company. The directors of the company are accountable to the shareholders, and both parties must play their part in making that accountability effective.

The directors of a limited company may comprise one or more professionally qualified accountants (usually including a finance director). The directors of the company necessarily delegate to middle managers and junior managers the responsibility for the day-to-day management of the business. It is certainly likely that this body of managers, who report to the board of directors, will include a further one or more qualified accountants responsible for managing the finance function.

Accountability is maintained by reporting on the financial performance and the financial position of the business to shareholders on both a yearly and an interim basis. The reporting made in the form of the financial statements includes the balance sheet, income statement, and statement of cash flows, which will be considered in detail throughout this book.

You may question why all the accounting regulation that we have discussed in the earlier sections of this chapter is necessary at all. Well, there are a number of arguments in favour of such regulation:

- It is very important that the credibility of financial statement reporting is maintained so that actual and potential investors are protected as far as possible against inappropriate accounting practices.
- Generally, being able to distinguish between the good and not so good companies also provides some stability in the financial markets.
- The auditors of companies must have some rules on which to base their true and fair view of financial position and financial performance, which they give to the shareholders and other users of the financial statements.

External auditors are appointed by, and report independently to, the shareholders. They are professionally qualified accountants who are required to provide objective verification to shareholders and other users that the financial statements have been prepared properly and in accordance with legislative and regulatory requirements; that they present the information truthfully and fairly; and that they conform to the best accounting practice in their treatment of the various measurements and valuations.

The audit is defined by the Auditing Practices Board (APB) as 'an independent examination of, and expression of an opinion on, the financial statements of the enterprise'. There is a requirement for all companies registered in the UK to have an annual audit, except for those companies that (currently) have annual sales revenue of less than £6.5m and a balance sheet total of less than £3.26m.

The financial reporting of the company includes preparation of the financial statements, notes and reports, which are audited and given an opinion on by the external auditors. A regulatory framework exists to see fair play, the responsibility for which is held jointly by the Government and the private sector, including the accountancy profession and the Stock Exchange.

The Government exercises influence through bodies such as the Department for Business, Innovation and Skills (BIS) and through Parliament by the enactment of legislation, for example the Companies Act. Such legal regulation began with the Joint Stock Companies Act 1844.

Subsequent statutes exerted greater influence on company reporting: the Companies Acts 1948, 1967, 1981 and 1985, amended in 1989. The provisions included in these Acts were consolidated into the Companies Act 2006. The Companies Act 2006 contains the overall current legal framework.

It may be argued that the increasing amount of accounting regulation itself stifles responses to changes in economic and business environments, and discourages the development of improved financial reporting. We have already seen that the development of various conceptual frameworks indicates that there is wide disagreement about what constitutes accounting best practice. The resistance to acceptance of international accounting standards may be for political reasons, the rules perhaps reflecting the requirements of specific interest groups or countries.

It is also true that despite increasing accounting regulation there have been an increasing number of well-publicised financial scandals in the USA in particular, where the accounting systems are very much 'rule-based', as well as in the UK, Italy and Japan. However, these scandals have usually been the result of fraudulent activity. This leads to another question as to why the auditors of such companies did not detect or prevent such fraud. The answer is that, despite the widespread perception of the general public to the contrary, auditors are not appointed to detect or prevent fraud. Rather, they are appointed by the shareholders to give their opinion as to whether the financial statements show a true and fair view and comply with statutory, regulatory, and accounting and financial reporting standards requirements.

Progress check 1.11

In what ways may the reliability of financial reporting be ensured?

Worked example 1.7

You are thinking of changing jobs (within marketing) and moving from a local, well-established retailer that has been in business for over 20 years. You have been asked to attend an interview at a new plc that started up around two years ago. The plc is a retailer via the Internet. Your family has suggested that you investigate the company thoroughly before your interview, paying particular attention to its financial resources. There is a chance the plc may not be a going concern if its business plan does not succeed.

You will certainly want to include the following questions at your interview.

(a) Are any published accounts available for review?

(b) What is the share capital of the company (for example, is it £50,000 or £1,000,000)?

(c) Is the company profitable?

(d) Does the company have loan commitments?

(e) Is the company working within its bank overdraft facilities?

(f) Are any press analyses of the company available?

(g) What is the current customer base?

The answers may suggest whether the company can continue trading for the foreseeable future.

Summary of key points

- The three main purposes of accounting are: to provide records of transactions and a scorecard of results; to direct attention to problems; to evaluate the best ways of solving problems.

- Accountancy is the practice of accounting.

- Conceptual frameworks of accounting have been developed in many countries and the UK conceptual framework is embodied in the Statement of Principles (SOP).

- The framework of accounting is bounded by concepts (or rules) and standards, covering what data should be included within an accounting system and how that data should be recorded.

- International Financial Reporting Standards (IFRSs) have been developed, which have been adopted by listed companies within the European Union with effect from 1 January 2005.

- The main branches of accounting within commercial and industrial organisations are financial accounting, management accounting, treasury management, financial management and corporate finance.

- The main services, in addition to accounting, that are provided by accountants to commercial and industrial organisations are auditing, corporate taxation, personal taxation, VAT advice and consultancy.

- The large variety of types of business entity includes profit and not-for-profit organisations, both privately and Government owned, involved in providing products and services.

- The four main types of profit-making businesses in the UK are sole traders, partnerships, limited companies (Ltd) and public limited companies (plc).

- Accounting processes follow a system of recording and classifying data, followed by a summarisation of financial information for subsequent interpretation and presentation.

- The three main financial statements that appear within a business's annual report and accounts, together with the chairman's statement, directors' report and auditors' report, are the balance sheet, income statement and statement of cash flows.

- There is a wide range of users of financial information external and internal to an organisation. External users include: potential investors; suppliers; financial analysts. Internal users include: managers; shareholders; employees.

- Accountability is maintained by the reporting to shareholders on a yearly and half-yearly basis of sales and other activities and profits or losses arising from those activities, and the audit function.

Assessment material

Questions

Q1.1 (i) How many different types of business entity can you think of?

(ii) In what respect do they differ fundamentally?

Q1.2 (i) Why are accountants required to produce financial information?

(ii) Who do they produce it for and what do they do with it?

Q1.3 Describe the broad regulatory, professional, and operational framework of accounting.

Q1.4 What are conceptual frameworks of accounting?

Q1.5 (i) What are accounting concepts?

(ii) What purpose do they serve?

Q1.6 What is the UK Statement of Principles (SOP)?

Q1.7 (i) What is accountancy?

(ii) What is an accountant?

(iii) What do accountants do?

Q1.8 What do accountants mean by SSAPs and FRSs, and what are they for?

Q1.9 What are IASs and IFRSs and why are they important?

Q1.10 (i) What is financial management?

(ii) How does financial management relate to accounting and perhaps other disciplines?

Q1.11 How do financial statements ensure accountability for the reporting of timely and accurate information to shareholders is maintained?

Discussion points

D1.1 The managing director of a large public limited company stated: 'I've built up my business over the past 15 years from a one man band to a large plc. As we grew we seemed to spend more and more money on accountants, financial managers and auditors. During the next few months we are restructuring to go back to being a private limited company. This will be much simpler and we can save a fortune on accounting and auditing costs.' Discuss.

(Hint: You may wish to research Richard Branson and, for example, Virgin Air, on the Internet to provide some background for this discussion.)

D1.2 The managing director of a growing private limited company stated: 'All these accounting concepts and standards seem like a lot of red tape to me, and we've got financial accountants and management accountants as well as auditors. Surely all I need to know at the end of the day is how much have we made.' Discuss.

D1.3 Is accounting objective? Discuss with reference to at least six different accounting concepts.

Exercises

Exercises E1.1 to E1.10 require an essay-type approach. You should refer to the relevant sections in Chapter 1 to check your solutions.

Level I

E1.1   *Time allowed – 15 minutes*

> **Discuss the implications of preparation of the income statement if there were no accounting concepts.**

E1.2   *Time allowed – 30 minutes*

At a recent meeting of the local branch of the Women's Institute they had a discussion about what sort of organisation they were. The discussion broadened into a general debate about all types of organisation, and someone brought up the term 'business entity'. Although there were many opinions, there was little sound knowledge about what business entities are. Jane Cross said that her husband was an accountant and she was sure he wouldn't mind spending an hour one evening to enlighten them on the subject. Chris Cross fished out his textbooks to refresh his knowledge of the subject and came up with a schedule of all the different business entities he could think of together with the detail of their defining features and key points of difference and similarity.

> **Prepare the sort of schedule that Chris might have drafted for his talk and identify the category that the Women's Institute might fall into.**

E1.3   *Time allowed – 30 minutes*

Mary Andrews was an accountant but is now semi-retired. She has been asked by her local comprehensive school careers officer to give a talk entitled: 'What is an accountant and what is accounting, and what are its use and its purpose?'.

> **Prepare a list of bullet points that covers everything necessary for Mary to give a comprehensive and easy-to-understand presentation to a group of sixth-formers at the school.**

Level II

E1.4   *Time allowed – 30 minutes*

Accounting standards in general are reasonably clear and unambiguous.

> **Are there any major areas where accountants may disagree in balance sheet accounting?**

E1.5   *Time allowed – 30 minutes*

Financial statements are produced each year by businesses, using prescribed formats.

> **Should major plcs be allowed to reflect their individuality in their own financial statements?**

E1.6 *Time allowed – 45 minutes*

Professionals in the UK, for example, doctors, solicitors, accountants etc., normally work within partnerships. Many tradesmen, such as plumbers, car mechanics, carpenters and so on, operate as sole traders. Software engineers seem to work for corporations and limited companies.

> **Consider the size of operation, range of products, financing, the marketplace and the geographical area served, to discuss why companies like Microsoft and Yahoo! should operate as plcs.**

E1.7 *Time allowed – 60 minutes*

Bill Walsh has just been appointed Finance Director of a medium-sized engineering company, Nutsan Ltd, which has a high level of exports and is very sensitive to economic changes throughout the UK and the rest of the world. One of the tasks on Bill's action list is a review of the accounting and finance function.

> **What are the senior financial roles that Bill would expect to be in place and what are the important functions for which they should be responsible?**

E1.8 *Time allowed – 60 minutes*

Wembley Stadium II (the Football Association's replacement for the original iconic Wembley Stadium) was planned to open in 2003 but due to numerous problems financing the construction, problems in the general day-to-day operations and changes of contractor, it finally opened in March 2007. There were many crises reported in the press during the course of the project and the development finally cost over £1 billion.

> **You are required to research into the Wembley Stadium II project using the BBC, *Financial Times*, other serious newspapers, and the Internet, and summarise the financial aspects of the project that you gather. You should focus on the attitudes expressed by the general public, Government ministers, and the Football Association management, and consider examples of bias, non-timeliness, and lack of transparency.**

E1.9 *Time allowed – 60 minutes*

Conceptual frameworks of accounting have been developed over many years and in many countries.

> **Explain how these culminated in the publication of the UK Statement of Principles (SOP) in 1999, and discuss the implications of each of the eight chapters.**

E1.10 *Time allowed – 60 minutes*

The International Accounting Standards Board (IASB) decreed the adoption of the International Financial Reporting Standards (IFRSs) by all listed companies within the European Union mandatory with effect from 1 January 2005.

> **Discuss the practical and political issues surrounding this decision.**

2

Classifying and recording financial transactions

Contents

Learning objectives

Completion of this chapter will enable you to:

- explain the convention of double-entry bookkeeping
- describe what is meant by 'debit' and 'credit'
- enter business transactions into accounts
- account for closing inventories and other accounting adjustments
- explain the balancing of accounts
- extract a trial balance from a company's accounts
- prepare an income statement, balance sheet and statement of cash flows from a trial balance
- appreciate the concepts of accrual accounting and cash accounting
- explain and account for payments in advance (prepayments) and charges not yet received (accruals)
- appreciate the importance of accounting periods.

Introduction

This chapter begins by explaining what is sometimes referred to as the dual aspect rule. This rule recognises that for all transactions there is a two-sided effect within the entity. A manager in a non-accounting role may not be expected to carry out the recording of transactions in this way, but an appreciation of how accounting data has been recorded will be extremely helpful in the interpretation of financial information. We will go on to describe the processes that deal with the two sides of each transaction, the 'debits' and 'credits' of double-entry bookkeeping.

Don't worry if at first these topics seem a little difficult and confusing. They will become clearer as we follow through some transactions step-by-step into the accounts of a business and show how these accounts are kept in balance.

The chapter continues with an introduction to the way in which each of the accounts is held in what are termed the books of account and ledgers of the business. The balances on all the accounts in an entity are summarised in what is called a trial balance. The trial balance may be adjusted to allow for payments in advance, charges not yet received, and other adjusting entries. From this information we will show how to prepare a simple income statement, balance sheet and statement of cash flows.

This chapter refers to some of the accounting concepts introduced in Chapter 1. In that context we will look at the time period chosen by a business, to which the financial reporting relates – the accounting period.

Theory and practice of double-entry bookkeeping

Double-entry bookkeeping has a long history, having been created by the father of modern accounting, the Franciscan monk Luca Pacioli in Italy in the late fifteenth century. His publication, *Summa de Arithmetica, Geometria, Proportioni et Proportionalita* (Everything about Arithmetic, Geometry and Proportion), published in 1494, was the first printed work dealing with algebra and also contained the first text on bookkeeping, entitled *Particularis de Computis et Scripturis*. Bookkeeping then spread throughout the world by a series of plagiarisms and imitations of Pacioli's work. If Pacioli were around today he would be very disappointed to see the extent to which double-entry has apparently not been practised in Greece in more recent times. During 2009 and 2010 the Greek economy was in severe economic difficulty. It may be significant that a large part of the Greek public sector does not use double-entry bookkeeping at all (see the press extract below).

It is important to remember that the idea of double-entry is a convention. There are two main objectives of bookkeeping: to have a permanent record of transactions; and show the effect of each transaction and the combined effect of all the transactions on the financial position of the entity.

The fundamental idea of double-entry bookkeeping is that all business transactions of a business entity, for example, cash and invoices, should be recorded twice in the entity's business records. It is based on the principle that every financial transaction involves the simultaneous receiving and giving of value, and is therefore recorded twice. Transactions of course involve both services and goods. We

Look what happens when you neglect double entry!

Standard & Poor's has become the second rating agency to downgrade Greek sovereign debt to near junk levels of BBB1, issuing a withering verdict on spartan plans unveiled this week by premier George Papandreou.

'The downgrade reflects our opinion that the measures to reduce the high fiscal deficit are unlikely, on their own, to lead to a sustainable reduction in the public debt burden. If political considerations and social pressures hamper progress, we could lower the ratings further', it said.

The move came as Spyros Papanikolaou, head of Greece's Public Debt Management Agency, held back-to-back meetings with bankers in London in a bid to stop the crisis spiralling out of control.

Yields on 10-year Greek bonds surged to 5.75pc, a spread of 254 basis points over German Bunds. Borrowing costs are nearing levels that risk setting off an interest compound spiral. The public debt is already 113pc of GDP. S&P said it is likely to reach 138pc by 2012. 'The increasing debt-service burden narrows the scope for debt stabilisation', it said.

Fitch Ratings precipitated the Greek crisis earlier this month with a surprisingly harsh downgrade to BBB1, accompanied by a 'negative outlook'.

It emerged yesterday that Greece had raised euro2bn (£1.77bn) at a premium of 30 basis points in a private placement shortly after the Fitch move, avoiding the public glare of an auction.

To make matters worse, there were fresh concerns yesterday about the true scale of Greek military spending, which is kept off the books of the debt agency.

'Greek military accounts seem to be regarded as a state secret', said Chris Pryce, Fitch's director of sovereign ratings.

'In every other EU country we can find out how much they spend on defence, but we don't know for Greece. All we know is that their military spending is very large, around 5pc of GDP', he said.

Analysts who have probed deeply into Greek accounts have been astonished to discover that parts of the public sector lack double-entry bookkeeping, 700 years after it was invented by the Venetians.

Given Greece has misled the bond markets and Brussels in the past over its deficits, analysts suspect that Athens may try to hide problems behind a military veil. Mr Papandreou admits that Greece has lost "every shred of credibility".

Greece has already cut defence this year. It announced in September that it would not take delivery of four submarines built by Thyssen-Krupp, alleging technical faults. This has led to accusations Athens is effectively defaulting on a euro520m contract. Last week it cancelled tenders for a flight of maritime aircraft worth up to euro250m.

Source: **Greek crisis deepens with S&P downgrade; worry about true scale of undisclosed military spending adds to concern**, by Ambrose Evans-Pritchard © *Daily Telegraph*, 17 December 2009

shall find out later in this chapter that there are other accounting entries which do not result directly from invoice or cash transactions but which also result in double-entry records being created. These **accounting adjustment** entries relate, for example, to accounting for depreciation, **bad debts**, and **doubtful debts**.

The convention of double-entry assumes that in all business transactions equal and opposite values are exchanged. For example, if a company purchases materials for £1,000 for cash it adds to its inventory of materials to the value of £1,000, but reduces its cash balance also to the value of £1,000. The convention uses two terms for convenience to describe the two aspects of each transaction. These terms are debit and credit.

There is sometimes confusion in the use of the terms debit and credit used in bookkeeping when they are compared with the same terms used on bank statements. Bank statements traditionally refer to a receipt of cash as a credit, whereas a receipt of cash in bookkeeping terms is referred to as a debit. The reason for this is that customer accounts are presented from the bank's point of view; as far as the bank is concerned, account holders are creditors, to whom the bank will eventually have to repay any money deposited by them.

Debits and credits

The explanation of debits and credits in terms of value received and value given respectively is not perhaps one that provides the clearest understanding. Neither is the explanation that debits are in the left-hand column and credits are in the right-hand column, or debits are on the side of the room closest to the window!

Debits and credits do represent certain types of account, as we will see later, in both the balance sheet: **assets** and **liabilities**, and the income statement: costs and sales. However, for the purpose of clarity of explanation we shall propose a couple of basic assumptions with which to work as we go through some elementary accounting entries.

If we initially consider all business transactions as either goods or services then it is reasonable to assume (unless we are in a barter society) that all these transactions will ultimately end up with cash (or cash equivalents, such as cheques, bank transfers, etc.) changing hands. We can also assume that all these transactions will involve a document being raised, as a record of the transaction and an indication of the amount of cash that will change hands, namely an invoice. A **purchase invoice** records a purchase from a third party and so it represents an account to be payable at some time. A **sales invoice** records a sale to a third party and so it represents an account to be receivable at some time.

Business entities themselves have a separate identity from the owners of the business. When we consider double-entry bookkeeping we will now assume that all the entries we are discussing relate to those of the business entity, in whatever form the entity takes: sole trader; partnership; limited company; public limited company (see Chapter 1).

For the business entity, we shall define the following business transactions:

Transaction		Accounting entries	
CASH RECEIPT	=	DEBIT CASH	and credit something else
CASH PAYMENT	=	CREDIT CASH	and debit something else
PURCHASE INVOICE	=	CREDIT ACCOUNTS PAYABLE	and debit something else
SALES INVOICE	=	DEBIT ACCOUNTS RECEIVABLE	and credit something else

These are definitions within the convention of double-entry bookkeeping, which may be usefully remembered as a basis for establishing whether all further subsequent transactions are either debits or credits. It is suggested that the above four statements are kept filed in permanent memory, as a useful aid towards the understanding of further accounting entries.

Progress check 2.1

Outline what is meant by double-entry bookkeeping.

An elementary method of representing and clarifying double-entry is known as the T account. We shall use this method to demonstrate double-entry in action using a simple example. (Note that in the UK there are many computerised accounting packages that automate the double-entry for a business, for example Sage. The purpose of this extensive worked example is to illustrate how such transactions take place.)

Worked example 2.1

Mr Bean decides to set up a wholesale business, Ayco, on 1 January 2010. He has his own cash resources available for the purpose of setting it up and has estimated that an initial £50,000 would be required for this purpose. During the first month in business, January 2010, *Ayco* (as distinct from Mr Bean) will enter into the following transactions:

	£
Receipt of cheque from Mr Bean	50,000
Purchase the freehold of a shop for cash	30,000
Purchase the shop fittings for cash	5,000
Cash expenses on printing and stationery	200
Purchases of inventory, from Beeco, of Aymen toys, payable two months later (12,000 toys at £1 each)	12,000
Sales of Aymen toys to Ceeco for cash (1,000 toys at £2 each)	2,000
Sales of Aymen toys to Deeco, receivable one month later (8,000 toys at £2 each)	16,000

We shall consider each of these transactions in detail and subsequently represent them in T account format for clarity, with debits on the left and credits on the right of the middle line of the T. We will repeatedly refer to the earlier four key double-entry definitions in order to establish the entries required for each transaction.

Receipt of cheque from Mr Bean £50,000 – transaction 1

Ayco will have needed to open a bank account to pay in the money received from Mr Bean. This represents a receipt of cash of £50,000 to Ayco, and so:

Debit cash account   **£50,000 and credit what?**

This money represents the capital that Mr Bean, as the sole investor in the business, has invested in Ayco and so the account is called the capital account. So:

Debit cash account   **£50,000**
Credit capital account   **£50,000**

Worked example 2.2

Purchase for cash the freehold of a shop £30,000 – transaction 2

This represents a cash payment for the purchase of a shop, something which is called a non-current asset: an asset acquired for retention by the entity for the purpose of providing a service to the business, and not held for resale in the normal course of trading.

Credit cash account	**£30,000 and debit what?**

A payment of cash of £30,000 is a credit to the cash account, and so:

Credit cash account	**£30,000**
Debit non-current assets – shop account	**£30,000**

Worked example 2.3

Purchase for cash the shop fittings £5,000 – transaction 3

This represents a cash payment for the shop fittings, which are also non-current assets, but a different category of non-current asset from the freehold shop.

A payment of cash of £5,000 is a credit to the cash account, and so:

Credit cash account	**£5,000**
Debit non-current assets – fittings account	**£5,000**

Worked example 2.4

Cash expenses on printing and stationery £200 – transaction 4
This represents a payment of cash of £200 by Ayco in the month, and so:

Credit cash account	**£200 and debit what?**

This money was paid out on day-to-day expenses that have been made to support the business, and is a charge for printing and stationery expenses. So:

Credit cash account	**£200**
Debit printing and stationery expenses account	**£200**

Worked example 2.5

Purchases of inventory, from Beeco, of Aymen toys, payable two months later £12,000 – transaction 5

This represents a purchase on credit from Beeco. An invoice is assumed to have been received from Beeco along with the receipt of inventory. The invoice from Beeco is a purchase invoice for £12,000 to Ayco, and so:

Credit accounts payable	**£12,000 and debit what?**

This represents a purchase of inventory which are goods held for resale, and so:

Credit accounts payable	£12,000
Debit inventories account	£12,000

a purchase of inventory may alternatively be initially debited to the purchases account and then subsequently transferred to the inventories account.

Worked example 2.6

Sales of Aymen toys to Ceeco for cash £2,000 – transaction 6

This represents a sale for cash to Ceeco. An invoice will be issued by Ayco to Ceeco along with the delivery of inventory. The invoice to Ceeco is a sales invoice for £2,000 from Ayco, and so:

Debit accounts receivable	£2,000	and credit what?

This represents sales of inventory which are called sales, or sales revenue, and so:

Debit accounts receivable	£2,000
Credit sales revenue account	£2,000

But as a cash sale this sales invoice is being paid immediately with a cash receipt of £2,000, and so:

Debit cash account	£2,000	and credit what?

This £2,000 is immediately paying accounts receivable, and so

Debit cash account	£2,000
Credit accounts receivable	£2,000

which means that on this transaction the net balance of accounts receivable is zero.

This transaction may be short cut by directly crediting the sales revenue account and debiting cash. However, it is normally recorded in the way described in order to create and record a value added tax (VAT) sales invoice.

Worked example 2.7

Sales of Aymen toys to Deeco, receivable one month later £16,000 – transaction 7

This represents sales on credit to Deeco. An invoice will be issued by Ayco to Deeco along with the delivery of inventory.

The invoice to Deeco is a sales invoice for £16,000 from Ayco, and so as above:

Debit accounts receivable	£16,000
Credit sales revenue account	£16,000

This is different from the transaction in Worked example 2.6 because the account receivable will not be paid until the following month.

Closing inventories adjustment

In the Ayco example, one further accounting entry needs to be considered, which relates to the inventory of toys sold during the period. It is called a **closing inventories** adjustment, which is illustrated in Worked example 2.8.

Worked example 2.8

We represented the purchase of 12,000 toys into the inventory of Ayco as a debit of £12,000 to the inventories account. Ayco sold 1,000 toys for cash and 8,000 toys on credit. The physical inventory of 12,000 toys at 31 January 2010 has therefore been reduced to only 3,000 (12,000 − 1,000 − 8,000). We may value these units that are left in inventory at cost, for the purpose of this example, at 3,000 × £1, or £3,000. Ayco sold a total of 9,000 units during January at a selling price of £2 per unit. These 9,000 units cost £1 each and so these sales have cost Ayco £9,000: cost of sales £9,000. A double-entry accounting transaction is necessary to represent this for two reasons: to show the cost of the 9,000 toys that matches the sale of 9,000 toys; to ensure that the inventories account represents only the physical toys that are actually held in inventory.

The entries for the original purchase of inventory were:

Credit accounts payable	£12,000
Debit inventories account	£12,000

We know that the inventories account should now be £9,000 less than the original £12,000, representing the £9,000 cost of sales. Therefore we need to credit the inventories account to reduce it and debit something else. The something else is the cost of sales account.

Transaction 8

Credit inventories account	£9,000
Debit cost of sales account	£9,000

Accounting adjustments

The diagram in Figure 2.1 includes all the main types of accounting transactions that may be recorded in an accounting system. The shaded items represent the prime entries (the first record of transactions) and cash entries. The non-shaded items are the five main accounting adjustment entries.

The closing inventories adjustment, illustrated in Worked example 2.8, is one of the five main accounting adjustment entries that are shown in Figure 2.2, which may or may not be incorporated into the **trial balance**.

Accounting adjustments are made to the trial balance and prior to preparation of the income statement and balance sheet. The other four adjusting entries are **accruals** and **prepayments** (covered later in this chapter), depreciation, and bad and doubtful debts and the **doubtful debt provision** (which are covered together with further detail on closing inventories in Chapter 4).

Each of the T accounts for Ayco in Figure 2.3 shows the detailed movement through the month and each account represents the balance on each account at the 31 January 2010, the end of the first month of trading.

Figure 2.1   Accounting transactions

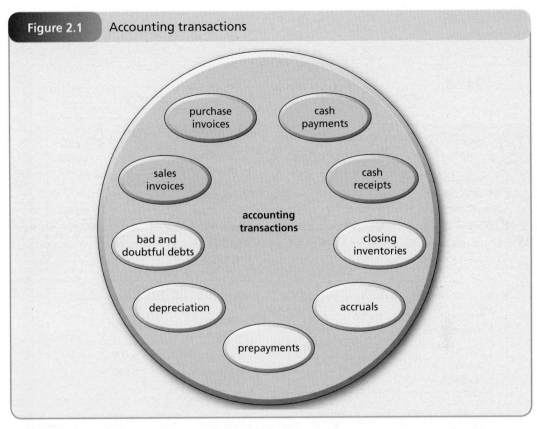

Figure 2.2   The five accounting adjustments and their impact on the profit and loss account and the balance sheet

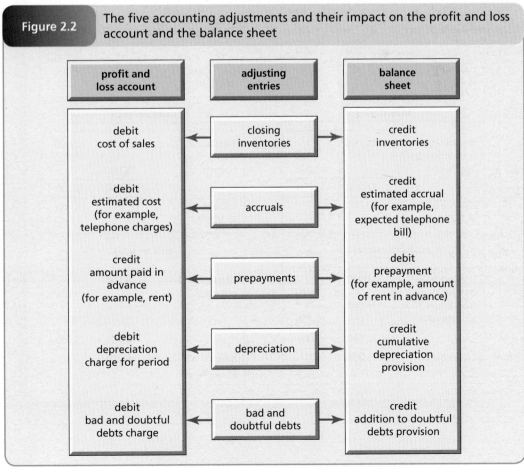

Figure 2.3	T account representation of the January 2010 transactions of Ayco

Figures in £

share capital

transaction 1		50,000
balance c/f	50,000	
	50,000	50,000
balance b/f @ 1/2/10		50,000

cash book

transaction 1	50,000	
transaction 2		30,000
transaction 3		5,000
transaction 4		200
transaction 6	2,000	
balance c/f		
		16,800
	52,000	52,000
balance b/f @ 1/2/10	16,800	

non-current assets – shop

transaction 2	30,000	
balance c/f		30,000
	30,000	30,000
balance b/f @ 1/2/10	30,000	

non-current assets – fittings

transaction 3	5,000	
balance c/f		5,000
	5,000	5,000
balance b/f @ 1/2/10	5,000	

printing and stationery – expenses

transaction 4	200	
balance c/f		200
	200	200
balance b/f @ 1/2/10	200	

accounts payable

transaction 5		12,000
balance c/f	12,000	
	12,000	12,000
balance b/f @ 1/2/10		12,000

inventories

transaction 5	12,000	
transaction 8		9,000
balance c/f		3,000
	12,000	12,000
balance b/f @ 1/2/10	3,000	

sales revenue

transaction 6		2,000
transaction 7		16,000
balance c/f	18,000	
	18,000	18,000
balance b/f @ 1/2/10		18,000

accounts receivable

transaction 6	2,000	
transaction 6		2,000
transaction 7	16,000	
balance c/f		16,000
	18,000	18,000
balance b/f @ 1/2/10	16,000	

cost of sales

transaction 8	9,000	
balance c/f		9,000
	9,000	9,000
balance b/f @ 1/2/10	9,000	

Progress check 2.2

Explain broadly what is meant by accounting adjustment entries.

Books of account and the ledgers in action

We saw in the previous section how the principle of double-entry bookkeeping operates to record the detail of transactions. We represented these records in T accounts to provide some clarity in seeing how each entry has been made and the interrelation of the entries. In practice, accounting records are kept along the same lines but in books of account and ledgers rather than T accounts on a piece of paper. The old-fashioned manually prepared ledgers maintained by companies have long since been superseded by **computerised accounting systems**. Nevertheless, the same principles apply and the same books of account and ledgers are maintained, albeit in an electronic format.

The chart in Figure 2.4 shows the relationship between the main ledger, the general ledger (or nominal ledger) and the other books of account, and subsidiary ledgers:

- **cash book** (receipts and payments)
- **purchase invoice daybook** and accounts payable (or purchase ledger)
- **sales invoice daybook** and accounts receivable (or sales ledger).

It also shows the main sources of data input for these ledgers and the basic reporting information produced out of these ledgers and books of account.

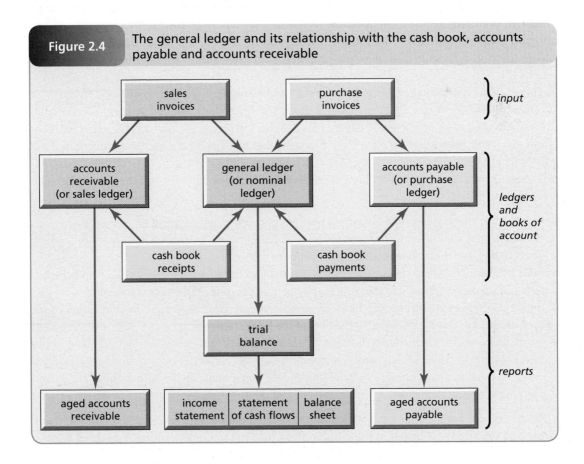

Figure 2.4 The general ledger and its relationship with the cash book, accounts payable and accounts receivable

General ledger

In smaller businesses, wages and salaries data are usually recorded in the cash book and subsequently posted to the general ledger. In larger companies, wages and salaries usually have their own ledgers and control accounts in the general ledger.

The main ledger of any company, in which the results of all transactions made by the entity are recorded, is called the **general ledger** or nominal ledger. This ledger is set up to include all accounts whether they are assets, liabilities, sales (or revenues), or costs (or expenses). The detail of every transaction finds its way into this ledger, or is posted to it (to use the technical term), in much the same way as we saw in the T accounts. The general ledger may be said to be the collection of every T account within the entity.

Within the general ledger one account or more will be established to represent cash transactions (including cheques, drafts, bank transfers, etc.). These entries are posted to the general ledger from the analysis of entries made into the cash book. The cash book is a book of original entry maintained to show the detail of all receipts and payments made by the entity; it records the dates, values and unique references of all receipts and payments, and what they are for. These include, for example, payment of salaries, receipts from customers, purchase of non-current assets, etc.

Cash book

The cash book is a book of account that in theory should match exactly with the regular statements issued by the entity's bank. In practice, the cash book is prepared partly from company internally generated **cash payments** information and available information relating to **cash receipts**. Some transactions may appear in the bank account without prior notification, for example bank charges, and so the cash book may also be partly prepared with reference to information from the bank statement.

There is a need to periodically check cash book balances against the balances shown on the bank statements supplied by the bank. The two numbers are rarely the same and so the differences between them need to be reconciled to ensure that cash book balances are correct. The regular preparation of a **bank reconciliation** on at least a monthly basis is therefore a necessary function of the finance department.

There are five main reasons for differences between cash book balances and the balances shown on bank statements:

- cash book arithmetic errors and incorrect postings of receipts and payments
- cash book omissions of items shown on the bank statements such as bank charges, standing orders, direct debits, and dishonoured (returned) cheques
- timing differences where cheques have been written and issued and entered in the cash book but have not yet been presented to the bank for payment at the date of the bank statement
- timing differences where cheques received have been entered in the cash book but have not yet been credited to the bank account at the date of the bank statement
- errors and overcharges made by the banks included in their statements but not reflected in the cash book (do not assume that bank statements are always correct: it is very important to always check interest and bank charges calculations in detail on a monthly basis, to identify errors and overcharges made by the banks).

All differences between the cash book and bank statement balance must be identified and any errors and omissions corrected in the cash book so that the updated cash book balance may be reconciled with the bank statement balance as follows:

	balance per cash book
plus:	**cheques paid but not yet presented**
minus:	**receipts not yet credited**
=	**balance per bank statement**

Each payment and each receipt is posted from the cash book to the cash account in the general ledger as a credit or debit to cash. The opposite entry, either debit or credit, is posted at the same time to its relevant account in the general ledger, for example accounts payable, printing and stationery expenses, accounts receivable, etc. In the days when accounting ledgers were maintained manually such postings were made weekly or monthly. With computerised, integrated accounting systems postings may be made simultaneously to the cash book and the general ledger from the same source but avoiding any duplication of effort.

It is most important that the balance on the cash book, the net of all receipts and payments, at all times equals the balance of the cash book represented in the cash account within the general ledger, and that all the opposite entries have also been posted to their relevant accounts. In this way, the equality of total debits and total credits is maintained. The use of computerised accounting systems should guarantee this.

Worked example 2.9

The debit balance on the cash book of Renfrew Ltd at 31 May 2010 is £4,800, but the bank statement at the same date shows a balance of £6,768. A comparison of the company's cash book with the bank statements has identified the following differences at 31 May 2010:

Cheques received amounting to £1,986 have been entered in the cash book prior to 31 May 2010 and paid into the bank but have not been credited to Renfrew's account until 5 June.

Cheques paid amounting to £4,364 have been entered in the cash book but not presented for payment and shown on the bank statement until after 31 May 2010.

Bank charges of £180 have been included in the bank statement but have not been entered in the cash book.

Dividends received of £220 appear on the bank statement but have not been entered into the cash book.

A cheque received from a credit customer for £450 was entered in the cash book and paid into the bank, but on 30 May this was returned unpaid because the customer had fled to South America.

First, we need to make the appropriate corrections to the cash book.

		£
	balance per cash book	4,800
plus:	dividends received	220
minus:	bank charges	180
	returned cheque	450
		4,390

We can now prepare a bank reconciliation as at 31 May 2010.

		£
	balance per cash book	4,390
plus:	cheques paid but not yet presented	4,364
minus:	receipts not yet credited	1,986
	balance per bank statement	6,768

Accounts payable

Payables are recorded in a ledger, the accounts payable account, which represents all supplier account balances owed by the entity. Within the general ledger one account or more (control accounts) will be established to represent trade payables transactions, the purchases by the entity for which invoices have been rendered by suppliers, or vendors. All supplier invoices are recorded in accounts payable and analysed into the various items of expense by allocating them to a specific general ledger control account. These entries are debited to the appropriate general ledger accounts from the analysis of supplier invoices that are posted to accounts payable. The totals of these entries are credited to the control account representing accounts payable in the general ledger.

The accounts payable ledger is maintained to show the detail of all invoices received from and cash paid to suppliers. In addition to its functions of posting the totals of invoices to the accounts payable control account in the general ledger, and the analysis of what the invoices represent to the appropriate accounts in the general ledger, accounts payable may be analysed to show all invoices, credit notes, cash payments, etc. and grouped by supplier.

Payments made to suppliers are recorded in the cash book, and are credited to the cash account and debited to the accounts payable control account in the general ledger. They are also recorded in detail by amount, date and supplier within the trade payables supplier accounts. In this way it can be seen that the total balances at any one time of all supplier accounts within accounts payable equal the balance on the accounts payable control account in the general ledger.

Accounts receivable

Receivables are recorded in another ledger – the accounts receivable account, which represents all customer account balances owed to the entity. Within the general ledger one account or more will be established (control accounts) to represent accounts receivable transactions – the sales by the entity for which invoices have been issued to customers. All customer invoices are recorded in accounts receivable and analysed into the various items of sale or revenue by allocating them to a specific general ledger control account. These entries are credited to the appropriate general ledger accounts from the analysis of customer invoices posted to accounts receivable. The totals of these entries are debited to the control account(s) representing accounts receivable in the general ledger.

The accounts receivable ledger is maintained to show the detail of all invoices issued to and cash received from customers. The totals of customer invoices are posted to the accounts receivable control account in the general ledger. The analyses of what the invoices represent are posted to the appropriate accounts in the general ledger. The sales ledger may also enable each invoice to be analysed and grouped by customer.

Receipts from customers are recorded in the cash book, and are debited to the cash account and credited to the accounts receivable control account in the general ledger. They are also recorded in detail by amount, date and customer within the accounts receivable customer accounts. In this way the total balances at any one time of all customer accounts within accounts receivable equal the balance on the accounts receivable control account in the general ledger.

The cash accounts, accounts payable and accounts receivable control accounts in the general ledger are referred to as control accounts because they provide control over the same transactions which are also represented in some further detail, and which must agree in total, in what are termed the books of account and subsidiary ledgers: the cash book, accounts payable (purchase ledger), and accounts receivable (sales ledger).

Progress check 2.3

What are the usual books of account and ledgers you would expect to be used in a company's accounting system?

The trial balance

A **trial balance** is a list of account balances in a double-entry system. If the records have been correctly maintained, the sum of the debit balance accounts will be equal and opposite to the sum of the credit balance accounts, although certain errors such as omission of a transaction or erroneous entries will not be apparent in the trial balance. The importance of the trial balance is illustrated in the press extract on the next page.

Worked example 2.10

If we turn again to the Ayco example, we can see that each of the T accounts we have prepared represents the general (or nominal) ledger balances of the entity. These balances may be listed to form a trial balance for Ayco as at 31 January 2010.

The trial balance for Ayco as at 31 January 2010:

	Debit £	Credit £
Capital		50,000
Cash	16,800	
Non-current assets – shop	30,000	
Non-current assets – fittings	5,000	
Printing and stationery expenses	200	
Accounts payable		12,000
Inventories	3,000	
Sales revenue		18,000
Accounts receivable	16,000	
Cost of sales	9,000	
	80,000	80,000

From this simple trial balance it is possible to derive three reports that tell us something about the business: the income statement; the balance sheet; the statement of cash flows.

Balancing becomes a trial for Birmingham City Council

For the first time in its long history, Birmingham City Council's annual accounts have not been given a clean bill of health by auditors.

Inspectors found the books littered with errors, in particular an asset register supposedly listing the value of buildings owned by the local authority.

District Auditor Mark Stocks wrote to the council in January saying that numerous errors and 'significant weaknesses' in checks and controls meant that he still could not approve the 2008–09 accounts, more than four months after the books should have been signed off.

It was the third successive year that problems in agreeing the finances of Britain's largest public body had arisen.

The council responded by suggesting that most of the errors were little more than mistakes on paper which had no impact on the authority's financial position.

Mr Stocks has now approved the accounts, but he issued a 'qualified opinion' adding that he had been unable to substantiate all aspects of the asset register.

That led Corporate Resources Director Paul Dransfield, the council official with overall responsibility for the accounts, to admit that things had to improve.

Mr Dransfield said: 'I am not happy that we are in this position. There is a big learning curve for the finance team.'

Mr Stocks released a report outlining 44 individual mistakes and raising questions about the efficiency of the council's controversial Voyager IT system, which the District Auditor found did not produce an accurate record of expenses and assets.

Buildings worth £10.5 million which have been demolished or which the council no longer owns, including Matthew Boulton College, were incorrectly listed as assets on the system.

The Rowans day nursery in Sutton Coldfield, worth £400,000, was shown on the records as having been sold but is still in the council's ownership.

Schools worth £20.5 million, which are being rebuilt through Private Finance Initiative programmes and should have been off the balance sheet, were incorrectly listed as council assets.

Mr Stocks said that proper checks were not being carried out and £30 million of assets had been double counted.

A further £11 million of capital receipts that the council claimed it possessed could not be traced on Voyager.

The District Auditor said: 'Summary and detailed trial balance reports are not routinely generated from the Voyager system on a monthly basis. Consequently, there is an increased risk of imbalanced trial-balance being undetected, including the potential build up of uncleared items within control and suspense accounts.

'I am unable to conclude as to whether the asset register accurately reflects the properties owned by the council and whether the properties have been appropriately valued either due to oversight or posting errors.

'I do not consider that I have sufficient assurances to state that the asset register presents fairly the council's asset base.'

Mr Stocks went on to warn that he encountered 'significant difficulties' in reconciling the draft accounts for 2009–09 presented to the cabinet in June 2008.

He added: 'I concluded that the council has not made appropriate arrangements for maintaining a sound system of internal controls and, due to the difficulties in auditing the financial statements outlined already in this report, that it had not made appropriate arrangements for financial reporting.

'I was unable to obtain sufficient evidence that Birmingham City Council had the control environments fully embedded for its new financial systems to maintain a sound system of internal control. Due to the delays in their production there is also presently insufficient evidence that the council can produce financial statements that are free from material error.'

In an improvement plan, Mr Stocks insists that all errors and adjustments must be posted on Voyager to ensure that the opening balances for 2009–10 are accurate.

The improvement plan states: 'To ensure that an accurate set of draft accounts is produced, the Corporate Finance Team should ensure that it produces both a detailed and summary trial balance report from the Voyager system at key stages throughout the year. The trial-balance reports should be filed and made available for audit inspection purposes.'

Source: **Imaginary assets on council's accounts**, by Paul Dale © *The Birmingham Post*, 11 February 2010

How do we know which items in the trial balance are balance sheet items and which are income statement items? Well, if an item is not a cost (expense) or a sales revenue item, then it must be an asset or a liability. The expenses and revenues must appear in the income statement and the assets and liabilities must appear in the balance sheet. Even a computerised accounting system must be told the specific classification of a transaction.

Worked example 2.11

Let's examine each of the items in the Ayco trial balance as at 31 January 2010.

	Debit £	Credit £
Capital account		50,000
This represents the original money that the investor Mr Bean put into Ayco – not revenue or expense.		
Cash account	16,800	
This represents the total cash that Ayco has at its disposal at 31 January, an asset – not revenue or expense.		
Non-current assets – shop account	30,000	
This represents assets purchased out of cash to help run the business – not revenue or expense.		
Non-current assets – fittings account	5,000	
This represents assets purchased out of cash to help run the business – not revenue or expense.		
Printing and stationery expenses account	200	
This represents costs incurred on disposable items used in running the business through January – expense.		
Accounts payable		12,000
This represents debts which Ayco must pay in the next two months, a liability – not revenue or expense.		
Inventories account	3,000	
This represents items held in inventory to sell to customers over future periods, an asset – not revenue or expense.		
Sales revenue account		18,000
This represents the value of toys delivered to customers in January – revenue.		
Accounts receivable	16,000	
This represents debts for which Ayco will receive payment next month, an asset – not revenue or expense.		
Cost of sales account	9,000	
This represents the cost of toys delivered to customers in January – expense.		
	80,000	80,000

Income statement

The income statement shows the profit or loss generated by an entity during an accounting period by deducting all costs from total sales. Within the trial balance we may extract the balances on the costs (expenses) and sales revenue accounts in order to construct the income statement. The total sum of these accounts will then result in a balance which is a profit or a loss, and which may be inserted back into a restated trial balance in summary form in place of all the individual profit and loss items which make up that balance.

Worked example 2.12

The expense and revenue items, or the income statement items, may be extracted from Ayco's trial balance and summarised as follows:

	Debit	Credit
	£	£
Sales		18,000
Cost of sales	9,000	
Printing and stationery expenses	200	
Balance representing a profit for January	8,800	
	18,000	18,000

Although the £8,800 is shown in the debit column to balance the account, it is in fact a credit balance that is carried forward, that is a balance resulting from £18,000 total credits less total debits of £9,200.

Ayco income statement for January 2010

	£	£
Sales	18,000	
less		
Cost of sales	9,000	
Gross profit (gross margin)		9,000
Printing and stationery expenses		200
Net profit for January 2010		8,800

Balance sheet

The balance sheet of an entity discloses the assets (debit balances), and liabilities and shareholders' capital (credit balances), and profits (gains) or losses as at a given date. A gain or profit is a credit balance, and a loss is a debit balance. The revised trial balance, which includes the net balance of profit or loss, then forms the basis for the balance sheet. The balance sheet may then be constructed by rearranging the balances into an established format.

Worked example 2.13

Ayco's profit for January 2010 is a credit balance of £8,800, and if we substitute this back into Ayco's trial balance to replace the individual revenue and expense items we have:

	Debit £	Credit £
Capital		50,000
Cash	16,800	
Non-current assets – shop	30,000	
Non-current assets – fittings	5,000	
Accounts payable		12,000
Inventory	3,000	
Accounts receivable	16,000	
Profit for January		8,800
	70,800	70,800

To construct a balance sheet this needs to be rearranged into a more usual sort of format:

Ayco balance sheet as at 31 January 2010

	£	£		£	£
Assets			**Liabilities**		
Non-current assets		35,000	**Owner's investment**		
			Capital	50,000	
			Profit and loss account	8,800	
					58,800
Current assets			**Short-term liabilities**		
Accounts receivable	16,000		Accounts payable		12,000
Inventories	3,000				
Cash	16,800				
		35,800			
		70,800			70,800

Progress check 2.6

Outline what a balance sheet tells us about a company.

Statement of cash flows

The final report, the **statement of cash flows**, is simply a report on the detail of the movement within the cash account in the trial balance. This starts with the opening balance, shows the receipts and payments during the accounting period, and results in the closing balance.

Worked example 2.14

The final report, the statement of cash flows, may be constructed by looking at the elements that are included in Ayco's cash T account, that is the elements which make up the total movements in the cash account in the general ledger:

	Debit £	Credit £
Cash balance at 1 January 2010	–	
Receipt from Mr Bean – capital for business	50,000	
Payment for freehold shop		30,000
Payment for shop fittings		5,000
Payment for printing and stationery expenses		200
Receipt from customers	2,000	
Cash balance at 31 January 2010		16,800
	52,000	52,000

The £16,800 debit balance brought forward represents a positive cash position of £16,800.

The aim of the last few sections has been to explain the basics of double-entry bookkeeping and the sources of accounting data, and to provide an introduction to the accounting ledgers and books of account. This begins to show how the information from double-entry bookkeeping records may be effectively used. The inclusion of the rudimentary financial statements shown above illustrates the importance of the:

- accuracy
- timeliness
- completeness

of the financial data included in the double-entry system.

Progress check 2.7

Outline what a statement of cash flows tells us about a company.

Accrual accounting and cash accounting

We have already covered a number of important accounting ideas and concepts, one of which is that profit does not necessarily equal cash. This was apparent from the Ayco worked examples. The net cash movement in the month of January was an inflow, a positive of £16,800. However, the income statement showed a gain, a profit of £8,800. The reason that they were not identical was first (as shown in the statement of cash flows) due to cash items other than those associated with trading, for example receipt of the original capital, and expenditure on non-current assets. Second, the trading or operational transactions were not all converted into cash within the month of January; they were held as trade payables, inventory and trade receivables.

The approach that we took in the Ayco examples demonstrated compliance with the accruals concept, or matching concept, the principle that revenues and costs are:

- recognised as they are earned or incurred
- matched with one another
- dealt with in the income statement of the period to which they relate, irrespective of the period of cash receipt or cash payment.

Progress check 2.8

In what way does a company's income statement differ from the movements on its cash account during an accounting period?

Accruals

It may be that an expense has been incurred within an accounting period, for which an invoice may or may not have been received. For example, electricity used, telephone charges incurred, or stationery supplies received and used. We have talked about the concept of matching costs with sales revenues. Costs not necessarily related to sales cannot be matched in that way. Such charges must be matched to the accounting period to which they relate, and therefore an estimate of the cost (an accrual) must be made and included as an accounting adjusting entry in the accounts for that period.

Figure 2.5 shows an invoice dated 15 April 2010 received by a company from its communications provider for charges of £2,000 for the period January to March 2010. At the end of April 2010 the company had not yet received its bill for the next quarter even though it had use of telephone lines and had incurred call charges. We may assume that the company's accounting year runs from January to December. Therefore, before finalising its income statement for January to April the company needed to estimate its telephone costs for April, which are shown as £700.

The estimate of £700 has been charged, or debited, to telephone costs in the profit and loss account, and a temporary payable, an accrual, credited in the balance sheet for £700. The total telephone costs charged to the profit and loss account for January to April 2010 are therefore £2,700. The accrual carried forward at the end of April would normally be reversed and the position assessed again at the end of May, and the same procedure followed at the end of June. By the end of July the invoice would normally be expected to have been received covering the period April to June and so no accrual will be necessary. However, an accrual will be required for the month of July.

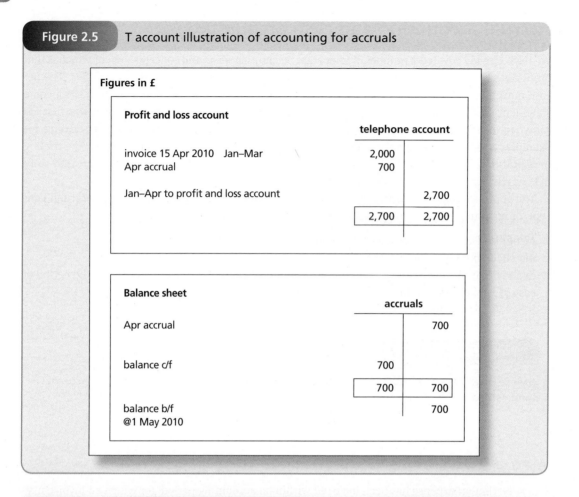

Figure 2.5   T account illustration of accounting for accruals

Worked example 2.15

From the following information we are required to prepare three-column accounts (in an Excel **spreadsheet** or in a Word table) to reflect the current balances on each account, which are then required to be adjusted for the accruals at 31 December 2010 to show the total transfer to the profit and loss account. We are also required to show a summary of the accruals as at 31 December 2010.

	£
Balances at 31 December 2010	
Electricity	10,000
Gas	11,000
Telephone	5,000
Interest on overdraft	6,000
Accruals required at 31 December 2010	
Electricity	500
Gas	600
Telephone	500
Interest on overdraft	600

Accruals adjustments at 31 December 2010:

	Debit £	Credit £	Balance £
Electricity			
31 December 2010			10,000
Accrual 31 December 2010	500		10,500
Transfer to profit and loss account		(10,500)	0
Gas			
31 December 2010			11,000
Accrual 31 December 2010	600		11,600
Transfer to profit and loss account		(11,600)	0
Telephone			
31 December 2010			5,000
Accrual 31 December 2010	500		5,500
Transfer to profit and loss account		(5,500)	0
Interest payable on overdraft			
31 December 2010			6,000
Accrual 31 December 2010	600		6,600
Transfer to profit and loss account		(6,600)	0
Accruals 31 December 2010			
Electricity		(500)	(500)
Gas		(600)	(1,100)
Telephone		(500)	(1,600)
Interest payable on overdraft		(600)	(2,200)

The same sort of exercise is carried out within a company for all the categories of expense for which accruals are likely to be required. Worked example 2.16 explains how accruals may have been dealt with in Ayco.

Worked example 2.16

The accruals concept could have been further illustrated in the Ayco scenario by the introduction of a number of additional factors. Assume, for example, that Ayco had used more than £200 of stationery in the month, say £1,000. We know that Ayco had been invoiced for and paid for £200 worth of stationery.

If £500 worth of the additional stationery had been used, and an invoice had been received but not processed through the ledgers, what would be the impact on Ayco? If £300 worth of the additional stationery had been used, and an invoice had not yet been received but was in the mail what would be the impact on Ayco?

The answer is that both would have to be debited to printing and stationery expenses for a total of £800, and credited not to accounts payable but to accruals.

Accruals are treated in a similar way to accounts payable but the invoices for these charges have not yet been processed by the entity. They are charges which are brought into the period because, although goods (or services) have been provided, they have not yet been included in the suppliers' accounts.

Expense recognition is an important concept. Expenses should be recognised immediately they are known about. Ayco knew they had used stationery for which there was a cost even though an invoice may not have been processed. On the other hand, revenues or profits should not be recognised until they are earned.

The net impact of the above on Ayco would have been a reduction in profit, a debit of £800 and an increase in liabilities, a credit of £800 to accruals. The accruals entries would need to be exactly reversed at the beginning of the following month to avoid a doubling up since the actual transactions will also be processed.

Prepayments

It may be that an expense has been incurred within an accounting period that related to future period(s). For example, property taxes, rents or vehicle licence fees paid in advance. As with accruals, these costs are not necessarily related to sales and cannot be matched with sales. Such charges must also be matched to the period to which they relate and therefore the proportion of the charges that relates to future periods (a prepayment) must be calculated and included as an adjustment in the accounts for that period. Figure 2.6 shows a charge of £6,000 that has been incurred by a company from its landlord on 1 January 2010 for rent for the period January to June 2010. At the end of

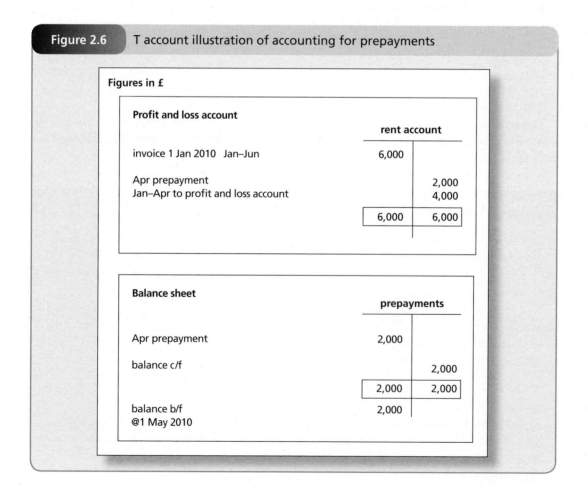

Figure 2.6 T account illustration of accounting for prepayments

Figures in £

Profit and loss account

	rent account	
invoice 1 Jan 2010 Jan–Jun	6,000	
Apr prepayment		2,000
Jan–Apr to profit and loss account		4,000
	6,000	6,000

Balance sheet

	prepayments	
Apr prepayment	2,000	
balance c/f		2,000
	2,000	2,000
balance b/f	2,000	
@1 May 2010		

April 2010 the company had paid rent not only for January to April, but rent in advance for May and June. Therefore, before finalising its profit and loss account for January to April the company needed to calculate the rent in advance for May and June, which is shown as £2,000.

The rent in advance of £2,000 has been credited to the rent account and a temporary receivable, a prepayment, created in the balance sheet for £2,000. The total rent costs charged to the profit and loss account for January to April 2010 are therefore £4,000. The prepayment carried forward at the end of April would normally be reversed and the position assessed again at the end of May, and the same procedure followed at the end of June. By the end of July a charge would normally be expected to have been received covering the period July to December and so a prepayment will be necessary at the end of July for the period August to December.

Worked example 2.17

From the following information we are required to prepare three-column accounts (in an Excel spreadsheet or in a Word table) to reflect the current balances on each account, which are then required to be adjusted for the prepayments, deferred income and accrued income at 31 December 2010, to show the total transfer to the profit and loss account. We are also required to show a summary of the prepayments and accrued income, and accruals and deferred income as at 31 December 2010.

	£
Balances at 31 December 2010	
Rent paid	12,000
Property taxes paid	13,000
Interest received	7,000 (credit)
Rent received	8,000 (credit)

Prepayments, accrued income, and deferred income required at 31 December 2010	
Rent paid	700 (normally paid in advance)
Property taxes paid	800 (normally paid in advance)
Interest receivable	700 (normally received in arrears)
Rent received	800 (normally received in advance)

Prepayments and accruals adjustments at 31 December 2010

	Debit £	Credit £	Balance £
Rent payable			
31 December			12,000
Prepayment 31 December 2010		(700)	11,300
Transfer to profit and loss account		(11,300)	0
Property taxes			
31 December			13,000
Prepayment 31 December 2010		(800)	12,200
Transfer to profit and loss account		(12,200)	0
Interest receivable			
31 December			(7,000)
Accrued income 31 December 2010		(700)	(7,700)
Transfer to profit and loss account	7,700		0

Rent receivable		
31 December		(8,000)
Deferred income 31 December 2010	800	(7,200)
Transfer to profit and loss account	7,200	0
Prepayments and accrued income		
31 December 2010		0
Rent paid	700	700
Property taxes paid	800	1,500
Interest receivable	700	2,200
Accruals and deferred income		
31 December 2010		0
Rent received	(800)	(800)

The same sort of exercise is carried out within a company for all the categories of expense for which prepayments are likely to be required. Worked example 2.18 explains how prepayments may have been dealt with in Ayco.

Worked example 2.18

Assume, for example, that Ayco had received an invoice for £2,000 for advertising in January to be paid in March, but the advertising was not taking place until February. An invoice may have been received and processed through the ledgers, but what would be the impact on Ayco?

The answer is that accounts payable would have been credited with £2,000 and advertising expenses debited with £2,000 in the month of January. However, because the advertising had not taken place, the charge of £2,000 would be considered as being in advance, or to use its technical term a prepayment. The accounts payable entry remains as a credit of £2,000, but an additional entry is required to credit advertising expenses with £2,000 and debit prepayments with £2,000.

A prepayment is expenditure on goods (or services) for future benefit, which is to be charged to future operations. Such amounts are similar to trade receivables and are included in current assets in the balance sheet.

The net impact of the above on Ayco would have been no charge to profit. The prepayment entry would need to be exactly reversed at the beginning of the following month.

Progress check 2.9

What are accruals and prepayments and why are such adjusting entries needed?

Accounting periods

In the Ayco worked examples we were introduced to the idea of an accounting period. An accounting period is that covered by the accounting statements of an entity. Different periods may be chosen within the financial year, for example 13 periods of four weeks, 12 periods using a four, four, five-week quarter basis, or 12 calendar periods. The Ayco worked examples assumed 12 periods on a calendar basis. Once an accounting period basis has been chosen, consistency must be maintained. This is an example of both the periodicity concept and the consistency concept (see Chapter 1).

Progress check 2.10

What is an accounting period?

Summary of key points

- Double-entry bookkeeping is a convention, the two main objectives of which are to have a permanent record of transactions, and to show the effect of each transaction and the combined effect of all the transactions upon the financial position of the entity.

- Double-entry bookkeeping data are recorded as transactions described as 'debits' and 'credits'.

- The meaning of a debit and a credit may most usefully be remembered using the following rule, applying to entries reflected in the accounts of a company:

Cash receipt	= debit cash account and credit another account
Cash payment	= credit cash account and debit another account
Purchase invoice	= credit accounts payable and debit another account
Sales invoice	= debit accounts receivable and credit another account.

- The main ledger held within the accounting system of a company is called the general ledger, or nominal ledger, in which the results of all transactions made by the company are recorded either in summary or in detail.

- The original books of account, and subsidiary ledgers: cash book (receipts and payments); purchase invoice daybook and accounts payable (or purchase ledger); sales invoice daybook and accounts receivable (or sales ledger), hold the details of transactions that are reflected in the general ledger.

- Wages and salaries data are recorded in the cash books and posted to the general ledger.

- Adjusting accounting entries, such as those relating to closing inventories valuations, are made to the accounts prior to preparation of the income statement and balance sheet.

- There are five main accounting adjustments that are made prior to preparation of the income statement and balance sheet:
  - closing inventories
  - accruals: charges not yet received
  - prepayments: payments in advance (and income accrued)
  - depreciation
  - bad and doubtful debts.

- The balances on the individual accounts recorded within the general ledger may be summarised in a trial balance, the total of the debit balances being equal to the total of the credit balances.

- The income statement of an entity shows the profit or loss generated by the entity during an accounting period by deducting all expenses from all revenues.

- The balance sheet of an entity discloses the assets (debit balances) and liabilities and shareholders' capital (credit balances), and gains (credits) or losses (debits) as at a given date.

- The statement of cash flows is a report on the detail of the movement within the cash account in the trial balance, starting with the opening balance and adding the receipts and deducting the payments during the accounting period, resulting in the closing balance.

- The accounting period chosen by a business is the period covered by its financial statements.

Assessment material

Questions

Q2.1 What are the four basic business transactions and what are their corresponding debit and credit accounting entries under the convention of double-entry bookkeeping?

Q2.2 (i) Name each of the books of account and ledgers in an accounting system.
(ii) What are they used for?

Q2.3 Describe the use and purpose of the five main accounting adjusting entries.

Q2.4 (i) At a specific point in time, what does a company's trial balance show?
(ii) What may the trial balance not show?

Q2.5 How may the financial performance of a company be ascertained from its trial balance?

Q2.6 How may the financial position of a company be ascertained from its trial balance?

Q2.7 How may the cash position of a company be ascertained from its trial balance?

Q2.8 Why is the profit made during an accounting period not necessarily equal to the cash flow during that period?

Q2.9 In what ways do businesses adjust their accounts for accruals and prepayments?

Q2.10 What is the relevance of the accounting period?

Discussion points

D2.1 'Managers who are non-accounting specialists don't need to learn about bookkeeping, debits and credits, etc.' Discuss.

D2.2 Computerised accounts and information systems have speeded up the recording of accounting data and the presentation of information. What are the other advantages over manual accounting systems and what are the disadvantages?

Exercises

Solutions are provided in Appendix 2 to all exercise numbers highlighted in colour.

Level I

E2.1 *Time allowed – 30 minutes*

Extracts from the ledgers of Hall Ltd have provided the following information for 2009 and 2010.

	£
Sales revenue 2009	11,000
Sales revenue 2010	12,000
Purchases 2009	7,100
Purchases 2010	8,300
Expenses 2009	2,500
Expenses 2010	2,800
Inventories 1 January 2009	600
Inventories 31 December 2009	700
Inventories 31 December 2010	800
Obsolete inventories included in 31 December 2010 inventories	200

You are required to prepare a basic income statement for the years ended 31 December 2009 and 2010.

E2.2 *Time allowed – 30 minutes*

(a) **Explain why there are always problems at the year end in the assessment of the costs associated with electricity, gas and telephone.**

(b) **Using the information below, prepare the appropriate year-end accounting entries.**

Electricity charges account balance at 15 December 2010: £10,000
Gas charges account balance at 20 December 2010: £5,000
Estimated consumption
Electricity 16 December to 31 December 2010: £300
Gas 21 December to 31 December 2010: £150

E2.3 *Time allowed – 30 minutes*

Arthur Moment set up a table-making business, Forlegco, on 1 July 2010. He had £10,000 available to invest, which is the amount he estimated was required for setting up costs. In the first month of trading Forlegco entered into the following transactions:

	£
£10,000 from Arthur Moment	10,000
Purchase of hand tools for cash	2,000
Purchase of lathe, power saw and drill on one month's credit	6,000
Purchase of printing and stationery – invoice received for half the order	100
The total order is £200, and it was all delivered in July and used	
Purchase of advertising flyers for cash 2,000 at 50p each, of which 1,000 will be used in July, and 500 in August and September	

Purchases of timber, glue and varnish, from Woodco, payable within the month £1,500 – half of this inventory will be on hand at 31 July 2010

Sales of tables to Gardenfurnco for settlement one month later (10 tables at £700 each)

> You are required to present these transactions in T account format, and then prepare a trial balance for Forlegco for 31 July 2010.

E2.4 *Time allowed – 30 minutes*

> From the trial balance for Forlegco for 31 July 2010 (Exercise E2.3)
>
> (i)   Prepare a simple income statement for the month of July 2010.
> (ii) Has Forlegco made a profit in July?
> (iii) If Forlegco has not made a profit, why not?

E2.5 *Time allowed – 30 minutes*

> From the trial balance for Forlegco for 31 July 2010 (Exercise E2.3) prepare a simple balance sheet at that date.

E2.6 *Time allowed – 30 minutes*

> From the trial balance for Forlegco for 31 July 2010 (Exercise E2.3) prepare a simple statement of cash flows for the month of July 2010.

E2.7 *Time allowed – 30 minutes*

> You are required to prepare the appropriate correcting entries in a company's accounts at 31 December 2010 for the following:
>
> (i)   A cheque paid for rent amounting to £2,400 has been entered into the car hire account in error.
> (ii)   A cheque for £980 was received from a customer in full settlement of a balance of £1,000, but no accounting entry for the discount has been made.
> (iii) A cheque paid for insurance on the company cars amounting to £1,200 has been entered in the cost of motor cars account in error.
> (iv)   An invoice from a builder for £3,500 has been entered in the buildings cost account, but in fact it related to redecoration of the reception area of the office and should be treated as a building repair.

Level II

E2.8 *Time allowed – 60 minutes*

David (Dai) Etcoak decided to set up a drinks wholesale business, Etcoakco, on 1 December 2009. He had £100,000 available to invest, which is the amount he felt was required to set up the business. In the first month of trading Etcoakco entered into the following transactions:

	£
£100,000 from Dai Etcoak	100,000
Purchase for cash the freehold of a shop	50,000
Purchase for cash the shop fittings	7,000

	£
Purchase of a labelling machine payable one month later	20,000
Cash expenses on printing and stationery	400
Purchases of inventory, from Gasco, of bottles of pop, payable three months later	
(25,000 bottles at £1.25 each)	31,250
Sales of bottles of Etcoak to Boozah for settlement one month later	
(10,000 bottles at £2.30 each)	23,000
Sales of bottles of Etcoak to Disco30, receivable in the month	
(12,000 bottles at £2.30 each)	27,600

You are required to:

(i)   look at these transactions in detail and then present them in T account format, and

(ii)   state any assumptions you have made particularly relating to how you have valued inventories transactions.

Also:

(iii) Do you think £100,000 was enough money or too much to invest in the business?

(iv) What alternative courses of action are open to Dai?

3

Financial statements of limited companies – balance sheet

Contents

Learning objectives

Completion of this chapter will enable you to:

■ explain the differences in accounting treatment of capital expenditure and revenue expenditure

■ identify the financial information shown in the financial statements of a company: balance sheet; income statement; statement of cash flows

■ construct simple financial statements

■ outline the structure of the balance sheet of a limited company

■ classify the broad balance sheet categories of shareholders' equity, liabilities, and assets

■ outline the alternative balance sheet formats

■ prepare a balance sheet

■ evaluate some of the alternative methods of asset valuation

■ appreciate the limitations of the conventional balance sheet.

Introduction

We talked about business entities in general in Chapter 1. The financial accounting and reporting of limited companies are similar to those of sole traders and partnerships, except that they are more detailed and require a greater disclosure of information. This is to comply with current legislation and the requirements for reporting of financial information to the owners of the business (the shareholders).

Each type of business is required to prepare periodic financial statements in one form or another for internal control purposes, the shareholders and, for example, HM Revenue & Customs. The current chapter and Chapters 4 and 5 provide a comprehensive coverage of financial statements, which are the basis for the subsequent chapters about business performance analysis and published reports and accounts.

We will be looking in a little more detail at the profit and loss account and income statement in Chapter 4 and the balance sheet later in this chapter. The terms income statement and profit and loss account have often been used interchangeably. To conform with International Accounting Standards (IASs) and International Financial Reporting Standards (IFRSs) requirements, the financial statement that companies in the UK and many other countries had hitherto called the profit and loss account is now called the income statement. The financial statements in this book comply with that requirement. However, the term profit and loss account is still used throughout this book but essentially to describe that part of the general ledger that includes all the revenue and cost accounts, as distinct from all the asset, liability and equity accounts which are included within the balance sheet part of the general ledger.

Each of the financial statements includes expenditure of one form or another. This chapter begins by broadly looking at types of expenditure and explaining what is meant by revenue expenditure and capital expenditure. Most items may be clearly identified in terms of revenue or capital expenditure, but there are also a number of uncertain areas in these classifications with regard to the rules used in accounting and in the way that expenditure may be analysed for taxation purposes.

Before dealing specifically with the balance sheets of limited companies we will discuss the subject of financial statements that was introduced in Chapter 1. We will see how these are constructed and interrelated, by working through a comprehensive example that illustrates how transactions are reflected in the income statement, balance sheet and statement of cash flows of a business.

This chapter deals with how balance sheets are structured and how the accounts within the balance sheet are categorised. Each of the items within each of the balance sheet categories will be described in detail and form the basis that enables the preparation of a balance sheet of a limited company in the appropriate format.

The chapter closes by illustrating the subjective nature of the balance sheet and considers the areas in which this is apparent through looking at examples of the alternative methods for valuation of assets that are available to companies.

Capital expenditure and revenue expenditure

Expenditure made by an entity falls generally within two types:

- **revenue expenditure**
- **capital expenditure**.

Revenue expenditure relates to expenditure incurred in the manufacture of products, the provision of services or in the general conduct of the company, which is normally charged to the profit and loss account in the accounting period in which it is incurred or when the products and services are sold. This expenditure includes repairs and depreciation of non-current assets as distinct from the provision of these assets. Revenue expenditure relates to expenditure on those items where the full benefit is received within the normal accounting period. The accruals (matching) concept says that sales must be recognised in the period in which they are earned, and the costs incurred in achieving those sales must also be recognised in the same period. Therefore the costs of revenue expenditure appear under the appropriate headings within the profit and loss account of the period in which the benefits are consumed and the costs are therefore incurred.

In some circumstances expenditure, which would normally be treated as revenue expenditure, is not written off in one period. This is called deferred revenue expenditure and relates to, for example, extensive expenditure on an advertising campaign over a period of months.

Capital expenditure (not to be confused with share capital or capital account, which are something completely different) relates to the cost of acquiring, producing or enhancing non-current assets. Capital expenditure is extremely important because it is usually much higher in value and follows the appropriate authorisation of expenditure on items of plant or equipment, or on a specific project. Such expenditure is usually expected to generate future earnings for the entity, protect existing revenue or profit levels, or provide compliance with, for example, health and safety or fire regulation requirements. Capital expenditure does not necessarily relate directly to sales derived in the period that the expenditure was made. It relates to expenditure on those items where the benefit from them is received over a number of future accounting periods. Therefore, capital expenditure items are held and carried forward to subsequent accounting periods until such time as their costs must be matched with sales or other benefits derived from their use. Accordingly, such items should appear in the balance sheet under the heading non-current assets. The values of these items are reduced during each subsequent accounting period as the appropriate portions of their cost are charged to the profit and loss account to match the sales or other benefits deriving from their use. Receipts from the disposal of non-current assets also appear under the non-current assets heading in the balance sheet. They are not treated as sales in the profit and loss account.

Control over capital expenditure is maintained through procedures for authorisation and subsequent monitoring of capital expenditure. Capital expenditure proposals are formal requests for authority to incur capital expenditure. Organisations usually require capital expenditure proposals to be supported by detailed qualitative and quantitative justifications for the expenditure, in accordance with the company's capital investment criteria. Levels of authority for expenditure must be clearly defined. The reporting structure of actual expenditure must also be aligned with the appropriate authority levels.

In addition to the actual plant or equipment cost some revenue-type expenditure such as delivery, installation and financing costs may also, where appropriate, be treated as capital expenditure. Such expenditure is described as being capitalised. In many circumstances revenue items must be capitalised as they are considered part of the acquisition cost, and in other circumstances revenue items may optionally be capitalised as part of the acquisition cost. In many circumstances it is not always possible to provide a clear ruling.

The general rule is that if the expenditure is as a result of: (a) a first-time acquisition, delivery and commissioning of a non-current asset; or relates to (b) improving the asset from when it was first acquired, then it is capital expenditure. If the expenditure is neither of these two types then it is normally revenue expenditure. The following examples of expenditure illustrate some of the circumstances that may prompt the question 'is it revenue or capital expenditure?'

Repairs are usually treated as revenue expenditure, but if, for example, some second-hand plant is purchased and some immediate repair costs are incurred which are necessary to make it efficient for the company's purpose, then such repairs become capital expenditure and are therefore added to the plant cost as part of the acquisition cost. Salaries and wages are revenue items. However, salaries and wages paid to employees to erect and fit some new machinery that has been acquired must be considered as an addition to the cost of the machinery.

Legal expenses are usually treated as revenue expenditure. But the legal expenses of conveyancing when purchasing a factory must be treated as part of the cost of the factory. Finance changes incurred during, say, the building of a factory or installation of plant and machinery may be capitalised so long as such a policy is applied consistently.

Apportionment of expenditure

Some items of expenditure require an apportionment of costs. This means that part of the cost is charged as capital expenditure and the balance is written off immediately as revenue expenditure. This is frequently the case within the uncertain area of improvements, alterations and extensions to plant and buildings. Capitalisation of the whole may not be prudent, since the value of the plant or building may not be enhanced to anything near the amount of money that may have been spent. The prudent policy may be not to permanently capitalise any expenditure that is not represented by assets, although legally this may be acceptable.

You may question why the distinction between capital and revenue expenditure is so important. We have already touched on the prudence concept and the consistency concept. The matching concept requires a company to match income, or sales revenue, and costs as closely as possible to the time period to which they relate. If the expected life of a non-current asset acquired to generate income is, say, five years then the costs of that asset should be spread over five years to match the realisation of the income it generates. It is therefore important to ensure that all the costs associated with the acquisition, installation and commissioning of the asset are included as part of its capitalised cost.

The amount of corporation tax that a company must pay on the profits it has generated is not computed simply as a percentage of profit. Depending on the tax rules currently in force, many revenue items may be disallowable expenses so far as taxable profit is concerned. In a similar way the treatment of capital expenditure in terms of allowances against taxation also has an impact on the amount of tax payable by the company.

Worked example 3.1

The following table illustrates how various items of expenditure are normally classified as either capital expenditure or revenue expenditure.

Revenue expenditure	Capital expenditure
Wages and salaries	Computer software
Interest payable	Goodwill
Travel expenses	Enhancement of a moulding machine
Repairs to the factory building	Patents
Professional fees	Office desk

Financial statements of limited companies

In Chapter 1 we introduced the topic of the financial statements that businesses need to prepare for each accounting period to provide adequate information about the financial performance and the financial position of the business.

We will now look in more detail at the three key financial statements (see Figure 3.1): balance sheet, income statement and statement of cash flows.

Balance sheet

The balance sheet summarises the financial position of the business; it is a financial snapshot at a moment in time. It may be compared to looking at a DVD. In 'play' mode the DVD is showing what is happening as time goes on second by second. If you press 'pause' the DVD stops on a picture. The

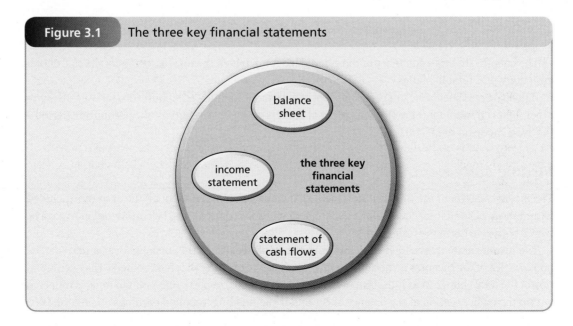

Figure 3.1   The three key financial statements

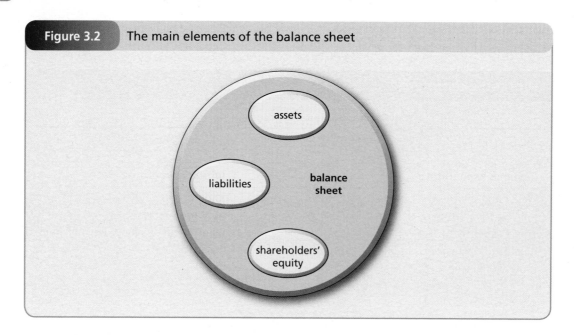

Figure 3.2   The main elements of the balance sheet

picture does not tell you what has happened over the period of time up to the pause (or what is going to happen after the pause). The balance sheet is the financial position of the company at the 'pause' position. It is the consequence of everything that has happened up to that time. It does not explain how the company got to that position, it just shows the results of financial impacts of events and decisions up to the balance sheet date. The year end may be 31 December, but other dates may be chosen. A company's year end date is (normally) the same date each year.

The balance sheet comprises a number of categories, within the three main elements (see Figure 3.2), which are labelled **assets, liabilities** or shareholders' equity (usually referred to as just **equity**). The assets are debit balances and the liabilities and shareholders' equity are credit balances. (Note: the concepts of debit and credit, and double-entry bookkeeping were fully covered in Chapter 2.) The balance sheet is always in balance so that

$$\text{total assets (TA)} = \text{equity (E)} + \text{total liabilities (TL)}$$

The balance sheet is a summary of the general ledger in which the total assets equal the shareholders' equity plus total liabilities.

If the balance sheet is the financial snapshot at a moment in time – the 'pause' on the DVD – the two other financial statements are the equivalent of what is going on throughout the accounting period – the 'play' mode on the DVD.

Income statement

The income statement is a financial statement that summarises the total of all the accounts included within the profit and loss section of the general ledger. Profit (or loss) may be considered in two ways, which both give the same result.

The income statement shows the change in the book wealth of the business over a period. The book wealth of the business is the amount it is worth to the owners, the shareholders. The accumulation of the total change in wealth since the business began, up to a particular point in time, is reflected within the equity section of the balance sheet under the heading 'retained earnings'. Using the DVD

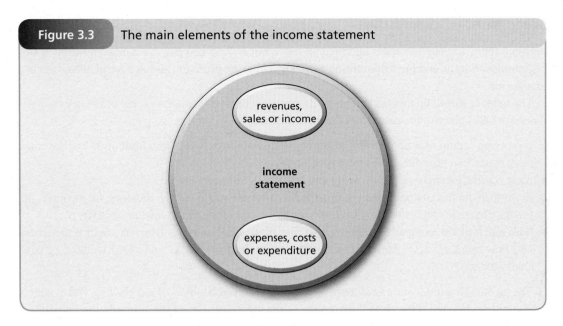

Figure 3.3   The main elements of the income statement

analogy, the income statement measures the change in the balance sheet from one 'pause' to another. An increase in equity is a profit and a decrease in equity is a loss.

The income statement may also be considered in its measurement of the trading performance of the business (see Figure 3.3). The income statement calculates whether or not the company has made a profit or loss on its operations during the period, through producing and selling its goods or services. The result, the earnings, net income or **profit** (or loss), is derived from deducting expenses incurred from revenues derived throughout the period between two 'pauses'. The income statement is dealt with in detail in Chapter 4.

The profit and loss account comprises the total of the expenses (debits) accounts and revenues (credits) accounts within the general ledger. The total of these may be a net debit or a net credit. A net debit represents a loss and a net credit represents a profit. The profit or loss is reflected in the balance sheet of the business under the heading retained earnings, which is part of shareholders' equity. All the other accounts within the general ledger, other than expenses and revenues, may be summarised into various other non-profit and loss account categories and these represent all the other balances that complete the overall balance sheet of the business.

There are three main points to consider regarding the income statement and how it differs from the statement of cash flows. First, revenues (or sales, or sales revenues, or income) and expenses (or costs or expenditure) are not necessarily accounted for when cash transfers occur. Sales are normally accounted for when goods or services are delivered and accepted by the customer. Cash will rarely be received immediately from the customer, except in businesses like high-street retailers and supermarkets; it is normally received weeks or months later.

Second, the income statement does not take into account all the events that impact on the financial position of the company. For example, an issue of new **shares** in the company, or a loan to the company, will increase cash but they are neither revenue nor expenses.

Third, non-cash flow items, for example depreciation and provisions for doubtful debts, reduce the profit, or increase the loss, of the company but do not represent outflows of cash. These topics will be covered in detail in the next chapter.

Therefore it can be seen that net profit is not the same as cash flow. A company may get into financial difficulties if it suffers a severe shortage of **cash and cash equivalents** even though it may have positive net earnings (profit).

Statement of cash flows

Between them, the balance sheet and income statement show a company's financial position at the beginning and at the end of an accounting period and how the profit or loss has been achieved during that period.

The balance sheet and income statement do not show or directly analyse some of the key changes that have taken place in the company's financial position, for example:

- how much capital expenditure (for example, equipment, machinery and buildings) has the company made, and how did it fund the expenditure?
- what was the extent of new borrowing and how much **debt** was repaid?
- how much did the company need to fund new **working capital** (which includes, for example, an increase in trade receivables and **inventories** as a result of increased business activity)?
- how much of the company's funding was met by funds generated from its trading activities, and how much by new external funding (for example, from banks and other lenders, or new shareholders)?

The income statement and the statement of cash flows (see Figure 3.4) are the two 'DVDs' which are running in parallel between the two 'pauses' – the balance sheets at the start and the finish of an accounting period. However, the statement of cash flows goes further in answering the questions like those shown above. The aim of the statement of cash flows is to summarise the cash inflows and outflows and calculate the net change in the cash position of the company throughout the period between two 'pauses'.

Progress check 3.1

Explain the fundamental differences between the types of information presented in each of the three key financial statements.

Figure 3.4   The main elements of the statement of cash flows

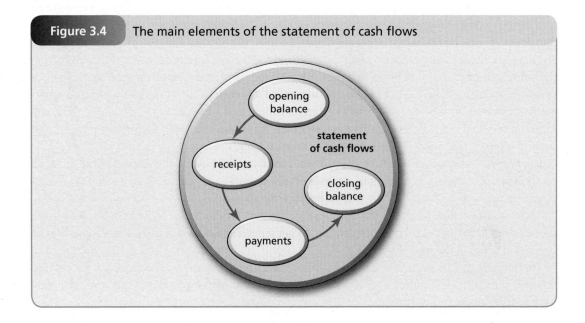

Construction and use of financial statements

An example will best illustrate how financial statements may be constructed. We will use the example of Mr Bean's business, Ayco (see also Worked example 2.1, Chapter 2), to track how some simple transactions are reflected in the income statement, statement of cash flows and balance sheet.

Worked examples 3.2 to 3.5 will look at the four one-week periods during Ayco's first month of trading and show the income statement reflecting the trading transactions of the business. The result, the change in wealth of the business, is shown as the resources held at the end of each period and reflected in the balance sheet. The example will show the statement of cash flows as movements in cash and changes to the cash balance, which is reflected in the balance sheet that gives a summary of the financial position of the company at the end of each period.

Worked example 3.2

Mr Bean decides to set up a wholesale business, Ayco, on 1 January 2010. He has his own cash resources for the purpose of setting up the business and has estimated that an initial £50,000 would be required for this purpose. During the first four-week period in business, January 2010, Ayco will enter into the following transactions:

		£
Week 1	Receipt of cheque from Mr Bean	50,000
Week 1	Purchase for cash the freehold of a shop	30,000
Week 1	Purchase for cash the shop fittings	5,000
Week 2	Cash paid for printing and stationery used	200
Week 3	Purchases of inventory, from Beeco Ltd, of Aymen toys, payable two months later (12,000 toys at £1 each)	12,000
Week 3	Sales of Aymen toys to Ceeco Ltd for cash (1,000 toys at £2 each)	2,000
Week 4	Sales of Aymen toys to Deeco Ltd, receivable one month later (8,000 toys at £2 each)	16,000

		Week 1 £	Total £
Profit and loss account	Sales revenue	0	0
	Cost of sales	0	0
	Gross profit	0	0
	Expenses	0	0
	Profit/(loss)	0	0
	Cumulative profit/(loss)	0	0
Cash flow	Opening balance	0	0
	Cash received ex Mr Bean	50,000	50,000
	Cash received from customers	0	0
	Cash paid for shop freehold	(30,000)	(30,000)
	Cash paid for shop fittings	(5,000)	(5,000)
	Cash paid for stationery	0	0
	Closing balance	15,000	15,000

		Week 1 £	Total £
Balance sheet	Cash closing balance	15,000	15,000
	Freehold shop	30,000	30,000
	Shop fittings	5,000	5,000
	Inventories	0	0
	Accounts receivable	0	0
	Accounts payable	0	0
	Total wealth	50,000	50,000
	Represented by:		
	Mr Bean's original capital	50,000	50,000
	Profit/(loss) to date	0	0
	Total capital	50,000	50,000

The statement above shows that no trading took place during the first week of January. Mr Bean paid £50,000 of his personal funds into the bank account of Ayco, representing his capital invested in Ayco. The company immediately used £35,000 of this to purchase the freehold of a shop together with shop fittings.

We can summarise the financial position at the end of the first week as follows:

- There was neither a profit nor a loss.
- Cash has been increased by Mr Bean's capital invested, less payments for the shop and fittings, to give a closing cash (bank) balance of £15,000.
- The wealth of the business at the end of the first week was Mr Bean's original capital of £50,000. Wealth had not been increased or decreased as there was no profit or loss.
- The wealth was represented by the shop, its fittings and the closing bank balance.
- Totals for the month to date are of course the same as for week 1.

Let's look at Ayco for the subsequent three weeks accounting periods, one week at a time, beginning with week 2.

Worked example 3.3

Accounting period week 2.

		Week 1 £	Week 2 £	Total £
Profit and loss account	Sales revenue	0	0	0
	Cost of sales	0	0	0
	Gross profit	0	0	0
	Expenses	0	(200)	(200)
	Profit/(loss)	0	(200)	(200)
	Cumulative profit/(loss)	0	(200)	(200)

		Week 1 £	Week 2 £	Total £
Cash flow	Opening balance	0	15,000	0
	Cash received ex Mr Bean	50,000	0	50,000
	Cash received from customers	0	0	0
	Cash paid for shop freehold	(30,000)	0	(30,000)
	Cash paid for shop fittings	(5,000)	0	(5,000)
	Cash paid for stationery	0	(200)	(200)
	Closing balance	15,000	14,800	14,800
Balance sheet	Cash closing balance	15,000	14,800	14,800
	Freehold shop	30,000	30,000	30,000
	Shop fittings	5,000	5,000	5,000
	Inventories	0	0	0
	Accounts receivable	0	0	0
	Accounts payable	0	0	0
	Total wealth	50,000	49,800	49,800
	Represented by:			
	Mr Bean's original capital	50,000	50,000	50,000
	Profit/(loss) to date	0	(200)	(200)
	Total capital	50,000	49,800	49,800

We can summarise the financial position at the end of the second week as follows:

- There was still no trading but printing and stationery had been used, and there was a charge for their expense to the profit and loss account, therefore there was a loss for the week. The cumulative two weeks is obtained by adding across each line in the profit and loss account, which is also the sum of the totals, to give a cumulative two-week loss of £200.
- Cash was reduced in week 2 by the cash paid for printing and stationery expenses to give a closing balance of £14,800. It can be seen that the two-week cumulative cash position is calculated by starting with the week 1 opening balance and then adding across all the payment and receipt elements. The sum of the total column will give the same closing balance as that shown for week 2.
- The book wealth of the business at the end of the second week was Mr Bean's original capital reduced by the cumulative loss of £200 to give £49,800. The wealth was represented by the shop, its fittings and the closing bank balance.

Note that the cumulative balance sheet at the end of week 2 is exactly the same as that shown in the week 2 column and not the totals of each of the elements added across in weeks 1 and 2. This is always true for however many weeks or any other period we may be looking at, which is what we would expect since the balance sheet does show the financial position at a point in time, in this example the position at the end of week 2.

Progress check 3.2

How can a business have made a loss during an accounting period if it hasn't been involved in any trading during the period?

Worked example 3.4

Let's now look at accounting period week 3.

		Week 1 £	Week 2 £	Week 3 £	Total £
Profit and loss account	Sales revenue	0	0	2,000	2,000
	Cost of sales	0	0	(1,000)	(1,000)
	Gross profit	0	0	1,000	1,000
	Expenses	0	(200)	0	(200)
	Profit/(loss)	0	(200)	1,000	800
	Cumulative profit/(loss)	0	(200)	800	800
Cash flow	Opening balance	0	15,000	14,800	0
	Cash received ex Mr Bean	50,000	0	0	50,000
	Cash received from customers	0	0	2,000	2,000
	Cash paid for shop freehold	(30,000)	0	0	(30,000)
	Cash paid for shop fittings	(5,000)	0	0	(5,000)
	Cash paid for stationery	0	(200)	0	(200)
	Closing balance	15,000	14,800	16,800	16,800
Balance sheet	Cash closing balance	15,000	14,800	16,800	16,800
	Freehold shop	30,000	30,000	30,000	30,000
	Shop fittings	5,000	5,000	5,000	5,000
	Inventories	0	0	11,000	11,000
	Accounts receivable	0	0	0	0
	Accounts payable	0	0	(12,000)	(12,000)
	Total wealth	50,000	49,800	50,800	50,800
	Represented by:				
	Mr Bean's original capital	50,000	50,000	50,000	50,000
	Profit/(loss) to date	0	(200)	800	800
	Total capital	50,000	49,800	50,800	50,800

We can summarise the financial position at the end of the third week as follows:

■ There was some trading, which gave a profit for the week of £1,000. The cumulative three weeks is obtained by adding across each line in the profit and loss account, which is also the sum of the totals, to give a cumulative three-week profit of £800.

- Cash was increased in week 3 by the cash received from customers, and with no cash payments the closing balance was £16,800. It can be seen that the three-week cumulative cash position is calculated by starting with the week 1 opening balance and then adding across all the payment and receipt elements. The sum of the total column will give the same closing balance as that shown for week 3.
- The book wealth of the business at the end of the third week was Mr Bean's original capital increased by the cumulative profit of £800 to give £50,800. The wealth was represented by the shop, its fittings, the closing bank balance, plus inventories less trade payables (two new categories introduced in this example). The first category is inventories. Inventories had been purchased in the month, but had been reduced by the amount used in trading. The second new category is the result of the purchase of inventory for £12,000, which had not yet been paid out in cash but nevertheless was a claim against the company. This claim is an amount due to be paid to suppliers – accounts payable by the business – and therefore a reduction in the wealth of the company.

The amount of inventories used in trading to provide the sales of £2,000 is called **cost of sales**, which in this example is £1,000. Note again that the cumulative balance sheet at the end of week 3 is exactly the same as that shown in the week 3 column and not the totals added across each of the elements in weeks 1, 2 and 3.

Worked example 3.5

Let's now look at the final accounting period, week 4.

		Week 1 £	Week 2 £	Week 3 £	Week 4 £	Total £
Profit and	Sales revenue	0	0	2,000	16,000	18,000
loss account	Cost of sales	0	0	(1,000)	(8,000)	(9,000)
	Gross profit	0	0	1,000	8,000	9,000
	Expenses	0	(200)	0	0	(200)
	Profit/(loss)	0	(200)	1,000	8,000	8,800
	Cumulative profit/ (loss)	0	(200)	800	8,800	8,800
Cash flow	Opening balance	0	15,000	14,800	16,800	0
	Cash received ex Mr Bean	50,000	0	0	0	50,000
	Cash received from customers	0	0	2,000	0	2,000
	Cash paid for shop freehold	(30,000)	0	0	0	(30,000)
	Cash paid for shop fittings	(5,000)	0	0	0	(5,000)
	Cash paid for stationery	0	(200)	0	0	(200)
	Closing balance	15,000	14,800	16,800	16,800	16,800

		Week 1 £	Week 2 £	Week 3 £	Week 4 £	Total £
Balance sheet	Cash closing balance	15,000	14,800	16,800	16,800	16,800
	Freehold shop	30,000	30,000	30,000	30,000	30,000
	Shop fittings	5,000	5,000	5,000	5,000	5,000
	Inventories	0	0	11,000	3,000	3,000
	Accounts receivable	0	0	0	16,000	16,000
	Accounts payable	0	0	(12,000)	(12,000)	(12,000)
	Total wealth	50,000	49,800	50,800	58,800	58,800
	Represented by:					
	Mr Bean's original capital	50,000	50,000	50,000	50,000	50,000
	Profit/(loss) to date	0	(200)	800	8,800	8,800
	Total capital	50,000	49,800	50,800	58,800	58,800

We can summarise the final financial position at the end of the fourth week as follows:

■ There was further trading, which gave a profit for the week of £8,000. The cumulative four weeks is obtained by adding across each line in the profit and loss account, which is also the sum of the totals, to give a cumulative four-week profit of £8,800.

■ No cash was received or paid during week 4, and so the closing balance remained at £16,800. It can be seen that the four-week cumulative cash position is calculated by starting with the week 1 opening balance and then adding across all the payment and receipt elements. The sum of the total column will give the same closing balance as that shown for week 4.

■ The book wealth of the business at the end of the fourth week was Mr Bean's original capital increased by the cumulative profit of £8,800 to give £58,800. The wealth was represented by the shop, its fittings, closing bank balance, inventories, less accounts payable, and now another additional element: accounts receivable. Sales of £16,000 had been made in the month, none of which had been paid in cash. The amount remaining due from customers – accounts receivable by the company – at the end of the week was £16,000 which represented an element of the wealth of Ayco. The inventories used for those sales had reduced the inventories from the end of the previous week £11,000 to £3,000 at the end of week 4.

Note again that the cumulative balance sheet at the end of week 4 is exactly the same as that shown in the week 4 column and not the totals of each of the elements added across in weeks 1, 2, 3 and 4.

Progress check 3.3

Why is there usually a difference between profit and cash in an accounting period?

Worked examples 3.2 to 3.5 introduced a number of terms relating to financial statements. Whilst they gave an introduction to the principles and put things in context they were by no means exhaustive. In this chapter and the next two, we will consider each of the financial statements in more detail, beginning with the balance sheet.

Balance sheet formats

IAS 1, Presentation of Financial Statements, allows considerable flexibility in the way that a balance sheet may be presented. The Companies Act 2006 indicates that the balance sheet and income statement for all reporting entities must comply with the current relevant accounting or financial reporting standards. The Companies Act 2006 does not specify the format of the financial statements. There is a general requirement for the reporting of comparative previous year numbers. These are normally shown in a column to the right of the current year's numbers.

Assets and liabilities must both be classified as current and non-current. IAS 1 provides a choice in presentation of the balance sheet between separating current and non-current assets and liabilities, or presenting assets and liabilities in order of their liquidity (or in reverse order of liquidity) without a current and non-current distinction. Liquidity presentation of assets and liabilities is required only when it provides a more relevant and reliable presentation.

Sometimes an asset or liability may be classified as current even if it is not due to be settled within 12 months of the balance sheet date, if it is expected to be settled within the company's normal operating cycle.

While IAS 1 does not stipulate the precise format of balance sheets, it does require a minimum of information that should be presented on the face of the balance sheet, which includes:

- property, plant and equipment
- investment property
- investments (financial assets, for example shares and loans)
- inventories
- **trade receivables** (accounts receivable net of any doubtful debt provision)
- other receivables
- cash and cash equivalents
- **trade payables** (net accounts payable)
- other payables
- provisions
- tax liabilities
- equity (issued share capital and retained earnings).

Additional items or sub-classification of items may need to be included because of their size or nature, or in order to comply with some other financial reporting standard or to present fairly the company's financial position or when such presentation is relevant to an understanding of the company's financial performance. This may include classifications of:

- assets, such as property, plant, equipment and inventories
- liabilities, such as provisions
- equity, such as share numbers and par values, retained earnings, and **reserves**.

In order to keep the balance sheet presentation clear, such additional information may be included in the notes on the accounts.

What does the balance sheet tell us?

In theory the balance sheet of a private limited company or a public limited company should be able to tell us all about the company's financial structure and liquidity – the extent to which its assets and liabilities are held in cash or in a near-cash form (for example, bank accounts and deposits). It should also tell us about the assets held by the company, the proportion of **current assets** and the extent to which they may be used to meet current obligations. In later chapters we will look at many of the important ratios used to evaluate the strength of a company's balance sheet. We will also see what the balance sheet tells us about the financial structure of companies and the sources of such financing.

An element of caution should be noted in analysing balance sheet information. The balance sheet is a historical document. It may have looked entirely different six months or a year ago, or even one week ago. There is not always consistency between the information included in one company's balance sheet and that of another company. Two companies even within the same industry are usually very difficult to compare. Added to that, different analysts very often use the same ratios in different ways.

We will look at some of the variety of methods used to value the various items contained in the balance sheet. However, in addition to the wide choice of valuation methods, the information in a typical published balance sheet does not tell us anything about the quality of the assets, their real value in money terms or their value to the business.

Off balance sheet financing and **window dressing** are two terms that often crop up in discussions about the accuracy of balance sheet information. The former relates to the funding of operations in such a way that the relevant assets and liabilities are not disclosed in the balance sheet of the company concerned. The latter is a **creative accounting** practice in which changes in short-term funding have the effect of disguising or improving the reported liquidity (cash and near-cash) position of the reporting organisation.

Structure of the balance sheet

Assets are acquired by a business to generate future benefits, for example from trading or whatever activities the business has been set up to provide. To acquire assets the business must first raise the necessary funds primarily from shareholders. In doing so the claims or obligations are created in the form of shareholders' equity.

Shareholders' equity and also **non-current liabilities** and **current liabilities** represent claims, or obligations, on the company to provide cash or other benefits to third parties. Equity, or shareholders' capital, represents a claim by the owners, or shareholders of the business, against the business.

Liabilities represent claims by persons, other than the owners of the business, against the business. These claims arise from transactions relating to the provision of goods or services, or lending money to the business.

An example of a balance sheet format adopted by a limited company, Flatco plc, is shown in Figure 3.5. It is shown in what is termed a horizontal format in order to illustrate the grouping of the assets categories, the total of which equals the total of the liabilities and equity categories. In practice, UK companies adopt the vertical format (see Figure 3.7), rather than the horizontal format balance sheet, which we shall discuss in a later section of this chapter.

Figure 3.5	A horizontal balance sheet format showing the balancing of assets with liabilities and equity

Flatco plc
Balance sheet as at 31 December 2010

	Assets	£000	Liabilities	£000	
	Non-current assets		**Equity**		
operational	Tangible	1,884	Share capital	1,200	financial
operational	Intangible	416	Share premium account	200	financial
operational	Investments	248	Retained earnings	1,594	financial
	Total non-current assets	2,548	**Total equity**	2,994	
			Non-current liabilities		
			Borrowings and finance leases	173	financial
			Trade and other payables	154	operational
			Deferred tax liabilities	–	operational
			Provisions	222	operational
			Total non-current liabilities	549	
	Current assets		**Current liabilities**		
operational	Inventories	311	Borrowings and finance leases	50	financial
operational	Trade and other receivables	1,162	Trade and other payables	553	operational
financial	Cash and cash equivalents	327	Current tax liabilities	50	operational
			Provisions	152	operational
	Total current assets	1,800	**Total current liabilities**	805	
	Total assets	4,348	**Total liabilities and equity**	4,348	

The detail of each of the categories within the balance sheet will be explained in the sections that follow. As we have shown in Figure 3.5, each balance sheet category, both assets and liabilities, may be described as either financial or operational. **Equity**, borrowings and finance leases, and cash and cash equivalents are financial resources, whereas **non-current assets**, inventories, trade and other receivables, non-current liabilities and current liabilities are operational, relating to the manufacturing, commercial and administrative activities of the company.

We will now look at each of the balance sheet categories in detail, beginning with shareholders' equity and liabilities.

Equity

Shareholders' equity is usually simply called equity. It represents the total investment of the shareholders in the company, the total book wealth of the business. Equity broadly comprises share capital, the share premium account and retained earnings. The cost of shareholders' equity is generally related to the **dividends** paid to shareholders, the level of which is usually dependent on how well the company has performed during the year.

Share capital

The nominal value of a share is the value of each share, decided at the outset by the promoters of the company. The nominal value is the same for each of the shares and may be, for example, 25p, 50p or £1 (the usual maximum). The initial **share capital** is the number of shares in the company multiplied by the nominal value of the shares (for example, two million shares at 50p per share is £1,000,000, or at £1 per share is £2,000,000). Each share is a title of ownership of the assets of the company. This is an important issue in respect of control and growth of the company.

Worked example 3.6

Arthur King is setting up a small limited company, Round Table Ltd, for which he needs initial capital of £10,000. Arthur creates 100 shares each having a nominal value of £100. Arthur decides to start off as king of his empire and keep 90% of the shares for himself and so buys 90 shares at £100 each and pays £9,000 out of his personal bank account into the bank account of the new company, Round Table Ltd. Arthur owns 90% of the company. The remaining 10 shares are purchased by 10 of Arthur's friends each for £100. Each friend owns 1% of the company, has 1% of the voting rights at shareholders' meetings and will receive 1% of dividends paid by the company.

Round Table Ltd does well and after some time considers that it needs additional capital of a further £10,000 to fund its growth. The company may issue 100 new shares at £100 each.

We may discuss the implications for Arthur if he is unable to afford any additional shares himself and the new shares are sold to new investors. The total number of shares will become 200, of which he will own 90, that is 45%.

Because Arthur will have less than 50% of the shares we may say that he therefore loses control of the company. There are two main considerations regarding the issue of shares and control.

The first point is that the founder of a growing business must face a difficult dilemma: growing but losing control, or keeping control but losing growth opportunities. An alternative may be to go to the bank and fund growth with a loan. However, along with this goes a vulnerability to failure at the first cash crisis the company may face.

The second point is that the issue of new shares at the same price as the existing original shares may be considered unfair. When Round Table Ltd was created it was worth only the money that the original shareholders invested in it. The company's credibility has now been built up through successful operations and an understanding of the market. Surely this must have a value so that the new share issue should be made at a higher price? The difference in price between the original nominal value and the price new investors will have to pay is the share premium.

Share premium account

The **share premium account** may be best illustrated with a worked example.

Worked example 3.7

Using the company in Worked example 3.6, let's assume that for potential investors the value of one share is now £400. This means that 25 shares of £400 would be needed to raise additional capital of £10,000.

We will look at how these new shares should appear in the company's balance sheet.

(i) These new shares cannot appear in the balance sheet with a nominal value of £400 because it would then mean that legally the shareholders would have voting and dividend rights four times those of the £100 nominal shares.

(ii) The capital in the balance sheet will need to be increased by 25 times £100, the nominal value of the shares, that is £2,500.

(iii) A new category, the share premium account, is required on the balance sheet.

(iv) The share premium account will have a value of 25 (£400 − £100), that is £7,500.

Retained earnings

Retained earnings is the final element within the equity of the company. The profit or net income generated from the operations of the company belongs to the shareholders of the company. It is the directors who recommend how much of those earnings are distributed to shareholders as dividends, the balance being held as retained earnings and reinvested in the business. The retained earnings of the company are increased by the annual net profit less any dividends payable; they are part of the wealth of the company and therefore appear within the equity of the company. Similarly, any losses will reduce the retained earnings of the company.

Liabilities

Current liabilities

Current liabilities are items that are expected to become payable within one year from the balance sheet date. These comprise borrowings and finance leases, trade and other payables, current tax liabilities and **provisions**.

Borrowings and finance leases

Borrowings and finance leases are the elements of bank overdrafts, loans and leases that are payable within one year of the balance sheet date.

Trade and other payables

Whereas there is a cost associated with equity and borrowings in the form of dividends and interest payable, trade payables are sometimes considered 'free' of such cost. This, however, is rarely true. Trade payables, the accounts payable to suppliers net of any adjustments such as credit notes due, are not a free source of finance. This is because when credit is extended this is usually accompanied by an increase in the price of the product or service being provided.

Worked example 3.8

A supplier may offer to a company payment terms of three months from delivery date.

We will look at the effect of the company proposing to the supplier payment terms of two months from delivery date, for which the supplier may for example offer 1% or 2% early settlement discount.

A discount of 1% for settlement one month early is equivalent to over 12% per annum. Consequently, it becomes apparent that the supplier's selling price must have included some allowance for financial charges; accounts payable to suppliers are therefore not a free debt.

Other payables include for example employee and social costs payable and also accruals, which are allowances made for costs and expenses incurred and payable within one year of the balance sheet date but for which no invoices have yet been processed through the accounts. This is in line with the matching (or accruals) concept we discussed in Chapter 1. Expense recognition is an important concept. Expenses should be recognised immediately they are known about. Accruals are treated in a similar way to payables but the invoices for these charges have not yet been processed by the entity. They are charges or expenses that are brought into the period because, although goods (or services) have been provided, they have not yet been included in the supplier's accounts. Some examples are telephone and electricity charges which are incurred but for which invoices may not normally be received until the end of each quarter. On the other hand, revenues or profits should not be recognised until they are earned.

Worked example 3.9

We know that in the Ayco example the business had used and had been invoiced for and paid for £200 worth of stationery. If we assume, for example, that more than £200 worth of stationery had been used in the month of January, say £1,000, we can consider:

(i)   What would be the impact on Ayco if £500 worth of the additional stationery had been used, and an invoice had been received but not processed through the ledgers?

(ii) What would be the impact on Ayco if £300 worth of the additional stationery had been used, and an invoice had not yet been received but was still in the mail?

Both amounts would have to be charged to printing and stationery expenses for a total of £800. The balancing entries that would have to be made would be to credit a total of £800 to accruals. Ayco knew they had used stationery for which there was a cost even though an invoice may not have been processed.

The net impact of the above on Ayco would have been a reduction in profit, a debit of £800 and an increase in liabilities, a credit of £800 to accruals.

Current tax liabilities

Corporation tax assessed on the current year profit is shown as a liability for tax to be paid within one year following the balance sheet date and may be shown as income tax payable. This is based on a tax computation that may not necessarily be agreed by HMRC and so the exact amount of tax paid may be more or less than that stated in the balance sheet.

Provisions

A provision that is classified as a current liability is an amount charged against profit to provide for an expected liability or loss even though the amount of the liability or loss is uncertain, but which is expected to materialise within the next year. This is in line with the prudence concept we discussed in Chapter 1.

Non-current liabilities

Non-current liabilities are items that are expected to become payable after one year from the balance sheet date. These comprise borrowings and finance leases, trade and other payables, deferred tax liabilities and provisions.

Borrowings and finance leases

Items included within the non-current liabilities category of borrowing and finance leases are the elements of loans and finance leases that are not payable within one year following the balance sheet date but are payable some time after that year. To help the company finance its operations it may take on further financial debt, or loans, for a limited period of time. The company has to pay interest on financial debt, over the period of the loan, regardless of how well or not the company performs, that is, regardless of whether it has made a profit or a loss.

Financial debt, provided by various financial institutions such as banks, may take the form of loans, **debentures** and leases. Interest rates vary according to the risk of the investment. The level of interest payable, and thus the choice of which type of debt the company may wish to take on, will be determined by how risky the potential lender regards this particular company.

A banker or investor may wish to invest in Government securities, which are risk-free, and receive the low rate of return offered by such investments. For a company, which is not risk-free, the investor will expect a higher rate of interest as an incentive or compensation for the risk being taken. The higher the risk of a security, the higher the expected rate of return (see Figure 3.6).

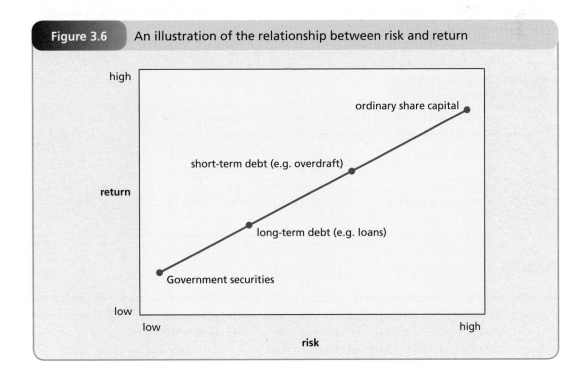

| Figure 3.6 | An illustration of the relationship between risk and return |

The difference between the interest rate paid on Government securities and the interest rate that a company pays on loans is called the risk premium. Shareholders' equity is even riskier than shorter-term corporate debt (for example, a loan made to the company). Therefore, the company should not only make a profit but the level of profit should be such that the shareholders get a return in line with their level of risk. This should be the return on Government securities plus a risk premium which is even higher than the risk premium payable on the corporate debt.

Trade and other payables

Trade and other payables after one year mainly comprise accounts payable to suppliers of goods and services provided to the company that may typically be, for example, relating to capital projects taking place over an extended period for which stage payments may have been agreed.

Deferred tax liabilities

Deferred tax is the difference between the tax ultimately payable on the profits recognised in an accounting period and the actual amount of tax payable for the same accounting period. The former figure will be based on the tax implications of accounting profit and the carrying amounts of assets and liabilities. The latter figure will be based on a calculation of profits as recognised by the tax authorities.

The deferred tax liability is the amount of income taxes payable in future periods in respect of taxable temporary differences. Similarly, a deferred tax asset is the amount of income taxes recoverable in future periods in respect of deductible temporary differences, carried forward unused tax losses, and unused tax credits (IAS 12, Income Taxes).

Provisions

A provision that is classified as a non-current liability is an amount charged against profit to provide for an expected liability or loss even though the amount and date of the liability or loss is uncertain. This is in line with the prudence concept we discussed in Chapter 1.

Progress check 3.4

Which of the following do you think may be classified as liabilities or shareholders' equity within a balance sheet, and under which headings should they appear?

- bank overdraft
- computer
- five-year bank loan
- amounts owed by customers
- accruals
- amounts owed to suppliers
- ordinary shares
- share premium

Assets

We have seen that assets are acquired by a business to generate future benefits, for example from trading or whatever activities the business has been set up to provide. In addition to providing benefits from transactions, accounting assets have a number of other characteristics: they must be capable of being measured in monetary units; the business must have exclusive control over such assets.

The assets sections of the balance sheet are more homogeneous than the equity and liabilities sections of the balance sheet. The liabilities sections of the balance sheet generally describe where the financing comes from, whereas the assets sections generally represent how the money has been used.

Non-current assets

Non-current assets include land and buildings, equipment, machinery, furniture, fittings, computers, software and motor vehicles, which the company has purchased to enable it to meet its strategic objectives. They have a very important common feature, namely that they are not renewed within the operating cycle (see current assets below), which may be measured in months, weeks, days, or even hours. Non-current assets have a longer life of usually much more than one year.

A building may have a life of 20 years, whereas a personal computer may have a life of three years, both being longer than the cycle in which raw materials and packaging are renewed, for example. Regardless of this, non-current assets are 'consumed' on a day-to-day basis. The measure of this consumption is called depreciation.

Non-current assets comprise tangible non-current assets, **intangible non-current assets** and long-term investments (or financial assets).

Tangible non-current assets

Tangible non-current assets are long-term assets that one can touch, for example land, buildings, equipment, machinery, computers, fixtures and fittings. Their costs are apportioned, or depreciated, over the estimated economic life of each asset.

Intangible non-current assets

Intangible non-current assets are the long-term assets that one cannot touch, for example computer software, patents, trademarks and **goodwill**. A business must decide if the useful lives of its intangible assets (other than goodwill) are indefinite or finite, in accordance with IAS 38, Intangible Assets. An indefinite life means that there is no foreseeable limit to the period over which the asset is expected to generate net cash inflows for the business. A finite life means there is a limited period of benefit to the business.

If a business decides that the useful economic life of the asset is finite then the costs, net of their residual values, are amortised (or apportioned) over the estimated economic life of each asset. The **amortisation** method used should reflect the time pattern over which the benefits are received from the use of the asset. If the asset is considered to have an indefinite life then it should not be amortised. Goodwill is always assumed to have an indefinite life, and both finite and indefinite life assets should be subject to annual **impairment** reviews (see page 102).

Investments

Investments are long-term financial assets that include loans to **subsidiary companies**, investments in associate companies and non-associated companies.

Current assets

In addition to the investment in its whole long-term, and relatively fixed, environment (buildings, equipment, machinery, computers and furniture), the company has to invest additional funds in its **operating cycle**. The operating cycle involves the management of the company's current assets and current liabilities, which may be measured in months, weeks, days, or even hours. The operating cycle is the period of time between the point at which cash starts to be spent on production and the collection of cash from customers who have been supplied with finished product.

Current assets comprise inventories, trade and other receivables, and cash and cash equivalents.

Inventories

Inventories generally include raw materials, work in progress and finished goods. They may also include sundry other consumable items purchased for use over a period of time such as stationery, replacement parts, spare parts and cleaning materials, if these are of any significant value, so that the inclusion of their total cost on acquisition would provide a distortion in the income statement.

Trade and other receivables

Trade and other receivables include accounts receivable, net of any doubtful debt provision, due from customers and others including subsidiaries, and also prepayments and accrued income.

A prepayment is expenditure on goods (or services) for future benefit, which is to be charged to future operations. Such amounts are similar to accounts receivable which is why they are included in the current assets section of the balance sheet.

Prepayments include prepaid expenses for services not yet used, for example rent, insurance, subscriptions, or electricity charges in advance, and also accrued income. Accrued income relates to sales of goods or services that have occurred and have been accounted for within the trading period but have not yet been invoiced to the customer. This is in accord with the matching (or accruals) concept discussed in Chapter 1.

Cash and cash equivalents

Cash and cash equivalents includes bank balances and deposits in addition to actual cash held in the form of notes and coins.

Other financial assets

Current assets may also include short-term financial assets such as foreign exchange contracts and options, currency swaps and other derivatives.

Worked example 3.10

In the Ayco example we may assume, for example, that Ayco had received an invoice in January for £2,000 for advertising to be paid in March, but the advertising was not taking place until February.

An invoice may have been received and processed through the ledgers, which has an additional impact on Ayco.

Accounts payable would be increased by (or credited with) £2,000 and advertising expenses charged with (or debited with) £2,000 in the month of January. However, because the advertising had not yet taken place the charge of £2,000 would be considered as being in advance, or to use its technical term, a prepayment. The accounts payable entry remains as a credit of £2,000, but an additional entry is required to credit advertising expenses with £2,000 and debit prepayments with £2,000.

The net impact of the above on Ayco would have been no change to profit.

Progress check 3.5

(i) Which of the following items do you think may be classified as assets within a balance sheet?

(ii) Which ones are non-current assets and which ones are current assets?

(iii) In which categories should the assets appear?

- long-term loan
- computer printer
- goodwill
- share premium

- water charges paid in advance
- an invoice not yet received for photocopy expenses already incurred
- materials held to be used in production
- products for sale to customers

The summary balance sheet that we saw in Figure 3.5 is known as the horizontal format. Although now rarely used in practice within businesses, it was a conventional format in which assets are shown in one column, and liabilities and shareholders' equity in the other column. Such a presentation clearly illustrated how total assets equalled the total of liabilities plus shareholders' equity.

The horizontal balance sheet format can be represented by the equation

$$\text{total assets (TA)} = \text{equity (E)} + \text{total liabilities (TL)}$$

$$\text{TA} = \text{E} + \text{TL}$$

or

$$\text{non-current assets (NCA)} + \text{current assets (CA)}$$
$$= \text{equity (E)} + \text{non-current liabilities (NCL)} + \text{current liabilities (CL)}$$

$$\text{NCA} + \text{CA} = \text{E} + \text{NCL} + \text{CL}$$

Using the above equation, companies generally present their balance sheets in a vertical format. IAS 1 does not prescribe the exact order or format in which a company presents individual items in the balance sheet and so companies may therefore present their balance sheets in a variety of different ways. A company arranges each item and presents its balance sheet in a way that it feels is most appropriate to its comprehensibility. A commonly used vertical format rearranges the above equation to become:

$$\text{NCA} + \text{CA} - \text{CL} - \text{NCL} = \text{E}$$

Each element in the equation is represented vertically with total assets minus total liabilities equal to net assets, and represented by the shareholders' equity of the company.

Using the data from Figure 3.5 the balance sheet for Flatco plc is shown in a vertical format in Figure 3.7. The total book wealth of the company is represented by the **net assets** of the business. Net assets is derived by deducting total liabilities from total assets, and therefore equals the shareholders' equity of the business. A balance sheet is probably easier to read down the page

| Figure 3.7 | A vertical format balance sheet |

Flatco plc

Balance sheet as at 31 December 2010

Assets	£000
Non-current assets	
Tangible	1,884
Intangible	416
Investments	248
Total non-current assets	2,548
Current assets	
Inventories	311
Trade and other receivables	1,162
Cash and cash equivalents	327
Total current assets	1,800
Total assets	4,348
Liabilities	
Current liabilities	
Borrowings and finance leases	50
Trade and other payables	553
Current tax liabilities	50
Dividends payable	70
Provisions	82
Total current liabilities	805
Non-current liabilities	
Borrowings and finance leases	173
Trade and other payables	154
Deferred tax liabilities	—
Provisions	222
Total non-current liabilities	549
Total liabilities	1,354
Net assets	2,994
Equity	
Share capital	1,200
Share premium account	200
Retained earnings	1,594
Total equity	2,994

rather than across, and the vertical format does clearly highlight each of the main sections of the balance sheet.

In Chapter 2, the concept of the trial balance, and its links with the income statement and balance sheet are examined in detail. Worked example 3.11 uses the trial balance of Perfecto Ltd to identify the various categories of assets, liabilities and shareholders' equity (the debits and the credits).

Worked example 3.11

The balances extracted from the trial balance of Perfecto Ltd at 30 September 2010 are presented in an alphabetical list:

	£000
Accruals	100
Bank and cash balances	157
Intangible non-current assets	203
Inventories of finished goods	95
Inventories of materials	37
Long-term loans	85
Prepaid expenses and accrued income	295
Profit and loss account to 30 September 2010 (profit)	130
Provisions	103
Retained earnings at 30 September 2009	525
Share capital	600
Share premium account	105
Tangible non-current assets	902
Trade payables due after one year	77
Trade payables due within one year	277
Trade receivables	284
Work in progress	29

It should be remembered that a loss is a debit. If the total of the debit balances is equal to the total of the credit balances it may be assumed that the information is complete.

- First, we need to identify which are assets (debit balances) and which are liabilities and shareholders' equity (credit balances).
- Second, we can check that the trial balance is actually in balance, and if there is any missing information.
- Third, we can prepare a balance sheet for Perfecto Ltd as at 30 September 2010 using a vertical format.

	Assets (debits) £000	Liabilities and equity (credits) £000
Accruals		100
Bank and cash balances	157	
Trade payables due within one year		277
Trade payables due after one year		77
Trade receivables	284	
Intangible non-current assets	203	
Long-term loans		85
Prepaid expenses and accrued income	295	
Profit and loss account year to September 2010 (profit)		130
Provisions		103
Retained earnings at 30 September 2009		525
Ordinary share capital		600
Share premium		105

	Assets (debits)	Liabilities and equity (credits)
	£000	£000
Inventories of finished goods	95	
Inventories of materials	37	
Tangible non-current assets	902	
Work in progress	29	
Total	2,002	2,002

The total of the assets is £2,002,000, which is equal to the total of the liabilities plus shareholders' equity. The trial balance is therefore in balance and there doesn't appear to be any information missing. However, errors of omission, for example, or transposed figures, may not be spotted from the information given. There could be equal and opposite debit and credit balances that have been excluded from the list in error.

Given that the data is correct, an accurate balance sheet for Perfecto Ltd as at 30 September 2010 may be prepared.

Perfecto Ltd
Balance sheet as at 30 September 2010

	£000
Non-current assets	
Tangible	902
Intangible	203
Total non-current assets	1,105
Current assets	
Inventories	161
Trade receivables	284
Prepayments	295
Cash and cash equivalents	157
Total current assets	897
Total assets	2,002
Current liabilities	
Trade payables	277
Accruals	100
Total current liabilities	377
Non-current liabilities	
Borrowings and finance leases	85
Trade and other payables	77
Provisions	103
Total non-current liabilities	265
Total liabilities	642
Net assets	1,360
Equity	
Share capital	600
Share premium account	105
Retained earnings	655
Total equity	1,360

Many of the larger businesses in the UK consist of a number of companies rather than just one company. The control of such companies, or groups of companies, rests with a parent company, which is called the holding company. The other companies within the group are called subsidiaries. The holding company holds the required number of shares in each of the subsidiaries to give it the required control.

Businesses operate in a group structure for a variety of reasons. It may be because they cover different countries, different products, or different market sectors; it may be to provide independence, or separate accountability, or may very often be a result of successive takeovers or mergers of businesses.

IAS 27, Consolidated and Separate Financial Statements, requires group accounts to be prepared for the holding company in addition to the accounts that are required to be prepared for each of the individual companies within the group. These **consolidated accounts** exclude all transactions between companies within the group, for example inter-company sales revenue and purchases, to avoid double counting of transactions. In most other respects, the group consolidated accounts reflect an amalgamation of each of the components of the balance sheets of all the companies within the group.

Valuation of assets

The question of valuation of assets at a specific balance sheet date arises in respect of choosing the most accurate methods relating to non-current assets, inventories and receivables (and similarly payables), which support the fundamental requirement to give a true and fair view. Companies must be very careful to ensure that their assets are valued in a way that realistically reflects their ability to generate future cash flows. This applies to both current assets such as inventories, and non-current assets such as land and buildings. The balance sheets of companies rarely reflect either the current market values of non-current assets, or their future earnings potential, since they are based on historical costs.

During 2008 the house building market suffered greatly as property prices fell and the demand for new housing diminished. We saw several house builders failing or being the subject of takeover bids. One of the UK's largest house builders, Persimmon (see the press extract below), recorded a loss of £780m in 2008. However, in 2009 they reported a profit of £77.8m.

In 2008 Persimmon had written down the value of the land they held by £664.1m, which largely explained the huge loss for that year. In 2009, following a review of the value of the company's land, the directors decided to reverse £74.8m of these write-offs, which was added back to profit. Directors of companies must take care in such valuation increases that reflect the impact of property price inflation, which may not be sustained, and which ignore the future earning potential of the assets. The effect on Persimmon was that the shareholders, and the market, were delighted at the tremendous reversal in fortunes in the year, particularly as rival house builder Taylor Wimpey reported a £640m pre-tax loss in 2009.

Differences between the methods chosen to value various assets (and liabilities) at the end of accounting periods may have a significant impact on the results reported in the income statement for those periods. Examples of this may be seen in:

- non-current assets and depreciation
- inventories valuations and cost of sales
- valuations of trade payables and trade receivables denominated in foreign currencies
- provisions for doubtful debts.

The real value of a company's assets

Britain's biggest house builder gave the troubled sector a lift yesterday by returning to profitability following a torrid period in which it was forced to wipe £600m off the value of its assets.

York-based Persimmon posted a profit of £77.8m – boosted by a windfall of £74.8m from a revaluation of its land bank – on sales of £1.42bn. This compares with a loss last year of £780m. The company also reported a sharp reduction in its debt – cut by more than half from £601m to £268m.

John White, the chairman, described the results as 'a major turnaround' and the market responded well to the news with Persimmon's share price rising 29 to 429p at one point, despite the lack of a dividend.

While Persimmon's profit would have been a modest £7m without the write-back – a steep fall on last year's pre-exceptionals profit of £127m – one analyst suggested that the company's revaluation veered on the side of caution.

Mike Farley, the group chief executive, agreed there was scope for further write-backs but was inclined to wait and see before making any further changes. 'We come into this year with a strong forward order book of £900m, up 29pc on the same period last year', he said. 'We are going to open 90 new sites in the first half of 2010 and, to put that into context, we opened 90 in the whole of 2009.

'That said, there's an election campaign coming up and whichever party gets in there could be cuts in Government spending and increases in taxation and they could have knock-on effects for the economy as a whole.'

Mr Farley does look forward to a further reduction in Persimmon's debts over the next 12 months, however. 'We'd like to see debt below £100m if things remain as they are', he said. 'If things improve, we may have to invest more cash. We're comfortable with our debt. Our gearing is at 16pc and we have £1bn of facilities and so have plenty of headroom.'

Both the chairman and chief executive yesterday failed to issue outright denials to speculation that they would use this 'headroom' to mount a takeover of smaller rival Bovis – expected to be at £600m – taking refuge in the line that their focus is on debt reduction.

But Mr Farley added fuel to the rumours by saying: 'You can never say never, can you?' He also held out hope for a dividend next year. 'That's not something we are going to decide at this point', he said. 'We recognise [the loyalty of] our shareholders and we are one of the few companies in our sector who haven't asked for extra cash. That's something we'll review as the year goes on.'

Source: **Persimmon returns to profit after revaluation,** by Dominic Midgley © *Daily Telegraph*, 3 March 2010

The valuation of assets and liabilities will all be covered in detail in Chapter 4 when we look at the income statement. The rules applicable to the valuation of balance sheet items are laid down in the international accounting standards and UK financial reporting standards (IASs and FRSs). These rules allow companies to prepare their financial statements under the historical cost convention (the gross value of the asset being the purchase price or production cost), or alternative conventions of historical cost modified to include certain assets at a revalued amount or current cost.

Under alternative conventions, the gross value of the asset is either the market value at the most recent valuation date or its current cost: tangible non-current assets should be valued at market value or at current cost; investments (non-current assets) are valued at market value or at any value considered appropriate by the directors; short-term investments are valued at current cost; inventories are valued at current cost. If a reduction in value of any non-current assets is expected to be permanent then provision for this must be made. The same applies to investments even if the reduction is not expected to be permanent.

Non-current assets with finite lives are subject to depreciation charges. Current assets must be written down to the amount for which they could be disposed of (their **net realisable value**), if that value is lower than cost or an alternative valuation. It should be noted that provisions for reductions in value no longer considered necessary must be written back to the profit and loss account.

There is an element of choice between alternative valuation methods that may be adopted by businesses. Because of this, difficulties may arise in trying to provide consistent comparisons of the performance of companies even within the same industrial sectors. If changes in accounting policies have been introduced, further inconsistencies arise in trying to provide a realistic comparison of just one company's performance between one accounting period and another.

The difficulty of accurately valuing assets was clearly made by a recent story in the *Daily Telegraph* shown below.

Accounting concepts and the IASs and UK FRSs provide rules and guidance for the valuation of balance sheet items. We will look at some of the most important valuation rules in respect of non-current assets and current assets.

Non-current assets

IAS 16, Property, Plant and Equipment, and IAS 38, Intangible Assets, and IAS 40, Investment Property, define non-current assets as those assets intended for use on a continuing basis in

---

The real value of an asset – priceless!

Its value as a 5,000-year-old monument to British heritage is priceless. But should Stonehenge be sold on the open market it would fetch £51million, according to estate agents. Ever willing to put a pound sign beside any available assets, property marketeers have valued a host of national landmarks, should the Government or the Crown be tempted to sell them.

According to a survey of 500 estate agents, 10 Downing Street is worth £5.2million and Windsor Castle £390.9million.

The exercise by the property website FindaProperty.com also valued Brighton's Royal Pavilion at £51.9million and Blackpool Tower at £60million.

Nigel Lewis, a property analyst at FindaProperty.com, said: 'Based on these valuations, the Government and Crown probably own enough land and property to pay down the national debt pretty significantly.

'Of course, we know these landmarks will never be put up for sale, but with property prices shooting up 10 per cent in value over the past year we thought it would be fun to see what the market consensus was about their values.

'It's quite a challenge for estate agents more used to valuing suburban semis to put an accurate valuation on a royal castle or ancient monument, but there was a surprising amount of agreement between the different agents we spoke to.' The valuations were based on location, transport links, available land and the potential for renovation and reuse.

Other landmarks valued included Birmingham's Bull Ring, which estate agents said would cost £750million; Coventry Cathedral, worth £50million, and Leeds Town Hall, which would be listed for an estimated £30million on the open market.

Source: **The value of 5,000 years of history? £51m,** by Myra Butterworth © *Daily Telegraph*, 25 May 2010

the company's activities. As we have already discussed, non-current assets comprise tangible assets, intangible assets and investments (financial assets). Within tangible non-current assets there are various categories of asset: land and buildings (freehold, long leasehold and short leasehold); plant and machinery; fixtures, fittings, tools and equipment; assets in the course of construction.

Capital expenditure relates to acquisition of non-current assets and includes all the costs of putting an asset into service with the company so that the company will benefit from the services of the asset for more than one trading period.

Interest charges incurred in the financing of the production of an asset may be added to and included in the total cost of the asset. Such charges are said to have been capitalised, and if they are included in the total non-current asset cost this must be disclosed in a note to the financial statements.

Which other acquisition costs should be added to the asset price to give the total acquisition cost? The total amount recorded in the accounts of a company, the capitalised cost, for each category of non-current asset, should include various acquisition costs in addition to the purchase price of the asset, as follows:

- land
  - agent's commissions
  - legal fees
  - survey fees
  - draining, clearing, landscaping, demolition costs
- buildings
  - repair, alteration and improvement costs
- other assets
  - freight costs
  - customs duty
  - installation charges
- building construction
  - subcontract work
  - materials costs
  - labour costs
  - direct construction overheads
  - excavation costs
  - construction offices
  - professional fees
- own-built plant and machinery
  - materials costs
  - labour costs
  - production overheads.

Overheads that may be capitalised relate to costs of wages, salaries and expenses not directly incurred in the construction of buildings or machinery, but which nevertheless are necessary costs incurred to enable construction to take place. Examples may be a proportion or the full costs of management and supervision of projects, and a share of electricity or similar charges incurred on such projects.

Worked example 3.12

We have been asked to decide which of the following items should be disclosed in the balance sheet and which should be disclosed in the income statement.

		£
1.	Extension to the factory	500,000
2.	New plant	100,000
3.	Architect's fee for supervising the building of the extension	10,000
4.	Haulier's invoice for delivering the plant	5,000
5.	Invoice from decorators for painting the reception area	2,000
6.	Insurance premium for twelve months on new cars	15,000
7.	Invoice from garage for ten new cars	200,000

The disclosure should be as follows:

		£
1.	Balance sheet – non-current assets	500,000
2.	Balance sheet – non-current assets	100,000
3.	Balance sheet – non-current assets	10,000
4.	Balance sheet – non-current assets	5,000
5.	Income statement – repairs	2,000
6.	Income statement – insurance	15,000
7.	Balance sheet – non-current assets	200,000

A valuation problem arises with regard to non-current assets because such assets have been 'consumed' over time and will currently be worth less than at the time of acquisition. The total cost of using a non-current asset over its life is generally defined as the original investment less a portion of its cost recovered (its residual value) at the end of the asset's useful life. Depreciation is allocated to charge a fair proportion of the total cost (or valuation) of the asset to each accounting period expected to benefit from its use. The net non-current asset figure reported in each period's balance sheet will reflect the reduction to the historical cost, or revalued amount, of the asset using the depreciation calculated for each period.

Intangible assets include: deferred development costs; concessions; patents; licences; trademarks; goodwill; brand names. Investments (financial assets) primarily include shares and loans in non-consolidated group companies.

Progress check 3.7

Does it really matter if the year-end balance sheet of a company shows non-current assets at cost, less depreciation and amortisation, but ignores any change in their value? This should be discussed from the points of view of an investor and a lender as two major users of financial statements.

Brand names

Some organisations have included brand names for products like cakes and beers in their balance sheets as intangible assets, therefore inflating the totals of their balance sheets. Examples of companies that have capitalised brand names have been:

- Ranks Hovis McDougall (1991) capitalised non-purchased brand names
- Guinness (1993) capitalised purchased brand names.

Capitalisation of purchased brand names is permitted under IAS 38. Although brands purchased by a company may be capitalised, non-purchased brands are specifically prohibited from being capitalised. The IASB has viewed the inclusion of non-purchased brands as undesirable because of the difficulty in ascertaining historical costs and the inappropriateness of trying to capitalise the earnings or cash flows which have been generated by the brand names. If the value of an intangible asset cannot be measured reliably it cannot be capitalised in the balance sheet. Purchased brands have proved to be as desirable as traditional tangible non-current assets, and so should be disclosed in the balance sheet.

Goodwill

IAS 22 provided for two methods of accounting for business combinations: the pooling of interests method or merger method; the purchase method or acquisition method. IFRS 3, Business Combinations, has replaced IAS 22. Under IFRS 3 the merger method is no longer used and it is only the acquisition method that should be applied.

IFRS 3 defines goodwill as the difference between the consideration (purchase price) paid for the business and the fair value of the assets acquired. It can only appear on the balance sheet if a business has been acquired for a value in either cash or shares, so a company may not capitalise internally generated goodwill. IFRS 3 explains that if the value of the assets acquired are greater than the consideration then the gain is recognised immediately as a 'bargain purchase' in the profit and loss account. If, as is more usual, the consideration paid has a greater value than the assets acquired then the difference (the goodwill) is capitalised in the balance sheet as an intangible non-current asset. Unlike other intangible non-current assets goodwill is not amortised over its useful economic life but is tested for impairment annually, or more frequently if events or changes in circumstances indicate that the asset might be impaired, in accordance with IAS 36 Impairment of Assets.

Impairment requires the goodwill to be evaluated to see if its value in the balance sheet is greater than the net income that could be derived from the goodwill either from its continued use in the business or from sale. It must then be reduced to the lower figure and the difference charged as an expense to the profit and loss account.

Research and development costs

Research and development are activities directed to the development of knowledge. Development costs do not include research costs.

A development cost is defined in IAS 38, Intangible Assets, as the cost of the application of research findings or other knowledge to a plan or design for the production of new or substantially improved materials, devices, products, processes, systems or services before the start of commercial production or use. Development expenditure on new products or services is normally undertaken with an expectation of future commercial benefits, from either increased profits or reduced costs. Development costs are therefore matched against future revenues. IAS 38 indicates that once an intangible asset arising from development activity can be recognised it is capitalised as an intangible asset in the balance sheet. The cost of the intangible asset is then charged in proportion to the revenues derived from this development activity period by period over the life of the project.

Examples of development activities that might create intangible assets include:

- design, construction and testing of pre-production prototypes
- design of equipment that uses new technology
- a pilot project involving design, construction and operation of a new plant.

Research costs are defined in IAS 38 as the costs of original and planned investigation undertaken with the prospect of gaining new scientific or technical knowledge and understanding.

Examples of activities classified as research include:

- activities aimed at obtaining new knowledge
- the search for applications of research findings or other knowledge
- the search for alternatives for materials, devices, products, processes, systems or services.

In general, no one particular period rather than another is expected to benefit from research activities and so their costs should be charged to the profit and loss account as they are incurred.

Inventories

Problems arise in the area of valuation of inventories for three main reasons. First, homogeneous items within various inventory categories are purchased continuously and consumed continuously in the manufacturing processes. The purchase prices of these homogeneous items may vary considerably. How do we know the specific prices of each item as we take them from inventory and use them?

The general rule is that inventories must be valued at the lower of purchase cost (or production cost) and their net realisable value. IAS 2, Inventories, allows alternative methods to be used to match the cost of inventory items with their usage: FIFO (first in first out, where the oldest items of inventory or their costs are assumed to be the first to be used); weighted average cost.

LIFO (last in first out, where the most recently acquired items of inventory or their costs are assumed to be the first to be used) is not permitted in IAS 2, and is not acceptable for taxation purposes in the UK.

Second, materials may be purchased from a variety of geographical locations. Additional costs such as duty, freight and insurance may be incurred. How should these be accounted for? The costs of inventories should comprise the expenditure that has been incurred in the normal course of business in bringing the product or service to its present location and condition.

Third, as materials, packaging and other consumable items are used during the production processes to manufacture work in progress, partly finished product and fully finished product, how should costs be correctly apportioned to give a true cost? Which costs should be included and which should be excluded?

Inventories are disclosed as a main heading in the balance sheet and comprise raw materials and consumables, work in progress, and finished goods. IAS 2 requires that companies must disclose accounting policies adopted in respect of inventories and work in progress.

Trade receivables

Trade receivables are normally paid to the company according to contractual terms of trading agreed at the outset with each customer. However, economic and trading circumstances may have changed.

Can the company be sure that it will receive payment in full against all outstanding receivables? If not, what is a more realistic valuation of such receivables?

Trade receivables may need to be reduced by an assessment of individual accounts receivable that will definitely not be paid (bad debts), or individual accounts receivable that are unlikely ever to be paid (doubtful debts). Bad and doubtful debts and their impact on profit and trade receivables will be examined in detail in Chapter 4, which looks at the income statement.

When goods or services are supplied to a customer they are invoiced at the agreed price and on the trading terms that have been contracted. The trading terms may be, for example 30 days. In this case the sales value will have been taken into the current period profit and loss account but the debt, or the account receivable, will remain unpaid in the accounts receivable ledger until it is settled after 30 days.

Foreign currency transactions

A general factor that may impact on the valuation of all asset types (and liability types) is foreign currency exchange rate risk. For example, a customer in the USA may insist on being invoiced by the company in US$, say 10,000 US$. At the time of delivery of the goods or services the value of the US$ sale in £ at the exchange rate on the day may be say £6,250 (£ = 1.60 US$). The sales invoice may be issued a few days later and the exchange rate may have changed, for example £6,173 (£ = 1.62 US$). The customer may have agreed to settlement two months later, by which time the exchange rate may have moved again, say £5,714 (£ = 1.75 US$). What value should have been attributed to the account receivable at the balance sheet date?

The value attributed to a sales invoice is its £ value on the day if invoiced in £ sterling. If a sales invoice is rendered in foreign currency IAS 21 requires it to be valued at the exchange rate at the date of the transaction, or at an average rate for the period if exchange rates do not fluctuate significantly. If the transaction is to be settled at a contracted exchange rate then the exchange rate specified in the contract should be used. Such a trading transaction is then said to be covered by a matching forward contract.

> ### Progress check 3.8
>
> UK International Ltd invoiced a customer in the USA for goods to the value of 100,000 US$ on 31 December 2009. The US$ cheque sent to UK International by the customer was received on 31 January 2010 and was converted into £ sterling by the bank at 1.55 US$ to £1. Discuss the two transactions, the invoice and its settlement, and their impact on UK International Ltd's income statement and its balance sheet as at 31 December 2009.

A foreign exchange forward contract is a contract, for example between a company and a bank, to exchange two currencies at an agreed exchange rate. Note also the foreign exchange forward option contract which extends this idea to allow the bank or the company to call for settlement of the contract, at two days' notice, between any two dates that have been agreed between the bank and the company at the time of agreeing the contract.

At the end of each accounting period, all receivables denominated in foreign currency should be translated, or revalued, using the rates of exchange ruling at the period-end date, or where appropriate, the rates of exchange fixed under the terms of the relevant transactions. Where there are related or matching forward contracts in respect of trading transactions, the rates of exchange specified in those contracts may be used. A similar treatment should be applied to all monetary assets and liabilities denominated in a foreign currency, that is cash and bank balances, loans, and amounts payable and receivable.

An exchange gain or loss will result during an accounting period if a business transaction is settled at an exchange rate which differs from that used when the transaction was initially recorded, or where appropriate that used at the last balance sheet date. An exchange gain or loss will also arise on unsettled transactions if the rate of exchange used at the balance sheet date differs from that used previously. Such gains and losses are recognised during each accounting period and included in the profit or loss from ordinary activities.

Summary of key points

- Items of expenditure may be generally classified as either capital expenditure or revenue expenditure, although some items may need to be apportioned between the two classifications.

- Limited companies are required to prepare periodically three main financial statements: balance sheet; income statement; statement of cash flows.

- Financial statements are required for the shareholders and the Registrar of Companies, and are also used by, for example, analysts, potential investors, customers, suppliers.

- Categories within the balance sheet are classified into shareholders' equity, liabilities and assets.

- With regard to the structure of the balance sheet, assets and liabilities must both be classified as current and non-current but IAS 1 provides a choice in presentation of the balance sheet between separating current and non-current assets and liabilities, or presenting assets and liabilities in order of their liquidity (or in reverse order of liquidity) without a current and non-current distinction.

- Valuation of the various items within the balance sheet is covered by the accounting concepts, International Accounting Standards (IASs) and UK Financial Reporting Standards (FRSs), but nevertheless gives rise to problems and differences in approach.

- Within the rules, alternative methods may be used to value the different categories of assets (and liabilities) within the balance sheet.

- There are limitations to the conventional balance sheet arising not only from the fact that it is a historical document, but from inconsistencies in its preparation between companies and industries, the employment of various asset valuation methods, off-balance sheet financing and window dressing.

Assessment material

Questions

Q3.1 (i)   What are the three main financial statements?
(ii) What is their purpose?
(iii) What does the statement of changes in equity show?

Q3.2 Consider two ways of looking at the profit of a business: an increase in the book wealth of the company; and the net result of the company's trading operations (revenue less expenses). What do these terms mean, and is the result different using the two approaches?

Q3.3   Explain the format and structure of the balance sheet of a typical limited company.

Q3.4   Explain what assets, liabilities and shareholders' equity are, and give some examples of the items included in each of these categories.

Q3.5   Illustrate the difference between current liabilities and non-current liabilities by giving some examples of each.

Q3.6   **(i)**   What accounting convention is generally used in the valuation of non-current assets?
(ii)   What additional costs may sometimes be included within non-current assets costs and to which assets may these be applied?

Q3.7   Why are current assets and non-current assets shown under different balance sheet classifications?

Q3.8   Describe what is meant by intangible assets and give some examples of how they may be valued.

Q3.9   What factors influence the accurate valuation of a company's trade receivables?

Q3.10   Why should a potential investor exercise caution when analysing the balance sheets of potential companies in which to invest?

Discussion points

D3.1   'Surely the purchase of non-current assets is expenditure just like spending on stationery or photocopy expenses so why should it appear as an entry in the balance sheet?' Discuss.

D3.2   'It has often been said that the value of every item in a balance sheet is a matter of opinion and the cash and bank balances are the only numbers that can truly be relied upon.' Discuss.

Exercises

Solutions are provided in Appendix 2 to all exercise numbers highlighted in colour.

Level I

E3.1   *Time allowed – 30 minutes*
Mr IM Green – Manager Ian admired the sign on the door to his new office, following his appointment as manager of the human resources department. The previous manager left fairly suddenly to join another company but had left Ian with some papers about the costs of his department, which showed a total of £460,000 together with a list of items of expenditure. This seemed rather a high figure to Ian for a department of five people. Ian's boss muttered something to him about capital expenditure and revenue expenditure, but this was an area about which Ian had never been very clear. The list left with Ian by his predecessor was as follows:

	£
Legal fees	42,000
Five personal computers	15,000
Specialist HR software	100,000

	£
Three laser printers	10,000
Salaries	158,000
Employee benefit costs	16,000
Pension costs	14,000
Building repairs	25,000
Equipment repairs	8,000
Health and safety costs	20,000
Staff recruitment fees	10,000
Training costs	20,000
Subsistence and entertaining	10,000
Office furniture	12,000
	460,000

Assume that you are the finance manager whom Ian has asked for advice and provide him with a list that separates the items into capital expenditure and revenue expenditure.

E3.2   *Time allowed – 30 minutes*

The balances in the accounts of Vertico Ltd at 31 July 2010 are as follows:

	£000
Accrued expenses	95
Bank overdraft	20
Accounts receivable	275
Plant and equipment	309
Inventories of finished products	152
Computer system	104
Petty cash	5
Equity share capital	675
Accounts payable	293
Final payment on computer system due 1 September 2011	52
Loan for a factory building	239
Buildings	560
Raw materials	195

(i)   An important number has been omitted. What is that?

(ii)   Using the data provided and the missing data prepare a balance sheet for Vertico Ltd as at 31 July 2010.

E3.3   *Time allowed – 45 minutes*

You are required to prepare a balance sheet for Trainer plc as at 31 December 2010 using the trial balance at 31 December 2010 and the additional information shown on the next page.

	Debit £000	Credit £000
Bank balance	73	
Ordinary share capital		320
Land and buildings at cost	320	
Plant and machinery at cost	200	
Cumulative depreciation provision (charge for year 2010 was £20,000)		80
Inventories	100	
Revenue		1,000
Cost of sales	600	
Operating expenses	120	
Depreciation	20	
Bad debts written off	2	
Accounts receivable	100	
Accruals		5
Accounts payable		130
	1,535	1,535

Additional information: the company will be paying £20,000 for corporation tax on the 2010 profit during 2011.

E3.4   *Time allowed – 45 minutes*

The following information relates to Major plc at 31 December 2010 and the comparative numbers at 31 December 2009.

	2009 £000	2010 £000
Accruals	800	1,000
Bank overdraft		16,200
Cash at bank	600	
Plant and machinery at cost	17,600	23,900
Debenture loan (interest at 15% per annum)	600	750
Plant and machinery depreciation	9,500	10,750
Proposed dividends	3,000	6,000
Ordinary share capital	5,000	5,000
Preference share capital	1,000	1,000
Prepayments	300	400
Retained earnings	3,000	10,100
Inventories	5,000	15,000
Tax payable	3,200	5,200
Accounts payable	6,000	10,000
Accounts receivable	8,600	26,700

Prepare a balance sheet in the format adopted by most of the leading UK plcs showing the previous year comparative figures.

E3.5   *Time allowed – 60 minutes*

From the trial balance of Gremlins plc at 31 March 2010 identify the assets and expenses (debit balances) and income, liabilities and equity (credit balances). Confirm that the trial balance is in balance, then prepare a balance sheet for Gremlins Ltd as at 31 March 2010.

	£000
Depreciation on office equipment and furnishings (administrative expenses)	156
Bank overdraft	609
Accountancy and audit fees	30
Electricity paid in advance	45
Computer system (net book value)	441
Advertising and promotion	135
Share premium account	240
Interest received	15
Plant and equipment (net book value)	927
Amount for final payment on factory machine due March 2012	252
Accounts receivable	1,110
Goodwill	204
Twelve-year lease on factory	330
Rents received	63
Prepaid expenses	885
Interest paid	120
Office electricity	66
Retained earnings at 1 April 2009	513
Inventories of materials at 31 March 2010	585
Telephone	87
Distribution costs	162
Other office utilities	72
Cost of goods sold	1,659
Administrative salaries	216
Sales department salaries	267
Furniture and fixtures (net book value)	729
Revenue	3,267
Office rent	165
Finished products at 31 March 2010	84
Debenture loan	750
Accounts payable	1,257
Bank and cash	51
Share capital	1,560

Level II

E3.6   *Time allowed – 60 minutes*

Prepare a balance sheet as at 31 December 2010 for Gorban Ltd based on the following trial balance, and the further information shown below.

	£	£
Equity share capital		200,000
Retained earnings		108,968
Building at cost	130,000	
Machinery at cost	105,000	
Provision for depreciation as at 31 December 2010		30,165
Provision for doubtful debts at 31 December 2010		1,725
Accounts payable		35,112
Accounts receivable	42,500	
Bank balance	67,050	
Loan		20,000
Inventories as at 31 December 2010	51,420	
	395,970	395,970

You are given the following additional information, which is not reflected in the above trial balance.

(a) The authorised and issued share capital is divided into 200,000 shares at £1 each.
(b) Wages unpaid at 31 December 2010 amounted to £1,173.
(c) Inventories at 31 December 2010 were found to have been undervalued by £48,000.
(d) The provision for doubtful debts is to be increased by £1,870.
(e) Additional machinery was purchased on 31 December 2010 for cash at a cost of £29,368.
(f) The company issued 50,000 £1 ordinary shares at par on 31 December 2010.
(g) A customer owing £10,342 went into liquidation on 9 January 2011 – a bad debt which had not previously been provided for.
(h) The loan was repaid on 31 December 2010.

E3.7 *Time allowed – 60 minutes*

> You are required to prepare a balance sheet as at 31 December 2010 from the following summary of Pip Ltd's financial position at 31 December 2010.

Brands worth £10,000 (directors' opinion)
Reputation in the local area £10,000 (directors' opinion)
Inventories at cost £50,000 and resale value £85,000, with obsolete inventories £5,000 within the £50,000
Bank overdraft facility £20,000 agreed by the bank manager
Cash in the office £1,000
Cash in the bank number one current account £10,000
Overdraft on the bank number two current account £10,000, per the bank statement
Land and buildings at cost £100,000
Plant and equipment at cost £150,000
Plant and equipment cumulative depreciation £50,000
Plant and equipment market value £110,000
Accounts payable £81,000
Invoices outstanding by all customers £50,000, including an invoice of £5,000 owed by a customer in liquidation (Pip Ltd has been advised by the receiver that 1p in the £1 will be paid to creditors)
Past profits reinvested in the business £110,000
Ordinary shares issued £100,000 (authorised ordinary shares £200,000)

4

Financial statements of limited companies – income statement

Contents

Learning objectives

Completion of this chapter will enable you to:

- describe what is meant by profit (or loss)
- outline the structure of the income statement of a limited company
- classify the categories of income and expenditure that make up the income statement
- appreciate the alternative income statement formats
- prepare an income statement
- explain the links between the income statement and the balance sheet, particularly with regard to the valuation of non-current assets and depreciation, inventory and cost of sales, and accounts receivable and the doubtful debt provision
- explain the links between the income statement and cash flow
- appreciate the subjective aspects of profit measurement.

Introduction

In Chapter 3 we looked at how to prepare simple financial statements from transactions carried out by a business during an accounting period. We then looked in a little more detail at the first of these financial statements, namely the balance sheet. This chapter will be concerned with the second of the financial statements, the income statement (or profit and loss account). Although income statements are prepared by all forms of business entity, this chapter, in a similar way to Chapter 3, deals primarily with the income statements of limited companies, both private and public.

This chapter deals with how income statements are structured and how the accounts within the income statement are categorised. Each of the items within each of the income statement categories will be described in detail and form the basis to enable the preparation of an income statement of a limited company in the appropriate format.

We will look at the relationship between the income statement and the balance sheet and provide an introduction to the relationship between profit (or loss) and cash flow. Like the balance sheet, the income statement is subjective largely because of the impact on costs of the variety of approaches that may be taken to the valuation of assets and liabilities.

What does the income statement tell us?

The income statement of a private limited company or a public limited company should be able to tell us all about the results of the company's activities over specified accounting periods. The income statement shows us what revenues have been generated and what costs incurred in generating those revenues, and therefore the increase or decrease in wealth of the business during the period.

The same note of caution we mentioned in Chapter 3 that should be exercised in the analysis of balance sheet information, applies to income statement information. The income statement is a historical statement and so it does not tell us anything about the ability of the business to sustain or improve upon its performance over subsequent periods.

There is not always consistency between the information included in one company's income statement and that of another company. As with the balance sheet, the income statements of two companies even within the same industry may be very difficult to compare. This will be illustrated by the wide variety of methods of depreciation calculations and inventory valuation methods examined in this chapter. In addition, the bases of financial ratios (to be examined in detail in Chapter 7) used by analysts in looking at a company's income statement may often be different.

It is often said of income statements, as well as of balance sheets, that the value of every item included in them is a matter of opinion. This is due not only to the alternative inventory valuation and depreciation methods, but also because of the subjective assessment of whether the settlement of a customer account is doubtful or not, and the sometimes imprecise evaluation of accruals and provisions.

What is profit?

We saw from the worked examples in Chapter 2 that profit (or loss) may be considered from two perspectives. We may consider these perspectives to illustrate the links between the income statement and the balance sheet.

The first perspective, which is not suggested as a method for calculating profit in practice, compares the balance sheet of an entity at the start of an accounting period with the balance sheet at the end of the accounting period. We may see from these that the values of each of the components of the balance sheet may have changed. For example, levels of inventory, accounts receivable, accounts payable, cash, non-current assets and accruals may have changed during an accounting period. We have seen that the net value of the assets and liabilities in the balance sheet represents the capital, or equity, or the wealth of the business at a point in time. The change in wealth over an accounting period between the beginning and end of the accounting period is the profit or loss for the period reflected in the retained earnings category in the balance sheet.

Profit (or loss) considered in this way can be represented in the equation:

total assets (TA) − total liabilities (TL) = equity (E) + retained profit (RP)

Worked example 4.1

Using the balance sheet as at 1 March 2010 below and the further transactions (a) and (b), we are able to:

(i) show how the balance sheet will appear at the end of March after these transactions and events have taken place

(ii) identify the profit which the shareholders should consider is potentially distributable as a dividend.

Balance sheet as at 1 March 2010	£
Non-current assets	100,000
Current assets	100,000
less	
Current liabilities	(100,000)
Net assets	100,000
Equity	100,000

During March

(a) the non-current assets were re-valued from £100,000 to £120,000
(b) all the inventories of £20,000 were sold for £40,000 cash (that is, not on credit).

(i)

Balance sheet as at 31 March 2010	£
Non-current assets [100,000 + 20,000]	120,000
Current assets [100,000 − 20,000 + 40,000]	120,000
less	
Current liabilities [no change]	(100,000)
	140,000
Equity [100,000 + 20,000 + 20,000]	140,000

(ii)

The revised balance sheet reflects two profits:

- The revaluation surplus of £20,000 is a paper profit; as no cash has been involved it is not prudent to pay a dividend from this profit (and legally it is not permitted).
- The other £20,000 profit is from trading and is a cash profit; it is quite prudent to pay a dividend from this profit.

The balance sheets show each of the categories of assets, liabilities and equity, but it can be seen there must be an analysis of the movements between the balance sheets to appreciate their fundamental nature.

The second perspective, as we discussed in Chapter 3, considers profit by summarising all the trading and non-trading transactions that have occurred during an accounting period (see Figure 4.1). This is the method used in practice to calculate the profit or loss for an accounting period. This gives the same result as that derived by simply looking at the change in wealth between the beginning and end of the accounting period. It is the same because all the transactions relating to items contained in the profit and loss account are also all reflected in some way within one or more balance sheet categories. For example, sales revenues are reflected in trade receivables, expenses are reflected in trade payables, cost of goods that have been sold are reflected as a reduction of inventories.

Figure 4.1   The main elements of the income statement

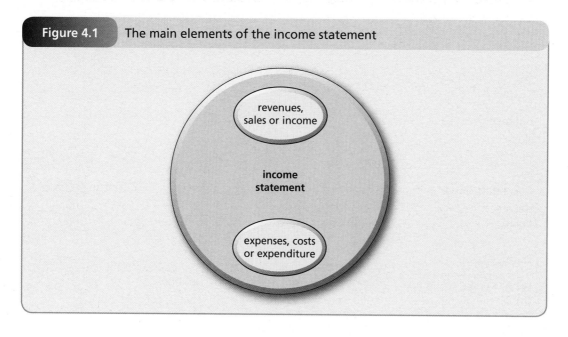

Profit (or loss) considered in this way can be represented in the equation:

profit (P) = total revenue (TR) − total costs (TC)

and it should be noted that

retained profit (RP) = profit (P) − dividends

Worked example 4.2

A trading company, Squirrel Ltd, has an accounting period that covers the 12 months to 31 December 2010. During that period the company entered into the following transactions:

Sales revenue of £1,300,000 included a sales invoice for January 2011 amounting to £100,000. Expenses of £1,000,000 included a payment of £60,000 for rent relating to the six months to 31 March 2011.

The expenses excluded some heating costs relating to the last two weeks of December 2010, for which the estimated cost was around £5,000. The quarterly invoice covering that period was not expected until late March 2011.

The above information may be used to look at why the annual net profit should be revenues less expenses, and why there should be accounting concepts applied to the treatment of those expenses.

The income statement for a year tries to match revenues and expenses for that year (complying with the matching concept – see Chapter 1). Profit means the difference between revenues and expenses. Gross profit or gross margin is derived from sales revenue less the costs of those sales, and profit is derived from deducting expenses from gross profit. Profit is not the difference between cash receipts and cash payments. Cash inflows and outflows suffer from timing differences.

The reported sales revenue for the year must relate only to the 12 months to 31 December. Sales revenue for Squirrel Ltd for the year 2010 is £1,200,000 (£1,300,000 less £100,000). Using the matching concept, the expenses must also be for 12 months. So the estimated heating costs of £5,000 for the last two weeks of December 2010 must be added, and the rent relating to January to March 2011 of £30,000 (£60,000/2) must be deducted from the total expenses of £1,000,000. Without these adjustments, the expenses would not represent 12 months' expenses.

Profit for the 12 months to 31 December 2010 for Squirrel Ltd is therefore:

Revenue	£1,200,000	[£1,300,000 less £100,000]
less		
Expenses	£975,000	[£1,000,000 plus £5,000 less £60,000 plus £30,000]
Which equals	£225,000	

There must be an application of accounting concepts and standard practices in arriving at profit, otherwise users of financial information would not have reasonable confidence in the amounts being shown in the financial statements reported by companies, large or small.

In this chapter we will look at the income statement from the second perspective. We will look at how an income statement is constructed and prepared by deducting total costs from total revenues, as the second of the three key financial statements that are required to be prepared by a limited company.

> **Progress check 4.1**
>
> Explain the perspectives from which we may consider the profit (or loss) of a business.

Income statement formats

The format of the income statement is explained in IAS 1 Presentation of Financial Statements. IAS 1 outlines the minimum information that should be disclosed on the face of the income statement, which gives a little flexibility to the ways in which individual companies report, rather than setting out a rigid format that must be adopted by every company.

IAS 1 does include the minimum information that should be disclosed on the face of the income statement, which includes:

■ revenue
■ finance costs
■ profits or losses arising from discontinued operations
■ income tax expense
■ profit or loss for the year.

IAS 1 recommends two alternative ways of presenting costs and expenses on the face of the income statement:

■ according to business functions, for example distribution costs and administrative expenses
■ according to their nature, for example employee expenses, depreciation etc.

The income statement in the example adopted by Flatco plc (see Figure 4.4) has been based on the format that presents expenses and costs according to business functions, and this format will be adopted generally throughout this book. Directors of companies will adopt this format if they believe that presenting how much of the revenue of the company was 'used' by particular functions of the business may provide more relevant and accurate information and a better impression of the efficiency of the business.

It is not always a straightforward matter to allocate costs within a company to specific functions. The costs of shared resources are often allocated between functions on a fairly arbitrary basis. The alternative presentation of the income statement which presents costs and expenses according to their nature, for example employee expenses, depreciation etc., may be adopted by companies. Certainly for management reporting within the company this analysis is far more useful in support of forecasting and planning.

Unlike FRS 3, Reporting Financial Performance, and UK GAAP, IAS 1 does not use the term 'exceptional items'. Exceptional items relate to material (significant), non-recurring items of income and expense of abnormal size and incidence arising from infrequent circumstances but which are derived from the ordinary activities of the business. FRS 3 required exceptional items to be included under the statutory format headings to which they relate and disclosed separately on the face of the income statement if necessary to give a true and fair view.

Although it does not refer to them as exceptional items, IAS 1 makes it clear that such material items of income and expense must be separately disclosed if they are relevant to an understanding of the financial performance of the business. These need not be shown on the face of the income statement so long as they appear within the notes on the financial statements. The material, non-recurring income and expense items that require separate disclosure include:

■ write-downs of inventories to net realisable value, and reversals of such write-downs
■ write-downs of property, plant and equipment to net realisable value, and reversals of such write-downs

- restructuring of the activities of the company
- reversals of provisions
- disposals of property, plant and equipment
- disposals of investments
- discontinued operations
- litigation settlements.

Another separate term, 'extraordinary items' as distinct from exceptional items, is defined as material income or costs which are derived or incurred from unusual events or transactions outside the ordinary activities of the company which like exceptional items are infrequent and therefore not expected to occur frequently or regularly. The costs resulting from the complete destruction of a factory may be sufficiently material and infrequent and possess such a high degree of abnormality as to warrant its disclosure as an extraordinary item.

Up until 2004, IAS 1 required extraordinary items to be disclosed in a separate line on the income statement. A company's ordinary activities have now been defined so broadly that the disclosure of extraordinary items is now expressly prohibited by IAS 1. US GAAP still requires extraordinary items to be disclosed in the income statement if they are unusual and infrequent.

Earnings per share (eps) are dealt with in IAS 33, Earnings per Share, which requires basic earnings per share and diluted earnings per share to be presented on the face of the income statement with equal prominence. Both should be presented relating to:

- the profit or loss from continuing operations attributable to ordinary equity shareholders of the parent company

and

- for total profit or loss attributable to such shareholders.

Earnings per share from discontinued operations should be shown either on the face of the income statement or in the notes on the accounts.

Basic earnings per share are calculated by dividing earnings, or profit of the year, by the weighted average number of ordinary shares in issue over the year. Diluted earnings per share are calculated by adjusting for a reduction in the earnings per share for the year caused by an increase or potential increase in the number of shares in issue, for example through the conversion of convertible securities into ordinary shares.

Earnings per share should also be presented for each class of ordinary shares that has a different right to participate in the profit of the company.

Group financial statements must to be prepared for the holding company in addition to the financial statements which are required to be prepared for each of the individual companies within the group. Consolidated financial statements exclude all transactions between companies within the group, for example inter-company sales and purchases. In most other respects the group consolidated financial statements reflect an amalgamation of each of the components of the income statements, balance sheets and statements of cash flows of all the companies within the group.

Progress check 4.2

There are broadly two income statement formats that are outlined in IAS 1. How do these formats differ? Which format appears to be favoured by the majority of large companies?

Structure of the income statement

As we have seen previously, the income statement measures whether or not the company has made a profit or loss on its operations during the period, through producing or buying and selling its goods or services. It measures whether total revenues are higher than the total costs (profit), or whether total costs are higher than total revenues (loss).

The total revenue of a business is generated from the provision of goods or services and may include, for example:

- sales of goods or services
- interest received (on loans)
- rents (from property)
- subscriptions (for example to TV channels)
- fees (for example professional subscriptions)
- royalties (payable on books and CDs)
- dividends received (from investments).

The total costs of a business include the expenditure incurred as a result of the generation of revenue. The total costs of a business include, for example:

- costs of goods purchased for resale
- costs of manufacturing goods for sale
- transport and distribution costs
- advertising
- promotion
- insurance
- costs of the 'consumption' of non-current assets over their useful lives (depreciation)
- wages and salaries
- interest paid
- stationery costs
- photocopy costs
- communications costs
- electricity
- water and effluent costs
- travel expenses
- entertaining expenses
- postage.

Each of the above examples of costs (which is by no means an exhaustive list) incurred in the generation of revenue by a business appears itself as a separate heading, or is grouped within one or other of the other main headings within the income statement. Figure 4.2 shows each of the levels of profit that are derived after allowing for the various categories of revenues and expenses.

We will look at how a basic income statement is constructed to arrive at the profit for the year after taxation (or net profit) for the company. Profit is also sometimes called earnings, or net income, from which may be deducted dividends payable to ordinary shareholders. The net result is then the retained earnings (or retained profit) for the financial year.

Each of the levels of profit shown in Figure 4.2 can be examined to show the categories of revenue and costs included in the income statement. These are illustrated in Figure 4.3, which is completely consistent with the headings shown in Figure 4.2.

Figure 4.2   Levels of profit within the income statement

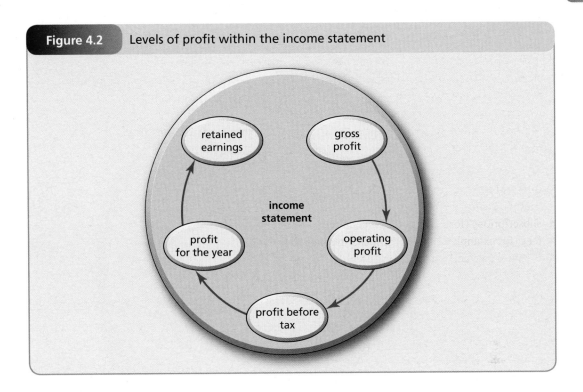

We will look at each of the headings included within the income statement as shown in Figures 4.2 and 4.3 in a little more detail.

Revenue

The main source of income for a company is its **revenue**, primarily comprising sales of its products and services to third-party customers. Revenues and costs are not necessarily accounted for when cash receipts and payments are made. Sales revenues are normally accounted for when goods or services are delivered and invoiced, and accepted by the customer, even if payment is not received until some time later, even in a subsequent trading period.

Cost of sales (COS)

It should be noted that a cost or expense is the financial result of the 'consumption' that occurred during the accounting period that relates directly or indirectly to the production or sales of the goods or services, and is accounted for as it is incurred rather than on a cash payment basis. Costs may be cash-related, invoiced costs such as raw materials, or non-cash items like depreciation charges.

The sum of direct costs of goods sold plus any manufacturing expenses relating to the sales revenue is termed cost of sales, or production cost of sales, or cost of goods sold. These costs include:

■ costs of raw material inventories used
■ costs of inward-bound freight paid by the company
■ packaging costs
■ direct production salaries and wages
■ production expenses, including depreciation of trading-related non-current assets.

| Figure 4.3 | Elements of the income statement |

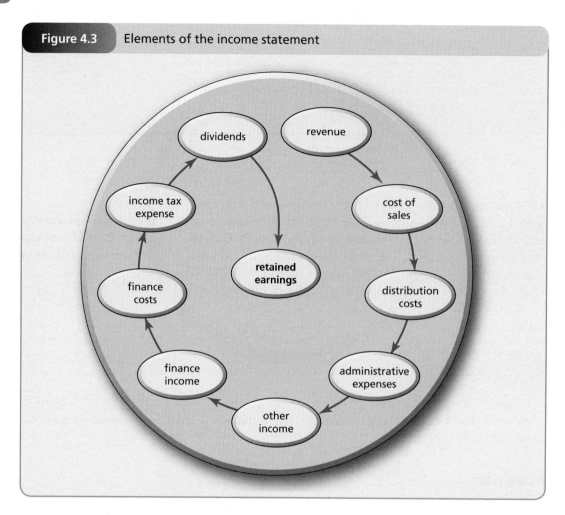

Gross profit (or gross margin)

The difference between revenue and cost of sales (COS) is **gross profit** or gross margin. It needs to be positive and large enough to at least cover all other expenses.

Distribution costs and administrative expenses

Although not directly related to the production process, but contributing to the activity of the company, there are further costs that are termed 'other operating expenses'. These include distribution costs and selling costs, administrative expenses, and research and development costs (unless they relate to specific projects and the costs may be deferred to future periods).

Distribution costs include the costs of selling and delivering goods and services. Such costs may include:

- advertising
- market research
- promotion
- costs of the sales department
- outbound freight costs
- delivery vehicles fleet costs
- costs of the warehouse and goods outward department.

Administrative expenses effectively include all costs not included in cost of sales, distribution costs and financial costs. They may include, for example:

- costs of service departments such as
  - finance
  - human resources
  - research and development
  - engineering
- telephone costs
- computer costs.

Distribution costs and administrative expenses include all expenses related to the 'normal' operations of the company, except those directly related to manufacturing like the costs of the purchasing department, logistics department and quality department. They also exclude the share of overhead costs, for example heating and lighting, business property taxes, water and effluent costs, relating to manufacturing activities. Administrative expenses exclude financial expenses and revenues, because these are really a function of the financial structure of the company (the extent of its funding by owners' share capital and by lenders' debt, or loans), and exclude any other non-operational expenses and revenues.

Other income

Other income includes all other revenues that have not been included in other parts of the income statement. It does not include sales of goods or services, reported within sales revenue, or any sort of interest receivable.

Operating profit (OP)

operating profit (OP)
= revenue − COS − distribution costs − administrative expenses + other income

The operating profit is the net of all operating revenues and costs, regardless of the financial structure of the company and whatever exceptional events occurred during the period that resulted in exceptional costs. The disclosure of operating profit is not listed as a requirement in IAS 1 but it is one of the specific recommendations within the UK standard FRS 3, Reporting Financial Performance.

Operating profit is a measure of the profitability of the operations of a company regardless of the amount of interest payable and receivable on overdrafts and loans, and regardless of the amount of corporation tax it may have to pay. It is therefore an extremely important profit or loss subtotal because it allows inter-company comparisons of companies operating in the same markets but having different financial policies.

Finance income

Finance income includes interest receivable, and dividends receivable from subsidiary companies and from **non-related companies**.

Finance costs

Finance costs include interest paid and interest payable, and other financial costs like bank charges and costs of transferring funds. The overall level of finance costs will be dependent on the type of company and level of interest rates and debt and equity mix within the funding of the company.

Profit before tax (PBT)

> **profit before tax (PBT) = OP + finance income − finance costs**

Income tax expense

Corporation tax is payable on profits of limited companies. The companies, as entities, are responsible for the tax, rather than individuals as with sole traders and partnerships. Tax is shown in the income statements, balance sheets and statements of cash flows of limited companies.

The corporation tax shown on the face of the income statement will have been based on a computation carried out prior to the exact amount payable having been agreed with HMRC. There may therefore be some differences from year to year between the tax payable numbers reported and tax actually paid.

Figure 4.4 shows an example of the income statement format adopted by a public limited company, Flatco plc.

Profit for the year

> **profit for the year = PBT − income tax expense**

Figure 4.4	Income statement format in compliance with IAS 1

Flatco plc
Income statement for the year ended 31 December 2010

	£000
Revenue	3,500
Cost of sales	(2,500)
Gross profit	1,000
Distribution costs	(300)
Administrative expenses	(250)
Other income	100
Operating profit	550
Finance income	111
Finance costs	(71)
Profit before tax	590
Income tax expense	(50)
Profit for the year from continuing operations	540
Profit for the year from discontinued operations	–
Profit for the year	540

Profit for the year is the net profit, or net income, or earnings, on ordinary activities after tax. The final charge that a company has to suffer, provided it has made sufficient profits, is therefore corporate taxation.

The profit for the year has resulted from the following processes. The assets, owned by the shareholders, have generated the operating profit. Operating profit has been used to pay interest to bankers and other lenders, and corporation tax to HMRC. What is left, the profit for the year, 'belongs' to the equity ordinary shareholders.

The directors of the company then recommend and propose to the shareholders how the profit for the year may be appropriated. It may be paid out to shareholders in dividends, or it may be held in equity as retained earnings for reinvestment in the operations of the company, or it may be appropriated in any combination of both dividends and retained earnings. The shareholders vote on whether to accept or reject the directors' proposal. The profit for the year is therefore used to provide the shareholders' returns in terms of the dividends they receive from their total investment in the equity of the company; so, not only does the profit of the year have to be positive, but it has to be high enough to reward the risk the shareholders took in investing in the company. In some circumstances a dividend may be paid out of retained earnings, even though the company may have made a loss during the period. This is obviously only acceptable in the short term and cannot be continued for successive accounting periods.

> ### Progress check 4.3
>
> What exactly do we mean by cost of sales? What types of expense does cost of sales include and what types of expense does it exclude?

Dividends on ordinary shares

Dividends for the year paid on equity shares are disclosed in the financial statement, Statement of Changes in Equity as a deduction from retained earnings. IAS 1, Presentation of Financial Statements, implies that dividends are usually deducted from the profit for the financial year in arriving at the profit retained for the year. Dividends include any interim payment that may have been made and any final dividend proposed by the directors to be paid to shareholders later in the year.

Dividends on preference shares

Some companies issue preference shares as well as equity shares. These pay a dividend at a set percentage on face value and payments are made to preference shareholders before the payment of equity dividends. IAS 32, Financial Instruments, requires that dividends paid on preference shares with a set maturity date be treated as a finance cost and charged directly to the income statement, whereas dividends paid on preference shares which do not have a maturity date are treated just like dividends paid on ordinary shares and deducted from retained earnings in the Statement of Changes in Equity.

Retained earnings

The **retained earnings** (or retained profit) for the year is what is left from profit for the year after deducting dividends for the year. The remainder is added to cumulative retained earnings and forms part of the total equity (or shareholders' funds) of the company. It is a requirement included in IAS 1, Presentation of Financial Statements, that the company's annual report and accounts includes a statement that discloses the reconciliation of the movement on shareholders' funds that has taken

Figure 4.5	Statement of changes in equity

Flatco plc
Statement of changes in equity
for the year ended 31 December 2010

	Share capital £000	Share premium £000	Revaluation reserve £000	Translation reserve £000	Retained earnings £000	Total £000
Balance at 1 January 2010	1,000	200	–	–	1,124	2,324
Changes in equity for 2010						
Gain on revaluation of property	–	–	–	–	–	–
Exchange differences on translation of foreign operations	–	–	–	–	–	–
Net income recognised directly to equity	–	–	–	–	–	–
Profit for the period	–	–	–	–	540	540
Total recognised income and expense for the period	–	–	–	–	540	540
Dividends	–	–	–	–	(70)	(70)
Issue of share capital	200	–	–	–	–	200
Balance at 31 December 2010	1,200	200	–	–	1,594	2,994

place between the beginning and the end of the financial year, called the Statement of Changes in Equity (see Figure 4.5). This financial statement is a combination of the two previously required statements in the UK called the statement of recognised gains and losses, and the reconciliation of movements in shareholders' funds.

Progress check 4.4

The profit or loss that a business has earned or incurred during an accounting period may be ascertained by deducting the total costs from the total revenues for the period. Identify in which category of the income statement the following items may appear.

- interest received
- share premiums
- interest paid
- depreciation of factory machinery for the year
- CD royalties received
- outward freight costs
- sales of redundant inventories
- travel and subsistence

- accountancy fees
- electricity standing charge
- rents received
- telephone charges
- advertising and promotion
- raw materials purchases
- inventory of work in progress
- sales of finished product

Worked example 4.3

The relevant profit and loss account balances, representing the costs and revenues for the year to date as extracted from the trial balance of Perfecto Ltd at 30 September 2010, are presented below in an alphabetical list:

	£000
Advertising and promotion	54
Corporation tax	70
Costs of administrative departments	146
Costs of production departments	277
Costs of purchasing and logistics departments	77
Depreciation of factory machinery	284
Depreciation of office equipment	35
Direct labour cost of sales	203
Freight out costs	230
Interest paid	20
Interest received	10
Materials cost of sales	611
Rent and utilities (2/3 factory, 1/3 office)	48
Sales revenue	2,279
Warehousing and goods outward costs	84

We will prepare an income statement for Perfecto Ltd for the year to 30 September 2010, using the format that presents expenses and costs according to business functions which complies as far as possible with the requirements of IAS 1.

Perfecto Ltd
Income statement for the year ended 30 September 2010

	£000
Revenue	2,279
Cost of sales [277 + 77 + 284 + 203 + 611 + 32 (2/3 of 48)]	(1,484)
Gross profit	795
Distribution costs [54 + 230 + 84]	(368)
Administrative expenses [146 + 35 + 16 (1/3 of 48)]	(197)
Operating profit	230
Finance income	10
Finance costs	(20)
Profit before tax	220
Income tax expense	(70)
Profit for the year	150

Profit and loss and the balance sheet

The balance sheet and the income statement, whilst they are both historical statements, are not alternatives or competing options. They show different financial information, as we have discussed. The balance sheet shows the financial position at the start and at the end of an accounting period, and the income statement shows what has happened during the period, the financial performance.

The income statement and the balance sheet are linked in two ways:

- the cumulative balance on the profit and loss account of the company is reflected within the equity, or the shareholders' funds, category of the balance sheet representing the increase in the book wealth of the business
- some of the items contained in the profit and loss account are also all reflected in some way within one or more balance sheet categories.

In Chapter 3 we saw how the balance on the profit and loss account was reflected in retained earnings, within the equity of the company. We will now look at some of the types of adjusting entries used to prepare the income statement, which are also reflected in the balance sheet. Two of these types of adjusting entries, accruals and prepayments, were described in Chapter 2.

In this chapter we will look at some further categories of adjusting entries:

- depreciation, the depreciation provision and non-current assets
- the cost of sales and the valuation of inventories
- bad and doubtful debts and accounts receivable.

Worked example 4.4

Ronly Bonly Jones Ltd, or RBJ, buys and sells giftware. It made a profit of £10,000 during the month of January 2010.

We will use the balance sheet as at 1 January 2010 as the starting point and then look at how each of the elements in the income statement for January is reflected in the balance sheet to derive the balance sheet as at 31 January 2010.

The income statement for January 2010 and the balance sheet as at 1 January 2010 are as follows:

Income statement for January 2010	£000	£000
Revenue		650
Cost of goods sold		
Opening inventories	45	
Purchases	424	
	469	
less: Closing inventories	79	(390)
Gross profit		260
Depreciation		(5)
Expenses		(245)
Profit for January [650 − 390 − 5 − 245]		10

Additional information

RBJ acquired non-current assets in January for £20,000 cash, and raised additional share capital of £10,000.

Suppliers (trade payables) were paid £422,000 in the month and £632,000 was received from customers (trade receivables). The bank account at the end of January 2010 was overdrawn by £39,000.

Balance sheet as at 1 January 2010	£000
Non-current assets at cost	130
Depreciation provision	(20)
Inventories	45
Trade receivables	64
Cash and bank	6
	225
Trade payables	(87)
Share capital	(50)
Retained earnings	(88)
	(225)

Let's derive the 31 January 2010 balance sheet from the information that has been provided.

Figures in £000	Non-curr. assets	Depn.	Inventories	Trade rec'bles	Cash	Trade payables	Equity share capital	Retained earnings
1 January 2010	130	(20)	45	64	6	(87)	(50)	(88)
Sales revenue				650				(650)
Cash from customers				(632)	632			0
Purchases			424			(424)		0
Cash to suppliers					(422)	422		0
Inventory sold			(390)					390
Depreciation		(5)						5
Expenses					(245)			245
Non-current asset additions	20				(20)			0
Issue of shares	—	—	—	—	10	—	(10)	0
31 January 2010	150	(25)	79	82	(39)	(89)	(60)	(98)

Ronly Bonly Jones Ltd

Balance sheet at 1 January 2010 and at 31 January 2010 is as follows:

	1 January 2010	31 January 2010
	£000	£000
Non-current assets at cost	130	150
Depreciation provision	(20)	(25)
Inventories	45	79
Trade receivables	64	82
Cash and bank	6	–
	225	286
Trade payables	(87)	(89)
Bank overdraft	–	(39)
Share capital	(50)	(60)
Retained earnings	(88)	(98)
	(225)	(286)

Worked example 4.4 shows the changes in the balance sheet that have taken place over the month of January. The 31 January 2010 balance sheet has been derived from considering each element in the income statement for January and the additional information we were given and their impact on the balance sheet, and movements between accounts within the balance sheet:

- sales to customers on credit are the starting point for the income statement, which also increase trade receivables
- cash received from customers increases cash and reduces trade receivables
- purchases of goods on credit for resale increase inventories and increase trade payables
- cash paid to suppliers reduces cash and reduces trade payables
- inventory sold reduces inventories and is a cost in the income statement
- depreciation of non-current assets increases the depreciation provision and is a cost in the income statement
- payments of expenses reduce cash and are a cost in the income statement
- payments for additions to non-current assets increase non-current assets and reduce cash
- issues of ordinary shares increase equity share capital and increase cash.

In Worked example 4.4, depreciation is a relatively small number. Normally, income statement movements may have significant impacts on the balance sheet in the areas of both inventories and depreciation. Real-life cases that illustrate this are:

- during the years 2009 and 2010 several major retailers had to announce that their profits would be lower due to their inventories having to be heavily discounted (for example, JJB Sports plc)
- depreciation of an automotive assembly line may need to be changed due to a revision in its estimated useful economic life following a reassessment of the life cycle of a vehicle.

Progress check 4.5

Describe the ways in which a company's income statement and its balance sheet are linked.

We have already discussed the links between the various categories in the income statement and those within the balance sheet. Consequently, the ways in which specific balance sheet items are valued have a significant impact on the profit reported for an entity for a particular period. The requirement for the valuation, or revaluation of, for example, assets like machinery, raw materials and finished product may be a result of their consumption or being used up; it may be because of their deterioration or obsolescence, or significant changes in their market value. For whatever reason, such changes in the valuation of assets must be reflected in the income statement in the period in which they occur. We will focus here on the valuation of the three key areas of:

- non-current assets, reflected in the income statement within *depreciation*
- inventories, reflected in the income statement within *cost of sales*
- trade receivables, reflected in the income statement within *bad and doubtful debts*.

Depreciation

Generally, the total cost of using a non-current asset over its life may be defined as the original investment less an estimate of the portion of its cost that may be recovered (its residual value) at the end of the asset's useful life. IAS 16 calls this the depreciable amount and defines depreciation as the systematic allocation of the depreciable amount of an asset over its useful life. In accordance with the accruals (matching) concept a fair proportion of the total cost (or valuation) of a non-current asset, its depreciation, should be charged to the profit and loss account during each period that sales revenue or other benefits are received from the use of that asset. At the same time as the depreciation charge is made to the profit and loss account, the value of the non-current asset is reduced by the same amount from a corresponding entry to credit the cumulative **depreciation provision** ◀|||| account. The cumulative balance at any point in time on the depreciation provision account for a non-current asset is deducted from its historical cost to provide its net value shown in the balance sheet at that time.

Worked example 4.5

Many companies operate and succeed in one market for many years. One of many business 'facts of life' is that recurring profits can come to an abrupt end, when a successful business model develops a basic flaw. Changes in technology can cause a change in trading or force a complete review of the equipment, systems or methods of trading that have been highly profitable in the past. In January 2008 William Hill plc (the sports betting company) brought in an outside technology company to install a system to allow customers to place bets on events that are in progress. William Hill had spent two years developing software in-house but it would have taken several more years to develop, while already available software could be installed within the year. The effect was that the company had to write off £26m already spent on the development against profits for the year. Had the company not cancelled its in-house development the £26m would have been recognised as an intangible non-current asset. The company blamed the pressure of the rapid growth in Internet betting which had caused their share of the market to decline over the previous 18 months.

There a number of reasons why this type of equipment review might affect the annual profits:

(i)   The income statement for a year aims to match revenues and expenses for that year, complying with the matching concept (see Chapter 1). Additionally, when it is clear that an asset is no longer capable of generating economic benefits it should be written out of the accounts immediately following the prudence principle (see Chapter 1).

(ii)   One of a company's expenses relates to the use of non-current assets, which aims to spread the economic use of the asset over its useful life, and is called depreciation.

(iii) The choice of method of depreciating an asset will result in differing amounts of depreciation for the year and so the annual income statement can be quite different because of this subjective decision (which involves opinions that may vary from manager to manager, and company to company).

(iv)   The International Accounting Standards Board (IASB) introduced IAS 36, Impairment of Assets, which requires companies to formally review their non-current assets for any changes in circumstances (impairment is not recurring, whereas depreciation is recurring).

(v)   In the William Hill circumstances outlined above, the company would have had to acknowledge that the development it had already paid for would not bring the future benefits it had anticipated because of the sudden and unexpected change in customer preferences. The company would have to reduce its asset values to reflect the fact that its software development no longer had value because market circumstances had changed significantly and the costs had therefore to be written off against the current profits.

The useful life of an asset is the period of its service relevant to the business entity. With regard to the useful life of the asset, there are a number of problems in dealing with depreciation of non-current assets:

- determining the useful life of the asset
- determining the correct way to spread the total cost of the asset over the useful life
- physical limitations regarding the useful life
  - intensity of use of the asset
  - the actions of the elements
  - adequacy of maintenance
  - the simple passage of time (e.g. legal rights or patents)
- economic limitations in respect of useful life
  - technological developments
  - business growth.

Three of the many depreciation methods include:

- straight line
- reducing balance
- sum of the digits.

We will consider each of these in detail in Worked example 4.6. However, the straight line and the reducing balance methods are the ones that are most frequently used by companies.

Straight-line depreciation is calculated by deducting the residual value from the acquisition cost to obtain the net cost of the asset (the depreciable amount) and then dividing the result by the life of the asset.

The reducing balance method is used to derive the rate required (d) to reduce the cost of the asset, period by period, to the residual value by the end of its life. This may be expressed as:

$$d = 1 - \sqrt[life]{\text{residual value/original cost}}$$

The sum of the digits method considers the life of the asset, say for example five years, and allocates the net cost of the asset (acquisition cost less residual value) over that period as follows:

For a five-year life the sum of digits is $5 + 4 + 3 + 2 + 1 = 15$

So each year's depreciation is calculated:

1st year $5/15 \times$ (acquisition cost − residual value)
2nd year $4/15 \times$ (acquisition cost − residual value)
3rd year $3/15 \times$ (acquisition cost − residual value)
4th year $2/15 \times$ (acquisition cost − residual value)
5th year $1/15 \times$ (acquisition cost − residual value)

Worked example 4.6

Castle Ltd purchased an item of equipment for £16,000 and estimated its residual value, at the end of its useful economic life of five years, at £1,000. At the start of year one the net book value (NBV) is the acquisition cost of the asset £16,000.

Annual depreciation charges and net book values may be derived by using each of the three methods:

- straight line
- reducing balance
- sum of the digits.

Straight line depreciation divides the acquisition cost less the residual value by the number of years of economic life, in this case 5.
    Reducing balance depreciation calculates:

$$d = 1 - \sqrt[5]{1,000/16,000} = 42.57\%$$

The sum of the digits is $(5 + 4 + 3 + 2 + 1) = 15$.

Figures in £000

	Straight line			Reducing balance			Sum of the digits		
	Start		End	Start		End	Start		End
Year	NBV	Depn	NBV	NBV	Depn	NBV	NBV	Depn	NBV
1	16,000	3,000	13,000	16,000	6,810	9,190	16,000	5,000	11,000
2	13,000	3,000	10,000	9,190	3,912	5,278	11,000	4,000	7,000
3	10,000	3,000	7,000	5,278	2,247	3,031	7,000	3,000	4,000
4	7,000	3,000	4,000	3,031	1,290	1,741	4,000	2,000	2,000
5	4,000	3,000	1,000	1,741	741	1,000	2,000	1,000	1,000

The resultant cost of £1,000 in the balance sheet under the non-current assets category at the end of year five is the same using each of the methods. This cost is likely to be offset exactly by the proceeds of £1,000 expected to be received on disposal of the asset.

In addition to the methods already discussed, it should be noted that there are many alternative methods that may be used to account for depreciation. We will not look at the detailed calculations of any further methods, but you may consider Worked example 4.7, which serves only to illustrate the wide variations in yearly depreciation (and therefore net book values) that may be derived from a selection of alternative methods, compared with the straight line method.

Worked example 4.7

Consider a company van, which cost £20,000 to purchase new. Its residual value is estimated to be zero at the end of its useful life of five years. The rate of inflation is 10% and the cost of capital (see Chapter 14) is 15%.

The depreciation for the first year and the net book value (NBV) at the end of year one may be evaluated using six alternative methods, including straight-line depreciation.

	Depreciation calculation	Depreciation in year 1	NBV at end of year 1
1. Straight-line depreciation over five years, i.e. 20% per annum using a historical cost of £20,000	£20,000 × 20%	£4,000	£16,000
2. Constant purchasing power, which means allowing for an inflationary price increase (in this case 10%), and using straight-line depreciation at 20% per annum	£20,000 × 1.10 × 20%	£4,400	£17,600
3. Replacement value for an identical one-year-old van based on used van market value of say £17,000	£20,000 − £17,000	£3,000	£17,000
4. Replacement cost of a new van less one year's depreciation based on an estimated replacement cost of say £21,600	£21,600 × 20%	£4,320	£17,280
5. Net realisable value; the net proceeds from a trade auction of say £16,000	£20,000 − £16,000	£4,000	£16,000
6. Economic value; the estimated future cash flows from using the van: £6,000 per year for years 1, 2, 3, and 4, and the calculation of the **present value** of each year's cash flow using a cost of capital of 15% per annum using the technique of **discounted cash flow (DCF)** £6,000/1.15 + £6,000/1.15^2 + £6,000/1.15^3 + £6,000/1.15^4 = £17,130	£20,000 − £17,130	£2,870	£17,130

We have already seen from Worked example 4.6 that there may be large variations in the amounts of depreciation charged to the profit and loss account, in each year, dependent on which method is adopted by a company. Worked example 4.7 further illustrates the wide variation in first-year depreciation, from £2,840 to £4,400 on an asset costing £20,000, using six alternative methods of calculation. The particular depreciation method used by a company, therefore, may result in widely differing levels of profit reported each year. This sometimes makes it difficult to compare the profit of a company from one year to the next on a like-for-like basis. Likewise, it may sometimes be diffi-cult to accurately compare the yearly performance of two or more businesses, which may be similar in every respect other than the difference in the methods they have used to depreciate their non-current assets.

Whichever method of depreciation is used, it must be consistent from one accounting period to an-other. The depreciation method adopted must be disclosed within the company's accounting policies that accompany the financial statements in its annual report and accounts and include the depreci-ation rates applied to each of the categories of non-current asset.

Progress check 4.6

What are the various methods that may be used to depreciate an asset? Describe two of the most commonly used methods.

The amount of depreciation calculated for an accounting period is charged as a cost reflected in the income statement, the depreciation charge. A corresponding amount is also reflected in an account in the balance sheet, the cumulative depreciation provision account, the effect of which is to reduce the original, historical cost of the non-current assets at the end of each accounting period.

The difference between depreciation cost and other costs such as wages and salaries is that it is not a cash expense, that is it does not represent a cash outflow. The only cash outflow relating to deprecia-tion took place when the asset was originally purchased. The depreciation is really only the 'memory' of that earlier cash outflow.

Progress check 4.7

Why are assets depreciated and what factors influence the decision as to how they may be depreciated?

Cost of sales

As we saw in Chapter 3, inventories of raw materials, **work in progress**, finished product, spare parts, consumable stores, etc., pose problems in their valuation for three main reasons:

- raw materials may be purchased from a variety of geographical locations, and additional costs such as duty, freight and insurance may be incurred – the costs of inventories should comprise the expenditure that has been incurred in the normal course of business in bringing the product or service to its present location and condition

- packaging and other consumable items, in addition to raw materials, are used during the production processes to manufacture work in progress, partly-finished product and fully-finished product, and such costs must be correctly apportioned to give a true cost – inventories are disclosed as a main heading in the balance sheet and comprise raw materials and consumables, work in progress, finished goods, and long-term contracts
- homogeneous items within various inventory categories are purchased continuously and consumed continuously in the manufacturing processes and the purchase prices of these homogeneous items may vary considerably – inventories must be valued at the lower of purchase cost (or production cost) and their net realisable value (IAS 2).

There are many alternative methods that may be used to determine the cost of inventories. Four methods that are most commonly used by businesses are:

- first in first out (FIFO)
- last in first out (LIFO)
- weighted average cost
- market value.

The choice of method adopted by individual companies depends largely on their particular requirements and will be influenced by a number of factors:

- ease of use
- volumes of inventories
- costs of inventories
- management information requirements.

The FIFO method of inventory valuation is by far the most popular and is permitted by IAS 2, Inventories. FIFO (first in first out, where the oldest items of inventory, and their costs, are assumed to be the first to be used) assumes that costs are matched with the physical flow of inventory (although this may not actually be true).

LIFO (last in first out, where the most recently acquired items of inventory, and their costs, are assumed to be the first to be used) matches current costs with current revenues. LIFO is not permitted by IAS 2, and is not acceptable for UK taxation purposes.

The weighted average cost method is permitted by IAS 2. This method smoothes income and inventory values and assumes that individual units cannot be tracked through the system. The use of market values begs the questions as to which market value is most appropriate and whether replacement or realisable values be used.

Progress check 4.8

What factors must be considered regarding the valuation of inventories?

The following worked example looks at the four main methods of inventory valuation to enable us to provide a comparison in numerical terms and represent this graphically.

Worked example 4.8

A retailing company at 1 January 2010 has 400 units in inventory of a product that cost £3 each, and therefore a total cost of £1,200. The company's purchases over January and February were:

	Units	Price £	Value £	
January	600	4.00	2,400	
	800	5.00	4,000	Total £6,400
February	200	6.00	1,200	
	1,000	4.00	4,000	Total £5,200

and its sales over the same periods were:

	Units	Price £	Value £
January	1,400	12.00	16,800
February	1,400	12.00	16,800

The market value of a unit of each product was:

	Price £
January	6.00
February	3.00

FIFO – first in first out, matching costs with physical inventory flows

	Units	£		Units	£
January opening inventories	400	1,200	Sales	1,400	16,800
Purchases	1,400	6,400			
	1,800	7,600			
January closing inventories	400	2,000			
Cost of goods sold	1,400	5,600			
Gross profit		11,200			
		16,800			16,800
February opening inventories	400	2,000	Sales	1,400	16,800
Purchases	1,200	5,200			
	1,600	7,200			
February closing inventory	200	800			
Cost of goods sold	1,400	6,400			
Gross profit		10,400			
		16,800			16,800

Note that purchases are always valued at their actual cost regardless of which inventory valuation method is used.

There were 400 units in inventory at the beginning of January that cost £3 each and then 600 units were purchased at £4 each and then 800 purchased at £5 each. On a FIFO basis it is assumed that the 1,400 units sold in January first used the 400 opening inventory and then the 600 units first purchased and then 400 of the 800 units next purchased. The cost of these units was (400 × £3) + (600 × £4) + (400 × £5) = £5,600. The 400 units of inventory remaining at the end of January (which becomes the opening inventory at the beginning of February) are the 400 units left from the purchase of 800 units at £5 each and so are valued at £2,000. Using the same basis, the cost of the 1,400 units sold in February was (400 × £5) + (200 × £6) + (800 × £4) = £6,400. The 200 units of inventory remaining at the end of February are the 200 units left from the purchase of 1,000 units at £4 each and so are valued at £800.

The result is a gross profit of £11,200 for January and £10,400 for February.

LIFO – last in first out, matching current costs with current revenues

	Units	£		Units	£
January opening inventories	400	1,200	Sales	1,400	16,800
Purchases	1,400	6,400			
	1,800	7,600			
January closing inventories	400	1,200			
Cost of goods sold	1,400	6,400			
Gross profit		10,400			
		16,800			16,800
February opening inventories	400	1,200	Sales	1,400	16,800
Purchases	1,200	5,200			
	1,600	6,400			
February closing inventories	200	600			
Cost of goods sold	1,400	5,800			
Gross profit		11,000			
		16,800			16,800

There were 400 units in inventory at the beginning of January that cost £3 each and then 600 units were purchased at £4 each and then 800 purchased at £5 each. On a LIFO basis it is assumed that the 1,400 units sold in January used the 800 last purchased at £5 each and then the 600 units purchased at £4 each. The cost of these units was (800 × £5) + (600 × £4) = £6,400. The 400 units of inventory remaining at the end of January (which becomes the opening inventory at the beginning of February) are the 400 units left from opening inventory at £3 each and so are valued at £1,200. Using the same basis, the cost of the 1,400 units sold in February was (1,000 × £4) + (200 × £6) + (200 × £3) = £5,800. The 200 units of inventory remaining at the end of February are the 200 units left from the opening inventory of 400 units at £3 each and so are valued at £600.

The result is a gross profit of £10,400 for January and £11,000 for February.

Weighted average cost – smoothing of revenues and inventories values, assuming that individual units purchased cannot be followed through to actual sales so total purchases are combined to calculate an average cost per unit

	Units	£		Units	£
January opening inventories	400	1,200	Sales	1,400	16,800
Purchases	1,400	6,400			
	1,800	7,600			
January closing inventories	400	1,689			
Cost of goods sold	1,400	5,911			
Gross profit		10,889			
		16,800			16,800

$$\text{Weighted average cost per unit for January} = \frac{(1{,}200 + 6{,}400)}{(400 + 1{,}400)} = \frac{7{,}600}{1{,}800} = £4.222$$

$$\text{January closing inventories} = 400 \times \frac{7{,}600}{1{,}800} = £1{,}689$$

	Units	£		Units	£
February opening inventories	400	1,689	Sales	1,400	16,800
Purchases	1,200	5,200			
	1,600	6,889			
February closing inventories	200	861			
Cost of goods sold	1,400	6,028			
Gross profit		10,772			
		16,800			16,800

$$\text{Weighted average cost per unit for February} = \frac{(1{,}689 + 5{,}200)}{(400 + 1{,}200)} = \frac{6{,}889}{1{,}600} = £4.305$$

$$\text{February closing inventories} = 200 \times \frac{6{,}889}{1{,}600} = £861$$

The result is a gross profit of £10,889 for January and £10,772 for February.

The lower of FIFO or market value

	Units	£		Units	£
January opening inventories	400	1,200	Sales	1,400	16,800
Purchases	1,400	6,400			
	1,800	7,600			
January closing inventories	400	2,000			
Cost of goods sold	1,400	5,600			
Gross profit		11,200			
		16,800			16,800
February opening inventories	400	2,000	Sales	1,400	16,800
Purchases	1,200	5,200			
	1,600	7,200			
February closing inventories	200	600			
Cost of goods sold	1,400	6,600			
Gross profit		10,200			
		16,800			16,800

The value of January closing inventories using FIFO is £2,000. Using market value, January closing inventory is 400 units at £6 per unit − £2,400. Using the lower value, inventory at the end of January is £2,000. February closing inventory using FIFO is £800. Using market value, February closing inventory is 200 units at £3 per unit − £600. Using the lower value, inventory at the end of February is £600.

The result is a gross profit of £11,200 for January and £10,200 for February.

Summary of inventory valuation methods

	FIFO £	LIFO £	Weighted average cost £	Lower of FIFO or market value £
Profit				
January	11,200	10,400	10,889	11,200
February	10,400	11,000	10,772	10,200
Inventories valuation				
January	2,000	1,200	1,689	2,000
February	800	600	861	600

Graphical representations of the summary of inventory valuation methods used in Worked example 4.8 are shown in Figure 4.6 and Figure 4.7.

Figure 4.6 Profit comparison from the use of various inventory valuation methods

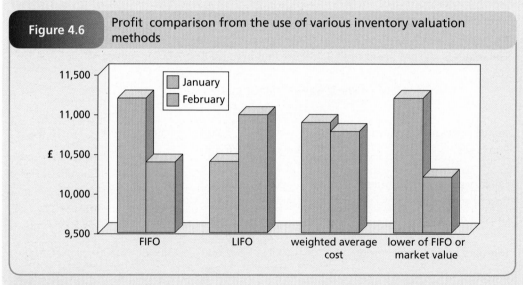

Figure 4.7 Inventory value comparison from the use of various inventory valuation methods

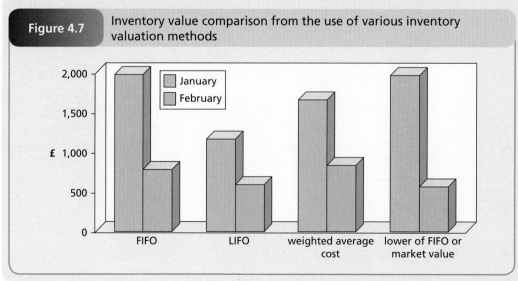

It can be seen from the summary of results in Worked example 4.8 that wide variations in profit may be reported from period to period. However, over the long run the total result will eventually be the same, when all inventories become used up. It is important to stress that a method may not be chosen to give, for example, a required result for one period. There must be consistency in the use of inventory valuation method from one period to the next.

Progress check 4.9

Why does inventory valuation cause such problems and why is it so very important?

Bad and doubtful debts

The term 'provision' often means very much the same thing as accrued expenses. The difference is that a provision is normally an amount charged against profit to provide for an expected liability or loss even though the amount or date of the liability or loss is uncertain. However, the word 'provision' is sometimes used in a different context, most commonly the depreciation provision relating to a non-current asset. It is also used in dealing with accounts receivable at the end of an accounting period.

When goods or services are sold to a customer on credit, an invoice is issued to record the transaction and to obtain settlement. The sale is reflected in the profit and loss account within the sales revenue of the business for the relevant period. The 'other side' of the accounting transaction is debited to accounts receivable, appearing as an amount due from the customer in line with the agreed payment terms. Most customers pay in accordance with their agreed terms, whether it is for example within 10 days, 1 month, or 2 months of invoice date. Unfortunately, there may sometimes be slow payers; there may be customers, for a variety of reasons, from whom payment will never be received. In the event of an invoice not being settled at all, as soon as this is known with reasonable certainty, the debt is deemed to be a bad debt and must be written off as a cost. The effect of this in the profit and loss account is not a reduction to sales revenue. It is a cost charged to the bad debt account. The accounting double entry is to the customer account to cancel the appropriate account receivable.

At the end of each accounting period accounts receivable still unpaid, falling outside their normal credit terms, must be reviewed as to the likelihood of their not paying in full or at all. If non-payment is certain then the debt must be written off. If there is uncertainty as to whether or not a debt will be settled then a provision for doubtful debts may be made on a specific basis, based on knowledge of particular customers, or on a general basis, say as a percentage of total accounts receivable, based on past trading experience.

An amount in respect of estimated doubtful debts that is charged to an account in the profit and loss account, the bad and doubtful debt account, is also reflected as a credit to an account in the balance sheet, the doubtful debt provision. The effect of the provision for doubtful debts is to reduce the value of accounts receivable in the balance sheet but without permanently eliminating any customer balances. Accounts receivable that are deemed to be bad debts are actually written off (charged as a cost in the profit and loss account) and the debts are permanently eliminated from accounts receivable.

Progress check 4.10

What are bad debts and doubtful debts and how are they reflected in the profit and loss account and balance sheet of a business?

Worked example 4.9

Accounts receivable on the books of Sportswear Wholesalers Ltd at 31 January 2010 were £429,378: current month £230,684, month two £93,812, three to six months £64,567, over six months £40,315. On 18 January 2010 one of Sportswear's customers, Road Runner Ltd, had gone into liquidation owing Sportswear £15,342, which had been invoiced over six months previously. Sportswear's policy was to provide for doubtful debts on the basis of three to six months' debts 5%, and over six months' debts 10%.

Let's consider what entries would appear in Sportwear's cumulative profit and loss account to January 2010 and its balance sheet at 31 January 2010 in respect of bad and doubtful debts. We may assume that no other debts have been written off during the year to date.

Road Runner Ltd had gone into liquidation owing Sportswear £15,342, of which it is assumed there was no chance of any recovery; therefore it had to be written off as a bad debt in the profit and loss account in January 2010.

The effect of the bad debt write-off was to reduce accounts receivable by £15,342, and the debts over six months old would reduce down to £24,973 [£40,315 − £15,342].

The doubtful debt provision at 31 January in line with Sportswear's policy was therefore:

5% × £64,567 = £3,228
10% × £24,973 = £2,497
Total   = £5,725 (assuming no opening doubtful debt provision at 1 January 2010)

Profit and loss account for the year to 31 January 2010:
Bad and doubtful debts

Road Runner Ltd write off 31 January 2010	£15,342
Doubtful debt provision at 31 January 2010	£5,725
Balance at 31 January 2010	£21,067

Balance sheet as at 31 January 2010:
Accounts receivable:

Balance 1 January 2010	£429,378
Road Runner Ltd write off 31 January 2010	£15,342
Balance at 31 January 2010	£414,036

Doubtful debt provision:

Doubtful debt provision at 31 January 2010	£5,725
Balance at 31 January 2010	£5,725

Trade receivables presented in Sportswear's published balance sheet as at 31 January 2010 would be £408,311 [£414,036 − £5,725].

Such bad and doubtful debt entries would not be individually apparent from inspection of Sportswear Wholesalers Ltd's financial statements. Bad and doubtful debt charges are normally included under the income statement heading *Distribution Costs*, and the corresponding balance sheet entries are reflected within the total *Trade Receivables* heading.

Profit and loss and cash flow

During the last decade of the twentieth century there was a great deal of activity in the birth and growth of so-called dot.com companies. Their aim was to exploit the use of the Internet to provide opportunities to sell products and services in wider markets and on an increasingly global basis.

The apparent success of the majority of these businesses was initially based on growth of potential in both market share and profitability reflected in the numbers of subscribers attracted to their websites. Actual and potential profitability do not necessarily inevitably result in a healthy cash position. Such companies invariably required large amounts of cash for them to continue operating for extended periods prior to achieving profitability and to generate their own cash flows. Many dot.com businesses from that era failed to survive and flourish, but there were also many successes, for example Google.com, Amazon.com, Sportingbet.com, and Lastminute.com.

In Chapter 3 we discussed how profit and cash flow do not mean the same thing. In fact, the profit earned and the net cash generated during an accounting period are usually very different, and often significantly different. How often do we see cases reported of businesses in serious financial difficulties because of severe cash shortages, even though they may appear to be trading profitably?

Profit is a matter of opinion. Cash flow is a matter of fact.

However, it is invariably the reported profits, or more usually estimated profits, that are closely monitored by investors and financial analysts. It is these numbers on which analysts base their business forecasts, and which influence investor confidence in a business, and therefore its share price.

While research by accountants Ernst & Young showed that profit warnings reached a six-year high in 2007, two years later the same researchers reported that profit warnings in 2009 had fallen to a six-year low. In spite of the reductions in the number of profit warnings issued, there were still some high-profile companies such as Aer Lingus, Sony Ericsson and National Express, who issued warnings. In 2010 the number of profit warnings began to rise again. Ernst & Young's research showed that 75 profit warnings were issued by 75 UK-listed companies in the first quarter of 2011, which was well up on the same period in 2010. The issue of a profit warning can have serious effects on the share values of the companies concerned, as illustrated by Thorntons in the press extract below.

Profit is important, but cash flow is very important. There is a relationship between cash and profit, and it is possible to identify and quantify the factors within this relationship. The profit or loss made by a business during an accounting period differs from the net cash inflows and outflows during the period because of:

■ cash expected to be paid or received relating to transactions during a period may in fact not be paid or received until the following or subsequent periods

■ cash may have been paid or received in advance of goods or services being received or provided and invoices being received or issued

Things get sticky for chocolate manufacturer

Sickly sweet chocolate, dull marketing, unappealing packaging, dismal displays . . . a steady stream of profit warnings from Thorntons has prompted a grandson of the confectionery firm's founder to deliver a scathing attack on management for 'wrecking' the 100-year-old business.

Blaming the unusually warm weather for putting children off their Easter eggs, Britain's biggest independent chocolate maker last week revealed it had suffered a 23% slump in chocolate sales over the financially crucial bank holiday as its 370 high-street shops and 229 franchise counters struggled to sell their sugary treats.

City analysts had a flash of déjà vu: just three months ago, Thorntons was blaming another climatic phenomenon – snow – for poor sales.

Thorntons' shares have fallen by 30% in 12 months and are down by two-thirds on their 2007 peak.

The firm has issued four profit warnings in little over a year and is on its fourth chief executive in 11 years. The City is running out of patience with the calamity-prone confectioner, and Peter Thornton, whose grandfather, Joseph, set up the company with a single sweetshop in Sheffield, is unimpressed.

'It's an old family business and I've been involved with it since I was 10 years old. I'm emotional about it,' says Thornton, who served as chairman until he was pushed out in a family rift in 1987. 'I hate to see it going downhill. I'd love to be able to put it right, which I don't think would be a very difficult job. I'm not very good at just letting go and letting somebody else wreck it.'

Thornton believes the 'theatre' of the company's chocolate shops has eroded as chocolates are sold in 'robot-packed' boxes designed to look fuller than they truly are. He reckons that the company's slogan – 'The Art of the Chocolatier' – is vacuous and that the stores are understaffed, and he complains that the once premium brand has been undermined by sales through supermarkets.

Last year, the scion of the chocolate dynasty teamed up with a group of associates including Peter Revers, a former Laura Ashley chief executive, to draw up a turnaround plan for Thorntons, which became Britain's biggest free-standing chocolate maker when Cadbury was snapped up by the US firm Kraft. But the six-page plan, obtained by the *Observer*, was rebuffed by Thorntons' chairman, former Budgens supermarket boss John von Spreckelsen, during a testy meeting at the Institute of Directors in London.

The changes prescribed by the septuagenarian Thornton are not to everybody's taste; he advocates a focus on British heritage, an end to drinks sales to concentrate on chocolate, and an ultimate push towards international expansion. But everybody agrees that troubled Thorntons can't carry on quite as it is.

The firm is one of the best-known brands on Britain's high streets, but it may not be as commonplace in future. Its new chief executive, Jonathan Hart, recruited from coffee chain Caffè Nero in January, has begun a strategic review that will involve a site-by-site examination of every shop.

Hart says Thorntons, which is likely to see its profits halved to £3m this year, is a victim of a high-street clearout in the wake of the recession. 'Some of the weaker high streets have become very weak, very quickly,' he says. 'One has to be grounded. We're all living in challenging times. The word "unprecedented" is perhaps overused.'

The chain, which employs 4,500 people, is hardly alone among retailers struggling in the recession. Woolworths, Borders, Zavvi, Threshers and Oddbins are among the many household names that have plunged into insolvency. Others, including HMV and All Saints, are facing a challenge to stay afloat.

Analysts believe that Hart must radically slim Thorntons down. David Stoddart, a retail expert at FinnCap, expects 'a couple of hundred' outlets to shut, partly because of cannibalisation as the chocolatier sells more of its produce in supermarkets. 'The more you can get your Thorntons' chocolate in your local Tesco or Sainsbury, the less you'll need to go to a Thorntons' shop,' Stoddart says.

One of Thorntons' challenges is that its factory at Alfreton, Derbyshire, was opened in more ambitious times, with capacity well beyond the amount of chocolate sold in the company's shops. Mail order is difficult because of the product's fragility and freshness. So the firm has made a conscious decision to push more of it through supermarkets.

Stoddart is also doubtful about Thorntons' positioning. He worries that it fails to distinguish itself in the premium category alongside names such as Green & Blacks and Hotel Chocolat, while still charging a higher price than mass-market Cadbury or Mars. 'It's probably not the present you'd give to impress a girlfriend.'

Few are optimistic about Thorntons' performance. The company is likely to cut its generous dividend payout this year to avoid dipping into reserves.

One previous chief executive, Peter Burdon, set a target of increasing the firm's market capitalisation to £1bn. That now seems laughable, with the figure down to £48m. Even Thorntons' house broker, Investec, is reluctant to advise clients to buy the shares; its recommendation was changed from 'hold' to 'under review' last week.

Some suggest that Thorntons' chocolate has failed to adapt to changing tastes towards darker, less sugary flavours. In a recession, though, treats ought still to prosper – Domino's Pizza has fared well from stay-at-home consumers seeking an inexpensive pick-me-up.

Clive Black, a food retailing analyst at Shore Capital in Liverpool, laments Thorntons' difficulties, recalling chewing its toffee as a child. 'In those days, Thorntons was a reasonably high-end brand and they had a real point of difference in their toffee,' he says.

Health concerns have taken their toll, Black says, as well as the firm's internal difficulties. 'I wish Thorntons well, because they're quite a nostalgic old British brand, but the fact is we've had more strategic reviews than I care to think of and they've seen off an awful lot of chief executives. They're the Coventry City of the confectionery world. No manager stays around long enough to prove whether they can be competitive.'

Source: **Anger grows at the Thorntons board as UK's famous chocolate brand goes stale**, by Andrew Clark © *The Observer*, 8 May 2011

■ cash may have been paid or received relating to non-manufacturing, non-trading or non-profit items – for example cash received for shares in the business and cash paid out on capital expenditure
■ profit will have been calculated to include the impact of non-cash items such as depreciation.

When we look at the statement of cash flows in the next chapter we shall see that one of the schedules that is required to be prepared in support of the statement of cash flows is in fact a reconciliation of profit to operating cash flow. Prior to that, we can consider the following example, which is not in strict compliance with the cash flow reconciliation schedule requirement, but will serve to illustrate how profit and cash flow are linked and how the links may be identified.

Worked example 4.10

In Worked example 4.4 we saw that Ronly Bonly Jones Ltd made a profit of £10,000 during the month of January 2010. A summary of its balance sheet at 1 January 2010, and the 31 January 2010 balance sheet that we derived, are as follows:

	1 January 2010 £000	31 January 2010 £000
Non-current assets at cost	130	150
Depreciation provision	(20)	(25)
Inventories	45	79
Trade receivables	64	82
Cash and bank	6	–
	225	286
Trade payables	(87)	(89)
Bank overdraft	–	(39)
Share capital	(50)	(60)
Retained earnings	(88)	(98)
	(225)	(286)

We can provide a reconciliation of Ronly Bonly Jones profit for the month of January with the cash flow for the same period.

	January 2010 £000
Profit for the month	10
Add back non-cash item:	
Depreciation for month	5
	15
Cash gained from:	
Increase in trade payables	2
Additional share capital	10
	27
Cash reduced by:	
Purchase of non-current assets	(20)
Increase in inventories	(34)
Increase in trade receivables	(18)
	(72)
Cash outflow for month	(45)
Cash and bank 1 January 2010	6
Cash outflow for month	(45)
Bank overdraft 31 January 2010	(39)

Despite making a profit of £10,000 during the accounting period the company in fact had a shortfall of cash of £45,000 for the same period. After adjusting profit for the non-cash item of depreciation and adding the increase in share capital it effectively had an increase in funds during the month of £25,000. It then had to finance the purchase of non-current assets of £20,000 and finance an increase in its working capital requirement of £50,000 (inventories £34,000 plus trade receivables £18,000 less trade payables £2,000). This resulted in its cash deficit for the month of £45,000. The company therefore went from having a positive cash balance of £6,000 at the start of the month to a bank overdraft of £39,000 at the end of the month.

Both the company and its bankers would obviously need to monitor RBJ's performance very closely over future months! A company will normally continuously review its cash, bank overdraft, trade payables and trade receivables position. The bank manager will regularly review a company's balances and require advance notice of potential breaches of its overdraft limits.

Progress check 4.11

In what way does the profit earned by a business during an accounting period differ from the cash generated during the same period? In what ways are profit and cash affected by the settlement (or not) of their accounts by the customers of the business?

Summary of key points

- An income statement is a summary report of the movements for the accounting period on each of the accounts in the profit and loss account section of the general ledger of a business.

- The profit (or loss) of an entity may be considered from two perspectives: by considering the change in book wealth between the start and end of an accounting period; by deducting total costs from total revenues (sales) generated during the accounting period.

- In accordance with IAS 1, costs and expenses on the face of the income statement may be presented according to business functions, and classified into revenue, cost of sales, other operating costs (distributions costs and administrative expenses), other income, finance costs, finance income and income tax expense.

- In accordance with IAS 1, costs and expenses on the face of the income statement may alternatively be presented according to their nature, and classified into revenue, employee expenses, depreciation etc.

- The profit for the year reported in the income statement 'belongs' to the equity shareholders and may be used either to pay dividends to shareholders or to retain as retained earnings. The company may use profit for either dividends or retained earnings or both.

- The profit and loss account (and therefore the income statement) is closely linked with the balance sheet in two ways: they both reflect the change in the book wealth of the business; most transactions are reflected once in the income statement and once in the balance sheet.

- Valuation of the various items within the balance sheet in accordance with accounting concepts and accounting and financial reporting standards has a significant impact on the level of profit (or loss) earned by a business during an accounting period.

■ The profit (or loss) earned during an accounting period is not the same as the cash flow generated during the period, but the links between the two measures may be quantified and reconciled.

■ There are limitations to the income statement, which like the balance sheet is a historical document, primarily due to the impact on costs of the employment of alternative methods of valuation of assets and liabilities.

Assessment material

Questions

Q4.1 How would you define the profit (or loss) earned by a business during an accounting period?

Q4.2 Outline an income statement showing each of the main category headings using the business functions format.

Q4.3 (i) Which accounting or financial reporting standard contains provisions relating to the format of the income statement?
(ii) What are the requirements that are relevant to the formats of the income statement of a limited company?

Q4.4 The income statement and the balance sheet report on different aspects of a company's financial status. What are these different aspects and how are they related?

Q4.5 (i) Why are the methods used for the valuation of the various types of assets so important?
(ii) Describe the three main categories of asset that are most relevant to asset valuation.

Q4.6 What is depreciation and what are the problems encountered in dealing with the depreciation of non-current assets?

Q4.7 Describe three of the most commonly used methods of accounting for depreciation.

Q4.8 Describe four of the most commonly used methods of valuing inventory.

Q4.9 How does the valuation of trade receivables impact on the income statement of a business?

Q4.10 Profit does not equal cash, but how can the one be reconciled with the other for a specific accounting period?

Discussion points

D4.1 'My profit for the year is the total of my pile of sales invoices less the cash I have paid out during the year.' Discuss.

D4.2 'The reason why companies make a provision for depreciation of their non-current assets is to save up enough money to buy new ones when the old assets reach the end of their lives.' Discuss.

D4.3 Why is judgement so important in considering the most appropriate method to use for valuing inventories? What are the factors that should be borne in mind and what are the pros and cons of the alternative methods?

Exercises

Solutions are provided in Appendix 2 to all exercise numbers highlighted in colour.

Level I

E4.1 *Time allowed – 30 minutes*

Mr Kumar's chemist shop derives income from both retail sales and from prescription charges made to the NHS and to customers. For the last two years to 31 December 2009 and 31 December 2010 his results were as follows:

	2009 £	2010 £
Sales and prescription charges to customers	196,500	210,400
Prescription charges to the NHS	48,200	66,200
Purchases of inventories	170,100	180,600
Opening inventories at the start of the year	21,720	30,490
Closing inventories at the end of the year	30,490	25,300
Wages	25,800	27,300
Mr Kumar's drawings*	20,500	19,700
Rent and property taxes	9,400	13,200
Insurance	1,380	1,620
Motor vehicle expenses	2,200	2,410
Other overheads	14,900	15,300

*Note that Mr Kumar's drawings are the amounts of money that he has periodically taken out of the business for his own use and should be shown as a deduction from the profits earned by the business rather than an expense in the income statement.

Rent for the year 2009 includes £2,400 paid in advance for the half year to 31 March 2010, and for 2010 includes £3,600 paid in advance for the half year to 31 March 2011. Other overheads for 2009 do not include the electricity invoice for £430 for the final quarter (included in 2010 other overheads). There is a similar electricity invoice for £510 for 2010. Depreciation may be ignored.

(i) Prepare an income statement for the two years to 31 December.
(ii) Why do you think that there is a difference in the gross profit to sales % between the two years?
(iii) Using Mr Kumar's business as an example, explain the accruals accounting concept and examine whether or not it has been complied with.

E4.2 *Time allowed – 30 minutes*

Discuss the concepts that may apply and practical problems that may be encountered when accounting for:

(i) the acquisition of desktop personal computers, and
(ii) popular brands of products supplied by retailers

with specific comments regarding their depreciation reported in the income statement and their net book values reported in the balance sheet.

E4.3   *Time allowed – 30 minutes*

A friend of yours owns a shop selling CDs and posters for the 12- to 14-year-old market. From the following information advise him on the potential problems that may be encountered in the valuation of such items for balance sheet purposes:

(a) greatest hits compilation CDs have sold consistently over the months and cost £5,000 with a retail value of £7,000
(b) sales of specific group CDs, which ceased recording in the previous year, have now dropped off to zero and cost £500 with a total retail value of £700
(c) specific band CDs, which are still constantly recording and selling in the shop every week cost £1,000 with a total retail value of £1,400
(d) specific artist posters are currently not selling at all (although CDs are), and cost £50 with a retail value of £100.

E4.4   *Time allowed – 30 minutes*

The Partex company began trading in 2008, and all sales are made to customers on credit. The company is in a sector that suffers from a high level of bad debts, and a provision for doubtful debts of 4% of outstanding accounts receivable is made at each year end.

Information relating to 2008, 2009 and 2010 is as follows:

	Year to 31 December		
	2008	2009	2010
Outstanding accounts receivable at 31 December*	£88,000	£110,000	£94,000
Bad debts to be written off during year	£4,000	£5,000	£4,000

*before bad debts have been written off

You are required to state the amount that will appear:

(i)   in the balance sheet for trade receivables, and
(ii) in the income statement for bad debts.

E4.5   *Time allowed – 45 minutes*

Tartantrips Ltd, a company in Scotland, operates several ferries and has a policy of holding several in reserve, due to the weather patterns and conditions of various contracts with local authorities. A ferry costs £5 million and has an estimated useful life of 10 years, at which time its realisable value is expected to be £1 million.

Calculate and discuss three methods of depreciation that the company may use:

(i)   sum of the digits
(ii)   straight line
(iii) reducing balance.

E4.6 *Time allowed – 60 minutes*

From the following financial information that has been provided by Lazydays Ltd, for the year ended 31 March 2010 (and the corresponding numbers for the year to 31 March 2009), construct an income statement, using the format adopted by the majority of UK plcs, including comparative figures.

	2010	2009
	£	£
Administrative expenses	22,000	20,000
Depreciation	5,000	5,000
Closing inventories	17,000	15,000
Distribution costs	33,000	30,000
Dividends paid	32,000	30,000
Dividends received from non-related companies	5,000	5,000
Interest paid	10,000	10,000
Interest received	3,000	3,000
Opening inventories	15,000	10,000
Purchases	99,000	90,000
Redundancy costs	5,000	–
Sales revenue	230,000	200,000
Taxation	25,000	24,000

(a) Depreciation is to be included in administrative expenses

(b) Redundancy costs are to be regarded as an exceptional item to be included in administrative expenses

Level II

E4.7 *Time allowed – 60 minutes*

Llareggyb Ltd started business on 1 January 2010 and its year ended 31 December 2010. Llareggyb entered into the following transactions during the year.

Received funds for share capital of £25,000

Paid suppliers of materials £44,000

Purchased 11,000 units of a product at £8 per unit, which were sold to customers at £40 per unit

Paid heating and lighting costs for cash £16,000

Further heating and lighting costs of £2,400 were incurred within the year, but still unpaid at 31 December 2010

Mr D Thomas loaned the company £80,000 on 1 January 2010 at 8% interest per annum

Loan interest was paid to Mr Thomas for January to June 2010

8,000 product units were sold to customers during 2010

Customers paid £280,000 to Llareggyb for sales of its products

Rent on the premises £60,000 was paid for 18 months from 1 January 2010, and local business property taxes of £9,000 were also paid for the same period

Salaries and wages were paid for January to November 2010 amounting to £132,000 but the December payroll cost of £15,000 had not yet been paid as at 31 December 2010

A lorry was purchased for £45,000 on 1 January 2010 and was expected to last for five years after which it was estimated that it could be sold for £8,000

The company uses the straight line method of depreciation.

Prepare an income statement for Llareggyb Ltd for the year ended 31 December 2010.

E4.8   *Time allowed — 60 minutes*

From the trial balance of Retepmal Ltd at 31 March 2010 shown below prepare an income statement for the year to 31 March 2010 and a balance sheet as at 31 March 2010 using the formats used by most UK companies.

	£
Premises (net book value)	95,000
Accounts receivable	75,000
Purchases of inventories	150,000
Retained earnings at 31 March 2009	130,000
Inventories at 31 March 2009	15,000
Furniture and fixtures	30,000
Sales revenue	266,000
Distribution costs	40,000
Administrative expenses	50,000
Accounts payable	54,000
Motor vehicles (net book value)	40,000
Cash and bank	35,000
Equity share capital	80,000

Additional information:

(a) Inventories at 31 March 2010 were £25,000.

(b) Dividend proposed for 2010 was £7,000.

(c) An accrual for distribution costs of £3,000 was required at 31 March 2010.

(d) A prepayment of administrative expenses of £5,000 was required at 31 March 2010.

(e) Corporation tax estimated to be payable on 2009/2010 profit was £19,000.

(f) Annual depreciation charges on premises and motor vehicles for the year to 31 March 2010 are included in administrative expenses and distribution costs, and in the cumulative depreciation provisions used to calculate the net book values of £95,000 and £40,000 respectively, shown in the trial balance at 31 March 2010.

The furniture and fixtures balance of £30,000 relates to purchases of assets during the year to 31 March 2010. The depreciation charge in administrative expenses and the corresponding depreciation provision are not included in the trial balance at 31 March 2010. They are required to be calculated on a straight line basis for a full year to 31 March 2010, based on a useful economic life of eight years and an estimated residual value of £6,000.

5

Financial statements of limited companies – statement of cash flows

Contents

Learning objectives

Completion of this chapter will enable you to:

- describe what is meant by cash flow
- outline the structure of the statement of cash flows for a limited company, and its supporting schedules
- classify the categories of cash inflows and cash outflows that make up the statement of cash flows
- illustrate how both the direct and indirect cash flow approaches are used to derive net cash flows from operating activities
- prepare a statement of cash flows
- explain the links between the statement of cash flows and the balance sheet
- explain the links between the statement of cash flows and the income statement
- consider the merits of cash flow versus profit as a measure of financial performance.

Introduction

Chapters 3 and 4 have been concerned with the first two of the three key financial statements required to be prepared periodically by limited companies: the balance sheet and the income statement. This chapter will be concerned with the third of the key financial statements, the statement of cash flows. It should be noted that IAS 7, Statement of Cash Flows, has now revised the formally reported heading of the **cash flow statement** to the statement of cash flows. Throughout this book, and in this chapter in particular we may use both headings interchangeably to mean exactly the same thing.

The statement of cash flows, in one form or another, is prepared and used as an important management tool by all businesses. However, as in the previous two chapters, this chapter deals primarily with the statement of cash flows of limited companies, both private and public.

Chapter 5 looks at how statements of cash flows are structured and how each of the different types of cash inflows and cash outflows are categorised. This forms the basis to enable the preparation of a statement of cash flows of a limited company, and its supporting schedules, in the appropriate format.

We will look at the relationship between the statement of cash flows and the balance sheet and the income statement. In Chapters 3 and 4 we have seen the subjective aspects of both the balance sheet and the income statement. Cash flow is not subjective in any way but is a matter of fact.

What does the statement of cash flows tell us?

Cash is a crucial requirement for any business to develop and survive, whether it is involved in the public services, retailing or manufacturing. The current serious economic recession clearly demonstrates the need for companies to undertake realistic and timely cash planning through the preparation of regular, clearly understood cash reports. Such cash planning and reporting can help managers to survive through the most difficult periods and to provide a solid financial base from which to take advantage of new projects and opportunities once the worst of the financial crisis is over. The importance of cash planning is emphasised by the Sheldon Clayton Logistics Group in the press extract on the following page.

Cash planning is crucial for success

A growing West Midlands-based logistics group has taken over a local rival – completing its eighth acquisition in the last two years.

The Sheldon Clayton Logistics Group has acquired established Willenhall firm Costin Logistics in a deal which has seen the West Bromwich-based company boost its annual turnover to £ 18 million.

The deal was completed with the support of Midlands-based chartered accountancy firm Spencer Gardner Dickins and comes after Sheldon Clayton took over FTG Logistics – another Midlands company which it merged with its European division over the summer.

Sheldon Clayton Logistics, which now has 170 employees, has been trading for more than 30 years and has its headquarters on Black Country New Road with its 12.5 acre site boasting over 300,000 sq ft of new build office and warehouse facilities.

The growth of the site and business from £5 million to £18 million in the last two years has been driven by chairman and founder Dave Sheldon.

The group's managing director Stephen Pollock said: 'Going into the recession our cash planning and investment strategy took the most important dimension in what we as a group did.

'Although, along with my chairman's support, we were hugely optimistic in our five-year plan.'

As well as the £12 million of local trade acquisitions in the last two years, the group has also acquired over £4 million of land to support its future growth plans.

David Thomas, partner at Coventry-based Spencer Gardner Dickins, said Sheldon Clayton Logistics has enjoyed tremendous growth in a short space of time.

'The group must and should remain focused on acquiring companies to complement the logistics infrastructure in the West Midlands when the time is right,' he said.

Source: **Firm acquires local rival as rapid growth continues** © *Birmingham Post*, 28 October 2010

The definition of cash includes not only cash in hand but also deposits and overdrafts, including those denominated in foreign currencies, with any bank or other financial institutions. A bank overdraft, which is **repayable on demand**, is a borrowing facility where interest is paid only to the extent of the facility that is actually used. Deposits repayable on demand include any kind of account where additional funds may be deposited at any time or funds withdrawn at any time without prior notice. All charges and credits on these accounts such as bank interest, bank fees, deposits or withdrawals, other than movements wholly within them, represent cash inflows and outflows of the reporting entity.

Virtually all transactions are conducted ultimately by cash or near cash (for example bank accounts and credit cards). Sales of goods or services, or any other business assets, whether they are settled immediately or settled at some future date, are settled by cash or cash equivalents. Cash is an asset like any other asset, such as a non-current asset like machinery, or current assets like accounts receivable. Cash has the same properties as other assets, but also many more.

Cash is:

■ a unit of measurement – we evaluate transactions and report financial information in £ sterling or whatever other foreign currency denominated

■ a medium of exchange – rather than using the exchange or barter of other assets, cash is used as the accepted medium, having itself a recognisable value

■ a store of value – cash may be used for current requirements or held for future use.

The inability of a business to pay its creditors and other claims on the business, is invariably the reason for that business to fail. Cash, therefore, is a key asset and different from all other assets, which is why the performance of cash as a measure of business performance is so important.

In Chapters 3 and 4 we have discussed how the balance sheet and the income statement do not show or directly deal with some of the key changes that have taken place in the company's financial position and financial performance. We will see in this chapter how the statement of cash flows addresses this shortfall of information seen from the other two key financial statements, by answering questions like:

- How much capital expenditure (for example on machines and buildings) has the company made, and how did it fund the expenditure?
- What was the extent of new borrowing and how much debt was repaid?
- How much did the company need to fund new **working capital requirements** (for example increases in trade receivables and inventory requirements as a result of increased business activity)?
- How much of the company's **financing** was met by funds generated from its trading activities, and how much was met by new external funding (for example, from banks and other lenders, or new shareholders)?

We introduced the DVD analogy in Chapters 3 and 4 with regard to the balance sheet and the income statement. In the same way as profit (or loss), cash represents the dynamic DVD of changes in the cash position of the business throughout the period between the two 'pauses' – the balance sheets at the start and the finish of an accounting period. The statement of cash flows summarises the cash inflows and outflows and calculates the net change in the cash position throughout the period. In this way it provides answers to the questions shown above. Analysis and summary of the cash inflows and outflows of the period answers those questions by illustrating:

- changes in the level of cash between the start and end of the period
- how much cash has been generated, and from where
- for what purpose cash has been used.

The basic purpose of a statement of cash flows, as we saw in Chapter 3, is to report the cash receipts and cash payments that take place within an accounting period (see Figure 5.1), and to show how the cash balance has changed from the start of the period to the balance at the end of the period. This can

Figure 5.1   The main elements of the statement of cash flows

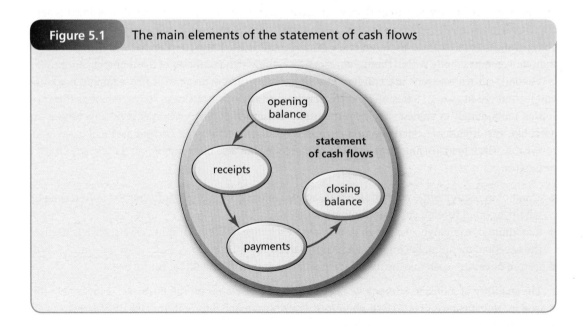

be seen to be objective and clearly avoids the problems of allocation associated with the preparation of a conventional income statement.

However, a more useful presentation would describe:

- how the company generated or lost cash
- how the company financed its growth and investments
- the extent to which the company was funded by debt and equity.

The statement of cash flows should ensure that companies:

- report their cash generation and cash absorption for a period by highlighting the significant components of cash flow in a way that facilitates comparison of the cash flow performances of different businesses
- provide information that assists in the assessment of their liquidity, solvency and financial adaptability.

Progress check 5.1

What questions should a statement of cash flows set out to answer?

Statement of cash flows format

The objective of IAS 7, Statement of Cash Flows, is the presentation of information about the historical changes in cash and cash equivalents of an entity by means of a statement of cash flows, which classifies cash flows during the period according to:

- operating activities
- investing activities
- financing activities.

Cash flows from operating activities are the main revenue-producing activities of the company that are not investing or financing activities, so operating cash flows include cash received from customers and cash paid to suppliers and employees. There are two methods of calculating cash flows from operating activities: the direct method; the indirect method. In IAS 7 the direct method of presentation is encouraged, but the indirect method is acceptable (see the section below about the direct method and indirect method of calculating operating cash flow).

Cash flows from investing activities are the acquisition and disposal of long-term assets and other investments that are not considered to be cash equivalents.

Cash flows from financing activities result from changes to the equity capital and borrowing structure of the company.

Interest and dividends received and paid may be classified as operating, investing, or financing cash flows, provided that they are classified consistently from period to period. Cash flows arising from taxes on income are normally classified as operating, unless they can be specifically identified with financing or investing activities.

All companies that prepare financial statements which conform with IFRSs are required to present a statement of cash flows.

The statement of cash flows analyses changes in cash and cash equivalents during a period. Cash and cash equivalents comprise cash on hand and demand deposits, together with short-term, highly liquid investments that are readily convertible to a known amount of cash, and that are subject to an insignificant risk of changes in value. An investment normally meets the definition of a cash equivalent when it has a maturity of three months or less from the date of acquisition. Equity investments are normally excluded, unless they are in substance a cash equivalent, for example preference shares acquired within three months of their specified redemption date. Bank overdrafts, which are repayable on demand, usually form an integral part of a company's cash position and are also included as a component of cash and cash equivalents.

The exchange rate used for translation of transactions denominated in a foreign currency should be the rate in effect at the date of the cash flows.

Aggregate cash flows relating to acquisitions and disposals of subsidiaries and other business units should be presented separately and classified as investing activities.

Investing and financing transactions which do not require the use of cash should be excluded from the statement of cash flows, but they should be separately disclosed elsewhere in the financial statements.

The components of cash and cash equivalents should be disclosed, and a reconciliation presented to amounts reported in the balance sheet.

The amount of cash and cash equivalents held by the entity that is not available for use by the group should be disclosed, together with a commentary by management.

Progress check 5.2

What are the aims and purposes of the statement of cash flows?

Direct and indirect cash flow

As we discussed earlier, the heading relating to cash flow from operating activities can be presented by using either the direct method or indirect method. We shall consider both methods in a little more detail, although the indirect method is by far the easier to use in practice and is the method used by most companies.

Cash flows from operating activities include the cash effects of transactions and other events relating to the operating or trading activities of the business. They are the movements in cash and cash equivalents of the operations that are included in the income statement to derive operating profit. Net cash flows from operating activities include the cash effects only and not all the revenues and costs that together represent the income statement.

Reference to the **direct method** and the **indirect method** relates to the choice of two options that are available for a business to derive the net cash flows from operating activities. Each method in one way or another involves individual identification of each of the cash items during the period that have been included in the income statement.

Direct method

The direct method provides an analysis of all the cash transactions for the appropriate period to identify all receipts and payments relating to the operating activities for the period. The analysis therefore shows the relevant constituent cash flows, operating cash receipts and cash payments including in particular cash receipts from customers, cash payments to suppliers, cash payments to and on behalf of employees, and other cash payments.

The direct method shows each major class of gross cash receipts and gross cash payments. The operating cash flows section of the statement of cash flows under the direct method would appear something like this:

Operating activities

Cash receipts from customers	xxx
Cash paid to suppliers	xxx
Cash paid to employees	xxx
Cash paid for other operating expenses	xxx
Cash generated from operations	xxx
Interest paid	xxx
Income taxes paid	xxx
Net cash generated from operating activities	xxx

Using data provided from Flatco plc's cash records for the year ended 31 December 2010 an example of the direct method is illustrated in Figure 5.2. IAS 7 requires a reconciliation between profit and cash flow from operating activities (using the indirect cash flow method – see below), even where the direct method is adopted. Because of the amount of time and other resources required to analyse the relevant cash information, the direct method has not been popular with many companies, although it does provide some very useful information.

Figure 5.2 shows cash generated from operations during the year ended 31 December 2010. Interest paid of £71,000 and tax paid of £44,000 must be deducted from cash generated from operations to determine cash flows from operating activities of £821,000.

Indirect method

The indirect method is by far the one more frequently adopted by UK companies. The basis of this approach is that operating revenues and costs are generally associated with cash receipts and cash payments and so profits earned from operating activities during an accounting period will approximate

---

Figure 5.2   Cash generated from operations – direct method

Flatco plc
Cash generated from operations for the year ended 31 December 2010
Direct cash flow method

	£000
Operating activities	
Cash receipts from customers	3,472
Cash paid to suppliers	(1,694)
Cash paid to employees	(631)
Cash paid for other operating expenses	(211)
Cash generated from operations	936
Interest paid	(71)
Income taxes paid	(44)
Net cash generated from operating activities	821

the net cash flows generated during the period. The cash generated from operations may be determined by adjusting the profit before tax reported in the income statement for non-cash items:

- depreciation
- amortisation

and also changes in working capital during the period:

- inventories
- trade receivables
- trade payables.

As we saw in the direct method, interest paid and tax paid during the accounting period must be deducted from the cash generated from operations to determine cash flows from operating activities.

The operating cash flows section of the statement of cash flows under the indirect method would appear something like this:

Operating activities	
Profit before tax	xxx
Add back depreciation and amortisation	xxx
Adjust net finance income/costs	xxx
Increase/decrease in trade and other receivables	xxx
Increase/decrease in inventories	xxx
Increase/decrease in trade and other payables	xxx
Cash generated from operations	xxx
Interest paid	xxx
Income taxes paid	xxx
Net cash generated from operating activities	xxx

Using the income statement for 2010 and balance sheet for the year ended 31 December 2010 for Flatco plc (see Figures 7.3, 7.4 and 7.5 in Chapter 7), an example of the indirect method is illustrated in Figure 5.3.

In the same way as in the direct method shown in Figure 5.2, the indirect method also shows cash generated from operations during the year ended 31 December 2010. Interest paid of £71,000 and tax paid of £44,000 must be deducted from cash generated from operations to determine cash flows from operating activities of £821,000.

Figure 5.3   Cash generated from operations – indirect method

Flatco plc
Cash generated from operations for the year ended 31 December 2010
Indirect cash flow method

	£000
Profit before tax	590
Depreciation and amortisation charges	345
Adjust finance (income)/costs [71 – 11 – 100]	(40)
Increase in inventories	(43)
Increase in trade and other receivables	(28)
Increase in trade and other payables, and provisions	112
Cash generated from operations	936
Interest paid	(71)
Income taxes paid	(44)
Net cash generated from operating activities	821

Worked example 5.1

Indirect Ltd earned profit before tax of £247,000 during 2009/2010, and its retained profit for the year was also £247,000. Indirect Ltd had acquired non-current assets totalling £290,000 during the year and had made no disposals of non-current assets. Indirect Ltd received no finance income and paid no interest or tax during the year ended 30 June 2010. Indirect Ltd's balance sheets as at 1 July 2009 and 30 June 2010 were as follows:

	1 July 2009 £000	30 June 2010 £000
Non-current assets	385	525
Inventories	157	277
Trade receivables	224	287
	766	1,089
Trade payables	(305)	(312)
Bank overdraft	(153)	(222)
Equity	(308)	(555)
	(766)	(1,089)

The indirect method may be used to calculate the net cash flow from operating activities:

Calculation of depreciation	£000
Non-current assets at the start of the year were	385
Additions during the year were	290
Disposals during the year were	zero
	675
Non-current assets at the end of the year were	525
Therefore, depreciation for the year was	150

Indirect Ltd
Cash generated from operations for the year ended 30 June 2010
Indirect cash flow method

	£000
Profit before tax	247
Depreciation charge	150
Adjust finance (income)/costs	–
Increase in inventories [277−157]	(120)
Increase in trade and other receivables [287−224]	(63)
Increase in trade and other payables [312−305]	7
Cash generated from operations	221
Interest paid	–
Income taxes paid	–
Net cash generated from operating activities	221

Worked example 5.1 shows how the cash generated from operations of £221,000 was calculated by starting with the profit before tax for the year of £247,000 and adjusting for changes in depreciation and working capital over the year. Because no interest or taxes were paid during the year net cash generated from operating activities is also £221,000. The only other cash activity during the year is the acquisition of non-current assets totalling £290,000. If we deduct that from the net cash generated from operating activities of £221,000 the result is the net decrease in cash and cash equivalents and bank overdrafts of £69,000. This agrees with the movement in the bank overdraft for the year, seen from the balance sheet, which has worsened from an overdraft of £153,000 at the beginning of the year to an overdraft of £222,000 at the end of the year.

Progress check 5.3

Describe the direct and the indirect cash flow methods that may be used to derive cash generated from operating activities, and their differences and their purpose.

Structure of the statement of cash flows

As we have seen, IAS 7 requires that a company's statement of cash flows should list its cash flows for the period and classify them under three standard headings. These headings and their detailed components are illustrated in Figure 5.4. We will look at each of these and how they are used to provide an analysis of the cash movements of the business over an accounting period.

Figure 5.4   Cash inflows and cash outflows reflected in the statement of cash flows

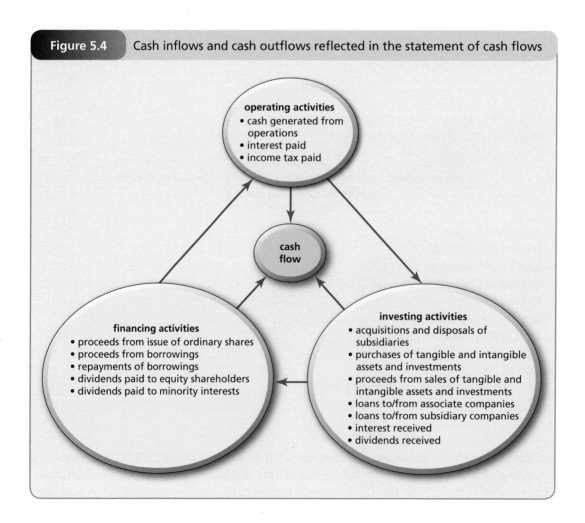

operating activities
• cash generated from operations
• interest paid
• income tax paid

cash flow

financing activities
• proceeds from issue of ordinary shares
• proceeds from borrowings
• repayments of borrowings
• dividends paid to equity shareholders
• dividends paid to minority interests

investing activities
• acquisitions and disposals of subsidiaries
• purchases of tangible and intangible assets and investments
• proceeds from sales of tangible and intangible assets and investments
• loans to/from associate companies
• loans to/from subsidiary companies
• interest received
• dividends received

Cash generated from operations

Cash generated from operations includes the cash effects of transactions and other events relating to the operating or trading activities of the business. We have seen above how this may be calculated using the direct method or indirect method.

Interest paid

Interest paid relates to payments of cash to providers of finance, and includes interest paid on bank overdrafts and long-term and short-term loans.

Income tax paid

Income tax paid includes all items in respect of taxes on revenue and capital profits. These include all payments relating to corporation tax, and receipts from rebate claims, overpayments, etc. Payments and receipts in respect of value added tax (VAT) are not included within the taxation heading. VAT payments and receipts are netted against the cash flows to which they relate, for example operating activities and non-current assets investments.

Acquisitions and disposals of subsidiaries

Cash payments and receipts for acquisitions and disposals of subsidiaries relate to the acquisition and sale of investments in subsidiary undertakings, or investment and sales of investments in other undertakings. This does not include any income derived from these investments, which is included within dividends received.

Purchases and sales of tangible and intangible assets and investments

Purchases and sales of tangible and intangible assets and investments relate to the acquisition and disposal of long-term assets and other investments not included in cash equivalents.

Loans to and from associate companies

Associate companies are companies in which a company has a substantial stake in the form of share ownership but does not have a controlling interest. Associate companies do not form part of a group for the purposes of consolidated accounts. This section of the statement of cash flows includes cash advances and loans made to associate companies and cash receipts from the repayment of advances and loans made to associate companies.

Loans to and from subsidiary companies

A parent company controls a subsidiary company by owning a majority of the voting shares in the subsidiary or by agreement to have the right to appoint or remove a majority of the board of directors. The parent company (the controlling company) and its subsidiary companies form a group for the purposes of consolidated accounts. This section of the statement of cash flows includes cash advances and loans made to subsidiary companies and cash receipts from the repayment of advances and loans made to subsidiary companies.

Interest received

This includes interest received on long-term and short-term loans.

Dividends received

Dividends received include receipts of cash that result from owning an investment and exclude all other returns included elsewhere in the statement of cash flows under operating activities, investing or financing activities.

Proceeds from issue of ordinary shares

These are the cash proceeds from issuing ordinary shares and the cash payments to shareholders to acquire or redeem the company's shares.

Proceeds from and repayments of borrowings

This includes cash proceeds from issuing debentures, loans, notes, bonds, mortgages and other short-term or long-term borrowings and cash repayments of amounts borrowed.

Loans are amounts borrowed that have fixed payments, and notes are borrowings that allow the lender to receive regular payments over a set time period ending on a specified date when the full amount is repaid. Bonds are debt instruments issued for periods of more than one year and mortgages are loans raised usually to purchase property with specified payment periods and interest rates. Short term generally means anything less than one year, whilst long term generally means anything more than one year. A debenture is a type of bond, which is made in writing and under the company's seal.

Dividends paid to ordinary shareholders

This heading includes all dividends actually paid in cash during the accounting period to ordinary shareholders. It does not include proposed dividends or dividends declared, which will not be paid until a subsequent accounting period, and it does not include preference share dividends.

Dividends paid to minority interests

This heading includes all dividends paid to other than ordinary shareholders, which are preference shareholders and minority interests.

Worked example 5.2

The following is a list of some of the different types of cash inflows and cash outflows of a typical plc. We will identify within which of the statement of cash flows headings they would normally be reported.

- sale of a subsidiary
- dividends paid to ordinary shareholders
- VAT
- interest paid
- purchase of a copyright (intangible non-current asset)
- interest received
- issue of debenture loans
- short-term Government loans (for example Treasury Stock)

- corporation tax
- purchase of a building
- income from investments
- receipts from customers (accounts receivable)
- payments to suppliers (accounts payable)
- purchase of factory machinery
- issue of ordinary shares

Cash flow from operating activities

Receipts from customers (trade receivables)

Payments to suppliers (trade payables)

Interest paid

Corporation tax

VAT? No, because VAT is netted against the cash flow to which it relates

Cash flow from investing activities

Purchase of a copyright

Purchase of a building

Purchase of factory machinery

Sale of a subsidiary

Short-term Government loans

Interest received

Income from investments

Cash flow from financing activities

Issue of ordinary shares

Issue of debenture loans

Dividends paid to ordinary shareholders

Progress check 5.4

Explain what cash inflows and outflows are reflected within each of the three main headings in the statement of cash flows.

Figures 5.5 and 5.6 illustrate the format of the statement of cash flows, and analysis of cash and cash equivalents and bank overdrafts, and have been prepared from the balance sheet and income statement for Flatco plc included in Chapter 7 (see Figures 7.3, 7.4 and 7.5). IAS 7 requires the comparative figures for the previous year to be disclosed in columns to the right of the current year's figures (although these are not shown in the Flatco illustration).

Figure 5.5   Statement of cash flows

Flatco plc
Statement of cash flows for the year ended 31 December 2010

	£000
Cash flows from operating activities	
Cash generated from operations	936
Interest paid	(71)
Income tax paid	(44)
Net cash generated from operating activities	821
Cash flows from investing activities	
Acquisition of subsidiary	–
Disposal of subsidiary	–
Purchases of tangible assets	(286)
Purchases of intangible assets	(34)
Proceeds from sales of intangible assets	21
Purchases of investments	–
Proceeds from sales of investments	–
Loans to/from associate companies	–
Loans to/from subsidiary companies	–
Interest received	11
Dividends received	100
Net cash outflow from investing activities	(188)
Cash flows from financing activities	
Proceeds from issue of ordinary shares	200
Proceeds from borrowings	173
Repayments of borrowings	–
Dividends paid to equity shareholders	(67)
Dividends paid to minority interests	–
Net cash inflow from financing activities	306
Increase in cash and cash equivalents in the year	939
Cash and cash equivalents and bank overdrafts at beginning of year	(662)
Cash and cash equivalents and bank overdrafts at end of year	277

Figure 5.6   Analysis of cash and cash equivalents and bank overdrafts

Flatco plc
Analysis of cash and cash equivalents and bank overdrafts
as at 31 December 2010

	At 1 January 2010 £000	At 31 December 2010 £000
Cash and cash equivalents	17	327
Bank overdrafts	(679)	(50)
Cash and cash equivalents and bank overdrafts	(662)	277

Worked example 5.3

The reconciliation of profit to net cash flow from operating activities shown below is an extract from the published accounts of BAE Systems plc, which is a global defence, security and aerospace company that places very strong emphasis on research and development. In the financial year 2009 BAE Systems spent £1,153m on research and development as well as unveiling a range of new products to the market.

We can use the reconciliation to identify a number of key aspects of the company's operations during the financial year 2009.

	2009 £m	2008 £m
(Loss)/profit for the year	(45)	1,768
Taxation expense	327	603
Share of results from investments	(203)	(139)
Net financing costs	700	(653)
Depreciation and impairment	1,600	755
Gains on disposals of assets	(33)	(225)
Changes in provisions	(605)	(387)
Decrease in inventories	6	46
Decrease/(increase) in receivables	52	(5)
Increase in payables	433	246
	2,232	2,009
Interest paid	(252)	(254)
Taxation paid	(350)	(261)
Net cash inflow from operating activities	1,630	1,494

The nature of BAE Systems' business means that much of the costs it incurs can be capitalised as intangible assets. According to IAS 38, development costs are capitalised only after technical and commercial feasibility of the asset for sale or use have been established. Once these costs are capitalised the asset must be amortised over the period from which economic benefit is estimated to flow from the asset. In 2009 a number of new products came on stream and we can see the impact of this in the very high depreciation charges in 2009. In addition, some products were developed but failed to gain sufficient orders and were subsequently cancelled. £592m is attributed to such write-offs. These costs are partly responsible for the dramatic change from a £1,768m profit in 2008 to a £45m loss in 2009.

It is important for any business to maintain a healthy cash flow from operations and the great change from profit to loss may deflect from the underlying health of the company. We can see from the reconciliation above that in fact BAE turned in a very healthy £1,630m cash inflow from operating activities (partly the result of the improved sales revenues generated by the new products). The net cash inflow actually increased by £136m over 2008 despite profits falling by £1,813m.

BAE Systems is a conservatively run company and its attention to sustainable cash flows from operations can clearly be seen from the reconciliation. Indeed, the company was able to increase its dividend payment to shareholders by 10% in 2009.

The nature of BAE Systems' business means that it maintains a relatively stable level of inventory and although contract work can lead to fluctuations in the levels of working capital, it can be seen that BAE Systems maintains relatively tight control over these fluctuations.

Worked example 5.4

The extract shown below is from the leading UK supermarket retailer, Tesco plc, for the year to 28 February 2009. It is an analysis of its net debt that supports its statement of cash flows.

Figures in £m	Opening balance 1 Mar 2008	Cash flow	Closing balance 28 Feb 2009
Cash and cash equivalents	1,788	1,721	3,509
Overdrafts	–	(37)	(37)
	1,788	1,684	3,472
Short-term investments	851	2,502	3,353
Short-term loans	(2,527)	(1,427)	(3,954)
Long-term loans	(6,294)	(6,177)	(12,471)
Net debt	(6,182)	(3,418)	(9,600)

We will discuss each of the elements in this analysis and comment briefly on the cash flow movements over the year.

(a) Cash and cash equivalents have almost doubled during the year. This apparent policy of increasing balances of cash and cash equivalents may be questioned. The actual policy may be established by looking at the trends over several years and any comments made by the company in its published report and accounts, but in an industry which generates substantial amounts of cash on a daily basis there seems little reason to hold large cash balances.

(b) The short-term investments were increased substantially, possibly to take advantage of the interest rates being paid on the money markets.

(c) The company is obviously making use of short-term loans to finance the business. The users of financial information usually require information on the timing of repayments of loans (in this case the bulk of the £3,954 million short-term debt is owed to banks), which plcs are required by the Companies Act to disclose in their published reports and accounts.

(d) The most striking aspect of this analysis is the increase in long-term debt during the financial year. The company now has over £12 billion of long-term debt, which would normally be used to fund long-term projects. The company has a policy of increasing debt to exploit new opportunities and then to reduce that debt when the new opportunities begin to deliver profits.

(e) All major UK plcs provide an overview of their treasury activities in their published reports and accounts, which links current policies with the components of net debt (for example, banking facilities).

(f) The financial press sometimes comment on companies' net debt movements. These may vary from year to year and comments vary from one analyst to another. A typical comment might be 'the increase in Tesco's net debt to £9.6bn was partly to finance higher capital expenditure, including overseas investments. The level of net debt was also affected by adverse currency movements and property market weakness, which made capital-raising measures more difficult.'

The Companies Act 2006 requires group financial statements to be prepared for the holding company in addition to the financial statements that are required to be prepared for each of the individual companies within the group. These 'consolidated' financial statements exclude all transactions between companies within the group, for example, inter-company sales and purchases. Undertakings preparing consolidated financial statements should prepare a consolidated statement of cash flows and related notes; they are not then required to prepare an entity statement of cash flows, that is the holding company (parent company) in isolation.

Progress check 5.5

Explain why the statement of cash flows is so important.

Worked example 5.5

We may use the following data, extracted from the financial records of Zap Electronics plc, to prepare a statement of cash flows in compliance with the provisions of IAS 7. The data relate to the financial statements prepared for the year ended 31 July 2010.

	£000
Dividends paid on ordinary shares	49
Purchases of Government bills (short-term investments)	200
Issue of ordinary share capital	100
Reduction in inventories	25
Corporation tax paid	120
Interest paid	34
Operating profit	830
Bank and cash balance 31 July 2010	527
Purchase of machinery	459
Sales of Government bills	100
Interest received	18
Purchase of a copyright (intangible non-current asset)	78
Depreciation charge for the year	407
Purchase of a building	430
Sale of a patent (intangible non-current asset)	195
Increase in trade receivables	35
Decrease in trade payables	85
Bank and cash balance 1 August 2009	342

Zap Electronics plc
Cash generated from operations for the year ended 31 July 2010
Indirect cash flow method

	£000
Profit before tax [830 − 34 + 18]	814
Depreciation charge	407
Adjust finance (income)/costs	16
Decrease in inventories	25
Increase in trade and other receivables	(35)
Decrease in trade and other payables	(85)
Cash generated from operations	1,142
Interest paid	(34)
Income taxes paid	(120)
Net cash generated from operating activities	988

Statement of cash flows for the year ended 31 July 2010

	£000
Cash flows from operating activities	
Cash generated from operations	1,142
Interest paid	(34)
Income tax paid	(120)
Net cash generated from operating activities	988
Cash flows from investing activities	
Purchases of tangible assets [430 + 459]	(889)
Purchases of intangible assets	(78)
Proceeds from sales of intangible assets	195
Purchases of investments	(200)
Proceeds from sales of investments	100
Interest received	18
Net cash outflow from investing activities	(854)
Cash flows from financing activities	
Proceeds from issue of ordinary shares	100
Dividends paid to equity shareholders	(49)
Net cash inflow from financing activities	51
Increase in cash and cash equivalents in the year	185
Cash and cash equivalents and bank overdrafts at beginning of year	342
Cash and cash equivalents and bank overdrafts at end of year	527

Analysis of cash and cash equivalents and bank overdrafts as at 31 December 2010

	At 1 August 2009 £000	At 31 July 2010 £000
Cash and cash equivalents	342	527
Bank overdrafts	–	–
Cash and cash equivalents and bank overdrafts	342	527

Worked example 5.6

Perfecto Ltd
Income statement for the year ended 30 September 2010

	£000
Revenue	2,279
Cost of sales	(1,484)
Gross profit	795
Distribution costs	(368)
Administrative expenses	(197)
Operating profit	230
Finance costs	(10)
Profit before tax	220
Income tax expense	(70)
Profit for the year	150

Perfecto Ltd
Balance sheet as at 30 September 2010

	2010 £000	2009 £000
Non-current assets		
Tangible	902	1,071
Intangible	203	193
Total non-current assets	1,105	1,264
Current assets		
Inventories	161	142
Trade receivables	284	193
Prepayments	295	278
Cash and cash equivalents	157	–
Total current assets	897	613
Total assets	2,002	1,877
Current liabilities		
Borrowings and finance leases	–	20
Trade payables (including income tax payable 2010: 70, 2009: 55)	277	306
Accruals	100	81
Total current liabilities	377	407
Non-current liabilities		
Borrowings and finance leases	85	126
Trade and other payables	77	184
Provisions	103	185
Total non-current liabilities	265	495
Total liabilities	642	902
Net assets	1,360	975
Equity		
Share capital	600	450
Share premium account	105	–
Retained earnings	655	525
Total equity	1,360	975

During the year Perfecto Ltd acquired new plant and machinery for £150,000, bought a patent for £10,000, and made no disposals of either tangible or intangible non-current assets.

Perfecto Ltd paid an interim dividend of £20,000 during the year and declared a final dividend of £20,000. Interest paid was £20,000 and interest received was £10,000. The company paid corporation tax of £55,000 during the year.

We have all the data required to prepare statement of cash flows and analysis of cash and cash equivalents and bank overdrafts for the year ended 30 September 2010 complying with IAS 7.

	£000
Non-current assets at the start of the year were	1,264
Additions during the year were [150 + 10]	160
Disposals during the year were	zero
	1,424
Non-current assets at the end of the year were	1,105
Therefore, depreciation for the year was	319

	30 Sep 2009 £000	30 Sep 2010 £000	Difference £000
Inventories	142	161	19 increase
Trade receivables, and prepayments	471 [193 + 278]	579 [284 + 295]	108 increase
Trade payables, accruals, and provisions	701 [306 − 55 + 81 + 184 + 185]	487 [277 − 70 + 100 + 77 + 103]	214 decrease

Perfecto Ltd
Cash generated from operations for the year ended 30 September 2010
Indirect cash flow method

	£000
Profit before tax	220
Depreciation charge	319
Adjust finance (income)/costs	10
Increase in inventories	(19)
Increase in trade and other receivables	(108)
Decrease in trade and other payables	(214)
Cash generated from operations	208
Interest paid	(20)
Income taxes paid	(55)
Net cash generated from operating activities	133

Statement of cash flows for the year ended 30 September 2010

	£000
Cash flows from operating activities	
Cash generated from operations	208
Interest paid	(20)
Income tax paid	(55)
Net cash generated from operating activities	133
Cash flows from investing activities	
Purchases of tangible assets	(150)
Purchases of intangible assets	(10)
Interest received	10
Net cash outflow from investing activities	(150)
Cash flows from financing activities	
Proceeds from issue of ordinary shares [600 + 105 − 450]	255
Repayments of borrowings [126 − 85]	(41)
Dividends paid to equity shareholders	(20)
Net cash inflow from financing activities	194
Increase in cash and cash equivalents in the year	177
Cash and cash equivalents and bank overdrafts at beginning of year	(20)
Cash and cash equivalents and bank overdrafts at end of year	157

Analysis of cash and cash equivalents and bank overdrafts as at 30 September 2010

	At 30 September 2009 £000	At 30 September 2010 £000
Cash and cash equivalents	–	157
Bank overdrafts	(20)	–
Cash and cash equivalents and bank overdrafts	(20)	157

Cash flow links to the balance sheet and income statement

The diagram shown in Figure 5.7 is a simple representation of the links between cash flow and the income statement, and their relationship with the balance sheet. It shows how for example:

■ a purchase of non-current assets for cash of £50 has
  – increased non-current assets in the balance sheet from the opening balance of £100 to the closing balance of £150
  – decreased the opening cash balance by £50
■ a profit of £100, that has been realised in cash, has
  – increased by £100 the opening cash balance of £100 which, less the outflow of £50 for non-current assets, gives a closing balance of £150
  – increased the profit and loss account from the opening balance of £100 to the closing balance of £200.

The effect of the above transactions is:

■ cash has increased by £50
■ non-current assets have been increased by £50
■ profit has increased by £100
■ the balance sheet is still in balance with increased total assets and total liabilities.

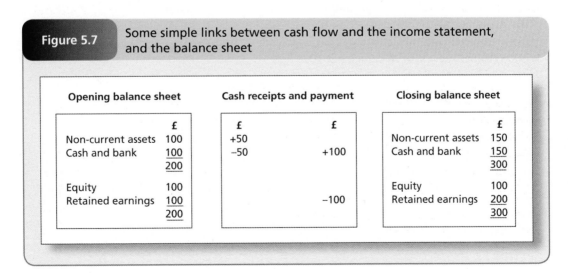

Figure 5.7 Some simple links between cash flow and the income statement, and the balance sheet

We may see from the more detailed information given as part of statement of cash flows reporting how cash flow may be appreciated in the context of the information given by the balance sheet and the income statement. IAS 7, Statement of Cash Flows, requires companies to provide two reconciliations included as part of the statement of cash flows reporting, between:

■ profit and the cash flow

and between:

■ cash and cash equivalents and bank overdrafts at the beginning and end of the accounting period,

which are provided in supporting schedules.

The reconciliation of cash flow and the income statement may be seen from profit adjusted for non-cash items and the changes in working capital to arrive at cash generated from operations.

The reconciliation of cash and cash equivalents and bank overdrafts at the beginning and end of the accounting period is a simple matter of adding the increase or decrease in cash during the accounting period to the opening balance of cash and cash equivalents and bank overdrafts to agree the closing balance of cash and cash equivalents and bank overdrafts.

Progress check 5.6

What are the schedules that are used to support the main statement of cash flows and what is their purpose?

Worked example 5.7

Detailed below are the direct method operating cash flow, indirect method operating cash flow and statement of cash flows for Ronly Bonly Jones Ltd for the month of January 2010, and its balance sheet as at 1 January 2010.

Rather than deriving a statement of cash flows from an income statement and a balance sheet this example aims to derive the following information from a statement of cash flows:

(i)   revenue, costs of sales, depreciation, and expenses for the month
(ii)   an income statement for the month
(iii) the changes in the balance sheet during the month from the 1 January balance sheet
(iv)   a balance sheet as at 31 January 2010.

Ronly Bonly Jones Ltd
Cash generated from operations for the month ended 31 January 2010
Direct cash flow method

	£000
Operating activities	
Cash receipts from customers	632
Cash paid to suppliers	(422)
Cash paid to employees	(190)
Cash paid for other operating expenses	(55)
Cash generated from operations	(35)

Cash generated from operations for the month ended 31 January 2010
Indirect cash flow method

	£000
Operating activities	
Profit before tax	10
Depreciation charge	5
Increase in inventories	(34)
Increase in trade and other receivables	(18)
Increase in trade and other payables	2
Cash generated from operations	(35)

Statement of cash flows for the month ended 31 January 2010

	£000
Cash flows from operating activities	
Cash generated from operations	(35)
Net cash generated from operating activities	(35)
Cash flows from investing activities	
Purchases of tangible assets	(20)
Net cash outflow from investing activities	(20)
Cash flows from financing activities	
Proceeds from issue of ordinary shares	10
Net cash inflow from financing activities	10
Decrease in cash and cash equivalents in the year	(45)

Balance sheet as at 1 January 2010

	£000
Non-current assets at cost	130
Depreciation provision	(20)
Inventories	45
Trade and other receivables	64
Cash and cash equivalents	6
	225
Trade and other payables	(87)
Equity share capital	(50)
Retained earnings	(88)
	(225)

(i) We may reconcile elements of cash flow for the month with the profit for the month as follows:

	January 2010 £000
Increase in trade and other receivables during the month	18
Cash received from customers	632
Revenue for the month	650

Increase in inventories during the month	(34)
Purchases from suppliers	424 [increase in trade and other payables 2 + cash paid to suppliers 422]
Cost of goods sold in the month	390
Depreciation charge in the month	5
Cash paid to employees	190
Cash paid for other operating expenses	55
Expenses for the month	245

(ii) Therefore:

Income statement for January 2010

	£000
Revenue	650
Cost of goods sold	(390)
Depreciation	(5)
Expenses	(245)
Profit for January	10

(iii) Let's derive the 31 January 2010 balance sheet from the information that has been provided:

Figures in £000

	Non-curr. assets	Depn.	Inventories	Trade & other rec'bles	Cash & cash equiv.	Trade & other payables	Equity share capital	Retained earnings
1 January 2010	130	(20)	45	64	6	(87)	(50)	(88)
Revenue				650				(650)
Cash from customers				(632)	632			0
Purchases			424			(424)		0
Cash to suppliers					(422)	422		0
Inventory sold			(390)					390
Depreciation		(5)						5
Expenses					(245)			245
Non-current asset additions	20				(20)			0
Issue of shares					10		(10)	0
31 January 2010	150	(25)	79	82	(39)	(89)	(60)	(98)

(iv) Therefore:

Balance sheets as at 1 January 2010 and at 31 January 2010

	1 January 2010 £000	31 January 2010 £000
Non-current assets at cost	130	150
Depreciation provision	(20)	(25)
Inventories	45	79
Trade and other receivables	64	82
Cash and cash equivalents	6	–
	225	286
Trade and other payables	(87)	(89)
Bank overdraft	–	(39)
Equity share capital	(50)	(60)
Retained earnings	(88)	(98)
	(225)	(286)

In Worked example 5.7, we have:

- used the statement of cash flows to derive the income statement for the month,

and we have then used the

- 1 January 2010 balance sheet
- income statement for the month of January 2010
- non-profit and loss items also shown in the January statement of cash flows

to derive the balance sheet for 31 January 2010.

In this way, we can see how the balance sheet, income statement and statement of cash flows of a business are inextricably linked.

Worked example 5.8

We can use the indirect cash flow analysis from Worked example 5.7 to provide an explanation to shareholders in Ronly Bonly Jones Ltd of the net cash outflow of £45,000.

During January 2010 there was a profit before depreciation of £15,000 (£10,000 + £5,000). This, together with the increase in share capital of £10,000, provided a total cash inflow for the month of £25,000. However, there was a net outflow of cash on increased working capital of £50,000 (£34,000 + £18,000 − £2,000) and capital expenditure of £20,000. This all resulted in a net cash outflow of £45,000 (£25,000 − £50,000 − £20,000).

The net cash outflow may be in line with what the company had planned or forecast for January 2010. Alternatively, the outflow may not have been expected. Changes in trading circumstances and management decisions may have been the reason for the difference between the actual and expected cash flow for January 2010.

The shareholders of Ronly Bonly Jones Ltd need to be reassured that the current cash position is temporary, and under control, and within the overdraft facility agreed with the company's bankers. The shareholders must also be reassured that the company is not in financial difficulty or that if problems are being experienced then the appropriate remedial actions are in place.

Progress check 5.7

How is the statement of cash flows of a business related to its other financial statements, the income statement and the balance sheet?

Summary of key points

- Cash flow includes not only cash in hand but also bank deposits and bank overdrafts (which are repayable on demand) with any bank or other financial institutions.

- The statement of cash flows lists the inflows and outflows of cash and cash equivalents for a period classified under the standard headings of: operating activities; investing activities; financing activities.

- IAS 7 requires all reporting entities that prepare financial statements which conform with IFRSs to prepare a statement of cash flows.

- There is only one standard format for the statement of cash flows prescribed by IAS 7, comprising a main statement of cash inflows and outflows (divided into those cash flows from operating activities, investing activities and financing activities), supported by a calculation of cash generated from operations, and an analysis of cash and cash equivalents and bank overdrafts.

- Cash generated from operations may be derived using the direct method or the indirect method, with both methods giving the same result.

- The statement of cash flows is directly related to both the income statement and the balance sheet and the links between them may be quantified and reconciled.

- The preparation of the statement of cash flows is a highly objective exercise, in which all the headings and amounts are cash based and therefore easily measured.

- The cash flow generated during an accounting period is a matter of fact and does not rely on judgement or the use of alternative conventions or valuation methods.

Assessment material

Questions

Q5.1 (i) How would you define cash generated by a business during an accounting period?
(ii) Which International Accounting Standard (IAS) deals with cash flow?

Q5.2 Give an example of a statement of cash flows showing each of the main categories.

Q5.3 Give an example of the supporting analyses and notes that are prepared in support of the main statement of cash flows.

Q5.4 Describe the ways in which both the direct method and the indirect method may be used by a business to derive cash generated from operations during an accounting period.

Q5.5 (i) Which cash analysis is used to link the statement of cash flows to the income statement?
(ii) How does it do that?

Q5.6 (i) Which cash analysis is used to link the statement of cash flows to the balance sheet?
(ii) What are the links?

Q5.7 Why is cash so important, compared to the other assets used within a business?

Q5.8 (i) What questions does the statement of cash flows aim to answer?
(ii) How far does it go towards answering them?

Discussion points

D5.1 Why is the information disclosed in the income statement and the balance sheet not considered sufficient for users of financial information? What is so important about cash flow that it has an International Accounting Standard, IAS 7, devoted to it?

D5.2 'Forget your income statements and balance sheets, at the end of the day it's the business's healthy bank balance that is the measure of its increase in wealth.' Discuss.

Exercises

Solutions are provided in Appendix 2 to all exercise numbers highlighted in colour.

Level I

E5.1 *Time allowed – 60 minutes*

Candice-Marie James and Flossie Graham obtained a one-year lease on a small shop which cost them £15,000 for the year 2010, and in addition agreed to pay rent of £4,000 per year payable one year in advance. Candyfloss started trading on 1 January 2010 as a florist, and Candice and Flossie bought a second-hand, white delivery van for which they paid £14,500. The business was financed by Candice and Flossie each providing £9,000 from their savings, and receipt of an interest-free loan from Candice's uncle of £3,000. Candice and Flossie thought they were doing OK over their first six months but they weren't sure how to measure this. They decided to try and see how they were doing financially and looked at the transactions for the first six months:

Cash transactions:

	£
Cash sales of flowers	76,000
Rent paid	4,000
Wages paid	5,000
Payments for other operating expenses	7,000
Purchases of inventories of flowers for resale	59,500
Legal expenses paid for the lease acquisition	1,000

In addition, at 30 June 2010:

The business owed a further £4,000 for the purchase of flowers and £1,000 for other operating expenses.

Customers had purchased flowers on credit and the sum still owed amounted to £8,000.

One customer was apparently in financial difficulties and it was likely that the £1,500 owed would not be paid.

Inventories of flowers at 30 June 2010 valued at cost were £9,500.

They estimated that the van would last four years, at which time they expected to sell it for £2,500, and that depreciation would be spread evenly over that period.

(i)   Prepare a statement of cash flows for Candyfloss for the first six months of the year 2010 using the direct method.

(ii) Prepare an income statement for Candyfloss for the first six months of the year 2010, on an accruals basis.

(iii) Why is the profit different from the cash flow?

(iv) Which statement gives the best indication of the first six months' performance of Candyfloss?

E5.2   *Time allowed – 60 minutes*

Using the information from Exercise E5.1 prepare a statement of cash flows for Candyfloss for the first six months of the year 2010, using the indirect method.

E5.3   *Time allowed – 60 minutes*

Jaffrey Packaging plc have used the following information in the preparation of their financial statements for the year ended 31 March 2010.

	£000
Dividends paid	25
Issue of a debenture loan	200
Reduction in inventories	32
Corporation tax paid	73
Interest paid	28
Operating profit for the year	450
Cash and cash equivalents 31 March 2010	376
Purchase of factory equipment	302
Dividends payable at 31 March 2010	25
Interest received	5
Depreciation charge for the year	195
Purchase of a new large computer system	204
Sale of a patent (intangible non-current asset)	29
Increase in trade and other receivables	43
Reduction in trade and other payables	62
Cash and cash equivalents 1 April 2009	202

You are required to prepare a cash generated from operations statement for Jaffrey Packaging Ltd using the indirect method, and a statement of cash flows for the year ended 31 March 2010 in compliance with the provisions of IAS 7, and also an analysis of cash and cash equivalents for the same period.

E5.4   *Time allowed – 60 minutes*

> From the income statement for the year ended 31 December 2010 and balance sheets as at 31 December 2009 and 31 December 2010, and the additional information shown below, prepare a statement of cash flows for Medco Ltd for the year to 31 December 2010.

Income statement	2010
	£
Operating profit	2,500
Interest paid	(100)
Profit before tax	2,400
Income tax paid	(500)
Profit for the year	1,900

Balance sheet as at 31 December	2010	2009
	£	£
Non-current assets	28,000	20,000
Current assets		
Inventories	6,000	5,000
Trade and other receivables	4,000	3,000
Investments	5,100	3,000
Cash and cash equivalents	2,150	5,000
Total current assets	17,250	16,000
Total assets	45,250	36,000
Current liabilities		
Borrowings and finance leases	(6,000)	(2,000)
Trade and other payables	(4,000)	(6,000)
Current tax liabilities	(500)	(400)
Dividend (proposed)	(600)	(450)
Total current liabilities	(11,100)	(8,850)
Non-current liabilities		
Borrowings and finance leases	(2,000)	(1,000)
Total liabilities	(13,100)	(9,850)
Net assets	32,150	26,150
Equity		
Ordinary share capital	14,000	10,000
Share premium account	6,000	5,000
Retained earnings	12,150	11,150
Total equity	32,150	26,150

During the year 2010 the company:

(a) acquired new non-current assets that cost £12,500
(b) issued new share capital for £5,000
(c) sold non-current assets for £2,000 that had originally cost £3,000 and had a net book value of £2,500
(d) depreciated its non-current assets by £2,000
(e) paid an interim dividend of £300,000 during the year and proposed a final dividend of £600,000.

Level II

E5.5   *Time allowed – 90 minutes*

Llareggyb Ltd started business on 1 January 2010 and its year ended 31 December 2010. Llareggyb entered into the following transactions during the year.

Received funds for share capital of £25,000

Paid suppliers of materials £44,000

Purchased 11,000 units of a product at £8 per unit, which were sold to customers at £40 per unit

Paid heating and lighting costs for cash £16,000

Further heating and lighting costs of £2,400 were incurred within the year, but still unpaid at 31 December 2010

Mr D Thomas loaned the company £80,000 on 1 January 2010 at 8% interest per annum

Loan interest was paid to Mr Thomas for January to June 2010

8,000 product units were sold to customers during 2010

Customers paid £280,000 to Llareggyb for sales of its products

Rent on the premises £60,000 was paid for 18 months from 1 January 2010, and local business property taxes of £9,000 were also paid for the same period

Salaries and wages were paid for January to November 2010 amounting to £132,000 but the December payroll cost of £15,000 had not yet been paid as at 31 December 2010

A lorry was purchased for £45,000 on 1 January 2010 and was expected to last for five years after which it was estimated that it could be sold for £8,000

The company uses the straight line method of depreciation.

> **You are required to:**
>
> (i)   prepare a balance sheet for Llareggyb Ltd as at 31 December 2010.
> (ii) prepare a statement of cash flows for Llareggyb Ltd for the year ended 31 December 2010.
>
> (Note: you may use the profit or loss figure calculated in Exercise E4.7 to complete this exercise.)

E5.6   *Time allowed – 90 minutes*

The balance sheets for Victoria plc as at 30 June 2009 and 30 June 2010 are shown below:

Victoria plc
Balance sheet as at 30 June

	£000 2009	£000 2010
Non-current assets		
Cost	6,900	9,000
Depreciation provision	900	1,100
Total non-current assets	6,000	7,900
Current assets		
Inventories	2,600	4,000
Trade and other receivables	2,000	2,680
Cash and cash equivalents	200	–
Total current assets	4,800	6,680
Total assets	10,800	14,580

Current liabilities

Borrowings and finance leases	–	600
Trade and other payables	2,000	1,800
Current tax liabilities	300	320
Dividend payable	360	480
Total current liabilities	2,660	3,200
Non-current liabilities		
Borrowings and finance leases	1,000	1,000
Total liabilities	3,660	4,200
Net assets	7,140	10,380
Equity		
Ordinary share capital	4,000	5,500
Share premium account	–	1,240
Retained earnings	3,140	3,640
Total equity	7,140	10,380

The following information is also relevant:

1. During the years 2009 and 2010 Victoria plc disposed of no non-current assets.
2. Interim dividends were not paid during the years ended 30 June 2009 and 2010.
3. Non-current liabilities borrowing is a 10% £1m debenture and loan interest was paid on 10 February in each year.

You are required to:

(i) Calculate:

    (a) profit before tax for the year ended 30 June 2010

    (b) operating profit for the year ended 30 June 2010

(ii) Prepare for Victoria plc for the year to 30 June 2010 a statement of cash generated from operations using the indirect method, and a statement of cash flows for the year ended 30 June 2010 in compliance with IAS 7, and also an analysis of cash and cash equivalents for the same period.

E5.7 *Time allowed – 90 minutes*

Sparklers plc have completed the preparation of their income statement for the year ended 31 October 2010 and their balance sheet as at 31 October 2010. During the year Sparklers sold some non-current assets for £2m that had originally cost £11m. The cumulative depreciation on those assets at 31 October 2009 was £7.6m.

You have been asked to prepare a statement of cash flows for the year ended 31 October 2010 in compliance with IAS 7. The directors are concerned about the large bank overdraft at 31 October 2010, which they believe is due mainly to the increase in trade receivables as a result of apparently poor credit control. What is your assessment of the reasons for the increased short-term borrowings?

Sparklers plc
Income statement for the year ended 31 October 2010

	£m	£m
	2010	2009
Operating profit	41.28	18.80
Interest paid	(0.56)	–
Interest received	0.08	0.20
Profit before tax	40.80	19.00
Income tax expense	(10.40)	(6.40)
Profit for the year	30.40	12.60
Dividends:		
Preference paid	(0.20)	(0.20)
Ordinary: interim paid	(4.00)	(2.00)
final proposed	(12.00)	(6.00)
Retained profit for the year	14.20	4.40

Sparklers plc
Balance sheet as at 31 October 2010

	2010	2009
	£m	£m
Non-current assets		
Tangible at cost	47.80	35.20
Depreciation provision	(21.50)	(19.00)
Total non-current assets	26.30	16.20
Current assets		
Inventories	30.00	10.00
Trade and other receivables	54.20	17.80
Cash and cash equivalents	–	1.20
Total current assets	84.20	29.00
Total assets	110.50	45.20
Current liabilities		
Borrowings and finance leases	32.40	–
Trade and other payables	22.00	13.60
Dividends payable	12.00	6.00
Income tax payable	10.40	6.40
Total current liabilities	76.80	26.00
Non-current liabilities		
Debenture loan	1.50	1.20
Total liabilities	78.30	27.20
Net assets	32.20	18.00
Equity		
Ordinary share capital – £1 ordinary shares	10.00	10.00
Preference share capital – £1 preferences shares 10%	2.00	2.00
Retained earnings	20.20	6.00
Total equity	32.20	18.00

E5.8   *Time allowed – 90 minutes*

Dimarian plc's income statement for the year ended 31 December 2010, and its balance sheets as at 31 December 2010 and 2009, are shown below. Dimarian plc issued no new ordinary shares during the year.

During 2010 Dimarian plc spent £100,000 on non-current assets additions. There were no non-current assets disposals during 2010.

Dimarian plc
Income statement for the year ended 31 December 2010

Figures in £000

Revenue	850
Cost of sales	(500)
Gross profit	350
Distribution costs and administrative expenses	(120)
	230
Other operating income	20
Operating profit	250
Interest paid	(30)
	220
Interest received	10
Profit before tax	230
Income tax expense	(50)
Profit for the year	180
Retained profit 1 January 2010	230
	410
Proposed dividends	(80)
Retained earnings 31 December 2010	330

Dimarian plc
Balance sheet as at 31 December 2010

Figures in £000	2010	2009
Non-current assets		
Tangible	750	800
Intangible	40	50
Total non-current assets	790	850
Current assets		
Inventories	50	60
Trade and other receivables	190	200
Cash and cash equivalents	20	10
Total current assets	260	270
Total assets	1,050	1,120

Current liabilities

Borrowings and finance leases	20	10
Trade and other payables	70	80
Dividends payable	80	70
Income tax payable	50	30
Total current liabilities	220	190
Non-current liabilities		
Debenture loan	100	300
Total liabilities	320	490
Net assets	730	630
Equity		
Share capital	260	260
Share premium account	50	50
Revaluation reserve	90	90
Retained earnings	330	230
Total equity	730	630

You are required to prepare:

(i)   An indirect statement of cash flows for the year to 31 December 2010.

(ii) A statement of cash flows for the year ended 31 December 2010, in the format required by IAS 7.

(iii) An analysis of cash and cash equivalents for the years ended 31 December 2009 and 31 December 2010.

Case Study I
BUZZARD LTD

The Buzzard Group is a first-tier global supplier to major passenger car and commercial vehicle manufacturers. As a first-tier supplier Buzzard provides systems that fit directly into motor vehicles, which they have manufactured from materials and components acquired from second, third, fourth-tier, etc., suppliers. During the 2000s, through investment in R&D and technology, Buzzard became regarded as one of the world's leaders in design, manufacture and supply of innovative automotive systems.

In the mid-2000s Buzzard started business in one of the UK's many development areas. It was established through acquisition of the business of Firefly from the Stonehead Group by a Buzzard subsidiary, Buzzard Ltd. Firefly was a traditional, mass production automotive component manufacturer, located on a brownfield site in Gentbridge, once a fairly prosperous mining area. Firefly had pursued short-term profit rather than longer-term development strategies, and had a poor image with both its customers and suppliers. This represented a challenge but also an opportunity for Buzzard Ltd to establish a world-class manufacturing facility.

A major part of Buzzard's strategic plan was the commitment to investing £30m to relocate from Gentbridge to a new fully equipped 15,000 square metre purpose-built factory on a 20-acre greenfield site in Bramblecote, which was finally completed during the year 2010. At the same time, it introduced the changes required to transform its culture and implement the operating strategies required to achieve the highest level of industrial performance. By the year 2010 Buzzard Ltd had become an established supplier of high quality and was close to achieving its aim of being a world-class supplier of innovative automotive systems.

In December 2010 a seven-year bank loan was agreed with interest payable half yearly at a fixed rate of 5% per annum. The loan was secured with a floating charge over the assets of Buzzard Ltd.

The financial statements of Buzzard Ltd, its accounting policies and extracts from its notes to the accounts, for the year ended 31 December 2010 are shown below, prior to the payment of any proposed dividend. It should be noted that note 3 to the accounts – profit for the year – reports on some of the key items included in the income statement for the year and is not a complete analysis of the income statement.

Required

(i) Prepare a strengths, weaknesses, opportunities, threats (SWOT) analysis for Buzzard Ltd based on the limited information available.

(ii) What do you consider to be the main risks faced by Buzzard Ltd, both internally and external to the business, based on your SWOT analysis and your own research about the automotive industry in the UK?

(iii) Prepare a report for shareholders that describes Buzzard Ltd's performance, supported by the appropriate profitability, efficiency, liquidity and investment ratios required to present as complete a picture as possible from the information that has been provided.

(iv) The company has demonstrated its achievement of high levels of quality and customer satisfaction but would you, as a shareholder, be satisfied with the financial performance of Buzzard Ltd?

Income statement
for the year ended 31 December 2010

	Notes	2010 £000	2009 £000
Revenue	1	115,554	95,766
Cost of sales		(100,444)	(80,632)
Gross profit		15,110	15,134
Distribution costs		(724)	(324)
Administrative expenses		(12,348)	(10,894)
Operating profit		2,038	3,916
Finance costs	2	(1,182)	(1,048)
Finance income	2	314	76
Profit for the year from continuing operations	3	1,170	2,944
Income tax expense		–	–
Profit for the year		1,170	2,944

The company has no recognised gains and losses other than those included above.

Balance sheet
as at 31 December 2010

	Notes	2010 £000	2009 £000
Non-current assets			
Tangible assets	8	42,200	29,522
Total non-current assets		42,200	29,522
Current assets			
Inventories	9	5,702	4,144
Trade and other receivables	10	18,202	16,634
Cash and cash equivalents		4	12
Total current assets		23,908	20,790
Total assets		66,108	50,312
Current liabilities	11	23,274	14,380
Non-current liabilities			
Borrowings and finance leases	12	6,000	–
Provisions	13	1,356	1,508
Accruals and deferred income	14	1,264	1,380
Total non-current liabilities		8,620	2,888
Total liabilities		31,894	17,268
Net assets		34,214	33,044
Equity			
Share capital	15	22,714	22,714
Retained earnings		11,500	10,330
Total equity	16	34,214	33,044

Statement of cash flows
for the year ended 31 December 2010

	2010 £000	2009 £000
Cash flows from operating activities		
Net cash generated from operating activities	11,742	2,578
Cash flows from investing activities		
Purchases of non-current assets	(20,490)	(14,006)
Proceeds from sales of non-current assets	12	30
Interest received	314	76
Proceeds from Government grants	1,060	1,900
Net cash outflow from investing activities	(19,104)	(12,000)
Cash flows from financing activities		
Proceeds from issue of ordinary shares	–	8,000
Proceeds from borrowings	6,000	–
Net cash inflow from financing activities	6,000	8,000
Decrease in cash and cash equivalents in the year	(1,362)	(1,422)
Cash and cash equivalents and bank overdrafts at beginning of year	(1,974)	(552)
Cash and cash equivalents and bank overdrafts at end of year	(3,336)	(1,974)

Accounting policies

The financial statements have been prepared in accordance with applicable financial reporting standards. A summary of the more important accounting policies which have been applied consistently is set out below.

Basis of accounting The accounts are prepared under the historical cost convention.

Research and development Expenditure on research and development is written off as it is incurred.

Tangible non-current assets Tangible non-current assets are stated at their purchase price together with any incidental costs of acquisition.

Depreciation is calculated so as to write off the cost of tangible non-current assets on a straight line basis over the expected useful economic lives of the assets concerned. The principal annual rates used for this purpose are:

Freehold buildings	20 years
Plant and machinery (including capitalised tooling)	4–8 years
Office equipment and fixtures and fittings	5–8 years
Motor vehicles	4 years

Freehold land is not depreciated.

Government grants Grants received on qualifying expenditure or projects are credited to deferred income and amortised in the income statement over the estimated useful lives of the qualifying assets or over the project life as appropriate.

Inventories and work in progress Inventories and work in progress are stated at the lower of cost and net realisable value. In general, cost is determined on a first in first out basis; in the case of manufactured products cost includes all direct expenditure and production overheads based on the normal level of activity. Net realisable value is the price at which inventories can be sold in the normal course of business after allowing for the costs of realisation and, where appropriate, the cost of conversion from their existing state to a finished condition. Provision is made where necessary for obsolescent, slow-moving and defective inventories.

Foreign currencies Assets, liabilities, revenues and costs denominated in foreign currencies are recorded at the rate of exchange ruling at the date of the transaction; monetary assets and liabilities at the balance sheet date are translated at the year-end rate of exchange or where there are related forward foreign exchange contracts, at contract rates. All exchange differences thus arising are reported as part of the results for the period.

Revenue Sales revenue represents the invoiced value of goods supplied, excluding value added tax.

Warranties for products Provision is made for the estimated liability arising on all known warranty claims. Provision is also made, using past experience, for potential warranty claims on all sales up to the balance sheet date.

Notes to the accounts

1 Segmental analysis

	Revenue		Profit before tax	
	2010	2009	2010	2009
	£000	£000	£000	£000
Class of business				
Automotive components	115,554	95,766	1,170	2,944
Geographical segment				
United Kingdom	109,566	92,020		
Rest of Europe	5,290	3,746		
Japan	698	–		
	115,554	95,766		

2 Finance costs/income

	2010	2009
	£000	£000
Interest payable on bank loans and overdrafts	(1,182)	(1,048)
Interest receivable	314	76
	(868)	(972)

3 Profit for the year from continuing operations

	2010	2009
	£000	£000
Profit for the year is stated after crediting:		
Amortisation of government grant	1,176	796
(Loss)/profit on disposal of non-current assets	(18)	10
and after charging:		
Depreciation charge for the year:		
Tangible non-current assets	7,782	4,742
Research and development expenditure	7,694	6,418
Auditors' remuneration for:		
Audit	58	58
Other services	40	52
Hire of plant and machinery – operating leases	376	346
Hire of other assets – operating leases	260	314
Foreign exchange losses	40	20

4 Directors and employees

The average weekly number of persons (including executive directors) employed during the year was:

	2010 number	2009 number
Production	298	303
Engineering, quality control and development	49	52
Sales and administration	56	45
	403	400

Staff costs (for the above persons):	2010 £000	2009 £000
Wages and salaries	6,632	5,837
Social security costs	562	483
Other pension costs	286	218
	7,480	6,538

8 Tangible non-current assets

	Freehold land and buildings £000	Motor vehicles £000	Plant, machinery and tooling £000	Office equipment, fixtures and fittings £000	Total £000
Cost					
At 1 January 2010	15,450	114	20,648	4,600	40,812
Additions	20	28	19,808	634	20,490
Disposals	–	–	(80)	(10)	(90)
At 31 December 2010	15,470	142	40,376	5,224	61,212
Depreciation					
At 1 January 2010	834	54	7,932	2,470	11,290
Charge for year	734	22	6,226	800	7,782
Eliminated in respect of disposals	–	–	(58)	(2)	(60)
At 31 December 2010	1,568	76	14,100	3,268	19,012
Net book value at					
31 December 2010	13,902	66	26,276	1,956	42,200
Net book value at 31 December 2009	14,616	60	12,716	2,130	29,522

9 Inventories

	2010 £000	2009 £000
Raw materials and consumables	4,572	3,274
Work in progress	528	360
Finished goods and goods for resale	602	510
	5,702	4,144

10 Trade and other receivables

	2010 £000	2009 £000
Trade receivables	13,364	8,302
Other receivables	4,276	7,678
Prepayments and accrued income	562	654
	18,202	16,634

11 Current liabilities

	2010 £000	2009 £000
Bank overdraft	3,340	1,986
Trade payables	13,806	8,646
Other taxation and social security payable	2,334	1,412
Other payables	122	350
Accruals and deferred income	3,672	1,986
	23,274	14,380

12 Borrowings and finance leases

	2010 £000	2009 £000
Bank and other loans repayable otherwise than by instalments		
Over five years	6,000	–

13 Provisions

	Pensions £000	Warranties for products £000	Total £000
At 1 January 2010	732	776	1,508
Expended in the year	(572)	(494)	(1,066)
Charge to profit and loss account	562	352	914
At 31 December 2010	722	634	1,356

14 Accruals and deferred income

	2010 £000	2009 £000
Government grants		
At 1 January 2010	1,380	2,176
Amount receivable	1,060	–
Amortisation in year	(1,176)	(796)
At 31 December 2010	1,264	1,380

15 Equity

	2010 £000	2009 £000
Authorised share capital		
28,000,000 (2009: 28,000,000) ordinary shares of £1 each	28,000	28,000
Issued and fully paid share capital		
22,714,000 (2009: 22,714,000) ordinary shares of £1 each	22,714	22,714

16 Reconciliation of movement in shareholders' funds

	2010 £000	2009 £000
Opening shareholders' funds	33,044	22,100
Issue of ordinary share capital	–	8,000
Profit for the year	1,170	2,944
Closing shareholders' funds	34,214	33,044

17 Capital commitments

	2010 £000	2009 £000
Capital expenditure that has been contracted for but has not been provided for in the financial statements	1,506	162
Capital expenditure that has been authorised by the directors but has not yet been contracted for	6,768	5,404

18 Financial commitments

At 31 December 2010 the company had annual commitments under non-cancellable operating leases as follows:

	Land and buildings 2010 £000	Other 2010 £000	Land and buildings 2009 £000	Other 2009 £000
Expiring within one year	–	96	112	210
Expiring within two to five years	–	254	–	360
Expiring after five years	–	120	–	90
	–	470	112	660

6

Corporate governance

Contents

Corporate Governance

Statement of Compliance with the Combined Code

This statement together with the Nomination Committee Report on page 66, the Audit Committee Report on page 67 and the Remuneration Report on pages 68 to 74, describes how the Main Principles of the Combined Code on Corporate Governance, issued by the Financial Reporting Council (FRC) dated June 2008 (the Code), have been applied during the year ended 31st March 2011. In June 2010 the FRC replaced the Code with the UK Corporate Governance Code which applies to accounting periods beginning on or after 29th June 2010 (the New Code). The board will report on compliance with the New Code in next year's annual report.

During the year ended 31st March 2011, the company has complied with all relevant provisions set out in Section 1 of the Code throughout the year except in respect of provision D.1.1 – *The senior independent director should attend sufficient meetings with a range of major shareholders to listen to their views in order to help develop a balanced understanding of the issues and concerns of major shareholders*. During the year the board has taken the view that it is not necessarily practical, efficient or desired by shareholders for the Senior Independent Director to attend meetings with major shareholders in order to learn their issues and concerns unless such discussions are requested by shareholders. The methods by which major shareholders' views are communicated to the board as a whole are discussed under 'Relations with Shareholders' on page 60.

The Role of the Board

The board is responsible to the company's shareholders for the group's long term success, its strategic objectives, its system of corporate governance and the stewardship of the group's resources and it is ultimately responsible for social, environmental and ethical matters. The board is also responsible for determining the nature and extent of the significant risks it is willing to take in order to achieve its strategic objectives.

Other key matters reserved for board decision include approval of the annual group operating and capital expenditure budgets, annual group three year plan and ten year strategy and of changes relating to the company's capital structure. The board also approves announcements of the group's results, the Annual Report and Accounts, the declaration of the interim dividend and recommendation of the final dividend. The board is responsible for considering and approving major capital projects, major acquisitions and major disposals of assets or operations. The board reviews the key activities of the business and receives papers and presentations to enable it to do so effectively.

In respect of board membership and other appointments, the board determines the structure, size and composition of the board, appointments to the board, selection of the Chairman of the board and the Chief Executive, appointment of the Senior Independent Director and membership and chairmanship of board committees.

The board held seven meetings in the year. In addition, the board met separately in the year to undertake a ten year strategy review.

The board delegates specific responsibilities to board committees, as described below.

Board Composition

The board comprises the Chairman (Sir John Banham), the Chief Executive (Mr N A P Carson), three other executive directors, the Chairman Designate (Mr T E P Stevenson) and six other independent non-executive directors. Sir John Banham will be retiring as Chairman with effect from the close of the 2011 Annual General Meeting, having served as Chairman for five years, and will be succeeded by Mr Stevenson who was appointed to the board on 29th March 2011. Sir John Banham's and Mr Stevenson's other commitments are disclosed on page 56.

Also with effect from the close of the 2011 Annual General Meeting, Mr A M Thomson and Mr R J W Walvis will be retiring from the board, each having served as a non-executive director for nine years. Mr A M Ferguson, who was appointed as a non-executive director on 13th January 2011, will succeed Mr Thomson as Chairman of the Audit Committee and Mr M J Roney, non-executive director, will be appointed the Senior Independent Director. Mr Roney will also take over the chairmanship of the Management Development and Remuneration Committee upon Mr Walvis' retirement. Following these changes, the board will comprise the Chairman, the Chief Executive, three other executive directors and four independent non-executive directors.

The roles of Chairman and Chief Executive are separate. The Chairman leads the board, ensuring that each director, particularly each non-executive director, is able to make an effective contribution. He is responsible for ensuring a culture of openness and debate and that adequate time is available for discussion. He monitors, with assistance from the Company Secretary, the information distributed to the board to ensure that it is sufficient, accurate, timely and clear.

Corporate Governance

The Role of the Board (continued)

Board Composition (continued)

The Chief Executive maintains day-to-day management responsibility for the group's operations, implementing group strategies and policies agreed by the board.

The three other executive directors, Mr R J MacLeod, Mr L C Pentz and Mr W F Sandford, have specific responsibilities, which are detailed on pages 56 and 57, and have direct responsibility for all operations and activities.

The role of the non-executive directors, who are appointed for specified terms subject to re-election and to the provisions of the Companies Act 2006 relating to the removal of a director, is to enhance independence and objectivity of the board's deliberations and decisions. Additionally, the non-executive directors play an important role in developing strategy. Each non-executive director (including, until his forthcoming appointment as Chairman, Mr Stevenson) is considered by the board to be independent in character and judgment and there are no relationships or circumstances which are likely to affect, or could appear to affect, the director's judgment.

Under the company's Articles of Association, all directors submit themselves for re-election at least once every three years. However, in accordance with the provisions of the New Code, all directors will retire at each Annual General Meeting and offer themselves for re-election. All directors except Sir John Banham, Mr Thomson and Mr Walvis, who are retiring from the board in July 2011, will be offering themselves for re-election at the 2011 Annual General Meeting. Mr Ferguson and Mr Stevenson will offer themselves for election having been appointed to the board since the 2010 Annual General Meeting.

Information and Support

Each board meeting includes a business or strategy presentation from senior managers. These presentations assist the non-executive directors in familiarising themselves with the group's businesses. The board also holds at least one board meeting per year at one of the group's operational sites and takes the opportunity to tour the site and discuss issues with local senior and middle management. During the year ended 31st March 2011, the board visited the Johnson Matthey Technology Centre in Sonning, UK where it toured the site and received presentations from management on the company's R&D organisation and on R&D long term trends. Individual non-executive directors also undertake site visits. Such presentations, meetings and site visits help to give a balanced overview of the company. They enable the non-executive directors to build an understanding of the company's businesses, the markets in which the company operates and its main relationships and to build a link with the company's employees. This is important in helping the non-executive directors to continually develop and refresh their knowledge and skills to ensure that their contribution to the board remains informed and relevant. Account is taken of environmental, social and governance matters in the training of directors.

The Company Secretary is responsible to the board, and is available to individual directors, in respect of board procedures. The Company Secretary is also responsible for keeping the board up to date on legislative, regulatory and corporate governance developments.

The company has in place formal induction programmes for new directors. Since their appointments, Mr Ferguson and Mr Stevenson have received a tailored induction programme which so far has included meetings with the Chief Executive, the executive directors and senior management in order to be briefed on the group strategy and individual businesses, briefing sessions with key group functions and visits to the principal UK sites. As part of his induction programme, Mr Stevenson has had meetings with several major shareholders. Mr Ferguson is available to attend meetings with major shareholders if requested.

Board and Committee Performance Evaluation

Following the appointment of Mr Stevenson as Chairman Designate on 29th March 2011, the board has instigated a formal evaluation of its performance and that of its committees and individual directors. This evaluation is being led by Mr Stevenson and is being externally facilitated. The external facilitator has no other connection with the company. The evaluation will allow Mr Stevenson to gain an objective view of the workings of the board and of its committees. The evaluation includes detailed interviews with each director covering the following key areas:

- overall board effectiveness,
- board composition and balance,
- succession planning,
- strategy process,
- financial and non-financial monitoring,
- risk and management systems, and
- the board development plan (including training and site visits).

This evaluation process is ongoing and will be reported on further in next year's annual report.

A full review of the Chairman's performance was undertaken in 2009/10 and the results were reported by the Senior Independent Director to the board in May 2010. In view of the forthcoming change in the chairmanship of the company, a separate formal review of the Chairman's performance has not been undertaken although the board expects feedback on the Chairman's performance to be reflected in the externally facilitated evaluation currently underway.

During the year ended 31st March 2011, the Chairman met with non-executive directors without the executive directors present.

Committees of the Board

The Chief Executive's Committee (CEC) is responsible for the recommendation to the board of strategic and operating plans and on making recommendations on matters reserved to the board where appropriate. It is also responsible for the executive management of the group's businesses. The Committee is chaired by the Chief Executive and meets monthly (except in August). During the year it comprised the Chief Executive, the three other executive directors and eight senior executives of the company including four division directors; the Group Director, Corporate and Strategic Development; the Director, Group Systems, EHS and HR; the Deputy Director, Group EHS and HR; and the Group Legal Director.

Johnson Matthey
Annual Report & Accounts 2011

REPORT OF THE DIRECTORS – CORPORATE GOVERNANCE

Corporate Governance

Committees of the Board (continued)

The Audit Committee is a committee of the board whose purpose is to assist the board in the effective discharge of its responsibilities for financial reporting and corporate control. The Audit Committee meets quarterly and is chaired by Mr Thomson. It comprises all the independent non-executive directors with the group Chairman, the Chief Executive, the Group Finance Director and the external and internal auditors attending by invitation. A report from the Audit Committee on its activities is given on page 67. Mr Thomson has recent and relevant financial experience as former Finance Director of Smiths Group plc and, until April 2011, as President of the Institute of Chartered Accountants of Scotland. As referred to above, Mr Thomson will be retiring from the board in July 2011 at which time Mr Ferguson will take over as Chairman of the Audit Committee. Mr Ferguson has recent and relevant financial experience as former Chief Financial Officer of Lonmin Plc.

The Nomination Committee is a committee of the board responsible for advising the board and making recommendations on the appointment and, if necessary, dismissal of executive and non-executive directors. The Nomination Committee is chaired by Sir John Banham, the group Chairman, and also comprises all the independent non-executive directors. Mr Stevenson will take over the chairmanship of the Nomination Committee upon his appointment as group Chairman in July 2011. A report from the Nomination Committee on its activities is given on page 66.

The Management Development and Remuneration Committee (MDRC) is a committee of the board which determines on behalf of the board the fair remuneration of the executive directors and the Chairman and assists the board in ensuring that the current and future senior management of the group is recruited, developed and remunerated in an appropriate fashion. The MDRC is chaired by Mr Walvis and comprises all the independent non-executive directors together with the group Chairman. The Chief Executive and the Director, Group EHS and HR attend by invitation except when their own performance and remuneration are discussed. Further details are set out in the Remuneration Report on pages 68 to 74. As referred to above, Mr Walvis will be retiring from the board in July 2011 at which time Mr Roney will take over as Chairman of the MDRC.

Board and Committee Attendance

Attendance at the board and board committee meetings in 2010/11 was as follows:

Director	Full Board		MDRC		Nomination Committee		Audit Committee	
	Eligible to attend	Attended	Eligible to attend	Attended	Eligible to attend	Attended	Eligible to attend	Attended
Sir John Banham	7	7	5	5	7	7	–	4[1]
N A P Carson	7	7	–	5[1]	–	7[1]	–	4[1]
A M Ferguson	2	2	1	1	2	2	1	1
Sir Thomas Harris	7	7	5	5	7	7	4	4
R J MacLeod	7	7	–	–	–	–	–	4[1]
L C Pentz	7	7	–	–	–	–	–	–
M J Roney	7	7	5	5	7	7	4	4
W F Sandford	7	7	–	–	–	–	–	–
T E P Stevenson	1	1	1	1	1	1	–	–
D C Thompson	7	7	5	5	7	7	4	4
A M Thomson	7	7	5	5	7	7	4	4
R J W Walvis	7	7	5	5	7	7	4	4

[1] Includes meetings attended by invitation for all or part of meeting.

Relations with Shareholders

The board considers effective communication with shareholders, whether institutional investors, private or employee shareholders, to be extremely important.

The company reports formally to shareholders when its full year and half year results are published. These results are posted on Johnson Matthey's website (www.matthey.com). At the same time, executive directors give presentations on the results to institutional investors, analysts and the media in London and other international centres. Live audiocasts of the results presentations in London and copies of major presentations are available on the company's website. The company also holds an annual investor day for its institutional investors and analysts. At the 2011 Investor Day, the company presented the results of its ten year strategy review. Copies of the Investor Day presentations are posted on the company's website.

Contact with Major Shareholders

Contact with major shareholders is principally maintained by the Chief Executive and the Group Finance Director, who ensure that their views are communicated to the board as a whole. The Chairman is also available to discuss governance and other matters directly with major shareholders. The board believes that appropriate steps have been taken during the year to ensure that the members of the board, and in particular the non-executive directors, develop an understanding of the views of major shareholders about the company. The board is provided with brokers' reports at every board meeting and feedback from shareholder meetings on a six-monthly basis. The canvassing of major shareholders' views for the board in a detailed investor survey is usually conducted every two years by external consultants. The board has taken the view that these methods, taken together, are a practical and efficient way both for the Chairman to keep in touch with major shareholder opinion on governance and strategy and for the Senior Independent Director to learn the views of major shareholders and to develop a balanced understanding of their issues and concerns. The Senior Independent Director and other non-executive directors are available to attend meetings with major shareholders if requested, however no such meetings were requested during the year.

Corporate Governance

Relations with Shareholders (continued)

Annual General Meeting

The company's Annual General Meeting takes place in London and formal notification is sent to shareholders at least 20 working days in advance of the meeting. The directors are available for questions, formally during the Annual General Meeting and informally afterwards. Details of the 2011 Annual General Meeting are set out in the circular accompanying this annual report.

Accountability, Audit and Control

In its reporting to shareholders, the board aims to present a balanced and understandable assessment of the group's financial position and prospects. The statement of the responsibility of directors for the preparation of the Annual Report and Accounts is set out on page 75.

The group's organisational structure is focused on its three divisions. These are all separately managed but report to the board through a board director. The CEC receives and reviews monthly summaries of financial results from each division through a standardised reporting process. The group has in place a comprehensive annual budgeting process including plans for the following two years. Variances from budget are closely monitored. In addition to the annual budgeting process, there is a ten year strategy review process.

The Group Control Manual, which is distributed to all group operations, clearly sets out the composition, responsibilities and authority limits of the various board and executive committees and also specifies what may be decided without central approval. It is supplemented by other specialist policy and procedures manuals issued by the group, divisions and individual businesses or departments. The high intrinsic value of many of the metals with which the group is associated necessitates stringent physical controls over precious metals held at the group's sites.

Internal Control and Risk Management

The board has overall responsibility for the group's systems of internal control, including in respect of the financial reporting process, and risk management systems and for reviewing their effectiveness. The internal control systems are designed to meet the group's needs and manage the risks to which it is exposed, although these cannot be eliminated. Such systems can only provide reasonable but not absolute assurance against material misstatement or loss.

The board has delegated responsibility for the review of the effectiveness of the group's internal financial control and risk management systems to the Audit Committee. The Audit Committee monitors and reviews the effectiveness of the group's systems for internal control and risk management, considering regular reports from management and Internal Audit. The internal audit function is responsible for monitoring the group's systems of internal financial controls. The Audit Committee approves the plans for internal audit reviews and receives the reports produced by the internal audit function on a regular basis. Actions are agreed with management in response to any issues raised by the internal audit reports produced. Internal Audit follows up the implementation of its recommendations, including any recommendations to improve internal controls, and reports the outcome to senior management and to the Audit Committee.

In addition, each year businesses are required to formally review their financial and non-financial controls and their compliance with group policies and statutory and regulatory obligations and to provide assurance on these. The results of these reviews are collated and summarised by the internal audit function and a report is made annually to the Audit Committee.

The Audit Committee also considers reports from the external auditors on their evaluation of the systems of internal financial control and risk management. Amongst other matters, the Audit Committee reviews the group's credit control procedures and risks, controls over precious metals, IT controls and the group's corporate social responsibility reporting arrangements and whistleblowing procedures. The Audit Committee also reviews the performance of both the internal and external auditors.

The Audit Committee reports to the board on the operation and effectiveness of internal financial controls and risk management systems. This is considered by the board in forming its own view of the effectiveness of the systems.

A report from the Audit Committee on its activities and on the work of Internal Audit is given on page 67.

There is a continuous process for identifying, evaluating and managing the significant risks faced by the company. This process, which is described on pages 38 and 39, has been in place during the year ended 31st March 2011 and up to the date of approval of the Annual Report and Accounts. The board regularly reviews this process.

The directors confirm that the system of internal controls for the year ended 31st March 2011 and the period up to 1st June 2011 has been established in accordance with the revised Turnbull Guidance on Internal Control published by the FRC included with the Code. The directors have reviewed the effectiveness of the group's system of internal controls, including financial, operational and compliance controls and risk management systems. No significant failings or weaknesses were identified.

Corporate Social Responsibility Risks

Measures to ensure responsible business conduct and the identification and assessment of risks associated with social, ethical and environmental matters are managed in conjunction with all other business risks and reviewed at regular meetings of the board, the Audit Committee and the CEC.

A review of the group's policies and targets for corporate social responsibility (CSR) is set out in the Sustainability section of the Business Review on pages 45 to 55. A full version of the Sustainability Report is available on the company's website.

The identification and monitoring of environment, health and safety (EHS), social and governance risks are the responsibility of the CSR Compliance Committee, which is a sub-committee of the CEC. It comprises the division directors, the Director, Group EHS and HR, the Group Legal Director and senior representatives of Internal Audit, Group EHS and other group functions. The Committee has specific responsibility for setting and overseeing compliance with the standards for group CSR performance through the development, dissemination, adoption and implementation of appropriate group policies and other operational measures. EHS performance is monitored using monthly statistics and detailed site audit reports. EHS performance is reviewed on a regular basis by the CEC and an annual review is undertaken by the board.

Risks from employment and employee issues are identified and assessed by the CEC and reported to the board.

Employment contracts, handbooks and policies specify acceptable business practices and the group's position on ethical issues. The Group Control Manual and security manuals provide further operational guidelines to reinforce these.

The Audit Committee reviews risks associated with corporate social responsibility on an annual basis and monitors performance through the annual control self-assessment process conducted by the internal audit function.

REPORT OF THE DIRECTORS – CORPORATE GOVERNANCE

Other Statutory Information

Annual General Meeting

The notice of the 2011 Annual General Meeting of the company to be held on Tuesday 19th July 2011 at 11.00 am at The Institution of Engineering and Technology (The Lecture Theatre), 2 Savoy Place, London WC2R 0BL is contained in the circular accompanying this annual report, together with an explanation of the resolutions to be considered at the meeting.

Dividends

The interim dividend of 12.5 pence per share (2010 11.1 pence) was paid in February 2011. The directors recommend a final dividend of 33.5 pence per share in respect of the year ended 31st March 2011 (2010 27.9 pence), making a total for the year of 46.0 pence per share (2010 39.0 pence), payable on 2nd August 2011 to shareholders on the register at the close of business on 10th June 2011.

A Dividend Reinvestment Plan is in place which allows shareholders to purchase additional shares in the company with their dividend payment. Further information and a mandate can be obtained from the company's registrars, Equiniti, whose details are set out on page 129.

Share Capital

The issued share capital of the company at 31st March 2011 was 214,675,736 ordinary shares of £1.00 each (excluding treasury shares). The company did not allot any shares during the year ended 31st March 2011. As at 31st March 2011, the company held 5,997,877 treasury shares. There were no purchases, sales or transfers of treasury shares during the year ended 31st March 2011.

At the 2010 Annual General Meeting, shareholders renewed the company's authority to make market purchases of up to 21,467,573 ordinary shares representing 10% of the issued share capital of the company (excluding treasury shares) as at 1st June 2010. The company did not make any purchases of its own shares during the year ended 31st March 2011. Authority to purchase up to 21,467,573 shares remained in place at 31st March 2011. At the forthcoming Annual General Meeting the board will again seek shareholders' approval to renew the annual authority for the company to make purchases of its own shares through the market.

The holders of ordinary shares are entitled to receive dividends when declared, to receive the company's Annual Report and Accounts, to attend and speak at general meetings of the company, to appoint proxies and to exercise voting rights.

There are no restrictions on the transfer of ordinary shares. The directors may, in certain circumstances, refuse to register the transfer of a share in certificated form which is not fully paid up, where the instrument of transfer does not comply with the requirements of the Articles of Association, or if entitled to do so under the Uncertificated Securities Regulations 2001. The directors may also refuse to register a transfer of ordinary shares in certificated form, which represent 0.25% or more of the issued share capital, following the failure by the member or any other person appearing to be interested in the shares to provide the company with information requested under section 793 of the Companies Act 2006. There are no limitations on the holding of ordinary shares and no requirements to obtain the company's or other shareholders' approval to any transfers.

There are no restrictions on voting rights except that a shareholder has no right to vote in respect of a share unless all sums due in respect of that share are fully paid. There are no arrangements by which, with the company's cooperation, financial rights carried by shares are held by a person other than the holder of the shares. There are no known agreements between holders of securities that may result in restrictions on the transfer of securities or on voting rights. No ordinary shares carry any special voting rights with regard to control of the company.

Shares acquired by employees through the Johnson Matthey employee share schemes rank equally with the other shares in issue and have no special rights. Voting rights in respect of shares held through the group's employee share schemes are not exercisable directly by employees however employees can direct the trustee of the schemes to exercise voting rights on their behalf.

Other Statutory Information

Employee Share Schemes

At 31st March 2011, 4,375 current and former employees, representing approximately 45% of employees worldwide, were shareholders in Johnson Matthey through the group's employee share schemes. Through these schemes, current and former employees held 3,944,966 shares (1.84% of issued share capital, excluding treasury shares). As at 31st March 2011, 408 current and former employees held options over 1,797,780 shares through the company's executive share option schemes. Also as at 31st March 2011, 2,402,541 shares had been allocated but had not yet vested under the company's long term incentive plan to 962 current and former employees.

Major Shareholders

As at 1st June 2011, the following information had been disclosed to the company under the Financial Services Authority's Disclosure and Transparency Rules in respect of holdings exceeding the 3% notification threshold:

	Nature of holding	Total voting rights	% of total voting rights[1]
BlackRock, Inc.	Indirect	20,570,656	9.58%
Financial Instrument (CFD)		578,823	0.27%
FIL Limited	Indirect	10,735,815	5.00%
Prudential plc	Direct	10,623,919	4.95%
	Indirect	77,634	0.03%
Lloyds Banking Group plc	Direct	1,142,771	0.53%
	Indirect	9,625,114	4.48%
Legal & General Group Plc	Direct	8,581,762	3.99%

[1] Total voting rights attaching to the issued ordinary share capital of the company (excluding treasury shares) at the date of disclosure.

Directors

The following served as directors during the year ended 31st March 2011:

Sir John Banham	Mr M J Roney
Mr N A P Carson	Mr W F Sandford
Mr A M Ferguson (appointed 13th January 2011)	Mr T E P Stevenson (appointed 29th March 2011)
Sir Thomas Harris	Mrs D C Thompson
Mr R J MacLeod	Mr A M Thomson
Mr L C Pentz	Mr R J W Walvis

Sir John Banham, Mr Thomson and Mr Walvis will be retiring from the board at the close of the forthcoming Annual General Meeting and therefore do not offer themselves for re-election. Mr Ferguson and Mr Stevenson, both of whom were appointed during the year, will retire at the forthcoming Annual General Meeting and, being eligible, offer themselves for election. In accordance with the provisions of the UK Corporate Governance Code, all the remaining directors will be offering themselves for re-election at the forthcoming Annual General Meeting.

The names and biographical details of all the directors are shown on pages 56 and 57.

Details of the constitution of the board and its committees are set out on pages 58 to 60.

Appointment and Replacement of Directors

The company's Articles of Association provide that the number of directors is not subject to any maximum but must not be less than six, unless otherwise determined by the company by ordinary resolution. Directors may be appointed by an ordinary resolution of the members or by a resolution of the directors. Under the company's Articles of Association, a director appointed by the directors must retire at the next following Annual General Meeting and is not taken into account in determining the directors who are to retire by rotation at the meeting.

Under the company's Articles of Association, at every Annual General Meeting at least one third of directors must retire by rotation. The directors to retire by rotation must include any director who has not been subject to election or re-election at the time of the two preceding Annual General Meetings and (if so required to constitute one third of directors) those directors who have been longest in office since their last appointment or reappointment. Notwithstanding this provision in the Articles of Association, all directors who served throughout the whole of the year ended 31st March 2011 (other than Sir John Banham and Messrs Thomson and Walvis who will be retiring from the board in July 2011) will be offering themselves for re-election at this year's Annual General Meeting in accordance with the UK Corporate Governance Code.

A director may be removed by a special resolution of the company. In addition, a director must automatically cease to be a director if (i) he or she ceases to be a director by virtue of any provision of the Companies Act 2006 or he or she becomes prohibited by law from being a director, or (ii) he or she becomes bankrupt or makes any arrangement or composition with his or her creditors generally, or (iii) he or she is suffering from a mental disorder, or (iv) he or she resigns from his or her office by notice in writing to the company or, in the case of an executive director, his appointment is terminated or expires and the directors resolve that his office be vacated, or (v) he or she is absent for more than six consecutive months without permission of the directors from meetings of the directors and the directors resolve that his or her office be vacated, or (vi) he or she is requested in writing, or by electronic form, by all the other directors to resign.

Powers of the Directors

The powers of the directors are determined by the company's Articles of Association, the Companies Act 2006 and any directions given by the company in general meeting. The directors have been authorised by the Articles of Association to issue and allot ordinary shares and to make market purchases of shares. These powers are referred to shareholders at the Annual General Meeting for renewal. Any shares purchased may be cancelled or held as treasury shares.

Directors' Conflicts of Interests

Procedures are in place to ensure compliance with the directors' conflict of interest duties set out in the Companies Act 2006. The company has complied with these procedures during the year ended 31st March 2011 and the board believes that these procedures operate effectively. During the year, details of any new conflicts or potential conflict matters were submitted to the board for consideration and, where appropriate, these were approved.

At the end of March 2011, the board undertook an annual review of previously approved conflict or potential conflict matters and, to the extent that these were still relevant, agreed that they should continue to be authorised on the terms previously set out. In each case, the review was undertaken by directors who were genuinely independent of the conflict matter. Authorised conflict or potential conflict matters will continue to be reviewed by the board on an annual basis.

REPORT OF THE DIRECTORS – CORPORATE GOVERNANCE

Other Statutory Information

Directors' Indemnities

Under Deed Polls the company has granted indemnities in favour of each director of the company in respect of any liability that he or she may incur to a third party in relation to the affairs of the company or any group member. These provisions were in force during the year ended 31st March 2011 for the benefit of all persons who were directors of the company at any time during the year ended 31st March 2011 and remain in force for the benefit of all persons who are directors of the company as at the date when this Report of the Directors was approved.

Under Deed Polls the company has also granted indemnities in favour of each director of its subsidiaries in respect of any liability that he or she may incur to a third party in relation to the affairs of any group member. These provisions were in force during the year ended 31st March 2011 for the benefit of all persons who were directors of the subsidiaries at any time during the year ended 31st March 2011 and remain in force for the benefit of all persons who are directors of the subsidiaries as at the date when this Report of the Directors was approved.

Copies of the Deed Polls and the company's Articles of Association are available for inspection during normal business hours at the company's registered office and will be available for inspection at the forthcoming Annual General Meeting from 10.00 am on Tuesday 19th July 2011 until the conclusion of the meeting.

Corporate Governance and Remuneration

The board's statement on corporate governance matters is given on pages 58 to 61 and its report on directors' remuneration, which includes details of service contracts and the directors' interests in the shares of the company, is set out on pages 68 to 74.

Other than service contracts, no director had any interest in any material contract with any group company at any time during the year ended 31st March 2011.

Articles of Association

The Articles of Association may only be amended by a special resolution at a general meeting of the company.

Change of Control

There are no significant agreements to which the company is a party that take effect following a change of control of the company, but the company and its subsidiaries are party to a number of commercial agreements that may allow the counterparties to alter or terminate the agreements on a change of control of the company following a takeover bid. Other than the matters referred to below, these are not deemed by the company to be significant in terms of their potential effect on the group as a whole.

The group has a number of loan notes and borrowing facilities which may require prepayment of principal and payment of accrued interest and breakage costs if there is change of control of the company. The group has also entered into a series of financial instruments to hedge its currency, interest rate and metal price exposures which provide for termination or alteration if a change of control of the company materially weakens the creditworthiness of the group.

The company is party to a marketing agreement with a subsidiary of Anglo Platinum Limited, originally entered into in 1992, under which the company was appointed as sales and marketing agent for refined platinum group metals worldwide excluding the US and the company agreed to provide certain marketing services. The agreement contains provisions under which the counterparty may have the right to terminate the agreement on a change of control of the company.

The rules of the company's employee share schemes set out the consequences of a change of control of the company on participants' rights under the schemes. Generally such rights will vest and become exercisable on a change of control subject to the satisfaction of relevant performance conditions.

The executive directors' service contracts each contain a provision to the effect that if the contract is terminated by the company within one year after a change of control of the company, the company will pay to the director as liquidated damages an amount equivalent to one year's gross basic salary and other contractual benefits less the period of any notice given by the company to the director. There are no other agreements between the company and its directors or employees providing for compensation for loss of office or employment (whether through resignation, purported redundancy or otherwise) on a change of control of the company following a takeover bid.

Other than the marketing agreement with a subsidiary of Anglo Platinum Limited referred to above, the group does not have any contractual or other arrangements with any persons which the directors consider are essential to the business of the company.

Disabled Persons

A description of the company's policy applied during the year ended 31st March 2011 relating to the recruitment, employment and training of disabled employees can be found on page 50.

Employee Involvement

A description of the action taken by the company during the year ended 31st March 2011 relating to employee involvement can be found on pages 45 to 55.

Use of Financial Instruments

Information on the group's financial risk management objectives and policies and its exposure to credit risk, liquidity risk, interest rate risk and foreign currency risk can be found on pages 111 to 115.

Branches

The company and its subsidiaries have established branches in a number of different countries in which they operate.

Policy on Payment of Commercial Debts

The group's policy in relation to the payment of all suppliers (set out in its Group Control Manual, which is distributed to all group operations) is that payment should be made within the credit terms agreed with the supplier, subject to the supplier having performed its obligations under the relevant contract. It is not the group's policy to follow any specific code or standard on payment practice in respect of its suppliers. At 31st March 2011, the company's aggregate level of 'creditor days' amounted to 8 days. Creditor days are calculated by dividing the aggregate of the amounts which were outstanding as trade payables at 31st March 2011 by the aggregate of the amounts the company was invoiced by suppliers during the year ended 31st March 2011 and multiplying by 365 to express the ratio as a number of days.

Charitable Donations

During the year ended 31st March 2011 the group donated £517,000 (2010 £458,000) to charitable organisations worldwide, of which £320,000 (2010 £298,000) was in the UK.

Further details of contributions made by the group worldwide are given on pages 52 and 53 and in the Sustainability Report which can be found on the company's website at www.matthey.com.

Other Statutory Information

Political Donations and Expenditure

It is the policy of the group not to make political donations. During the year ended 31st March 2011, no donations were made by the company or its subsidiaries to any EU political party, EU political organisation or to any EU independent election candidate (2010 £ nil), no EU political expenditure was incurred (2010 £ nil) and no contributions to political parties outside the EU were made within the meaning of Part 14 of the Companies Act 2006 (2010 £ nil).

Management Report

The Report of the Directors is the 'management report' for the purposes of the Financial Services Authority's Disclosure and Transparency Rules (DTR 4.1.8R).

Auditors and Disclosure of Information

In accordance with section 489 of the Companies Act 2006, resolutions are to be proposed at the forthcoming Annual General Meeting for the reappointment of KPMG Audit Plc as auditors of the company and to authorise the directors to determine their remuneration.

So far as each person serving as a director of the company at the date this Report of the Directors was approved by the board is aware, there is no relevant audit information of which the company's auditors are unaware. Each such director hereby confirms that he or she has taken all the steps that he or she ought to have taken as a director in order to make himself or herself aware of any relevant audit information and to establish that the company's auditors are aware of that information.

The Report of the Directors was approved by the Board of Directors on 1st June 2011 and is signed on its behalf by:

Simon Farrant
Company Secretary

REPORT OF THE DIRECTORS – CORPORATE GOVERNANCE

Nomination Committee Report

Role of the Nomination Committee

The Nomination Committee is a committee of the board whose purpose is to advise the board on the appointment and, if necessary, dismissal of executive and non-executive directors. The full terms of reference of the Nomination Committee are provided on the company's website at www.matthey.com.

Composition of the Nomination Committee

The Nomination Committee comprises all the independent non-executive directors together with the group Chairman. The quorum necessary for the transaction of business is two, each of whom must be an independent non-executive director. Biographical details of the independent directors and the group Chairman are set out on pages 56 and 57. Their remuneration is set out on page 71.

The group Chairman acts as the Chairman of the Nomination Committee, although he may not chair the Nomination Committee when it is dealing with the matter of succession to the chairmanship of the company. A non-executive director may not chair the Nomination Committee when it is dealing with a matter relating to that non-executive director.

Only members of the Nomination Committee have the right to attend Nomination Committee meetings. However, the Chief Executive, the Director, Group EHS and HR, external advisers and others may be invited to attend for all or part of any meeting as and when appropriate.

The Company Secretary is secretary to the Nomination Committee.

The Nomination Committee has the authority to seek any information that it requires from any officer or employee of the company or its subsidiaries. In connection with its duties, the Nomination Committee is authorised by the board to take such independent advice (including legal or other professional advice, at the company's expense) as it considers necessary, including requests for information from or commissioning investigations by external advisers.

Main Activities of the Nomination Committee

The Nomination Committee met seven times during the year ended 31st March 2011; on 5th May, 1st June, 20th July, 29th September and 23rd November 2010 and on 1st February and 29th March 2011.

At its prior meetings on 2nd February and 30th March 2010, the Committee had discussed the forthcoming retirement of the Chairman, Sir John Banham, after the Annual General Meeting in July 2011, and had considered the appointment of a successor and a draft specification for the role together with initial proposals from a number of executive search consultants to assist in the recruitment process. The Committee had agreed that the selection process, including the selection of executive search consultants, should be led by the Senior Independent Director and the Chief Executive, assisted by the Director, Group EHS and HR.

The Committee met on 5th May 2010 to further discuss the process for the selection and appointment of a new group Chairman. The Committee considered the specification for the role based on the skills and experience required and assessed the time commitment expected. It also reviewed external search consultancies proposed to be used in the selection process. The Committee reviewed progress at its meeting on 1st June 2010 and considered shortlisted external and internal candidates at its meetings on 20th July and 29th September 2010. Also at its meeting on 29th September 2010, the Committee considered fully the respective merits of the remaining external and internal candidates, including their other significant commitments. After full consideration, the Committee agreed to recommend the appointment of Mr T E P Stevenson as Chairman Designate and for him to take over as Chairman on Sir John Banham's retirement. At its meeting on 1st February 2011, the Committee noted that Mr Stevenson would join the board as Chairman Designate on 29th March 2011. At each of the aforementioned meetings, the Senior Independent Director chaired the discussions relating to the Chairman's successor.

At its prior meetings on 2nd February and 30th March 2010, the Nomination Committee had discussed the prospective retirement of Mr A M Thomson, the Senior Independent Director and Chairman of the Audit Committee, after serving as a non-executive director for nine years, and of Mr R J W Walvis, Chairman of the Management Development and Remuneration Committee, also after serving as a non-executive director for nine years. It was agreed that the process for appointment of successors should be instigated later in the year.

At its meeting on 5th May 2010, the Committee discussed further the need to appoint an additional non-executive director / chair of the Audit Committee following the forthcoming retirement of Mr Thomson. The Committee agreed that the process for selection would be instigated later in the year. On 29th September 2010, the Committee considered a description for the role based on the balance of skills, experience, independence and knowledge on the board and an assessment of the time commitment expected. Profiles were received from external search consultants in respect of several candidates. At its meeting on 23rd November 2010, the Committee reviewed progress, noting the outcome of interviews of the shortlisted candidates. After full consideration, the Committee agreed to recommend the appointment of Mr A M Ferguson as a new non-executive director and prospective Chairman of the Audit Committee.

At its meeting on 29th March 2011, the Committee discussed the need for the board to appoint one of the independent non-executive directors to be the Senior Independent Director following the forthcoming retirement of Mr Thomson. It also discussed the need to appoint a chair of the Management Development and Remuneration Committee following the forthcoming retirement of Mr Walvis. The Committee agreed to consider these matters again at its next meeting.

At its meeting after the year end on 10th May 2011, the Committee noted that Mr M J Roney had agreed to take on the role of Senior Independent Director and the chairmanship of the Management Development and Remuneration Committee upon the retirement of Mr Thomson and Mr Walvis respectively. The Committee recommended these appointments to the board. The board subsequently approved these appointments.

On behalf of the Nomination Committee:

Sir John Banham
Chairman of the Nomination Committee

Audit Committee Report

Role of the Audit Committee

The Audit Committee is a committee of the board whose responsibilities include:

- Reviewing the group's half-yearly and full year accounts and results announcements and any other formal announcements relating to the group's financial performance and recommending them to the board for approval.

- Reviewing the group's systems for internal financial control, financial reporting and risk management.

- Monitoring and reviewing the effectiveness of the group's internal audit function and considering regular reports from Internal Audit on internal financial controls and risk management.

- Considering the appointment of the external auditors, overseeing the process for their selection and making recommendations to the board in relation to their appointment to be put to shareholders for approval at a general meeting.

- Monitoring and reviewing the effectiveness and independence of the external auditors, agreeing the nature and scope of their audit, recommending their remuneration, and considering their reports on the group's accounts, their reports to shareholders and their evaluation of the systems of internal financial control and risk management.

The full terms of reference of the Audit Committee are provided on the company's website at www.matthey.com.

Composition of the Audit Committee

The Audit Committee comprises all the independent non-executive directors. Biographical details of the independent directors are set out on pages 56 and 57. Their remuneration is set out on page 71. The Chairman of the Audit Committee is Mr A M Thomson, who was formerly Finance Director of Smiths Group plc and, until April 2011, was President of the Institute of Chartered Accountants of Scotland. Mr A M Ferguson, who joined the board on 13th January 2011, will take over chairmanship of the Audit Committee in July 2011 when Mr Thomson retires. Mr Ferguson was formerly the Chief Financial Officer of Lonmin Plc and is a chartered accountant.

The group Chairman, Chief Executive, Group Finance Director, Head of Internal Audit and external auditors (KPMG Audit Plc) attend Audit Committee meetings by invitation. The Committee also meets separately with the Head of Internal Audit and with the external auditors without management being present. The Company Secretary is secretary to the Audit Committee.

Main Activities of the Audit Committee

The Audit Committee met four times during the financial year ended 31st March 2011. At its meeting on 27th May 2010 the Committee reviewed the group's preliminary announcement of its results for the financial year ended 31st March 2010, and the draft report and accounts for that year. The Committee received reports from the external auditors on the conduct of their audit, their review of the accounts, including accounting policies and areas of judgment, and their comments on risk management and control matters.

The Audit Committee met on 20th July 2010 to receive reports on internal controls from both the internal and external auditors. The external auditors also presented their proposed fees and scope for the forthcoming year's audit. The Committee also assessed the performance of both the internal and external auditors. The review of the external auditors was used to confirm the appropriateness of their reappointment and included assessment of their independence, qualification, expertise and resources, and effectiveness of the audit process. The Committee recommended to the board the reappointment of KPMG Audit Plc as auditors. The group's Sustainability Report 2010/11 was also reviewed, which is available on the company's website at www.matthey.com.

At its meeting on 22nd November 2010 the Audit Committee reviewed the group's half-yearly results, the half-yearly results announcement and the external auditors' review and also papers on key accounting judgments, credit control and credit risk and on litigation affecting the group. The Committee received a presentation on the risks facing the Catalysts, Chemicals and Refining business from its Finance Director. The Committee also reviewed the Audit

Inspection Unit's Public Report on the 2009/10 inspection of KPMG Audit Plc.

At its meeting on 1st February 2011 the Audit Committee reviewed the group's risk register and management's and Internal Audit's reports on the effectiveness of the group's systems for internal financial control and risk management. The group's whistleblowing procedures were also reviewed. Changes to the Group Control Manual were ratified. The Committee also approved the internal audit plan for 2011/12.

Since the year end the Committee has met to review the group's preliminary announcement of its results and draft report and accounts for the financial year ended 31st March 2011, and also the group's assessment of going concern.

Independence of External Auditors

Both the board and the external auditors have for many years had safeguards in place to avoid the possibility that the auditors' objectivity and independence could be compromised. Our policy in respect of services provided by the external auditors is as follows:

- Audit related services – the external auditors are invited to provide services which, in their position as auditors, they must or are best placed to undertake. This includes formalities relating to borrowings, shareholders' and other circulars, various other regulatory reports and work in respect of acquisitions and disposals.

- Tax compliance and advice – the auditors may provide such services where they are best suited, but otherwise such work is put out to tender.

- Other services – these may not be provided where precluded by ethical standards or where we believe it would compromise their audit independence and objectivity.

To the extent consistent with the above policy, services likely to cost less than £25,000 may be approved by the Group Finance Director. Services above this amount must be approved by the Chairman of the Audit Committee, unless they are likely to be in excess of £100,000 when they must be approved by the Audit Committee.

The split between audit and non-audit fees for the year ended 31st March 2011 and information on the nature of non-audit fees appear in note 5 on the accounts.

Internal Audit

During the year the Audit Committee reviewed the performance of the internal audit function, the findings of the audits completed during the year and the department's resource requirements and also approved the internal audit plan for the year ending 31st March 2012.

Internal Audit independently reviews the risks and control processes operated by management. It carries out independent audits in accordance with an internal audit plan which is agreed with the Audit Committee before the start of the financial year.

The plan provides a high degree of financial and geographical coverage and devotes significant effort to the review of the risk management framework surrounding the major business risks.

Internal audit reports include recommendations to improve internal controls together with agreed management action plans to resolve the issues raised. Internal Audit follows up the implementation of recommendations and reports progress to senior management and the Audit Committee.

The Audit Committee receives reports from the Head of Internal Audit on the department's work and findings.

The effectiveness of the internal audit function is reviewed and discussed on an annual basis with the Head of Internal Audit.

On behalf of the Audit Committee:

Alan Thomson
Chairman of the Audit Committee

REPORT OF THE DIRECTORS – CORPORATE GOVERNANCE

Remuneration Report

Remuneration Report to Shareholders for the Year Ended 31st March 2011

Management Development and Remuneration Committee and its Terms of Reference

The Management Development and Remuneration Committee of the board comprises all the independent non-executive directors of the company as set out on pages 56 and 57 and the group Chairman. The Chairman of the Committee throughout the year was Mr R J W Walvis.

The Committee's terms of reference include determination on behalf of the board of fair remuneration for the Chief Executive, the other executive directors and the group Chairman (in which case the group Chairman does not participate), which, while set in the context of what the company can reasonably afford, recognises their individual contributions to the company's overall performance. In addition, the Committee assists the board in ensuring that the company has well developed plans for management succession, including the recruitment and development of senior management, along with appropriate remuneration policies to ensure that management are retained and motivated.

The Director, Group EHS and HR acts as secretary to the Committee. The full terms of reference of the Committee are available on the company's website at www.matthey.com.

Non-executive directors' remuneration is determined by the board, within the limits prescribed by the company's Articles of Association. The remuneration consists of fees, which are set following advice taken from independent consultants and are reviewed at regular intervals.

Executive Remuneration Policy

The key goal in the remuneration policy remains to obtain the best value for shareholders. This requires that the pay and benefits structure is competitive within the sector, whilst simultaneously providing stretching targets that require significant outperformance to maximise incentive payments. The general remuneration policy is to have base salaries reflective of median levels within an appropriate benchmark group and with due consideration given to the performance and growth of the company. Further incentives are available with the potential to lift earnings towards the upper quartile, but only on the achievement of superior performance. The Committee considers the balance between fixed elements of remuneration, such as base salaries, and the performance related aspects of the complete remuneration package, and seeks to ensure that any earnings beyond base salaries are fully reflected in increased shareholder value through higher profits and earnings per share.

The Committee also recognises that there is a competitive market for successful executives and that the provision of appropriate rewards for superior performance is vital to the continued growth of the business.

In determining the remuneration structure, the Committee appoints and receives advice from independent remuneration consultants on the pay and incentive arrangements prevailing in comparably sized industrial companies in each country in which Johnson Matthey has operations. During the year, such advice was received from the Hay Group, which also provided advice on job evaluation, and PricewaterhouseCoopers LLP. PricewaterhouseCoopers LLP also provided expatriate tax advice and other tax advice, tax audit work, completion of overseas tax returns, advice on set up of new overseas operations, some overseas payroll services and a review of some financial controls. A statement regarding the use of remuneration consultants for the year ended 31st March 2011 is available on the company's website at www.matthey.com. The Committee also receives recommendations from the Chief Executive on the remuneration of those reporting to him as well as advice from the Director, Group EHS and HR.

To ensure the interests of the executive directors remain aligned with those of the shareholders, they are encouraged to build up over time and hold a shareholding in the company equal to at least their basic salary. Details of directors' shareholdings are set out on page 72.

Pay and Employment Conditions Across the Group

The remuneration policy of the company remains consistent in all countries and at all levels of the company with the overriding consideration being to pay competitive median level salaries and to provide opportunities to increase earnings to higher levels through superior performance. Almost all Johnson Matthey employees are able to earn bonuses based on business performance and around 900 employees are able to earn bonuses based on individual, team and business performance, including personal objectives. Around 900 employees are eligible to participate in the Johnson Matthey Long Term Incentive Plan (LTIP).

In setting executive director basic salaries, annual bonus awards and LTIP allocations, the Committee is made aware of comparative data relating to the pay and benefits of other group employees. Pay awards throughout Johnson Matthey's global operations have generally ranged between 0% and 10% in the last year, depending on local pay conditions and on local business and economic conditions. International data provided by the Hay Group is also utilised in considering and determining local settlements.

Remuneration Report

Executive Remuneration Policy (continued)

2010/11 Review of Executive Remuneration Policy – Triennial Review

Executive remuneration policy is normally reviewed by the Committee annually and a formal review is undertaken every three years. The previous formal review took place in 2006/07 and the review due in 2009/10 was delayed due to the uncertain market conditions prevailing at that time. Therefore, during 2010/11 the Committee undertook a comprehensive review of executive director and senior management remuneration arrangements within the group, which included advice from PricewaterhouseCoopers LLP and consultation with the company's major institutional shareholders.

The major inputs to the review were benchmarking data from an appropriate group of companies and a review of the group's performance and growth since the last review. For the purposes of the triennial review, the benchmark peer group comprised 20 adjacent industrial and service companies, with ten either side of Johnson Matthey, as measured by market capitalisation. In determining the overall remuneration package, due cognisance was also taken of the general performance of the group through the recession and in the return to more normal market conditions during the last year. Additionally, a consultation exercise on the changes was carried out with major shareholders in early 2011 and all changes to the remuneration structure remain within the parameters agreed under previous shareholder approvals.

Changes with Effect from 1st April 2011

As a result of the review undertaken in 2010/11, the Committee has approved the following changes to executive remuneration with effect from 1st April 2011:

1. Change in level of annual bonus, including deferral and clawback

   - The Chief Executive's maximum annual bonus opportunity is now set at 150% of basic salary, but one third of the achieved bonus is to be deferred for three years.

   - The executive directors' maximum annual bonus opportunity is now set at 125% of basic salary, but one fifth of the achieved bonus is to be deferred for three years.

   - The deferred element of the annual bonus will be converted into shares and held for three years before release.

   - The annual bonus will continue to be based on consolidated underlying profit before tax (PBT) compared with the annual budget.

   - The deferred element of the annual bonus is subject to clawback in the case of misstatement or misconduct, or other relevant reason as determined by the Committee.

2. Change in allocation levels under the LTIP

   - The Chief Executive's annual allocation level is increased to 175% of basic salary.

   - The executive directors' annual allocation levels are increased to 140% of basic salary.

   - The underlying earnings per share (EPS) performance target remains unchanged and requires annual compound growth in EPS of 6% per annum for threshold vesting and 15% compound for maximum vesting. The Committee also retains discretion to vary the award if the return on invested capital (ROIC) underpin over the performance period is not achieved in line with planned expectations.

Johnson Matthey and FTSE 100 Total Shareholder Return rebased to 100

The following graph charts total cumulative shareholder return of the company for the five year period from 31st March 2006 to 31st March 2011 against the FTSE 100 as the most appropriate comparator group, rebased to 100 at 1st April 2006. The graph shows significant outperformance by Johnson Matthey against the FTSE 100 group over the five year period.

As at 31st March 2011, Johnson Matthey was ranked 74th by market capitalisation in the FTSE 100.

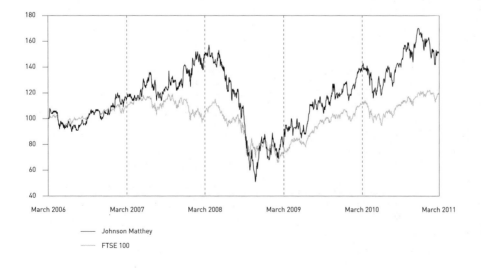

Johnson Matthey

FTSE 100

Remuneration Report

Executive Remuneration for the Year Ended 31st March 2011

Executive directors' remuneration consists of the following:

- **Basic Salary** – in setting the level of basic salaries there are a number of key determinants, the first of which is the performance of the individual executive. Performance is considered against a broad set of parameters including financial, environmental, social and governance issues. The second factor taken into account is the length of time that the executive director has been in post. For example, where an internal promotion has taken place, the median salary relative to the market would usually be reached over a period of a few years which can give rise to higher than normal salary increases while this is being achieved. The third important factor is the relevant comparator with the equivalent posts in appropriate benchmark companies. For the purposes of benchmarking, the remuneration comparator used by the Committee during 2010/11 for executive directors was drawn from FTSE 100 and 250 industrial and service companies (excluding the oil and financial sectors) with market capitalisation of around £2.25 billion and with over 40% of revenue coming from overseas. Further independent benchmark data was sourced from the Hay Group. Basic salary is normally reviewed on 1st August each year.

- **Annual Bonus** – is paid as a percentage of basic salary under the terms of the company's Executive Compensation Plan (which also applies to the group's 190 or so most senior executives). The executive directors' bonus award is based on PBT compared with the annual budget. The board rigorously reviews the annual budget to ensure that the budgeted PBT is sufficiently stretching. An annual bonus payment of 50% of basic salary (prevailing at 31st March) is paid if the group meets the annual budget. This bonus may rise on a straight line basis to a maximum 100% of basic salary if 110% of budgeted PBT is achieved. PBT must reach 95% of budget for a minimum bonus of 15% to be payable. The Committee has discretion in awarding annual bonuses and is able to consider corporate performance on environmental, social and governance issues when awards are made to executive directors. The Committee ensures that the incentive structure for senior management does not raise environmental, social and governance risks by inadvertently motivating irresponsible behaviour. The bonus awarded to executive directors for 2010/11 was 100% of basic salary at 31st March 2011 based on achieved PBT levels. Details of changes in the level of annual bonus, with effect from 1st April 2011, can be found on page 69.

- **LTIP** – is designed to achieve above average performance and growth over the long term. Shares allocated under the terms of the LTIP (which also applies to the group's 900 senior and middle managers) are released on the third anniversary of the allocation date and are subject to an EPS performance target. The LTIP allows share allocations of up to a maximum of 200% of basic annual salary each year (to take account of evolution of market practice if required). Share allocations made in 2008, 2009 and 2010 (all of which are still outstanding) were 150% of basic annual salary for the Chief Executive and 120% for executive directors. In 2009, there was a one-off allocation of 170% of basic salary to the then newly appointed Group Finance Director to ensure close alignment of his objectives with those of shareholders. Details of changes in LTIP allocation levels, with effect from 1st April 2011, are given on page 69.

  The release of the share allocation is subject to the achievement of a performance target measured over a three year performance period commencing in the year of allocation. The performance target is based on the compound annual growth in the company's underlying EPS. The minimum release, of 15% of the allocation, requires underlying EPS growth of 6% compound per annum over the three year period. For the maximum release of 100% of the allocation, underlying EPS must have grown by at least 15% compound per annum over the three year performance period.

The number of allocated shares released will vary on a straight line basis between these points. There is no retesting of the performance target and so allocations will lapse if underlying EPS growth is less than 6% compound per annum over the three year performance period.

In 2009 the Committee approved an adjustment to the performance targets for one year only to reflect the market conditions prevailing at the time of allocation. The top ten major shareholders were consulted regarding this adjustment. For the 2009 allocation only, the minimum release, of 15% of the allocation, requires underlying EPS growth of 3% compound per annum over the three year period, with no retesting of the performance target. For the maximum release of 100% of the allocation, underlying EPS must have grown by at least 10% compound per annum over the three year performance period. As a result of this adjustment, the level of award was reduced to 120% of basic annual salary for the Chief Executive and 100% for executive directors.

Although growth in underlying EPS is the primary financial measure, it is also a key objective of the company to achieve earnings growth only in the context of a good performance on ROIC. Accordingly, the Committee is required to make an assessment of the group's ROIC over the performance period to ensure underlying EPS growth has been achieved with ROIC in line with the group's planned expectations. The Committee may scale back vesting to the extent that ROIC has not developed appropriately.

- **Share Options** – the LTIP is now the company's single means for the provision of long term awards and from 2007 replaced the granting of share options under the Johnson Matthey 2001 Share Option Scheme (the 2001 Scheme). From 2001 to 2006 options were granted each year under the 2001 Scheme. There have been no option grants since 2006. Options were granted at the market value of the company's shares at the time of grant and were subject to performance targets over a three year period. Options may be exercised upon satisfaction of the relevant performance targets. Approximately 800 employees were granted options under the 2001 Scheme each year.

  Options granted from 2004 to 2006 – Grants made in 2004, 2005 and 2006 were subject to a three year performance target of EPS growth of UK RPI plus 3% per annum. If the performance target was not met at the end of the three year performance period, the options lapsed as there was no retesting of the performance target. In addition, to reduce the cost calculated under the International Financial Reporting Standard 2 – 'Share-based Payment', gains made on the exercise of options are capped at 100% of the grant price.

  The Committee had the discretion to award grants greater than 100% of basic annual salary. Grants which were made above this threshold were, however, subject to increasingly stretching performance targets. Grants between 100% and 125% of basic annual salary were subject to EPS growth of UK RPI plus 4% per annum and grants between 125% and 150% of basic annual salary were subject to EPS growth of UK RPI plus 5% per annum. The executive directors were granted options equal to 150% of basic annual salary. All the options, other than those granted in 2006 which were subject to EPS growth of UK RPI plus 5% per annum, have met their performance targets. The 2006 options which did not meet their performance targets have lapsed.

Remuneration Report

Executive Remuneration for the Year Ended 31st March 2011 (continued)

Options granted prior to 2004 – Prior to 2004, options granted to the executive directors under the 2001 Scheme were up to a maximum of 100% of basic annual salary each year. Such options were subject to a performance target of EPS growth of UK RPI plus 4% per annum over any three consecutive years during the life of the option. The performance target was subject to annual retesting until the lapse of the options on the tenth anniversary of grant. All of these options have met their performance targets.

- **Pensions** – all the executive directors are members of the Johnson Matthey Employees Pension Scheme (JMEPS) in the UK.

  Full disclosure of the pension arrangements are set out on pages 73 and 74.

- **Other Benefits** – which are available to the executive directors are private medical insurance, a company car and membership of the group's employee share incentive plans which are open to all employees in the countries in which the group operates such schemes.

- **Service Contracts** – the executive directors are employed on contracts subject to one year's notice at any time. On early termination of their contracts the directors would normally be entitled to 12 months' salary and benefits. The contracts of service of the executive directors and the terms and conditions of appointment of the non-executive directors are available for inspection at the company's registered office during normal business hours and at the forthcoming Annual General Meeting.

Directors' Emoluments 2010/11

	Date of service agreement	Date of appointment	Basic salary £'000	Payment in lieu of pension[1] £'000	Annual bonus £'000	Benefits £'000	Total excluding pension £'000	Total prior year excluding pension £'000
Executive								
N A P Carson [2]	1.8.99	1.8.99	733	183	750	21	1,687	1,596
R J MacLeod [3]	3.2.09	22.6.09	398	–	407	17	822	591
L C Pentz [4]	1.1.06	1.8.03	382	–	390	38	810	787
W F Sandford	21.7.09	21.7.09	330	83	345	16	774	471
Total Directors			**1,843**	**266**	**1,892**	**92**	**4,093**	**3,445**[5]

	Date of letter of appointment	Date of appointment	Fees £'000	Total excluding pension £'000	Total prior year excluding pension £'000
Non-Executive [6]					
Sir John Banham (Chairman)	10.12.05	1.1.06	293	293	280
A M Ferguson	10.1.11	13.1.11	11	11	–
Sir Thomas Harris	22.1.09	1.4.09	50	50	45
M J Roney	29.3.07	1.6.07	50	50	45
T E P Stevenson (Chairman Designate)	10.1.11	29.3.11	–[7]	–[7]	–
D C Thompson	22.5.07	1.9.07	50	50	45
A M Thomson	1.8.02	24.9.02	60[8]	60	50
R J W Walvis	1.8.02	24.9.02	58[9]	58	50
Total			**572**	**572**	**515**

The aggregate amount of remuneration receivable by directors and non-executive directors totalled £4,665,000 (2010 £5,721,000).

Notes

[1] Messrs Carson and Sandford ceased to accrue pensionable service in the Johnson Matthey Employees Pension Scheme with effect from 31st March 2006. They received an annual cash payment in lieu of pension equal to 25% of basic salary. This is taxable under the PAYE system.

[2] Mr Carson is a non-executive director of AMEC plc. His fees in respect of this non-executive directorship were £31,201 from the date of his appointment on 31st August 2010. This amount is excluded from the table above and retained by him.

[3] Mr MacLeod is a non-executive director of Aggreko plc. His fees for the year in respect of this non-executive directorship were £51,000. This amount is excluded from the table above and retained by him.

[4] Mr Pentz is a non-executive director of Victrex plc. His fees for the year in respect of this non-executive directorship were £44,000. This amount is excluded from the table above and retained by him.

[5] The total prior year relates to continuing directors only. Two of the continuing directors, Messrs MacLeod and Sandford, only served part of the prior year. Emoluments of former directors who left during the prior year were £1,761,000 including £833,000 compensation for loss of office.

[6] Non-executive fees (other than for the Chairman) were reviewed on 1st April 2010 for the period from 1st April 2010 to 31st March 2013. The fees are £50,000 per annum, with the fee for chairmanship of the Audit Committee being £10,000 per annum and the Management Development and Remuneration Committee being £8,000 per annum. The Chairman's fees were reviewed on 1st August 2010 for the period 1st August 2010 to 19th July 2011 (the date of his retirement). The Chairman and the non-executive directors do not receive any pension benefits, LTIP allocations, share option grants or bonus payments. The Chairman's fees include £25,000 per annum to cover his administrative and secretarial support costs.

[7] Mr Stevenson was appointed to the board on 29th March 2011 and his fees from the date of appointment to 31st March 2011 were £400.

[8] Includes £10,000 per annum for chairmanship of the Audit Committee.

[9] Includes £8,000 per annum for chairmanship of the Management Development and Remuneration Committee.

Remuneration Report

Directors' Interests

The interests (in respect of which transactions are notifiable to the company under the Financial Services Authority's Disclosure and Transparency Rules) of the directors as at 31st March 2011 in the shares of the company were:

1. Ordinary Shares

	31st March 2011	31st March 2010
Sir John Banham	18,400	18,400
N A P Carson	174,374	174,027
A M Ferguson	1,000	– [1]
Sir Thomas Harris	1,807	1,180
R J MacLeod	3,368	3,400
L C Pentz	25,383	24,968
M J Roney	3,000	3,000
W F Sandford	5,091	4,839
T E P Stevenson	–	– [1]
D C Thompson	9,721	9,721
A M Thomson	2,435	2,383
R J W Walvis	1,000	1,000

[1] At date of appointment.

All of the above interests were beneficial. The executive directors are also deemed to be interested in shares held by an employee share ownership trust (see note 31 on page 118).

Directors' interests as at 31st May 2011 were unchanged from those listed above, other than that the trustees of the Johnson Matthey Share Incentive Plan have purchased on behalf of Messrs Carson, MacLeod, Pentz and Sandford a further 39 shares each.

2. Share Options

As at 31st March 2011, individual holdings by the directors under the company's executive share option schemes were as set out below. Options are not granted to non-executive directors.

	Date of grant	Ordinary shares under option	Exercise price (pence)	Date from which exercisable	Expiry date	Total number of ordinary shares under option
N A P Carson	18.7.01	19,391	1,083.00	18.7.04	18.7.11	
	17.7.02	28,901	865.00	17.7.05	17.7.12	
	17.7.03	33,407	898.00	17.7.06	17.7.13	
	20.7.05	77,102	1,070.00	20.7.08	20.7.15	
	26.7.06	59,481	1,282.00	26.7.09	26.7.16	218,282
						(2010 218,282)
L C Pentz	17.7.02	17,730	865.00	17.7.05	17.7.12	
	17.7.03	17,185	898.00	17.7.06	17.7.13	
	20.7.05	37,850	1,070.00	20.7.08	20.7.15	
	26.7.06	28,765	1,282.00	26.7.09	26.7.16	101,530
						(2010 114,482)
W F Sandford	26.7.06	18,868	1,282.00	26.7.09	26.7.16	18,868
						(2010 18,868)

Between 1st April 2010 and 31st March 2011 the following options were exercised by directors:

	Date of grant	Date of exercise	Options exercised	Exercise price (pence)	Market price on exercise (pence)
L C Pentz	18.7.01	16.9.10	12,952	1,083.00	1,763.50

Gains made on exercise of options by the directors during the year totalled £88,138 (2010 £2,106,852).

The closing market price of the company's shares at 31st March 2011 was 1,860 pence. The highest and lowest closing market prices during the year ended 31st March 2011 were 2,100 pence and 1,460 pence respectively.

Remuneration Report

Directors' Interests (continued)

3. LTIP Allocations

Number of allocated shares:

	As at 31st March 2010	Allocations during the year	Market price at date of allocation (pence)	Lapsed during the year [1]	As at 31st March 2011
N A P Carson	184,554	72,393	1,554.00	56,704	200,243
R J MacLeod	55,072	31,397	1,554.00	–	86,469
L C Pentz	75,296	30,115	1,554.00	22,327	83,084
W F Sandford	56,161	26,640	1,554.00	15,268	67,533

[1] On 25th July 2010 shares allocated under the LTIP on 25th July 2007 lapsed as the relevant performance target was not met.

Pensions

Pensions and life assurance benefits for the executive directors are provided through the company's single occupational pension scheme for UK employees – the Johnson Matthey Employees Pension Scheme (JMEPS) – which is constituted under a separate Trust Deed. JMEPS is an exempt approved scheme under Chapter I of Part XIV of the Income & Corporation Taxes Act 1988. It is a registered scheme for the purposes of the Finance Act 2004.

Pensions that accrued in respect of service up to 31st March 2010 are based on a member's final salary at the point of retirement, or earlier date of withdrawal from employment. Pensions that accrue in respect of service from 1st April 2010 are based on career average salaries. Members are not required to pay contributions for these defined benefits. Members may pay contributions to a defined contribution account and the company will match the first 3% of pensionable pay each year.

Under the provisions of the Finance Act 2004 benefits from a registered pension scheme that exceed a Life Time Allowance, currently £1.8 million, will be subject to an additional tax charge of 25%. Any such tax charge arising out of membership of JMEPS will be paid by the Trustees at the point of retirement and the member's benefits will be reduced accordingly. Employees, including executive directors, whose retirement benefits are valued in excess of the Life Time Allowance may withdraw from pensionable service and receive instead a supplemental payment of 25% of basic salary each year.

Messrs Carson and Sandford withdrew from pensionable service and ceased paying member contributions on 31st March 2006. No pensionable service in JMEPS has been accrued by these directors since those dates. The increase in accrued pension in the tables below is attributable solely to the increase in basic salary in 2010/11. The supplemental payments received by Messrs Carson and Sandford are reflected in the table on page 71.

The Finance Act 2009 restricted tax relief to the basic rate of income tax on any contributions paid by "high earners" that exceed a Special Annual Allowance. Tax relief at the top rate of income tax is achieved at source, but the difference is repaid to HM Revenue & Customs through self assessment. This is the personal responsibility of individuals. These regulations were replaced by a reduced Annual Allowance for tax relief on pension savings with effect from 6th April 2011.

Disclosure of directors' pension benefits has been made under the requirements of the Financial Services Authority's Listing Rules and in accordance with the Companies Act 2006. The information below sets out the disclosures under the two sets of requirements.

a. Financial Services Authority's Listing Rules

	Age as at 31st March 2011	Years of JMEPS pensionable service at 31st March 2011	Directors' contributions to JMEPS during the year[1,2] £'000	Increase in accrued pension during the year (net of inflation)[3] £'000 pa	Total accrued pension as at 31st March 2011[4] £'000 pa	Total accrued pension as at 31st March 2010 £'000 pa	Transfer value of increase in accrued pension[5] £'000
N A P Carson [4]	53	25	–	8	353	329	152
R MacLeod [2]	46	2	–	5	9	4	46
L C Pentz [6]	55	26	–	7	90	83	139
W F Sandford [4]	57	28	–	16	179	155	342

b. Companies Act 2006

	Directors' contributions to JMEPS in the year[1,2] £'000	Increase in accrued pension in the year £'000 pa	Total accrued pension as at 31st March 2011[4] £'000 pa	Transfer value of accrued pension as at 31st March 2011[5] £'000	Transfer value of accrued pension as at 31st March 2010[5] £'000	Increase in transfer value £'000
N A P Carson [4]	–	24	353	6,402	4,952	1,450
R MacLeod [2]	–	5	9	81	27	54
L C Pentz [6]	–	7	90	1,371	1,052	319
W F Sandford [4]	–	24	179	3,779	2,734	1,045

Remuneration Report

Pensions (continued)

Notes

(1) No members are required to pay contributions for the career average salary defined benefits.

(2) Messrs Macleod and Pentz paid contributions on a voluntary basis into the defined contribution account at the rate of 3% of basic salary. The company paid a matching contribution for each.

(3) The disclosure regulations require the pension accrued to the end of the previous year to be adjusted for inflation. Inflation was 4.6% for the year to 30th September 2010 as prescribed in the Revaluation Order issued under the Pensions Act 1993.

(4) The entitlement shown under "Total accrued pension at 31st March 2011" is the pension which would be paid annually on retirement, based on pensionable service to 31st March 2011 (except in the case of Messrs Carson and Sandford whose pensionable service ceased on 31st March 2006). The final salary related pension accrued to 31st March 2010 would be subject to an actuarial reduction for each month that retirement precedes age 60. All pensions accrued in respect of service from 1st April 2010 will be reduced if taken before age 65.

(5) The transfer values have been calculated on the basis of actuarial advice in accordance with the transfer value regulations. No allowance has been made in the transfer values for any discretionary benefits that have been or may be awarded under JMEPS. The transfer value disclosed under the Financial Services Authority's Listing Rules is the value of the increase in the accrued pension as at 31st March 2011 (net of inflation). The transfer values disclosed under the Companies Act 2006 have been calculated at the start and the end of the year and, therefore, also take account of market movements.

(6) Mr Pentz is a US citizen but became a member of JMEPS on 1st January 2006. Prior to that he was a member of the Johnson Matthey Inc. Salaried Employees Pension Plan (a non-contributory defined benefit arrangement) and also of a US savings plan (401k). He also has benefits in a Senior Executive Retirement Plan. The pension values reported above are the aggregate for his separate membership of the UK and US pension schemes and the Senior Executive Retirement Plan. US entitlements have been converted to sterling by reference to exchange rates on 31st March 2010 and 31st March 2011. Mr Pentz's US pension was fixed on 31st December 2005. The sterling equivalent of it has fluctuated over the year as a result of exchange rate movements. This is reflected in the transfer values.

The Remuneration Report was approved by the Board of Directors on 1st June 2011 and signed on its behalf by:

Robert Walvis
Chairman of the Management Development and Remuneration Committee

Responsibility of Directors

Statement of Directors' Responsibilities in Respect of the Annual Report and Accounts

The directors are responsible for preparing the annual report and the group and parent company accounts in accordance with applicable law and regulations.

Company law requires the directors to prepare group and parent company accounts for each financial year. Under that law they are required to prepare the group accounts in accordance with International Financial Reporting Standards (IFRS) as adopted by the European Union (EU) and applicable law and have elected to prepare the parent company accounts on the same basis.

Under company law the directors must not approve the accounts unless they are satisfied that they give a true and fair view of the state of affairs of the group and parent company and of their profit or loss for that period. In preparing each of the group and parent company accounts, the directors are required to:

- select suitable accounting policies and then apply them consistently;
- make judgments and estimates that are reasonable and prudent;
- state whether they have been prepared in accordance with IFRS as adopted by the EU; and
- prepare the accounts on the going concern basis unless it is inappropriate to presume that the group and the parent company will continue in business.

The directors are responsible for keeping adequate accounting records that are sufficient to show and explain the parent company's transactions and disclose with reasonable accuracy at any time the financial position of the parent company and enable them to ensure that its accounts comply with the Companies Act 2006. They have general responsibility for taking such steps as are reasonably open to them to safeguard the assets of the group and to prevent and detect fraud and other irregularities.

Under applicable law and regulations the directors are also responsible for preparing a directors' report, directors' Remuneration Report and Corporate Governance statement that comply with that law and those regulations.

The directors are responsible for the maintenance and integrity of the corporate and financial information included on the company's website. Legislation in the UK governing the preparation and dissemination of accounts may differ from legislation in other jurisdictions.

Responsibility Statement of the Directors in Respect of the Annual Report and Accounts

Each of the directors as at the date of the Annual Report and Accounts, whose names and functions are set out on pages 56 and 57, states that to the best of his or her knowledge:

- the group and parent company accounts, prepared in accordance with the applicable set of accounting standards, give a true and fair view of the assets, liabilities, financial position and profit or loss of the company and the undertakings included in the consolidation taken as a whole; and
- the management report (which comprises the Report of the Directors) includes a fair review of the development and performance of the business and the position of the company and the undertakings included in the consolidation taken as a whole, together with a description of the principal risks and uncertainties that they face.

This responsibility statement was approved by the Board of Directors on 1st June 2011 and is signed on its behalf by:

Sir John Banham
Chairman

ACCOUNTS

Independent Auditor's Report

to the members of Johnson Matthey Public Limited Company

We have audited the group and parent company accounts of Johnson Matthey Plc for the year ended 31st March 2011 which comprise the Consolidated Income Statement, the Consolidated Statement of Total Comprehensive Income, the Consolidated and Parent Company Balance Sheets, the Consolidated and Parent Company Cash Flow Statements, the Consolidated Statement of Changes in Equity, the Parent Company Statement of Changes in Equity and the related notes. The financial reporting framework that has been applied in their preparation is applicable law and International Financial Reporting Standards (IFRS) as adopted by the EU and, as regards the parent company accounts, as applied in accordance with the provisions of the Companies Act 2006.

This report is made solely to the company's members, as a body, in accordance with Chapter 3 of Part 16 of the Companies Act 2006. Our audit work has been undertaken so that we might state to the company's members those matters we are required to state to them in an auditor's report and for no other purpose. To the fullest extent permitted by law, we do not accept or assume responsibility to anyone other than the company and the company's members, as a body, for our audit work, for this report, or for the opinions we have formed.

Respective Responsibilities of Directors and Auditor

As explained more fully in the directors' responsibilities statement set out on page 75, the directors are responsible for the preparation of the accounts and for being satisfied that they give a true and fair view. Our responsibility is to audit, and express an opinion on, the accounts in accordance with applicable law and International Standards on Auditing (UK and Ireland). Those standards require us to comply with the Auditing Practices Board's (APB's) Ethical Standards for Auditors.

Scope of the Audit of the Accounts

A description of the scope of an audit of accounts is provided on the APB's website at www.frc.org.uk/apb/scope/private.cfm.

Opinion on Accounts

In our opinion:

- the accounts give a true and fair view of the state of the group's and of the parent company's affairs as at 31st March 2011 and of the group's profit for the year then ended;

- the group accounts have been properly prepared in accordance with IFRS as adopted by the EU;

- the parent company accounts have been properly prepared in accordance with IFRS as adopted by the EU and as applied in accordance with the provisions of the Companies Act 2006; and

- the accounts have been prepared in accordance with the requirements of the Companies Act 2006 and, as regards the group accounts, Article 4 of the IAS Regulation.

Opinion on Other Matters Prescribed by the Companies Act 2006

In our opinion:

- the part of the directors' Remuneration Report to be audited has been properly prepared in accordance with the Companies Act 2006; and

- the information given in the directors' report for the financial year for which the accounts are prepared is consistent with the accounts.

Matters on Which we are Required to Report by Exception

We have nothing to report in respect of the following:

Under the Companies Act 2006 we are required to report to you if, in our opinion:

- adequate accounting records have not been kept by the parent company, or returns adequate for our audit have not been received from branches not visited by us; or

- the parent company accounts and the part of the directors' Remuneration Report to be audited are not in agreement with the accounting records and returns; or

- certain disclosures of directors' remuneration specified by law are not made; or

- we have not received all the information and explanations we require for our audit.

Under the Listing Rules we are required to review:

- the directors' statement, set out on page 37, in relation to going concern; and

- the part of the Corporate Governance statement on page 58 relating to the company's compliance with the nine provisions of the June 2008 Combined Code specified for our review; and

- certain elements of the report to shareholders by the board on directors' remuneration.

D V Matthews (Senior Statutory Auditor)
for and on behalf of KPMG Audit Plc, Statutory Auditor
Chartered Accountants
15 Canada Square, London E14 5GL

1st June 2011

Learning objectives

Completion of this chapter will enable you to:

- describe the agency problem and how the framework for establishing good corporate governance and accountability has been established in the UK Corporate Governance Code, developed from the work of the Cadbury, Greenbury, Hampel and Turnbull Committees

- explain the statutory requirement for the audit of limited companies, the election by shareholders of suitably qualified, independent auditors, and the role of the auditors

- outline directors' specific responsibility to shareholders, and responsibilities to society in general, for the management and conduct of companies

- recognise the fiduciary duties that directors have to the company, and their duty of care to all stakeholders and to the community at large, particularly with regard to the Companies Act 2006, Health and Safety at Work Act 1974, Health and Safety (Offences) Act 2008, and Financial Services Act 1986

- explain the implications for companies and their directors that may arise from the UK Government's newly-enacted legislation on the issue of corporate manslaughter

- appreciate the importance of directors' duties regarding insolvency, the Insolvency Act 1986 and the Enterprise Act 2002

- consider the implications for directors of wrongful trading, and recognise the difference between this and the offence of fraudulent trading, and the possibility of criminal penalties

- outline the implication for directors of the Company Directors Disqualification Act 1986

- explain the actions that directors of companies should take to ensure compliance with their obligations and responsibilities, and to protect themselves against possible non-compliance.

Introduction

In Chapter 6 we will see that a large part of Johnson Matthey Plc's report and accounts 2011 is devoted to the subject of corporate governance, the systems by which companies are directed and controlled. Before the start of this chapter you will have already seen pages 58 to 75, and page 125 of Johnson Matthey's report and accounts 2011 reproduced on pages 194 to 212. This chapter will refer to these extracts when it turns to the statutory and non-statutory rules that surround the accounting for limited companies.

In earlier chapters we discussed the way in which the limited company exists in perpetuity as a legal entity, separate from the lives of those individuals who both own and manage it. The limited company has many rights, responsibilities and liabilities in the same way as individual people. As a separate legal entity the company is responsible for its own liabilities. These liabilities are not the obligations of the shareholders who have paid for their shares, this being the limit of their obligations to the company.

The directors of a limited company are appointed by, and are responsible to, the shareholders for the management of the company, maintained through their regular reporting on the activities of the business. The responsibilities of directors, however, are wider than to just the shareholders. They are also responsible for acting correctly towards their employees, suppliers and customers, and to the public at large. Indeed these responsibilities are considered so vital that the Companies Act 2006 introduces the legal requirement that 'a director of a company must exercise reasonable care, skill and diligence'.

> The annual audit of the accounts is a statutory requirement for all limited companies, excluding smaller limited companies. As with directors, the auditors of a limited company are also appointed by, and are responsible to, the shareholders. Their primary responsibility is to make an objective report to shareholders and others as to whether, in their opinion, the financial statements show a true and fair view, and compliance with statutory, regulatory and accounting standard requirements. Therefore, the management and regulation of a company as a separate legal entity lies with the directors and the auditors. The directors are within, and part of, the company, and the auditors are external to, and not part of, the company.
>
> This chapter will look at roles and responsibilities of directors and auditors. It will also consider the obligations of directors, who are the agents of the shareholders (who are the principals). We will consider this agent–principal relationship and where it breaks down – the agency problem – and particularly with regard to the UK Corporate Governance Code, and the many Acts that are now in place to regulate the behaviour of directors of limited companies. The chapter closes with a look at some of the steps that directors may take to protect themselves against possible non-compliance.

The agency problem

Shareholder wealth maximisation is the primary objective of a business, reflected in increases in share prices and dividends. But can we assume that the managers and **directors** of the business are making decisions and taking actions that are consistent with the objective of maximising shareholder wealth? Certainly managers and directors should make decisions consistent with the objective of shareholder wealth maximisation, because that is what they are appointed to do by the shareholders. In practice, this may not actually happen, because their goals may be different and they may be seeking to enhance their status, secure their positions, or maximise their own wealth rather than that of the shareholders.

The agency problem occurs when directors and managers are not acting in the best interests of shareholders. Directors and managers of a company run the business day to day and have access to internal management accounting information and financial reports, but shareholders only see the external annual and six-monthly reports. Annual and interim reporting may also, of course, be subject to manipulation by management.

The agency problem of directors not acting in the best interests of shareholders may be seen in, for example:

- a high retention of profits and cash by directors to provide a cushion for easier day-to-day management of operations, rather than for investment in new projects
- an unwillingness by directors to invest in risky projects in line with shareholders' required returns, because of fear of failure and possibly losing their jobs, particularly if they are close to retirement age and wish to protect their pension benefits
- receipt of high salaries, benefits and perks by directors and chief executives, regardless of how well, or not, the business has performed
- participation by directors and managers in profit or eps-related bonus and incentive schemes, which encourage short-term profit maximisation rather than creation of shareholder wealth.

Why should the agency problem exist? Well, it is management who are in the position, and who have the opportunity, to pursue the maximisation of their own wealth without detection by the owners of the business. Additionally, both financial analysts and managers and directors of companies have an obsession with profit as the measure of financial performance. This is despite the fact that profit is a totally subjective measure and that it is future cash flows and not short-term profit from which the real value of a business is determined.

A growth in profit does not necessarily translate into a sustained increase in shareholder wealth. For example, diversified multinational companies, conglomerates, have in the past acquired many businesses to effectively 'buy' additional profits. This has invariably not resulted in an increase in the share prices of such conglomerates.

The agency problem manifests itself through a conflict of interest. There may be different views about risks and returns, for example. The shareholders may be interested in the long term, whereas the rewards paid to managers, for example, may be based on short-term performance. To address the agency problem between agents and principals – managers and shareholders – a number of initiatives may be implemented to encourage the achievement of goal congruence:

- audit of results
- reporting of manager performance
- work shadowing of managers and directors
- the use of external analysts.

Worked example 6.1

Directors of companies are concerned with the important issues of agency-related problems and their impact. What is the basis of discussions they may have to consider what actions they may implement to try and minimise the impact of such problems?

Their discussions may include the following:

- The agency problem emerges when directors or managers make decisions that are inconsistent with the objective of shareholder wealth maximisation.
- There are a number of alternative approaches a company can adopt to minimise the possible impact of such a problem, which may differ from company to company. In general, such approaches would range between:
  - the encouragement of goal congruence between shareholders and managers through the monitoring of managerial behaviour and the assessment of management decision outcomes and
  - the enforcement of goal congruence between shareholders and managers through the incorporation of formalised obligations and conditions of employment into management contracts.

Any such approach would invariably be associated with some form of remuneration package to include an incentive scheme to reward managers, such as performance-related pay, or executive share options.

Progress check 6.1

What are the conflicts that may arise between the directors and the shareholders of a business?

In addition to the agency problem relating to the directors and shareholders of a company, there may be a conflict between shareholders, and the lenders to a company, who may try to exploit their relationship with lenders. The agency problem here is that shareholders may prefer the use of debt for investments by the company in new high-risk projects. Shareholders then subsequently benefit from the rewards gained from the success of such investments, but it is the debt holders (lenders) who bear the risk. Debt holders may protect their interests by having security over specific assets or the assets in general of the company. They may also include restrictive covenants in their loan agreements with the company, for example with regard to decision-making, and levels of debt taken on by the company.

Progress check 6.2

Outline how the agency problem may occur between the shareholders, directors and lenders of a business.

There has been an increasing influence of institutional investors in the UK, which to some degree has helped in dealing with the agency problem. Institutional shareholders like banks, pension funds and fund management companies have been getting tougher with companies who do not comply with the appropriate standards of behaviour, and in particular with the appropriate **corporate governance** requirements.

Corporate governance is concerned with the relationship between company management, its directors, and its owners, the shareholders. It is the structure and the mechanisms by which the owners of the business 'govern' the management or the directors of the business. Its importance has been highlighted as a result of the increasing concern about the conduct of companies, following the spate of financial scandals, but also by concerns about senior executive remuneration.

Corporate governance code of practice

Concerns about financial reporting and accountability, and the impact on the business community (see Figure 6.1), grew during the 1980s following increasing numbers of company failures and financial scandals.

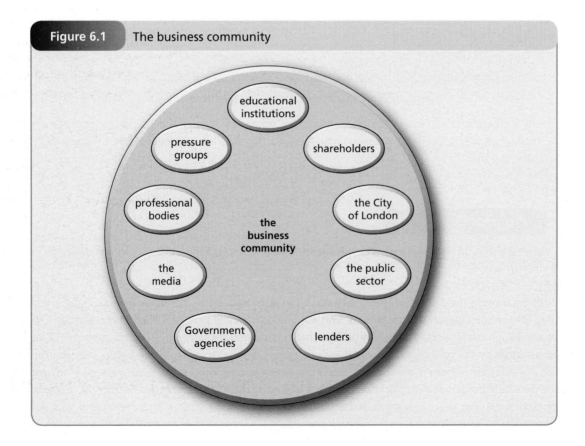

Figure 6.1   The business community

During the 1980s and 1990s there was huge concern within the business community following the financial scandals surrounding for example Polly Peck (1990), the Robert Maxwell companies (1991), BCCI (1991), and Barings Bank – Nick Leeson (1995).

The concerns increased as we saw in the 2000s even larger scandals involving companies such as Enron (2001), Marconi (2001), WorldCom (2002) and Parmalat (2004) and particularly the involvement of the consulting arms of major accounting firms like Arthur Andersen. These concerns resulted in a growing lack of confidence in financial reporting, and in shareholders and others being unable to rely on auditors to provide the necessary safeguards for their reliance on company annual reports.

The main factors underlying the lack of confidence in financial reporting were:

- loose accounting standards, which allowed considerable latitude (an example has been the treatment of extraordinary items and exceptional items in financial reporting)
- lack of a clear framework to ensure directors were able to continuously review business controls
- competitive pressure within companies and on auditors, making it difficult for auditors to maintain independence from demanding boards
- lack of apparent accountability regarding directors' remuneration and compensation for loss of office.

The Cadbury Committee, chaired by Sir Adrian Cadbury, was set up in May 1991 by the Financial Reporting Council, the London Stock Exchange, and the accounting profession, to address these concerns and make recommendations on good practice.

The Cadbury Committee defined corporate governance (see Figure 6.2) as

the system by which companies are directed and controlled. Boards of directors are responsible for the governance of their companies. The shareholders' role in governance is to appoint the directors and the auditors and to satisfy themselves that an appropriate governance structure is in place. The responsibilities of the board include setting the company's strategic aims, providing the leadership to put them into effect, supervising the management of the business and reporting to shareholders on their stewardship. The board's actions are subject to laws, regulations and the shareholders in general meeting.

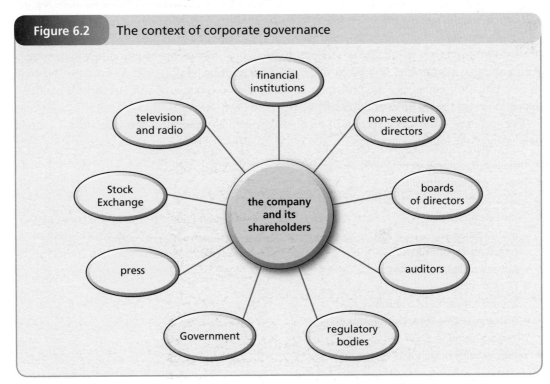

Figure 6.2   The context of corporate governance

The financial aspects within the framework described by Cadbury are the ways in which the company's board sets financial policy and oversees its implementation, the use of financial controls, and how the board reports on activities and progress of the company to shareholders.

The framework for establishing good corporate governance and accountability set up by the Cadbury Committee was formulated as the Committee's Code of Best Practice, published in December 1992. This provided a benchmark against which to assess compliance. The Cadbury Code was updated in 1998 by the **Hampel Committee**, to include their own Committee's work, and the Greenbury Committee report on directors' remuneration (published July 1995). In September 1999 the Turnbull Committee report on *Internal Control: Guidance for Directors on the Combined Code* was published by the ICAEW.

In May 2000 the original Cadbury Code and subsequent reports were all consolidated by the Committee on Corporate Governance and published in the **Combined Code of Practice**.

The underlying principles of the Code are:

- openness
- integrity
- accountability.

Openness

Openness from companies is constrained within the limits of their competitive position but is the basis for the confidence that needs to exist between business and all those who have a stake in its success. Openness in disclosure of information adds to the effectiveness of the market economy. It forces boards to take action and allows shareholders and others to be able to look more closely and thoroughly into companies.

Integrity

Integrity means straightforward dealing and completeness. Financial reporting should be honest and present a balanced view of the state of the company's affairs. The integrity of the company's reports will depend on the integrity of the people responsible for preparing and presenting them.

The annual reports and financial statements of the majority of UK plcs now include a section headed *Corporate Governance*. These sections of the annual reports are required to aim to comply with provisions set out in a Combined Code of Practice (principles of good governance and code of best practice), embracing the principles of the Cadbury, Greenbury and Hampel Committees, appended to the Listing Rules of the London Stock Exchange.

The corporate governance section of a company's annual report and accounts should contain details under the following headings:

- directors' biographies
- board responsibilities
- board composition and functions
- board committees
  - audit committee
  - nomination committee
  - remuneration committee
  - IT committee
  - capital expenditure committee
  - **non-executive directors'** committee
- directors' remuneration
- relations with shareholders

- internal financial control
- incentive compensation
- directors' pensions
- corporate strategy.

This may not be a complete list but it gives a broad indication of the areas of compliance under the Combined Code of Practice. This compliance can be seen as set out in the annual reports and accounts of UK plcs.

Accountability

Accountability of boards of directors to their shareholders requires the commitment from both to make the accountability effective. Boards of directors must play their part by ensuring the quality of information that is provided to shareholders. Shareholders must exercise their responsibilities as owners of the business. The major investing institutions (for example, pension funds and insurance companies) are in regular contact with the directors of UK plcs to discuss past, current and future performance.

Subsequent to 1998, further reviews of various aspects of corporate governance were set up:

- *Review of the role and effectiveness of non-executive directors*, by Derek Higgs and published January 2003
- *Audit Committees Combined Code guidance*, by a group led by Sir Robert Smith and published January 2003.

The above reviews were undertaken during a period in which investor confidence had been badly shaken both by lapses in corporate governance and by the high-profile failure of some corporate strategies, and were very much in response to these events. The reviews were reflected in a revision to the 2000 Combined Code of Practice, which was published by the Financial Reporting Council (FRC) in July 2003 – the Combined Code on Corporate Governance.

The Combined Code on Corporate Governance was revised by the FRC several times up to June 2008. Following an extensive consultation process, in June 2010 the FRC issued a new code of corporate governance entitled the **UK Corporate Governance Code**. This Code was to be effective for the financial years beginning after 29 June 2010.

The consultation was initiated by the world-wide financial crisis. The FRC, whilst it acknowledges the quality of the Combined Code, highlights an increasing problem within organisations in that 'it seems that there is almost a belief that complying with the Code in itself constitutes good governance'. The FRC, therefore, insists that to 'follow the spirit of the Code to good effect, boards must think deeply, thoroughly and on a continuing basis, about their overall tasks and the implications of these for the roles of their individual members'. The new Code then follows a 'comply or explain' approach to corporate governance that was introduced by the Cadbury Committee, and concentrates on developing sound mechanisms which the FRC believes to be central to effectively following the five key principles of corporate governance. These five key principles, which all listed companies must report to shareholders on how they have applied them, are: leadership; effectiveness; accountability; remuneration; relations with shareholders.

Companies listed on the London Stock Exchange are requested to comply with the Code, but other companies may also benefit from compliance. It is not compulsory for any company, but rather a target of best practice to aim for. The Combined Code on Corporate Governance also promoted the 'comply or explain' approach. This meant that companies listed on the London Stock Exchange were required to include in their annual report and accounts a statement to confirm that they had complied with the relevant provisions throughout the accounting period, or to provide an explanation if that were not the case.

Progress check 6.3

What is corporate governance and how is it implemented?

Let's take a look at the Johnson Matthey section on corporate governance, included in pages 58 to 75 of their report and accounts 2011, and reproduced on pages 194 to 211 of this book. This section includes the corporate governance report itself, and the audit committee report, remuneration committee report, remuneration of the directors, and the responsibility of the directors' report. This section also includes other statutory information (pages 62 to 65), which covers details about the annual general meeting, dividends, shareholders and share capital, directors, employees, commercial debt, donations, and auditors. Johnson Matthey's corporate governance report states that 'During the year ended 31st March 2011, the company has complied with all relevant provisions set out in Section 1 of the Code (the Combined Code on Corporate Governance) throughout the year except in respect of provision D.1.1.' Provision D.1.1 relates to the attendance by a senior independent director at sufficient meetings with a range of major shareholders to listen to their views and concerns. Johnson Matthey's report also says that the company will be reporting on compliance with the new UK Corporate Governance Code in its next year's annual report.

A number of the headings required as part of corporate governance reporting are not included within Johnson Matthey Plc's main corporate governance report, but are shown elsewhere in the report and accounts. For example, the composition and functions of the board, and directors' biographies are shown on pages 56 to 57 of the report and accounts 2011, and are not reproduced in this book.

Worked example 6.2

What are the basic problems that may be encountered by shareholders with small shareholdings as they enter a new relationship with the company they effectively part-own?

Most of the major UK plcs are owned by both individual and institutional shareholders. Some shareholders have large shareholdings, and some have small shareholdings, the analysis of which can be found in their companies' annual reports and accounts.

Usually within a very short time of acquiring their shares, most new small shareholders realise they have neither influence nor power.

As plcs have increasingly engaged in wider ranges of activities and become global businesses, so their directors have become more and more distanced from their shareholders. Compare the large multinational banks, for example, with locally based building societies.

During the move towards growth and expansion by companies, particularly throughout the 1980s, considerable disquiet regarding accountability emerged in the business community. In response to this the UK Government appointed the Committee on the Financial Aspects of Corporate Governance (Cadbury Committee), which produced its report in December 1992.

At the same time, there was also a great deal of unease regarding remuneration, bonus schemes, option schemes and contracts. Various other committees on corporate governance, subsequent to Cadbury, such as the Greenbury, Hampel and Turnbull committees, have reviewed each of these areas.

Non-executive directors are represented on all Johnson Matthey's main committees, except the chief executive's committee. The company does not appear to have an information technology (IT) committee or a capital expenditure committee, and so IT and capital expenditure are presumably the responsibility of the chief executive's committee.

The importance of **corporate social responsibility (CSR)** is emphasised in the business review section of the report and accounts 2011 headed sustainability on pages 44 to 55, which are not reproduced in this book.

Together with the section covering corporate governance, the reports of Johnson Matthey Plc's nomination committee, audit committee, remuneration committee, and the sustainability report are included in this book for reference.

The audit and the role of auditors

As we have noted earlier, an annual audit of the accounts is a statutory requirement for most limited companies. However, for accounting periods starting on or after 6 April 2008, companies satisfying at least two of the following three limits qualify for the small company annual audit requirement exemption: an annual sales revenue of less than £6.5 million; a balance sheet total of less than £3.26 million; number of employees less than 50 (refer to the Department for Business Innovation and Skills website *www.bis.gov.uk* for changes to these limits). The shareholders of a limited company are responsible for appointing suitably qualified, independent persons, either individually or as a firm, to act as auditors. The external auditors are not part of the company but are responsible to the shareholders, with a main duty of objectively reporting to shareholders and others as to whether, in their opinion, the financial statements show a true and fair view, and comply with statutory, regulatory and accounting standard requirements. Such an opinion is referred to as an unqualified opinion.

The report of the auditors is usually very short and additionally includes:

■ reference to the directors' responsibility for preparation of the annual report and accounts
■ reference to the responsibility as auditors being established by
  – UK statute
  – the **Auditing Practices Board (APB)**
  – the Listing Rules of the Financial Services Authority
  – the accountancy profession's ethical guidance.

The auditors are required to explain the basis of the audit, and report if in their opinion:

■ the directors' report is not consistent with the accounts
■ the company has not kept proper accounting records
■ they have not received all the information and explanations required for the audit
■ information specified by law, or the Listing Rules regarding directors' remuneration and transactions with the company, is not disclosed
■ company policies are appropriate and consistently applied and adequately disclosed
■ all information and explanations considered necessary provide sufficient evidence to give reasonable assurance that the accounts are free from material misstatement
■ the overall presentation of information in the accounts is adequate.

There may very occasionally be circumstances when the financial statements may be affected by an inherent and fundamental uncertainty. In such cases the auditors are obliged to draw attention to the fundamental uncertainty. If the fundamental uncertainty is adequately accounted for and disclosed in the financial statements then the opinion of the auditors may remain unqualified. If there is inadequate disclosure about the fundamental uncertainty then the auditors must give what is termed

➠ a qualified opinion. A qualified **audit report** is something that may destroy company credibility and create uncertainty, and is obviously something to be avoided.

In addition to their reporting on the financial statements of the company, the auditors' reports now include a statement of the company's corporate governance compliance with the provisions of the UK Corporate Governance Code (prior to 29 June 2010 the Combined Code on Corporate Governance). This review is in accordance with guidelines issued by the Auditing Practices Board. The auditors are not required to:

- consider whether the statements by the directors on internal control cover all risks and controls
- form an opinion on the effectiveness of the company's corporate governance procedures or its risk management and internal control procedures
- form an opinion on the ability of the company to continue in operational existence.

The audit and the perceived role of auditors has been the subject of much criticism over the years. The responsibility of the auditors does not include guarantees that:

- the financial statements are correct
- the company will not fail
- there has been no fraud.

This gap, 'the expectations gap', between public expectation and what the audit actually provides is understandable in the light of the numerous examples of company failures and financial scandals from the 1980s to date. These have led to a lack of confidence of the business community in financial reporting, and in shareholders being unable to rely on safeguards they assumed would be provided by their auditors.

The problem is that 'correctness' of financial statements is an unachievable result. We have seen from our consideration of both the balance sheet and income statement the inconsistency in asset valuation and the level of subjective judgement required in their preparation. Directors are required to prepare, and auditors give an opinion on, accounts that give a true and fair view rather than accounts that are deemed 'correct'.

Companies increasingly face a greater diversity and level of risk:

- financial risk
- commercial risk
- operational risk

and the increasing possibility of corporate failure is very real. Although the financial statements of companies are based on the going concern concept, the directors and auditors cannot realistically give any assurance that those businesses will not fail.

An area of risk that is of increasing concern to companies is fraud. This is perhaps due to the:

- increasing pace of change
- widespread use of computer systems
- ease and speed of communications and transfer of funds
- use of the Internet
- increase in staff mobility
- increasing dependence on specific knowledge (for example, Nick Leeson and Barings, and dot.com companies' IT experts).

Fraud is perhaps something on which auditors may arguably be expected to give an opinion. This is not something that is currently required from an external audit. It is something for which ➠ an **internal audit** department may be responsible. In the same way, external auditors could be requested to report on the adequacy or otherwise of systems of internal control.

Most major corporate fraud is now associated with communications and information technology systems. The use of internal (or external) audit for the:

■ detection of fraud
■ minimisation of fraud
■ elimination of fraud

therefore tends to be specialised and is something for which the costs and benefits must be carefully evaluated.

Progress check 6.4

What is the audit and to whom are the auditors responsible, and for what?

The report of the independent auditors to the shareholders of Johnson Matthey Plc, included in the report and accounts 2011 on page 125, is reproduced on page 212 of this book. It can be seen to have complied with the standard audit reporting requirements outlined above. It may be interesting to compare the auditors' report for say 1990 with the same report for the year 2011, in which so many more areas are covered, and to appreciate the importance of corporate governance.

Worked example 6.3

The audit is the objective review (or sometimes the detailed examination) of business systems of internal control, risk management and corporate governance and the company's financial transactions. A business may employ internal and external auditors. The latter are considered the more independent, although both are paid by the business. External auditors are appointed by, and report to, the shareholders, whereas the internal auditors report to the company's audit committee.

(i) Why should the external auditors of a plc report direct to the shareholders and not to the chairman of the company?

(ii) Why should the internal auditors of a plc report to the audit committee and not to the finance director?

(iii) In what ways may the independence of a company's audit committee be demonstrated?

The answers to these questions are:

(i) The external auditors are appointed by and are responsible to the shareholders. The annual general meeting (AGM) is the formal meeting of directors, shareholders and auditors. Conceivably, the chairman could shelve the report, with shareholders unaware of the contents. The law is quite strict on auditors' right to communicate directly with shareholders.

(ii) The finance director is responsible for the system of recording transactions. The finance director could prevent vital information from the internal auditors being distributed to others in the organisation.

(iii) The audit committee may request the non-executive directors to review specific areas, for example, the output from the internal auditors. The audit committee meets many times during the year and it offers a degree of objectivity. The careers of its members do not depend on the continuance of their directorship.

The directors of a company may not be accountants and they very rarely have any hands-on involvement with the actual putting-together of a set of accounts for the company. However, directors of companies must make it their business to be fully conversant with the content of the accounts of their companies. Directors are responsible for ensuring that proper accounting records are maintained, and for ensuring reasonably accurate reporting of the financial position of their company, and ensuring their compliance with the Companies Act 2006. Immediately following the remuneration committee report, Johnson Matthey Plc's report and accounts 2011 includes on page 75 a section headed responsibility of directors (reproduced on page 211 of this book), which details the responsibilities of its directors in the preparation of its accounts.

We will now consider the role of directors and their responsibilities in more detail, and with regard to the UK Corporate Governance Code. We will also look at some of the circumstances in which directors of limited companies are particularly vulnerable, and how these may lead to disqualification of directors.

The fact that a corporate governance code of practice exists or even that the appropriate corporate governance committees have been established is not necessarily a guarantee of effective corporate governance. There have been many examples of companies that have had corporate governance committees in place relating to directors and their remuneration, relations with shareholders, accountability and audit. Nevertheless, these companies have given cause for great concern from shareholders following much-publicised revelations about financial scandals and apparent loosely-adhered-to corporate governance practices.

Such examples have by no means been confined to the UK. Vivendi Universal, a French music and media company which grew out of a privatised water company in the mid 1990s, almost became bankrupt in the early 2000s. Under its then chairman Jean-Marie Messier it entered a period of massive expansion. However, the expansion was driven by numerous acquisitions funded by vast amounts of debt which started to become unsustainable when profits failed to match expectations. Although Vivendi had become the world's second biggest media company after AOL Time Warner, a 13.6bn euro loss for 2001 threatened to reveal the perilous financial position of the company. It was during that time that Messier, and others, were accused of share price manipulation, misleading the stock market about Vivendi's finances and misappropriation of company funds. Vivendi survived the mismanagement and buoyed by their strong games division in 2010 reported revenues up 4.2% to 8.9bn euro and an earnings increase of 4.5% to 5.7bn euro.

Another non-UK example is illustrated in the press extract on page 226. Bernie Madoff, founder and principal of Bernard L Madoff Investment Securities, had traded on Wall Street for 40 years, where he was described as a 'legend'. He seemed to epitomise probity and honesty in the sometimes murky world of financial dealings. Madoff's investment fund consistently outperformed similar funds and demonstrated remarkably little volatility of returns irrespective of market conditions. With his apparent astute financial skills and quiet authority there was no shortage of investors eager to increase their savings in Madoff's fund. The bad news was that Madoff's fund was a US$65bn fraud, a Ponzi scheme which paid returns to investors from their own investments or from the money from other investors.

The USA Securities and Exchange Commission (SEC) defines a Ponzi scheme as an investment fraud that involves the payment of purported returns to existing investors from funds contributed by new investors. Ponzi scheme organisers often solicit new investors by promising to invest funds in opportunities claimed to generate high returns with little or no risk. In many Ponzi schemes, the fraudsters focus on attracting new money to make promised payments to earlier-stage investors and to use for personal expenses, instead of engaging in any legitimate investment activity. The SEC further states that

> The schemes are named after Charles Ponzi, who duped thousands of New England residents into investing in a postage stamp speculation scheme back in the 1920s. At a time when the annual interest rate for bank accounts was five per cent per annum, Ponzi promised investors that he could provide a 50 per cent return in just 90 days.

Bernie Madoff was sentenced to 150 years in prison in June 2009 for his part in what is probably the biggest financial fraud ever perpetrated. However, it is most unlikely that much of the investors' money embezzled will ever be recovered.

Directors' responsibilities

The responsibilities of directors, in terms of the UK Corporate Governance Code, can be seen to be important and far-reaching. It has been said that being a director is easy, but being a responsible director is not. It is important for all directors to develop an understanding and awareness of their ever-increasing legal obligations and responsibilities to avoid the potential personal liabilities, and even disqualification, which are imposed if those obligations are ignored.

It can be seen that the aims of most of the codes of practice and legislation have been to promote better standards of management in companies. This has also meant penalising irresponsible directors, the effect of which has been to create an increasingly heavy burden on directors regardless of the size or nature of the business they manage. The Government is actively banning offending directors.

Directors' duties are mainly embodied in the:

■ Companies Act 2006
■ Insolvency Act 1986 (as amended by the Enterprise Act 2002)
■ Company Directors Disqualification Act 1986 (as amended by the Enterprise Act 2002)
■ Enterprise Act 2002
■ Health and Safety at Work Act 1974
■ Health and Safety (Offences) Act 2008
■ Financial Services Act 1986
■ Corporate Manslaughter and Corporate Homicide Act 2007.

In addition, it should be noted that further statutory provisions giving rise to vicarious liability of directors for corporate offences are included in Acts of Parliament, which currently number well over 200! Directors can be:

■ forced to pay a company's losses
■ fined
■ prevented from running businesses
■ imprisoned.

The Directors' Remuneration Report Regulations 2002 (Statutory Instrument 2002 No. 1986) are now in force and require the directors of a company to prepare a remuneration report that is clear, transparent and understandable to shareholders. Many smaller companies without continuous legal advice are unaware about how much the rules have tightened. It is usually not until there is wide publicity surrounding high-profile business problems that boards of directors are alerted to the demands and penalties to which they may be subjected if things go wrong.

It was not only the 1980s and early 1990s that saw corporate scandals and irregularities (for example, Polly Peck and the Maxwell companies). At the end of 1999, accounting irregularities caused trading in engineering company TransTec shares to be suspended, with Arthur Andersen called in as administrative receiver. The case was fuelled by the revelation by former TransTec chief accountant Max Ayris that nearly £500,000 of a total of £1.3m in grants from the Department of Trade and Industry was obtained fraudulently. TransTec, founded by former Government minister Geoffrey Robinson, collapsed in December 1999, after the accounting irregularities were discovered, with debts of more than £70m. Following the collapse of the company the role of the auditors to the

Anything you can do I can do better

On Mar. 12, victims of Bernard Madoff's Ponzi scheme finally had one of their wishes come true. After a judge denied bail, Madoff is going directly to jail, and he isn't passing 'go'. But Madoff's victims still want answers.

They want to know where the money went. They want to know who else was involved. And they want to know how they got scammed.

At the courthouse, many victims said there were no warning signs and Madoff himself, in his courtroom statement, backed them up on at least one count. 'The clients receiving trade confirmations and account statements had no way of knowing by reviewing these documents that I had never engaged in the transactions', Madoff said during his guilty plea.

Maybe not. But to Harry Markopolos, the risk manager who alerted the SEC to Madoff's fraud in 1999 to no avail, the foul play seemed obvious. Madoff was supposedly using a complex trading system to generate returns, a strategy he dubbed the 'split-strike conversion strategy'. He would buy stocks in the Standard & Poor's 100 and sell options to reduce volatility. But Markopolos' firm was running a similar strategy and couldn't match the returns. A look at the returns was all it took for Markopolos to know something was up.

Preying on a Community

Markopolos had plenty of incentive to doubt Madoff; he was a competitor irked by Madoff's claims of too-good-to-be-true returns. For most of Madoff's clients, the math that Markopolos employed would have been out of their league. Some Madoff investors were sophisticated enough that they might have dug deeper into their statements and trade confirmations. A quick comparison of their returns with those of the actual markets might have been enough to tip them off that at least some of the trades were phony. Some of them might have realized that the average returns were too high and too constant, based on the mathematical probabilities. 'If the standard deviation is too low and the mean too high, something is wrong', says Utpal Bhattacharya, finance professor at the Indiana University Kelley School of Business. Still, 'the retail investor would need some help.'

Experts say investors can avoid Ponzi schemes and other scams without relying on math. The first step: Take a look around; who are your fellow investors? Often in a scam, a pattern emerges. There's a reason why many Madoff-like scams are called 'affinity crimes'. Charles Ponzi, for whom the scam is named, targeted Italians. Joseph Forte ripped off his friends. And before Madoff branched out into Europe in recent years, his clients were primarily Jews and Jewish foundations.

'Ponzis involve preying on people who have some association. The same clubs, religion, geographic location', says Tim Kochis, chief executive of financial advisory firm Aspiriant. 'Madoff's investors all trusted each other. They assumed that was good enough.' If investors get a sense that their adviser caters to a very narrow group, they should probably dig a little deeper.

Do Your Own Due Diligence

That starts with doing your own due diligence. Scamsters often make claims to bolster the confidence of investors that they're dealing with a heavyweight. Allen Stanford built an image of a successful businessman whose family's financial-services roots went back to 1932. In fact, his banking empire consisted of a Montserrat bank founded in 1986 that had its license revoked by the local government. Go back further, and Stanford filed for bankruptcy not once, but twice.

Victims of Tom Petters, the mastermind behind another recent Ponzi scheme in Minnesota that cost investors $2 billion, didn't check out basic claims, such as Petters' assertion that he was a major supplier to Sam's Club. He wasn't, which the investors could have figured out if they'd picked up the phone and made a call.

Madoff's investors might have been able to determine if their trades were legitimate if they'd checked how a stock or option traded on any given day. Even something as trivial as the accounting firm can be a tip-off. Both Madoff and Stanford used tiny accounting firms that would have been hard-pressed to handle the job. 'Investors have to do their own due diligence', says Gregory Hays, managing principal of Atlanta-based Hays Financial Consulting. 'They need to make sure what they're investing in is accurate.'

Investors also should dig into the firm and the background of its managers. A quick check on the Financial Industry Regulatory Authority, or FINRA, Web site could alert investors to a black mark on an adviser's record. Its Broker Check function alerts investors to any regulatory proceedings against an adviser, from bad record-keeping to misuse of client funds for firms and advisers. If the firm doesn't have a solid explanation, it could be time to look elsewhere.

The Defense of Skepticism

Even a quick search of Google can be revealing, yet it's a step few victims take. It would have revealed accusations from the 1990s that Madoff was front-running his customers, that is, buying or selling shares before filling their orders. The charges may amount to nothing. 'But', says Billy Procida, founder of William Procida Inc., a turnaround management firm for middle-market real estate companies, 'do I really want to take that chance?'

Still, the best defense may be a healthy dose of skepticism. Most people with money to invest with people like Madoff worked very hard for it. In business, they wouldn't have taken anybody's word for something. They'd have checked it out. But they didn't do the same with their advisers.

Richard Friedland, a CPA and Madoff investor, said on Mar. 12 that he could have recognized the scam if he had been looking for it. But he saw no reason to look for it. 'Madoff was the chairman of Nasdaq', Friedland said.

And that's what the Madoffs of the world depend on to build their webs of deception. They have fancy offices, fancy cars, and travel in private jets. They have pictures of governors, mayors, movie stars, and athletes.

'People love that', Procida says. 'They want to be with a star.'

Source: **Madoff: Lessons from a Disaster**, by Ben Levisohn
© *BusinessWeek Online*, 16 March 2009

company, PricewaterhouseCoopers, was also to be examined by the Joint Disciplinary Scheme, the accountancy profession's senior watchdog.

Also during 1999, the trade finance group Versailles discovered that there had been some double counting of transactions, which prompted the Department of Trade and Industry to take a close interest in its affairs. Actual and apparent corporate misdemeanours continued, on an even larger scale, through the late 1990s and on into the twenty-first century (note the Barings debacle, Enron, World-Com and Tyco).

Non-executive directors are legally expected to know as much as executive directors about what is going on in the company. Ignorance is not a defence. Directors must be aware of what is going on and have knowledge of the law relating to their duties and responsibilities. Fundamentally, directors must:

- use their common sense
- be careful in what they do
- look after shareholders
- look after creditors
- look after employees.

Progress check 6.5

What are the main responsibilities of directors with regard to the accounting and financial reporting of their companies?

Duty of care

It is the duty of a director to exercise his or her powers in the best interests of the company, which includes not acting for his or her personal benefit, nor for an improper use. In the year 2000, Greg Hutchings, the chairman of a major plc, Tomkins, was criticised for alleged excessive perks, unauthorised donations, and inclusion of members of his family and household staff on the company payroll, without proper disclosure. Investors' concern over corporate governance practices at the group had been triggered by a fall in the share price of over 50% in two years. The resignation of the chairman followed an initial investigation. The new chairman very quickly launched a full inquiry into executive perks within the group, overseen by him personally.

Duty of care means doing the job with the skill and care that somebody with the necessary knowledge and experience would exercise if they were acting on their own behalf. Delegation of directors' power must be 'properly and sensibly done'. If a director of a company does not choose the right people or supervise them properly, all the directors may be liable for the misdeeds and mistakes of the people they have appointed.

When a company fails and is found to be insolvent, the **receiver** appointed will leave no stone unturned to identify whether any money may be recovered in order to pay off creditors. This will include checking for any oversights by directors for items they should have spotted 'if they had exercised their proper level of skill'.

Fiduciary duty

Directors must act in the best interests of the company. Courts will support directors who act honestly and in good faith. Acting in the best interests of the company includes not making personal profit at the company's expense, not letting personal interest interfere with the proper running of the business, or doing business which favours directors or their close associates. In the late 1990s and early

2000s there were several business failures within the dot.com sector, where directors did act in the best interests of the company although their business plans may not have been commercially successful (for example, *www.breathe.com*).

Corporate manslaughter

There is an offence of corporate manslaughter, which a company may be guilty of if a failure by its management is the cause of a person's death, and their failure is because their conduct is well below what can be reasonably expected. Before 1999 there were only five prosecutions in the UK for corporate manslaughter, resulting in two convictions. The risk for companies and their directors is remote but very real, and should therefore be managed in terms of awareness, training, preventative measures and liability insurance.

In earlier years companies were outside the criminal law. As one judge put it, 'a company had a soul to damn and no body to kick' – meaning that because a company did not have an actual existence it could not be guilty of a crime because it could not have a guilty will. In 1965 a case established the validity of the indictment of a company for manslaughter. Since then over 19,000 people have been killed as a result of corporate activity, but no company stood trial for manslaughter, apart from P&O European Ferries (Dover) Ltd after the capsize and sinking of the *Herald of Free Enterprise* off Zeebrugge in 1987. The directors of P&O Ferries did stand trial, but were acquitted because the trial collapsed halfway through. Currently, to succeed in a case of corporate manslaughter against a company there is a need to prove gross negligence and to prove that at least one sufficiently senior official was guilty of that same gross negligence.

Although each year hundreds of people are killed at work or in commercially related activity, if companies have been prosecuted at all they have been charged under the Health and Safety at Work Act (1974) and other regulatory legislation. Many of the companies implicated in work fatalities and public transport disasters operate with diffuse management systems and much delegated power. Such systems that appear to have no 'controlling mind' make it difficult to meet the requirement of the law because of the difficulty in identifying the individual(s) who may possess the mental element for the crime.

A case that was successfully prosecuted involved a small company, OLL Ltd, which organised a canoe expedition at Lyme Bay in 1993, in which four teenage schoolchildren died. In 1994 the jury in the case found OLL Ltd guilty of manslaughter – a historic decision. Peter Kite, the managing director of the activity centre responsible for the canoeing disaster, was jailed for three years for manslaughter, and OLL Ltd was fined £60,000. OLL Ltd was the first company in the UK ever to be found guilty of manslaughter, in a decision that swept away 400 years of legal history.

The Lyme Bay case was atypical of corporate homicide incidents. The company was small, so it was relatively easy to discover the 'controlling mind'; the risks to which pupils were exposed were serious and obvious and, critically, they were not technical or esoteric in any way. However, in the case of a large corporation with many levels of management it is virtually impossible to identify a controlling mind. The Corporate Manslaughter and Corporate Homicide Act (2007) replaces the concept of the controlling mind with a consideration of the way in which an organisation's activities were managed or organised. The Act puts emphasis on examining management systems and practices across the organisation to establish whether an adequate standard of care was applied to the fatal situation. At the time of writing this book the first attempted prosecution under the rules of the new Act was being tried in the courts, following several adjournments (the importance of this landmark case is illustrated in the press extract on the next page). The defendant was found guilty on 15 February 2011.

Great Western Trains was fined £1.5m over the Southall (1997) rail crash in which seven people were killed, following a Health and Safety Executive (HSE) prosecution. But no individual within the company was charged with manslaughter.

A new chapter in English law on corporate manslaughter?

In law, small cases often mark major milestones. When the prosecution of Cotswold Geotechnical Holdings begins next week at Stroud Magistrates' Court, a new chapter in English law will begin. It will be the first case brought under the Corporate Manslaughter and Corporate Homicide Act 2007 and it signifies a new approach to prosecuting companies for alleged crimes.

The case concerns the death of Alexander Wright, 27, a geologist, who was taking soil samples from a pit that had been excavated as part of a site survey when the sides collapsed, crushing him.

The first chapter of corporate manslaughter law began on February 2, 1965, but it was rather an empty one. The Times reported what was then an innovation in English law: a company had stood trial for manslaughter. Glanville Evans, a 27-year-old welder, had been killed when the bridge at Boughrood that he was demolishing collapsed and he fell into the River Wye. The company had evidently been reckless in instructing him to work in a perilous way but an attempt to convict it for manslaughter at Glamorgan Assizes failed on the evidence.

Nonetheless, the court accepted that a company could be prosecuted for manslaughter. A new crime was recognised. Since then more than 40,000 people have been killed at work or in commercial disasters, such as those involving ferries and trains, while prosecutions for corporate manslaughter have totalled just 38.

The old common law made it very difficult to prosecute companies because the doctrine of identification required the prosecution to pin all the blame on at least one director whose will was identified as the "mind" of the company. As companies commonly had responsibility for safety matters distributed across more than one directorial portfolio, pinning all the blame on one person was difficult. Various directors claimed to know only a fragment of the lethal danger that materialised. It was not permissible to incriminate the company by aggregating the fragmented faults of several directors.

The new law aims to criminalise corporate killing without the need to find all the blame in one individual. The offence is committed where an organisation owes a duty to take reasonable care for a person's safety but the way in which its business has been 'managed or organised' amounts to a gross breach of that duty and causes death.

The law says that, for a conviction, a 'substantial element' of the gross negligence must come from 'senior management' (as opposed to a maverick worker) but any company trying to evade the law by not making safety the responsibility of a senior manager would, by virtue of that very stratagem, be open to legal attack.

Companies convicted of manslaughter can be made to publicise their wrongdoing in the national press and are subject to an unlimited fine. The Sentencing Advisory Panel has suggested a level of fine of between 2.5 and 10 per cent of a convicted company's average annual turnover during the three years before the offence. This is a dramatic change. Most large companies convicted of fatal safety crimes are now fined at a level that is less than one 700th of annual turnover.

Directors can be prosecuted for safety offences alongside a corporate manslaughter prosecution and the Health and Safety (Offences) Act 2008 has widened the range of offences for which prison is a possible punishment.

The new corporate manslaughter law obliges the jury to consider whether a company is guilty by looking at what happened in the context of general safety law. Jurors are also invited to consider how far the evidence shows that there were 'attitudes, policies, systems or accepted practices within the organisation' that were likely to have encouraged the safety failures that resulted in death.

Historically, the law was chiselled to govern individuals accused of homicide and it could not properly be adapted to prosecute corporations. That became more problematic once companies became so powerful – of the world's 100 largest economic entities today, 49 are countries and 51 are companies. Having corporate citizens that are more powerful than governments is a challenge for good social governance.

Globally, more people are killed each year at work or through commercial enterprise – more than two million – than die in wars. If the Act works well in the United Kingdom it will be a good template to be adopted in other countries, and that would confer a substantial social benefit.

Source: **The small cases that will have a big influence on the way we work; Gary Slapper reflects on the deaths that have led to changes in corporate manslaughter law**
© The Times, 11 July 2009

The Paddington (1999) rail crash case, again brought by the HSE, resulted in 31 people killed and over 400 injured. The company, Thames Trains, was fined £2m in April 2004, but even though the HSE said its enquiries had revealed 'serious failing in management', there was no prosecution for corporate manslaughter.

A few years ago the legal profession considered that the promised review of the Law Commission's recommendation for an involuntary homicide Act 'could result in company directors being made personally responsible for safety and therefore potentially liable in cases of avoidable accidents'. The Corporate Manslaughter and Corporate Homicide Act 2007 is now expected to dramatically increase the level of directors' accountability to ensure the provision of safe work environments for their employees.

Other responsibilities

Directors do not owe a direct duty to shareholders, but to the company itself. Directors have no contractual or fiduciary duty to outsiders and are generally not liable unless they have acted in breach of their authority. Directors must have regard to the interests of employees but this is enforceable against directors only by the company and not by the employees.

Progress check 6.6

What is meant by a duty of care and fiduciary duty with regard to company directors?

Insolvency

Insolvency, or when a company becomes insolvent, is when the company is unable to pay creditors' debts in full after realisation of all the assets of the business. The penalties imposed on directors of companies continuing to trade while insolvent may be disqualification and personal liability. Many directors have lost their houses (as well as their businesses) as a result of being successfully pursued by the receivers appointed to their insolvent companies.

The Insolvency Act 1986 (as amended by the Enterprise Act 2002) provides guidance on matters to be considered by liquidators and receivers in the reports that they are required to prepare on the conduct of directors. These matters include:

- breaches of fiduciary and other duties to the company
- misapplication or retention of monies or other property of the company
- causing the company to enter into transactions which defrauded the creditors
- failure to keep proper accounting and statutory records
- failure to make annual returns to the Registrar of Companies and prepare and file annual accounts.

If a company is insolvent, the courts assess the directors' responsibility for:

- the cause of the company becoming insolvent
- the company's failure to supply goods or services which had been paid for
- the company entering into fraudulent transactions or giving preference to particular creditors
- failure of the company to adhere to the rules regarding creditors' meetings in a creditors' **voluntary winding-up**
- failure to provide a **statement of affairs** or to deliver up any proper books or information regarding the company.

Progress check 6.7

How does insolvency impact on directors and what are their responsibilities in this regard?

Wrongful trading

A major innovation of the Insolvency Act 1986 was to create the statutory tort (civil wrong) of **wrongful trading**. It occurs where a director knows or ought to have known before the commencement of winding up that there was no reasonable prospect of the company avoiding insolvency and he or she does not take every step to minimise loss to creditors. If the court is satisfied of this it may:

- order the director to contribute to the assets of the business, and
- disqualify him or her from further involvement in corporate management for a specified period.

A director will not be liable for wrongful trading if he or she can show that from the relevant time he or she 'took every step with a view to minimising the potential loss to the company's creditors as (assuming him or her to have known that there was no reasonable prospect that the company would avoid going into insolvent liquidation) he or she ought to have taken'. A company goes into insolvent liquidation, for this purpose, if it does so at a time when its assets are insufficient for the payment of its debts and other liabilities and the expenses of winding-up.

Both subjective tests and objective tests are made with regard to directors. A director who is responsible, for example, for manufacturing, quality, purchasing, or human resources, is likely to have less skill and knowledge regarding the financial affairs of the company than the **finance director**, unless otherwise fully briefed. Directors with financial or legal experience will certainly be expected to bear a greater responsibility than other directors because of their specialist knowledge.

Fraudulent trading

Fraudulent trading is an offence committed by persons who are knowingly party to the continuance of a company trading in circumstances where creditors are defrauded, or for other fraudulent purposes. Generally, this means that the company incurs more debts at a time when it is known that those debts will not be met. Persons responsible for acting in this way are personally liable without limitation for the debts of the company. The offence also carries criminal penalties.

The offence of fraudulent trading may apply at any time, not just in or after a winding-up. If a company is wound up and fraudulent trading has taken place, an additional civil liability arises in respect of any person who was knowingly a party to it.

> **Progress check 6.8**
>
> Are there any differences between wrongful trading and fraudulent trading? If so, what are they?

Disqualification of directors

Disqualification means that a person cannot be, for a specified period of time, a director or manager of any company without the permission of the courts. Disqualification is governed under the Company Directors (Disqualification) Act 1986, and may result from breaches under:

- the Companies Act 2006
    - from cases of fraud or other breaches of duty by a director
- the Insolvency Act 1986 (as amended by the Enterprise Act 2002)
    - if the courts consider that the conduct of a director makes him or her unfit to be concerned in the future management of a company.

Whilst there are serious implications for directors of companies under the Company Directors (Disqualification) Act 1986, it should be noted that the Act is not restricted to company directors.

Over one half of the liabilities fall on 'any persons' as well as company directors. 'Any persons' in this context potentially includes any employee within the organisation.

The following offences, and their penalties, under the Act relate to any persons:

- being convicted of an indictable offence – disqualification from company directorships for up to five years, and possibly for up to 15 years
- fraud in a winding-up – disqualification from company directorships for up to 15 years
- participation in fraudulent or wrongful trading – disqualification from company directorships for up to 15 years
- acting as a director while an undischarged bankrupt, and failure to make payments under a county court administration order – imprisonment for up to two years, or a fine, or both
- personal liability for a company's debts where the person acts while disqualified – civil personal liability.

The following offences, and their penalties, under the Act relate to directors (but in some instances include other managers or officers of the company):

- persistent breaches of company legislation – disqualification from company directorships for up to five years
- convictions for not less than three default orders in respect of a failure to comply with any provisions of companies' legislation requiring a return, account or other document to be filed, delivered, sent, etc., to the Registrar of Companies (whether or not it is a failure of the company or the director) – disqualification from company directorships for up to five years
- finding of unfitness to run a company in the event of the company's insolvency – disqualification from company directorships for a period of between 2 years and 15 years
- if after investigation of a company the conduct of a director makes him or her unfit to manage a company – disqualification from company directorships for up to 15 years
- attribution of offences by the company to others if such persons consent, connive or are negligent – imprisonment for up to two years, or a fine, or both, or possibly imprisonment for not more than six months, or a fine.

Worked example 6.4

In February 2010 it was reported that five former directors of a timeshare firm Worldwide International UK Limited had been disqualified for a total of 32 years following an investigation by the Companies Investigation Branch (CIB). Mr Bruce Goss, the controlling director of the family firm, was disqualified for eight years after the CIB investigation found that the company, which marketed timeshare and holiday products, was run with a 'serious lack of commercial probity', leading to several complaints to trading standards. The CIB suggested he caused the company to trade while insolvent and was responsible for 'intermingling' the accounts of several different companies. There was also a failure to keep proper accounts and failure to pay debts. In addition, it was claimed that the family had a 'propensity' to transfer surplus funds to their own accounts. In the judgement disqualifying Mr Goss, the High Court Registrar said, 'I am therefore satisfied that the allegations made against Mr Goss disclose persistent and serious dishonesty. Even when the company's financial situation was clearly hopeless he allowed it to continue to take money from customers and those customers who sought explanations were lied to and deceived.'

Let's look at the important implications of this case and the way in which the law protects society from the actions of unscrupulous directors.

There are some fundamental reasons why it is necessary for society to ban certain individuals from becoming directors of limited companies.

■ The limited liability company is a very efficient means of conducting business, but if used by unscrupulous persons then innocent people can lose money, through no fault of their own.
■ The limited liability company can offer a financial shield to protect employees and investors if things go wrong and the company ceases trading, and is unable to pays its creditors.

UK law is now quite strict and will attack an obviously unscrupulous person who takes advantage of the protection of the limited liability company and leaves various creditors out of pocket.

In recent times the UK government has banned an increasing number of persons from becoming directors, as well as publishing their names in the public domain (for example, on the Internet). Almost certainly the recently introduced regime is showing its teeth and punishing guilty directors in a most practical manner.

In some circumstances directors may be disqualified automatically. Automatic disqualification occurs in the case of an individual who revokes a county court administration order, and in the case of an undischarged bankrupt unless **leave of the court** is obtained. In all other situations the right to act as a director may be withdrawn only by an order of the court, unless a company through its Articles of Association provides for specific circumstances in which a director's appointment may be terminated. The City of London has seen a major toughening of the regime where persons have found themselves unemployable (for example, the fallout from the Baring Bank debacle in the mid-1990s).

Progress check 6.9

In what circumstances may a director be disqualified?

Summary of directors' obligations and responsibilities

In summary, the following may serve as a useful checklist of directors' obligations and responsibilities:

■ both executive and non-executive directors must act with care, look after the finances and act within their powers, and look after employees
■ directors are responsible for keeping proper books of account and presenting shareholders with accounts, and failure to do so can result in disqualification
■ directors should understand the accounts and be able to interpret them
■ the board of directors is responsible for filing accounts with the Registrar of Companies and must also notify changes to the board of directors and changes to the registered address
■ shareholders must appoint auditors
■ the directors are responsible for calling and holding annual general meetings, and ensuring minutes of all meetings are appropriately recorded
■ directors are responsible for ensuring that the company complies with its memorandum and articles of association
■ if a company continues to trade while technically insolvent and goes into receivership a director may be forced to contribute personally to repaying creditors
■ a director trading fraudulently is liable to be called on for money
■ any director who knew or ought to have known that insolvency was unavoidable without minimising loss to the creditors becomes liable
■ directors can be disqualified for paying themselves too much

- inadequate attention paid to the financial affairs of the company can result in disqualification
- directors are required to prepare a remuneration report.

We have seen the onerous burden of responsibility placed on directors of limited companies in terms of compliance with guidelines and legislation. The obligations of directors continue to grow with the increase in government regulation and legislation. Sixteen new directives were introduced in the UK during the two years to 2001, relating to such issues as employee working conditions, health and safety and, for example, administration of a minimum wage policy.

How can directors make sure that they comply and cover themselves in the event of things going wrong?

Actions to ensure compliance

Directors of companies need to be aware of the dividing line between the commission of a criminal offence and the commission of technical offences of the Companies Act. Directors should take the necessary actions to ensure compliance with their obligations and responsibilities, and to protect themselves against possible non-compliance:

- directors may delegate their responsibilities within or outside the company and in such circumstances they must ensure that the work is being done by competent, able and honest people
- directors of small companies in particular should get professional help to ensure compliance with statutory responsibilities
- directors must ensure that they are kept fully informed about the affairs of the company by having regular meetings and recording minutes and material decisions
- directors should ensure they have service contracts that cover the company's duties, rights, obligations and directors' benefits
- directors must ensure that detailed, timely management accounts are prepared, and, if necessary, professional help sought to provide, for example, monthly reporting systems and assistance with interpretation of information produced and actions required.

It is essential that directors carefully watch for warning signs of any decline in the company's position, for example:

- falling sales or market share
- overdependence on one product or customer or supplier
- overtrading
- pressure on bank borrowings
- increases in trade payables
- requirements for cash paid in advance
- increasing inventory levels
- poor financial controls.

The protection that directors may obtain is extremely limited. All directors should certainly take out individual professional liability insurance. But above all it is probably more important that all directors clearly understand their obligations and responsibilities, closely watch company performance, and take immediate, appropriate action as necessary, to ensure compliance and minimise their exposure to the type of personal risks we have discussed above.

Progress check 6.10

What actions should directors take to ensure they meet their obligations, and to protect themselves should things go wrong?

Summary of key points

- The framework for establishing good corporate governance and accountability has been established in a UK Corporate Governance Code, developed from the work of the Cadbury, Greenbury, Hampel, and Turnbull Committees.

- There is a statutory requirement for the audit of the accounts of limited companies, except for smaller limited companies.

- The election of suitably qualified, independent auditors is the responsibility of the shareholders, to whom they are responsible.

- Directors of limited companies have a specific responsibility to shareholders, and general responsibilities to all stakeholders and the community, for the management and conduct of companies. (Note the continued activities of pressure groups such as Greenpeace and Friends of the Earth.)

- Directors of limited companies have a fiduciary duty to act in the best interests of the company, and a duty of care to all stakeholders and to the community at large, particularly with regard to the Companies Act 2006, Health and Safety at Work Act 1974, Health and Safety (Offences) Act 2008, Financial Services Act 1986, Insolvency Act 1986, and Enterprise Act 2002.

- The risk for companies and their directors from the Corporate Manslaughter and Homicide Act 2007 has become very real, and should therefore be managed in terms of awareness, training, preventative measures and liability insurance.

- The implications for directors for wrongful trading may be to contribute to the assets of the business, and disqualification from further involvement in corporate management for a specified period.

- The implications for directors for fraudulent trading may be to contribute to the assets of the business without limit, disqualification, and possible criminal and civil penalties.

- The implications of the Company Directors (Disqualification) Act 1986 (as amended by the Enterprise Act 2002) apply not only to company directors, and over 50% of the provisions relate to any persons.

- Directors of limited companies, in addition to taking out individual professional liability insurance, must ensure that they clearly understand their obligations and responsibilities.

Assessment material

Questions

Q6.1   **(i)**   How was the UK Corporate Governance Code developed?
          (ii)   Why was it considered necessary?

Q6.2   Refer to the Johnson Matthey section on corporate governance in their annual report and accounts 2011, shown on pages 194 to 210, and illustrate their areas of compliance (or not) under the UK Corporate Governance Code (as distinct from the previous Combined Code of Practice).

Q6.3   **(i)**   Which areas of the business do auditors' opinions cover?
          (ii)   What happens if there is any fundamental uncertainty as to compliance?

Q6.4 Explain the implications of the 'expectation gap' with regard to external auditors.

Q6.5 Explain the obligations of directors of limited companies in terms of their duty of care, their fiduciary duty, and the Corporate Manslaughter and Corporate Homicide Act (2007).

Q6.6 If the severity of the penalty is determined by the seriousness of the offence, describe the half dozen or so most serious offences under the Company Directors (Disqualification) Act 1986 (as amended by the Enterprise Act 2002), which relate to directors of limited companies.

Q6.7 Outline the general responsibilities of a director of a limited company with regard to the company, its shareholders and other stakeholders.

Q6.8 What are the key actions that a director of a limited company may take to ensure compliance with his or her obligations and responsibiiities?

Discussion points

D6.1 Discuss, and illustrate with some examples, how far you think the UK Corporate Governance Code goes to preventing the kind of corporate excesses we have seen in the recent past.

D6.2 'I pay my auditors a fortune in audit fees. I look upon this almost as another insurance premium to make sure that I'm protected against every kind of financial risk.' Discuss.

D6.3 'Everyone who embarks on a career in industry or commerce aspires to become a director of their organisation, because then all their troubles are over! Directors just make a few decisions, swan around in their company cars, and pick up a fat cheque at the end of each month for doing virtually nothing.' Discuss.

D6.4 In an age of increasingly sophisticated computer systems is the traditional role of the auditor coming to an end?

Exercises

Solutions are provided in Appendix 2 to all exercise numbers highlighted in colour.

Level I

E6.1 *Time allowed – 30 minutes*

Discuss why users of financial statements should have information on awards to directors of share options, allowing them to subscribe to shares at fixed prices in the future.

E6.2 *Time allowed – 30 minutes*

Outline the basic reasons why there should be openness regarding directors' benefits and 'perks'.

E6.3 *Time allowed – 30 minutes*

Can you think of any reasons why directors of UK plcs found that their contracts were no longer to be open-ended under the new regime of corporate governance?

E6.4   *Time allowed – 60 minutes*

> William Mason is the managing director of Classical Gas plc, a recently formed manufacturing company in the chemical industry, and he has asked you as finance director to prepare a report that covers the topics, together with a brief explanation, to be included in a section on corporate governance in their forthcoming annual report and accounts.

Level II

E6.5   *Time allowed – 60 minutes*

After the birth of her twins Vimla Shah decided to take a couple of years away from her career as a company lawyer. During one of her coffee mornings with Joan Turnbull, Joan confided in her that although she was delighted at her husband Ronnie's promotion to commercial director of his company, which was a large UK plc in the food industry, she had heard many horror stories about problems that company directors had encountered, seemingly through no fault of their own. She was worried about the implications of these obligations and responsibilities (whatever they were) that Ronnie had taken on. Vimla said she would write some notes about what being a director of a plc meant, and provide some guidelines as to the type of things that Ronnie should be aware of, and to include some ways in which Ronnie might protect himself, that may all offer some reassurance to Joan.

> Prepare a draft of what you think Vimla's notes for Joan may have included.

E6.6   *Time allowed – 60 minutes*

Li Nan has recently been appointed managing director of Pingers plc, which is a company that supplies table tennis equipment to clubs and individuals throughout the UK and Europe. Li Nan is surprised at the high figure that appeared in last year's accounts under audit fees.

> Li Nan is not completely familiar with UK business practices and has requested you to prepare a detailed report on what the audit fees cover, and to include the general responsibilities of directors in respect of the external audit.

E6.7   *Time allowed – 60 minutes*

> Use the following information, extracted from Tomkins plc report and accounts for 2000, as a basis for discussing the users of financial information's need for information on directors' remuneration.

	Basic salary	Benefits in kind	Bonuses
G Hutchings, executive director	£975,000	£45,000	£443,000
G Gates (USA), non-executive director	nil, but has a 250,000 US$ consultancy agreement		
R Holland, non-executive director	£23,000	Nil	Nil

E6.8   *Time allowed – 60 minutes*

> Explain what is meant by insolvency and outline the responsibilities of receivers appointed to insolvent companies.

7

Financial statements analysis

Contents

Learning objectives

Completion of this chapter will enable you to:

■ carry out a performance review of a business, including the use of SWOT analysis

■ critically evaluate the limitations of the performance review process

■ differentiate between divisional manager performance measurement and economic performance measurement

■ analyse business performance through the use of ratio analysis of profitability; efficiency; liquidity; investment; financial structure

■ use both profit and cash flow in the measurement of business performance

■ critically compare the use of cash flow versus profit as the best measure in the evaluation of financial performance

■ use earnings before interest, tax, depreciation and amortisation (EBITDA) as a close approximation of a cash flow performance measure.

Introduction

Chapters 2, 3, 4 and 5 introduced us to the financial statements of limited companies that are prepared with regard to the accountability we discussed in Chapter 6. This chapter is concerned with how the performance of a business may be reviewed through analysis and evaluation of the balance sheet, the income statement and the statement of cash flows. Business performance may be considered from outside or within the business for a variety of reasons. The performance review process provides an understanding of the business which, together with an analysis of all the relevant information, enables interpretation and evaluation of its financial performance during successive accounting periods and its financial position at the end of those accounting periods.

The chapter begins with an outline of the steps involved in the performance review process and also considers the limitations of such a process. The main body of this chapter is concerned with ratio analysis. Financial ratio analysis looks at the detailed use of profitability, efficiency, liquidity, investment and financial structure ratios in the evaluation of financial performance.

The chapter closes with a discussion about which is the best measure of performance – cash or profit. The use of earnings per share and cash flow in performance measurement are discussed along with the measurement of earnings before interest, tax, depreciation and amortisation (EBITDA) as an approximation of cash flow. The debate continues as to whether cash flow or profit represents the best basis for financial performance measurement.

In Chapter 8 we shall build on the knowledge gained from the current chapter when we examine the published report and accounts of a major UK plc, Johnson Matthey.

The performance review process

A performance review using financial statements may be undertaken for a number of reasons, for example:

■ to assist in investment decisions
■ to identify possible takeover targets
■ to evaluate the financial strength of potential or existing customers or suppliers.

The main aim of a performance review is to provide an understanding of the business, and, together with an analysis of all the relevant information, provide an interpretation of the results. A performance review is generally undertaken using a standard format and methodology. The most effective performance review is provided from a balanced view of each of the activities of the organisation, which necessarily involves the close co-operation of each role: marketing; research and development; design; engineering; manufacturing; sales; logistics; finance; human resources management.

The performance review process begins with a SWOT analysis and works through a number of steps to the conclusions, as outlined in Figure 7.1. A SWOT analysis includes an internal analysis of the company and an analysis of the company's position with regard to its external environment.

1. SWOT analysis

SWOT is shorthand for strengths, weaknesses, opportunities and threats. The first look at a company's performance usually involves listing the key features of the company by looking internally at its particular strengths and weaknesses, and externally at risks or threats to the company and opportunities that it may be able to exploit. The SWOT analysis may give some indication of, for example, the strength of the company's management team, how well it is doing on product quality, and areas as yet untapped within its marketplace.

To keep the analysis focused, a cruciform chart may be used for SWOT analysis. An example is outlined in Figure 7.2, relating to the position in 2010 of the low-budget airline, Ryanair.

2. Consideration of major features

The increasing amount of information now provided in published financial statements enables the analyst to look in detail at the various industrial and geographical sectors of the business, the trends

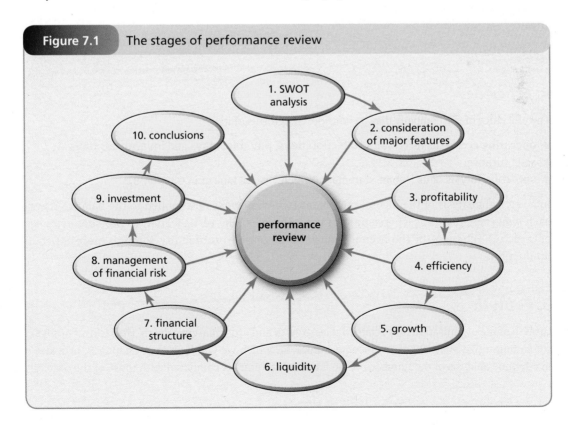

Figure 7.1   The stages of performance review

Figure 7.2	An example of a SWOT analysis

Strengths	**Weaknesses**
Firm operating strategy Robust route network Strong fleet operations	Declining profitability Legal proceedings Unfunded employee post-retirement benefits
Opportunities	**Threats**

Accelerating UK airlines industry
Positive outlook for the European online
    travel market
Growing global travel and tourism industry
	Intense competition and price discounting
	EU regulations on denied boarding
	    compensation

within these and the business in general. Further background information may be extracted from the accounting policies, the auditors' report, chairman's report and details of any significant events that have been highlighted.

3. Profitability

A number of financial indicators and ratios may be considered to assess the profitability of the company, which may include:

- gross profit (or gross margin) to sales
- return on sales (ROS)
- **return on capital employed (ROCE)**, or **return on investment (ROI)**.

4. Efficiency

The efficiency of the company may be considered in terms of its:

- **operating cycle** – its receivables **collection days**, **payables days** and **inventories days**
- asset turnover
- **vertical analysis** of its income statement (which we will look at in Chapter 8).

In a vertical analysis of the income statement (which may also be applied to the balance sheet) each item is expressed as a percentage of the total sales. The vertical analysis provides evidence of structural changes in the accounts such as increased profitability through more efficient production.

5. Growth

Growth of the organisation may relate to sales growth and gross margin growth. **Horizontal analysis** (or common size analysis) of the income statement, which we will look at in Chapter 8, provides a line-by-line analysis of the numbers in the financial statements compared with those of the previous year. It may provide over a number of years a trend of changes showing either growth or decline in these numbers by calculation of annual percentage growth rates in profits, sales, inventories or any other item.

6. Liquidity

Liquidity is concerned with the short-term solvency of the company. It is assessed by looking at a number of key ratios, for example:

- **current ratio**
- **acid test**
- **defensive interval**
- cash ROCE
- **cash interest cover.**

7. Financial structure

How the company is financed is concerned with the long-term solvency of the company. It is assessed by looking at a number of other key ratios, for example:

- **gearing** – the proportion of capital employed financed by lenders rather than shareholders, expressed in a number of ways, for example the **debt/equity ratio** (long-term loans and preference shares/ordinary shareholders' funds)
- **dividend cover** (eps/dividend per share)
- **interest cover** (profit before interest and tax (PBIT)/interest payable)
- various forms of off balance sheet financing.

Off balance sheet financing is defined as the funding or refinancing of a company's operations in such a way that, under legal requirements and existing accounting conventions, some or all of the finance may not be disclosed in its balance sheet. The International Accounting Standards Board (IASB) has tried (and indeed continues to try) to introduce regulations forcing the exclusion of this type of financing.

8. Management of financial risk

The global market is here. Companies increasingly trade globally with greater levels of sophistication in products, operations and finance. Risk assessment and the management of risk are therefore now assuming increasing importance. The main areas of financial risk are in investment, foreign currency exchange rates and interest rates, and levels of trade credit.

9. Investment

Investment ratios examine whether or not the company is undertaking sufficient investment to ensure its future profitability. These ratios include, for example:

- earnings per share (eps)
- **price earnings ratio (P/E)**
- capital expenditure/sales revenue
- capital expenditure/gross non-current assets.

10. Conclusions

The conclusion of the performance review will include consideration of the company's SWOT analysis and the main performance features. It will consider: growth and profitability, and whether or not these are maintainable; levels of finance and investment, and whether there is sufficient cash flow; the future plans of the business.

All performance reviews must use some sort of benchmark. Comparisons may be made against past periods and against budget; they may also be made against other companies and using general data relating to the industry within which the company operates. Later in this chapter we will look in more detail at the use of profitability, efficiency, liquidity, and investment ratios, and ratios relating to financial structure.

> ### Progress check 7.1
>
> Describe each of the stages in a business performance review process.

Limitations of the performance review process

There are many obvious limitations to the above approach. In comparing performance against other companies (and sometimes within the company in comparing past periods), or looking at industrial data, it should be borne in mind that:

- there may be a lack of uniformity in accounting definitions and techniques
- the balance sheet is only a snapshot in time, and only represents a single estimate of the company's position
- there may actually be no standards for comparison
- changes in the environment and changes in money values, together with short-term fluctuations, may have a significant impact
- the past should really not be relied on as a good predictor of the future.

The speed of change in the computer peripherals market is well known to manufacturers. Some components may have been large revenue generators for many years yet even they finally cease to have a market. Sony had sold 3.5 inch floppy disks (invented by IBM in 1971) since 1983 and in 2002 sold 47 million of them in Japan. Inevitably, new technologies eventually superseded the floppy disk, leading to its decline in sales (see the press extract on the next page). Even a product which currently provides a strong income stream will not do so indefinitely.

Diversified companies present a different set of problems. Such companies by their very nature comprise companies engaged in various industrial sectors, each having different market conditions, financial structures and expectations of performance. The notes to the accounts, which appear in each company's annual report and accounts, invariably present a less than comprehensive picture of the company's position.

As time goes by, and accounting standards and legislation get tighter and tighter, the number of loopholes which allow any sort of window dressing of a company's results are reduced. Inevitably,

The past is not a good predictor of the future

They were once the stalwarts of the techno-logical era. But the humble floppy disk is about to bite the dust once and for all. The un-wieldy storage devices have been shown the door by their biggest manufacturer, Sony, which has announced that production will cease next year.

The plastic storage 'disks' have been usurped by smaller USB drives, which have more space for data and are far easier to transport. To tell the truth, we thought sales of floppy disks had nose-dived years ago. Yet, incredibly, Sony still sold 12 million floppy disks last year in Japan.

The first floppy was invented by IBM in 1971 and was eight wobbly inches wide. And while most people thought the floppiness of the whole thing gave the product its name, it was actually the circular magnetic disk inside that was technically the 'floppy' bit. This pioneering technology allowed information to be passed between computers – but heaven forbid you forgot to slap a brightly coloured sticky label on your anonymous-looking disk to remind you of the contents.

Later, the more common 3.5in disks weren't floppy at all, but the name stuck – though some show-offs called them 'diskettes'. Hundreds of millions of floppy disks have been sold since 1971 – until now.

But although computers don't have built in floppy drives any more, the floppy's legacy will live on – we still click on a little icon of one to save a document when we're using most computer software today.

Source: **Farewell then ... floppy disks**, by Chris Beanland
© *Daily Mail*, 28 April 2010

however, there will always remain the possibility of the company's position being presented in ways that may not always represent the 'truth'. We will now look at the type of information that may be used and the important financial ratios and their meaning and relevance.

> ### Progress check 7.2
>
> What are the main limitations encountered in carrying out the performance review of a business?

Economic performance measurement

Most large organisations are divided into separate divisions in which their individual managers have autonomy and total responsibility for investment and profit. Within each division there is usually a functional structure comprising many departments. Divisionalisation is more appropriate for com-panies with diversified activities. The performance of the managers of each division may be measured in a number of ways, for example return on investment (ROI) and **residual income (RI)**.

The relationships between divisions should be regulated so that no division, by seeking to increase its own profit, can reduce the profitability of the company as a whole. Therefore, there are strong arguments for producing two broad types of performance measure. One type of measure is used to evaluate managerial performance and the other type of measure is used to evaluate economic performance. In the current chapter we are primarily concerned with the performance of the organi-sation as a whole. We will look at ratios that measure economic performance, which focus not only on profit and profitability, but on a range of other areas of performance that include, for example, cash and working capital.

Ratio analysis

The reasons for a performance review may be wide and varied. Generally, it is required to shed light on the extent to which the objectives of the company are being achieved. These objectives may be:

- to earn a satisfactory return on capital employed (ROCE)
- to maintain and enhance the financial position of the business with reference to the management of working capital, non-current assets and bank borrowings
- to achieve cost targets and other business targets such as improvements in labour productivity.

Ratio analysis is an important area of performance review. It is far more useful than merely considering absolute numbers, which on their own may have little meaning. Ratios may be used:

- for a subjective assessment of the company or its constituent parts
- for a more objective way to aid decision-making
- to provide **cross-sectional analysis** and **inter-company comparison**
- to establish models for loan and credit ratings
- to provide equity valuation models to value businesses
- to analyse and identify underpriced shares and takeover targets
- to predict company failure.

There are various models that may be used to predict company failure such as those developed by John Argenti (*Corporate Collapse: The Causes and Symptoms*, McGraw-Hill 1976), and Edward Altman (*Corporate Financial Distress: A Complete Guide to Predicting, Avoiding and Dealing with Bankruptcy*, John Wiley & Sons 1983). Altman's model is sometimes used for prediction of corporate failure by calculating what is called a *Z score* for each company. For a public industrial company, if the *Z score* is greater than 2.99 then it is unlikely to fail, and if the score is less than 1.81 then it is likely to fail. Statistical analyses of financial ratios may further assist in this area of prediction of corporate failure, using for example time series and line of business analyses.

As we saw in our examination of the performance review process, the key ratios include the following categories:

- profitability
- efficiency
- liquidity
- investment
- financial structure.

We will use the financial statements of Flatco plc, an engineering company, shown in Figures 7.3 to 7.8, to illustrate the calculation of the key financial ratios. The income statement and statement of cash flows are for the year ended 31 December 2010 and the balance sheet is as at 31 December 2010. Comparative figures are shown for 2009.

Profitability ratios

It is generally accepted that the primary objective for the managers of a business is to maximise the wealth of the owners of the business. To this end there are a number of other objectives, subsidiary to the main objective. These include:

- survival
- stability
- growth
- maximisation of market share

- maximisation of sales
- maximisation of profit
- maximisation of return on capital.

Each group of financial ratios is concerned to some extent with survival, stability, growth and maximisation of shareholder wealth. We will first consider ratios in the broad area of profitability (see Figure 7.9), which give an indication of how successful the business has been in its achievement of the wealth maximisation objective.

$$\text{gross profit \%} = \frac{\text{gross profit}}{\text{revenue}} = \frac{\text{revenue} - \text{cost of sales (COS)}}{\text{revenue}}$$

Figure 7.3	Flatco plc balance sheets as at 31 December 2009 and 2010

Flatco plc
Balance sheet as at 31 December 2010

	2010 £000	2009 £000
Assets		
Non-current assets		
Tangible	1,884	1,921
Intangible	416	425
Investments	248	248
Total non-current assets	2,548	2,594
Current assets		
Inventories	311	268
Trade and other receivables	1,162	1,134
Cash and cash equivalents	327	17
Total current assets	1,800	1,419
Total assets	4,348	4,013
Liabilities		
Current liabilities		
Borrowings and finance leases	50	679
Trade and other payables	553	461
Current tax liabilities	50	44
Dividends payable	70	67
Provisions	82	49
Total current liabilities	805	1,300
Non-current liabilities		
Borrowings and finance leases	173	–
Trade and other payables	154	167
Deferred tax liabilities	–	–
Provisions	222	222
Total non-current liabilities	549	389
Total liabilities	1,354	1,689
Net assets	2,994	2,324
Equity		
Share capital	1,200	1,000
Share premium account	200	200
Retained earnings	1,594	1,124
Total equity	2,994	2,324

Figure 7.4	Flatco plc income statements for the years ended 31 December 2009 and 2010

Flatco plc
Income statement for the year ended 31 December 2010

	2010 £000	2009 £000
Revenue	3,500	3,250
Cost of sales	(2,500)	(2,400)
Gross profit	1,000	850
Distribution costs	(300)	(330)
Administrative expenses	(250)	(160)
Other income	100	90
Operating profit	550	450
Finance income	111	80
Finance costs	(71)	(100)
Profit before tax	590	430
Income tax expense	(50)	(44)
Profit for the year from continuing operations	540	386
Profit for the year from discontinued operations	–	–
Profit for the year	540	386

Figure 7.5	Flatco plc additional information to the financial statements 2010

Additional information

Administrative expenses for 2010 include an exceptional item of £95,000 redundancy costs.

Dividends were £70,000 for 2010 (2009: £67,000) and retained earnings were £470,000 (2009: £319,000).

Authorised and issued share capital 31 December 2010 was 1,200,000 £1 ordinary shares (2009: 1,000,000).

Total assets less current liabilities 31 December 2008 were £2,406,000.

Trade receivables 31 December 2010 were £573,000 (2009: £517,000, 2008: £440,000).

The market value of ordinary shares in Flatco plc on 31 December 2010 was £2.75 (£3.00 2009).

During the year 2010 tangible non-current assets were acquired at a cost of £286,000, and intangible non-current assets were acquired at a cost of £34,000. During 2010 intangible non-current assets were sold for £21,000, generating neither a profit nor a loss.

Tangible non-current assets depreciation provision at 31 December 2010 was £1,102,000 (£779,000 2009).

Current liabilities: Provisions for 2010 include Accruals £82,000, and for 2009 include Accruals £49,000. Trade and other payables for 2010 include Trade payables £553,000 and other payables zero, and for 2009 include Trade payables £461,000 and other payables zero.

Figure 7.6	Flatco plc cash generated from operations for the years ended 31 December 2009 and 2010

Flatco plc
Cash generated from operations for the year ended 31 December 2010

	2010 £000	2009 £000
Profit before tax	590	430
Depreciation and amortisation charges	345	293
Adjust finance (income)/costs	(40)	20
Increase in inventories	(43)	(32)
Increase in trade and other receivables [1,134 − 1,162]	(28)	(25)
Increase in trade and other payables, and provisions [461 − 553 + 49 − 82 + 167 − 154]	112	97
Cash generated from operations	936	783

Figure 7.7	Flatco plc statement of cash flows for the years ended 31 December 2009 and 2010

Flatco plc
Statement of cash flows for the year ended 31 December 2010

	2010 £000	2009 £000
Cash flows from operating activities		
Cash generated from operations	936	783
Interest paid	(71)	(100)
Income tax paid	(44)	(40)
Net cash generated from operating activities	821	643
Cash flows from investing activities		
Purchases of tangible assets	(286)	(170)
Purchases of intangible assets	(34)	–
Proceeds from sales of intangible assets	21	–
Interest received	11	–
Dividends received	100	80
Net cash outflow from investing activities	(188)	(90)
Cash flows from financing activities		
Proceeds from issue of ordinary shares	200	290
Proceeds from borrowings	173	–
Dividends paid to equity shareholders	(67)	(56)
Net cash inflow from financing activities	306	234
Net increase in cash and cash equivalents in the year	939	787
Cash and cash equivalents and bank overdrafts at beginning of year	(662)	(1,449)
Cash and cash equivalents and bank overdrafts at end of year	277	(662)

Figure 7.8	Flatco plc analysis of cash and cash equivalents and bank overdrafts as at 31 December 2009 and 2010

Flatco plc
Analysis of cash and cash equivalents and bank overdrafts as at 31 December 2010

	At 1 January 2010 £000	At 31 December 2010 £000
Cash and cash equivalents	17	327
Bank overdrafts	(679)	(50)
Cash and cash equivalents and bank overdrafts	(662)	277

	At 1 January 2009 £000	At 31 December 2009 £000
Cash and cash equivalents	–	17
Bank overdrafts	(1,449)	(679)
Cash and cash equivalents and bank overdrafts	(1,449)	(662)

Figure 7.9	Profitability ratios

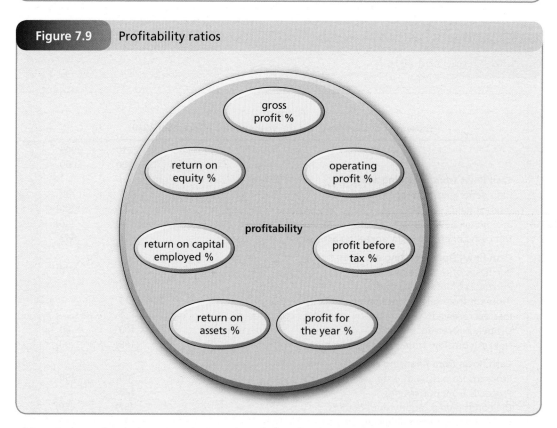

This ratio is used to gain an insight into the relationship between production and purchasing costs and sales revenue. The gross profit (or gross margin) needs to be high enough to cover all other costs incurred by the company, and leave an amount for profit. If the gross profit percentage is too low then sales prices may be too low, or the purchase costs of materials or production costs may be too high.

$$\text{operating profit \%} = \frac{\text{operating profit}}{\text{revenue}} = \frac{\text{revenue} - \text{COS} - \text{other operating expenses}}{\text{revenue}}$$

The operating profit (or profit before interest and tax (PBIT) excluding other operating income) ratio is a key ratio that shows the profitability of the business before incurring financing costs. If the numerator is not multiplied by 100 to give a percentage, it shows the profit generated by each £1 of sales revenue.

$$\text{profit before tax (PBT) \%} = \frac{\text{profit before tax}}{\text{revenue}} = \frac{\text{operating profit} +/- \text{net interest}}{\text{revenue}}$$

This is the profit ratio that uses profit after financing costs, that is, having allowed for interest payable and interest receivable. It should be remembered that profit before tax (PBT) is a profit measure that goes further than dealing with the trading performance of the business, in allowing for net financing costs. It provides an indication of pre-tax profit-earning capability from the sales for the period.

$$\text{profit for the year \%} = \frac{\text{net profit}}{\text{revenue}} = \frac{\text{profit before tax (PBT)} - \text{corporate income tax}}{\text{revenue}}$$

This is the final profit ratio after allowing for financing costs and corporation tax. The net profit for the year (or profit after tax) or **return on sales (ROS)** ratio is the profit available for distribution to shareholders in the form of dividends and/or future investment in the business.

$$\text{return on assets (ROA) \%} = \frac{\text{operating profit}}{\text{total assets}}$$

Return on assets (ROA) compares operational income with the total assets used to generate that income. Profit is calculated before net financing costs and tax.

$$\frac{\text{return on capital employed (ROCE)}}{\text{or return on investment (ROI) \%}} = \frac{\text{operating profit}}{\text{total assets} - \text{current liabilities}\\ \text{(usually averaged)}}$$

This is a form of return on capital employed (using pre-tax profit) which compares income with the net operational assets used to generate that income. Profit is calculated before net financing costs and tax. This is because the introduction of interest charges introduces the effect of financing decisions into an appraisal of operating performance, and tax levels are decided by external agencies (governments).

The average cost of a company's finance (equity, debentures, loans), weighted according to the proportion each element bears to the total pool of capital, is called the **weighted average cost of capital (WACC)**. The difference between a company's ROI and its WACC is an important measure of the extent to which the organisation is endeavouring to optimise its use of financial resources. In their 2009 annual report, Sainsbury's plc reported on the improvement in their ROCE versus WACC gap, stating that 'the pre-tax return on average capital employed continued to improve significantly, increasing by 85 basis points in the year to 11.0 per cent, around 70 basis points above the company's weighted average cost of capital'.

A company manages its ROCE through monitoring its operating profit as a percentage of its capital employed. A company manages its WACC by planning the proportions of its financing through either equity (ordinary shares) or debt (loans), with regard to the relative costs of each, based on dividends and interest.

WACC is an important measure when companies are considering acquisitions. This is emphasised by the Rio Tinto Group plc in their 2009 annual report, where the company identified how WACC is used in determining the potential future benefits that may be derived from investments:

Forecast cash flows are discounted to present values using Rio Tinto's weighted average cost of capital with appropriate adjustment for the risks associated with the relevant cash flows, to the extent that such risks are not reflected in the forecast cash flows. For final feasibility studies and ore reserve estimation, internal hurdle rates are used which are generally higher than the weighted average cost of capital.

This refers to the importance of WACC as a factor used in the evaluation of investment in projects undertaken (or not) by a business (see Chapter 9).

$$\text{return on equity (ROE)} = \frac{\text{net profit}}{\text{equity}}$$

Another form of return on capital employed, **return on equity (ROE)** measures the return to the owners on the book value of their investment in a company. The return is measured as the residual profit after all expenses and charges have been made, and after corporate income tax has been deducted. The equity comprises share capital, retained earnings and reserves.

The profitability performance measures discussed above consider the general performance of organisations as a whole. It is important for managers also to be aware of particular areas of revenue or expenditure that may have a significant importance with regard to their own company and that have a critical impact on the net profit of the business. Companies may, for example:

■ suffer large warranty claim costs
■ have to pay high royalty fees
■ receive high volumes of customer debit notes (invoices) for a variety of product or service problems deemed to be their fault.

All managers should fully appreciate such key items of cost specific to their own company and be innovative and proactive in identifying ways that these costs may be reduced and minimised.

Managers should also be aware of the general range of costs for which they may have no direct responsibility, but nevertheless may be able to reduce significantly by:

■ improved communication
■ involvement
■ generation of ideas for waste reduction, increased effectiveness and cost reduction.

Such costs may include:

■ the cost of the operating cycle
■ costs of warehouse space
■ project costs
■ costs of holding inventories
■ depreciation (as a result of capital expenditure)
■ warranty costs
■ repairs and maintenance
■ stationery costs
■ telephone and fax costs
■ photocopy costs.

The relative importance of these costs through their impact on profitability will of course vary from company to company.

Worked example 7.1

We will calculate the profitability ratios for Flatco plc for 2010 and the comparative ratios for 2009, and comment on the profitability of Flatco plc.

Gross profit

$$\text{gross profit \% 2010} = \frac{\text{gross profit}}{\text{revenue}} = \frac{£1,000 \times 100\%}{£3,500} = 28.6\%$$

$$\text{gross profit \% 2009} = \frac{£850 \times 100\%}{£3,250} = 26.2\%$$

Profit before interest and tax, PBIT (PBIT is operating profit plus finance income)

$$\text{PBIT \% 2010} = \frac{\text{PBIT}}{\text{revenue}} = \frac{£661 \times 100\%}{£3,500} = 18.9\%$$

$$\text{PBIT \% 2009} = \frac{£530 \times 100\%}{£3,250} = 16.3\%$$

Profit for the year (or profit after tax, PAT), or return on sales (ROS)

$$\text{PAT \% 2010} = \frac{\text{net profit}}{\text{revenue}} = \frac{£540 \times 100\%}{£3,500} = 15.4\%$$

$$\text{PAT \% 2009} = \frac{£386 \times 100\%}{£3,250} = 11.9\%$$

Return on assets, ROA

$$\text{ROA \% 2010} = \frac{\text{operating profit}}{\text{total assets}} = \frac{£550 \times 100\%}{£4,348} = 12.6\%$$

$$\text{ROA \% 2009} = \frac{£450 \times 100\%}{£4,013} = 11.2\%$$

Return on capital employed, ROCE (or return on investment, ROI)

$$\text{ROCE \% 2010} = \frac{\text{operating profit}}{\substack{\text{total assets} - \text{current liabilities} \\ \text{(average capital employed)}}}$$

$$= \frac{£550 \times 100\%}{(£3,543 + £2,713)/2} = \frac{£550 \times 100\%}{£3,128} = 17.6\%$$

$$\text{ROCE \% 2009} = \frac{£450 \times 100\%}{(£2,713 + £2,406)/2} = \frac{£450 \times 100\%}{£2,559.5} = 17.6\%$$

Return on equity, ROE

$$\text{ROE \% 2010} = \frac{\text{PAT}}{\text{equity}} = \frac{£540 \times 100\%}{£2,994} = 18.0\%$$

$$\text{ROE \% 2009} = \frac{£386 \times 100\%}{£2,324} = 16.6\%$$

Report on the profitability of Flatco plc

Sales revenue for the year 2010 increased by 7.7% over the previous year, partly through increased volumes and partly through higher selling prices.

Gross profit improved from 26.2% to 28.6% of sales, as a result of increased selling prices but also lower costs of production.

PBIT improved from 16.3% to 18.9% of sales (and operating profit, which is calculated as operating profit × 100/sales, improved from 13.8% to 15.7%). If the one-off costs of redundancy of £95,000 had not been incurred in the year 2010 operating profit would have been £645,000 (£550,000 + £95,000) and the operating profit ratio would have been 18.4% of sales, an increase of 4.6% over 2009. The underlying improvement in operating profit performance (excluding the one-off redundancy costs) was achieved from the improvement in gross profit and from the benefits of lower distribution costs and administrative expenses.

ROA increased from 11.2% to 12.6%. This was because although the total assets of the company had increased by 8.3%, operating profit had increased by 22.2% in 2010 compared with 2009.

ROCE was static at 17.6% because the increase in capital employed as a result of additional share capital of £200,000 and long-term loans of £173,000 was matched by a similar increase in operating profit.

Return on equity increased from 16.6% to 18%, despite the increase in ordinary share capital. This was because of improved profit after tax (up 3.5% to 15.4%) arising from increased income from non-current asset investments and lower costs of finance. Corporation tax was only marginally higher than the previous year despite higher pre-tax profits.

Progress check 7.3

How may financial ratio analysis be used as part of the process of review of business performance?

Efficiency ratios

The regular monitoring of efficiency ratios by companies is crucial because they relate directly to how effectively business transactions are being converted into cash. For example, if companies are not regularly paid in accordance with their terms of trading:

- their profit margins may be eroded by the financing costs of funding overdue accounts
- cash flow shortfalls may put pressure on their ability to meet their day-to-day obligations to pay employees, replenish inventory, etc.

Despite the introduction of legislation to combat slow payments to suppliers, the general situation in the UK still remains poor, although there are some signs of improvement, as can be seen from the extract on the next page from the *Daily Telegraph*.

The range of efficiency ratios is illustrated in Figure 7.10.

Efficiency generally relates to the maximisation of output from resources devoted to an activity or the output required from a minimum input of resources. Efficiency ratios measure the efficiency with which such resources have been used.

$$\text{collection days} = \frac{\text{trade receivables} \times 365}{\text{revenue}}$$

Companies that fail to pay suppliers on time

Small businesses are being forced to write off debt at a faster rate because they are struggling to reduce a near £63bn mountain of unpaid bills, say bankers.

Nearly three out of four **small and medium-sized enterprises (SMEs)** have been hit by late payments over the past year but less than half have taken steps to reduce the pressure, according to research among 500 companies by NatWest and its Royal Bank of Scotland parent. Invoices for £15.7bn are more than 120 days in arrears.

The banks estimate 235,000 SMEs have been wasting time chasing overdue invoices. The problem has been most acute among wholesalers where 93pc have suffered considerable delays, while retailers have fared better with 66pc troubled by late payments.

Other research from Barclays based on data from 1,000 companies suggests many businesses are taking active steps to reduce the pressure on cash flow with extensive debt write-offs.

Around 720,000 SMEs wrote off an average of £2,529 last year, double the 2008 figure of £1,133, according to Barclays.

NatWest and RBS estimate less than half of SMEs have taken action, with 11pc hiring an in-house credit controller, 9pc using invoice discounting and 8pc factoring to ease cashflow pressures.

Peter Ibbetson, chairman of NatWest and RBS small business operations, is concerned that so few SMEs are using banking services to alleviate the problem, but small business organisations believe companies are reluctant to incur extra charges after their bank borrowing experiences.

Barclays believes late payment pressures are easing with 18pc saying their survival is threatened compared with 32pc in 2008. The proportion worried about the impact on cash flow is down from 61pc to 26pc over the period.

Source: **Late payments mean bigger write-offs for small businesses**, by Roland Gribben © *Daily Telegraph*, 15 April 2010

Figure 7.10 Efficiency ratios

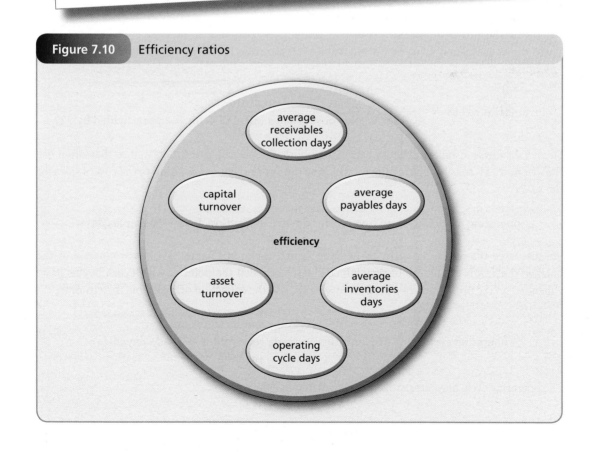

Collection days indicate the average time taken, in calendar days, to receive payment from credit customers. Adjustment is needed if the ratio is materially distorted by VAT (or other taxes). This is because sales invoices to customers, and therefore trade receivables, may include the net sales value plus VAT. However, sales revenue is reported net of VAT. To provide a more accurate ratio, VAT may be eliminated from the trade receivables numbers as appropriate. (Note: for example, export and zero-rated sales invoices, which may be included in trade receivables, do not include VAT and so an adjustment to total trade receivables by the standard percentage rate for VAT may not be accurate.)

$$\text{payables days} = \frac{\text{trade payables} \times 365}{\text{cost of sales (or purchases)}}$$

Payables days indicate the average time taken, in calendar days, to pay for supplies received on credit. For the same reason, as in the calculation of collection days, adjustment is needed if the ratio is materially distorted by VAT or other taxes.

$$\text{inventories days} = \frac{\text{inventories}}{\text{average daily cost of sales in period}} \quad \text{or} \quad \frac{\text{inventories} \times 365}{\text{cost of sales}}$$

Inventories days or inventory turnover is the number of days that inventories could last at the forecast or most recent usage rate. This may be applied to total inventory, finished goods, raw materials, or work in progress. The weekly internal efficiency of inventory utilisation is indicated by the following ratios:

$$\frac{\text{finished goods}}{\text{average weekly}} \qquad \frac{\text{raw materials}}{\text{average weekly raw}} \qquad \frac{\text{work in progress}}{\text{average weekly}}$$
$$\text{despatches} \qquad \qquad \text{material usage} \qquad \qquad \text{production}$$

These ratios are usually calculated using values but may also be calculated using quantities where appropriate.

$$\text{inventories weeks} = \frac{\text{inventories}}{\text{average weekly cost of sales (total COS for the year divided by 52)}}$$

Financial analysts usually only have access to published reports and accounts and so they often use the inventories weeks ratio using the total closing inventories value in relation to the cost of sales for the year.

$$\text{operating cycle (days)} = \text{inventories days} + \text{collection days} - \text{payables days}$$

We discussed the operating cycle, or working capital cycle, in Chapter 3 when we looked at the balance sheet. It is the period of time which elapses between the point at which cash begins to be expended on the production of a product or service, and the collection of cash from the customer.

$$\text{operating cycle \%} = \frac{\text{working capital requirement}}{\text{revenue}} = \frac{\text{(inventories} + \text{trade receivables} - \text{trade payables)}}{\text{revenue}}$$

The operating cycle may alternatively be calculated as a percentage.

$$\text{asset turnover (times)} = \frac{\text{revenue}}{\text{total assets}}$$

Asset turnover measures the performance of the company in generating sales revenue from the assets under its control. The denominator may alternatively be average net total assets.

$$\text{capital turnover} = \frac{\text{revenue}}{\text{average capital employed in year}}$$

The capital turnover expresses the number of times that capital is turned over in the year, or alternatively the sales revenue generated by each £1 of capital employed. This ratio will be affected by capital additions that may have taken place throughout a period but have not impacted materially on the performance for that period. Further analysis may be required to determine the underlying performance.

Worked example 7.2

We will calculate the efficiency ratios for Flatco plc for 2010 and the comparative ratios for 2009, and comment on the efficiency of Flatco plc.

Receivables collection days

$$\text{collection days 2010} = \frac{\text{trade receivables} \times 365}{\text{revenue}} = \frac{£573 \times 365}{£3,500} = 60 \text{ days}$$

$$\text{collection days 2009} = \frac{£517 \times 365}{£3,250} = 58 \text{ days}$$

Payables days

$$\text{payables days 2010} = \frac{\text{trade payables} \times 365}{\text{cost of sales}} = \frac{£553 \times 365}{£2,500} = 81 \text{ days}$$

$$\text{payables days 2009} = \frac{£461 \times 365}{£2,400} = 70 \text{ days}$$

Inventories days (or inventory turnover)

$$\text{inventories days 2010} = \frac{\text{inventories}}{\text{average daily cost of sales in period}} = \frac{£311}{£2,500/365}$$

$$= 45 \text{ days (6.5 weeks)}$$

$$\text{inventories days 2009} = \frac{£268}{£2,400/365} = 41 \text{ days (5.9 weeks)}$$

Operating cycle days

$$\text{operating cycle 2010} = \text{inventories days} + \text{collection days} - \text{payables days}$$
$$= 45 + 60 - 81 = 24 \text{ days}$$

$$\text{operating cycle 2009} = 41 + 58 - 70 = 29 \text{ days}$$

Operating cycle %

$$\text{operating cycle \% 2010} = \frac{\text{working capital requirement}}{\text{revenue}}$$

$$= \frac{(£311 + £573 - £553) \times 100\%}{£3,500} = 9.5\%$$

$$\text{operating cycle \% 2009} = \frac{(£268 + £517 - £461) \times 100\%}{£3,250} = 10.0\%$$

Asset turnover

$$\text{asset turnover 2010} = \frac{\text{revenue}}{\text{total assets}} = \frac{£3,500}{£4,348} = 0.80 \text{ times}$$

$$\text{asset turnover 2009} = \frac{£3,250}{£4,013} = 0.81 \text{ times}$$

Capital turnover

$$\text{capital turnover 2010} = \frac{\text{revenue}}{\text{average capital employed in year}} = \frac{£3,500}{£3,128} = 1.1 \text{ times}$$

$$\text{capital turnover 2009} = \frac{£3,250}{£2,559.5} = 1.3 \text{ times}$$

Report on the efficiency of Flatco plc

A major cash improvement programme was introduced by the company late in the year 2010, which began with the implementation of new cash collection procedures and a reinforced credit control department. This was not introduced early enough to see an improvement in the collection days for the year 2010. Average receivables collection days actually worsened from 58 to 60 days.

The purchasing department negotiated terms of 90 days with a number of key large suppliers. This had the effect of improving the average payables period from 70 to 81 days.

A change in product mix during the latter part of the year 2010 resulted in a worsening of the average inventory turnover period from 41 to 45 days. This is expected to be a temporary situation. An improved just in time (JIT) system and the use of **vendor-managed inventory (VMI)** with two main suppliers in the year 2011 are expected to generate significant improvements in inventory turnover.

Despite the poor inventory turnover, the operating cycle improved from 29 days to 24 days (operating cycle % from 10.0% to 9.5%). Operating cycle days are expected to be zero or better by the end of year 2011.

Asset turnover dropped from 0.81 in 2009 to 0.80 times in the year 2010. New capital was introduced into the company in 2010 to finance major new projects which are expected to result in significant increases in sales levels over the next few years which will result in improvements in asset turnover over and above 2009 levels.

Capital turnover for 2010 dropped to 1.1 times from 1.3 times in 2009. As with asset turnover, the new capital introduced into the company in the year 2010 to finance major new projects is expected to result in significant increases in sales revenue levels over the next few years, which will be reflected in improvements in capital turnover over and above 2009 levels.

Progress check 7.4

What do the profitability and efficiency ratios tell us about the performance of a business?

Liquidity ratios

The degree to which assets are held in a cash or near-cash form is determined by the level of obligations that need to be met by the business. Liquidity ratios (see Figure 7.11) reflect the health or otherwise of the cash position of the business and its ability to meet its short-term obligations.

Figure 7.11   Liquidity ratios

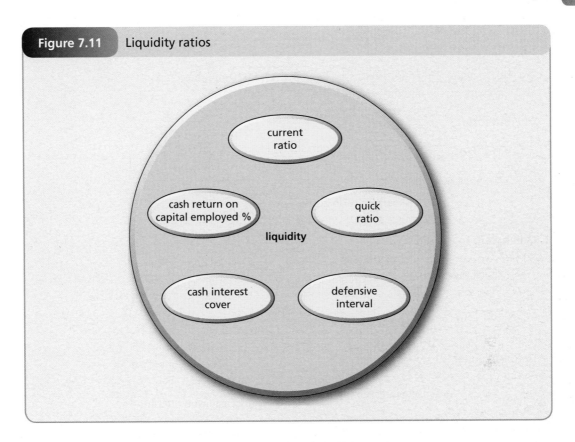

$$\text{current ratio (times)} = \frac{\text{current assets}}{\text{current liabilities}}$$

The current ratio is an overall measure of the liquidity of the business. It should be appreciated that this ratio will be different for different types of business. For example, an automotive manufacturer may have a higher ratio because of its relatively high level of inventories (mainly work in progress) compared with a supermarket retailer which holds a very high percentage of fast-moving inventories.

$$\text{quick ratio (times)} = \frac{\text{current assets} - \text{inventories}}{\text{current liabilities}}$$

The **quick ratio** (or **acid test**) excludes inventories from current assets. While trade receivables and trade payables are just one step away from being converted into cash, inventories are two or more steps away from being converted into cash; they need to be worked on and processed to produce products which are then sold to customers. Therefore, the quick ratio indicates the ability of the company to pay its trade payables out of its trade receivables in the short term. This ratio may be particularly meaningful for supermarket retailers because of the speed with which their inventories are converted into cash.

$$\text{defensive interval (days)} = \frac{\text{quick assets (current assets} - \text{inventories)}}{\text{average daily cash from operations}}$$

The defensive interval shows how many days a company could survive at its present level of operating activity if no inflow of cash were received from sales revenue or other sources.

We will consider some of the other ratios outlined in Figure 7.11 later in this chapter.

Worked example 7.3

We will calculate the liquidity ratios for Flatco plc for 2010 and the comparative ratios for 2009, and comment on the liquidity of Flatco plc.

Current ratio

$$\text{current ratio 2010} = \frac{\text{current assets}}{\text{current liabilities}} = \frac{£1{,}800}{£805} = 2.2 \text{ times}$$

$$\text{current ratio 2009} = \frac{£1{,}419}{£1{,}300} = 1.1 \text{ times}$$

Quick ratio (or acid test)

$$\text{quick ratio 2010} = \frac{\text{current assets} - \text{inventories}}{\text{current liabilities}} = \frac{£1{,}800 - £311}{£805} = 1.8 \text{ times}$$

$$\text{quick ratio 2009} = \frac{£1{,}419 - £268}{£1{,}300} = 0.9 \text{ times}$$

Defensive interval

$$\text{defensive interval 2010} = \frac{\text{quick assets}}{\text{average daily cash from operations}}$$
$$(\text{opening trade receivables} + \text{sales revenue} - \text{closing trade receivables})/365$$

$$= \frac{£1{,}800 - £311}{(£517 + £3{,}500 - £573)/365} = 158 \text{ days}$$

$$\text{defensive interval 2009} = \frac{£1{,}419 - £268}{(£440 + £3{,}250 - £517)/365} = 132 \text{ days}$$

Report on the liquidity of Flatco plc

From the statement of cash flows we can see that cash generated from operations improved from £783,000 in 2009 to £936,000 in 2010. Investments in non-current assets were more than covered by increases in long-term financing in both years. Operational cash flow improvement was reflected in the increase in net cash flow of £939,000 from £787,000 in 2009.

The improved cash flow is reflected in increases in the current ratio (1.1 to 2.2 times) and the quick ratio (0.9 to 1.8 times). The increase in the defensive interval from 132 to 158 days has strengthened the position of the company against the threat of a possible downturn in activity.

Although there has been a significant improvement in cash flow, the increase in investment in working capital is a cause for concern. Three key actions have already been taken since the year end 31 December 2010 to try and maximise the returns on investment: reduction in inventories levels (noted above); further reductions in trade receivables; investment of surplus cash in longer-term investments.

Progress check 7.5

What are liquidity ratios and why are they so important?

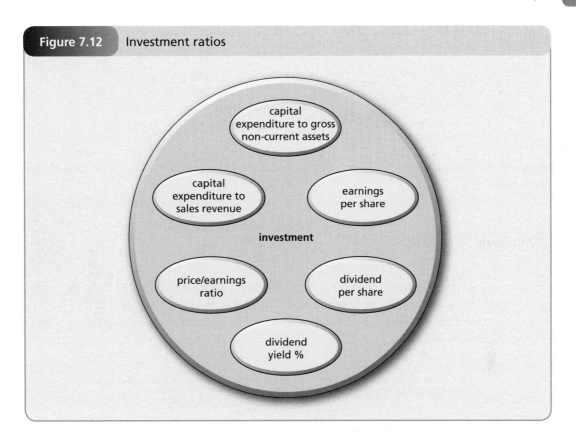

Figure 7.12 Investment ratios

Investment ratios

Investment ratios (see Figure 7.12) generally indicate the extent to which the business is undertaking capital expenditure to ensure its survival and stability, and its ability to sustain current revenue and generate future increased revenue.

$$\text{earnings per share (or eps)} = \frac{\text{profit for the year} \; - \; \text{preference share dividends}}{\text{number of ordinary shares in issue}}$$

Earnings per share, or eps, measures the return per share of earnings available to shareholders. The eps of companies may be found in the financial pages sections of the daily press.

$$\text{dividend per share} = \frac{\text{total dividends paid to ordinary shareholders}}{\text{number of ordinary shares in issue}}$$

Dividend per share is the total amount declared as dividends per each ordinary share in issue. It is the dividend per share actually paid in respect of the financial year. The amount must be adjusted if additional equity shares are issued during the financial year.

$$\text{dividend cover} = \frac{\text{earnings per share}}{\text{dividend per share}}$$

Dividend cover shows the number of times the profit attributable to equity shareholders covers the dividends payable for the period, and conversely also indicates the level of profit being retained by the company, the retention ratio.

$$\text{dividend yield \%} = \frac{\text{dividend per share}}{\text{current share price}}$$

The dividend yield shows the dividend return on the market value of the shares, expressed as a percentage.

$$\text{price/earnings (P/E) ratio} = \frac{\text{current share price}}{\text{eps}}$$

The price/earnings or P/E ratio shows the number of years it would take to recoup an equity investment from its share of the attributable equity profit. The P/E ratio values the shares of the company as a multiple of current or prospective earnings, and therefore gives a market view of the quality of the underlying earnings.

$$\text{capital expenditure to sales revenue \%} = \frac{\text{capital expenditure for year}}{\text{revenue}}$$

This ratio gives an indication of the level of capital expenditure incurred to sustain a particular level of sales revenue.

$$\text{capital expenditure to gross non-current assets \%} = \frac{\text{capital expenditure for year}}{\text{gross value of tangible non-current assets}}$$

This is a very good ratio for giving an indication of the replacement rate of new for old non-current assets.

Worked example 7.4

We will calculate the investment ratios for Flatco plc for 2010 and the comparative ratios for 2009, and comment on the investment performance of Flatco plc.

Earnings per share, eps

$$\text{eps 2010} = \frac{\text{profit for the year} - \text{preference share dividends}}{\text{number of ordinary shares in issue}} = \frac{£540,000}{1,200,000} = 45\text{p}$$

$$\text{eps 2009} = \frac{£386,000}{1,000,000} = 38.6\text{p}$$

Dividend per share

$$\text{dividend per share 2010} = \frac{\text{total dividends paid to ordinary shareholders}}{\text{number of ordinary shares in issue}}$$

$$= \frac{£70,000}{1,200,000} = 5.8\text{p per share}$$

$$\text{dividend per share 2009} = \frac{£67,000}{1,000,000} = 6.7\text{p per share}$$

Dividend cover

$$\text{dividend cover 2010} = \frac{\text{earnings per share}}{\text{dividend per share}}$$

$$= \frac{45\text{p}}{5.8\text{p}} = 7.8\text{ times}$$

$$\text{dividend cover 2009} = \frac{38.6\text{p}}{6.7\text{p}} = 5.8\text{ times}$$

Dividend yield %

$$\text{dividend yield 2010} = \frac{\text{dividend per share}}{\text{share price}}$$

$$= \frac{5.8\text{p} \times 100\%}{£2.75} = 2.11\%$$

$$\text{dividend yield 2009} = \frac{6.7\text{p} \times 100\%}{£3.00} = 2.23\%$$

Price/earnings ratio, P/E

$$\text{P/E ratio 2010} = \frac{\text{current share price}}{\text{eps}} = \frac{£2.75}{45\text{p}} = 6.1\text{ times}$$

$$\text{P/E ratio 2009} = \frac{£3.00}{38.6\text{p}} = 7.8\text{ times}$$

Capital expenditure to sales revenue %

$$\text{capital expenditure to sales revenue 2010} = \frac{\text{capital expenditure for year}}{\text{revenue}} = \frac{£286 \times 100\%}{£3,500} = 8.2\%$$

$$\text{capital expenditure to sales revenue 2009} = \frac{£170 \times 100\%}{£3,250} = 5.2\%$$

Capital expenditure to gross non-current assets %

$$\text{capital expenditure to gross non-current assets 2010} = \frac{\text{capital expenditure for year}}{\text{gross value of tangible non-current assets}}$$

$$= \frac{£286 \times 100\%}{(£1,884 + £1,102)} = 9.6\%$$

(net book value + cumulative depreciation provision)

$$\text{capital expenditure to gross non-current assets 2009} = \frac{£170 \times 100\%}{(£1,921 + £779)} = 6.3\%$$

Report on the investment performance of Flatco plc

The improved profit performance in 2010 compared to 2009 was reflected in improved earnings per share from 38.6p to 45p.

The price/earnings ratio dropped from 7.8 to 6.1 times, indicating that an investment in the company's shares may be recovered in 6.1 years from its current level of net profit.

The board of directors reduced the dividend for the year to 5.8p per share from 6.7p per share in 2009, establishing a dividend cover, or profit retention ratio, of 7.8 times. The increased profit retention provided internal financing in addition to its external financing to fund the company's increase in capital expenditure.

The increase in the capital expenditure to sales revenue ratio from 5.2% to 8.2% indicates the company's ability to both sustain and improve upon current sales revenue levels.

The increase in the capital expenditure to gross non-current assets ratio from 6.3% to 9.6% illustrates Flatco's policy of ongoing replacement of old assets for new in order to keep ahead of the technology in which the business is engaged.

Each of the above four ratios indicate that Flatco is a growth company, from which increased sales revenues and profits may be expected in future years.

The dividend yield reduced from 2.23% at 31 December 2009 to 2.11% at 31 December 2010.

Progress check 7.6

What are investment ratios and what is their purpose?

Financial ratios

Financial ratios (see Figure 7.13) are generally concerned with the relationship between debt and equity capital, the financial structure of an organisation. This relationship is called gearing. Gearing is discussed in further detail in Chapter 9. The ratios that follow are the two most commonly used. Both ratios relate to financial gearing, which is the relationship between a company's borrowings, which includes both prior charge capital and long-term debt, and its shareholders' funds (share capital plus reserves).

$$\text{gearing} = \frac{\text{long-term debt}}{\text{equity } + \text{ long-term debt}}$$

and

$$\text{debt/equity ratio (D/E or leverage)} = \frac{\text{long-term debt}}{\text{equity}}$$

These ratios are both equally acceptable in describing the relative proportions of debt and equity used to finance a business. Gearing calculations can be made in other ways, and in addition to those based on capital values may also be based on earnings/interest relationships, for example:

$$\text{dividend cover (times)} = \frac{\text{earnings per share (eps)}}{\text{dividend per share}}$$

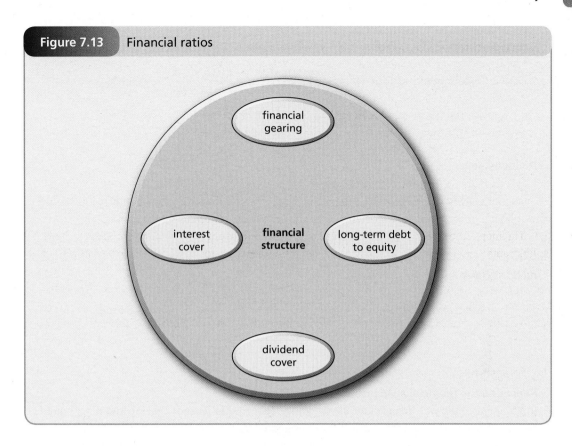

Figure 7.13 Financial ratios

This ratio indicates the number of times the profits attributable to the equity shareholders covers the actual dividends paid and payable for the period. Financial analysts usually adjust their calculations for any exceptional or extraordinary items of which they may be aware.

$$\text{interest cover (times)} = \frac{\textbf{profit before interest and tax}}{\textbf{interest payable}}$$

This ratio calculates the number of times the interest payable is covered by profits available for such payments. It is particularly important for lenders to determine the vulnerability of interest payments to a fall in profit.

Worked example 7.5

We will calculate the financial ratios for Flatco plc for 2010 and the comparative ratios for 2009, and comment on the financial structure of Flatco plc.

Gearing

$$\text{gearing 2010} = \frac{\text{long-term debt}}{\text{equity + long-term debt}} = \frac{£173 \times 100\%}{(£2,994 + £173)} = 5.5\%$$

$$\text{gearing 2009} = \frac{£0 \times 100\%}{(£2,324 + £0)} = 0\%$$

Debt/equity ratio

$$\text{debt/equity ratio } 2010 = \frac{\text{long-term debt}}{\text{equity}} = \frac{£173 \times 100\%}{£2,994} = 5.8\%$$

$$\text{debt/equity ratio } 2009 = \frac{£0 \times 100\%}{£2,324} = 0\%$$

Dividend cover

$$\text{dividend cover } 2010 = \frac{\text{earnings per share (eps)}}{\text{dividend per share}} = \frac{45p}{5.8p} = 7.8 \text{ times}$$

$$\text{dividend cover } 2009 = \frac{38.6p}{6.7p} = 5.8 \text{ times}$$

Interest cover

$$\text{interest cover } 2010 = \frac{\text{profit before interest and tax}}{\text{interest payable}} = \frac{£661}{£71} = 9.3 \text{ times}$$

$$\text{interest cover } 2009 = \frac{£530}{£100} = 5.3 \text{ times}$$

Report on the financial structure of Flatco plc

In 2009 Flatco plc was financed totally by equity, reflected in its zero gearing and debt/equity ratios for that year. Flatco plc was still very low geared in 2010, with gearing of 5.5% and debt/equity of 5.8%. This was because the company's debt of £173,000 at 31 December 2010 was very small compared with its equity of £2,994,000 at the same date.

Earnings per share increased by 16.6% in 2010 compared with 2009. However, the board of directors reduced the dividend, at 5.8p per share for 2010, by 13.4% from 6.7p per share in 2009. This provided an increase in retained earnings (retained profit), shown by the increase in dividend cover from 5.8 times in 2009 to 7.8 times in 2010.

Interest payable was reduced by £29,000 in 2010 from the previous year, but PBIT was increased by £120,000 year on year. The result was that interest cover nearly doubled from 5.3 times in 2009 to 9.3 times in 2010. This ratio may drop again in 2011 as a result of an increase in interest payable in 2011 because of the loan taken by the company late in 2010.

Progress check 7.7

What are financial ratios and how may they be used to comment on the financial structure of an organisation?

In this chapter we have looked at most of the key ratios for review of company performance, and their meaning and relevance. However, the limitations we have already identified generally relating to performance review must always be borne in mind. In addition, it should be noted that the calculations used in business ratio analysis are based on past performance. These may not, therefore, reflect the current or future position of an organisation. Performance ratio analyses can also sometimes be misleading if their interpretation does not also consider other factors that may not always be easily quantifiable, and may include non-financial information, for example customer satisfaction, and delivery performance (see the section about non-financial performance indicators in Chapter 10). There may be inconsistencies in some of the measures used in ratio analysis; for example, sales revenue numbers being reported net of VAT, but trade receivable and trade payables numbers normally including VAT. Extreme care should therefore be taken with the conclusions used in any performance review to avoid reaching conclusions that may perhaps be ambiguous or erroneous.

If all the financial literature were thoroughly researched the number of different ratios that would be discovered may run into thousands. It is most helpful to use a limited set of ratios and to fully understand their meaning. The ratios will certainly help with an understanding of the company but do not in themselves represent the complete picture.

Calculation of the ratios for one company for one year is also very limited. It is more relevant to compare companies operating in the same market and to analyse how a company has changed over the years. However, difficulties inevitably arise because it is sometimes impossible to find another company that is strictly comparable with the company being analysed. In addition, the company itself may have changed so much over recent years as to render meaningless any conclusions drawn from changes in ratios.

The best performance measure – cash or profit?

The importance of cash flow versus profit (or earnings per share) as a measure of company performance has increased over the past few years. The advantages and disadvantages in the use of each are shown in Figures 7.14 and 7.15.

Cash flow has assumed increasing importance and has gained popularity as a measure of performance because the income statement has become somewhat discredited due to the unacceptable degree of subjectivity involved in its preparation. Some of the financial ratios that we have already looked at may be considered in cash terms, for example:

$$\text{cash ROCE \%} = \frac{\text{net cash flow from operations}}{\text{average capital employed}}$$

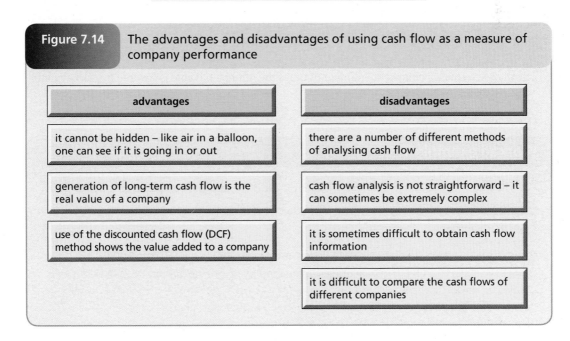

Figure 7.14   The advantages and disadvantages of using cash flow as a measure of company performance

advantages	disadvantages
it cannot be hidden – like air in a balloon, one can see if it is going in or out	there are a number of different methods of analysing cash flow
generation of long-term cash flow is the real value of a company	cash flow analysis is not straightforward – it can sometimes be extremely complex
use of the discounted cash flow (DCF) method shows the value added to a company	it is sometimes difficult to obtain cash flow information
	it is difficult to compare the cash flows of different companies

---

Figure 7.15   The advantages and disadvantages of using earnings per share (eps) as a measure of company performance

advantages	disadvantages
simple method to use	the 1980s boom led to some creative accounting, e.g. Coloroll, Polly Peck, Maxwell, all based on accounting conventions
easy to compare companies	different bases are used from one company to another
possible to see the company relative to the market	use of the historical cost concept means that there is no account taken of expected growth or inflation
profit is easily identifiable	there is no account taken of market risk
	the numbers are too easy to manipulate
	the imprecise area of the treatment of extraordinary items and provisions has now been resolved but there still remain dubious areas such as derivatives, depreciation rates, and provisioning

---

and

$$\text{cash interest cover} = \frac{\text{net cash inflow from operations} + \text{interest received}}{\text{interest paid}}$$

which, in cash terms, calculates the number of times the interest payable is covered by cash available for such payments.

Worked example 7.6

We will calculate the cash ROCE % for Flatco plc for 2010 and the comparative ratio for 2009, and compare with the equivalent profit ratio for Flatco plc.

Cash ROCE %

$$\text{cash ROCE \% 2010} = \frac{\text{net cash flow from operations}}{\text{average capital employed}} = \frac{£936 \times 100\%}{(£3,543 + £2,713)/2}$$

$$= \frac{£936 \times 100\%}{£3,128} = 29.9\%$$

$$\text{cash ROCE \% 2009} = \frac{£783 \times 100\%}{(£2,713 + £2,406)/2} = \frac{£783 \times 100\%}{£2,559.5} = 30.6\%$$

Report on the cash and profit ROCE of Flatco plc

While the profit ROCE % was static at 17.6% for 2009 and 2010, the cash ROCE % reduced from 30.6% to 29.9%. Operating cash flow for 2010 increased by only 19.5% over 2009, despite the fact that operating profit for 2010 increased by 22.2% over 2009.

Operating profit before depreciation (EBITDA) was £895,000 [£550,000 + £345,000] for 2010, which was an increase of 20.5% over 2009 [£450,000 + £293,000 = £743,000]. If pre-depreciation operating profit had been used to calculate ROCE, it would have been 28.6% for 2010 compared with 29.0% for 2009, a reduction of 0.4% and more in line with the picture shown by the cash ROCE.

The chairman of Flatco plc expects that ROCE will be improved in 2011 as a result of:

- increased profitability resulting from higher sales revenues generated from the investments in new projects
- reduction in levels of working capital, with more efficient use of company resources.

Progress check 7.8

What are the benefits of using cash flow instead of profit to measure financial performance? What are the disadvantages of using cash flow?

The increasing importance of cash flow as a measure of performance has led to new methods of measurement:

- the Rappaport method uses DCF looking 10 years ahead as a method of valuing a company
- the **economic value added (EVA™)** method, which we will discuss in Chapter 9 (pages 365 to 370) ◀▥
- enterprise value, a very similar method to EVA, which excludes the peripheral activities of the company.

The profit-based measure of financial performance **EBITDA**, or earnings before interest, tax, depre- ◀▥ ciation and amortisation, has become widely used as an approximation to operational cash flow. Amortisation, in the same way as depreciation applies to tangible non-current assets, is the systematic write-off of the cost of an intangible asset. The way in which EBITDA may be used has been illustrated in the Flatco plc Worked example 7.6.

Graphs showing BT plc's EBITDA and free cash flows cash flows derived from EDITDA for the years 2006 to 2010, which were included in the group's annual report for the year 2010, are shown in Figure 7.16.

In their 2010 annual report and accounts, BT plc commented on their use of EBITDA as a performance measure:

> EBITDA is a common measure used by investors and analysts to evaluate the operating financial performance of companies, particularly in the telecommunications sector. We consider EBITDA to be a useful measure of our operating performance because it reflects the underlying operating cash costs, by eliminating depreciation and amortisation. EBITDA is not a direct measure of our liquidity, which is shown by our statement of cash flows, and it needs to be considered in the context of our financial commitments.

We have seen that the method of performance measurement is not a clear-cut cash or profit choice. It is generally useful to use both. However, many analysts and the financial press in general continue to depend heavily on profit performance measures with a strong emphasis on earnings per share (eps) and the price/earnings ratio (P/E).

Figure 7.16 BT plc EBITDA and free cash flow for 2006 to 2010

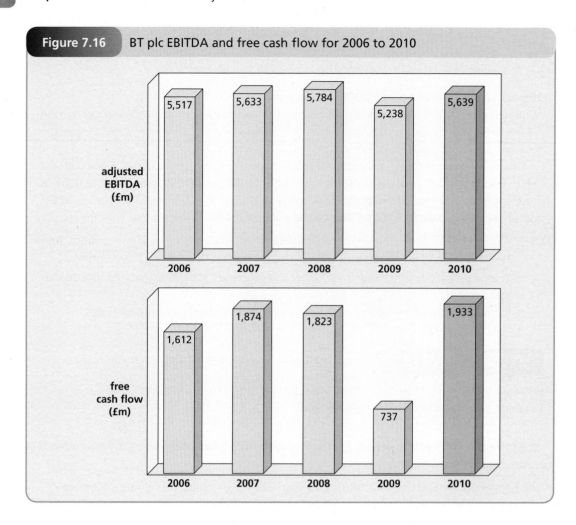

Summary of key points

- The main aims of a business performance review are to provide an understanding of the business and provide an interpretation of results.
- Care must be taken in reviewing business performance, primarily because of lack of consistency in definitions and changes in economic conditions.
- An important area of business performance review is the use of ratio analysis looking at profitability, efficiency, liquidity, investment and growth, and financial structure.
- Cash flow and cash ratios are becoming increasingly as important as profit and profitability ratios in the measurement of business performance.
- There is no best way of evaluating financial performance and there are advantages and disadvantages in using earnings per share or cash flow as the basis of measurement.
- Earnings before interest, tax, depreciation and amortisation (EBITDA) is sometimes used as an approximate measure of a cash flow performance.

Assessment material

Questions

Q7.1 **(i)** Who is likely to carry out a business performance review?
(ii) Describe what may be required from such reviews giving some examples from different industries and differing perspectives.

Q7.2 **(i)** Outline how the business performance review process may be used to evaluate the position of a dot.com company like Amazon UK.
(ii) What are the limitations to the approach that you have outlined?

Q7.3 How is ratio analysis, in terms of profitability ratios, efficiency ratios, liquidity ratios, investment ratios and financial structure ratios used to support the business review process?

Q7.4 Why should we be so careful when we try to compare the income statement of a limited company with a similar business in the same industry?

Q7.5 **(i)** Why does profit continue to be the preferred basis for evaluation of the financial performance of a business?
(ii) In what ways can cash flow provide a better basis for performance evaluation, and how may cash flow be approximated?

Discussion points

D7.1 In what ways may the performance review process be used to anticipate and react to change?

D7.2 'Lies, damned lies, and statistics.' In which of these categories do you think ratio analysis sits, if at all?

Exercises

Solutions are provided in Appendix 2 to all exercise numbers highlighted in colour.

Level I

E7.1 *Time allowed – 30 minutes*
The information below relates to Priory Products plc's actual results for 2009 and 2010 and their budget for the year 2011.

	2009 £000	2010 £000	2011 £000
Cash and cash equivalents	100	0	0
Overdraft	0	50	200
Loans	200	200	600
Ordinary share capital	100	200	400
Retained earnings	200	300	400

You are required to calculate the following financial ratios for Priory Products for 2009, 2010, and 2011:

(i)   debt/equity ratio (net debt to equity)

(ii) gearing (long-term loans to equity and long-term loans).

E7.2   *Time allowed – 60 minutes*

From the financial statements of Freshco plc, a Lancashire-based grocery and general supplies chain supplying hotels and caterers, for the year ended 30 June 2010, prepare a report on performance using appropriate profitability ratios for comparison with the previous year.

Freshco plc
Balance sheet as at 30 June 2010

	2010	2009
	£m	£m
Non-current assets	146	149
Current assets		
Inventories	124	100
Trade receivables	70	80
Cash and cash equivalents	14	11
Total current assets	208	191
Total assets	354	340
Current liabilities		
Trade payables	76	74
Dividends payable	20	13
Income tax payable	25	20
Total current liabilities	121	107
Non-current liabilities		
Debenture loan	20	67
Total liabilities	141	174
Net assets	213	166
Equity		
Share capital	111	100
General reserve	14	9
Retained earnings	88	57
Total equity	213	166

Freshco plc
Income statement for the year ended 30 June 2010

	2010	2009
	£m	£m
Revenue	894	747
Cost of sales	(690)	(581)
Gross profit	204	166
Distribution costs and administrative expenses	(121)	(84)

Operating profit	83	82
Net interest	(2)	(8)
Profit before tax	81	74
Income tax expense	(25)	(20)
Profit for the year	56	54
Retained profit brought forward	57	16
	113	70
Dividends for the year	(20)	(13)
	93	57
Transfer to general reserve	(5)	–
Retained profit carried forward	88	57

Additional information:

(i)   Authorised and issued share capital 30 June 2010, £222m £0.50 ordinary shares (£200m, 2009).

(ii) Total assets less current liabilities 30 June 2008, £219m. Trade receivables 30 June 2008, £60m.

(iii) Market value of ordinary shares in Freshco plc 30 June 2010, £3.93 (£2.85, 2009).

(iv) Non-current assets depreciation provision 30 June 2010, £57m (£44m, 2009).

(v)   Depreciation charge for the year to 30 June 2010, £13m (£10m, 2009).

Freshco plc
Cash generated from operations for the year ended 30 June 2010

	2010 £m	2009 £m
Profit before tax	81	74
Depreciation charge	13	10
Adjust finance costs	2	8
Increase in inventories	(24)	(4)
Decrease/(increase) in trade receivables	10	(20)
Increase in trade payables	2	9
Cash generated from operations	84	77

Freshco plc
Statement of cash flows for the year ended 30 June 2010

	2010 £m	2009 £m
Cash flows from operating activities		
Cash generated from operations	84	77
Interest paid	(2)	(8)
Income tax paid	(20)	(15)
Net cash generated from operating activities	62	54

Freshco plc
Statement of cash flows for the year ended 30 June 2010 (*continued*)

	2010 £m	2009 £m
Cash flows from investing activities		
Purchases of tangible assets	(10)	(40)
Net cash outflow from investing activities	(10)	(40)
Cash flows from financing activities		
Proceeds from issue of ordinary shares	11	0
Proceeds from borrowings	0	7
Repayments of borrowings	(47)	0
Dividends paid to equity shareholders	(13)	(11)
Net cash outflow from financing activities	(49)	(4)
Increase in cash and cash equivalents in the year	3	10

E7.3   *Time allowed – 60 minutes*

Using the financial statements of Freshco plc from Exercise E7.2, for the year ended 30 June 2010, prepare a report on performance using appropriate efficiency ratios for comparison with the previous year.

E7.4   *Time allowed – 60 minutes*

Using the financial statements of Freshco plc from Exercise E7.2, for the year ended 30 June 2010, prepare a report on performance using appropriate liquidity ratios for comparison with the previous year.

E7.5   *Time allowed – 60 minutes*

Using the financial statements of Freshco plc from Exercise E7.2, for the year ended 30 June 2010, prepare a report on performance using appropriate investment ratios for comparison with the previous year.

E7.6   *Time allowed – 60 minutes*

Using the financial statements of Freshco plc from Exercise E7.2, for the year ended 30 June 2010, prepare a report on performance using appropriate financial ratios for comparison with the previous year.

Level II

E7.7   *Time allowed – 60 minutes*

The summarised income statement for the years ended 31 March 2009 and 2010 and balance sheets as at 31 March 2009 and 31 March 2010 for Boxer plc are shown below:

Boxer plc
Income statement for the year ended 31 March

Figures in £000	2009	2010
Revenue	5,200	5,600
Cost of sales	(3,200)	(3,400)
Gross profit	2,000	2,200
Expenses	(1,480)	(1,560)
Profit before tax	520	640

Boxer plc
Balance sheet as at 31 March

	2009 £000	2010 £000
Non-current assets	4,520	5,840
Current assets		
Inventories	1,080	1,360
Trade receivables	680	960
Cash and cash equivalents	240	–
Total current assets	2,000	2,320
Total assets	6,520	8,160
Current liabilities		
Borrowings and finance leases	–	160
Trade payables	360	520
Income tax payable	240	120
Dividends payable	280	384
Total current liabilities	880	1,184
Non-current liabilities		
Debenture loan	1,200	1,200
Total liabilities	2,080	2,384
Net assets	4,440	5,776
Equity		
Ordinary share capital	4,000	5,200
Retained earnings	440	576
Total equity	4,440	5,776

Required:

(i)   Calculate the following ratios for the years 2009 and 2010:
  (a) gross profit percentage of sales
  (b) profit before tax percentage of sales
  (c) return on capital employed
  (d) collection days
  (e) payables days
  (f) inventory turnover
  (g) current ratio
  (h) quick ratio.

(ii) Comment on Boxer plc's financial performance over the two years and explain the importance of effective management of working capital (net current assets).

E7.8   *Time allowed – 90 minutes*

The chief executive of Laurel plc, Al Chub, wants to know the strength of the financial position of Laurel's main competitor, Hardy plc. Using Hardy's financial statements for the past three years he has asked you to write a report that evaluates the financial performance of Hardy plc and to include:

(i)   a ratio analysis that looks at profitability, efficiency and liquidity
(ii) an identification of the top five areas which should be investigated further
(iii) details of information that has not been provided, but if it were available would improve your analysis of Hardy's performance.

Hardy plc
Balance sheet as at 31 March 2010

	2008 £m	2009 £m	2010 £m
Non-current assets	106	123	132
Current assets			
Inventories	118	152	147
Trade receivables	53	70	80
Cash and cash equivalents	26	29	26
Total current assets	197	251	253
Total assets	303	374	385
Current liabilities			
Trade payables	26	38	38
Other payables	40	52	55
Total current liabilities	66	90	93
Non-current liabilities			
Debenture loan	38	69	69
Total non-current liabilities	38	69	69
Total liabilities	104	159	162
Net assets	199	215	223
Equity			
Share capital	50	50	50
Retained earnings	149	165	173
Total equity	199	215	223

Hardy plc
Income statement for the year ended 31 March 2010

	2008 £m	2009 £m	2010 £m
Revenue	420	491	456
Cost of sales	(277)	(323)	(295)
Gross profit	143	168	161
Distribution costs and administrative expenses	(93)	(107)	(109)
Operating profit	50	61	52
Net interest	(3)	(7)	(9)
Profit before tax	47	54	43
Income tax expense	(22)	(26)	(23)
Profit for the year	25	28	20
Dividends	(12)	(12)	(12)
Retained profit for the year	13	16	8

E7.9   *Time allowed – 120 minutes*

Locate the website for HSBC Bank plc on the Internet. Use their most recent annual report and accounts to prepare a report that evaluates their financial performance, financial position and future prospects. Your report should include calculations of the appropriate ratios for comparison with the previous year.

E7.10   *Time allowed – 120 minutes*

Locate the websites for Tesco plc and Morrisons plc on the Internet. Use their most recent annual report and accounts to prepare a report that evaluates and compares their financial performance and financial position. Your report should include calculations of the appropriate ratios for comparing the two groups, and an explanation of their differences and similarities.

Case Study II
DESIGN PIERRE LTD

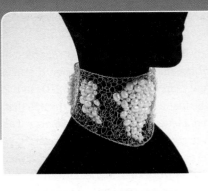

Design Pierre Ltd is a designer and manufacturer of gift and presentation packaging, aimed particularly at the mass market, via jewellery shops, large retail chains and mail order companies. The company was founded many years ago by Pierre Girault, who was the managing director and was involved in the sales and marketing side of the business.

Towards the end of 2007 when Pierre was due to retire, Marie Girault, Pierre's daughter, joined the company as managing director, along with Erik Olsen as marketing director. Marie had worked as a senior manager with Saturn Gifts plc, a large UK designer and manufacturer of giftware, of which Erik had been a director. Marie and Erik capitalised on their experience with Saturn to present some very innovative ideas for developing a new product range for Design Pierre. However, Marie and Erik's ideas for expanding the business required additional investment, the majority of which was spent during the financial year just ended on 31 March 2010.

The share capital of Design Pierre Ltd, 800,000 £1 ordinary shares, had all been owned by Pierre himself. On retirement he decided to transfer 390,000 of his shares to his daughter Marie, and to sell 390,000 shares to Erik Olsen (to help fund his pension). Pierre gifted his remaining 20,000 shares to Nigel Finch, who was the production director and had given the company many years of loyal service. Although Marie had received her share in the company from her father, Erik had used a large part of his personal savings and had taken out an additional mortgage on his house to help finance his investment in the business. This was, of course, paid to Pierre Girault and did not provide any additional capital for the business.

In order to raise additional share capital, Marie and Erik asked Pierre's advice about friends, family and business contacts who may be approached. Pierre suggested approaching a venture capital company, Fishtale Ltd, which was run by a friend of his, Paul Fish. Fishtale already had a wide portfolio of investments in dot.com and service businesses, and Paul was interested in investing in this type of growing manufacturing business. He had known Pierre and the Girault family for many years, and was confident that Marie and Erik would make a success of the new ideas that they presented for the business. Additional capital was therefore provided from the issue of 800,000 new £1 shares at par to Fishtale Ltd, to become the largest shareholder of Design Pierre Ltd. Design Pierre Ltd also had a bank loan, which it increased during 2009/10, and had a bank overdraft facility.

The directors of the newly structured Design Pierre Ltd, and its shareholders were as follows:

Marie Girault	Managing director	390,000 shares
Erik Olsen	Marketing director	390,000 shares
Nigel Finch	Production director	20,000 shares
Paul Fish	Non-executive director	800,000 shares
Fishtale Ltd		

As a non-executive director of Design Pierre Ltd, Paul Fish attended the annual general meetings, and review meetings that were held every six months. He didn't have any involvement with the day-to-day management of the business.

The new range at Design Pierre did quite well and the company also began to export in a small way to the USA and Canada. Marie and Erik were pleased by the way in which the sales of the business had grown, and in the growth of their customer base. They had just received a large order from Norbox, a Swedish company, which was regarded as an important inroad into the Scandinavian market. If Norbox became a regular customer, the sales of the company were likely to increase rapidly over the next few years and would establish Design Pierre as a major player in the market.

In the first week of May 2010, the day that Design Pierre received the order from Norbox, Marie also received a letter from the bank manager. The bank manager requested that Design Pierre Ltd immediately and considerably reduce its overdraft, which he felt was running at a level which exposed the bank and the company to a higher level of risk then he was prepared to accept. Marie Girault was very angry and felt very frustrated. Marie, Erik and Nigel agreed that since they had just had such a good year's trading and the current year looked even better, the reduction in the overdraft facility was going to seriously jeopardise their ability to meet the commitments they had to supply their customers.

When they joined the company, Marie and Erik decided that Design Pierre, which had always been production led, would become a design- and marketing-led business. Therefore, a great deal of the strategic planning was concerned with integrating the product design and development with the sales and marketing operations of the business. Over the past three years Marie and Erik had invested in employing and training a young design team to help continue to develop the Design Pierre brand. The marketing team led by Erik had ensured that the enthusiasm of their key customers was converted into new firm orders, and that new orders were received from customers like Norbox. The order book grew until it had now reached the highest level ever for the company.

In addition to his role as production director, Nigel had always tended to look after the books and any financial matters. Nigel wasn't an accountant and he hadn't had any formal financial training. But, as he said, he had a small and experienced accounts team who dealt with the day-to-day transactions; if ever there had been a problem, they would ask Design Pierre's auditors for some advice.

As soon as she received the letter from the bank, Marie called the bank manager to try and persuade him to continue to support the overdraft facility at the current level, but with no success. Marie also convened an urgent meeting of the directors, including Paul Fish, to talk about the letter and the draft accounts of the business for the year ended 31 March 2010. The letter from the bank was distributed to all the directors before the meeting.

Erik Olsen was very worried about his investment in the company. He admitted that his accounting knowledge was fairly limited. He thought that the company was doing very well, and said that the draft accounts for the year to 31 March 2010 seemed to confirm their success. Profit before tax was more than double the profit for 2009. He couldn't understand why the cash flow was so bad. He appreciated that they had spent a great deal of money on the additional plant and equipment, but they had already had a bank loan to help with that. He thought that the cash situation should really be even better than the profit because the expenses included £1.5m for depreciation, which doesn't involve any cash at all.

Marie Girault still appeared very angry at the lack of support being given by the bank. She outlined the impact that the overdraft reduction would have on their ability to meet their commitments over the next year. She said that the bank's demand to cut their overdraft by 50% over the next three months put them in an impossible position with regard to being able to meet customer orders. Design Pierre Ltd couldn't find an alternative source of such a large amount of money in such a short time.

Erik, Marie and Nigel had, before the meeting, hoped that Paul Fish would be prepared to help out by purchasing further additional new shares in the company or by making a loan to the company. However, it was soon made clear by Paul that further investment was not a possible option. Fishtale Ltd had made a couple of new investments over the past few months and so did not have the money to invest further in Design Pierre. As a venture capitalist, Fishtale had actually been discussing the possible exit from Design Pierre by selling and trying to realise a profit on the shares. Finding a prospective buyer for their shares, or floating Design Pierre on the alternative investment market (AIM), did not currently appear to be a realistic option.

Paul Fish had been so much involved in running his own business, Fishtale Ltd, that he had neglected to monitor the financial position of Design Pierre Ltd as often and as closely as he should have done. At the directors' meeting he realised that he should have been much more attentive and there was now a possibility that Design Pierre would not provide the returns his company expected, unless things could be drastically improved.

The accounts of Design Pierre Ltd for the past two years are shown below:

Income statement for the year ended 31 March

	2009	2010
	£000	£000
Revenue	7,000	11,500
Cost of sales	3,700	5,800
Gross profit	3,300	5,700
Operating expenses	2,200	3,100
Operating profit	1,100	2,600
Interest paid	200	500
Profit before tax	900	2,100
Income tax expense	200	400
Profit for the year	700	1,700
Dividend	200	300
Retained earnings for the year	500	1,400
Retained earnings brought forward	1,100	1,600
Retained earnings carried forward	1,600	3,000

Balance sheet as at 31 March

	2009	2010
	£000	£000
Non-current assets	4,300	7,200
Current assets		
Inventories	1,200	2,900
Trade receivables	800	1,900
Other receivables	100	200
Cash and cash equivalents	100	–
Total current assets	2,200	5,000
Total assets	6,500	12,200
Current liabilities		
Borrowings and finance leases	–	2,100
Trade payables	600	1,300
Other payables	100	200
Income tax payable	200	400
Dividends payable	200	300
Total current liabilities	1,100	4,300
Non-current liabilities		
Loan	2,200	3,300
Total liabilities	3,300	7,600
Net assets	3,200	4,600

Equity

Ordinary shares (£1)	1,600	1,600
Retained earnings	1,600	3,000
Total equity	3,200	4,600

The directors of Design Pierre Ltd were unable to agree on a way of dealing with the financial problem faced by the company. Marie thought it best that she continue to try and negotiate with the bank manager, and believed that she could change the bank manager's mind if she:

- presented him with the accounts for 31 March 2010, which showed such good results, and
- made him fully aware of the implications of the reduction in the overdraft facility on the future of Design Pierre.

However, Erik and Nigel said that they were aware that Design Pierre Ltd had exceeded its agreed overdraft limit a few times over the past two years and so they were not confident that Marie could persuade the bank to change its mind. They suggested that they should try and find another investor prepared to provide additional funds for the business, to keep the business going. They really believed that the year-end accounts showed how successful Design Pierre had been over the past two years and that their track record was sufficient to attract a potential new investor in the business. Paul didn't agree. He felt that this would not be a practical solution. More importantly, Fishtale didn't want to have another large shareholder in the company because it would dilute its shareholding, and also reduce its influence over the future direction of the business. However, Paul agreed that immediate and radical action was necessary to be taken by the company.

After hours of argument and discussion, it became apparent that the problem would not be resolved at the meeting. Therefore, it was agreed by all present that expertise from outside the company should be sought to help the company find an acceptable and viable solution to the problem. The directors decided to approach Lucis Consulting, which specialises in helping businesses with financial problems, and to ask them to produce a plan of action for their consideration.

Required

As a member of the Lucis team, prepare a report for the board of directors of Design Pierre Ltd which analyses the problems faced by the company and which sets out a detailed plan of action for dealing with its financing problem.

Your report should be supported by the appropriate analyses, and a full statement of cash flows for the year ended 31 March 2010.

8

Annual report and accounts

Contents

Chairman's Statement

Sir John Banham
Chairman

I am delighted to report, in what will be my final statement to you as Chairman, that Johnson Matthey performed very well in 2010/11 benefiting from good demand for its products, strong precious metal prices and the actions that the management team took during the recession to reduce costs and improve the efficiency of your company's operations.

As I outlined in my statement to you last year, the board, the executive management team and employees at all levels seized the opportunities presented by the economic crisis. As a result Johnson Matthey not only performed relatively well during the downturn but returned to strong growth in 2010/11, with underlying earnings per share up 38% to a record 119.0 pence. This represents a compound annual growth rate of more than 10% over the five years that I have been Chairman, despite the impact of the recession in 2008 and 2009.

Our strategy has served us well and I have no doubt that this year's strong performance results from the fundamental strength of your company and the actions that we have taken over several years. Johnson Matthey has stuck to its global organic growth strategy, underpinned by heavy and increasing investment in research and development. This has been complemented by a number of successful bolt-on acquisitions that have expanded the group's product portfolio and the range of industries and markets that it serves and have made an important contribution to our growth.

Despite the recession, we have continued to invest in new, highly efficient manufacturing capacity, for example completing our emission control catalyst manufacturing plants in Macedonia, to supply both light and heavy duty catalysts to the European market, and Smithfield, Pennsylvania, to serve the North American heavy duty diesel market. As markets have recovered, we are now seeing the benefits of our investments in world class manufacturing facilities to meet the demand for our products around the world.

During the recession, the company took early and decisive action to reduce costs. However, this was not done at the expense of research and development, which provides the high technology products and manufacturing processes that enable us to maintain market leadership and underpins the future growth of our business. Rather than cutting our R&D investment we have continued to increase it. Over the next few years our R&D spend is targeted to rise from £109.8 million to around £135 million a year. As you will see in the Group Strategy section on pages 8 to 13, part of this additional investment is to generate major new business opportunities.

02

Sustainability 2017, our group wide programme to make Johnson Matthey more sustainable, is also playing an important role in the success of your company. It provides a focus for improving the performance of our operations, the development of new sustainable products and for investment in our people and culture around the world. As I have travelled around the company, I continue to be impressed by the commitment of Johnson Matthey's employees at all levels to Sustainability 2017. We have set some very challenging targets, for example to halve the key resources that we use per unit of output, but given the dedication of our people and the spirit of innovation that is evident throughout the group, I believe that our sustainability efforts will underpin future business growth. You can read a summary of progress towards our Sustainability 2017 goals on pages 45 to 55. Full details will be presented in the group's Sustainability Report which will be published on our website in July.

My term of office as Chairman of Johnson Matthey comes to an end at the close of this year's Annual General Meeting (AGM) in July. In January 2011 we announced the appointment of my successor, Tim Stevenson OBE, who joined the board as a non-executive director and Chairman Designate with effect from 29th March 2011. He will be standing for election at the AGM. Tim has had a most distinguished career and is a very experienced chairman; he is currently Chairman of The Morgan Crucible Company plc and was Chairman of Travis Perkins plc from November 2001 to May 2010. He is ideally qualified to chair the board through the next phase of your company's development and will continue its successful record of delivering superior value to shareholders.

In January the company also announced the appointment of Alan Ferguson as a non-executive director with effect from 13th January 2011. He was previously Chief Financial Officer and an executive director of Lonmin Plc and prior to that was Group Finance Director of The BOC Group. Alan has a wealth of international financial experience including in the precious metals and automotive industries and he is already making a strong contribution to the work of the board. Full biographical details of both Tim Stevenson and Alan Ferguson are shown on pages 56 and 57.

With effect from the close of this year's AGM, Alan Thomson and Robert Walvis will retire from the board, both of them having served as non-executive directors of Johnson Matthey for nine years. Since joining the board both Alan and Robert have made invaluable contributions to the strategic development and governance of the company. Alan Thomson has served as Chairman of the Audit Committee for eight years and has also been our Senior Independent Director for the last three years.

Robert Walvis has served as the Chairman of the company's Management Development and Remuneration Committee for the last three years. We are extremely fortunate to have had the benefit of their vast experience of both UK and international business and I would like to thank them for the valuable contributions that they have both made to the work of the board. On behalf of all of us at Johnson Matthey I would like to wish Alan and Robert all the very best for the future.

Following these retirements, Alan Ferguson will succeed Alan Thomson as Chairman of the Audit Committee and Michael Roney, who has been a non-executive director since June 2007, will be appointed the Senior Independent Director and will also take over chairmanship of the Management Development and Remuneration Committee.

It has always been my belief that the most important investment that a company makes is the one that it makes in its people. I have never ceased to be impressed by the enthusiasm, professionalism and dedication of Johnson Matthey's employees at all levels of the organisation. On your behalf I would like to thank all of them, around the world, for their contribution to the success of your company.

It has been a privilege to be Chairman of Johnson Matthey over the last five years. It is a great company with strong market and technology drivers, excellent people and a robust strategy that will ensure continued growth. Johnson Matthey is well positioned to grow in the next five years supported by strong positions in our core markets. The drivers for our business remain firmly in place and the group is committed to continue to invest in both infrastructure and R&D. The outlook beyond five years is also positive.

Sir John Banham
Chairman

REPORT OF THE DIRECTORS – BUSINESS REVIEW

Chief Executive's Statement

Neil Carson
Chief Executive

I am pleased to say that Johnson Matthey performed strongly in 2010/11, recovering throughout the year from the effects of the recession that impacted the first half of last year's results. All of the group's businesses performed well with sales excluding precious metals (sales) substantially ahead of last year. Underlying operating profit was also well up and 2010/11 marked a return to strong growth for the group.

Our Environmental Technologies Division performed well in the year. The division's Emission Control Technologies business benefited from good growth in light duty vehicle production around the world and the recovery in the proportion of diesel cars produced in Europe. Its heavy duty diesel (HDD) business recovered very well with robust sales throughout 2010/11 in Europe and strong growth in the United States in the second half as the truck market recovered. Our Process Technologies business performed well with good growth in its Ammonia, Methanol and Gas business. Intercat, Inc., which was acquired in November 2010, made a good contribution to sales in the final quarter and Davy Process Technology (DPT) had another strong year.

Precious Metal Products Division also achieved very good results. Its Services businesses benefited from robust precious metal prices throughout the year and its Manufacturing businesses saw strong demand across the wide range of industries that they serve.

Fine Chemicals Division performed well with good sales growth in its Active Pharmaceutical Ingredient (API) Manufacturing businesses. Its global Research Chemicals business also grew well in the year.

For the group as a whole, revenue was up 27% on last year at £10.0 billion and sales were 21% higher than last year at £2.3 billion. Underlying profit before tax was 36% up at £345.5 million. The group's underlying return on sales increased to 16.1% from 14.4% last year, benefiting from operational leverage as plant utilisation across the group increased as a result of the strong demand for our products and from the continued management actions that we have taken to reduce costs.

During the summer and autumn of 2010 we carried out a comprehensive review of the group's strategy for the next ten years.

As a result of this review process, the board agreed a ten year strategy to deliver superior growth in value for Johnson Matthey shareholders. Importantly, the key elements of our strategy remain unchanged: continued focus on leading edge catalysis, maintaining differentiation through technology, recognition that our strong position in platinum group metals remains an intrinsic part of the group and the maintenance of a primary focus on organic growth. However, following this strategy review, we are increasing our efforts to identify new opportunities underpinned by our core chemistry, recognising that Johnson Matthey's key attributes provide a focus for investment, placing increased emphasis on manufacturing excellence and focusing further on tackling the challenge of integrating Johnson Matthey's culture across our expanding global operations. Further details of the review process and of our group strategy are presented on pages 8 to 13.

Sustainability

Sustainability remains a key element of our strategy for future growth and we have continued to focus on sustainability efforts across our businesses this year. Our Sustainability 2017 Vision sets out our direction and aspirations in this area and includes challenging targets to support business growth. It is now just over three years since the launch of our vision and during the year we undertook a detailed review of our sustainability strategy. The review confirmed support throughout the company for Sustainability 2017 and highlighted several areas where we are now working to evolve the strategy, as detailed on page 48 of this annual report.

We have continued to realise considerable savings through our sustainability programme and maintain our focus on developing the next generation of products to enable our customers to improve their sustainability footprint and their competitiveness. Many of Johnson Matthey's products and technologies have a beneficial impact on the environment, human health and wellbeing and these products generated a major proportion of Johnson Matthey's profit this year. The sustainability benefit of our products is an important aspect of our sustainability strategy and work is underway to better assess the impact of our products in the market place.

Our employees continue to show great enthusiasm for Sustainability 2017 and there are a huge number of initiatives underway at sites around the world. Thanks to their efforts we have continued to make steady progress towards our Sustainability 2017 aspirations and remain committed to building a sustainable business for the future.

Outlook

At this time last year we commented on the short term uncertainties in our markets. This year confidence in our markets is more robust and after our strong performance in 2010/11, the group is expected to make further good progress in the current year.

Environmental Technologies Division is well placed for continued growth. For the year as a whole, Emission Control Technologies should benefit from higher global car production, particularly in Asia, but there may be a temporary hiatus in the first half of our year following the Japanese earthquake and its consequences on our customers' supply chain. This is however expected to reverse by the second half of 2011/12. The increasingly important North American HDD truck market has started 2011/12 well and is expected to continue to improve. In addition, the action commenced this year to reduce our autocatalyst manufacturing capacity in Europe will lower our costs. Higher rare earth prices will however adversely impact the business, particularly in the first half of the year. Process Technologies will benefit from a full year's contribution from the Intercat business. Furthermore, demand for its syngas catalysts and DPT's licensing services remains strong, particularly in China.

Precious Metal Products Division supplies products and services to a wide range of industries and therefore its performance is influenced by a number of different market drivers. The Manufacturing businesses have started the year well with good demand across our markets, particularly from the automotive, LED and glass sectors. In 2010/11 the division's Services businesses benefited from higher pgm and gold prices and while they have been quite volatile recently, they remain strong. Indeed, platinum, palladium and gold in the first two months of 2011/12 have averaged $1,795/oz, $756/oz and $1,493/oz respectively, approximately 7%, 47% and 27% higher than in the same period last year. The division delivered very strong growth in 2010/11 and with demand expected to remain robust this year, we expect it to show further growth in 2011/12.

We also expect that Fine Chemicals Division will continue to grow steadily in 2011/12 benefiting from increasing demand for our APIs, new product introductions and the additional capacity following the acquisition of the Conshohocken, USA plant in November 2010.

As we detailed in our presentation to analysts and investors in February 2011, the drivers that will provide superior earnings growth for the group in our existing markets are expected to remain strong for at least the next five years. Beyond that, we are confident that these markets will continue to deliver growth. As a technology company, being at the forefront of research and development is vital to satisfy our customers' needs and to exploit new market opportunities. We are increasing our investment in R&D in order to target new areas of future growth for our business. We are confident that the combination of our existing strengths and the investments that we are making now will position the group well for longer term growth.

Neil Carson
Chief Executive

Group Performance Review

Business Review

	Year to 31st March		
	2011	2010	%
	£ million	£ million	change
Revenue	**9,985**	7,839	+27
Sales excluding precious metals	**2,280**	1,886	+21
Operating profit	**281.2**	250.6	+12
Profit before tax	**260.6**	228.5	+14
Total earnings per share	**85.6p**	77.6p	+10
Underlying*:			
Operating profit	**366.2**	271.8	+35
Profit before tax	**345.5**	254.1	+36
Earnings per share	**119.0p**	86.4p	+38

* Before amortisation of acquired intangibles, major impairment and restructuring charges, profit or loss on disposal of businesses and, where relevant, related tax effects.

Sales

Revenue for the year ended 31st March 2011 was 27% up on last year at £10.0 billion driven by good sales activity and robust metal prices. The group's sales excluding precious metals (sales) were 21% higher than last year at £2.3 billion. Translated at constant exchange rates (last year's results translated at this year's average exchange rates), revenue for the year was 26% ahead and sales grew by 19%.

Operating Profit

For the group as a whole, underlying operating profit (before amortisation of acquired intangibles, major impairment and restructuring charges) was 35% higher than last year at £366.2 million, while underlying profit before tax was 36% up at £345.5 million. At constant exchange rates underlying

operating profit would have been 33% higher than last year. The group's underlying return on sales increased to 16.1% from 14.4% last year, benefiting from operational leverage as plant utilisation across the group increased as a result of the strong demand for our products and from continued management actions to reduce costs.

This year we have taken an impairment and restructuring charge of £71.8 million in respect of the closure of Environmental Technologies' autocatalyst manufacturing facility in Brussels, Belgium to reduce overcapacity in our European autocatalyst business and also of the closure of the Vertec business, which ceased operation on 31st March 2011. This charge has been excluded from underlying profit.

The performance of the individual businesses is explained in more detail on pages 19 to 31 in the Operations Review.

Sales Excluding Precious Metals by Division

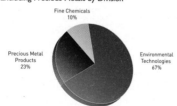

Sales Excluding Precious Metals by Destination

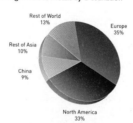

Divisional Sales Excluding Precious Metals

£ million

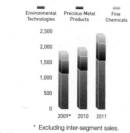

* Excluding inter-segment sales.

Divisional Underlying Operating Profit

£ million

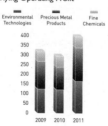

Group Key Performance Indicators

Business Review

→ Johnson Matthey uses a range of key performance indicators (KPIs) to monitor the group's performance over time in line with its strategy.

These principal KPIs, together with the group's performance against them in 2010/11, are described below:

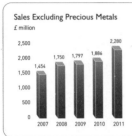

Sales Excluding Precious Metals
£ million

Monitoring sales provides a measure of the growth of the business. In measuring the growth of the group, we focus on sales excluding the value of precious metals because total revenue can be heavily distorted by year on year fluctuations in precious metal prices. Not only that, in many cases variations in the value of the precious metal contained within our products are passed directly on to our customers.

In 2010/11 sales excluding precious metals grew by 21% reflecting good growth in our markets as described in the Operations Review on pages 19 to 31.

Underlying Earnings per Share
Pence

Underlying earnings per share is the principal measure used by the board to assess the overall profitability of the group. The following items are excluded from underlying earnings because they can distort the trend in measuring results:

- Amortisation and impairment of intangible assets arising on acquisition of businesses (acquired intangibles).
- Major impairment or restructuring charges.
- Profit or loss on disposal of businesses.
- Tax on the above and major tax items arising from changes in legislation.

This year underlying earnings per share rose by 38% to 119.0 pence supported by a strong performance across the group. Further details are provided in the Operations Review on pages 19 to 31.

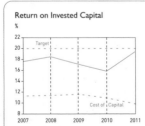

Return on Invested Capital
%

In a business as capital intensive as Johnson Matthey's, profitability alone is a poor measure of performance; it is possible to generate good operating margins but poor value for shareholders if assets are not used efficiently. Return on invested capital (ROIC) is therefore used alongside profit measures to ensure focus upon the efficient use of the group's assets. ROIC is defined for the group as underlying operating profit divided by average capital employed (equity plus net debt). ROIC for individual divisions is calculated using average segmental net assets as the denominator.

The group's ROIC increased from 15.8% to 19.4%, close to our target of 20%.

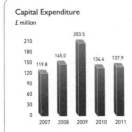

Capital Expenditure
£ million

To enable the group to continue to grow, Johnson Matthey invests significant amounts in maintaining and improving our existing plants and in adding new facilities to provide additional capacity where necessary. All new capital expenditure is subject to detailed review to ensure that its investment case passes internal hurdles. Annual capital expenditure is measured as the cost of property, plant and equipment and intangible assets purchased during the year. The ratio of capital expenditure to depreciation gives an indication of the relative level of investment.

In 2010/11 the group's capital expenditure was £137.9 million which represented 1.1 times depreciation (2009/10 1.2).

Gross Research and Development Expenditure

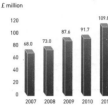

£ million

Johnson Matthey is fundamentally a technology company. To maintain our competitive position, we need to keep investing in research and development. Whilst absolute levels of research and development expenditure do not necessarily indicate how successful we are, that success rapidly feeds through to higher sales as lead times in our business can be quite short.

In 2010/11 the group increased its research and development expenditure by 20% to £109.8 million. Further details are given in the Research and Development section on pages 42 and 43.

Sustainability – Global Warming Potential

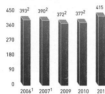

Tonnes CO_2 equivalent ('000)

¹ Calendar year.   ² Restated.

We measure our progress towards achieving carbon neutrality by looking at the group's total global warming potential (GWP). Total GWP is based on our direct and indirect energy usage and CO_2 equivalence which provide a strong platform for monitoring the impacts associated with energy use in our operations. We are working to broaden the scope of our GWP measurement to include all aspects of our business and to consider the beneficial impacts of our products and services.

This year the group's GWP increased from 377,000 to 415,000 tonnes CO_2 equivalent as a result of increased production and the addition of new manufacturing facilities. Further information on the group's GWP is given in the Sustainability section on pages 45, 46, 48, 54 and 55.

Safety – Annual Rate of >3 Day Accidents per 1,000 Employees

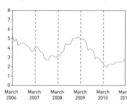

Johnson Matthey is a manufacturing business and a significant proportion of our employees work in production environments with chemicals and process machinery. Rigorous safety systems apply across all facilities and are essential if the group is to avoid accidents which could cause injury to people or damage to our property, both of which can impact the group's performance. We actively manage our safety performance through monitoring the incidence and causes of accidents that result in more than three days lost time.

The group's annual accident rate of greater than three day accidents increased slightly during the year to 2.88 per 1,000 employees. Actions taken to improve our safety performance are described in more detail in the Sustainability section on pages 53 to 55.

Occupational Health – Annual Incidence of Occupational Illness Cases per 1,000 Employees

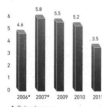

* Calendar year.

The health and wellbeing of our employees is a priority for Johnson Matthey and we are committed to minimising workplace related negative health effects. We manage our performance in this area by measuring the number of occupational illness cases arising as a result of exposure to workplace health hazards.

The annual incidence of occupational illness cases fell this year to 3.5 per 1,000 employees as a result of initiatives underway to promote employee wellbeing across the group. Further details are provided in the Sustainability section on pages 54 and 55.

Voluntary Employee Turnover

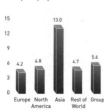

%

The success of Johnson Matthey is partly dependent upon the extent that we are able to attract and retain talented employees. This means that being an attractive employer is a prerequisite in a competitive environment. We monitor our success in retaining our staff using voluntary employee turnover statistics.

In 2010/11 the group's voluntary employee turnover increased very slightly to 5.6% from 5.4% in 2009/10. This remains low compared to industry standards.

Financial Review

Business Review

Robert MacLeod
Group Finance Director

Profit before Tax

Underlying profit before tax rose by 36% to £345.5 million. Profit before tax was 14% higher at £260.6 million. Items excluded from underlying operating profit were:

- an impairment and restructuring charge of £71.8 million in respect of the closure of ECT's manufacturing facility in Brussels and the Vertec business. On 31st January 2011 it was announced that ECT had entered into statutory formal consultation with the employees at its Brussels facility regarding the closure of its manufacturing plant there. On 31st March 2011, the group formally closed the Vertec business on the Haverton manufacturing site in Billingham, UK; and

- amortisation of acquired intangibles of £13.2 million. This was £3.3 million higher than 2009/10 mainly following the acquisition of Intercat.

Underlying Profit Reconciliation

	Year to 31st March 2011			Year to 31st March 2010		
	Profit before tax £ million	Income tax expense £ million	Profit from continuing operations £ million	Profit before tax £ million	Income tax expense £ million	Profit from continuing operations £ million
Underlying basis	**345.5**	**(91.7)**	**253.8**	254.1	(71.2)	182.9
Amortisation of acquired intangibles	**(13.2)**	**4.1**	**(9.1)**	(9.9)	2.7	(7.2)
Major impairment / restructuring:						
Closure of autocatalyst facility in Brussels	**(57.0)**	**8.1**	**(48.9)**	–	–	–
Closure of Vertec business	**(14.8)**	**3.5**	**(11.3)**	–	–	–
Impairment loss in Fine Chemicals facility in USA	**–**	**–**	**–**	(11.3)	4.2	(7.1)
Dissolution of associate	**0.1**	**–**	**0.1**	(4.4)	–	(4.4)
Reported basis	**260.6**	**(76.0)**	**184.6**	228.5	(64.3)	164.2

Exchange Rates

The main impact of exchange rate movements on the group's results comes from the translation of foreign subsidiaries' profits into sterling as the group does not hedge the impact on the income statement or balance sheet of these translation effects. The group's underlying operating profit at constant exchange rates is shown in the table below:

Underlying Operating Profit

| | Year to 31st March | | | 2010 at 2011 exchange | |
	2011 £ million	2010 £ million	change %	rates £ million	change %
Environmental Technologies	164.7	120.9	+36	123.4	+33
Precious Metal Products	172.9	116.7	+48	117.5	+47
Fine Chemicals	56.2	55.8	+1	56.5	-1
Corporate	(27.6)	(21.6)		(21.5)	
Total group	**366.2**	271.8	+35	275.9	+33

During the year, sterling weakened against both the US dollar and the Chinese renminbi and this increased reported group underlying operating profit for the year by £1.8 million and £1.0 million respectively. Sterling, on the other hand, strengthened against the euro and this decreased reported group underlying operating profit by £1.1 million.

Sterling also weakened in the year against the South African rand. However, the catalysts manufactured by our South African business are ultimately for export and the impact of movements in the rand on margins more than offsets the translational effect.

Overall, excluding the South African rand, exchange translation increased the group's underlying operating profit by £4.1 million compared with 2009/10.

Of the group's underlying operating profit that is denominated in overseas currencies the average exchange rates during 2010/11 were:

	Share of 2010/11 non-sterling denominated underlying operating profit	Average exchange rate 2010/11	2009/10
US dollar	40%	1.555	1.595
Euro	26%	1.176	1.129
Chinese renminbi	12%	10.43	10.89
South African rand	6%	11.18	12.46

Going forward, each one cent change in the average US dollar exchange rate and each one cent change in the euro exchange rate have approximately a £0.6 million and £0.5 million effect respectively on underlying operating profit in a full year.

Return on Sales

The group's return on sales benefited from higher returns generated by Environmental Technologies and Precious Metal Products Divisions. However, higher corporate costs and lower returns from Fine Chemicals Division resulted in a net increase in the group's return on sales of 1.7% to 16.1%.

Return on Sales

| | Sales excluding precious metals | | Return on sales [1] | |
	2011 £ million	2010 £ million	2011 %	2010 %
Environmental Technologies	1,566	1,252	10.5	9.7
Precious Metal Products	541	454	31.9	25.7
Fine Chemicals	245	221	22.9	25.3
Less inter-segment sales	(72)	(41)	n/a	n/a
Total group	**2,280**	1,886	16.1	14.4

[1] Underlying operating profit divided by sales excluding precious metals.

Return on Invested Capital

The group's return on invested capital (ROIC) improved significantly from 15.8% to 19.4%. Underlying operating profit was £94.4 million higher than last year at £366.2 million and average invested capital was £168 million higher at £1,885 million. At 19.4%, the group's ROIC is well ahead of our pre-tax cost of capital, which we estimate to be 9.7%.

Our target is to achieve a group ROIC above 20% on a pre-tax basis. This year we made very good progress towards that target as the group's profitability increased substantially. Looking forward, the outlook for the group remains encouraging and, as we have already invested in the plants necessary to meet much of the expected demand across our markets, we are well placed to achieve our ROIC target as plant utilisation increases.

Return on Invested Capital

| | Average invested capital [1] | | Return on invested capital [2] | |
	2011 £ million	2010 £ million	2011 %	2010 %
Environmental Technologies	1,435	1,281	11.5	9.4
Precious Metal Products	309	249	55.9	46.8
Fine Chemicals	409	417	13.7	13.4
Corporate / other	(268)	(230)	n/a	n/a
Total group	**1,885**	1,717	19.4	15.8

[1] Average of opening and closing segmental net assets as shown in note 1 on the accounts on pages 86 and 87. For the group, the average of opening and closing equity plus net debt.

[2] Underlying operating profit divided by average invested capital.

Interest

The group's net finance costs increased by £1.3 million to £20.7 million as a result of higher average borrowings in the year.

Approximately 54% of the group's net debt at 31st March 2011 has fixed interest rates averaging approximately 5.1%.

REPORT OF THE DIRECTORS – BUSINESS REVIEW

Financial Review

Business Review

Taxation

The group's total tax charge for the year was £76.0 million, a tax rate of 29.2% on profit before tax (2009/10 28.1%).

The effective tax rate on underlying profit before tax was 26.5% (2009/10 28.0%). This reduction was primarily due to the continued increase in the share of profit from lower tax jurisdictions.

Earnings per Share

Underlying earnings per share (before amortisation of acquired intangibles, major impairment and restructuring charges, profit or loss on disposal of businesses and related tax effects) increased by 32.6 pence, or 38%, to 119.0 pence. Total earnings per share were 85.6 pence, 10% up on last year.

Dividend

In view of the group's strong performance in 2010/11 the board is recommending an 18% increase in the total dividend for the year. This comprises of a final dividend of 33.5 pence which, together with the interim dividend of 12.5 pence, gives a total dividend for the year of 46.0 pence (2009/10 39.0 pence). At this level, the dividend would be covered by underlying earnings per share 2.6 times, up from 2.2 times last year. Subject to approval by shareholders, the final dividend will be paid on 2nd August 2011 to ordinary shareholders on the register as at 10th June 2011, with an ex-dividend date of 8th June 2011.

Pensions

At 31st March 2011 the group's principal defined benefit pension scheme in the UK was in deficit by £60.6 million (94% funded) on an IFRS basis compared with a deficit of £156.9 million at 31st March 2010. The £96.3 million decrease in the deficit was principally due to an increase in the market value of the scheme's assets. Worldwide, the group has other similar defined benefit pension scheme arrangements, some of which are in deficit (total deficit £35.0 million) and others in surplus (total surplus £3.8 million).

Worldwide, including provisions for the group's post-retirement healthcare schemes, the group had a net deficit of £130.4 million on employee benefit obligations at 31st March 2011 (2010 £245.7 million).

In 2010/11 the company commenced deficit funding contributions to the UK scheme under a ten year recovery plan agreed last year with the Trustees. During the year the company made deficit funding payments of £28.1 million to the scheme, which included an accelerated payment of £5.0 million in respect of contributions planned for 2011/12 in order to take advantage of certain tax benefits. The group's normal ongoing contribution to the UK scheme in 2010/11 was £22.0 million (2009/10 £23.1 million), making total cash contributions to the scheme in the year of £50.1 million.

In July 2010, the UK government announced a change in the measure of inflation used to determine statutory minimum increases to pensions from RPI to CPI. The effect of this change on the benefits of deferred pensioners, the only group impacted, is to reduce the UK scheme's liabilities as at 31st March 2011 by approximately £13 million before tax. This change has been accounted for within equity.

Cash Flow

During the year ended 31st March 2011 net cash flow from operating activities was £123.9 million (2009/10 £275.7 million). Demand for our products and the price of precious metals continued to grow and as a result the group's working capital requirement increased substantially. Working capital, excluding the element that relates to precious metals, increased by £67.4 million. Working capital days at 31st March 2011 increased to 60 days from 57 days last year. Higher precious metal prices and increased activity also increased working capital by £215.9 million.

During the year our capital expenditure was £137.9 million (of which £137.4 million was cash spent in the year) which equated to 1.1 times depreciation. In the year, £90.1 million, or 65% of the total, was incurred by Environmental Technologies Division with the principal investments being to increase autocatalyst manufacturing capacity and to add testing facilities in Shanghai, China and to add additional capacity at our manufacturing plants in the UK and India to make process catalysts for our Ammonia, Methanol and Gas business. In Precious Metal Products Division, the largest investment is the construction of a new pgm catalyst plant in Shanghai, China, to support the anticipated future growth in the Chinese pharmaceutical market.

We anticipate that capital expenditure will average approximately 1.3 times depreciation for the next few years. However, we retain the capacity to invest in further growth opportunities as they arise.

The group's free cash flow was an outflow of £25.5 million (2009/10 an inflow of £123.7 million).

Capital Structure

In the year ended 31st March 2011 net debt rose by £166.0 million to £639.4 million and the group's EBITDA (on an underlying basis) rose by 28% from £382.7 million to £489.4 million. Net debt / EBITDA for the year was 1.3 times but if the post tax pension deficit of £70.0 million is included within net debt, the ratio would increase to 1.4 times. Interest cover (underlying operating profit / net finance costs) was 17.7 times (2009/10 14.0 times).

Borrowings	31st March 2011		31st March 2010	
	£ million	%	£ million	%
Five to ten years	181.0	24	99.6	15
Two to five years	330.4	44	383.3	59
One to two years	40.6	5	56.1	9
Within one year	206.3	27	113.5	17
Gross borrowings (net of swaps)	758.3	100	652.5	100
Less: cash and deposits	118.9		179.1	
Net debt	639.4		473.4	

Treasury Policies

Financial Risk Management and Treasury Policies

The group uses financial instruments, in particular forward currency contracts and currency swaps, to manage the financial risks associated with its underlying business activities and the financing of those activities. The group does not undertake any speculative trading activity in financial instruments. Our treasury department is run as a service centre rather than a profit centre.

Interest Rate Risk

At 31st March 2011 the group had net borrowings of £639.4 million. Some 54% of this debt was at fixed rates with an average interest rate of 5.1%. The remaining 46% of the group's net borrowings was funded on a floating rate basis. A 1% change in all interest rates would have a 0.9% impact on underlying profit before tax. This is within the range the board regards as acceptable.

Foreign Currency Risk

Johnson Matthey's operations are located in over 30 countries, providing global coverage. The significant amount of its profit is earned outside the UK. In order to protect the group's sterling balance sheet and reduce cash flow risk the group has financed most of its investment in the USA and Europe by borrowing US dollars and euros respectively. Although much of this funding is obtained by directly borrowing the relevant currency, a part is achieved through currency swaps which can be more efficient and reduce costs. To a lesser extent the group has also financed a portion of its investment in China, Japan and South Africa using currency borrowings and swaps. The group uses forward exchange contracts to hedge foreign exchange exposures arising on forecast receipts and payments in foreign currencies. Currency options are occasionally used to hedge foreign exchange exposures, usually in a bid situation. Details of the contracts outstanding on 31st March 2011 are shown on pages 110 and 111.

Precious Metal Prices

Fluctuations in precious metal prices can have a significant impact on Johnson Matthey's financial results. Our policy for all manufacturing businesses is to limit this exposure by hedging against future price changes where such hedging can be done at acceptable cost. The group does not take material exposures on metal trading.

All the group's stocks of gold and silver are fully hedged by leasing or forward sales. Currently the majority of the group's platinum stocks are unhedged because of the lack of liquidity in the platinum market.

Liquidity and Going Concern

The group's policy on funding capacity is to ensure that we always have sufficient long term funding and committed bank facilities in place to meet foreseeable peak borrowing requirements. At 31st March 2011 the group had cash and deposits of £118.9 million and £169.7 million of undrawn committed bank facilities available to meet future funding requirements. The group also has a number of uncommitted facilities, including overdrafts and metal lease lines, at its disposal.

Gross borrowings (net of related swaps) of £758.3 million at 31st March 2011 included £554.6 million of debt arranged under long term bond issues and long term funding from the European Investment Bank (EIB). Of this, only £5.3 million falls due to be repaid in the 15 months to 30th June 2012 (the going concern period). The group's committed bank facilities have a range of maturities with £141.2 million expiring after 30th June 2012. The maturity dates of the group's debt and borrowing facilities are illustrated in the table on page 36 and the chart below.

Maturity Profile of Debt Facilities
At 31st March 2011 exchange rates
£ million

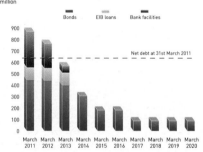

The directors have assessed the future funding requirements of the group and the company and compared it to the level of long term debt and committed bank facilities for the 15 months from the balance sheet date. The assessment included a sensitivity analysis on the key factors which could affect future cash flow and funding requirements. Having undertaken this work the directors are of the opinion that the group has adequate resources to fund its operations for the foreseeable future and so determine that it is appropriate to prepare the accounts on a going concern basis.

Johnson Matthey
Annual Report & Accounts 2011

REPORT OF THE DIRECTORS - BUSINESS REVIEW

Risks and Uncertainties

Business Review

The effective identification and management of risks and opportunities across the group is necessary to ensure the delivery of the group's strategic objectives. The group's approach to risk management is aimed at the early identification of key risks and the taking of action to remove or reduce the likelihood of those risks occurring and their effect.

The board has overall responsibility for ensuring that risk is effectively managed across the group. However, the board has delegated to the Audit Committee the responsibility for reviewing the effectiveness of the group's system of internal control and procedures for the identification, assessment, management and reporting of risk.

Risk Description	Description	Impact
STRATEGIC		
Failure to identify new business opportunities	The group's existing activities are well placed to deliver good growth over the coming years. New business areas could help to sustain the group's growth beyond that period.	Failure to identify new business areas may impact the ability of the group to continue to grow in the long term.
Inability to deliver anticipated benefits from acquisitions	The group's strategy is based upon organic growth. However, acquisitions may help to accelerate the achievement of strategic goals. The realisation of anticipated benefits depends upon the performance of acquired businesses after acquisition and their successful integration into the group.	A successful acquisition requires significant management attention on its integration. This diversion of management could adversely impact the rest of the business. In addition, an unsuccessful integration of the acquired business could result in the failure to realise the expected benefits and hence impact the group's results.
Changes to future environmental legislation	Approximately 50% of the group's revenue is driven by environmental legislation, particularly legislation over emissions from light and heavy duty vehicles. Further tightening of global emissions legislation generally requires improved technological solutions and the extension of emissions legislation to new applications can create opportunities for the group.	A curtailment in environmental legislation around the world could limit the group's growth potential and undermine profit margins.
Technological change	Johnson Matthey operates in highly competitive markets in which technology is a key to success. Constant product innovation is critical to maintain competitive advantage.	Failure to keep up with changes in the market place could result in a lack of competitive products and erosion of margins and / or loss of market share.
MARKET		
Global political and economic conditions	The global nature of the group's business exposes it to risk arising from economic, political and legislative change in the countries in which we operate.	A sustained period of economic weakness in our markets could have a material adverse effect upon the group's results. The group has no influence upon changes in inflation, interest rates or other economic factors affecting its business. In addition, the possibility of political unrest and legal or regulatory changes also exist in countries in which the group operates.
Commercial relationships	The group has well established long term relationships with a number of customers and suppliers. Maintaining good relationships with customers and suppliers enables the group to enhance the quality of service to its customers.	The group has high market shares in many of the markets in which it operates. The deterioration in the relationship with, or ultimately the loss of, a key customer or supplier could have a material impact on the group's results.

The group has in place a process for the continuous review of its risks. As part of that process, each business reviews its risks and its mitigation strategies. Each risk is allocated an owner who has the authority and responsibility for assessing, monitoring and managing it. The most significant risks identified are then collated into a Group Risk Register. The Group Risk Register is reviewed by the Chief Executive's Committee. Each individual risk is considered and the status and progression of mitigation plans are monitored. The Group Risk Register is reviewed by the board twice a year.

The table below sets out what the board believes to be the principal risks and uncertainties facing the group, the mitigating actions for each, and an update on any change in the profile of each risk during the course of 2010/11.

Mitigation	Changes since 2010 Annual Report
• Each business prepares a ten year strategic plan to review demand in existing markets and potential new opportunities. • The group continues to invest in research for new products and technologies. • Following the ten year strategy review, a new team has been established to review larger scale potential opportunities.	The group's investment in R&D has increased during the year by £18.1 million to £109.8 million. The new team has been established with the remit of identifying new business areas with significant long term growth potential that are consistent with the group's existing core competencies.
• The group has clearly defined criteria for suitable acquisition targets and substantial due diligence is carried out before any acquisition is made. • A dedicated team is appointed to manage the integration process and regular monitoring of the performance of newly acquired businesses is carried out.	The only significant acquisition made during the year was the purchase of Intercat, Inc. in November 2010. This has strengthened the group's position in the petroleum refining catalyst market and has a clear fit with our Process Technologies business. The integration is going well but it is too early to assess whether the business will realise the anticipated benefits.
• The group maintains a diverse product portfolio. • Forthcoming changes in emissions regulations are well understood and our products are designed to meet these increased requirements. • Profit margins can be maintained with ongoing improvements in technology to reduce the cost and improve the effectiveness of our products. • Regular reviews are undertaken to monitor areas of new potential legislation.	There has been no material change in emissions regulations in any of the group's major markets.
• The group continues to invest in its products through research and development. • There is constant innovation and development in cooperation with our key customers. • The group invests in its people to ensure that it maintains a high level of relevant scientific expertise.	There has been no major change in the risk profile during the year.
• The group maintains a balanced portfolio of businesses to reduce the impact of a change to any one market. • Management monitors the performance of our businesses across the world at both business and group level.	The group's strong performance this year reflects the continuing recovery of its businesses since the recession in the group's developed markets. The political unrest in the Middle East could disrupt our Process Technologies businesses. There has, however, been no material impact in the current year and any potential long term impact is still unknown.
• Some of the group's key relationships are supported by long term contracts, notably the group's relationship with Anglo Platinum. • A broad customer base is maintained to prevent the group from becoming unduly dependent on any single customer. • Industry developments and market shares are constantly monitored. • We actively manage our customer relationships at all levels to ensure a high quality of service.	No significant changes have arisen in this risk.

REPORT OF THE DIRECTORS – BUSINESS REVIEW

Risks and Uncertainties

Business Review

Risk Description	Description	Impact
FINANCIAL		
Movements in raw material prices	The group uses a variety of raw materials, including precious metals, in its products. In some circumstances, in the short term it may not be possible to pass on higher raw material prices to our customers. In addition, higher prices that are passed on to our customers could result in substitution or replacement of our products with cheaper alternatives.	Raw material prices can fluctuate significantly and have an impact on Johnson Matthey's results.
Pension scheme funding	The group operates a number of defined benefit pension schemes. In some cases, the schemes' actuaries have estimated that actuarial deficits exist and in those cases the group has agreed deficit recovery plans.	Actuarial deficits could be adversely affected by changes in interest rates, the market values of investments, as well as inflation and increasing longevity of the schemes' members. A further increase in actuarial deficits could result in increased costs to meet the pension schemes' liabilities.
OPERATIONAL		
Changes to health, safety, environment and other regulations and standards	In common with similar manufacturing companies, the group operates in an environment that is subject to numerous health, safety and environmental laws, regulations and standards.	Changes made to applicable laws, regulations or standards could adversely impact the group's manufacturing capability or indeed, the marketability of our products.
Availability of raw materials	The group uses many raw materials within its manufacturing processes. Several raw materials are available from only a limited number of countries and / or suppliers.	Disruption to the supply of raw materials, most notably platinum group metals, rare earths or narcotic raw materials, could adversely affect the group's profit. This may be due to increased prices or because our ability to manufacture and supply product to customers may be impacted.
Recruitment and retention of high quality staff	The group relies upon its ability to recruit, train and develop employees around the world with the necessary range of skills and experience to meet its stated objectives.	The lack of an appropriately skilled workforce could adversely impact the group's ability to perform in line with expectations.
Security	On any given day the group has significant quantities of high value precious metals or highly regulated substances on site and in transit, the security of which is critical.	The value of any precious metal process losses could be material to the group and any loss of a highly regulated substance could result in the removal of our licence to operate. In addition, in both cases there remains the possibility of theft or fraud.
Intellectual property	The group operates in markets in which the generation and application of technology and know how can give competitive advantage. The protection of that intellectual property allows that advantage to be maintained. Careful monitoring of competitors' intellectual property is required to ensure that breaches of their rights are not made by the group.	Failure to establish the group's intellectual property rights or to identify third parties' intellectual property rights could undermine the group's competitive advantage. Alternatively, not noting the expiration of patents held by third parties could mean the loss of potential business opportunities.

Mitigation	Changes since 2010 Annual Report
• The cost of precious metals that are used as raw materials in the group's products is generally passed directly on to customers and any price exposure is hedged. • Innovation that allows ongoing thrifting of precious metals in our products limits the impact of higher prices on our customers.	The most significant change since last year concerns rare earth materials. Supply constraints have resulted in price rises for these commodities, which have exposed the group to reduced margins on some products although these were not material to the group's results. Going forward, the group is reviewing its supply arrangements with customers to identify the most cost effective solutions for both them and Johnson Matthey.
• The performance of the group's pension schemes are regularly reviewed by both the company and the trustees of the schemes, taking actuarial and investment advice as applicable. • Where possible, appropriate pension scheme assets are held to match movements in the schemes' liabilities.	The deficit on the group's principal defined benefit pension scheme in the UK was £60.6 million in 2010/11, compared to £156.9 million last year.
• The group carries out regular internal reviews to ensure compliance with group policies and applicable laws, regulations and standards. • Changes in legislation are carefully monitored and if required, the composition of our products is amended to comply with latest legislation.	The registration deadline for REACH phase I came into effect from 1st December 2010 and the group materially met the requirements for its qualifying products. The group is also reviewing its products containing vanadium, primarily in its Colour Technologies business, to identify potential alternatives in the event of any tightening of regulations in this area.
• Although most of the world's platinum is mined in South Africa, the group has access to world markets for platinum and other precious metals and is not dependent on any one source for obtaining supplies. • Appropriate sourcing arrangements are in place for other key raw materials to ensure that the group is not dependent on any one supplier. • Where possible the group enters into long term supply arrangements to limit the exposure to significant movements in raw material prices.	As mentioned above, the supply of rare earth materials has been constrained during the year although this has only had a price impact on the group and has not affected our ability to manufacture. No other material changes to raw material supply have arisen.
• The group has a targeted graduate recruitment programme. • Global training and management development processes are in place. • Regular reviews of management succession plans are carried out. • Global remuneration policies are in place to ensure appropriate rewards to motivate and retain staff.	The group has a low level of voluntary employee turnover. A triennial review of executive remuneration has recently been completed to ensure that our executive remuneration packages are competitive. Global graduate recruitment processes are being reviewed in 2011/12.
• The group has highly developed security, assay and other process controls. • Annual security audits are carried out across the group. • Insurance cover is maintained for losses from theft or fraud.	There has been no evidence of any material losses in the year and the group's security processes remain robust.
• The group has established policies for registering patents and for monitoring its existing patent portfolio and those of third parties. • A substantial part of the group's intellectual property is know how and this is protected through non-disclosure agreements and other legal measures.	There has been no change in the year.

REPORT OF THE DIRECTORS – BUSINESS REVIEW

Consolidated Income Statement

for the year ended 31st March 2011

	Notes	2011 £ million	2010 £ million
Revenue	1,2	**9,984.8**	7,839.4
Cost of sales		**(9,328.2)**	(7,325.4)
Gross profit		**656.6**	514.0
Distribution costs		**(121.2)**	(103.6)
Administrative expenses		**(169.2)**	(138.6)
Major impairment and restructuring charges	3	**(71.8)**	(11.3)
Amortisation of acquired intangibles	4	**(13.2)**	(9.9)
Operating profit	1,6	**281.2**	250.6
Finance costs	7	**(33.1)**	(30.5)
Finance income	8	**12.4**	11.1
Share of profit of associate	19	**–**	1.7
Dissolution of associate	19	**0.1**	(4.4)
Profit before tax		**260.6**	228.5
Income tax expense	9	**(76.0)**	(64.3)
Profit for the year from continuing operations		**184.6**	164.2
Loss for the year from discontinued operations	40	**(1.9)**	–
Profit for the year		**182.7**	164.2
Attributable to:			
Owners of the parent company		**182.3**	164.2
Non-controlling interests		**0.4**	–
		182.7	164.2

		pence	pence
Earnings per ordinary share attributable to the equity holders of the parent company			
Continuing operations			
Basic	11	**86.5**	77.6
Diluted	11	**86.0**	77.3
Total			
Basic	11	**85.6**	77.6
Diluted	11	**85.1**	77.3

Consolidated Statement of Total Comprehensive Income

for the year ended 31st March 2011

	Notes	2011 £ million	2010 £ million
Profit for the year		**182.7**	164.2
Other comprehensive income:			
Currency translation differences	32	**(7.9)**	(5.7)
Cash flow hedges	32	**3.7**	27.0
Fair value gains on net investment hedges		**2.2**	32.8
Actuarial gain / (loss) on post-employment benefits assets and liabilities	14	**85.4**	(124.6)
Share of other comprehensive income of associate		**–**	0.2
Tax on above items taken directly to or transferred from equity	33	**(30.0)**	34.1
Other comprehensive income / (expense) for the year		**53.4**	(36.2)
Total comprehensive income for the year		**236.1**	128.0
Attributable to:			
Owners of the parent company		**235.7**	127.9
Non-controlling interests		**0.4**	0.1
		236.1	128.0

The notes on pages 86 to 124 form an integral part of the accounts.

Consolidated and Parent Company Balance Sheets

as at 31st March 2011

	Notes	Group 2011 £ million	Group 2010 £ million	Parent company 2011 £ million	Parent company 2010 £ million
Assets					
Non-current assets					
Property, plant and equipment	15	**907.7**	921.6	**230.8**	245.3
Goodwill	16	**529.5**	513.8	**110.5**	110.5
Other intangible assets	17	**152.9**	131.6	**6.4**	6.3
Investments in subsidiaries	18	**–**	–	**1,506.2**	1,518.7
Investment in associate	19	**–**	3.4	**–**	–
Deferred income tax assets	30	**39.7**	57.1	**19.9**	49.1
Available-for-sale investments	20	**8.0**	7.5	**–**	–
Swaps related to borrowings	25	**23.7**	19.3	**23.7**	19.3
Other receivables	23	**3.0**	3.1	**524.0**	466.4
Post-employment benefits net assets	14	**3.8**	4.6	**–**	–
Total non-current assets		**1,668.3**	1,662.0	**2,421.5**	2,415.6
Current assets					
Inventories	21	**556.3**	390.1	**154.8**	101.2
Current income tax assets		**9.4**	12.9	**–**	–
Trade and other receivables	23	**892.2**	639.3	**793.3**	637.5
Cash and cash equivalents – cash and deposits	25	**118.9**	179.1	**23.1**	88.4
Other financial assets	27	**6.9**	6.5	**7.2**	9.0
Total current assets		**1,583.7**	1,227.9	**978.4**	836.1
Total assets		**3,252.0**	2,889.9	**3,399.9**	3,251.7
Liabilities					
Current liabilities					
Trade and other payables	24	**(662.4)**	(527.2)	**(1,286.3)**	(1,372.0)
Current income tax liabilities		**(113.8)**	(91.0)	**(15.4)**	(17.9)
Cash and cash equivalents – bank overdrafts	25	**(24.5)**	(14.7)	**(74.1)**	(10.3)
Other borrowings and finance leases	25	**(181.8)**	(98.8)	**(146.8)**	(84.7)
Other financial liabilities	26	**(6.5)**	(8.0)	**(7.8)**	(9.2)
Provisions	29	**(59.7)**	(8.7)	**(2.5)**	(0.4)
Total current liabilities		**(1,048.7)**	(748.4)	**(1,532.9)**	(1,494.5)
Non-current liabilities					
Borrowings, finance leases and related swaps	25	**(575.7)**	(558.3)	**(575.0)**	(551.7)
Deferred income tax liabilities	30	**(60.3)**	(56.5)	**–**	–
Employee benefits obligations	14	**(134.2)**	(250.3)	**(73.2)**	(171.5)
Provisions	29	**(22.7)**	(19.6)	**(13.3)**	(9.5)
Other payables	24	**(4.8)**	(6.0)	**(0.2)**	–
Total non-current liabilities		**(797.7)**	(890.7)	**(661.7)**	(732.7)
Total liabilities		**(1,846.4)**	(1,639.1)	**(2,194.6)**	(2,227.2)
Net assets		**1,405.6**	1,250.8	**1,205.3**	1,024.5
Equity					
Share capital	31	**220.7**	220.7	**220.7**	220.7
Share premium account		**148.3**	148.3	**148.3**	148.3
Shares held in employee share ownership trust (ESOT)		**(35.8)**	(30.7)	**(35.8)**	(30.7)
Other reserves	34	**69.3**	73.4	**1.8**	0.2
Retained earnings		**1,002.0**	837.7	**870.3**	686.0
Total equity attributable to owners of the parent company		**1,404.5**	1,249.4	**1,205.3**	1,024.5
Non-controlling interests		**1.1**	1.4	**–**	–
Total equity		**1,405.6**	1,250.8	**1,205.3**	1,024.5

The accounts were approved by the Board of Directors on 1st June 2011 and signed on its behalf by:

N A P Carson
R J MacLeod   Directors

The notes on pages 86 to 124 form an integral part of the accounts.

Johnson Matthey
Annual Report & Accounts 2011

77

ACCOUNTS

Consolidated and Parent Company Cash Flow Statements

for the year ended 31st March 2011

	Notes	Group 2011 £ million	2010 £ million	Parent company 2011 £ million	2010 £ million
Cash flows from operating activities					
Profit before tax		**260.6**	228.5	**231.1**	376.9
Adjustments for:					
Share of profit of associate	19	**–**	(1.7)	**–**	–
Dissolution of associate	19	**(0.1)**	4.4	**–**	–
Discontinued operations	40	**(1.9)**	–	**–**	–
Depreciation, amortisation, impairment losses and profit on sale of non-current assets and investments		**167.5**	140.3	**41.9**	41.2
Share-based payments		**11.3**	4.7	**6.7**	4.2
(Increase) / decrease in inventories		**(159.6)**	(22.1)	**(53.4)**	12.0
Increase in receivables		**(250.1)**	(123.1)	**(215.3)**	(53.9)
Increase / (decrease) in payables		**113.3**	47.1	**(96.6)**	(90.7)
Increase in provisions		**52.0**	2.5	**5.8**	1.1
Contributions in excess of employee benefit obligations charge		**(26.8)**	(24.9)	**(23.4)**	(7.9)
Changes in fair value of financial instruments		**1.7**	1.3	**1.0**	1.6
Dividends received from subsidiaries		**–**	–	**(123.3)**	(276.8)
Net finance costs		**20.7**	19.4	**(20.0)**	(11.5)
Income tax (paid) / received		**(64.7)**	(0.7)	**(16.0)**	41.1
Net cash inflow / (outflow) from operating activities		**123.9**	275.7	**(261.5)**	37.3
Cash flows from investing activities					
Dividends received from associate	19	**3.5**	0.6	**–**	–
Dividends received from subsidiaries		**–**	–	**123.3**	276.8
Purchases of non-current assets and investments	35	**(137.4)**	(131.8)	**(29.1)**	(239.8)
Proceeds from sale of non-current assets and investments		**3.9**	0.3	**3.8**	–
Purchases of businesses	35	**(53.1)**	(5.7)	**–**	–
Net proceeds from sale of businesses	35	**–**	–	**–**	56.3
Net cash (outflow) / inflow from investing activities		**(183.1)**	(136.6)	**98.0**	93.3
Cash flows from financing activities					
Net (cost of) / proceeds on ESOT transactions in own shares	35	**(9.1)**	18.4	**(9.1)**	18.4
Proceeds from borrowings and finance leases	35	**95.2**	30.1	**101.0**	31.9
Dividends paid to equity holders of the parent company	10	**(86.1)**	(78.4)	**(86.1)**	(78.4)
Dividends paid to non-controlling interests		**(0.5)**	–	**–**	–
Settlement of currency swaps for net investment hedging		**7.4**	(25.3)	**7.4**	(25.3)
Proceeds from non-controlling interest on share issue		**–**	0.3	**–**	–
Interest paid		**(33.1)**	(31.5)	**(42.0)**	(46.7)
Interest received		**13.7**	10.4	**63.2**	52.6
Net cash (outflow) / inflow from financing activities		**(12.5)**	(76.0)	**34.4**	(47.5)
(Decrease) / increase in cash and cash equivalents in the year		**(71.7)**	63.1	**(129.1)**	83.1
Exchange differences on cash and cash equivalents		**1.7**	1.5	**–**	–
Cash and cash equivalents at beginning of year		**164.4**	99.8	**78.1**	(5.0)
Cash and cash equivalents at end of year	36	**94.4**	164.4	**(51.0)**	78.1
Reconciliation to net debt					
(Decrease) / increase in cash and cash equivalents in the year		**(71.7)**	63.1	**(129.1)**	83.1
Proceeds from borrowings and finance leases		**(95.2)**	(30.1)	**(101.0)**	(31.9)
Change in net debt resulting from cash flows		**(166.9)**	33.0	**(230.1)**	51.2
Borrowings acquired with subsidiaries		**(21.5)**	–	**–**	–
Exchange differences on net debt		**22.4**	28.0	**20.0**	26.7
Movement in net debt in year		**(166.0)**	61.0	**(210.1)**	77.9
Net debt at beginning of year		**(473.4)**	(534.4)	**(539.0)**	(616.9)
Net debt at end of year	25	**(639.4)**	(473.4)	**(749.1)**	(539.0)

The notes on pages 86 to 124 form an integral part of the accounts.

Consolidated Statement of Changes in Equity

for the year ended 31st March 2011

	Share capital £ million	Share premium account £ million	Shares held in ESOT £ million	Other reserves (note 34) £ million	Retained earnings £ million	Total attributable to equity holders £ million	Non-controlling interests £ million	Total equity £ million
At 1st April 2009	220.7	148.3	(61.8)	18.5	849.6	1,175.3	0.8	1,176.1
Profit for the year	–	–	–	–	164.2	164.2	–	164.2
Actuarial loss on post-employment benefits	–	–	–	–	(124.6)	(124.6)	–	(124.6)
Cash flow hedges	–	–	–	27.0	–	27.0	–	27.0
Associate's cash flow hedges	–	–	–	0.2	–	0.2	–	0.2
Net investment hedges	–	–	–	32.8	–	32.8	–	32.8
Currency translation differences	–	–	–	(5.8)	–	(5.8)	0.1	(5.7)
Tax on other comprehensive income	–	–	–	0.7	33.4	34.1	–	34.1
Total comprehensive income	–	–	–	54.9	73.0	127.9	0.1	128.0
Dividends paid (note 10)	–	–	–	–	(78.4)	(78.4)	(0.2)	(78.6)
Acquisition of non-controlling interest	–	–	–	–	–	–	0.4	0.4
Share issue to non-controlling interest	–	–	–	–	–	–	0.3	0.3
Share-based payments	–	–	–	–	10.4	10.4	–	10.4
Cost of shares transferred to employees	–	–	31.1	–	(18.4)	12.7	–	12.7
Tax on share-based payments	–	–	–	–	1.5	1.5	–	1.5
At 31st March 2010	220.7	148.3	(30.7)	73.4	837.7	1,249.4	1.4	1,250.8
Profit for the year	–	–	–	–	182.3	182.3	0.4	182.7
Actuarial gain on post-employment benefits	–	–	–	–	85.4	85.4	–	85.4
Cash flow hedges	–	–	–	3.7	–	3.7	–	3.7
Net investment hedges	–	–	–	2.2	–	2.2	–	2.2
Currency translation differences	–	–	–	(7.9)	–	(7.9)	–	(7.9)
Tax on other comprehensive income	–	–	–	(2.1)	(27.9)	(30.0)	–	(30.0)
Total comprehensive income	–	–	–	(4.1)	239.8	235.7	0.4	236.1
Dividends paid (note 10)	–	–	–	–	(86.1)	(86.1)	(0.7)	(86.8)
Purchase of shares by ESOT	–	–	(16.7)	–	–	(16.7)	–	(16.7)
Share-based payments	–	–	–	–	17.1	17.1	–	17.1
Cost of shares transferred to employees	–	–	11.6	–	(10.3)	1.3	–	1.3
Tax on share-based payments	–	–	–	–	3.8	3.8	–	3.8
At 31st March 2011	220.7	148.3	(35.8)	69.3	1,002.0	1,404.5	1.1	1,405.6

The notes on pages 86 to 124 form an integral part of the accounts.

Johnson Matthey
Annual Report & Accounts 2011

ACCOUNTS

Parent Company Statement of Changes in Equity

for the year ended 31st March 2011

	Share capital £ million	Share premium account £ million	Shares held in ESOT £ million	Other reserves (note 34) £ million	Retained earnings £ million	Total equity £ million
At 1st April 2009	220.7	148.3	(61.8)	(19.5)	485.1	772.8
Profit for the year	–	–	–	–	374.9	374.9
Actuarial loss on post-employment benefits	–	–	–	–	(122.0)	(122.0)
Cash flow hedges	–	–	–	26.6	(0.2)	26.4
Currency translation differences	–	–	–	0.5	–	0.5
Tax on other comprehensive income	–	–	–	(7.4)	33.6	26.2
Total comprehensive income	–	–	–	19.7	286.3	306.0
Dividends paid (note 10)	–	–	–	–	(78.4)	(78.4)
Share-based payments	–	–	–	–	8.0	8.0
Cost of shares transferred to employees	–	–	31.1	–	(16.0)	15.1
Tax on share-based payments	–	–	–	–	1.0	1.0
At 31st March 2010	220.7	148.3	(30.7)	0.2	686.0	1,024.5
Profit for the year	–	–	–	–	210.6	210.6
Actuarial gain on post-employment benefits	–	–	–	–	74.8	74.8
Cash flow hedges	–	–	–	0.6	–	0.6
Currency translation differences	–	–	–	1.2	–	1.2
Tax on other comprehensive income	–	–	–	(0.2)	(23.8)	(24.0)
Total comprehensive income	–	–	–	1.6	261.6	263.2
Dividends paid (note 10)	–	–	–	–	(86.1)	(86.1)
Purchase of shares by ESOT	–	–	(16.7)	–	–	(16.7)
Share-based payments	–	–	–	–	15.3	15.3
Cost of shares transferred to employees	–	–	11.6	–	(8.5)	3.1
Tax on share-based payments	–	–	–	–	2.0	2.0
At 31st March 2011	**220.7**	**148.3**	**(35.8)**	**1.8**	**870.3**	**1,205.3**

The notes on pages 86 to 124 form an integral part of the accounts.

Accounting Policies

for the year ended 31st March 2011

The group's and parent company's significant accounting policies, together with the judgments made by management in applying those policies which have the most significant effect on the amounts recognised in the accounts, are:

Basis of accounting and preparation

The accounts are prepared in accordance with International Financial Reporting Standards (IFRS) and interpretations issued by the International Financial Reporting Interpretations Committee (IFRIC) or the Standing Interpretations Committee (SIC) as adopted by the European Union. For Johnson Matthey, there are no differences between IFRS as adopted by the European Union and full IFRS as published by the International Accounting Standards Board (IASB) and so the accounts comply with IFRS.

The accounts are prepared on the historical cost basis, except for certain assets and liabilities which are measured at fair value as explained below.

The parent company has not presented its own income statement, statement of total comprehensive income and related notes as permitted by section 408 of the Companies Act 2006.

Basis of consolidation

The consolidated accounts comprise the accounts of the parent company and all its subsidiaries, including the employee share ownership trust, and included the group's interest in its associate until the date of its dissolution. They will include the group's interest in its joint venture when its formation is complete.

Entities over which the group has the ability to exercise control are accounted for as subsidiaries. Entities that are not subsidiaries or joint ventures but where the group has significant influence (i.e. the power to participate in the financial and operating policy decisions) are accounted for as associates.

The results and assets and liabilities of the associate were included in the consolidated accounts using the equity method of accounting.

The results and assets and liabilities of the joint venture will be included in the consolidated accounts using the equity method of accounting.

The results of businesses acquired or disposed of in the year are consolidated from or up to the effective date of acquisition or disposal respectively. The net assets of businesses acquired are incorporated in the consolidated accounts at their fair values at the date of acquisition.

Transactions and balances between group companies are eliminated. No profit is taken on transactions between group companies and the group's share of profits on transactions with its associate was also eliminated.

In the parent company balance sheet, businesses acquired by the parent company from other group companies are incorporated at book value at the date of acquisition. Where the consideration given exceeds the book value of the net assets acquired this difference is accounted for as goodwill.

Revenue

Revenue comprises all sales of goods and rendering of services at the fair value of consideration received or receivable after the deduction of any trade discounts and excluding sales taxes. Revenue is recognised when it can be measured reliably and the significant risks and rewards of ownership are transferred to the customer. With the sale of goods, this occurs when the goods are despatched or made available to the customer, except for the sale of consignment products located at customers' premises where revenue is recognised on notification that the product has been used. With the rendering of services, revenue is recognised by reference to the stage of completion as measured by the proportion that costs incurred to date bear to the estimated total costs. With royalties and licence income, revenue is recognised in accordance with the substance of the relevant agreement.

Long term contracts

Where the outcome of a long term contract can be estimated reliably, revenue and costs are recognised by reference to the stage of completion. This is measured by the proportion that contract costs incurred to date bear to the estimated total contract costs.

Where the outcome of a long term contract cannot be estimated reliably, contract revenue is recognised to the extent of contract costs incurred that it is probable will be recoverable. Contract costs are recognised as expenses in the period in which they are incurred.

When it is probable that the total contract costs will exceed total contract revenue, the expected loss is recognised as an expense immediately.

Finance costs and finance income

Finance costs that are directly attributable to the construction of an asset that necessarily takes a substantial period of time to get ready for its intended use and for which construction was commenced after 1st April 2007 are capitalised as part of the cost of that asset. Other finance costs and finance income are recognised in the income statement in the year incurred.

Research and development

Research expenditure is charged to the income statement in the year incurred.

Development expenditure is charged to the income statement in the year incurred unless it meets the IFRS recognition criteria for capitalisation. When the recognition criteria have been met any further development expenditure is capitalised as an intangible asset.

ACCOUNTS

Accounting Policies

for the year ended 31st March 2011

Foreign currencies

Foreign currency transactions are recorded in the functional currency of the relevant subsidiary, associate or branch at the exchange rate at the date of transaction. Foreign currency monetary assets and liabilities are retranslated into the relevant functional currency at the exchange rate at the balance sheet date.

Income statements and cash flows of overseas subsidiaries, associates and branches are translated into sterling at the average rates for the year. Balance sheets of overseas subsidiaries, associates and branches, including any fair value adjustments and including related goodwill, are translated into sterling at the exchange rates at the balance sheet date.

Exchange differences arising on the translation of the net investment in overseas subsidiaries, associates and branches, less exchange differences arising on related foreign currency financial instruments which hedge the group's net investment in these operations, are taken to a separate component of equity. The group has taken advantage of the exemption allowed in IFRS 1 – 'First-time Adoption of International Reporting Standards' to deem the cumulative translation difference for all overseas subsidiaries, associates and branches to be zero at 1st April 2004.

Other exchange differences are taken to operating profit.

Property, plant and equipment

Property, plant and equipment are stated at cost less accumulated depreciation and any provisions for impairment. Finance costs that relate to an asset that takes a substantial period of time to construct and for which construction was started after 1st April 2007 are capitalised as part of the cost of that asset. Other finance costs are not capitalised.

Depreciation is provided at rates calculated to write off the cost less estimated residual value of each asset over its useful life. Certain freehold buildings and plant and equipment are depreciated using the units of production method, as this more closely reflects their expected consumption. All other assets are depreciated using the straight line method. The useful lives vary according to the class of the asset, but are typically: leasehold property 30 years (or the life of the lease if shorter); freehold buildings 30 years; and plant and equipment 4 to 10 years. Freehold land is not depreciated.

Goodwill

Goodwill arises on the acquisition of a business when the fair value of the consideration given exceeds the fair value attributed to the net assets acquired (including contingent liabilities). It is subject to annual impairment reviews. Acquisition-related costs arising on acquisitions made after 31st March 2010 are charged to the income statement as incurred. Acquisition-related costs arising on acquisitions made on or before 31st March 2010 were regarded as a component of consideration and therefore increased goodwill.

The group and parent company have taken advantage of the exemption allowed under IFRS 1 and so goodwill arising on acquisitions made before 1st April 2004 is included at the carrying amount at that date less any subsequent impairments. Up to 31st March 1998 goodwill was eliminated against equity.

Intangible assets

Intangible assets are stated at cost less accumulated amortisation and any provisions for impairment. They are amortised in accordance with the relevant income stream or by using the straight line method over their useful lives from the time they are first available for use. The estimated useful lives vary according to the specific asset but are typically: 1 to 12 years for customer contracts and relationships; 3 to 8 years for capitalised software; 3 to 20 years for patents, trademarks and licences; and 3 to 8 years for capitalised development currently being amortised.

Intangible assets which are not yet being amortised are subject to annual impairment reviews.

Investments in subsidiaries

Investments in subsidiaries are stated in the parent company's balance sheet at cost less any provisions for impairment. If a distribution is received from a subsidiary then the investment in that subsidiary is assessed for an indication of impairment.

Leases

Leases are classified as finance leases whenever they transfer substantially all the risks and rewards of ownership to the group. The assets are included in property, plant and equipment and the capital elements of the leasing commitments are shown as obligations under finance leases. The assets are depreciated on a basis consistent with similar owned assets or the lease term if shorter. The interest element of the lease rental is included in the income statement.

All other leases are classified as operating leases and the lease costs are expensed on a straight line basis over the lease term.

Grants

Grants related to assets are included in deferred income and released to the income statement in equal instalments over the expected useful lives of the related assets.

Grants related to income are deducted in reporting the related expense.

Accounting Policies

for the year ended 31st March 2011

Precious metal inventories

Inventories of gold, silver and platinum group metals are valued according to the source from which the metal is obtained. Metal which has been purchased and committed to future sales to customers or hedged in metal markets is valued at the price at which it is contractually committed or hedged, adjusted for unexpired contango and backwardation. Other precious metal inventories owned by the group, which are unhedged, are valued at the lower of cost and net realisable value using the weighted average cost formula.

Other inventories

Non-precious metal inventories are valued at the lower of cost, including attributable overheads, and net realisable value. Except where costs are specifically identified, the first-in, first-out or weighted average cost formulae are used to value inventories.

Cash and cash equivalents

Cash and deposits comprise cash at bank and in hand, including short term deposits with a maturity date of three months or less from the date of acquisition. The group and parent company routinely use short term bank overdraft facilities, which are repayable on demand, as an integral part of their cash management policy. Therefore cash and cash equivalents in the cash flow statements are cash and deposits less bank overdrafts. Offset arrangements across group businesses have been applied to arrive at the net cash and overdraft figures.

Derivative financial instruments

The group and parent company use derivative financial instruments, in particular forward currency contracts and currency swaps, to manage the financial risks associated with their underlying business activities and the financing of those activities. The group and parent company do not undertake any trading activity in derivative financial instruments.

Derivative financial instruments are measured at their fair value. Derivative financial instruments may be designated at inception as fair value hedges, cash flow hedges or net investment hedges if appropriate. Derivative financial instruments which are not designated as hedging instruments are classified under IFRS as held for trading, but are used to manage financial risk.

Changes in the fair value of any derivative financial instruments that are not designated as or are not determined to be effective hedges are recognised immediately in the income statement.

Changes in the fair value of derivative financial instruments designated as fair value hedges are recognised in the income statement, together with the related changes in the fair value of the hedged asset or liability. Fair value hedge accounting is discontinued if the hedging instrument expires or is sold, terminated or exercised, the hedge no longer meets the criteria for hedge accounting or the designation is revoked.

Changes in the fair value of derivative financial instruments designated as cash flow hedges are recognised in equity, to the extent that the hedges are effective. Ineffective portions are recognised in the income statement immediately. If the hedged item results in the recognition of a non-financial asset or liability, the amount recognised in equity is transferred out of equity and included in the initial carrying amount of the asset or liability. Otherwise, the amount recognised in equity is transferred to the income statement in the same period that the hedged item is recognised in the income statement. If the hedging instrument expires or is sold, terminated or exercised, the hedge no longer meets the criteria for hedge accounting or the designation is revoked, amounts previously recognised in equity remain in equity until the forecast transaction occurs. If a forecast transaction is no longer expected to occur, the amounts previously recognised in equity are transferred to the income statement.

For hedges of net investments in foreign operations, the effective portion of the gain or loss on the hedging instrument is recognised in equity, while the ineffective portion is recognised in the income statement. Amounts taken to equity are transferred to the income statement when the foreign operations are sold.

Other financial instruments

All other financial instruments are initially recognised at fair value plus transaction costs. Subsequent measurement is as follows:

- Unhedged borrowings are measured at amortised cost.

- Available-for-sale investments are investments in equity instruments that do not have a quoted market price in an active market and whose fair value cannot be measured reliably and so are measured at cost.

- All other financial assets and liabilities, including short term receivables and payables, are measured at amortised cost less any impairment provision.

Taxation

Current and deferred tax are recognised in the income statement, except when they relate to items recognised directly in equity when the related tax is also recognised in equity.

Current tax is the amount of income tax expected to be paid in respect of taxable profits using the tax rates that have been enacted or substantively enacted at the balance sheet date.

Deferred tax is provided in full, using the liability method, on temporary differences arising between the tax bases of assets and liabilities and their carrying amount in the balance sheet. It is provided using the tax rates that are expected to apply in the period when the asset or liability is settled, based on tax rates that have been enacted or substantively enacted at the balance sheet date.

Deferred tax assets are recognised to the extent that it is probable that future taxable profits will be available against which the temporary differences can be utilised. No deferred tax asset or liability is recognised in respect of temporary differences associated with investments in subsidiaries, branches and associates where the group is able to control the timing of the reversal of the temporary difference and it is probable that the temporary difference will not reverse in the foreseeable future.

Accounting Policies

for the year ended 31st March 2011

Provisions and contingencies

Provisions are recognised when the group has a present obligation as a result of a past event and a reliable estimate can be made of a probable adverse outcome, for example warranties, environmental claims and restructurings. Otherwise, material contingent liabilities are disclosed unless the transfer of economic benefits is remote. Contingent assets are only disclosed if an inflow of economic benefits is probable.

The group considered financial guarantees of its share of the borrowings and precious metal leases of its associate to be insurance contracts. The parent company considers financial guarantees of its subsidiaries' borrowings and precious metal leases to be insurance contracts. These are treated as contingent liabilities unless it becomes probable that it will be required to make a payment under the guarantee.

Share-based payments and employee share ownership trust (ESOT)

The fair value of outstanding share options granted to employees after 7th November 2002 was calculated using an adjusted Black-Scholes options valuation model and the fair value of outstanding shares allocated to employees under the long term incentive plans after 7th November 2002 is calculated by adjusting the share price on the date of allocation for the present value of the expected dividends that will not be received. The resulting cost is charged to the income statement over the relevant vesting periods, adjusted to reflect actual and expected levels of vesting where appropriate.

The group and parent company provide finance to the ESOT to purchase company shares in the open market. Costs of running the ESOT are charged to the income statement. The cost of shares held by the ESOT are deducted in arriving at equity until they vest unconditionally in employees.

Pensions and other post-employment benefits

The group operates a number of contributory and non-contributory plans, mainly of the defined benefit type, which require contributions to be made to separately administered funds.

The costs of the defined contribution plans are charged to the income statement as they fall due.

For defined benefit plans, the group and parent company recognise the net assets or liabilities of the schemes in their balance sheets. Obligations are measured at present value using the projected unit credit method and a discount rate reflecting yields on high quality corporate bonds. Assets are measured at their fair value at the balance sheet date. The changes in scheme assets and liabilities, based on actuarial advice, are recognised as follows:

- The current service cost is spread over the period during which benefit is expected to be derived from the employees' services based on the most recent actuarial valuation and is deducted in arriving at operating profit.
- The interest cost, based on the discount rate at the beginning of the year and the present value of the defined benefit obligation during the year, is included in operating profit.
- The expected return on plan assets, based on market expectations at the beginning of the year for returns over the entire life of the related obligation and amended for changes in the fair value of plan assets as a result of contributions paid in and benefits paid out, is included in operating profit.
- Actuarial gains and losses, representing differences between the expected return and actual return on plan assets and reimbursement rights, differences between actuarial assumptions underlying the plan liabilities and actual experience during the year, and changes in actuarial assumptions, are recognised in the statement of total comprehensive income in the year they occur.
- Past service costs are spread evenly over the period in which the increases in benefit vest and are deducted in arriving at operating profit. If an increase in benefits vests immediately, the cost is recognised immediately.
- Gains or losses arising from settlements or curtailments are included in operating profit.

Standards and interpretations adopted in the year

During the year, the following new and amendments to accounting standards and interpretations were adopted:

The January 2008 revision to IFRS 3 – 'Business Combinations' and amendment to IAS 27 – 'Consolidated and Separate Financial Statements' required changes to the accounting of business combinations, transactions with non-controlling interests and the accounting in the event of the loss of control over a subsidiary which occur from 1st April 2010. No restatement of prior years is required. Acquisitions during the year disclosed in note 39 have been accounted for in accordance with the revised IFRS 3.

'Improvements to IFRSs' issued in April 2009 made some minor amendments to a number of standards, including minor revisions to the disclosure requirements of IFRS 8 – 'Operating Segments'. The requirement to disclose a measure of total assets even if it is not provided to the chief operating decision maker has been removed and so this disclosure has been deleted. The amendments have no impact on the reported results or financial position of the group and parent company.

Amendment to IAS 39 – 'Eligible Hedged Items', IFRIC 17 – 'Distributions of Non-cash Assets to Owners', Amendment to IFRS 2 – 'Group Cash-settled Share-based Payment Transactions', Amendments to IFRS 1 – 'Additional Exemptions for First-time Adopters' and Amendment to IAS 32 – 'Classification of Rights Issues' have all been adopted during the year. There was no material impact on the reported results or financial position of the group and parent company.

Accounting Policies

for the year ended 31st March 2011

Standards and interpretations issued but not yet applied

IFRS 9 – 'Financial Instruments' was originally issued in November 2009 as the first stage of the IASB's project to review and replace IAS 39 – 'Financial Instruments: Recognition and Measurement', focusing on the classification and measurement of financial assets. In October 2010 the IASB issued an expanded and amended version which also addresses financial liabilities and derecognition. The standard will be applicable for annual periods beginning on or after 1st January 2013. The effect on the group and parent company is still being evaluated.

IAS 24 – 'Related Party Disclosures' was issued in November 2009 and is applicable for annual periods beginning on or after 1st January 2011. The revision clarifies the definition of a related party for disclosure purposes and so will not result in any impact on the reported results or net assets of the group and parent company.

Amendments to IFRIC 14 – 'Prepayments of a Minimum Funding Requirement' was issued in November 2009 and is required to be applied for annual periods beginning on or after 1st January 2011. This will not affect the reported results or net assets of the group and parent company.

IFRIC 19 – 'Extinguishing Financial Liabilities with Equity Instruments' was issued in November 2009 and is applicable for annual periods beginning on or after 1st July 2010. This will not affect the reported results or net assets of the group and parent company.

Amendments to IFRS 1 – 'Limited Exemption from Comparative IFRS 7 Disclosures for First-time Adopters' was issued in January 2010 and is required to be applied for annual periods beginning on or after 1st July 2010. This will not affect the reported results or net assets of the group and parent company.

'Improvements to IFRSs' was issued in May 2010 making minor amendments to a number of standards and is required to be applied mainly for annual periods beginning on or after 1st January 2011, with some amendments for annual periods beginning on or after 1st July 2010. The effect on the group and parent company is still being evaluated.

Amendments to IFRS 7 – 'Disclosures – Transfers of Financial Assets' was issued in October 2010 and is required to be applied for annual periods beginning on or after 1st July 2011. It requires a number of changes to disclosures but will not affect the reported results or net assets of the group and parent company.

Amendments to IFRS 1 – 'Severe Hyperinflation and Removal of Fixed Dates for First-time Adopters' was issued in December 2010 and is required to be applied for annual periods beginning on or after 1st July 2011. This will not affect the reported results or net assets of the group and parent company.

Amendments to IAS 12 – 'Deferred Tax: Recovery of Underlying Assets' was issued in December 2010 and is applicable for periods beginning on or after 1st January 2012. This will not affect the reported results or net assets of the group and parent company.

The effect of standards and interpretations amended or issued after 30th April 2011 have not yet been evaluated.

ACCOUNTS

Notes on the Accounts

for the year ended 31st March 2011

1   Segmental information

For management purposes, the group is organised into three operating divisions – Environmental Technologies, Precious Metal Products and Fine Chemicals and each division is represented by a director on the Board of Directors. These operating divisions represent the group's segments. Their principal activities are described on pages 19 to 31. The performance of the divisions is assessed by the Board of Directors on underlying operating profit, which is before amortisation of acquired intangibles, major impairment and restructuring charges and profit or loss on disposal of businesses. Each division is also now assessed on sales excluding precious metals including inter-segment sales as this is believed to be a better measure of each division's performance than external sales excluding precious metals and so the segmental information has been expanded to include this. Sales between segments are made at market prices, taking into account the volumes involved.

Year ended 31st March 2011

	Environmental Technologies £ million	Precious Metal Products £ million	Fine Chemicals £ million	Eliminations £ million	Total £ million
Revenue from external customers	2,703.4	7,028.3	253.1	–	9,984.8
Inter-segment revenue	4.6	1,241.3	1.9	(1,247.8)	–
Total revenue	2,708.0	8,269.6	255.0	(1,247.8)	9,984.8
External sales excluding the value of precious metals	1,561.3	475.4	243.6	–	2,280.3
Inter-segment sales	4.5	65.8	1.8	(72.1)	–
Sales excluding the value of precious metals	1,565.8	541.2	245.4	(72.1)	2,280.3
Segmental underlying operating profit	164.7	172.9	56.2	–	393.8
Unallocated corporate expenses					(27.6)
Underlying operating profit					366.2
Major impairment and restructuring charges (note 3)					(71.8)
Amortisation of acquired intangibles (note 4)					(13.2)
Operating profit					281.2
Net finance costs					(20.7)
Dissolution of associate (note 19)					0.1
Profit before tax					260.6
Segmental net assets	1,535.6	357.3	417.5	–	2,310.4
Net debt					(639.4)
Post-employment benefits net assets and liabilities					(130.4)
Deferred income tax assets and liabilities					(20.6)
Provisions and non-current other payables					(87.2)
Unallocated corporate net assets					(27.2)
Total net assets					1,405.6
Segmental capital expenditure	90.1	26.1	16.0	–	132.2
Other additions to non-current assets (excluding financial assets, deferred tax assets and post-employment benefits net assets)	42.5	2.1	10.9	(0.3)	55.2
Segmental total additions to non-current assets	132.6	28.2	26.9	(0.3)	187.4
Corporate capital expenditure					5.7
Total additions to non-current assets					193.1
Segmental depreciation and amortisation	78.8	24.3	17.2	–	120.3
Corporate depreciation					2.9
Amortisation of acquired intangibles (note 4)					12.3
Total depreciation and amortisation					135.5

Notes on the Accounts
for the year ended 31st March 2011

1   Segmental information (continued)
Year ended 31st March 2010

	Environmental Technologies £ million	Precious Metal Products £ million	Fine Chemicals £ million	Eliminations £ million	Total £ million
Revenue from external customers	2,056.4	5,561.8	221.2	–	7,839.4
Inter-segment revenue	5.2	636.5	1.8	(643.5)	–
Total revenue	2,061.6	6,198.3	223.0	(643.5)	7,839.4
External sales excluding the value of precious metals	1,246.5	419.9	219.1	–	1,885.5
Inter-segment sales	5.2	34.3	1.6	(41.1)	–
Sales excluding the value of precious metals	1,251.7	454.2	220.7	(41.1)	1,885.5
Segmental underlying operating profit	120.9	116.7	55.8	–	293.4
Unallocated corporate expenses					(21.6)
Underlying operating profit					271.8
Major impairment and restructuring charges (note 3)					(11.3)
Amortisation of acquired intangibles (note 4)					(9.9)
Operating profit					250.6
Net finance costs					(19.4)
Share of profit of associate					1.7
Dissolution of associate (note 19)					(4.4)
Profit before tax					228.5
Segmental net assets excluding investment in associate	1,333.7	257.8	400.8		1,992.3
Investment in associate	–	3.4	–	–	3.4
Segmental net assets	1,333.7	261.2	400.8	–	1,995.7
Net debt					(473.4)
Post-employment benefits net assets and liabilities					(245.7)
Deferred income tax assets and liabilities					0.6
Provisions and non-current other payables					(34.3)
Unallocated corporate net assets					7.9
Total net assets					1,250.8
Segmental capital expenditure	93.8	15.9	22.0	–	131.7
Other additions to non-current assets (excluding financial assets, deferred tax assets and post-employment benefits net assets)	3.5	1.0	0.3	(0.3)	4.5
Segmental total additions to non-current assets	97.3	16.9	22.3	(0.3)	136.2
Corporate capital expenditure					2.7
Total additions to non-current assets					138.9
Segment depreciation and amortisation	69.3	23.1	15.8	–	108.2
Corporate depreciation					2.7
Amortisation of acquired intangibles (note 4)					9.9
Total depreciation and amortisation					120.8

The group received £1,196.8 million of revenue from one external customer (2010 £1,030.5 million) which is 12% (2010 13%) of the group's revenue from external customers. The revenue is reported in Precious Metal Products as it is generated by the group's platinum marketing and distribution activities and so has a very low return on sales.

ACCOUNTS

Notes on the Accounts

for the year ended 31st March 2011

1 Segmental information (continued)

The group's country of domicile is the UK. Revenue from external customers is based on the customer's location. Non-current assets are based on the location of the assets and excludes financial assets, deferred tax assets and post-employment benefits net assets.

	Revenue from external customers		Non-current assets	
	2011 £ million	2010 £ million	2011 £ million	2010 £ million
UK	2,442.0	2,192.6	665.0	676.7
Germany	762.1	659.5	242.8	250.9
Rest of Europe	1,242.3	713.4	105.3	122.2
USA	2,690.5	1,928.1	351.3	309.8
Rest of North America	105.0	122.6	14.2	14.3
China (including Hong Kong)	1,197.9	1,138.5	53.1	42.9
Rest of Asia	965.1	547.3	118.6	105.2
Rest of World	579.9	537.4	42.7	51.3
Total	9,984.8	7,839.4	1,593.0	1,573.3

2 Revenue

	2011 £ million	2010 £ million
Sale of goods	9,801.1	7,682.7
Rendering of services	145.0	119.8
Royalties and licence income	38.7	36.9
Total revenue	9,984.8	7,839.4

3 Major impairment and restructuring charges

On 27th May 2010 the group entered into consultation with employees of its Vertec business to look at the future options for that business. On 19th November 2010 the Office of Fair Trading announced that it proposed to refer the sale of Vertec to Dorf Ketal Chemicals AG to the UK Competition Commission for further review. As a result, the group terminated its agreement with Dorf Ketal and commenced a structured closure of the group's Haverton manufacturing site in Billingham, UK, which was complete by 31st March 2011. The closure of the site gives rise to a pre-tax impairment and restructuring charge of £14.8 million. This is excluded from underlying operating profit.

On 31st January 2011 the group announced it was starting consultation with the Works Council about the closure of its autocatalyst facility in Brussels. The closure of the site is expected to be completed during the year ending 31st March 2012 and gives rise to a pre-tax impairment and restructuring charge which is estimated to be £57.0 million. This is excluded from underlying operating profit.

During the year ended 31st March 2010 the carrying amount of the group's Fine Chemicals facility in Massachusetts, USA was impaired as a result of the global recession. This gave rise to a pre-tax impairment loss of £11.3 million in that year, which was excluded from underlying operating profit.

4 Amortisation of acquired intangibles

The amortisation of intangible assets which arise on the acquisition of businesses, together with any subsequent impairment of these intangible assets, is shown separately on the face of the income statement. It is excluded from underlying operating profit.

Five Year Record

	2007 £ million	2008 £ million	2009 £ million	2010 £ million	**2011 £ million**
Revenue	6,151.7	7,498.7	7,847.8	7,839.4	**9,984.8**
Sales excluding the value of precious metals	1,454.2	1,750.2	1,796.9	1,885.5	**2,280.3**
EBITDA	329.9	374.1	398.1	382.7	**489.4**
Depreciation	(68.6)	(68.3)	(88.7)	(97.3)	**(108.3)**
Amortisation	(6.1)	(9.0)	(10.9)	(13.6)	**(14.9)**
Underlying operating profit	255.2	296.8	298.5	271.8	**366.2**
Amortisation of acquired intangibles	(2.8)	(3.1)	(9.1)	(9.9)	**(13.2)**
Major impairment and restructuring charges	–	–	(9.4)	(11.3)	**(71.8)**
Operating profit	252.4	293.7	280.0	250.6	**281.2**
Net finance costs	(26.8)	(30.3)	(32.6)	(19.4)	**(20.7)**
Share of profit / (loss) of associates	0.9	(1.1)	2.0	1.7	**–**
Dissolution of associate	–	–	–	(4.4)	**0.1**
Profit before tax	226.5	262.3	249.4	228.5	**260.6**
Income tax expense	(64.7)	(77.2)	(76.7)	(64.3)	**(76.0)**
Profit after taxation	161.8	185.1	172.7	164.2	**184.6**
Profit / (loss) for the year from discontinued operations	43.7	0.3	1.2	–	**(1.9)**
Non-controlling interests	1.0	0.8	0.2	–	**(0.4)**
Profit attributable to owners of the parent company	206.5	186.2	174.1	164.2	**182.3**
Underlying earnings per ordinary share	82.2p	89.5p	89.6p	86.4p	**119.0p**
Earnings per ordinary share	96.9p	88.5p	82.6p	77.6p	**85.6p**
Dividend per ordinary share	33.6p	36.6p	37.1p	39.0p	**46.0p**
Summary Balance Sheet **Assets employed:**					
Goodwill	399.2	480.4	516.0	513.8	**529.5**
Property, plant and equipment / other intangible assets	640.8	827.9	1,060.5	1,053.2	**1,060.6**
Non-current investments / associates	9.6	8.9	12.1	10.9	**8.0**
Inventories	362.7	380.4	371.7	390.1	**556.3**
Receivables / current investments / tax assets / financial assets	549.2	712.4	585.9	718.9	**951.2**
Payables / provisions / tax liabilities / financial liabilities	(519.5)	(655.7)	(684.1)	(717.0)	**(930.2)**
Post-employment benefits net assets / employee benefits obligations	0.9	16.4	(151.6)	(245.7)	**(130.4)**
	1,442.9	1,770.7	1,710.5	1,724.2	**2,045.0**
Financed by:					
Net debt	364.8	610.4	534.4	473.4	**639.4**
Retained earnings	783.7	879.1	849.6	837.7	**1,002.0**
Share capital, share premium, shares held in ESOTs and other reserves	292.0	279.8	325.7	411.7	**402.5**
Non-controlling interests	2.4	1.4	0.8	1.4	**1.1**
Capital employed	1,442.9	1,770.7	1,710.5	1,724.2	**2,045.0**
Return on invested capital (Underlying operating profit / average capital employed)	17.6%	18.5%	17.1%	15.8%	**19.4%**

The balance sheet for 2008 has been restated for the changes to Argillon Group's fair value at acquisition and goodwill on acquisition.

Learning objectives

Completion of this chapter will enable you to:

- explain why annual reports and accounts of limited companies are filed and published
- recognise the key elements of the contents of the annual report and accounts of a typical public limited company
- evaluate the information disclosed within the annual report and accounts
- carry out a horizontal analysis of the income statement and the balance sheet
- carry out a vertical analysis of the income statement and the balance sheet
- interpret the information provided by segmental reporting
- critically evaluate the quality of sustainability reporting within annual reports
- appreciate the impact of inflation on the financial performance of companies
- prepare and describe an alternative perception of the income statement illustrated by the value added statement.

Introduction

This chapter builds on the business performance analysis techniques we introduced in Chapter 7. It is concerned with the type of information, both financial and non-financial, that is included in a company's annual report and accounts. We will use the annual report and accounts of Johnson Matthey Plc for the year 2011 to illustrate the financial statements of a large UK plc. Before the start of this chapter you will have already seen pages 2 to 5, pages 15 to 17, pages 34 to 41, pages 76 to 88, and page 126 of Johnson Matthey's report and accounts 2011 reproduced on pages 282 to 310. This chapter will refer to these extracts but we will not consider the whole of the Johnson Matthey Plc annual report, a copy of which may be obtained from their head office at 40–42 Hatton Garden, London EC1N 8EE, UK. Further information about the company and copies of its report and accounts 2011 may be obtained from the Johnson Matthey website which is linked to the website accompanying this book at *www.pearsoned.co.uk/daviestony.*

We will look at extracts from Johnson Matthey Plc's report and accounts 2011, which are split into three main sections:

- Report of the directors, which includes the business review and corporate governance (see Chapter 6)
- Accounts
- Other information.

Within the report of the directors we will look at the business review section that includes:

- Financial highlights
- Chairman's statement
- Chief executive's statement
- Financial review
- Treasury policies
- Liquidity and going concern
- Sustainability.

An area of increasing importance appears in a section of the annual reports and accounts of UK plcs called sustainability. Corporate governance is an important area within this section, which is reported on and audited, and was discussed in Chapter 6.

Within the Accounts section we will look at the:

■ Accounting policies
■ Financial statements
■ Notes on the accounts
■ Segmental reporting.

Two further areas within this section, responsibility of directors and the independent auditors' report, were included in Chapter 6.

We will use Johnson Matthey's five-year record and other shareholder information, contained in the final section, other information, in Worked examples and Exercises later in this chapter.

The information disclosed in Johnson Matthey Plc's report and accounts 2011 provides us with a broad picture of what sort of company Johnson Matthey is. The report and accounts includes not only Johnson Matthey's historical financial performance, but also an indication of Johnson Matthey's prospects for the future. Included within the financial review is an example of how such a group manages risk.

In Chapter 7 we considered ratio analysis in our review of business performance. In this chapter we will look at some further tools of analysis. The first is horizontal analysis, or common size analysis, which provides a line-by-line comparison of the financial statements of a company (income statement and balance sheet) with those of the previous year. The second approach is the vertical analysis, where each item in the income statement and balance sheet is expressed as a percentage of the total.

The report and accounts of companies are now including more and more non-financial information, for example employee accident rates. Companies are also increasing generally their reporting on their sustainability performance. This includes areas such as health and safety, the environment, equal opportunities, employee development, and ethical issues. Johnson Matthey's report and accounts 2011 includes a comprehensive report on its sustainability performance, which is reproduced within this chapter.

The chapter closes with a look at the nature and purpose of the value added statement and its preparation. The value added statement is a variation on the income statement and is concerned with measuring the value added by a business rather than the profit earned by the business.

Why are annual accounts filed and published?

After each year end, companies prepare their annual report and accounts, which include the financial statements and the auditors' report, for their shareholders. Copies of the annual report and accounts must be filed with the Registrar of Companies (or Chambers of Commerce in some countries), and presented for approval by the shareholders at the company's annual general meeting (AGM). Further copies are usually made available to other interested parties such as financial institutions, major suppliers and other investors. The annual report and accounts of a plc usually takes the form of a glossy booklet which includes photographs of the directors, products and activities and other promotional material, and many non-financial performance measures, as well as the statutory legal and financial information. Large companies also issue half-yearly, or interim reports, which include the standard financial information, but the whole report is on a much smaller scale than the annual report.

Interim financial reporting

The market seemed a little surprised at the strength of Johnson Matthey's halfway figures, which itself is a surprise. This is one of those world-beating British companies with huge technical expertise and a commanding position in growth markets that should be emerging well from the recession.

Both its main divisions, environmental technologies and precious metals, have a significant exposure to automotive markets that are recovering strongly and to heavy-duty vehicles increasingly bound by environmental legislation that requires them to fit the sort of products that JM produces.

Add to that the fact that the first half of the previous financial year was inevitably depressed and a sharp rebound in the half-year to the end of September was to be expected. In the event, underlying operating profits from precious metals rebounded by 65 per cent on sales up 25 per cent. These go into cars and industries such as electronics, a substantial user of palladium.

At environmental technologies, the bounce-back was almost as pronounced, profits up 41 per cent on sales up 29 per cent. This takes precious metals such as platinum and palladium, the core of the original Johnson Matthey business, for use in the catalytic converters fitted into cars and, increasingly, heavy-duty diesel vehicles.

The market for HDD catalysts is worth about $600 million today but is expected to grow to $2.5 billion within about four years. JM has 65 per cent of this. Pre-tax profits for the first half were up by 32 per cent to £144 million and analysts are being guided towards the same again in the second half. The dividend is increased by a hefty 13 per cent to 12½p and would have been higher but for the need to rebuild dividend cover, 2.2 times' earnings last year, to a more healthy 2.5 times.

The problem for bulls of the stock is that Johnson Matthey shares are trading on about 17 times' this year's earnings, which does not suggest much growth in the share price short-term, however fast its core markets may be expanding. Analysts expect a clearer idea of the long-term strategy at the investors' day in February.

One route to growth, suggested by the most recent acquisition, would be to find further industrial applications for its existing process technology business, which falls within environmental technologies and makes refineries and other heavy plant more efficient. Until the long-term outlook is clearer, the shares remain a strong hold.

Source: **Cars and the road to growth: Johnson Matthey**, by Martin Waller © *The Times*, 25 November 2010

The press extract above includes comments on the interim financial report published by Johnson Matthey Plc for the six months to 30 September 2010, the first half of their 2010/11 financial year. Johnson Matthey Plc's pre-tax profits rose by 32% for the first six months of its financial year to 31 March 2011, which was broadly in line with an anticipated increase in global car production by over 25%. Although there was a slowing down in European markets there was strong growth in emerging markets, with China having become the world's largest car market in 2009. In response to the reported improved performance for the period to 30 September 2010, and an increase by 13% of its interim dividend to 12.5p, the company's share price rose 37p to £18.77 (*Financial Times*, 24 November 2010).

The publication of the annual report and accounts is always the time, of course, when forecasts may be seen to have been justified or not. There was uncertainty in 2010 and 2011 following the end of the Government scrappage scheme on new car sales on 31 March 2010, which did have an impact as new car sales in the UK fell by 11.5% between January 2010 and January 2011 (*http://www.am-online.com/NewCarSalesFigures/index.asp*).

The improvements in the first six months were expected to continue throughout the financial year and indeed pre-tax profit for the year ended 31 March 2011 for the Johnson Matthey group as a whole rose by 14% to £260.6m, from a 27% increase in sales revenue to £9.99bn. Johnson Matthey stated that they had performed strongly with a return to strong growth in their major markets after a disappointing performance in the year ended 31 March 2010.

With governments around the world continuously tightening emissions levels, companies and individuals are seeking to live and work in a cleaner and more energy-efficient way. This has created new opportunities for Johnson Matthey particularly in the area of hydrogen catalysts. Johnson Matthey already has a 35% average share of the market and expects to see the market grow by 6 to 8% over the next five years particularly in Asia, generating further demand for the company's products.

Johnson Matthey also identified another opportunity for its catalysts in China as a result of China's desire to use its coal reserves to produce cleaner fuel rather than burning it in coal-fired power stations. China has low natural gas reserves but lots of coal and has a great interest in blending methanol produced from coal with petrol which can then be used to power motor vehicles.

Platinum prices increased by 24% during the 2010/11 financial year, driven primarily by demand from India and China. Platinum is a precious metal used in catalytic converters and other oil and gas processes. Johnson Matthey's biggest business by sales revenue is its precious metals products division, which provided over 70% (£8.27bn) of its total sales revenue (£9.98bn) in the year ended 31 March 2011.

Following publication of the end of year results, analysts felt that the long-term health of the Johnson Matthey business looked assured as a reduction in the impact of energy use on the environment becomes ever more important. Signs for continued strong growth appeared in the catalyst market and, in anticipation of new emissions legislation in China and India, Johnson Matthey is already shipping products to these markets. However, analysts warn that a massive increase in the price of cerium oxide, a key component in car catalytic converters, which by April 2011 had already risen 20-fold on 2010 prices (see the report issued by Industrial Minerals, a non-metallic minerals service at *http://www.indmin.com/Article/2811393/RE-up-over-19-times-from-2010-market-says-hike-to-continue.html*) could dent profits in the medium term. In its annual report Johnson Matthey say that they believe that the risk will have been mitigated by March 2012. Johnson Matthey predicted continued growth but suggest that European manufacturing will be scaled down in order to reduce costs.

Financial statements, whether for internal or external parties, are defined as summaries of accounts to provide information for interested parties. The key reports and statements within the published annual report and accounts are illustrated in Figure 8.1.

In 1993 the Accounting Standards Board (ASB) issued a statement of good practice that supported the earlier suggestion made in the report of the **Cadbury Committee** (1992) that companies should include in their annual reports an operating and financial review (OFR) of the business. The reason for this suggestion was that businesses had become increasingly diversified and complex, and it had become increasingly difficult to understand information contained in financial reporting. Complex financial and organisational structures made it difficult to analyse and interpret financial information. It was felt that the OFR was needed to provide a greater insight into the affairs of the company, in addition to the information traditionally already provided by the chairman's statement and the directors' report.

The OFR was intended to cover the business as a whole for the year under review, and to include issues relevant to the assessment of future prospects. The OFR should include:

- brief reports that are easy to understand
- reports on each of the individual aspects of the business
- explanations of non-recurring aspects of the business
- discussion of matters that underpin the financial results for the period
- consideration of factors that might impact on the future performance of the business.

Figure 8.1	The key reports and statements within a company's annual report and accounts

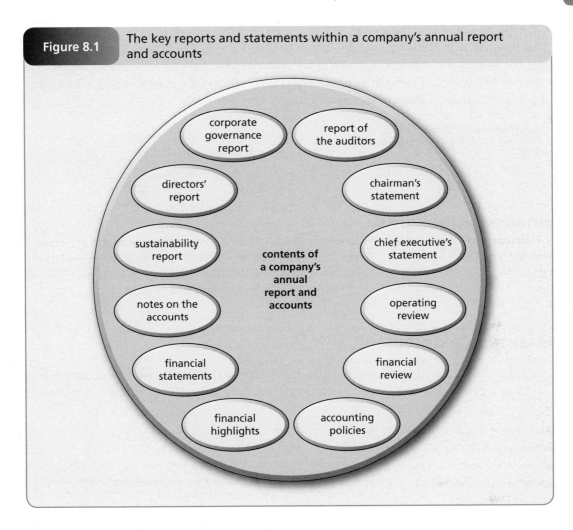

The OFR includes two separate reports which Johnson Matthey Plc includes within its business review:

■ an operations review, which includes:
  – new product development information
  – details of shareholders' returns
  – sensitivities of the financial results to specific accounting policies
  – risks and uncertainties
  – future investment

■ a financial review, which includes:

  – current cash position
  – sources of funding
  – treasury policy
  – capital structure
  – confirmation that the business is a going concern
  – factors outside the balance sheet impacting on the value of the business
  – taxation.

We will look at each of the reports and statements included in Figure 8.1 in this chapter, using the annual report and accounts 2011 of Johnson Matthey Plc as an illustration, except for the operations review, and also the corporate governance report and the report of the auditors, which were discussed in Chapter 6. With regard to the notes on the accounts, in this chapter we will consider only Note 1, which relates to **segmental reporting**.

> ### Progress check 8.1
>
> Why are annual accounts filed and published?

Financial highlights

The section headed financial highlights serves to focus on the headline numbers of revenue, profit before tax, earnings per share and dividends. Johnson Matthey's financial highlights are shown inside the front cover of its annual report and accounts 2011 and are illustrated on page 317.

Chairman's statement

In addition to the income statement and statement of cash flows for the year and the balance sheet as at the year-end date, the annual report and accounts includes much more financial and non-financial information such as:

- company policies
- financial indicators
- directors' remuneration
- employee numbers
- business analysis.

The annual report and accounts includes the chairman's statement. This offers an opportunity for the chairman of the company to report in unquantified and unaudited terms on the performance of the company during the past financial period and on likely future developments. Let's take a look at the Johnson Matthey chairman's statement from Sir John Banham, in his final year as chairman (see pages 282 to 283).

Sir John comments on the great improvement in performance of the company over the past year and his positive outlook for the future. He reports on the return to strong growth through seizing opportunities presented by the economic crisis and a 38% increase in earnings per share to a record 119.0 pence. During his period as chairman, earnings per share have seen a compound annual growth of over 10% over the past five years. He emphasises the importance of the robust global organic growth strategy that Johnson Matthey has maintained over several years, supported by heavy and increasing investment in research and development.

The main themes of Johnson Matthey's chairman's statement are the company's focus on its:

- global organic strategy
- worldwide investment in new highly-efficient capacity, particularly emission control catalyst manufacturing plants
- early action to reduce operating costs
- past and future high research and development expenditure
- group-wide sustainability initiatives through Sustainability 2017.

JOHNSON MATTHEY PERFORMED STRONGLY IN 2010/11 with good growth in its major markets. All of the group's businesses performed well, marking a return to strong growth for the group.

Financial Highlights 2011

	Year to 31st March		%
	2011	2010	change
Revenue	**£9,985m**	£7,839m	+27
Sales excluding precious metals	**£2,280m**	£1,886m	+21
Profit before tax	**£260.6m**	£228.5m	+14
Total earnings per share	**85.6p**	77.6p	+10
Underlying*:			
Profit before tax	**£345.5m**	£254.1m	+36
Earnings per share	**119.0p**	86.4p	+38
Dividend per share	**46.0p**	39.0p	+18

* Before amortisation of acquired intangibles, major impairment and restructuring charges, profit or loss on disposal of businesses and, where relevant, related tax effects.

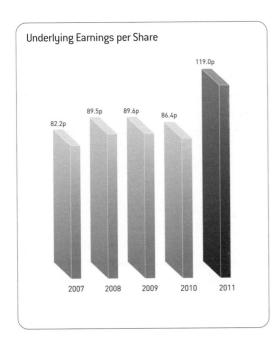

Underlying Earnings per Share

82.2p (2007), 89.5p (2008), 89.6p (2009), 86.4p (2010), 119.0p (2011)

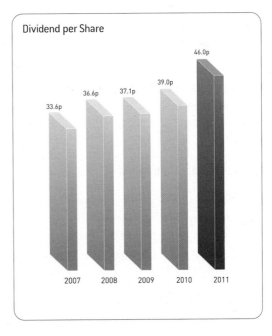

Dividend per Share

33.6p (2007), 36.6p (2008), 37.1p (2009), 39.0p (2010), 46.0p (2011)

Sir John also comments about the retirements from and replacements to the group's board of directors, and the appointment of his successor as chairman, Tim Stevenson OBE. As in previous years, Sir John affirms his belief that the most important investment that a company makes is the one that it makes in its people. He emphasises the enthusiasm, professionalism and dedication of Johnson Matthey's employees at all levels of the organisation.

Progress check 8.2

What is the purpose of a chairman's statement?

Chief executive's statement

Chief executives' statements generally include detail on the performance of the business particularly relating to products, markets, technology and the various geographical areas of activity. These statements include brief comments on the financial highlights of the preceding year and the recommended dividend payable to shareholders. The chief executive's statement includes a review of operations, which outlines the main factors underlying the business and identifies any changes or expected future changes which may impact on the business. It normally concludes with an outlook on the future prospects of the business.

The Johnson Matthey chief executive's statement for 2011, presented by Neil Carson (see pages 284 to 285), reinforces the chairman's statement with regard to recovery during 2011 from the 2010 effects of the economic recession and provides details about developments in the various divisions of the company including acquisitions. The report provides a great deal of information of particular interest to current and potential new shareholders relating to future growth opportunities, planned major investments, the development of new and existing technologies, and new product development. The importance of Johnson Matthey's ten-year strategy with its primary focus on organic growth, and sustainability as a key element of that strategy, are again emphasised. Neil Carson's report includes some detail of the headline financial results, but its main focus is on strategy and operations, and an outlook for the business over the next few years. Further detail is provided in the reports that follow the chief executive's statement that cover group activities, group strategy to deliver superior growth, group performance review (see page 286), group key performance indicators (see pages 287 to 288), operations review, and strategy in action with regard to the various technologies in which the group is engaged.

Financial review

The financial review goes into further financial detail than the chief executive's statement. It is normally prepared by the finance director. In the case of Johnson Matthey, the financial review has been prepared by its group finance director, Robert MacLeod. The purpose of the financial review is to review the results for the past year and to provide an overview of financial policy. Let's look at the Johnson Matthey financial review, included within the business review section of its annual report and accounts for the year 2011 (see pages 289 to 291).

The Johnson Matthey financial review begins with a review of the results for the year to 31 March 2011, with an initial focus on profit before tax. The financial review looks in detail at:

- profit before tax
- return on invested capital
- exchange rates
- interest
- return on sales
- taxation
- earnings per share
- cash flow
- dividend
- capital structure
- pensions
- borrowings

We can see that the financial review includes many of the financial performance measures we have discussed in Chapter 7; for example return on sales and return on investment, which are analysed by each area of business activity.

Johnson Matthey commented on the weakness of £ sterling during 2010/11 against most major currencies. Each one cent change in the average US$/£ exchange rate had an approximate £0.6m effect on the year's operating profit and a one cent change in the euro/£ exchange rate affected the year's operating profit by £0.5m. The group benefited by £1.8m from the fall in sterling against the US$, and by £1.0m from the fall in sterling against the Chinese renminbi. However, a strengthening **euro** caused a decrease of £1.1m in reported profits. Sterling fell against the South African rand but any impact was mitigated by operational factors. Exchange rate gains were responsible for increasing the group's operating profit for the year by £4.1m compared with 2009/10.

Further sections that follow the financial review are headed treasury policies, liquidity and going concern, risks and uncertainties, and research and development (see pages 292 to 296). The treasury policies section explains the group's policies with regard to financial **risk management** and treasury policies. Risk management is a key strategic area for the type of business in which Johnson Matthey is involved. This section also covers the group's approach and policies relating to interest rate risk and foreign currency risk; it also includes the **financial instruments** that are used by Johnson Matthey to manage financial risks. Risk relating to fluctuations in precious metal prices, which have a significant impact on Johnson Matthey's results, is also outlined in terms of policy and the way in which that area of risk is managed. The group finance director indicated in an outline of its policy the extent to which the group is risk averse. The group hedges against future changes in precious metal prices where such hedging can be done at acceptable cost.

The liquidity and going concern section explains the group's policy on funding, its group borrowings, and future funding requirements. The group undertakes sensitivity analyses of the key factors which could affect cash flow and funding requirements to ensure adequate resources to fund its operations for the foreseeable future and to be able to prepare its accounts on a going concern basis.

Johnson Matthey reported on its share price performance and other shareholder information on page 128 of its report and accounts for the year 2011 which is not reproduced in this book.

Johnson Matthey's share price each 31 March from 2002 to 2011 is shown in the chart below and illustrated in Figure 8.2.

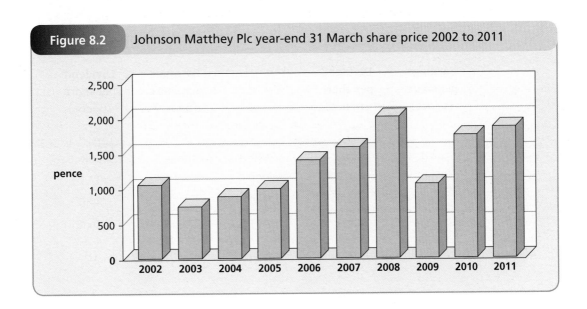

Figure 8.2 Johnson Matthey Plc year-end 31 March share price 2002 to 2011

	Share price		Share price
2002	1,046.0	2007	1,576.0
2003	737.0	2008	2,005.0
2004	879.5	2009	1,053.0
2005	989.0	2010	1,746.0
2006	1,396.0	2011	1,860.0

Accounting policies

The statement of accounting policies informs readers of the policies the company has pursued in preparation of the report and accounts, and of any deviation from the generally accepted fundamental accounting concepts and conventions. Johnson Matthey devotes a large part of its statement of accounting policies to its application of IFRSs and IASs (see pages 302 to 306).

Progress check 8.3

What information do the chief executive's statement and the financial review provide and how do these reports differ?

Worked example 8.1

We can use the Johnson Matthey Plc five-year record, which you will find on page 310, and the company's past years annual reports and accounts to present earnings per share and dividends per share for 2002 to 2011 in:

tabular form
    and
bar chart for comparison (see Figure 8.3).

	Earnings per share (pence)	Dividend per share (pence)		Earnings per share (pence)	Dividend per share (pence)
2002	49.0	24.6	2007	96.9	33.6
2003	55.4	25.5	2008	88.5	36.6
2004	56.0	26.4	2009	82.6	37.1
2005	53.2	27.7	2010	77.6	39.0
2006	70.8	30.1	2011	85.6	46.0

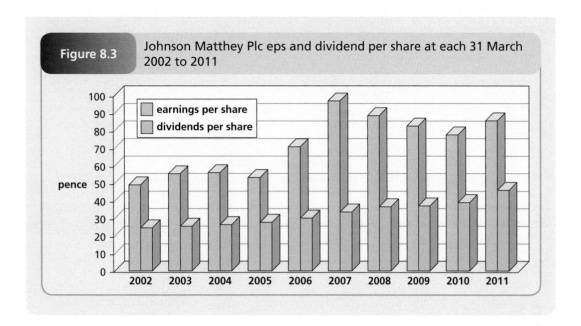

Figure 8.3 Johnson Matthey Plc eps and dividend per share at each 31 March 2002 to 2011

Income statement, balance sheet and statement of cash flows

The financial statements that are shown on pages 297 to 300 illustrate Johnson Matthey Plc's consolidated income statement, statement of cash flows, and statement of changes in equity for the year to 31 March 2011, and its consolidated balance sheet as at 31 March 2011.

The income statement is consolidated to include the results of all the companies within the group, together with the parent company, Johnson Matthey Plc. The consolidated income statement also shows previous year comparative numbers.

The balance sheet is presented in consolidated form, also showing previous year comparative numbers.

The statement of cash flows is consolidated to include the cash flows of all the companies within the group, and includes the parent company, Johnson Matthey Plc.

We will look at the financial performance of Johnson Matthey in Worked examples 8.2 and 8.3 using the two approaches to ratio analysis that were mentioned in the introduction to this chapter:

- horizontal analysis, or common size analysis, which provides a line-by-line comparison of the income statement (and balance sheet) with those of the previous year
- vertical analysis, where each item in the income statement (and balance sheet) is expressed as a percentage of the total sales (and total assets).

Horizontal analysis

We introduced the technique of horizontal analysis in Chapter 7. The following example illustrates the technique applied to a summary of the Johnson Matthey Plc income statement for the years to 31 March 2010 and 31 March 2011.

Worked example 8.2

We can prepare a horizontal analysis using a summary of the income statement results for Johnson Matthey Plc for 2010 and 2011, using 2010 as the base year.

(You may note that a part of the income statement refers to profit for the year from **continuing operations**, as distinct from **discontinued operations**, which are defined in the glossary at the end of this book.)

Johnson Matthey Plc
Consolidated income statement for the year ended 31 March 2011

	2011 £m	2010 £m
Revenue	9,984.8	7,839.4
Cost of sales	(9,328.2)	(7,325.4)
Gross profit	656.6	514.0
Distribution costs	(121.2)	(103.6)
Administrative expenses	(169.2)	(138.6)
Restructuring charge	(71.8)	(11.3)
Amortisation of acquired intangibles	(13.2)	(9.9)
Operating profit	281.2	250.6
Finance costs	(33.1)	(30.5)
Finance income	12.4	11.1
Share of profit/(loss) of associate	–	1.7
Dissolution of associate	0.1	(4.4)
Profit before tax	260.6	228.5
Income tax expense	(76.0)	(64.3)
Profit for the year from continuing operations	184.6	164.2
Profit for the year from discontinued operations	(1.9)	–
Profit for the year	182.7	164.2
Attributable to:		
Equity holders of the parent company	182.3	164.2
Minority interests	0.4	–
	182.7	164.2

Worked example 8.2 considers only two years, and has used 2010 as the base year 100. This means, for example:

If

$$\text{revenue for 2010 of } £7,839.4m = 100$$

Then

$$\text{revenue for 2011 of } £9,984.8m = \frac{£9,984.m \times 100}{£7,839.4m} = 127.4$$

Subsequent years may similarly be compared with 2010 as base 100, using the same sort of calculation.

Johnson Matthey Plc
Consolidated income statement for the year ended 31 March 2011

Horizontal analysis	2010	2011
Revenue	100.0	127.4
Cost of sales	100.0	127.3
Gross profit	100.0	127.7
Distribution costs	100.0	117.0
Administrative expenses	100.0	122.1
Restructuring charge	100.0	635.4
Amortisation of acquired intangibles	100.0	133.3
Operating profit	100.0	112.2
Finance costs	100.0	108.5
Finance income	100.0	111.7
Share of profit/(loss) of associate	100.0	–
Dissolution of associate	100.0	(2.3)
Profit before tax	100.0	114.0
Income tax expense	100.0	118.2
Profit for the year from continuing operations	100.0	112.4
Profit for the year from discontinued operations	100.0	–
Profit for the year	100.0	111.3
Attributable to:		
Equity holders of the parent company	100.0	111.0
Minority interests	100.0	–

The horizontal analysis technique is particularly useful to make a line-by-line comparison of a company's accounts for each accounting period over say 5 or 10 years, using the first year as the base year. When we look at a set of accounts we may by observation automatically carry out this process of assessing percentage changes in performance over time. However, presentation of the information in tabular form, for a number of years, gives a very clear picture of trends in performance in each area of activity and may provide the basis for further analysis.

We can easily see from the above horizontal analysis how the profit for 2011 compares with that for 2010. Sales increased by 27.4% in 2011 compared to 2010, and operating profit was 112.2% of the 2010 level. Profit for the year 2011 was 111.3% of the previous year.

Progress check 8.4

What can a horizontal analysis of the information contained in the financial statements of a company add to that provided from ratio analysis?

Vertical analysis

Worked example 8.3 uses total revenue as the basis for calculation. The following analysis confirms the conclusions drawn from the horizontal analysis.

Worked example 8.3

We can prepare a vertical analysis using the summary of the consolidated income statement results for Johnson Matthey Plc for 2010 and 2011 shown in Worked example 8.2.

Johnson Matthey Plc
Consolidated income statement for the year ended 31 March 2011

Vertical analysis	2010	2011
Revenue	100.0	100.0
Cost of sales	(93.5)	(93.4)
Gross profit	6.5	6.6
Distribution costs	(1.3)	(1.2)
Administrative expenses	(1.8)	(1.7)
Restructuring charge	(0.1)	(0.7)
Amortisation of acquired intangibles	(0.1)	(0.2)
Operating profit	3.2	2.8
Finance costs	(0.4)	(0.3)
Finance income	0.1	0.1
Share of profit/(loss) of associate	–	–
Dissolution of associate	–	–
Profit before tax	2.9	2.6
Income tax expense	(0.8)	(0.8)
Profit for the year from continuing operations	2.1	1.8
Profit for the year from discontinued operations	–	–
Profit for the year	2.1	1.8
Attributable to:		
Equity holders of the parent company	2.1	1.8
Minority interests	–	–

Operating profit fell from 3.2% of sales revenue in 2010 to 2.8% in 2011. Profit before tax fell from 2.9% of sales revenue in 2010 to 2.6% in 2011. Profit for the year fell from 2.1% of sales revenue in 2010 to 1.8% in 2011.

Progress check 8.5

What can a vertical analysis of the information contained in the financial statements of a company add to the information provided from a horizontal analysis and a ratio analysis?

Notes on the accounts

The section headed notes on the accounts in the annual report and accounts contains information that must be reported additional to, and in support of, the financial statements. This may be used to comment on financial performance. Generally, the information disclosed in notes to the accounts includes:

- segmental information – analysis by business and geographical area relating to revenue and net assets
- revenue
- exceptional items

- fees payable to auditors
- operating profit
- finance costs
- finance income
- taxation
- dividends
- earnings per share
- employee numbers
- employee costs
- post-employment benefits
- incentive schemes
- non-current assets
- goodwill
- other intangible assets
- investments in subsidiaries
- investments in associates
- other investments
- inventories
- construction contracts
- trade and other receivables
- trade and other payables
- other liabilities and assets held for sale
- net debt
- other financial assets
- other financial liabilities
- financial risk management: interest rate; foreign currency; liquidity; trade credit; capital management
- provisions
- **contingent liabilities**
- deferred taxation
- share capital
- reserves
- minority interests
- cash flow
- commitments
- acquisitions
- discontinued operations
- related parties transactions
- **post balance sheet events**
- estimation uncertainty.

Segmental reporting

The first note in the notes on the accounts in Johnson Matthey's report and accounts for 2011 is headed segmental information. International Financial Reporting Standard IFRS 8, Operating Segments, requires large companies to disclose segmental information by each operating segment, which could be a type of activity, a class of product or service or a geographical region. This analysis is required in order that users of financial information may carry out more meaningful financial analysis.

Most large companies usually comprise diverse businesses supplying different products and services, rather than being engaged in a single type of business. Each type of business activity may have:

- a different structure
- different levels of profitability
- different levels of growth potential
- different levels of risk exposure.

The financial statements of such diversified companies are consolidated to include all business activities, which is a potential problem for the users of financial information. For analysis and interpretation of financial performance, aggregate figures are not particularly useful for the following reasons:

- difficulties in evaluation of performance of a business which has interests that are diverse from the aggregated financial information
- difficulties of comparison of trends over time and comparison between companies because the various activities undertaken by the company are likely to differ in size and range in comparison with other businesses
- differences in conditions between different geographical markets, in terms of levels of risk, profitability and growth
- differences in conditions between different geographical markets, in terms of political and social factors, environmental factors, currencies and **inflation** rates.

Segmental reporting analysis enables:

- the further analysis of segmental performance to determine more accurately the likely growth prospects for the business as a whole
- evaluation of the impact on the company of changes in conditions relating to particular activities
- improvements in internal management performance, because it may be monitored through disclosure of segmental information to shareholders
- evaluation of the acquisition and disposal performance of the company.

An operating segment is a component of a company that engages in business activities from which it earns revenues and incurs expenses and for which discrete financial information is available.

Worked example 8.4

The information in the table below relates to global sales by Nestlé SA, the Swiss nutrition and foods giant, for the years 2009 and 2008.

Figures in Swiss francs (CHF) millions

	Europe 2009	Americas 2009	Asia and Africa 2009	Europe 2008	Americas 2008	Asia and Africa 2008
Beverages	5,362	3,746	5,331	5,072	3,830	5,576
Milk products	3,147	9,884	5,228	2,708	9,698	5,013
Prepared dishes	7,243	5,291	2,565	6,288	5,414	2,680
Confectionery	5,416	4,632	1,850	4,686	4,831	1,852
Pet care	3,930	7,804	733	3,774	8,395	770
Total sales	25,098	31,357	15,707	22,528	32,168	15,891

(i) Using the information provided we may prepare a simple table that compares the sales for 2009 with the sales for the year 2008.

(ii) We can also consider how a simple sales analysis can provide an investor with information that is more useful than just global sales for the year.

(i)

	Europe			Americas			Asia and Africa		
	2009		2008	2009		2008	2009		2008
Beverages	5,362	+5.72%	5,072	3,746	−2.19%	3,830	5,331	−4.39%	5,576
Milk products	3,147	+16.21%	2,708	9,884	+1.92%	9,698	5,228	+4.29%	5,013
Prepared dishes	7,243	+15.19%	6,288	5,291	−2.27%	5,414	2,565	−4.29%	2,680
Confectionery	5,416	+15.58%	4,686	4,632	−4.12%	4,831	1,850	−0.01%	1,852
Pet care	3,930	+4.13%	3,774	7,804	−7.04%	8,395	733	−4.81%	770
Total sales	25,098	+11.41%	22,528	31,357	−2.52%	32,168	15,707	−1.16%	15,891

(ii) Numbers that are blandly presented in a global format do not usually reveal trends. Analysis of information year on year by area and by percentage, for example, may reveal trends and may illustrate the impact of new policies or the changes in specific economic environments. The analysis of the Nestlé SA sales for the two years shows:

■ in which geographical area sales have increased or decreased
■ which products' sales have increased or decreased.

Analysis of the results over several years is usually needed to provide meaningful trend information as a basis for investigation into the reasons for increases and decreases.

For each operating segment of a company IFRS 8 requires information to be provided about

■ how the business identifies its operating segments
■ the types of products and services from which it earns revenues in each operating segment
■ the reported profit or loss of each segment.

Also required is an analysis of revenues and non-current assets by geographical area irrespective of the identification of operating segments and a requirement to disclose information about transactions with major customers.

Let's take a look at Johnson Matthey's segmental reporting (see pages 307 to 309). This may be used to provide even more useful information through horizontal and vertical analysis of the numbers. Such an analysis over a 5- or 10-year period would be particularly useful to identify trends in performance, and changes that may have taken place in the activities of the business and the areas of the world in which the company has operated.

Worked example 8.5

If we refer to note 1 in the Johnson Matthey Plc notes on the accounts in their annual report and accounts 2011 we can identify total sales revenue for each global division for 2011 and 2010. We can use this to present the data in both pie chart format (see Figure 8.4 and Figure 8.5) and bar chart format (see Figure 8.6) and more clearly explain JM's sales results for 2011 and 2010.

Figure 8.4   Johnson Matthey Plc sales revenue 2011

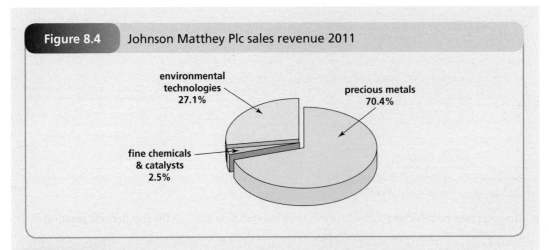

Figure 8.5   Johnson Matthey Plc sales revenue 2010

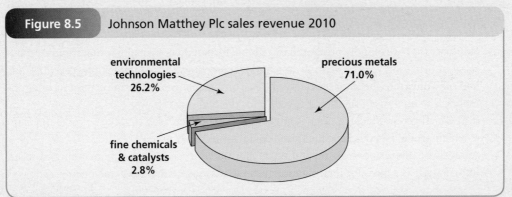

Figure 8.6   Johnson Matthey Plc sales revenue 2011 and 2010

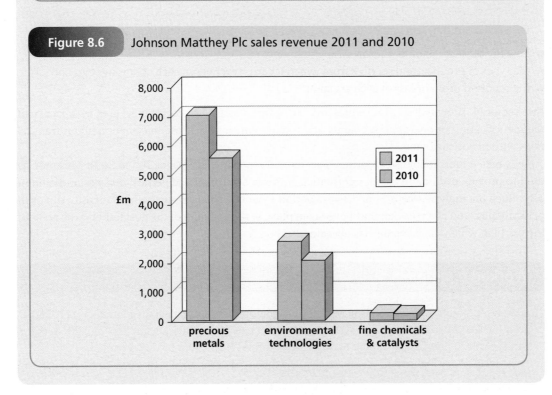

The pie charts give a broad indication of sales revenue by type of business, and show that for both years precious metals provide over two-thirds of the sales revenue and is increasing, and environmental technologies provide over one quarter of sales revenue. Fine chemicals and catalysts is the smallest sector that provides the balance.

The bar chart is probably more useful in showing more clearly that sales revenue from the largest sector has increased in 2011 over 2010, that the next largest sector has decreased, and the smallest sector has remained at around the same volume.

There are many problems relating to the principle of disclosure of segmental information, some of which we have already identified:

- directors may be reluctant to disclose information that may damage the competitive position of the company – foreign competitors may not have to disclose similar data
- segmental information may not be useful since the total company results are what should be relevant to shareholders
- some users of information may not be sufficiently financially expert to avoid being confused by the segmental information
- conglomerates may choose not to disclose segmental information, whereas a single-activity company by definition is unable to hide anything.

There are, in addition, some accounting problems concerned with the preparation of segmental reports:

- identification of operating segments is not defined in IFRS 8, but is left to the judgement of the directors of the company
- lack of definition of segments results in difficulty in comparison of companies
- difficulties in analysis and apportionment of costs that are common between operating segments
- difficulties in the treatment of costs of transfers of goods and services between segments.

Progress check 8.6

Describe what is meant by segmental reporting and to whom it is useful.

Sustainability reporting

An inspection of Johnson Matthey's report and accounts 2011 will reveal that sustainability, and health and safety issues with regard to its employees, customers and the community, rank highly amongst the company's priorities. This is demonstrated in the coverage given to such issues in the section of the business review headed sustainability (see pages 45 to 55 of Johnson Mathey's annual report and accounts 2011, not reproduced in this book).

Throughout the past 10 years or so companies have started to show greater interest in their position with regard to environmental and social issues. General corporate awareness has increased as to how the adoption of particular policies may have adverse social and environmental effects. Environmental issues naturally focus on our inability to sustain our use of non-renewable resources, the disappearance of the ozone layer and forestation, pollution and waste treatment. Social issues may include problems associated with race, gender, disability, sexual orientation and age, and the way that companies manage bullying, the incidence of accidents, employee welfare, training and development.

The increase in awareness of environmental and social issues has followed the concern that the focus of traditional reporting has been weighted too heavily towards the requirements of shareholders, with too little regard for the other stakeholders. That led to an over-emphasis on the financial performance, particularly the profitability, of the business. The accountancy profession and other interested parties have given thought to the widening of the annual report and accounts to meet the requirements of all stakeholders, and not just the shareholders of the business.

In March 2000, the UK Government appointed a Minister for Corporate Social Responsibility, and subsequently produced two reports on CSR:

- Business and Society, developing corporate social responsibility in the UK (2001)
- Business and Society – corporate social responsibility report (2002).

The UK Government, prior to May 2010, viewed CSR as the business contribution to sustainable development goals. They regarded CSR as essentially about how business takes account of its economic, social and environmental impacts in the way it operates – maximising the benefits and minimising the downsides. Indeed, the role played by businesses was clearly put at the centre of the Government's vision for the development of sustainable CSR, which saw 'UK businesses taking account of their economic, social and environmental impacts, and acting to address the key sustainable development challenges based on their core competences wherever they operate – locally, regionally and internationally'. However, following the general election of May 2010, the UK has been without a minister for CSR, thus putting the responsibility to continue its development firmly with businesses in the private sector.

CSR is about companies moving beyond a base of legal compliance to integrating socially responsible behaviour into their core values, and in recognition of the sound business benefits in doing so. In principle, CSR applies to SMEs as well as to large companies.

There is currently no consensus of 'best practice' in the area of social and **environmental reporting**. Nor is there a compulsory requirement for companies to include such statements in their annual reports and accounts. The Government's approach has been to encourage the adoption and reporting of CSR through best practice guidance, including development of a Corporate Responsibility Index and, where appropriate, intelligent regulation and fiscal incentives. Most large companies have reacted positively to the need for such reporting, although the quality, style and content, and the motives for inclusion, may vary from company to company. Motives may range from a genuine wish to contribute to the goal of sustainable development to simple reassurance, or attempts to mould and change opinion, and political lobbying.

While CSR does not currently appear one of the UK Government's top priorities, the European Union remains strongly supportive of CSR initiatives. The EU defines CSR as 'a concept whereby companies integrate social and environmental concerns in their business operations and in their interaction with their stakeholders on a voluntary basis'. The EU material on CSR may be viewed on its website at: *http://ec.europa.eu/enterprise/policies/sustainable-business/corporate-social-responsibility*.

Companies that include CSR reporting in their annual reports and accounts now endeavour to go beyond a simple outline of their environmental and social policies. Many companies include reports expanding on these policies in qualitative ways that explain the performance of the business in its compliance with national and international standards. Some companies (for example, Johnson Matthey Plc) have taken the next step to provide detailed quantitative reports of targets, performance, and the financial impact of social and environmental issues.

CSR performance reporting is still in its infancy. Although there has not been a great deal of work on what really constitutes best practice in CSR reporting, some research has suggested that the higher standards of quality in CSR reporting are to be found in large companies which have the potential for greater impacts on the environment. Companies engaged in CSR may benefit from improvements in their image and reputation, and in the longer term perhaps their profitability. As the focus on standardisation of targets, indicators and audit of social and environmental performance increases, then the pressure for wider reporting may increase, and perhaps may be supported by a CSR financial reporting standard.

Progress check 8.7

What is sustainability reporting and why is it becoming increasingly important to companies?

Responsibility of directors' report

The responsibility of directors' report included in Johnson Matthey's report and accounts 2011 (see page 211 in Chapter 6) emphasises the responsibility that directors of companies have for the preparation of the annual report and accounts. The report states that the directors are responsible for preparing the annual report and the group and parent company accounts in accordance with company law requirements for each financial year. Under that law they are required to prepare the group accounts in accordance with International Financial Reporting Standards (IFRSs) as adopted by the European Union (EU) and applicable law and have elected to prepare the parent company accounts on the same basis. The group and parent company accounts are required by law and IFRSs as adopted by the EU to present fairly the financial position of the group and the parent company and the performance for that period; the Companies Act 2006 provides in relation to such accounts that references in the relevant part of that Act to accounts giving a true and fair view are references to their achieving a fair presentation.

The directors are required to:

- select suitable accounting policies and apply them consistently
- make judgements and estimates that are reasonable and prudent
- state whether they have been prepared in accordance with IFRSs as adopted by the EU
- prepare the accounts on the going concern basis unless it is inappropriate to presume that the group and parent company will continue in business.

Each of the directors of a company whose names and functions are listed within the annual report and accounts, are required to confirm that:

- they have complied with applicable UK law and in conformity with IFRSs in preparation of their financial statements
- the financial statements give a true and fair view of the assets, liabilities, financial position and profit or loss of the company and all companies included within their consolidated group accounts as a whole
- they have provided a fair review of the development and performance of the business and the position of the company and all companies included within their consolidated group accounts as a whole, together with a description of the principal risks and uncertainties they face.

Progress check 8.8

What purpose does the responsibility of directors report serve and what information does it usually include?

Inflation and reporting

Inflation is a general increase in the price level over time. We will consider the impact of inflation on the financial statements prepared under the traditional, historical cost convention. In this book we will not cover in detail the alternative approaches to reporting the effect of inflation, other than to highlight the level of awareness of the problem. The accountancy profession has, over the years, considered many proposals for methods to try and deal with inflation-related problems requiring financial reports to reflect the effects of inflation. The proposals relating to the treatment of inflation in financial reporting have revolved around two schools of thought:

■ the purchasing power approach, using a price index like the Retail Price Index (RPI), to adjust the historical costs of transactions

■ the current cost accounting approach, which requires non-current assets and inventories to be included in the accounts at their current value rather than their historical cost.

We have previously discussed the reasons for using money as the unit of measurement, which include its properties as a medium of exchange and a store of value. Its use implies some stability in its value, which in the real world is patently not the case. One £ held today does not have the same value as one £ held in a year's time; it will purchase less in a year's time despite the relatively low levels of inflation prevailing in the UK over recent years – but note how in the mid-1970s the inflation level reached nearly 25% per annum!

The basic problem of inflation in financial reporting is that it tends to overstate profit calculated using traditional historical costs. In periods of inflation the impact on profit is seen in four key areas:

■ borrowing and extended credit received are worth less in real terms when settled compared to when the borrowing took place or the credit was received, which is a gain for the business

■ financial investments made and extended credit allowed are worth less in real terms when settled compared to when the investments took place or the credit was granted, which is a loss for the business

■ depreciation of non-current assets is understated, being based on non-current assets' historical costs and so when assets eventually have to be replaced the replacement cost will be higher, for which the company may have provided insufficient cash resources

■ closing inventories will be more likely to have higher values, on a like-for-like basis, compared with opening inventories and so profit may be overstated, but the pressure on cash resources will be felt when inventories have been sold and then need to be replaced at higher prices.

It is important for the non-accounting specialist to be aware that the published financial statements of UK limited companies have not been adjusted to allow for the effects of inflation. Over extended periods there is therefore significant distortion in the accounting information that has been presented based on historical costs. However, the non-specialist may be assured that the accountancy profession continues to grapple with the problem of inflation in financial reporting.

> ### Progress check 8.9
>
> Why should users of financial information be aware of the effects of inflation on financial reporting?

Value added statements

Value added is a measure of the wealth created by a company through its activities. It is the difference between the value of its sales and the cost of the materials and services that it has bought in.

The **value added statement** is effectively a rearrangement of the income statement. It shows how value added is distributed among the relevant parties:

■ employees
■ lenders

- shareholders
- government

and the amount to provide maintenance and expansion of the business.

The value added statement has often been compared with a cake or a pie, with interested parties asking 'are we getting our fair share of the cake?' This question is often the basis of trades union employee wage negotiations with companies.

The Accounting Standards Committee in 1975 published *The Corporate Report*, which described the value added statement as 'the simplest and most immediate way of putting profit into a proper perspective vis-à-vis the whole enterprise as a collective effort of capital, management and employees'. The value added statement has certain advantages as a business performance measure as it:

- is simple to calculate
- enables comparison between companies with different activities
- improves relationships between shareholders, managers and employees
- cannot be manipulated to the same extent as accounting profit
- enables further analysis, for example vertical analysis against revenue
- lends itself to integration with employee incentive schemes.

The value added statement for Johnson Matthey Plc shown in Worked example 8.6 illustrates how value added has been derived and how it has been applied in absolute terms for the years 2010 and 2011. A vertical analysis of the numbers perhaps provides a better basis for comparison, which is illustrated in Worked example 8.7.

Worked example 8.6

We can prepare a value added statement for Johnson Matthey Plc using the consolidated income statements, the notes on the accounts for 2011 and 2010, and the five-year record.

Johnson Matthey Plc
Consolidated value added statement for the year ended 31 March 2011

Figures in £m	2011	2010
Sales revenue (from the consolidated income statement)	9,984.8	7,839.4
Bought in materials and services (balancing number)	8,926.3	7,140.5
Value added	1,058.5	698.9
Applied as follows:		
To pay employees		
Employees' compensation (from the notes on the accounts, 12b)	492.3	405.9
Key management personnel compensation (from the notes on the accounts, 12c)	10.9	10.7
To pay providers of capital		
Net interest on loans (from the consolidated income statement)	20.7	19.4
Dividends to shareholders (from the notes on the accounts, 10)	86.1	78.4
To pay Government		
Income tax (from the consolidated income statement)	76.0	64.3
To provide maintenance and expansion		
Depreciation, amortisation and impairment (from the five-year record)	208.2	132.1
Retained earnings (from the five-year record)	164.3	(11.9)
	1,058.5	698.9

Worked example 8.7

We can use the value added statement from Worked example 8.6 to:

prepare a vertical analysis of the data, and

present the results in a pie chart format (see Figures 8.7 and 8.8).

Johnson Matthey Plc
Consolidated vertical analysis value added statement
for the year ended 31 March 2011

	2011	2010
Value added	100.0	100.0
Applied as follows:		
To pay employees		
Employees' compensation	46.5	58.1
Key management personnel compensation	1.0	1.5
To pay providers of capital		
Net interest on loans	2.0	2.8
Dividends to shareholders	8.1	11.2
To pay Government		
Income tax	7.2	9.2
To provide maintenance and expansion		
Depreciation	19.7	18.9
Retained earnings	15.5	(1.7)

Figure 8.7   Johnson Matthey Plc % distribution of value added for the year 2011

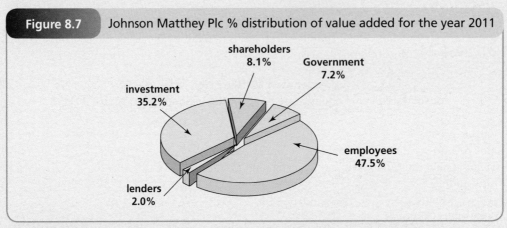

Figure 8.8   Johnson Matthey Plc % distribution of value added for the year 2010

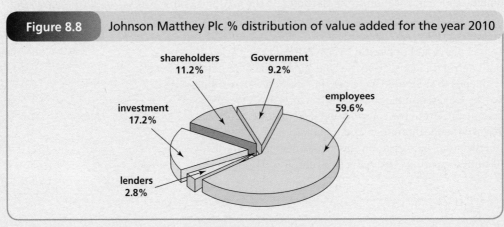

The vertical analysis of the value added statement for Johnson Matthey Plc shows us that about one half of the value generated by the business is distributed to employees in the form of salaries, wages and benefits (59.6% for 2010 down to 47.5% for 2011). The proportion of value added distributed to the providers of capital (lenders and shareholders) was 10.1% for 2011 (14.0% for 2010), and the proportion paid to lenders was lower in 2011 than 2010 (2.0% compared with 2.8%). Corporation tax fell from 9.2% in 2010 to 7.2% in 2011.

The remainder of value added is retained for maintenance and expansion of assets. This increased from 17.2% in 2010 to 35.2% in 2011, indicating an increase in the financing of growth of the business through internally generated sources. This resulted primarily from a large increase in the retained earnings of the business.

The value added statement provides a great deal of clarification on company performance, but, of course, also has disadvantages:

- some difficulty encountered in measurement and reporting
- classification of items – for example taxation, which normally excludes employee tax and National Insurance, and business rates
- unstandardised format with varying treatment of items in the value added statement
- current lack of popularity among companies, despite the inclusion of a value added statement by a large percentage of large companies up to the early 1980s in their annual reports and accounts.

The value added statement seems unlikely to replace the conventional income statement or statement of cash flows as a decision-making tool or as a measure of business performance. However, it may continue to be useful for internal communication of company financial performance to employees, and in support of employee incentive schemes.

Progress check 8.10

What is a value added statement and what does it tell us?

Summary of key points

- Limited companies prepare their annual reports and accounts to keep shareholders informed about financial performance and the financial position of the business.
- The annual report and accounts of a public limited company requires disclosure of a great deal of both financial and non-financial information in addition to the financial statements.
- The annual report and accounts allows evaluation of a public limited company in a wider context than was possible from the sort of financial information traditionally required by the shareholders.
- Horizontal analysis of the income statement (which may also be applied to the balance sheet) for two or more years starts with a base year 100 and shows each item, line-by-line, indexed against the base year, and is particularly useful in looking at performance trends over a number of years.
- Vertical analysis of the income statement (which may also be applied to the balance sheet) shows every item as a percentage of revenue (or in the balance sheet – total assets), and is also particularly useful in looking at performance trends over a number of years.
- Segmental reporting provides a further dimension to the financial statements through analysis of revenues and expenses by operating segment and analysis of geographical results.

- The quality and depth of sustainability reporting, in both qualitative and quantitative terms, is becoming increasingly important as annual reports and accounts are required to meet the needs of all stakeholders, not just the shareholders.

- Although the financial statements of limited companies are not adjusted for the effects of inflation, the impact of inflation is a factor that must be considered in evaluation of business performance.

- The value added statement, which is an alternative presentation of the traditional income statement, measures wealth as the value added by the business rather than the profit earned by the business.

Assessment material

Questions

Q8.1 **(i)** Why, and for whom, do the annual reports and accounts of limited companies have to be prepared?

(ii) Where do they have to be filed?

(iii) Who are the main users of the information contained in the annual report and accounts?

(iv) How do they use the information?

Q8.2 **(i)** Why do you think that the directors, chairman, chief executive and finance director of a plc each need to provide a statement or report for inclusion in the annual report and accounts?

(ii) What purpose do these reports serve and in what ways do they differ?

Q8.3 **(i)** Describe the key elements of Johnson Matthey's financial review that are included in their report and accounts for 2011, and what these indicate about the performance of the business.

(ii) Why do you think that about a third of this report is devoted to financial risk management?

(iii) What does risk management mean?

(iv) What are the financial risks faced by Johnson Matthey?

Q8.4 Describe the technique of horizontal analysis and how it may be used to evaluate, explain and compare company performance.

Q8.5 Describe the technique of vertical analysis and how it may be used to evaluate, explain and compare company performance.

Q8.6 **(i)** What were the inadequacies in financial statement reporting that IFRS 8, Operating Segments, sought to address and how did it do this?

(ii) What are the practical problems that companies face associated with their compliance with IFRS 8?

Q8.7 **(i)** Why do you think that sustainability reporting has become increasingly important in terms of corporate awareness, and with regard to the awareness of the non-business community?

(ii) Examine the annual reports and accounts of a number of large UK plcs to critically evaluate and compare their sustainability reporting with that provided by Johnson Matthey in its 2011 report and accounts.

Q8.8　**(i)**　How does inflation distort accounting information that has been prepared under the historical cost convention?

　　　　(ii)　In what ways has the accountancy profession considered some alternative approaches to try and deal with the problem of inflation?

Q8.9　**(i)**　Explain what is meant by a value added statement.

　　　　(ii)　In what ways may a value added statement be used to measure financial performance?

　　　　(iii)　What are the disadvantages in using value added statements?

　　　　(iv)　Why do you think the levels of popularity they enjoyed in the 1980s have not been maintained?

Q8.10　What information included in the annual report and accounts of UK public listed companies (plcs) may influence prospective investors and in what ways? How impartial do you think this information is?

Discussion points

D8.1　'The annual reports and accounts prepared by the majority of UK plcs serve to ensure that shareholders, and other stakeholders, are kept very well informed about the affairs of their businesses.' Discuss.

D8.2　'In the global competitive world in which we live, company directors should be able to exercise their full discretion as to the amount of information they disclose in their annual reports and accounts. If they are not allowed this discretion in disclosure, their companies may be driven out of business by their competitors, particularly foreign competitors who may not have the restriction of such extensive reporting requirements.' Discuss.

D8.3　'The main reason that companies increasingly include sustainability reports in their annual reports and accounts is to change the views of users and regulators about the activities in which their businesses are engaged, in order to pre-empt and avoid any negative or harmful reactions.' Discuss this statement by drawing on examples of the type of businesses to which this might apply.

　　　　(Hint: You may wish to research British Gas, as well as Johnson Matthey Plc, to provide material for this discussion.)

Exercises

Solutions are provided in Appendix 2 to all exercise numbers highlighted in colour.

Level I

E8.1　*Time allowed – 60 minutes*

Refer to note 1 in Johnson Matthey Plc's notes on the accounts in their annual report and accounts 2011 and identify the geographical analysis by origin for 2011 and 2010 for:

(a)　total revenue

(b)　non-current assets.

> **(i)**　Present each of the data from (a) and (b) in both pie chart and bar chart format.
>
> **(ii)**　What do the charts you have prepared tell you about Johnson Matthey's revenue and non-current assets for 2011 and 2010?

E8.2 *Time allowed – 60 minutes*

(i) Use the five-year record of Johnson Matthey (see page 310) to prepare a horizontal analysis of the income statement for the five years 2007 to 2011, using 2007 as the base year.

(ii) What does this analysis tell us about Johnson Matthey's financial performance over that period?

E8.3 *Time allowed – 60 minutes*

(i) Use the five-year record of Johnson Matthey (see page 310) to prepare a horizontal analysis of the balance sheet for the five years 2007 to 2011, using 2007 as the base year.

(ii) What does this analysis tell us about Johnson Matthey's financial position over that period?

Level II

E8.4 *Time allowed – 60 minutes*

(i) Use the five-year record of Johnson Matthey (see page 310) to prepare a vertical analysis of the income statement for the five years 2007 to 2011.

(ii) What does this analysis tell us about Johnson Matthey's financial performance over that period?

E8.5 *Time allowed – 60 minutes*

Note 1 in the Johnson Matthey Plc notes on the accounts in their annual report and accounts 2011 provides a segmental analysis for the years 2011 and 2010.

Prepare a horizontal analysis from this information, with 2010 as the base year, and use it to explain the appropriate elements of financial performance and the changes in the financial position of the business.

E8.6 *Time allowed – 60 minutes*

Refer to the financial statements included in Johnson Matthey's report and accounts 2011 to calculate the appropriate ratios for comparison with the previous year, and include them in a report on the profitability of the group (see Chapter 7).

E8.7 *Time allowed – 60 minutes*

Refer to the financial statements included in Johnson Matthey's report and accounts 2011 to calculate the appropriate ratios for comparison with the previous year, and to give your assessment of the company's sources and uses of cash, and include them in a report on the group's cash position (see Chapter 7).

E8.8 *Time allowed – 60 minutes*

Refer to the financial statements included in Johnson Matthey's report and accounts 2011 to calculate the appropriate ratios for comparison with the previous year, and include them in a report on the working capital of the group (see Chapter 7).

E8.9   *Time allowed – 60 minutes*

> Refer to the financial statements included in Johnson Matthey's report and accounts 2011 to calculate the appropriate ratios for comparison with the previous year, and include them in a report on the investment performance of the group (see Chapter 7).

E8.10   *Time allowed – 60 minutes*

> Refer to the financial statements included in Johnson Matthey's report and accounts 2011 to calculate the appropriate ratios for comparison with the previous year, and include them in a report on the financial structure of the group (see Chapter 7).

E8.11   *Time allowed – 90 minutes*

The notes and five-year income statement extracts from the financial statements of an alcoholic drinks group are shown below.

> You are required to use these to carry out an appropriate analysis and provide a report on the likely explanations of differences in performance over the five years.

Notes:

- The group sells alcohol-based products to consumers and operates in nearly every major country throughout the world.
- Local and global competition is intense in many markets.
- Brands have been sold during the five years.
- New products are invariably variants on the group's basic products of beers, wines and spirits.
- The group share price had been relatively static due to the maturity of the market and the pattern of profits.
- Other investment income shown in the five-year analysis related to an investment in a French luxury goods group.
- Soon after year six the group merged with another international food and drinks business, which also had an extensive portfolio of own and purchased brands.
- After the merger several brands were sold to competitors.
- After the merger many of the directors left the group's management team.
- Exchange rates over the five-year period in several of the group's markets were quite volatile.
- The group had £1.4 billion of brands in its balance sheet.

Five-year income statement

	Year 5 £m	Year 4 £m	Year 3 £m	Year 2 £m	Year 1 £m
Sales revenue	4,730	4,681	4,690	4,663	4,363
Gross profit	961	943	956	938	1,023
Other investment income	113	47	89	(48)	(24)
Operating profit	1,074	990	1,045	890	999
Finance cost	(99)	(114)	(130)	(188)	(204)
Profit before tax	975	876	915	702	795
Income tax expense	(259)	(251)	(243)	(247)	(242)
Profit after tax	716	625	672	455	553
Minority interests	(31)	(30)	(31)	(22)	(29)
Profit for the year	685	595	641	433	524
Dividends	(295)	(302)	(279)	(258)	(237)

	Year 5 £m	Year 4 £m	Year 3 £m	Year 2 £m	Year 1 £m
Retained earnings	390	293	362	175	287
Earnings per share	35.1p	29.4p	31.8p	22.9p	28.1p
Interest cover	10.8	8.7	8.0	4.7	4.9
Dividend cover	2.2	2.0	2.3	1.8	2.3

E8.12   *Time allowed – 90 minutes*

The BOC Group is a company in the chemical industry, and is in the same industrial sector as Johnson Matthey Plc. Locate the website for BOC Group plc on the Internet. Review their most recent annual report and accounts and prepare a report that compares it with Johnson Matthey Plc's report and accounts for the same year. Your report should include comments that relate to specific points that have been covered in Chapter 8, and also the differences and the similarities between the two companies.

9

Financing the business

Contents

Learning objectives

Completion of this chapter will enable you to:

- identify the different sources of finance available to an organisation
- explain the concept of gearing, and the debt/equity ratio
- explain what is meant by the weighted average cost of capital (WACC)
- calculate the cost of equity and the cost of debt
- appreciate the concept of risk with regard to capital investment
- outline the capital asset pricing model (CAPM) and the β factor
- analyse return on equity as a function of financial structure
- explain the use of economic value added (EVA™) and market value added (MVA) as performance measures and value creation incentives.

Introduction

This chapter begins with an outline of the types of finance available to organisations to fund their long-term capital investment and short-term requirement for working capital. Financing may be internal or external to the organisation, and either short-term (shorter than one year) or medium- to long-term (longer than one year).

This chapter will consider a number of financing options such as leasing and Government grants, but will focus on the main sources of long-term external finance available to an entity to finance such investments: loans (or debt) and ordinary shares (or equity). We shall also discuss gearing or financial structure, which relates to the relationship between the debt and equity of the entity.

The appraisal of investment projects by a company inevitably involves calculations that use some sort of discount rate. The discount rate that is normally used is based on the company's cost of capital. A company's cost of capital is dependent on the financial structure of the entity, its relative proportions and cost of debt (loans) and cost of equity capital (shares). In Chapter 7 we introduced WACC and in this chapter we will consider its calculation and application.

We will look at how the costs of equity and debt may be determined. One of the fundamental differences between equity and debt is the risk associated with each type of financing and its impact on their cost. The capital asset pricing model (CAPM) is introduced to show how risk impacts on the cost of equity.

This chapter looks briefly at the relationship between the return on equity and the financial structure of the company. The chapter closes with an introduction to economic value added (EVA) and market value added (MVA). These measures are increasingly replacing traditional performance measures in many large companies. An outline of these recently developed techniques is considered in terms of their use as both performance measures and motivational tools.

Sources of finance

In Chapter 3 we considered some of the various types of business finance when we looked at the balance sheet. Organisations require finance for both short- and medium- to long-term requirements and the financing is usually matched with the funding requirement. Longer-term finance (longer than one year) is usually used to fund capital investment in non-current assets and other longer-term projects. Short-term finance (shorter than one year) is usually used to fund the organisation's requirement for working capital.

Both short- and long-term finance may be either internal or external to the organisation.

Internal finance may be provided from:

- retained earnings
- trade credit
- cash improvements gained from the more effective management of working capital.

Retained earnings

Retained earnings are the funds generated that are surplus to:

- the costs of adding to or replacing non-current assets
- the operational costs of running the business
- net interest charges
- tax charges
- dividend payments.

There is statistical evidence which shows that through the 2000s the majority of capital funding of UK companies continued to be derived from internal sources of finance. However, this is not free. The profit or net earnings generated from the operations of the company belongs to the shareholders of the company. There is a cost, an opportunity cost, which is the best alternative return that shareholders could obtain on these funds elsewhere in the financial markets.

It is the directors who recommend and the shareholders who vote at the annual general meeting (AGM) how much of those earnings is distributed to shareholders as dividends, the balance being held and reinvested in the business. The retained earnings of the company are increased by net profit less any dividends payable; they are part of the shareholders' funds and therefore appear within the equity of the company. Similarly any losses will reduce the retained earnings of the company. The cost of shareholders' equity is reflected in the level of dividends paid to shareholders, which is usually dependent on how well the company has performed during the year.

The main source of external short-term funding is short-term debt.

Short-term debt

Short-term financial debts are the elements of overdrafts, loans and leases that are repayable within one year of the balance sheet date. Short-term finance tends to be more expensive but more flexible than long-term debt. Short-term debt is therefore normally matched to finance the fluctuations in levels of the company's net current assets, its working capital.

Such short-term finance represents a higher risk for the borrower. Interest rates can be volatile, and an overdraft, for example, is technically repayable on demand. The company may finance its operations by taking on further short-term debt, as levels of working capital increase. Because of the higher risk associated with short-term debt, many companies adopting a conservative funding policy may accept a reduction in profitability and use long-term debt to finance not only non-current assets, but also a proportion of the company's working capital. Less risk-averse companies may use short-term debt to finance both working capital and non-current assets; such debt provides increased profitability because of its lower cost.

We will discuss each of the other sources of external finance, which are primarily long-term, and include:

- **ordinary shares** (or equity shares)
- **preference shares**
- **loan capital** (financial debt that includes bank loans, debentures and other loans)
- **hybrid finance** (for example, convertible loans)
- leasing
- UK Government funding
- European Union funding.

The two main primary sources of long-term finance available to a company, which are both external, are broadly:

- equity share capital (ordinary shares)
- debt (long-term loans, bonds and debentures).

Both types of financing have a unique set of characteristics and rights. The main ones are shown in the table in Figure 9.1.

Figure 9.1   The main characteristics and rights of equity capital compared with debt capital

equity (ordinary shares)	debt (loans)
the term is unlimited, i.e. for life	the term is fixed and has a maturity date
ordinary shares have a nominal or par value	loans require security, e.g. debentures
ordinary shares have voting rights	loans have no voting rights
dividends are payable on ordinary shares, the values of which are dependent on company performance	interest is payable on loans: it may be fixed; variable; rolled over
dividends are an appropriation or a use of profits, and are therefore payable after corporation tax	interest on loans is an allowable expense for corporation tax
if a company is wound up the ordinary shareholders are the last to be considered — it is capital having the highest risk	if a company is wound up, lenders appear near the top of the list for consideration

Share capital

The share capital of a company may comprise ordinary shares and preference shares (although there are other classes of shares, which are not covered in this book). The company determines the maximum share capital that it is ever likely to need to raise and this level is called its authorised share capital. The amount of shares actually in issue at any point in time is normally at a level for the company to meet its foreseeable requirements. These shares are called the company's issued share capital which, when all the shareholders have paid for them, are referred to as fully paid-up issued share capital. Ordinary shares represent the long-term capital provided by the owners of a company, both new and existing.

In start-up businesses the ordinary shares are usually owned by the founder(s) of the business, and possibly by family and friends, or by investors seeking a gain in their value as the business grows. As a company grows it may decide:

- to raise further equity share capital, in order to finance its growth, at levels much higher than the founders of the business and/or their friends and family are willing or able to afford, or
- to sell its shares by making them publicly available and freely traded, to realise gains in their value for the founders or other investors.

The way that such businesses action these decisions is by making what are termed **initial public ◀‖‖** **offerings (IPOs)** of shares in their companies. This means that shares are offered for sale to the general public and to financial institutions and are then traded (in the UK) on the London Stock Exchange or the Alternative Investment Market (AIM).

The online dating company EasyDate (see the press extract on page 346) grew rapidly from its foundation in 2005. The company listed on the AIM on 30 June 2010, raising £45m by issuing 75 million shares at 60p each. After having made a number of successful acquisitions to improve its market share, the company decided that its key strategy should be to continue to make more substantial acquisitions. For that it needed more capital, and because of the relative ease with which companies were able to raise funds on the AIM, the EasyDate founders decided that such a listing was the best strategic option for their company.

Ordinary shareholders receive a dividend at a level determined usually by company performance and not as a specific entitlement. The level of dividends is usually based on the underlying profitability of the company (Tesco plc actually advised its shareholders of this relationship in the late 1990s). Preference shareholders receive a dividend at a level that is fixed, subject to the conditions of issue of the shares, and have priority over the ordinary shareholders if the company is wound up. In addition, ordinary shareholders normally have voting rights, whereas preference shareholders do not.

If a company goes into liquidation the ordinary shareholders are always last to be repaid. Ordinary shareholders are paid out of the balance of funds that remain after all other creditors have been repaid.

Additional equity capital may be raised through increasing the number of shares issued by the company through **rights issues**. A **scrip issue** (or bonus issue) increases the number of shares with ◀‖‖ the additional shares going to existing shareholders, in proportion to their holdings, through capitalisation of the reserves of the company. No cash is called for from the shareholders.

Rights issues

In a rights issue, the right to subscribe for new shares (or debentures) issued by the company is given to existing shareholders. The 'rights' to buy the new shares are usually fixed at a price discounted to below the current market price (see Worked examples 9.1 and 9.2). A shareholder not wishing to take up a rights issue may sell the rights.

Floating on the AIM

Online dating agency EasyDate is planning for a big year. The Edinburgh-based business, which last year made £11.5m of sales and cash before charges of just under £3m, is looking to expand internationally, raise funds – possibly from a flotation – and launch a revolutionary new website that will allow those seeking a new partner to browse all the available online dating tools.

'It'll be a bit like a comparison site', says the internet, telecoms and technology entrepreneur Bill Dobbie, the 51-year-old chairman and founder of EasyDate.

The business was formed in 2005 when Dobbie teamed up with software writer Max Polyakov and has been growing steadily ever since. Last year it realised a 7pc average monthly revenue growth. But the size, scope and opportunities from the rapidly expanding global markets mean Dobbie has his sights set on still further rapid expansion. And he thinks EasyDate is well placed to capitalise on the potential due to its niche approach to online dating.

'Unlike our competition such as Match and Dating Direct, we operate a portfolio of sites and we are a niche operator', says Dobbie.

The idea is that with its basic model, systems and structure – built over five years by a team of 20 working on it full time, says Dobbie – EasyDate can launch both new niche sites itself or, as a white-label site provider, with a partner. Each will target a specific sector of society. The thinking, explains Dobbie, is that singles in their 20s, for example, need a different dating site to other demographic groups.

'There is consolidation going on in the marketplace and niches are emerging. Even companies like Match realise they can't be all things to all men. It's analogous to the drinks industry – not every pub is a Wetherspoons', he says.

The market is growing by about 20pc a year, says Dobbie, and is estimated to be worth $1bn – just over half coming from Europe. There is, he believes, still huge growth potential.

'At $20 per head per month, which is what everybody charges, that's not that many people.

'Online dating is becoming increasingly socially acceptable. People are more readily willing to say they met someone through an online dating site. There is no longer a social stigma attached to it at all. I guess it's fuelled by people being more comfortable being online and the whole social network thing.'

Alongside the niche and comparison site approach comes global growth. EasyDate's international expansion began last year.

'We are now in all the English-speaking countries and beginning to look at Spanish-speaking and others such as Sweden, Netherlands and Thailand.'

He plans to launch in Brazil this year. 'We have done some testing on the internet and if there is uptake then we'll push a little harder.

'We are test-marketing Spain now and are about to buy a Spanish database that will accelerate that expansion.'

Language is not so much an issue. 'We have an international staff and we like to keep everything in-house', he said.

The approach works. EasyDate sees £150,000 a month income from its Australian site, for example, without any of EasyDate's team of 80 having set foot in the country, says Dobbie.

'You need a critical mass', he says. 'The database is really the only barrier to entry and once you get a bit of momentum, and your database grows, it's an exponential effect.'

Buying that information by acquiring other dating companies is the fastest way to get a foothold in a new territory. And for that, EasyDate needs funds.

'We are looking at raising institutional finance – an Alternative Investment Market flotation,' says Dobbie. 'We are weighing up the options. That will give us the capital to make acquisitions, which will allow us to accelerate our foreign growth.'

Source: **Online dating site seeks to woo investors**, by Philip Smith © *Daily Telegraph*, 18 May 2010

Worked example 9.1

A company that achieves a profit after tax of 20% on capital employed has the following capital structure:

400,000 ordinary shares of £1	£400,000
Retained earnings	£200,000

In order to invest in some new profitable projects the company wishes to raise £252,000 from a rights issue. The company's current ordinary share price is £1.80.

The company would like to know the number of shares that must be issued if the rights price is: £1.60; £1.50; £1.40; £1.20.

Capital employed is £600,000 [£400,000 + £200,000]

Current earnings are 20% of £600,000 = £120,000

$$\text{Therefore, earnings per share (eps)} = \frac{£120,000}{400,000} = 30p$$

After the rights issue earnings will be 20% of £852,000 [£400,000 + £200,000 + £252,000], which equals £170,400.

Rights price £	Number of new shares £252,000/ rights price £	Total shares after rights issue £	Eps £170,400/ total shares pence
1.60	157,500	557,500	30.6
1.50	168,000	568,000	30.0
1.40	180,000	580,000	29.4
1.20	210,000	610,000	27.9

We can see that at a high rights issue share price the earnings per share are increased. At lower issue prices eps are diluted. The 'break-even point', with no dilution, is where the rights price equals the pre-rights issue capital employed per share £600,000/400,000 = £1.50.

Worked example 9.2

A company has 1,000,000 £1 ordinary shares in issue with a market price of £2.10 on 1 June. The company wished to raise new equity capital by a 1 for 4 share rights issue at a price of £1.50. Immediately the company announced the rights issue the price fell to £1.92 on 2 June. Just before the rights issue was due to be made, the share price had recovered to £2 per share, the cum rights price (the share price that includes the associated rights).

The company may calculate the theoretical ex rights price (the new market price that excludes the associated rights) as

1,000,000 shares × the cum rights price of £2	£2,000,000
250,000 shares × the issue price of £1.50	375,000
Theoretical value of 1,250,000 shares	£2,375,000

Therefore, the theoretical ex rights price is $\dfrac{£2,375,000}{1,250,000}$ = £1.90 per share

Or to put it another way

Four shares at the cum rights value of £2	£8.00
One new share issued at £1.50	£1.50
	£9.50

Therefore, the theoretical ex rights price is $\dfrac{£9.50}{5}$ = £1.90 per share

Long-term debt

Generally, companies try and match their financing with what it is required for, and the type of assets requiring to be financed:

- non-current assets
- long-term projects.

Long-term debt is usually less expensive and less flexible, but has less risk, than short-term debt. Long-term debt is therefore normally matched to finance the acquisition of non-current assets, which are long-term assets from which the company expects to derive benefits over several future periods.

Long-term financial debts are the elements of loans and leases that are payable after one year of the balance sheet date. Debt capital may take many forms: loans, debentures, Eurobonds, mortgages, etc. We will look at debentures, but we will not delve into the particular attributes of every type of debt capital. Suffice to say, each involves interest payment, and capital repayment and security for the loan is usually required. Loan interest is a fixed commitment, which is usually payable once or twice a year. But although debt capital is burdened with a fixed commitment of interest payable, it is a tax-efficient method of financing.

Debentures

Debentures and long-term loans are both debt, and are often taken to mean the same thing. However, loans may be either unsecured, or secured on some or all of the assets of the company. Lenders to a company receive interest, payable yearly or half-yearly, the rate of which may vary with market conditions. A debenture is a type of bond and more specifically refers to the written acknowledgement of a debt by a company, usually given under its seal, and is secured on some or all of the assets of the company or its subsidiaries. A debenture agreement normally contains provisions as to payment of interest and the terms of repayment of the principal. Other long-term loans are usually unsecured.

Security for a debenture may be by way of a floating charge, without attachment to specific assets, on the whole of the business's assets. If the company is not able to meet its obligations the floating charge will crystallise on specific assets like accounts receivable or inventories. Security may alternatively, at the outset, take the form of a fixed charge on specific assets like land and buildings.

Debentures are a tax-efficient method of corporate financing, which means that interest payable on such loans is an allowable deduction in the computation of taxable profit. For example, if corporation tax were at 30%, a 10% debenture would actually cost the company 7%, that is {10% − (10% × 30%)}.

Debentures, and other loans, may be redeemable, in which case the principal, the original sum borrowed, will need to be repaid on a specific date.

Hybrid finance

Loans may sometimes be required by companies as they move through their growth phase, and for them to finance specific asset acquisitions or projects. Disadvantages of loans are:

- the financial risk resulting from a reduction in the amount of equity compared with debt
- the commitment to fixed interest payments over a number of years
- the requirement of a build-up of cash with which to repay the loan on maturity.

Alternatively, if an increase in equity is used for this type of funding, eps (earnings per share) may be immediately 'diluted'. However, some financing is neither totally debt nor equity, but has the characteristics of both. Such hybrid finance, as it is called, includes financial instruments like convertible loans. A **convertible loan** is a 'two-stage' financial instrument. It may be a fixed interest debt or preference shares, which can be converted into ordinary shares of the company at the option of the lender. Eps will therefore not be diluted until a later date. The right to convert may usually be exercised each year at a predetermined conversion rate up until a specified date, at which time the loan must be redeemed if it has not been converted. The conversion rate may be stated as:

- a conversion price (the amount of the loan that can be converted into one ordinary share), or
- a conversion ratio (the number of ordinary shares that can be converted from one unit of the loan).

The conversion price or ratio will be specified at the outset and may change during the term of the loan. Convertibles tend to pay a lower rate of interest than straight loans, which is effectively charging lenders for the right to convert to ordinary shares. They therefore provide an additional benefit to company cash flow and cost of financing.

> ### Progress check 9.1
>
> What makes convertible loans attractive to both investors and companies?

Leasing

Leases are contracts between a lessor and lessee for the hire of a specific asset. Why then is leasing seen as a source of long-term financing? There are two types of leases, **operating leases** and **finance leases**, and the answer to the question lies in the accounting treatment of the latter.

Under both types of leasing contract the lessor has ownership of the asset but gives the lessee the right to use the asset over an agreed period in return for rental payments.

An operating lease is a rental agreement for an asset, which may be leased by one lessee for a period, and then another lessee for a period, and so on. The lease period is normally less than the economic life of the asset, and the lease rentals are charged as a cost in the profit and loss account as they occur. The leased asset does not appear in the lessee's balance sheet. The lessor is responsible for maintenance and regular service for assets like photocopiers, cars and PCs. The lessor therefore retains most of the risk and reward of ownership.

A finance lease relates to an asset where the present value of the lease rentals payable amounts to at least 90% of the fair market value of the asset at the start of the lease. Under a finance lease the legal title to the asset remains with the lessor, but the difference in accounting treatment, as defined by IAS 17, Leases, is that a finance lease is capitalised in the balance sheet of the lessee. A value of the finance lease is shown under non-current assets, based on a calculation of the present value of the capital part (excluding finance charges) of the future lease rentals payable. The future lease rentals are also shown as long- and short-term payables in the balance sheet. The lessee, although not the legal owner, therefore takes on the risks and rewards of ownership.

The leasing evaluation process involves appraisal of the investment in the asset itself, its outright purchase or lease, and an evaluation of leasing as the method of financing. These two decisions may be made separately in either order or they may form a combined decision, and take account of a number of factors:

- asset purchase price and residual value
- the lease rental amounts and the timing of their payments
- service and maintenance payments
- tax
  - capital allowances for purchased non-current assets
  - tax allowable expenses of lease rentals
- VAT (relating to the asset purchase and the lease rentals)
- interest rates – the general level of rates of competing financing options.

Apart from this outline of the process, the evaluation of leasing as a source of finance is beyond the scope of this book.

UK Government and European Union funding

Businesses involved in certain industries or located in specific geographical areas of the UK may from time to time be eligible for assistance with financing. This may be by way of grants, loan guarantees, and subsidised consultancy. Funding may be on a national or a regional basis from various UK Government or European Union sources.

By their very nature, such financing initiatives are continually changing in format and their areas of focus. For example, funding assistance has been available in one form or another for SMEs, the agriculture industry, tourism, former coal and steel producing areas, and parts of Wales.

This type of funding may include support for the following:

- business start-ups
- new factories
- new plant and machinery
- research and development
- IT development.

There are many examples of funding schemes that operate currently. For example, the Government, via the Department for Business, Innovation and Skills (BIS), can provide guarantees for loans from banks and other financial institutions for small businesses that may be unable to provide the security for conventional loans. Via the various regional development agencies, they may also provide discretionary selective financial assistance, in the form of grants or loans, for businesses that are willing to invest in 'assisted areas'. The BIS and Government Business Link websites, *www.bis.gov.uk* and *www.businesslink.gov.uk*, provide up-to-date information on all current funding initiatives.

The Welsh Assembly's use of European Structural Funds (ESFs) assists businesses in regenerating Welsh communities. For example, through a scheme called match funding, depending on the type of business activity and its location, ESFs can contribute up to 50% of a project's funding. The balance of the funding is provided from the business's own resources or other public or private sector funding. Websites like the Welsh European Funding Office website, *www.wefo.wales.gov.uk*, provide information on this type of funding initiative.

> ### Progress check 9.2
>
> Describe what is meant by debt and equity and give some examples of each. What are the other sources of long-term, external finance available to a company?

Gearing

In Chapter 7 when we looked at financial ratios we introduced gearing, the relationship between debt and equity capital that represents the financial structure (or capital structure) of an organisation. We will now take a look at the application of gearing and then consider worked examples that compare the use of debt capital with ordinary share capital.

The relationship between the two sources of finance, loans and ordinary shares, or debt and equity gives a measure of the gearing of the company. A company with a high proportion of debt capital to share capital is highly geared, and a company with a low proportion of debt capital to share capital is low geared. Gearing (leverage, or debt/equity) has important implications for the long-term stability of a company because of, as we have seen, its impact on financial risk.

Companies closely monitor their gearing ratios to ensure that their capital structure aligns with their financial strategy. Various alternative actions may be taken by companies, as necessary, to adjust their capital structures by increasing or decreasing their respective levels of debt and equity. An example of one of the ways in which this may be achieved is to return cash to shareholders through share repurchases. Domino's Pizza plc has had a programme of buying back shares since 2004. In November 2009 it announced a new share-repurchasing phase and had repurchased 500,000 shares by 15 February 2010. The company's annual report and accounts for the year ended 27 December 2009 reported £18.1m of cash returned to shareholders in the year through a combination of dividends and share repurchases; the company had been very cash-generative and had created £35.6m of cash in the year. Indeed the group has returned £31.7m of cash to shareholders through repurchases over the past five years. The company noted in its annual report that it monitors its overall level of financial gearing on a monthly basis to keep gearing levels within targets.

The extent to which the debt/equity is high or low geared has an effect on the earnings per share (eps) of the company:

- if profits are increasing, then higher gearing is preferable
- if profits are decreasing, then lower gearing or no gearing is preferred.

Similarly, the argument applies to the riskiness attached to capital repayments. If a company goes into liquidation, lenders have priority over shareholders with regard to capital repayment. So, the more highly geared the company the less chance there is of ordinary shareholders being repaid in full.

The many types of short- and long-term capital available to companies leads to complexity, but also the expectation that overall financial risks may be reduced through improved matching of funding with operational needs. The gearing position of the company may be considered in many ways depending on whether the long-term or overall capital structure is being analysed. It may also be analysed by concentrating on the income position rather than purely on the capital structure.

Financial gearing relates to the relationship between a company's borrowings, which includes debt, and its share capital and reserves. Concerning capital structure, gearing calculations may be based on a number of different capital values. All UK plcs disclose their net debt to equity ratio in their annual reports and accounts.

The two financial ratios that follow are the two most commonly used (see also Chapter 7). Both ratios relate to financial gearing, which is the relationship between a company's borrowings, which includes both prior charge capital and long-term debt, and shareholders' funds (share capital plus reserves).

$$\text{gearing} = \frac{\text{long-term debt}}{\text{equity} + \text{long-term debt}}$$

$$\text{debt equity ratio, or leverage} = \frac{\text{long-term debt}}{\text{equity}}$$

Worked example 9.3 illustrates the calculation of both ratios.

Worked example 9.3

Two companies have different gearing. Company A is financed totally by 20,000 £1 ordinary shares, whilst company B is financed partly by 10,000 £1 ordinary shares and a £10,000 10% loan. In all other respects the companies are the same. They both have assets of £20,000 and both make the same profit before interest and tax (PBIT).

	A	B
	£	£
Assets	20,000	20,000
less 10% loan	–	(10,000)
	20,000	10,000
Ordinary shares	20,000	10,000

$$\text{gearing} = \frac{\text{long-term debt}}{\text{equity} + \text{long-term debt}} \qquad \frac{0}{20,000 + 0} = 0\% \qquad \frac{10,000}{10,000 + 10,000} = 50\%$$

$$\text{debt equity ratio} = \frac{\text{long-term debt}}{\text{equity}} \qquad \frac{0}{20,000} = 0\% \qquad \frac{10,000}{10,000} = 100\%$$

Company B must make a profit before interest of at least £1,000 to cover the interest cost of the 10% loan. Company A does not have any minimum PBIT requirement because it has no debt.

Company A is lower geared and considered less risky in terms of profitability than company B which is a more highly geared company. This is because PBIT of a lower geared company is more likely to be sufficiently high to cover interest charges and provide a return for equity shareholders.

As we have seen, gearing calculations can be made in a number of ways, and may also be based on earnings and interest relationships in addition to capital values. For example:

$$\text{dividend cover (times)} = \frac{\text{earnings per share (eps)}}{\text{dividend per share}}$$

This ratio indicates the number of times the profits attributable to the equity shareholders covers the actual dividends paid and payable for the period. Financial analysts usually adjust their calculations for any exceptional items of which they may be aware.

$$\text{interest cover (times)} = \frac{\text{profit before interest and tax}}{\text{interest payable}}$$

This ratio calculates the number of times the interest payable is covered by profits available for such payments. It is particularly important for lenders to determine the vulnerability of interest payments to a drop in profit. The following ratio determines the same vulnerability in cash terms.

$$\text{cash interest cover} = \frac{\text{net cash inflow from operations} + \text{interest received}}{\text{interest paid}}$$

Progress check 9.3

What is gearing? Outline some of the ways in which it may be calculated.

Worked example 9.4

Swell Guys plc is a growing company that manufactures equipment for fitting out small cruiser boats. Its planned expansion involves investing in a new factory project costing £4m. Chief Executive, Guy Rope, expects the 12-year project to add £0.5m to profit before interest and tax each year. Next year's operating profit is forecast at £5m, and dividends per share are forecast at the same level as last year. Tax is not expected to be payable over the next few years due to tax losses that have been carried forward.

Swell Guys last two years' results are as follows:

	Last year £m	Previous year £m
Income statement for the year ended 31 December		
Revenue	18	15
Operating costs	16	11
Operating profit	2	4
Finance costs	1	1
Profit before tax	1	3
Income tax expense	0	0
Profit after tax	1	3
Dividends	1	1
Retained profit	0	2

	Last year £m	Previous year £m
Balance sheet as at 31 December		
Non-current assets	8	9
Current assets		
Inventories	7	4
Trade and other receivables	4	3
Cash and cash equivalents	1	2
Total current assets	12	9
Total assets	20	18
Current liabilities		
Borrowings and finance leases	4	2
Trade and other payables	5	5
Total current liabilities	9	7
Non-current liabilities		
Loan	6	6
Total liabilities	15	13
Net assets	5	5
Equity		
Share capital (25p ordinary shares)	2	2
Retained earnings	3	3
Total equity	5	5

Swell Guys is considering two options:

(a) Issue of £4m 15% loan stock repayable in five years' time.
(b) Rights issue of 4m 25p ordinary shares at £1 per share after expenses.

For each of the options the directors would like to see:

(i) how the retained earnings will look for next year
(ii) how earnings per share will look for next year
(iii) how the capital and reserves will look at the end of next year
(iv) how long-term loans will look at the end of next year
(v) how gearing will look at the end of next year.

(i) **Swell Guys plc forecast income statement for next year ended 31 December**
Operating profit £5m + £0.5m from the new project

		New debt £m	New equity £m
Operating profit		5.5	5.5
Interest payable	[1.0 + 0.6]	1.6	1.0
Profit before tax		3.9	4.5
Income tax expense		0.0	0.0
Profit after tax		3.9	4.5
Dividends		1.0	1.5
Retained profit		2.9	3.0

(ii) Earnings per share

$$\frac{\text{Profit available for ordinary shareholders}}{\text{Number of ordinary shares}} \quad \frac{£3.9m}{8m} = 48.75p \qquad \frac{£4.5m}{12m} = 37.5p$$

(iii) Capital and reserves

		As at 31 December		
		New debt		**New equity**
		£m		**£m**
Share capital (25p ordinary shares)	(8m shares)	2.0	(12m shares)	3.0
Share premium account		0.0		3.0
Retained earnings		5.9		6.0
		7.9		12.0
		10.0		

(iv) Long-term loans $\quad$ [6 + 4] $\qquad\qquad\qquad\qquad\qquad\qquad\qquad\qquad$ 6.0

(v) Gearing

$$\frac{\text{long-term debt}}{\text{equity + long-term debt}} \quad \frac{£6m + £4m}{£7.9m + £6m + £4m} = 55.9\% \quad \frac{£6m}{£12m + £6m} = 33.3\%$$

Progress check 9.4

Explain how a high interest cover ratio can reassure a prospective lender

---

The weighted average cost of capital (WACC)

The weighted average cost of capital (WACC) may be defined as the average cost of the total financial resources of a company, i.e. the shareholders' equity and the financial debt.

If we represent the market value of shareholders' equity as E and the market value of financial debt as D then the relative proportions of equity and debt to the total are:

$$\frac{E}{E + D} \text{ and } \frac{D}{E + D}$$

The cost of equity to the company is also the expected return on equity, the return the shareholders expect from their investment. If we represent the cost of shareholders' equity as e and the cost of financial debt as d, and t is the rate of corporation tax, then we can provide a formula to calculate WACC. The return on shareholder equity comprises both cash flows from dividends and increases in the share price. We will return to how the cost of equity may be derived from these in a later section in this chapter.

Interest on debt capital is an allowable deduction for purposes of corporate taxation and so the cost of share capital and the cost of debt capital are not properly comparable costs. The tax relief on debt interest should be recognised in calculating the cost of debt capital, to arrive at an after-tax cost of debt. Therefore the cost of debt d, must be multiplied by $(1 - t)$, which is called the **tax shield**, to reflect the tax benefit. The weighted average cost of capital is therefore:

$$\text{WACC} = \left\{ \frac{E}{(E + D)} \times e \right\} + \left\{ \frac{D}{(E + D)} \times d\,(1 - t) \right\}$$

The real value of a company may be determined by its WACC. The lower the WACC then the higher the net present values of its future cash flows and therefore the higher its market value. The determination of the optimum D/E ratio is one of the most difficult tasks facing the finance director.

Worked example 9.5

Fleet Ltd has the following financial structure:

$$\frac{E}{E + D} = 60\% \text{ equity to debt plus equity ratio}$$

$$\frac{D}{E + D} = 40\% \text{ debt to debt plus equity ratio}$$

$e = 15\%$ return on equity (this may be taken as given for the purpose of this example)
$d = 10\%$ lower risk, so lower than the return on equity
$t = 30\%$ rate of corporation tax

We can calculate the WACC for Fleet Ltd, and evaluate the impact on WACC of a change in capital structure to equity 40% and debt 60%.

Calculation of WACC for Fleet Ltd with the current financial structure:

$$\text{WACC} = \left\{ \frac{E}{(E + D)} \times e \right\} + \left\{ \frac{D}{(E + D)} \times d\,(1 - t) \right\}$$

$$\text{WACC} = (60\% \times 15\%) + \{40\% \times 10\%\,(1 - 30\%)\} = 11.8\%$$

If the company decides to change its financial structure so that equity is 40% and debt is 60% of total financing, then WACC becomes:

$$(40\% \times 15\%) + \{60\% \times 10\%\,(1 - 30\%)\} = 10.2\%$$

So it appears that the company has reduced its WACC by increasing the relative weight from 40% to 60% of the cheapest financial resource, debt, in its total financing. However, this may not be true in practice because as the debt/equity ratio of the company increased from 0.67 (40/60) to 1.50 (60/40) the company's financial risk has also increased. Therefore the providers of the financial resources will require a higher return on their investment. There is a well-established correlation between risk and return. So, it may not be correct to calculate the WACC using the same returns on equity and debt, as both may have increased.

One of the consequences of this is the problem for a company of calculating an accurate WACC. WACC is based on the relative proportions and costs of debt and equity capital that are continually changing as the company takes on additional debt or repays debt or issues additional share capital.

The risks and costs associated with debt capital and equity capital are different and subject to continual change, and may vary from industry to industry and between different types of business. Measurement of the D/E ratio may therefore not be a straightforward task, particularly for diversified groups of companies. Companies in different markets and indeed diversified companies that have trading divisions operating within different markets and producing different products face different levels of risk. If division A operates with a higher risk than division B then the required rate of return on A's investments should be higher than the hurdle rate of return on B's investments. The difference is 'paying' for the difference in risk. This is an important principle but very difficult to implement in practice.

In a later section, we will look at ways in which both the cost of equity and the cost of debt to the company may be determined.

There are many arguments for and against the use of WACC for investment appraisal. Its use is argued on the basis that:

■ new investments must be financed by new sources of funds – retained earnings, new share issues, new loans, and so on
■ the cost of capital to be applied to new project evaluation must reflect the cost of new capital
■ the WACC reflects the company's long-term future capital structure, and capital costs; if this were not so, the current WACC would become irrelevant because eventually it would not relate to any actual cost of capital.

It is argued that the current WACC should be used to evaluate projects, because a company's capital structure changes only very slowly over time; therefore, the marginal cost of new capital should be roughly equal to the WACC. If this view is correct, then by undertaking investments that offer a return in excess of the WACC, a company will increase the market value of its ordinary shares in the long run. This is because the excess returns would provide surplus profits and dividends for the shareholders.

The arguments against the use of WACC are based on the criticisms of the assumptions made that justify the use of WACC:

■ new investments have different risk characteristics from the company's existing operations therefore the return required by investors may go up or down if the investments are made, because their business risk is perceived to be higher or lower
■ finance raised to fund a new investment
　– may substantially change the capital structure and perceived risk of investing in the company
　– may determine whether debt or equity used to finance the project will change the perceived risk of the entire company, which
　– must be taken into account in the investment appraisal
■ many companies raise floating rate debt capital as well as fixed rate debt capital, having a variable rate that changes every few months in line with current market rates; this is difficult to include in a WACC calculation, the best compromise being to substitute an 'equivalent' fixed debt rate in place of the floating rate.

Progress check 9.5

What is WACC and why is it so important?

Cost of debt and equity capital

We have introduced the concept of risk and its correlation with returns on investments. The relationship between risk and return is also one of the key concepts relating to determination of the cost of debt and equity capital. It is an important concept and so we will briefly explore risk a little further, with regard to investments in companies. We shall discuss the cost of debt based on future income flows, that is, interest. We shall similarly discuss the cost of equity based on future income flows, that is, dividends. This will also provide an introduction to risk and the **beta factor (β)** and the **capital asset pricing model (CAPM)**.

The interest rate paid on a loan is known almost with certainty. Even if the debt carries a floating or variable interest rate it is far easier to estimate than the expected dividend flows on ordinary shares. Debt comprises debentures, loans etc., and may be corporate or government debt. Their levels of risk are different, and some debt may be secured on specific assets or the assets of a company in general.

The cost of debt is generally based on the current market rate for debt having a specific level of risk. Two of the main differences between the cost of equity and the cost of debt are:

- the different levels of risk between debt and equity
- the tax shield is applicable to interest paid on debt, but not to equity dividends paid.

The cost of servicing debt capital is based on the yearly or half-yearly interest payment, which is an allowable expense for tax. The cost of repayment of a loan, or debt, depends on the type of loan. Loans may be irredeemable and traded on the stock market, with a market value like any other security. Or loans may be redeemable at a specific date. We will look at the calculation of the cost to a company of a redeemable loan and also the cost of an irredeemable loan.

If

d = cost of debt capital
i = annual loan interest rate
L = the current market value of the loan

then, if the loan is redeemable, and if R is the loan value at redemption after n years, then:

$$L = i/(1 + d) + i/(1 + d)^2 + i/(1 + d)^3 + \cdots + (i + R)/(1 + d)^n$$

The cost of debt in the above equation can be calculated by trial and error, by interpolation, or using the appropriate Excel function.

For an irredeemable loan the interest is payable in perpetuity (for ever), so:

$$L = i/(1 + d) + i/(1 + d)^2 + i/(1 + d)^3 + \cdots \textbf{ to infinity}$$

which simplifies to:

$$L = i/d$$

Because interest payable on loans is an allowable deduction for corporation tax the cost of debt d is calculated by adjusting the interest rate by $(1 - t)$, the tax shield, to provide an after-tax rate of interest.

Therefore, if t = the rate of corporation tax and we rearrange the above equation then:

$$d = \frac{i \times (1 - t)}{L}$$

The value of L, the market value of the debt, is generally stated as a percentage of the nominal value of the debt.

By rearranging the formula it can be seen that L, market value of the debt, is dependent on the level of future returns, the interest rate paid, which is determined by the level of risk associated with the investment, and the rate of corporation tax:

$$L = \frac{i \times (1 - t)}{d}$$

Worked example 9.6

Owen Cash plc pays 12% interest (i) per annum on an irredeemable debt of £1m, with a nominal value of £100. The corporation tax rate (t) is currently 50%. The market value of the debt is currently £90, and therefore L, expressed as a percentage of the nominal value, is 90%.
What is Owen Cash plc's cost of debt?

$$d = \text{cost of debt capital}$$

$$d = \frac{i \times (1 - t)}{L} = \frac{12\% \times (1 - 50\%)}{90\%}$$

$$d = \frac{12\% \times 50\%}{90\%} = 6.7\%$$

In a similar way to cost of debt, the cost of equity to a company may be determined by looking at future income flows. In the case of equity or ordinary shares this future income is dividends. A difference between this method and the method applied to debt is that there is no tax relief for dividend payments.

The value of an ordinary share may be simply expressed as the present value of its expected future dividend flows:

$$S = v_1/(1 + e) + v_2/(1 + e)^2 + v_3/(1 + e)^3 + \cdots + v_n/(1 + e)^n$$

where
e = cost of equity capital
v = expected future dividends for n years
S = the current market value of the share

If dividends are expected to remain level over a period of time the formula may be simplified to:

$$S = \frac{v}{e}$$

Therefore, the cost of equity to the company would be:

$$e = \frac{v}{S}$$

Dividends payable on a particular share rarely stay constant from year to year. They may be assumed to grow at a regular rate. This so-called dividend growth model approach to the cost of equity may then be used with the above formula revised as:

$$S = v/(e - G)$$

where G = the expected future dividend growth rate, and v = next year's dividend.
The cost of equity may then be stated as:

$$e = \frac{v}{S} + G$$

Worked example 9.7

Cher Alike plc has 3m ordinary shares in issue that currently have a market price (S) of £2.71. The board have already recommended next year's dividend (v) at 17p per share. The chairman, Sonny Daze, is forecasting that dividends will continue to grow (G) at 4.2% per annum for the foreseeable future.

What is Cher Alike plc's cost of equity?

$$e = \text{cost of equity capital}$$

$$e = \frac{v}{S} + G = \frac{0.17}{2.71} + 4.2\%$$

$$e = 0.063 + 0.042 = 10.5\%$$

The cost of equity to a company may alternatively be derived using the capital asset pricing model (CAPM). We will look at this approach to risk, and at how some risk may be diversified away by using a spread (or portfolio) of investments.

Progress check 9.6

In broad terms how are the costs of debt and equity determined?

Cost of equity and risk, CAPM and the β factor

Whenever any investment is made there will be some risk involved. The actual return on investment in ordinary shares (equity capital) may be better or worse than hoped for. Unless the investor settles for risk-free securities a certain element of risk is unavoidable.

However, investors in companies or in projects can diversify their investments in a suitably wide portfolio. Some investments may do better and some worse than expected. In this way, average returns should turn out much as expected. Risk that can be diversified away is referred to as **unsystematic risk**.

Some investments are by their very nature more risky than others. This is nothing to do with chance variations in actual compared with expected returns, it is inherent risk that cannot be diversified away. This type of risk is referred to as **systematic risk** (or **market risk**). The investor must therefore accept this risk, unless he or she invests entirely in risk-free investments. In return for accepting systematic risk an investor will expect to earn a return, which is higher than the return on a risk-free investment.

The amount of systematic risk depends, for example, on the industry or the type of project. If an investor had a completely balanced portfolio of shares he or she would incur exactly the same systematic risk as the average systematic risk of the stock market as a whole, which of course is highly unlikely in practice. The capital asset pricing model (CAPM) is mainly concerned with how systematic risk is measured and how systematic risk affects required returns and share prices. It was first formulated for investments in shares on the stock exchange, but is now also used for company investments in capital projects.

CAPM considers the market return, and also the risk-free return and volatility of a share. Share-holders expect returns that are in terms of dividends and capital growth in the share price. However, actual shareholder returns may be higher or lower than expected, because of risk. Systematic risk is measured using what are known as beta factors. A beta factor (β) is the measure of the volatility of a share in terms of systematic or market risk.

CAPM is a statement of the principles outlined above. The relationship between the expected return on a company's shares, its cost of equity, and the average market return may be measured by its beta (note that $\beta = 1$ for the stock market as a whole). An investor can use the beta factor in such a way that a high factor will automatically suggest a share is to be avoided because of considerably high risk in the past. For example, a share with a β of 0.8 means less systematic risk than the market – if the market increases by 10% the share price increases by 8%; a share with a β of 1.5 means more systematic risk than the market – if the market increases by 10% the share price increases by 15%. Consider the impact on the beta factor of a company caused by the resignation from the board of the chief financial officer, together with the issue of a profits warning by the company.

CAPM may be used to calculate the return on a company's shares while making some allowance for the systematic risk relating to that company. CAPM can be stated as follows:

> **the expected return from a security = the risk-free rate of return, plus a premium for market risk, adjusted by a measure of the volatility of the security**

If

R_s	is the expected return from an individual security
β_e	is the equity beta factor for the individual security
R_f	is the risk-free rate of return
R_m	is the return from the market as a whole
$(R_m - R_f)$	is the market risk premium

$$R_s = R_f + \{\beta_e \times (R_m - R_f)\}$$

It should be remembered that CAPM considers systematic risk only, and is based on an assumption of market equilibrium.

The β factor of a security may be calculated using the market and an individual company's information over an extended period of time as follows:

> $$\frac{\text{covariance of the returns of the security and the market}}{\text{standard deviation of the returns of the market squared}}$$

which equals

> $$\frac{\text{standard deviation of the security's returns} \times}{}$$
> $$\frac{\text{correlation coefficient between the security's returns and the market returns}}{\text{standard deviation of the returns of the market}}$$

This method involves collecting data on the periodic returns of the market and the particular security and using regression analysis or plotting security returns (y axis) against market returns (x axis) over a period of time. The β_e of the security is the slope of the line of best fit.

Alternatively, β values are obtainable from a variety of sources and it is perhaps easier to leave it to the experts. There are many analysts that specialise in the charting of the volatility of shares and markets, and their findings may regularly be found in the UK financial press. The Risk Measurement Service of the London Business School publishes a quarterly report of companies' beta coefficients. They calculate the betas of all major companies by regressing their monthly returns against the monthly returns of the Financial Times actuaries' all-share index over the previous five years.

A variation of the above β relationship may be used to establish an equity cost of capital to use in project appraisal. The cost of equity e, equates to the expected return from an individual security R_s, and the beta value for the company's equity capital β_e equates to the beta factor for the individual security β. CAPM is an alternative method to the dividend growth model that we discussed above, which may be used to calculate the cost of equity:

$$e = R_f + \{\beta_e \times (R_m - R_f)\}$$

Worked example 9.8

Bittaboth plc has ordinary shares in issue with a market value four times the value of its debt capital. The debt is considered to be risk-free and pays 11% (R_f) before tax. The beta value of Bittaboth's equity capital has been estimated at 0.9 (β_e) and the average market return on equity capital is 17% (R_m). Corporation tax is at 50% (t).

We can calculate Bittaboth plc's WACC.

$$e = \text{cost of equity capital}$$

$$e = R_f + \{\beta_e \times (R_m - R_f)\} = 11\% + \{0.9 \times (17\% - 11\%)\}$$

$$e = 0.11 + (0.9 \times 0.06) = 0.164 = 16.4\%$$

$$d = \text{cost of debt capital}$$

which after tax is $i \times (1 - t)$ or 11% $\times$ 50% = 5.5%

Any capital projects that Bittaboth may wish to consider may be evaluated using its WACC, which may be calculated as:

{equity/(debt + equity) ratio $\times$ return on equity} + {debt/(debt + equity) ratio $\times$ after tax cost of debt}

$$(4/5 \times 16.4\%) + (1/5 \times 5.5\%) = 14.2\%$$

14.2% is Bittaboth's weighted average cost of capital (WACC).

Progress check 9.7

Describe what is meant by systematic risk and unsystematic risk.

Return on equity and financial structure

The important formula that follows shows the return on equity (ROE) as a function of return on investment (ROI) and the financial structure, leverage or gearing of the company, where:

D = debt capital
E = equity capital
t = corporation tax rate
i = interest rate on debt
ROI = return on investment
ROE = return on equity

$$\mathbf{ROE = \{ROI \times (1 - \mathit{t})\} + \{(ROI - \mathit{i}) \times (1 - \mathit{t}) \times D/E\}}$$

Worked example 9.9 illustrates the use of this relationship and also gives a general rule derived from it.

Worked example 9.9

A hospital equipment manufacturing company, Nilby Mouth plc, makes an operating profit (PBIT) of £10m on sales of £100m and with a total investment of £60m. The investment is financed by equity (E) of £40m and debt (D) of £20m with an interest rate (i) of 10%. Assume the corporation tax rate (t) is 50%.

We will calculate:

(i)   the current return on equity (ROE)
(ii)   the ROE if financing were changed so that debt was £40m and equity was £20m
(iii)   the current ROE if operating profit were reduced to £4m
(iv)   the ROE if operating profit were reduced to £4m and if financing were changed so that debt was £40m and equity was £20m.

(Figures in £m)

(i) Calculation of return on equity (ROE)

Profit before interest and tax, or operating profit PBIT = 10

Profit before tax PBT = $10 - (20 \times 10\%) = 8$

Profit after tax PAT = $8 \times (1 - 50\%) = 4$

Return on sales ROS = $4/100 = 4\%$

Return on investment ROI (before interest and tax) = $10/60 = 16.7\%$

Debt/equity ratio D/E = $20/40 = 50\%$

ROE = $ROI \times (1 - t) + \{(ROI - i) \times (1 - t) \times D/E\}$

Return on equity ROE = $\{16.7\% \times (1 - 50\%)\} + \{(16.7\% - 10\%) \times (1 - 50\%) \times 50\%\}$
$$= 0.10025 \text{ or } 10\%$$

(ii) Calculation of ROE if financing is changed so that debt is £40m and equity is £20m

PBIT = 10   PBT = 10 − (40 × 10%) = 6   PAT = 6 × (1 − 50%) = 3
ROS = 3/100 = 3%
ROI (before interest and tax) = 10/60 = 16.7%
D/E = 40/20 = 200%
ROE = {16.7% × (1 − 50%)} + {(16.7% − 10%) × (1 − 50%) × 200%}
     = 0.15050 or 15%
Return on sales has reduced, whereas return on equity has increased.

(iii) Calculation of ROE if the operating profit were reduced to £4m

PBIT = 4 PBT = 4 − (20 × 10%) = 2   PAT = 2 × (1 − 50%) = 1
ROS = 1/100 = 1%
ROI (before interest and tax) = 4/60 = 6.7%
D/E = 20/40 = 50%
ROE = {6.7% × (1 − 50%)} + {(6.7% − 10%) × (1 − 50%) × 50%} = 0.02525 or 2.5%

(iv) Calculation of ROE if financing is changed so that debt is £40m and equity is £20m

PBIT = 4 PBT = 4 − (40 × 10%) = 0   PAT = 0 × (1 − 50%) = 0
ROS = 0/100 = 0%
ROI (before interest and tax) = 4/60 = 6.7%
D/E = 40/20 = 200%
ROE = {6.7% × (1 − 50%)} + {(6.7% − 10%) × (1 − 50%) × 200%} = 0.00050 or 0.05%
Return on sales and return on equity are both zero.

The general rule apparent from the relationships outlined in Worked example 9.9 is:

- when ROI is greater than *i*   the higher the D/E, the higher the ROE
- when ROI is less than *i*   the higher the D/E, the lower the ROE.

However, even if the ROI is greater than the debt interest the company's bankers may not automatically allow the D/E to increase indefinitely. The company's risk increases as the D/E or leverage increases, in terms of its commitment to high levels of interest payments, and bankers will not tolerate too high a level of risk; they will also be inclined to increase the debt interest rate as D/E increases. Shareholders will have the same reaction – they are happy with an increase in ROE but realise that they also have to face a higher risk.

For a high-growth company, to limit the shareholders' investment, the company will have a tendency to increase D/E and therefore ROE, but also the financial risk. The press (for example Questor in the *Daily Telegraph*) usually comments when a plc is seen to embark on a policy of increased borrowings and increasing its gearing ratio, which alerts the reader to 'increased financial risk'. Plcs are usually prepared and ready for such comments in order to respond with their 'defence' of such a policy.

Progress check 9.8

Discuss why bankers may refuse additional lending to a company as its debt/equity ratio increases.

Growth of a company may be looked at using income statement horizontal analyses. Use of this technique, which was covered in Chapter 8, presents all numbers in the income statement as a percentage using a base year, which is 100, for year-on-year comparison. Financial commentators usually begin articles on the performance of plcs by comparing the current year performance with the previous year, and then attempt a forecast of future performance. This is an example of a basic horizontal analysis that focuses on sales revenues and profits. Only a few companies actually succeed in growing year on year over an extended period (for example, 10 years).

Economic value added (EVA™) and market value added (MVA)

Maximisation of shareholder wealth continues to be the prime objective with which managers of companies are charged. We have considered various ways to measure managers' financial performance. The extent to which success in particular performance measures aligns with shareholder wealth is particularly relevant. Equally important are the ways in which managers are motivated to maximise shareholder wealth. In most organisations managerial remuneration provides the link between the measures of financial performance and shareholder value.

Financial performance measures such as a company's share price are commonly used to indicate how well the company is doing. However, it may be questioned how directly the share price reflects decisions that have been taken by management. In the context of managers' performance against budget targets, and the company's overall financial performance, we have previously discussed the merits and otherwise of other performance measures such as profit after tax, earnings per share, dividends, return on capital employed, and cash flow, etc. Each has its limitations, but measures based on cash flow are now becoming accepted as perhaps better indicators than profit-related measures.

During the mid-1980s, Rappaport developed shareholder value analysis, from which the American firm Stern Stewart Management Services evolved concepts known as economic value added (EVA), and **market value added (MVA)**. Through EVA, Stern Stewart attempted to reconcile the need for a performance measure correlated with shareholder wealth, and a performance measure which was also responsive to actions taken by managers. By the mid-1990s over 200 global companies had been in discussion with Stern Stewart with regard to adoption of EVA; Lucas Varity in the UK and Coca-Cola in the USA were already successful users of EVA.

If we assume that the organisation's objective is to maximise shareholder wealth then this will be achieved if new projects are taken on and existing projects are allowed to continue only if they create value. Investment in capital projects may be made only on the basis of choosing those with a positive **net present value (NPV)**. However, NPV cannot be applied to remuneration schemes because it is a summary measure based on projected cash flows and not realised performance.

Companies usually turn to company earnings and cash flow (which are termed flow measures) for management remuneration schemes. EVA supports the same sort of recommendations that NPV provides at the project level, but also provides a better measure of management performance because it rewards for earnings generated, whilst also including charges for the amount of capital employed to create those earnings.

If profit after tax = PAT
weighted average cost of capital = WACC
adjusted book value of net assets = NA
then we may define EVA as:

$$\textbf{EVA} = \textbf{PAT} - (\textbf{WACC} \times \textbf{NA})$$

It should be noted that to calculate EVA the PAT should be adjusted by adding back interest paid. Profit before interest paid is therefore used to calculate EVA to avoid double counting because a charge for financing is being made by deducting WACC in the calculation.

Worked example 9.10 will illustrate the calculation of EVA and its relationship with NPV.

Worked example 9.10

A manager has to choose between three mutually exclusive projects. The company may invest:

£50,000 in project A, or
£110,000 in project B, or
£240,000 in project C

Project A is expected to generate incremental profits after tax (PAT) of £50,000 in year one, £40,000 in year two (total £90,000), after which the project is terminated.

Project B is expected to generate incremental PATs of £45,000 in year one, £70,000 in year two, £70,000 in year three (total £185,000), after which the project is terminated.

Project C is expected to generate incremental PATs of £55,000 in year one, £75,000 in year two, £80,000 in year three (total £210,000), after which the project is terminated.

The company's WACC is 10% per annum. Capital levels may be assumed to be maintained throughout the life of each project. That is, each year's new capital investment equals depreciation in that year.

Capital items are sold at their book value in the final year of each project, so free cash flow (operating cash flow less capital expenditure) will be equal to PAT each year except the final years when the capital costs are recovered.

We will assess which project the manager will choose if:

(i)   his remuneration is tied to the NPV of the project
(ii) his remuneration is based on IRR
(iii) his remuneration is based on project earnings
(iv) his remuneration is based on EVA.

Using a discount rate of WACC at 10% per annum, we first calculate the NPVs of each project.

Year	Cash outflows £000	Cash inflows £000		Net cash flow £000	Discount factor at 10%	Present values £000
Project A						
0	−50			−50	1.00	−50.0
1		50		50	0.91	45.5
2		90	[40 + 50]	90	0.83	74.7
3		0		0	0.75	0.0
Total	−50	140		90		+70.2
Project B						
0	−110			−110	1.00	−110.0
1		45		45	0.91	40.9
2		70		70	0.83	58.1
3		180	[70 + 110]	180	0.75	135.0
Total	−110	295		185		+124.0

Project C

0	−240		−240	1.00	−240.0
1		55	55	0.91	50.0
2		75	75	0.83	62.3
3		320 [80 + 240]	320	0.75	240.0
Total	−240	450	210		+112.3

The IRR is the rate of return that would give an NPV of zero.

Interpolation or extrapolation techniques may be used to derive the internal rate of return of each project.

For project C, if we assume a discount rate of 30%, we may calculate a revised NPV as follows:

Year	Cash outflows £000	Cash inflows £000	Net cash flow £000	Discount factor at 30%	Present values £000
0	−240		−240	1.00	−240.0
1		55	55	0.77	42.4
2		75	75	0.59	44.3
3		320	320	0.46	147.2
Total	−240	450	210		−6.1

We have already calculated the positive NPV for project C of £112,300 using a cost of capital of 10%. The IRR of project C must be at some point between 30% and 10% (difference 20%).

Using interpolation:

$$\frac{£6,100}{x} = \frac{£112,300}{(20 - x)}$$

$$(£6,100 \times 20) - £6,100x = £112,300x$$

$$£122,000 = £118,400x$$

$$x = \frac{£122,000}{£118,400}$$

$$x = 1.03$$

Therefore, interpolation gives us an IRR of 30% less 1.03%, which equals 28.97% and may be rounded to 29%.

The IRRs of projects A and B may be calculated in the same way.

The cash flows, NPVs and IRRs of the three projects may be summarised as:

Project	PAT Year 1 £000	Year 2 £000	Year 3 £000	Cash out £000	Cash in Year 1 £000	Year 2 £000	Year 3 £000	Total cash flow £000	IRR %	NPV £000
A	50	40		−50	50	90 [40 + 50]		90	93	70.2
B	45	70	70	−110	45	70	180 [70 + 110]	185	53	124.0
C	55	75	80	−240	55	75	320 [80 + 240]	210	29	112.3

(i) Based on the highest NPV, project B at £124,000 is best for the company shareholders.

(ii) But if the manager's remuneration is based on IRR then he will choose project A at 93%.

(iii) If the manager is remunerated on total project earnings then he will choose project C at £210,000.

(iv) We can calculate the EVA for each project, which equals profit after tax for each period, less capital employed at the start of each period multiplied by the weighted average cost of capital.

	Project A		Project B		Project C	
		EVA		EVA		EVA
Year	£000	£000	£000	£000	£000	£000
1	50 − (50 × 10%)	45	45 − (110 × 10%)	34	55 − (240 × 10%)	31
2	40 − (50 × 10%)	35	70 − (110 × 10%)	59	75 − (240 × 10%)	51
3			70 − (110 × 10%)	59	80 − (240 × 10%)	56
Total		80		152		138

We may also calculate the NPV of the EVAs of each project, the present values of the EVAs:

	Discount	Project A		Project B		Project C	
	factor	EVA	NPV	EVA	NPV	EVA	NPV
Year	at 10%	£000	£000	£000	£000	£000	£000
1	0.91	45	41.0	34	30.9	31	28.2
2	0.83	35	29.1	59	48.9	51	42.3
3	0.75			59	44.2	56	42.0
Total		80	+70.1	152	+124.0	138	+112.5

This illustrates that EVAs actually equate to cash flows because their present values are the same as the NPV of each project. The small differences between the totals calculated for Project A and Project C are as a result of rounding differences.

If the manager is remunerated based on EVA it will be consistent with maximising NPV, which is best for shareholders.

We have seen from Worked example 9.10 that an earnings-based remuneration scheme may result in over-investment of capital whereas a scheme based on IRR may result in under-investment of capital. Use of EVA as a basis for management remuneration takes account of the fact that the use of capital is charged for by using WACC; additionally, at the project level, the present value of the EVAs gives the same result as NPVs derived from free cash flows. Compare the results in the project NPV tables with the NPVs of the EVAs of each project in Worked example 9.10.

Although the free cash flow NPVs gives the same result as the present values of the EVAs, EVA is more appropriate for remuneration schemes because, as well as being fundamentally related to shareholder value, it is a flow measure of performance. The reason is that flow measures of performance are needed for periodic remuneration because remuneration is designed to provide a flow of rewards. The other flow measure is cash flow. EVA is a better measure than that because it takes into account the cost of capital invested in the project.

Worked example 9.11

We will compute the EVA for 2008, 2009 and 2010 for a major plc from the following information.

			£m
Group cost of capital	5%		
Adjusted net assets		2010	750
		2009	715
		2008	631
Profit after tax		2010	550
		2009	526
		2008	498
Equity		2010	100
		2009	48
		2008	115
Net debt		2010	800
		2009	802
		2008	546

Year	Profit after tax £m	Adjusted net assets £m	5% cost of capital × net assets £m	EVA £m	EVA % of net profit
2010	550	750	37.50	512.50	93%
2009	526	715	35.75	490.25	93%
2008	498	631	31.55	466.45	94%

Note how the profits are being earned using borrowed funds to finance the group. The plc can earn a very high EVA by using borrowed funds.

We have talked about EVA in respect of projects, and that the present value of future EVAs equals the NPV derived from future free cash flows. At a company level, the present value of EVAs equals the market value added (MVA) of a business. This is defined as the difference between the market value of the company and the adjusted book values of its net assets.

EVA is a good financial performance measure because it answers the question of how well the company has performed in generating profits over a period, given the amount of capital tied up to generate those profits. However, the capital base is a difficult element to estimate in calculating EVA. The total net assets value on a balance sheet is not an accurate representation of either the liquidation value or the replacement cost value of the business. Stern Stewart considered more than 250 possible accounting adjustments to profit and the balance sheet to arrive at a valuation of the company's assets. In practice, most organisations find that no more than a dozen or so adjustments are truly significant, for example adding back interest to profit, and those relating to inventory valuations, depreciation calculations, goodwill and impairment, doubtful debt provision, leasing, deferred tax, and closure costs.

Further information about EVA may be obtained from the Stern Stewart's weblink at: *www.sternstewart.com/index.php?content=main*.

Worked example 9.12

We will compute the MVA for 2009 and 2010 from the following extracts from the annual report and accounts of a major plc, using the unadjusted value of net assets.

	2010	2009
Number of shares (5p)	950.2m	948.9m
Share price	278p	268p
Net assets	£1,097m	£1,437m

	2010	2009
Net assets	£1,097m	£1,437m
Market value	£2,641m	£2,543m
MVA	£1,544m	£1,106m

Progress check 9.9

What is economic value added (EVA) and what is it used for?

EVA probably does not change or add anything to the conclusions reached on the basis of conventional valuation analysis based on cash flow. EVA is primarily a behavioural tool that corrects possible distortions. However, along with most other financial measures, it fails to measure on an *ex post* basis. EVA is undoubtedly a very useful concept for measuring and evaluating management and company performance. It is not a cure for poor management and poor investment decisions but it raises the profile and the awareness of the costs of capital involved in undertaking projects and in running the business.

Summary of key points

- Sources of finance internal to a company are its retained earnings, extended credit from suppliers, and the benefits gained from the more effective management of its working capital.

- Short-term, external sources of finance include bank overdrafts and short-term loans.

- The two main sources of long-term, external finance available to a company are equity (ordinary shares), preference shares and debt (loans and debentures).

- Other sources of long-term, external finance available to UK companies include hybrid finance, leasing, and UK Government and European funding.

- Gearing, or the debt/equity ratio, is the relationship between the two sources of finance, loans and ordinary shares – a company having more debt capital than share capital is highly geared, and a company having more share capital than debt capital is low geared.

- The weighted average cost of capital (WACC) is the average cost of the total financial resources of a company, i.e. the shareholders' equity and the net financial debt, which may be used as the discount rate to evaluate investment projects, and as a measure of company performance.

- Both the cost of debt and the cost of equity are based on future income flows and the risk associated with such returns.

- A certain element of risk is unavoidable whenever any investment is made, and unless a market investor settles for risk-free securities, the actual return on investment in equity (or debt) capital may be better or worse than hoped for.

- Systematic risk may be measured using the capital asset pricing model (CAPM) and the β factor, in terms of its effect on required returns and share prices.

- The return on equity may be considered as a function of the gearing, or financial structure, of the company.

- The recently developed techniques of economic value added (EVA) and market value added (MVA) are widely becoming used in business performance measurement and as value creation incentives.

Assessment material

Questions

Q9.1 (i) What are the main sources of long-term, external finance available to an organisation?

(ii) What are their advantages and disadvantages?

Q9.2 What are the advantages and disadvantages of convertible loans?

Q9.3 Why may leasing be considered as a long-term source of finance?

Q9.4 What are the implications for a company of different levels of gearing?

Q9.5 What are the advantages and disadvantages for a company in using WACC as a discount factor to evaluate capital projects?

Q9.6 Describe the ways in which the costs of debt and equity capital may be ascertained.

Q9.7 How does risk impact on the cost of debt and equity?

Q9.8 What is the β factor, and how may it be related to WACC?

Q9.9 How may a company's return on equity (ROE) be related to its financial structure?

Q9.10 In what way is company growth of such interest to shareholders?

Q9.11 Business performance may be evaluated to determine ways in which it can be improved upon. If managers are capable of delivering improved performance how can EVA be used to support this?

Discussion points

D9.1 The former owner and manager of a private limited company recently acquired by a large plc, of which he is now a board member, said: 'This company has grown very quickly over the past few years so that our sales revenue is now over £20m per annum. Even though we expect our revenue to grow further and double in the next two years I cannot see why we need to change our existing financing arrangements. I know we need to make some large investments in new machinery over the next two years but in the past we've always operated successfully using our existing bank overdraft facility, which has been increased as required, particularly when we've needed new equipment. I don't really see the need for all this talk about additional share capital and long-term loans.' Discuss.

D9.2 In the long run does it really matter whether a company is financed predominantly by ordinary shares or predominantly by loans? What's the difference?

D9.3 The marketing manager of a large UK subsidiary of a multinational plc: 'Surely the interest rate that we should use to discount cash flows in our appraisal of new capital investment projects should be our bank overdraft interest rate. I don't really see the relevance of the weighted average cost of capital (WACC) to this type of exercise.' Discuss.

D9.4 'Economic value added (EVA) is nothing more than just flavour of the month.' Discuss.

Exercises

Solutions are provided in Appendix 2 to all exercise numbers highlighted in colour.

Level I

E9.1   *Time allowed – 30 minutes*

A critically important factor required by a company to make financial decisions, for example the evaluation of investment proposals and the financing of new projects, is its cost of capital. One of the elements included in the calculation of a company's cost of capital is the cost of equity.

> **(i) Explain in simple terms what is meant by the 'cost of equity capital' for a company.**

The relevant data for Normal plc and the market in general are given below.

Normal plc

Current price per share on the London Stock Exchange	£1.20
Current annual dividend per share	£0.10
Expected average annual growth rate of dividends	7%
β beta coefficient for Normal plc's shares	0.5

The market

Expected rate of return on risk-free securities	8%
Expected return on the market portfolio	12%

> **(ii) Calculate the cost of equity capital for Normal plc, using two alternative methods:**
> **(a) the Capital Asset Pricing Model (CAPM)**
> **(b) a dividend growth model of your choice.**

E9.2   *Time allowed – 30 minutes*

Normal plc pays £20,000 a year interest on an irredeemable debenture, which has a nominal value of £200,000 and a market value of £160,000. The rate of corporation tax is 30%.

You are required to:

(i)   calculate the cost of the debt for Normal plc
(ii)   calculate the weighted average cost of capital for Normal plc using the cost of equity calculated in Exercise E9.1 (ii) if Normal plc has ordinary capital of 300,000 £1 shares
(iii) comment on the impact on a company's cost of capital of changes in the rate of corporation tax
(iv)   calculate Normal plc's WACC if the rate of corporation tax were increased to 50%.

Level II

E9.3   *Time allowed – 30 minutes*

Lucky Jim plc has the opportunity to manufacture a particular type of self-tapping screw, for a client company, that would become indispensable in a particular niche market in the engineering field.

Development of the product requires an initial investment of £200,000 in the project. It has been estimated that the project will yield cash returns before interest of £35,000 per annum in perpetuity.

Lucky Jim plc is financed by equity and loans, which are always maintained as two-thirds and one-third of the total capital respectively. The cost of equity is 18% and the pre-tax cost of debt is 9%. The corporation tax rate is 40%.

If Lucky Jim plc's WACC is used as the cost of capital to appraise the project, should the project be undertaken?

E9.4   *Time allowed – 30 minutes*

You are required to compute the MVA for 2009, 2010 and 2011 from the estimated information for a large supermarket group.

	2011	2010	2009
Number of shares	6.823m	6.823m	6.776m
Share price	261p	169p	177p
Adjusted net assets	£5,000m	£4,769m	£4,377m

E9.5   *Time allowed – 60 minutes*

Yor plc is a fast-growing, hi-tech business. Its income statement for the year ended 30 September 2010 and its balance sheet as at 30 September 2010 are shown below. The company has the opportunity to take on a major project that will significantly improve its profitability in the forthcoming year and for the foreseeable future. The cost of the project is £10m, which will result in large increases in sales, which will increase profit before interest and tax by £4m per annum. The directors of Yor plc have two alternative options of financing the project: the issue of £10m of 4% debentures at par, or a rights issue of 4m ordinary shares at a premium of £1.50 per share (after expenses).

Regardless of how the new project is financed, the directors will recommend a 10% increase in the dividend for 2010/2011. You may assume that the effective corporation tax rate is the same for 2010/2011 as for 2009/2010.

Yor plc
Income statement for the year ended 30 September 2010

	£m
PBIT	11.6
Finance costs	(1.2)
Profit before tax	10.4
Income tax expense	(2.6)
Profit for the year	7.8
Retained earnings 1 October 2009	5.8
	13.6
Dividends	(3.0)
Retained earnings 30 September 2010	10.6

Yor plc
Balance sheet as at 30 September 2010

	£m
Non-current assets	
Tangible	28.8
Current assets	
Inventories	11.2
Trade and other receivables	13.8
Cash and cash equivalents	0.7
Total current assets	25.7
Total assets	54.5
Current liabilities	
Trade and other payables	9.7
Dividends payable	1.6
Income tax payable	2.6
Total current liabilities	13.9
Non-current liabilities	
6% loan	20.0
Total liabilities	33.9
Net assets	20.6
Equity	
Share capital (£1 ordinary shares)	10.0
Retained earnings	10.6
Total equity	20.6

The directors of Yor plc would like to see your estimated income statement for 2010/2011, and a summary of the equity and debt at 30 September 2011, assuming:

(i)   the new project is financed by an issue of the debentures
(ii) the new project is financed by the issue of new ordinary shares

To assist in clarification of the figures, you should show your calculations of:

(iii) eps for 2009/2010
(iv) eps for 2010/2011, reflecting both methods of financing the new project

(v)   dividend per share for 2009/2010

(vi)   dividend per share for 2010/2011, reflecting both methods of financing the new project

Use the information you have provided in (i) and (ii) above to:

(vii)   calculate Yor plc's gearing, reflecting both methods of financing the new project, and compare with its gearing at 30 September 2010

(viii)   summarise the results for 2010/2011, recommend which method of financing Yor plc should adopt, and explain the implications of both on its financial structure.

E9.6   *Time allowed – 90 minutes*

Sparks plc is a large electronics company that produces components for CD players and iPods. It is close to the current year end and Sparks is forecasting profit after tax at £60m. The following two years' post-tax profits are each expected to increase by another £15m, and years four and five by another £10m each.

The forecast balance sheet for Sparks plc as at 31 December is as follows:

	£m
Non-current assets	500
Current assets	
Inventories	120
Trade and other receivables	160
Total current assets	280
Total assets	780
Current liabilities	
Borrowings and finance leases	75
Trade and other payables	75
Total current liabilities	150
Non-current liabilities	150
Total liabilities	300
Net assets	480
Equity	
Share capital (£1 ordinary shares)	220
Share premium account	10
Retained earnings	250
Total equity	480

Sparks plc has a large bank overdraft of £75m on which it pays a high rate of interest at 15%. The board would like to pay off the overdraft and obtain cheaper financing. Sparks also has loan capital of £150m on which it pays interest at 9% per annum. Despite its high level of debt Sparks is a profitable organisation. However, the board of directors is currently planning a number of new projects for the next year, which will cost £75m. These projects are expected to produce profits after tax of £8m in the first year and £15m a year ongoing for future years.

The board has discussed a number of financing options and settled on two of them for further consideration:

(1)   a one for four rights issue at £3.00 a share to raise £150m from the issue of 50m £1 shares

(2)   a convertible £150m debenture issue at 12% (pre tax) that may be converted into 45m ordinary shares in two years' time.

The equity share index has risen over the past year from 4,600 to the current 5,500, having reached 6,250. Sparks plc's ordinary shares are currently at a market price of £3.37. Gearing of companies in the same industry as Sparks plc ranges between 25% and 45%. In two years' time it is expected that all Sparks debenture holders will convert to shares or none will convert.

The rate of corporation tax is 50%. Repayment of the bank overdraft will save interest of £5.625m a year after tax.

The board requires some analysis of the numbers to compare against the current position:

(i)   if they make the rights issue
(ii) if they issue debentures
(iii) if the debentures are converted.

The analysis should show:

(a)   the impact on the balance sheet
(b)   the impact on the profit after tax
(c)   earnings per share
(d)   gearing
(e)   which option should be recommended to the board and why.

Case Study III
BUZZARD (1) LTD

The Buzzard Group is a first-tier global supplier to major passenger car and commercial vehicle manu-facturers. As a first-tier supplier Buzzard provides systems that fit directly into motor vehicles, which they have manufactured from materials and components acquired from second, third, fourth-tier, etc., suppliers. During the 2000s, through investment in R&D and technology, Buzzard became re-garded as one of the world's leaders in design, manufacture and supply of innovative automotive systems.

In the mid-2000s Buzzard started business in one of the UK's many development areas. It was established through acquisition of the business of Firefly from the Stonehead Group by a Buzzard sub-sidiary, Buzzard Ltd. Firefly was a traditional, mass production automotive component manufacturer, located on a brownfield site in Gentbridge, once a fairly prosperous mining area. Firefly had pursued short-term profit rather than longer-term development strategies, and had a poor image with both its customers and suppliers. This represented a challenge but also an opportunity for Buzzard Ltd to establish a world class manufacturing facility.

A major part of Buzzard's strategic plan was the commitment to investing £30m to relocate from Gentbridge to a new fully equipped 15,000 square metre purpose-built factory on a 20-acre green-field site in Bramblecote, which was finally completed during the year 2010. At the same time, it introduced the changes required to transform its culture and implement the operating strategies re-quired to achieve the highest level of industrial performance. By the year 2010 Buzzard Ltd had be-come an established supplier of high quality and was close to achieving its aim of being a world class supplier of innovative automotive systems.

In December 2010 a seven-year bank loan was agreed with interest payable half yearly at a fixed rate of 5% per annum. The loan was secured with a floating charge over the assets of Buzzard Ltd.

The financial statements of Buzzard Ltd, its accounting policies and extracts from its notes to the accounts, for the year ended 31 December 2010 are shown in Case Study I on pages 186 to 191. It should be noted that note 3 to the accounts – profit for the year – reports on some of the key items included in the income statement for the year and is not a complete analysis of the income statement.

Required

Use the financial statements of Buzzard Ltd and the other financial information given in Case Study I:

(i)   Prepare a vertical analysis of the income statement and balance sheet of Buzzard Ltd based on sales revenue and net assets respectively, for 2009 and 2010.

(ii) Prepare a horizontal analysis of the income statement, balance sheet, and the segmen-tal analysis from note 1 to the accounts, using 2009 as base 100.

(iii) Prepare a value added statement for 2009 and 2010 and a vertical analysis of the value added statement for both years.

(iv) Prepare a report on the financial performance and the financial position of Buzzard Ltd that makes extensive use of the analyses that have been prepared in (i), (ii), and (iii) above.

APPENDICES

Outline of Appendices

Appendix 1 includes schedules of all current International Accounting Standards (IASs) and International Financial Reporting Standards (IFRSs).

Appendix 2 contains solutions to around 45% of the chapter-end exercises, which include a mix of both Level I and Level II exercises. They refer to the chapter-end exercise numbers which are highlighted in colour. This allows you to attempt the exercises at the end of each chapter and then check on your understanding of the key points and how well you have been able to apply the various learning topics and techniques. Further exercises are included on the book's accompanying website.

Appendix 1

IFRSs and IASs

International Financial Reporting Standards (IFRSs) in force in the year 2012

IFRS 1   First-time adoption of international financial reporting standards
IFRS 2   Share-based payment
IFRS 3   Business combinations
IFRS 4   Insurance contracts
IFRS 5   Non-current assets held for sale and discontinued operations
IFRS 6   Exploration for and evaluation of mineral resources
IFRS 7   Financial instruments: disclosures
IFRS 8   Operating segments (to replace IAS 14)
IFRS 9   Financial instruments (with effect from 1 January 2013 to replace IAS 39)

International Accounting Standards (IASs) in force in the year 2012

IAS 1   Presentation of financial statements
IAS 2   Inventories
IAS 7   Statement of cash flows
IAS 8   Accounting policies, changes in accounting estimates, and errors
IAS 10   Events after the reporting period
IAS 11   Construction contracts
IAS 12   Income taxes
IAS 16   Property, plant and equipment
IAS 17   Leases
IAS 18   Revenue
IAS 19   Employee benefits
IAS 20   Accounting for Government grants and disclosure of Government assistance
IAS 21   The effects of changes in foreign exchange rates
IAS 23   Borrowing costs
IAS 24   Related party disclosures
IAS 26   Accounting and reporting by retirement benefit plans
IAS 27   Consolidated and separate financial statements
IAS 28   Investments in associates
IAS 29   Financial reporting in hyperinflationary economies
IAS 31   Interests in joint ventures
IAS 32   Financial instruments: presentation
IAS 33   Earnings per share
IAS 34   Interim financial reporting
IAS 36   Impairment of assets
IAS 37   Provisions, contingent liabilities and contingent assets
IAS 38   Intangible assets
IAS 39   Financial instruments: recognition and measurement
IAS 40   Investment property
IAS 41   Agriculture

Appendix 2

Solutions to selected exercises

Solutions are provided for the chapter-end exercise numbers highlighted in colour.

Chapter 2

E2.1 Hall

Hall Ltd
Income statement for the years ended 31 December 2009 and 2010

	2010	2009
	£	£
Sales revenue	12,000	11,000
Cost of sales	8,000	7,000
Gross profit	4,000	4,000
Expenses	3,000	2,500
Net profit	1,000	1,500

Working
2009
Cost of sales: opening inventories £600 + purchases £7,100 less closing inventories £700.

2010
Cost of sales: opening inventories £700 + purchases £8,300 less closing inventories £800 less the obsolete inventories of £200.

Cost of sales for 2010 must exclude obsolete inventories as it has not been sold.

Expenses £2,800 plus the obsolete inventories £200.

E2.2 Accruals

(i)
The invoices for the common utilities rarely coincide with accounting period ends. To ensure that costs up to the year end are appropriately included, an adjustment is required for the consumption between the invoice date and year end.

(ii)

	Debit	Credit
	£	£
Profit and loss account		
Electricity to 15 December 2010	10,000	
Accruals for charges 16 to 31 December 2010	300	
Total electricity costs for the year 2010	10,300	
Gas to 20 December 2010	5,000	
Accruals for charges 21 to 31 December 2010	150	
Total gas costs for the year 2010	5,150	
Balance sheet		
Electricity accrual at 31 December 2010		300
Gas accrual at 31 December 2010		150
Total accruals at 31 December 2010		450

E2.7 Correcting entries

31 December 2010

	Debit £	Credit £
(i)		
Profit and loss account		
Rent	2,400	
Profit and loss account		
Car hire		2,400
Correction of account error		
(ii)		
Profit and loss account		
Discount allowed		20
Balance sheet		
Accounts receivable control account	20	
Customer settlement discount		
(iii)		
Profit and loss account		
Car insurance	1,200	
Balance sheet		
Motor vehicle non-current assets account		1,200
Correction of account error		
(iv)		
Profit and loss account		
Building repairs	3,500	
Balance sheet		
Buildings non-current assets account		3,500
Correction of account error		

E2.8 Etcoakco

(i)

	Debit £	Credit £
	Capital	
Transaction 1		100,000
Balance c/f	100,000	
	100,000	100,000
Balance b/f		100,000
@ 1/1/10		

	Debit £	Credit £
	Cash	
Transaction 1	100,000	
Transaction 2		50,000
Transaction 3		7,000
Transaction 5		400
Transaction 10	27,600	
Balance c/f		70,200
	127,600	127,600
Balance b/f	70,200	
@ 1/1/10		

	Debit £	Credit £		Debit £	Credit £
	Non-current assets – shop			**Non-current assets – fittings and equipment**	
Transaction 2	50,000		Transaction 3	7,000	
			Transaction 4	20,000	
Balance c/f		50,000	Balance c/f		27,000
	50,000	50,000		27,000	27,000
Balance b/f @ 1/1/10	50,000		Balance b/f @ 1/1/10	27,000	
	Printing and stationery expenses			**Payables**	
Transaction 5	400		Transaction 4		20,000
			Transaction 6		31,250
Balance c/f		400	Balance c/f	51,250	
	400	400		51,250	51,250
Balance b/f @ 1/1/10	400		Balance b/f @ 1/1/10		51,250
	Inventories			**Sales revenue**	
Transaction 6	31,250		Transaction 7		23,000
Transaction 9		27,500	Transaction 8		27,600
Balance c/f		3,750	Balance c/f	50,600	
	31,250	31,250		50,600	50,600
Balance b/f @ 1/1/10	3,750		Balance b/f @ 1/1/10		50,600
	Receivables			**Cost of sales**	
Transaction 7	23,000		Transaction 9	27,500	
Transaction 8	27,600		Balance c/f		27,500
Transaction 10		27,600		27,500	27,500
Balance c/f		23,000	Balance b/f @ 1/1/10	27,500	
	50,600	50,600			
Balance b/f @ 1/1/10	23,000				

Solutions to parts **(ii)**, **(iii)** and **(iv)** may provide an introduction to inventories valuation, cost of sales and alternative uses of funds, covered in Chapters 3, 4 and 5 of this book.

Chapter 3

E3.3 Trainer

Trainer plc
Balance sheet as at 31 December 2010

	£000
Non-current assets	
Land and buildings	320
Plant and machinery cost	200
Plant and machinery depreciation provision	(80)
Total non-current assets	440
Current assets	
Inventories	100
Trade receivables	100
Cash and cash equivalents	73
Total current assets	273
Total assets	713
Current liabilities	
Trade payables	130
Accruals	5
Income tax payable	20
Total current liabilities	155
Net assets	558
Equity	
Ordinary shares	320
Retained earnings	238
Total equity	558

Working	£000
Revenue	1,000
Cost of sales	600
Gross profit	400
Expenses	(120)
Bad debt	(2)
Depreciation	(20)
Profit before tax	258
Income tax expense (also within *Current Liabilities*)	(20)
Net profit	238

E3.6 Gorban

Gorban Ltd
Balance sheet as at 31 December 2010

	Per TB £					£
Non-current assets						
Tangible assets	235,000		29,368			264,368
Depreciation provision	(30,165)					(30,165)
Total non-current assets	204,835					234,203
Current assets						
Inventories	51,420		48,000			99,420
Trade receivables	42,500				(10,342)	32,158
Doubtful debts provision	(1,725)			(1,870)		(3,595)
Cash and cash equivalents	67,050	(20,000)	(29,368)	50,000		67,682
Total current assets	159,245					195,665
Total assets	364,080					429,868
Current liabilities						
Trade payables	35,112					35,112
Accruals		1,173				1,173
Total current liabilities	35,112					36,285
Non-current liabilities						
Loan	20,000	(20,000)				
Total liabilities	55,112					36,285
Net assets	308,968					393,583
Equity						
Share capital	200,000			50,000		250,000
Retained earnings	108,968	(1,173)	48,000	(1,870)	(10,342)	143,583
Total equity	308,968					393,583

E3.7 Pip

Pip Ltd
Balance sheet as at 31 December 2010

	£000	Working
Non-current assets		
Land and buildings	100,000	
Plant and equipment	100,000	[150,000 − 50,000]
Total non-current assets	200,000	
Current assets		
Inventories	45,000	[50,000 − 5,000]
Trade receivables	45,000	[50,000 − 5,000]
Cash and cash equivalents	11,000	[10,000 + 1,000]
Total current assets	101,000	
Total assets	301,000	

Current liabilities

Borrowings	10,000
Trade payables	81,000
Total liabilities	91,000
Net assets	210,000

Equity

Ordinary shares (issued)	100,000
Retained earnings	110,000
Total equity	210,000

Note that the intangible assets, brands worth £10,000 in the opinion of the directors, have not been included in the balance sheet on the assumption that they are not purchased brands. Under IAS 38, Intangible Assets, only brand names that have been purchased may be capitalised and included in the balance sheet.

Chapter 4

E4.3 CDs

Overview

Inventories are dealt with in IAS 2, Inventories, which states that they should be valued at the lower of cost and net realisable value. Retailers can (and do) take the retail value of their inventories (by category) and deduct the gross profit (by category) as an estimate of cost.

(i)   This inventory should be valued at £5,000 (cost) as it is selling consistently.

(ii)   This inventory should not be in the balance sheet at any value, as it will not generate any cash in the future.

(iii) As in (i) above this inventory can be valued at £1,000 (cost) for balance sheet purposes. As there are more risks associated with holding single artist CDs the inventory levels should be continually reviewed.

(iv)   In this situation the selling pattern has changed and the posters have stopped selling. The posters must not appear in the balance sheet as they will not generate any future cash.

E4.4 Partex

	2008 £	2009 £	2010 £
(i) Balance sheet as at 31 December – accounts receivable			
Accounts receivable including debts to be written-off	88,000	110,000	94,000
Write-off of debts to profit and loss account (1)	(4,000)	(5,000)	(4,000)
	84,000	105,000	90,000
	–	3,360	4,200
Doubtful provision at 4% of accounts receivable (2)	(3,360)	(4,200)	(3,600)
Trade receivables at end of year	80,640	104,160	90,600

(ii) Profit and loss account year ended 31 December – bad and doubtful debts

Bad debts written-off (1)	4,000	5,000	4,000
$\{$	–	(3,360)	(4,200)
Doubtful debt provision at 4% of accounts receivable (2)	3,360	4,200	3,600
Bad and doubtful debts charge for year	7,360	5,840	3,400

E4.5 Tartantrips

(i) Sum of the digits depreciation

The company needs to decide on the economic life of the asset (say 10 years in this example) and its estimated residual value at the end of its life (£1m in this example).

Cost	£5,000,000
Residual value	£1,000,000
Amount to be written-off over 10 years	£4,000,000

Over 10 years the digits $10 + 9 + 8 \ldots 2 + 1$ add up to 55

Depreciation in year 1 is 10/55 × £4,000,000	=	£727,272
Depreciation in year 2 is 9/55 × £4,000,000	=	£654,545
Depreciation in year 3 is 8/55 × £4,000,000	=	£581,818
and so on until		
Depreciation in year 9 is 2/55 × £4,000,000	=	£145,546
Depreciation in year 10 is 1/55 × £4,000,000	=	£72,727
Total depreciation for 10 years		£4,000,000

(ii) Straight line depreciation

This method is very simple to operate. The company needs to decide on the economic life of the asset and its residual value at the end of its life (as above). The annual depreciation will be:

Depreciation per year is £4,000,000 divided by 10 years = £400,000 per year

It can be seen that there is a constant charge to the annual profit and loss account for the systematic allocation of the depreciable amount of the non-current asset.

(iii) Reducing balance depreciation

This method is quite different to the straight line method because the depreciation charge is much higher in the earlier years of the life of the asset. The same sort of estimates are required: economic life, residual value, which are used in a reducing balance formula to calculate each year's depreciation.

The reducing balance formula where d is the percentage depreciation to charge on the written down value of the asset at the end of each year is:

$$d = 1 - \sqrt[10]{1,000,000/5,000,000} = 14.9\%$$ (which may also be calculated using the Excel DB function)

Depreciation in year 1 is 14.9% of £5,000,000	=	£745,000
Depreciation in year 2 is 14.9% of £4,255,000	=	£633,995
Depreciation in year 3 is 14.9% of £3,621,005	=	£539,530
and so on until year 10		
The total depreciation for 10 years is		£4,000,000

E4.8 Retepmal

			£	£
Revenue				266,000
Cost of sales				
		Opening inventories 31 March 2009	15,000	
	plus	Purchases	150,000	
	less	Closing inventories 31 March 2010	(25,000)	140,000
Gross profit				126,000
Distribution costs [40,000 + 3,000]				43,000
Administrative expenses [50,000 − 5,000 + 3,000]				48,000
Profit before tax				35,000
Income tax expense				19,000
Profit for the year				16,000
Dividend				7,000
Retained earnings				9,000

Balance sheet as at 31 March 2010

	£
Non-current assets [95,000 + 40,000 + 30,000 − 3,000]	162,000
Current assets	
Inventories	25,000
Trade receivables	75,000
Prepayments	5,000
Cash and cash equivalents	35,000
Total current assets	140,000
Total assets	302,000
Current liabilities	
Trade payables	54,000
Accruals	3,000
Income tax payable	19,000
Dividends payable	7,000
Total current liabilities	83,000
Net assets	219,000
Equity	
Share capital	80,000
Retained earnings [130,000 + 9,000]	139,000
Total equity	219,000

Chapter 5

E5.1 Candyfloss

(i)   Candyfloss cash flow six months to 30 June 2010 using the direct method

	£000
Operating activities	
Receipts from customers	76.0
Payments	
Flowers suppliers	59.5
Employees	5.0
Other overheads:	
Rent	4.0
Operating expenses	7.0
	75.5
Cash inflow from operating activities	0.5
Investing activities	
Purchase of lease	15.0
Lease fees	1.0
Purchase of van	14.5
Cash outflow from investing activities	30.5
Financing activities	
Loan	3.0
Issue of shares	18.0
Cash inflow from financing activities	21.0
Decrease in cash and cash equivalents for the period	(9.0)

(ii)   Candyfloss income statement for the 6 months to 30 June 2010

	£000	
Revenue	84.0	[76.0 + 8.0]
Cost of flowers	54.0	[59.5 + 4.0 − 9.5]
Operating expenses	8.0	[7.0 + 1.0]
Wages	5.0	
	67.0	
Gross profit	17.0	
Overheads		
Rent	2.0	
Depreciation	1.5	[(14.5 − 2.5)/4 × 50% for the half year]
Bad debts	1.5	
	5.0	
Profit for period	12.0	

(iii) The difference between the cash flow and profit for the period is

−£9,000 − £12,000 = −£21,000

Both cash and profit give an indication of performance.

The profit of £12,000 may be compared with the cash inflow from operating activities of £500.

	Profit	Operating cash flow	Differences
	£000	£000	
Revenue/receipts	84.0	76.0	sales 8 not yet paid by customers
Bad debts	(1.5)		sales assumed will never be paid
Flowers	(54.0)	(59.5)	9.5 in inventory and 4 not yet paid for
Wages	(5.0)	(5.0)	
Operating expenses	(8.0)	(7.0)	1 not yet paid
Rent	(2.0)	(4.0)	2 rent paid in advance
Depreciation	(1.5)		1.5 not cash
	12.0	0.5	

(iv) **A number of items in the income statement are subjective and open to various different methods of valuation:**

Bad debts	1.5	different subjective views as to whether customers may pay or not
Inventories	9.5	different valuation methods
Depreciation	1.5	different bases may be used

- additionally cash flow shows how much was paid out for the lease and for the van and what financing was obtained
- cash flow gives a clear picture of the financial performance, looked at alongside the balance sheet which shows the financial position at a point in time
- looking at the income statement from period to period it is difficult to compare performance with that of similar businesses because of different approaches to asset valuation.

E5.4 Medco

Medco Ltd
Cash generated from operations for the year ended 31 December 2010
Indirect cash flow method

	£
Profit before tax	2,400
Depreciation charge	2,000
Loss on disposal of tangible asset	500
Adjust finance (income)/costs	100
Increase in inventories	(1,000)
Increase in trade and other receivables	(1,000)
Decrease in trade and other payables	(2,000)
Cash generated from operations	1,000
Interest paid	(100)
Income tax paid	(400)
Net cash inflow from operating activities	500

Statement of cash flows for the year ended 31 December 2010

	£000
Cash flows from operating activities	
Cash generated from operations	1,000
Interest paid	(100)
Income tax paid	(400)
Net cash inflow from operating activities	500
Cash flows from investing activities	
Purchases of tangible assets	(12,500)
Proceeds from sales of tangible assets	2,000
Net cash outflow from investing activities	(10,500)
Cash flows from financing activities	
Proceeds from issue of ordinary shares [20,000 − 15,000]	5,000
Proceeds from borrowings [2,000 − 1,000]	1,000
Dividends paid to equity shareholders	(750)
Net cash inflow from financing activities	5,250
Decrease in cash and cash equivalents in the year	(4,750)
Cash and cash equivalents and bank overdrafts at beginning of year	6,000
Cash and cash equivalents and bank overdrafts at end of year	1,250

E5.6 Victoria

(i)

(a)

	£000
Increase in retained earnings 2010 over 2009 from balance sheet	500
Add tax payable	320
Add dividends payable	480
Therefore profit before tax is	1,300

(b)

	£000
Profit before tax	1,300
Add debenture interest	100
Therefore operating profit is	1,400

(ii)

Victoria plc
Cash generated from operations for the year ended 30 June 2010
Indirect cash flow method

	£000
Profit before tax	1,300
Depreciation charge	200
Adjust finance (income)/costs	100
Increase in inventories	(1,400)

Increase in trade and other receivables	(680)
Decrease in trade and other payables	(200)
Cash used from operations	(680)
Interest paid	(100)
Income tax paid	(300)
Net cash outflow from operating activities	(1,080)

Statement of cash flows for the year ended 30 June 2010

	£000
Cash flows from operating activities	
Cash used from operations	(680)
Interest paid	(100)
Income tax paid	(300)
Net cash outlow from operating activities	(1,080)
Cash flows from investing activities	
Purchases of tangible assets	(2,100)
Net cash outflow from investing activities	(2,100)
Cash flows from financing activities	
Proceeds from issue of ordinary shares	2,740
Dividends paid to equity shareholders	(360)
Net cash inflow from financing activities	2,380
Decrease in cash and cash equivalents in the year	(800)
Cash and cash equivalents and bank overdrafts at beginning of year	200
Cash and cash equivalents and bank overdrafts at end of year	(600)

Analysis of cash and cash equivalents and bank overdrafts as at 30 June 2010

	At 30 June 2009 £000	At 30 June 2010 £000
Cash and cash equivalents	200	–
Bank overdrafts	–	(600)
Cash and cash equivalents and bank overdrafts	200	(600)

E5.7 Sparklers

Sparklers plc
Cash generated from operations for the year ended 31 October 2010
Indirect cash flow method

	£m
Profit before tax	40.80
Depreciation charge	10.10
Loss on disposal of tangible asset	1.40

Adjust finance (income)/costs	0.48
Increase in inventories	(20.00)
Increase in trade and other receivables	(36.40)
Decrease in trade and other payables	8.40
Cash generated from operations	4.78
Interest paid	(0.56)
Income tax paid	(6.40)
Net cash outflow from operating activities	(2.18)

Statement of cash flows for the year ended 31 October 2010

	£m
Cash flows from operating activities	
Cash generated from operations	4.78
Interest paid	(0.56)
Income tax paid	(6.40)
Net cash outflow from operating activities	(2.18)
Cash flows from investing activities	
Purchases of tangible assets	(23.60)
Proceeds from sales of tangible assets	2.00
Interest received	0.08
Net cash outflow from investing activities	(21.52)
Cash flows from financing activities	
Proceeds from borrowings	0.30
Dividends paid to equity shareholders	(10.20)
Net cash outflow from financing activities	(9.90)
Decrease in cash and cash equivalents in the year	(33.60)
Cash and cash equivalents and bank overdrafts at beginning of year	1.20
Cash and cash equivalents and bank overdrafts at end of year	(32.40)

Analysis of cash and cash equivalents and bank overdrafts as at 31 October 2010

	At 31 October 2009	At 31 October 2010
	£000	£000
Cash and cash equivalents	1.20	–
Bank overdrafts	–	(32.40)
Cash and cash equivalents and bank overdrafts	1.20	(32.40)

Working

	£m	£m
Depreciation		
Depreciation 31 October 2010		21.50
Depreciation 31 October 2009	19.00	
Depreciation on assets sold in 2010	(7.60)	(11.40)
Charge for the year 2010		10.10
Loss on sale of assets		
Proceeds on sale		2.00
Net book value: cost	11.00	
depreciation	(7.60)	(3.40)
Loss on sale		(1.40)
Dividends paid		
Dividends payable at 31 October 2009		6.00
Dividends declared for 2010: preference		0.20
ordinary interim		4.00
ordinary final		12.00
		22.20
Less dividends payable at 31 October 2010		12.00
Dividends paid during 2010		10.20
Purchase of non-current assets		
Non-current assets 31 October 2010		47.80
Non-current assets 31 October 2009	35.20	
Cost of non-current assets sold	(11.00)	(24.20)
Non-current assets purchased 2010		23.60

You should refer to the relevant sections in Chapter 5 to check your assessment of the reasons for the increased overdraft.

Chapter 6

E6.1 Share options

Past governments have made employee share option schemes tax efficient and therefore schemes are now very common amongst plcs.

Many plcs have found that their share prices react to specific management policies and decisions, for example takeovers and disposals of businesses. Users of financial information can assess these decisions, knowing of the options awarded to the directors.

Many plcs have found that they can only keep and attract high-calibre managers by including share options in their remuneration packages.

Investing institutions demand more and more information regarding directors' remuneration. This can influence their basic hold or buy or sell decisions. The financial press frequently includes criticism of specific companies.

E6.2 Perks

Directors are not the owners of the company (although sometimes directors may own shares in the company). The shareholders own the company and appoint the directors to manage it on their behalf.

Any monies (expenses) that a director takes from the company will affect the annual profit.

Annual dividends are paid from the annual profits. The shareholders approve the accounts at the AGM, which includes remuneration of the directors.

If the directors hide information regarding their remuneration and benefits from the shareholders, then that part of the accounts may not show a true and fair view of the situation.

E6.3 Contracts

Before the UK Corporate Governance Code of Practice was introduced, shareholders found that their directors had powers that were increasing, especially regarding length of contract and compensation for loss of office.

The Cadbury and Greenbury committees recommended that directors' contracts should be no longer than (first) three years (Cadbury) and then one year (Greenbury). These committees had looked at the evidence presented to them. Hampel (1998) provided that the contracts should be one year or less.

The financial press regularly comments on the compensation paid to a director, where company performance has been acknowledged to be poor. There is always reference to the length of outstanding directors' contracts.

Shareholders can decide whether to hold or buy or sell shares if they have advance information on the type of contracts being awarded to the executive directors of their company.

UK financial institutions have also become proactive regarding the length of directors' contracts issue. They have noted that in the past too many highly paid directors were awarding themselves contracts in which compensation for loss of office was very expensive to pay. Currently it often costs companies potentially many millions of pounds to buy out a chief executive from just a one-year contract.

E6.7 Tomkins

Equity shareholders are the owners of the company, and the level of their dividends usually varies with levels of profits earned by the company.

Directors are appointed by the shareholders, and remunerated for their efforts. Major multinational companies are difficult to manage successfully over a long period of time. The remuneration of directors should reflect that difficulty.

The information that has been given about Tomkins plc shows that there was an executive director who earned a basic salary of just below £1 million a year, an amount which most shareholders would like to see disclosed in the accounts and discussed at the AGM.

The bonus of £443,000 would also have generated some interest amongst the institutions and individual shareholders. Institutions (and the UK Government) are seen to put pressure on directors if they feel pay awards are excessive.

The consultancy agreement for a non-executive director may also have been of interest to the various users of the notes to the accounts.

Chapter 7

E7.1 Priory

(i) Net debt to equity

	2009	2010	2011
Net debt	100	250	800
Equity	300	500	800
Debt/equity (%)	33%	50%	100%

(ii) Long-term loans to equity and long-term loans – gearing

	2009	2010	2011
Long-term loans	200	200	600
Equity plus long-term loans	500	700	1,400
Gearing (%)	40%	29%	43%

E7.2 Freshco

Profitability ratios for Freshco plc for 2010 and the comparative ratios for 2009
Gross profit (or gross margin, GM)

$$\text{Gross profit \%} \atop 2010 = \frac{\text{gross profit}}{\text{revenue}} = \frac{£204 \times 100\%}{£894} = 22.8\%$$

$$\text{Gross profit \%} \atop 2009 = \frac{£166 \times 100\%}{£747} = 22.2\%$$

Profit before interest and tax, PBIT (or operating profit)

$$\text{PBIT \%} \atop 2010 = \frac{\text{operating profit}}{\text{revenue}} = \frac{£83 \times 100\%}{£894} = 9.3\%$$

$$\text{PBIT \%} \atop 2009 = \frac{£82 \times 100\%}{£747} = 11.0\%$$

Profit for the year (profit after tax, PAT, or return on sales, ROS)

$$\text{PAT \%} \atop 2010 = \frac{\text{net profit}}{\text{revenue}} = \frac{£56 \times 100\%}{£894} = 6.3\%$$

$$\text{PAT \%} \atop 2009 = \frac{£54 \times 100\%}{£747} = 7.2\%$$

Return on capital employed, ROCE (return on investment, ROI)

$$\text{ROCE \%} \atop 2010 = \frac{\text{operating profit}}{\text{total assets} - \text{current liabilities} \atop \text{(average capital employed)}} = \frac{£83 \times 100\%}{(£233 + £233)/2} = \frac{£83 \times 100\%}{£233} = 35.6\%$$

$$\text{ROCE \%} \atop 2009 = \frac{£82 \times 100\%}{(£233 + £219)/2} = \frac{£82 \times 100\%}{£226} = 36.3\%$$

Return on equity, ROE

$$\text{ROE \%} \atop 2010 = \frac{\text{PAT}}{\text{equity}} = \frac{£56 \times 100\%}{£213} = 26.3\%$$

$$\text{ROE \%} \atop 2009 = \frac{£54 \times 100}{£166} = 32.5\%$$

Capital turnover

$$\text{Capital turnover} \atop 2010 = \frac{\text{revenue}}{\text{average capital employed in year}} = \frac{£894}{£233} = 3.8 \text{ times}$$

$$\text{Capital turnover} \atop 2009 = \frac{£747}{£226} = 3.3 \text{ times}$$

Report on the profitability of Freshco plc
Sales for the year 2010 increased by 19.7% over the previous year, but it is not clear whether from increased volumes, new products, or higher selling prices.

Gross profit improved by 0.6% to 22.8% of sales revenue, possibly from increased selling prices and/or from lower costs of production.

Operating profit dropped by 1.7% to 9.3% of sales despite the improvement in gross profit, because of higher levels of distribution costs and administrative expenses.

ROCE declined from 36.3% to 35.6%, indicating a less effective use of funds by Freshco.

Return on equity dropped by 6.2% to 26.3%. This was because the profit for the year after tax remained fairly static but equity was increased through an issue of shares and increases in general reserves and retained earnings.

Capital turnover for 2010 increased to 3.8 times from 3.3 in 2009, reflecting the significant increases in sales levels in 2010 over 2009.

E7.4 Freshco

Liquidity ratios for Freshco plc for 2010 and the comparative ratios for 2009

Current ratio

$$\text{Current ratio} \atop 2010 = \frac{\text{current assets}}{\text{current liabilities}} = \frac{£208}{£121} = 1.7 \text{ times}$$

$$\text{Current ratio} \atop 2009 = \frac{£191}{£107} = 1.8 \text{ times}$$

Quick ratio

$$\text{Quick ratio} \atop 2010 = \frac{\text{current assets} - \text{inventories}}{\text{current liabilities}} = \frac{£208 - £124}{£121} = 0.7 \text{ times}$$

$$\text{Quick ratio} \atop 2009 = \frac{£191 - £100}{£107} = 0.8 \text{ times}$$

Defensive interval

$$\text{Defensive interval} \atop 2010 = \frac{\text{quick assets}}{\text{average daily cash from operations}} = \frac{£208 - £124}{(£80 + £894 - £70)/365} = 34 \text{ days}$$

$$\text{Defensive interval} \atop 2009 = \frac{£191 - £100}{(£60 + £747 - £80)/365} = 46 \text{ days}$$

Report on the liquidity of Freshco plc
The current ratio and the quick ratio have both dropped slightly to 1.7 times and 0.7 times respectively. However, the defensive interval has dropped significantly from 46 days to 34 days at which level the company could potentially survive if there were no further cash inflows.

Net cash flow from operations improved from £54m in 2009 to £62m in 2010. Investments in non-current assets were at lower levels in 2010 and matched by a reduction in long-term financing (debentures).

E7.8 Laurel

(i)

Profitability ratios for Hardy plc for 2010 and the comparative ratios for 2009 and 2008
Gross profit

$$\text{Gross profit \%} \atop 2010 = \frac{\text{gross profit}}{\text{revenue}} = \frac{£161 \times 100\%}{£456} = 35.3\%$$

$$\text{Gross profit \%}_{2009} = \frac{£168 \times 100\%}{£491} = 34.2\%$$

$$\text{Gross profit \%}_{2008} = \frac{£142 \times 100\%}{£420} = 34.0\%$$

Profit before interest and tax, PBIT (or operating profit)

$$\text{PBIT \%}_{2010} = \frac{\text{operating profit}}{\text{revenue}} = \frac{£52 \times 100\%}{£456} = 11.4\%$$

$$\text{PBIT \%}_{2009} = \frac{£61 \times 100\%}{£491} = 12.4\%$$

$$\text{PBIT \%}_{2008} = \frac{£50 \times 100\%}{£420} = 11.9\%$$

Profit for the year, or profit after tax, PAT

$$\text{PAT \%}_{2010} = \frac{\text{net profit}}{\text{revenue}} = \frac{£20 \times 100\%}{£456} = 4.4\%$$

$$\text{PAT \%}_{2009} = \frac{£28 \times 100\%}{£491} = 5.7\%$$

$$\text{PAT \%}_{2008} = \frac{£25 \times 100\%}{£420} = 6.0\%$$

Return on capital employed, ROCE (return on investment, ROI)

$$\text{ROCE \%}_{2010} = \frac{\text{operating profit}}{\text{total assets} - \text{current liabilities}} = \frac{£52 \times 100\%}{(£284 + £292)/2} = \frac{£52 \times 100\%}{£288} = 18.1\%$$

$$\text{ROCE \%}_{2009} = \frac{£61 \times 100}{(£237 + £284)/2} = \frac{£61 \times 100\%}{£260.5} = 23.4\%$$

ROCE % 2008 is not available because we do not have the capital employed number for 31 March 2007.

Return on equity, ROE

$$\text{ROE \%}_{2010} = \frac{\text{PAT}}{\text{equity}} = \frac{£20 \times 100\%}{£223} = 9.0\%$$

$$\text{ROE \%}_{2009} = \frac{£28 \times 100\%}{£215} = 13.0\%$$

$$\text{ROE \%}_{2008} = \frac{£25 \times 100\%}{£199} = 12.6\%$$

Capital turnover

$$\text{Capital turnover}_{2010} = \frac{\text{revenue}}{\text{average capital employed in year}} = \frac{£456}{£288} = 1.6 \text{ times}$$

$$\text{Capital turnover}_{2009} = \frac{£491}{£260.5} = 1.9 \text{ times}$$

Capital turnover 2008 is not available because we do not have the capital employed number for 31 March 2007.

Report on the profitability of Hardy plc

Sales for the year 2010 were 7.1% lower than sales in 2009, which were 16.9% above 2008. It is not clear whether these sales reductions were from lower volumes, fewer products, or changes in selling prices.

Gross profit improved from 34.0% in 2008 to 34.2% in 2009 to 35.3% in 2010, possibly from increased selling prices and/or from lower costs of production.

Operating profit to sales increased from 11.9% in 2008 to 12.4% in 2009 but then fell to 11.4% in 2010, despite the improvement in gross profit, because of higher levels of distribution costs and administrative expenses.

ROCE dropped from 23.4% to 18.1%, reflecting the lower level of operating profit. Return on equity increased from 12.6% in 2008 to 13.0% in 2009 but then fell sharply in 2010 to 9.0%. This was because of the large fall in profit after tax in 2010.

Capital turnover was reduced from 1.9 times in 2009 to 1.6 in 2010, reflecting the fall in sales levels in 2010 compared with 2009.

Efficiency ratios for Hardy plc for 2010 and the comparative ratios for 2009 and 2008

Collection days

$$\text{Collection days } 2010 = \frac{\text{trade receivables} \times 365}{\text{revenue}} = \frac{£80 \times 365}{£465} = 63 \text{ days}$$

$$\text{Collection days } 2009 = \frac{£70 \times 365}{£491} = 52 \text{ days}$$

$$\text{Collection days } 2008 = \frac{£53 \times 365}{£420} = 46 \text{ days}$$

Payables days

$$\frac{\text{Payables days}}{2010} = \frac{\text{trade payables} \times 365}{\text{cost of sales}} = \frac{£38 \times 365}{£295} = 47 \text{ days}$$

$$\frac{\text{Payables days}}{2009} = \frac{£38 \times 365}{£323} = 43 \text{ days}$$

$$\frac{\text{Payables days}}{2008} = \frac{£26 \times 365}{£277} = 34 \text{ days}$$

Inventories days (inventory turnover)

$$\frac{\text{Inventory days}}{2010} = \frac{\text{inventories}}{\text{average daily cost of sales in period}} = \frac{£147}{£295/365} = 182 \text{ days (26.0 weeks)}$$

$$\frac{\text{Inventories days}}{2009} = \frac{£152}{£323/365} = 172 \text{ days (24.5 weeks)}$$

$$\frac{\text{Inventories days}}{2008} = \frac{£118}{£277/365} = 155 \text{ days (22.2 weeks)}$$

Operating cycle days

$$\text{Operating cycle } 2010 = \text{inventories days} + \text{collection days} - \text{payables days} = 182 + 63 - 47$$
$$= 198 \text{ days}$$

$$\text{Operating cycle } 2009 = 172 + 52 - 43 = 181 \text{ days}$$

$$\text{Operating cycle } 2008 = 155 + 46 - 34 = 167 \text{ days}$$

Operating cycle %

$$\text{Operating cycle \%} \atop 2010 = \frac{\text{working capital requirement}}{\text{revenue}}$$

$$= \frac{(£147 + £80 - £38) \times 100\%}{£456} = 41.4\%$$

$$\text{Operating cycle \%} \atop 2009 = \frac{(£152 + £70 - £38) \times 100\%}{£491} = 37.5\%$$

$$\text{Operating cycle \%} \atop 2008 = \frac{(£118 + £53 - £26)}{£420} = 34.5\%$$

Asset turnover

$$\text{Asset turnover} \atop 2010 = \frac{\text{revenue}}{\text{total assets}} = \frac{£456}{£385} = 1.18 \text{ times}$$

$$\text{Asset turnover} \atop 2009 = \frac{£491}{£374} = 1.31 \text{ times}$$

$$\text{Asset turnover} \atop 2008 = \frac{£420}{£303} = 1.39 \text{ times}$$

Report on the efficiency performance of Hardy plc

Average collection days worsened successively over the years 2008, 2009 and 2010 from 46 to 52 to 63 days. This was partly mitigated by some improvement in the average payables days which increased from 34 to 43 to 47 days over the same period. The average inventories days worsened from 155 to 172 to 182 days over 2008, 2009 and 2010. Therefore, mainly because of the poor receivables collection performance and increasingly high inventories levels, the operating cycle worsened from 167 days in 2008 to 181 days in 2009 and to 198 days in 2010 (operating cycle 34.5% to 37.5% to 41.4%). Asset turnover reduced from 1.39 to 1.31 times from 2008 to 2009 and then to 1.18 in 2010, reflecting the degree to which sales revenue had dropped despite increasing levels of total assets.

Liquidity ratios for Hardy plc for 2010 and the comparative ratios for 2009 and 2008

Current ratio

$$\text{Current ratio} \atop 2010 = \frac{\text{current assets}}{\text{current liabilities}} = \frac{£253}{£93} = 2.7 \text{ times}$$

$$\text{Current ratio} \atop 2009 = \frac{£251}{£90} = 2.8 \text{ times}$$

$$\text{Current ratio} \atop 2008 = \frac{£197}{£66} = 3.0 \text{ times}$$

Quick ratio

$$\text{Quick ratio} \atop 2010 = \frac{\text{current assets} - \text{inventories}}{\text{current liabilities}} = \frac{£253 - £147}{£93} = 1.1 \text{ times}$$

$$\text{Quick ratio} \atop 2009 = \frac{£251 - £152}{£90} = 1.1 \text{ times}$$

$$\text{Quick ratio} \atop 2008 = \frac{£197 - £118}{£66} = 1.2 \text{ times}$$

Defensive interval

$$\text{Defensive interval} \atop 2010 = \frac{\text{quick assets}}{\text{average daily cash from operations}}$$

$$= \frac{£253 - £147}{(£70 + £456 - £80)/365} = 87 \text{ days}$$

$$\text{Defensive interval} \atop 2009 = \frac{£251 - £152}{(£53 + £491 - £70)/365} = 76 \text{ days}$$

The defensive interval for 2008 is not available because we do not have the trade receivables number for 31 March 2007.

Report on the liquidity of Hardy plc

The current ratio and the quick ratio have both dropped over the 3 years from 3.0 to 2.7 times, and 1.2 times to 1.1 times respectively. The defensive interval has increased from 76 days to 87 days at which level the company could potentially survive if there were no further cash inflows.

(ii)   There are a number of areas that require further investigation. The following five ratios may be particularly useful to assist this investigation:

■ return on capital employed, ROCE
■ receivables collection days
■ payables days
■ inventories days
■ current ratio.

(iii) The relevant information has not been provided to enable the following investment ratios to be calculated for Hardy plc, which would have improved the analysis of Hardy plc's performance:

Earnings per share, eps

Cannot be calculated because we do not have details of the number of ordinary shares in issue.

Dividend per share

Cannot be calculated because we do not have details of the number of ordinary shares in issue.

Dividend cover

Cannot be calculated because we have not been able to calculate earnings per share, eps, and dividend per share.

Dividend yield %

Cannot be calculated because we have not been able to calculate dividend per share, and we do not have the market prices of the company's shares.

Price/earnings ratio, P/E

Cannot be calculated because we have not been able to calculate earnings per share, and we do not have the market prices of the company's shares.

Capital expenditure to sales %

Cannot be calculated because we do not have details of capital expenditure.

Capital expenditure to gross non-current assets %

Cannot be calculated because we do not have details of capital expenditure.

Chapter 8

E8.11 Alcoholic drinks group

Five-year income statement

Horizontal analysis

	Year 5	Year 4	Year 3	Year 2	Year 1
Revenue	108.4	107.3	107.5	106.9	100.0
Gross profit	93.9	92.2	93.5	91.7	100.0
Other investment income	(470.8)	(195.8)	(370.8)	200.0	100.0
Operating profit	107.5	99.1	104.6	89.1	100.0
Finance cost	48.5	55.9	63.7	92.2	100.0
Profit before tax	122.6	110.2	115.1	88.3	100.0
Income tax expense	107.0	103.7	100.4	102.1	100.0
Profit after tax	129.5	113.0	121.5	82.3	100.0
Minority interests	106.9	103.4	106.9	75.9	100.0
Profit for the year	130.7	113.5	122.3	82.6	100.0
Dividends	124.5	127.4	117.7	108.9	100.0
Retained earnings	135.9	102.1	126.1	61.0	100.0
Earnings per share	124.9	104.6	113.2	81.5	100.0
Interest cover	220.4	177.6	163.3	95.9	100.0
Dividend cover	95.7	87.0	100.0	78.3	100.0

Vertical analysis

	Year 5	Year 4	Year 3	Year 2	Year 1
Revenue	100.0	100.0	100.0	100.0	100.0
Gross profit	20.3	20.1	20.4	20.1	23.4
Other investment income	2.4	1.0	1.9	(1.0)	(0.6)
Operating profit	22.7	21.1	22.3	19.1	22.9
Finance cost	(2.1)	(2.4)	(2.8)	(4.0)	(4.7)
Profit before tax	20.6	18.7	19.5	15.1	18.2
Income tax expense	(5.5)	(5.4)	(5.2)	(5.3)	(5.5)
Profit after tax	15.1	13.4	14.3	9.8	12.7
Minority interests	(0.7)	(0.6)	(0.7)	(0.5)	(0.7)
Profit for the year	14.5	12.7	13.7	9.3	12.0
Dividends	(6.2)	(6.5)	(5.9)	(5.5)	(5.4)
Retained earnings	8.2	6.3	7.7	3.8	6.6

Revenue

The horizontal analysis shows an increase in sales of 8.4% over the five years, most of which was gained from year two over year one. Since year two, sales have not increased materially.

Gross profit

The horizontal analysis shows a drop in gross profit of 6.1% of sales over the five years. The vertical analysis shows that gross profit at 23.4% of sales in year one has dropped to 20.3% of sales in year five. The group may have been suffering from increased competition as its brands failed to continue to maintain their profitability.

Operating profit

The horizontal analysis shows an increase in operating profit of 7.5% of sales over the five years, despite the drop in gross profit levels. This is due to the extremely large gains in investment income. The vertical analysis shows that operating profit has been maintained fairly level over the five years at 22.9% of sales in year one to 22.7% of sales in year five.

Finance cost

The horizontal analysis shows a drop in interest paid by year five to less than half the level in year one. The vertical analysis bears this out, showing interest paid of 2.1% of revenue in year five compared with 4.7% of sales in year one. The group's borrowings were probably significantly reduced as little expansion has taken place, indicated by a reliance on mature markets and a lack of new ideas. The increased interest cover confirms the loan repayments.

Profit for the year

The horizontal analysis reflects a small increase in profit levels from 12.0% of revenue in year one to 14.5% of revenue in year five. The vertical analysis shows a steady increase in profit over the years except for a drop in year two, because of the negative investment income and high interest payments in that year.

Dividends

The level of dividends has been up and down over the years but year five is slightly higher at 6.2% of sales than year one which was 5.4% of sales, as shown in the vertical analysis. Dividend cover has been maintained at around two times.

Earnings per share

The horizontal analysis shows an increase of almost 25% in earnings per share in year five compared with year one, having recovered from a dip in earnings in year four.

Chapter 9

E9.3 Lucky Jim

If shareholders' equity is E and the financial debt is D then the relative proportions of equity and debt in the total financing are:

$$\frac{E}{E + D} \text{ and } \frac{D}{E + D}$$

$$\frac{E}{E + D} = 2/3$$

$$\frac{D}{E + D} = 1/3$$

Cost of equity $e = 18\%$
Return on financial debt $d = 12\%$
WACC $= (2/3 \times 18\%) + ((1/3 \times 9\% (1 - 40\%))$
$\qquad = 12\% + 1.8\% = 13.8\%$

The present value of future cash flows in perpetuity $= \dfrac{\text{annual cash flows}}{\text{annual discount rate \%}}$

$$\frac{£35,700}{0.138} = £253,623$$

Net present value, NPV = £253,623 − £200,000 = £53,623

Using WACC to discount the cash flows of the project, the result is a positive NPV of £53,623 and therefore the project should be undertaken.

E9.4 Supermarket

	2011	2010	2009
Adjusted net assets	£5,000m	£4,769m	£4,377m
Market value	£17,808m	£11,531m	£11,995m
MVA	£12,808m	£6,762m	£7,618m

E9.5 Yor

(i)

Yor plc
Income statement for the year ended 30 September 2011

	using debentures £m	using shares £m
PBIT	15.6	15.6
Finance costs	(1.6)	(1.2)
Profit before tax	14.0	14.4
Income tax expense	(3.5)	(3.6)
Profit for the year	10.5	10.8
Retained earnings 1 October 2010	10.6	10.6
	21.1	21.4
Dividends	(3.3)	(4.6)
Retained earnings 30 September 2011	17.8	16.8

(ii)

Yor plc
Equity and debt as at 30 September 2011

	using debentures £m	using shares £m
Share capital (£1 ordinary shares)	10.0	14.0
Share premium account (4m × £1.50)		6.0
Retained earnings	17.8	16.8
	27.8	36.8
Loans	30.0	20.0

(iii)

$$\text{earnings per share 2010} = \frac{\text{profit available for ordinary shareholders}}{\text{number of ordinary shares in issue}} = \frac{£7.8m}{10m}$$

$$= 78p$$

(iv)
using debentures

$$\text{earnings per share 2011} = \frac{£10.5m}{10m} = £1.05$$

using shares

$$\text{earnings per share 2011} = \frac{£10.8m}{14m} = 77p$$

(v)

$$\text{dividend per share 2010} = \frac{\text{total dividends paid to ordinary shareholders}}{\text{number of ordinary shares in issue}} = \frac{£3.0m}{10m}$$

$$= 30p$$

(vi)
using debentures

$$\text{dividend per share 2011} = \frac{£3.3m}{10m} = 33p$$

using shares

$$\text{dividend per share 2011} = \frac{£4.6m}{14m} = 33p$$

(vii)

$$\text{gearing} = \frac{\text{long-term debt}}{\text{equity} + \text{long-term debt}}$$

	using debentures	using shares
2010	**2011**	**2011**
$\dfrac{£20.0m}{£20.6m + £20.0m} = 49.3\%$	$\dfrac{£30.0m}{£27.8m + £30.0m} = 51.9\%$	$\dfrac{£20.0m}{£36.8m + £20.0m} = 35.2\%$

(viii)
Summary of results

Figures in £m

	2010	using debentures 2011	using shares 2011
Profit for the year	7.8	10.5	10.8
Dividends	(3.0)	(3.3)	(4.6)
Retained earnings for year	4.8	7.2	6.2

The use of debentures to finance the new project will increase the 2010/2011 profit for the year after tax, available for dividends, by £2.7m or 34.6%, whereas if shares were used the increase would be £3.0m or 38.5%. Earnings per share will be increased to £1.05 (+27p) and decreased to 77p (−1p) respectively. However, retained earnings would be increased by £2.4m (50%) and £1.4m (29.2%) respectively. The difference is because the gain from the lower interest cost in using shares is more than offset by the increase in dividends.

Dividend per share will be increased from 30p to 33p per share regardless of which method of financing is used.

Gearing at 30 September 2010 was 49.3%. If debentures are used to finance the new project then gearing will increase to 51.9%, but if shares are used to finance the new project then gearing will decrease to 35.2%. This represents a higher financial risk for the company with regard to its commitments to making a high level of interest payments. The company is therefore vulnerable to a downturn in business and also the possibility of its loans being called in and possible liquidation of the company.

Glossary of key terms

accountancy The practice or profession of accounting.

accounting The classification and recording of monetary transactions, the presentation and interpretation of the results of those transactions in order to assess performance over a period and the financial position at a given date, and the monetary projection of future activities arising from alternative planned courses of action.

accounting adjustments Accounting entries that do not arise from the basic transactions of cash and invoices. Adjusting entries are made for depreciation, bad and doubtful debts, closing inventories, prepayments, and accruals.

accounting concepts The principles underpinning the preparation of accounting information. Fundamental accounting concepts are the broad basic assumptions which underlie the periodic financial statements of business enterprises.

accounting period The time period covered by the accounting statements of an entity.

accounting policies The specific accounting bases selected and consistently followed by an entity as being, in the opinion of the management, appropriate to its circumstances and best suited to present fairly its results and financial position (FRS 18 and Companies Act).

Accounting Standards Board (ASB) A UK standard-setting body set up in 1990 to develop, issue and withdraw accounting standards. Its aims are to 'establish and improve standards of financial accounting and reporting, for the benefit of users, preparers and auditors of financial information'.

accounts payable (or **purchase ledger**) A subsidiary ledger that contains all the personal accounts of each individual supplier or vendor, and records every transaction for goods and services with each supplier since the start of their relationship with the company. The total of the balances on each individual supplier account at any time is reflected in an accounts payable control account within the general ledger, and is reported in the balance sheet as trade payables.

accounts receivable (or **sales ledger**) A subsidiary ledger that contains all the personal accounts of each individual customer, and records every transaction for goods and services with each customer since the start of their relationship with the company. The total of the balances on each individual customer account at any time is reflected in an accounts receivable control account within the general ledger, and is reported in the balance sheet as trade receivables.

accruals Allowances made for costs and expenses payable within one year of the balance sheet date but for which no invoices have yet been recorded.

accruals concept The principle that revenues and costs are recognised as they are earned or incurred, and so matched with each other, and dealt with in the profit and loss account of the period to which they relate, irrespective of the period of receipt or payment. Where a conflict arises, this concept is subservient to the prudence concept.

acid test ratio See quick ratio.

amortisation In the same way that depreciation applies to the charging of the cost of tangible non-current assets over their useful economic lives, amortisation is the systematic write-off of the cost of an intangible asset, relating particularly to the passage of time, for example leasehold premises (IAS 38 and IFRS 3).

annual report and accounts A set of statements which may comprise a management report (in the case of companies, a directors' report), an operating and financial review (OFR), and the financial statements of the entity.

asset A right or other access to future economic benefits which can be measured reliably and are controlled by an entity as a result of past transactions or events (IAS 16).

audit A systematic examination of the activities and status of an entity, based primarily on investigation and analysis of its systems, controls and records. A statutory annual audit of a company is defined by the APB as an independent examination of, and expression of an opinion on, the financial statements of the enterprise.

Auditing Practices Board (APB) A body formed in 1991 by an agreement between the six members of the Consultative Committee of Accountancy Bodies, to be responsible for developing and issuing professional standards for auditors in the United Kingdom and the Republic of Ireland.

auditor A professionally qualified accountant who is appointed by, and reports independently to, the shareholders, providing an objective verification to shareholders and other users that the financial statements have been prepared properly and in accordance with legislative and regulatory requirements; that they present the information truthfully and fairly; and that they conform to the best accounting practice in their treatment of the various measurements and valuations.

audit report An objective verification to shareholders and other users that the financial statements have been prepared properly and in accordance with legislative and regulatory requirements; that they present the information truthfully and fairly; and that they conform to the best accounting practice in their treatment of the various measurements and valuations.

bad debt A debt which is considered to be uncollectable and is, therefore, written off either as a charge to the profit and loss account or against an existing doubtful debt provision.

balance sheet The balance sheet is a section of the general ledger that records all asset, liability and shareholders' equity account transactions. The balance sheet report is a statement of the financial position of an entity at a given date disclosing the assets, liabilities and accumulated funds such as shareholders' contributions and reserves, prepared to give a true and fair view of the financial state of the entity at that date. The balance sheet is one of the three key financial statements.

bank reconciliation A detailed statement reconciling, at a given date, the cash balance in an entity's cash book with that reported in a bank statement.

beta factor (ß) The measure of the volatility of the return on a share relative to the market. If a share price were to rise or fall at double the market rate, it would have a beta factor of 2. Conversely, if the share price moved at half the market rate, the beta factor would be 0.5.

bonus issue See scrip issue.

bookkeeping Recording of monetary transactions, appropriately classified, in the financial records of an entity, either by manual means or otherwise.

business entity concept The concept that financial accounting information relates only to the activities of the business entity and not to the activities of its owners.

Cadbury Committee Report of the Cadbury Committee (December 1992) on the Financial Aspects of Corporate Governance, set up to consider issues in relation to financial reporting and accountability, and to make recommendations on good practice, relating to:

- responsibilities of executive and non-executive directors
- establishment of company audit committees
- responsibility of auditors
- links between shareholders, directors and auditors
- any other relevant matters.

The report established a Code of Best Practice, now succeeded by the UK Corporate Governance Code.

capital asset pricing model (CAPM) A theory which predicts that the expected risk premium for an individual share will be proportional to its beta, such that the expected risk premium on a share is equal to beta multiplied by the expected risk premium in the market. Risk premium is defined as the expected incremental return for making a risky investment rather than a safe one.

capital expenditure The cost of acquiring, producing or enhancing non-current assets.

cash and cash equivalents Cash and cash equivalents comprise cash on hand and demand deposits, together with short-term, highly liquid investments that are readily convertible to a known amount of cash (IAS 7).

cash book A book of original entry that includes details of all receipts and payments made by an entity. The details normally include transaction date, method of payment or receipt, amount paid or received, bank statement value (if different), name of payee or payer, general ledger allocation and coding.

cash flow statement See statement of cash flows.

cash interest cover Net cash inflow from operations plus interest received, divided by interest paid, calculates the number of times the interest payable is covered by cash flow available for such payments.

cash payment A cash payment is the transfer of funds from a business to a recipient (for example, trade creditor or employee).

cash receipt A cash receipt is the transfer of funds to a business from a payer (for example, a customer).

closing inventories All trading companies buy inventories with the intention of reselling, at a profit, to a customer. At the end of each accounting period, the company will have unsold inventories that will be sold during a subsequent accounting period. Unsold inventories are termed 'closing inventory' which is deducted from opening inventory plus purchases (to derive cost of sales), and will appear in the balance sheet as inventories (within current assets).

collection days Average trade receivables divided by average daily sales on credit terms indicates the average time taken, in calendar days, to receive payment from credit customers.

Combined Code of Practice The successor to the Cadbury Code, established by the Hampel Committee. The code consists of a set of principles of corporate governance and detailed code provisions embracing the work of the Cadbury, Greenbury and Hampel Committees. It was, itself, succeeded by the UK Corporate Governance Code in 2010.

common size analysis See horizontal analysis.

computerised accounting system This is a system that maintains business transactions on a computer on a long-term basis.

conceptual frameworks of accounting The statements of principles, which provide generally accepted guidance for the development of new financial information reporting practices and the review of current reporting practices.

consistency concept The principle that there is uniformity of accounting treatment of like items within each accounting period and from one period to the next.

consolidated accounts The consolidated financial statements which present financial information for the group as a single economic entity, prepared using a process of adjusting and combining financial information from the individual financial statements of a parent undertaking and its subsidiary undertakings (IAS 27).

contingent liability A possible obligation that arises from past events and whose existence will be confirmed only by the occurrence of one or more uncertain future events not wholly within the entity's control; or a present obligation that arises from past events but is not recognised because:
- it is not probable that a transfer of benefits will be required to settle the obligation or
- the amount of the obligation cannot be measured with sufficient reliability (IAS 37).

continuing operations Operations not satisfying all the conditions relating to discontinued operations (see below).

convertible loan A loan which gives the holder the right to convert to other securities, normally ordinary shares, at a predetermined date and at a predetermined price or ratio.

corporate governance The system by which companies are directed and controlled. Boards of directors are responsible for the governance of their companies. The shareholders' role in governance is to appoint the directors and the auditors and to satisfy themselves that an appropriate governance structure is in place.

corporate social responsibility (CSR) Corporate social responsibility is the decision-making and implementation process that guides all company activities in the protection and promotion of international human rights, labour and environmental standards and compliance with legal requirements within its operations and in its relations to the societies and communities where it operates. CSR involves a commitment to contribute to the economic, environmental and social sustainability of communities through the ongoing engagement of stakeholders, the active participation of communities impacted by company activities and the public reporting of company policies and performance in the economic, environmental and social arenas (*www.bench-marks.org*).

corporation tax Tax chargeable on companies resident in the UK, or trading in the UK through a branch or agency, as well as on certain unincorporated associations (FRS 16 and IAS 12).

cost of sales The sum of direct cost of sales, adjusted for closing inventories, plus manufacturing overhead attributable to the sales. Direct costs include the wages and salaries costs of time worked on products, and the costs of materials used in production. Manufacturing overheads include the wages and salaries costs of employees not directly working on production, and materials and expenses incurred on activities not directly used in production but necessary to carry out production. Examples are cleaning materials and electricity costs.

creative accounting A form of accounting which, while complying with all regulations, nevertheless gives a biased (generally favourable) impression of a company's performance.

cross-sectional analysis Cross-sectional analysis provides a means of providing a standard against which performance can be measured and uses ratios to compare different businesses at the same points in time (see inter-company comparison).

current assets Cash or other assets, for example inventories, receivables and short-term investments, held for conversion into cash in the normal course of trading.

current liabilities Liabilities which fall due for payment within one year. They include that part of long-term loans due for repayment within one year.

current ratio Current assets divided by current liabilities is an overall measure of liquidity.

debenture The written acknowledgement of a debt by a company, usually given under its seal, and normally containing provisions as to payment of interest and the terms of repayment of principal. A debenture may be secured on some or all of the assets of the company or its subsidiaries.

debt One of the alternative sources of capital for a company, also called long-term debt or loans.

debt/equity ratio A gearing ratio that relates to financial gearing, which is the relationship between a company's borrowings, which includes both prior charge capital and long-term debt, and its ordinary shareholders' funds (share capital plus reserves).

defensive interval Quick assets (current assets excluding inventories) divided by average daily cash from operations, shows how many days a business could survive at its present level of operating activity if no inflow of cash was received from sales or other sources.

depreciation The systematic allocation of the depreciable amount of an asset over its useful life (IAS 16). Depreciation should be allocated so as to charge a fair proportion of the total cost (or valuation) of the asset to each accounting period expected to benefit from its use.

depreciation provision The amount of depreciation that has cumulatively been charged to the profit and loss account, relating to a non-current asset, from the date of its acquisition. Non-current assets are stated in the balance sheet at their net book value (or written-down value), which is usually their historical cost less the cumulative amount of depreciation at the balance sheet date.

direct method A method of calculating cash flow from operating activities as the net of operating cash receipts and payments that is summarised for inclusion in the statement of cash flows. It is a time-consuming process that is not as straightforward as the indirect method.

director A person elected under the company's articles of association to be responsible for the overall direction of the company's affairs. Directors usually act collectively as a board and carry out such functions as are specified in the articles of association or the Companies Acts, but they may also act individually in an executive capacity.

discontinued operations A discontinued operation is a component of an entity that either has been disposed of or is classified as held for sale and: represents either a separate major line of business or a geographical area of operations, and:

– is part of a single coordinated plan to dispose of a separate major line of business or geographical area of operations

or

– is a subsidiary acquired exclusively with a view to resale and the disposal involves loss of control (IFRS 5).

discounted cash flow (DCF) The discounting of the projected net cash flows of a capital project to ascertain its present value, using a yield or internal rate of return (IRR), net present value (NPV) or discounted payback.

dividend An amount payable to shareholders from profits or distributable reserves. Dividends are normally paid in cash, but scrip dividends, paid by the issue of additional shares, are permissible. Listed companies usually declare two dividends each year, an interim dividend based on the mid-year profits and a final dividend based on annual profit.

dividend cover Earnings per share divided by dividend per share indicates the number of times the profits attributable to the equity shareholders cover the actual dividends payable for the period.

double-entry bookkeeping The system of bookkeeping based on the principle that every financial transaction involves the simultaneous receiving and giving of value, and is therefore recorded twice.

doubtful debt A debt for which there is some uncertainty as to whether or not it will be settled, and for which there is a possibility that it may eventually prove to be bad. A doubtful debt provision may be created for such a debt by charging it as an expense to the profit and loss account.

doubtful debt provision An amount charged against profit and deducted from trade receivables to allow for the estimated non-recovery of a proportion of the debts.

dual aspect concept The rule that provides the basis for double-entry bookkeeping, reflecting the practical reality that every transaction always includes both the giving and receiving of something.

earnings per share (eps) Profit after tax less preference share dividends divided by the number of ordinary shares in issue measures the return per share of earnings available to shareholders.

EBITDA Earnings before interest, tax, depreciation and amortisation.

economic value added (EVA™) EVA is a measure developed by the US consultancy firm Stern Stewart. EVA equals profit after tax (plus interest payable) adjusted for distortions in operating performance (such as goodwill, extraordinary losses and operating leases) minus a charge for the use of the capital employed to create that profit (calculated by multiplying the adjusted book value of net assets of the company by its weighted average cost of capital).

environmental reporting A statement included within the annual report and accounts that sets out the environmental policies of the company and an explanation of its environmental management systems and responsibilities. The environmental report may include reporting on the performance of the business on environmental matters in qualitative terms regarding the extent to which it meets national and international standards. It may also include a quantitative report on the performance of the business on environmental matters against targets, together with an assessment of the financial impact.

equity The total investment of the shareholders in the company, the total value of book wealth. Equity comprises capital, share premiums and retained earnings.

euro The common currency that is used in most of the member countries of the European Union, which came into being on 1 January 1999. Financial transactions and/or financial reporting of member states may now be undertaken in either the functional domestic currencies, or in euros.

finance director The finance director of an organisation is actively involved in broad strategic and policy-making activities involving financial considerations. The finance director provides the board of directors with advice on financing, capital expenditure, acquisitions, dividends, the implications of changes in the economic environment, and the financial aspects of legislation. The finance director is responsible for the planning and control functions, the financial systems, financial reporting, and the management of funds.

finance lease A lease is a contract between a lessor and a lessee for the hire of a specific asset. The lessor retains ownership of the asset but gives the right to the use of the asset to the lessee for an agreed period in return for the payment of specified rentals (IAS 17). A finance lease transfers substantially all the risks and rewards of ownership of the asset to the lessee.

financial accounting Financial accounting is the function responsible for the periodic external reporting, statutorily required, for shareholders. It also provides such similar information as required for Government and other interested third parties, such as potential investors, employees, lenders, suppliers, customers and financial analysts.

financial instrument Any contract that gives rise to both a financial asset of one entity and a financial liability or equity instrument of another entity. Financial instruments include both primary financial instruments – such as bonds, debtors, creditors and shares – and derivative financial instruments whose value derives from the underlying assets.

financial management The management of all the processes associated with the efficient acquisition and deployment of both short- and long-term financial resources. Within an organisation, financial management assists operations management to reach their financial objectives.

Financial Reporting Standards (FRSs) The accounting standards of practice published by the Accounting Standards Board since 1 August 1990, and which gradually replaced the Standard Statements of Accounting Practice (SSAPs), which were published by the Accounting Standards Committee up to 1 August 1990.

financial statements Summaries of accounts, whether to internal or external parties, to provide information for interested parties. The three key financial statements are: income statement; balance sheet; statement of cash flows. Other financial statements are: report of the auditors; statement of recognised gains and losses; statement of changes in equity.

financing The section of the statement of cash flows that shows the long-term funds raised by or repaid by the company during an accounting period.

flotation A flotation is the obtaining of a listing by a company on a stock exchange, through the offering of its shares to the general public, financial institutions or private-sector businesses.

fraudulent trading An offence committed by persons who are knowingly party to the continuance of a company trading in circumstances where creditors are defrauded or for other fraudulent purposes. Generally, this means that the company incurs more debts at a time when it is known that those debts will not be met. Persons responsible for so acting are personally liable without limitation for the debts of the company. The offence also carries criminal penalties.

gearing Financial gearing calculations can be made in a number of ways. Gearing is generally seen as the relationship between a company's borrowings, which include both prior charge capital (capital having a right of interest or preference shares having fixed dividends) and long-term debt, and its ordinary shareholders' funds (share capital plus reserves).

general ledger Also called the nominal ledger, contains all accounts and transactions relating to assets, expenses, revenue and liabilities.

going concern concept The assumption that the entity will continue in operational existence for the foreseeable future.

goodwill The difference between the consideration transferred and the net of the acquisition-date amounts of the identifiable assets acquired and the liabilities assumed (IFRS 3). If the difference above is negative, the resulting gain is recognised as a bargain purchase in the income statement.

gross profit (or gross margin) Gross profit is the difference between sales revenue and the total cost of sales.

Hampel Committee The 1998 report of the Hampel Committee on Corporate Governance was set up to conduct a review of the Cadbury Code and its implications:
- review of the role of directors
- matters arising from the Greenbury Study Group on directors' remuneration
- role of shareholders and auditors
- other relevant matters.

The Hampel Committee was responsible for the corporate governance Combined Code of Practice.

historical cost concept The normal basis of accounting prescribed by IAS 16 for published accounts that uses a system of accounting in which all values are based on the historical costs incurred.

horizontal analysis (or **common size analysis**) An analysis of the income statement (or balance sheet) that allows a line-by-line analysis of the accounts with those of the previous year. It may provide over a number of years a trend of changes showing either growth or decline in these elements of the accounts through calculation of annual percentage growth rates in profits, sales revenue, inventories or any other item.

hybrid finance A financial instrument that has the characteristics of both debt and equity.

impairment In accordance with IAS 36, an asset is impaired when its book value exceeds its recoverable amount. The recoverable amount is the greater of the net selling price of the asset and the discounted cash flow expected to arise from the use of the asset over its remaining life. If the recoverable amount is less than the book value then the asset's value should be impaired with the loss of value being charged to the income statement. The asset must then be depreciated for future periods on its revised carrying amount, which is the amount at which the asset is recognised in the balance sheet after deducting accumulated depreciation and accumulated impairment losses.

income statement The income statement shows the profit or loss generated by an entity during an accounting period by deducting all expenses from all revenues, its financial performance. It measures whether or not the company has made a profit or loss on its operations during the period, through producing and selling its goods or services. The income statement is one of the three key financial statements.

indirect method A method of calculating cash flow from operating activities which uses the starting point of profit before tax. Profit before tax for the period must then be adjusted for depreciation, as well as movements in inventories, receivables and payables over the same period to derive the net cash flow from operating activities.

inflation A general increase in the price level over time. In a period of hyperinflation the rate at which the price level rises has become extremely high, and possibly out of control.

initial public offering (IPO) An IPO is a company's first public sale of its shares. Shares offered in an IPO are often, but not always, those of young, small companies seeking outside equity capital and a public market for their shares. Investors purchasing shares in IPOs generally must be prepared to accept considerable risks for the possibility of large gains.

insolvency The inability of a company, partnership or individual to pay creditors' debts in full after realisation of all the assets of the business.

intangible non-current assets Intangible non-current assets are identifiable non-monetary assets without physical substance that are controlled by the entity as a result of past events (for example, purchase or self-creation), and from which future economic benefits are expected to flow. These assets include computer software, patents and copyrights (IAS 38).

inter-company comparison Systematic and detailed comparison of the performance of different companies generally operating in a common industry. Normally the information distributed by the scheme administrator (to participating companies only) is in the form of ratios, or in a format that prevents the identity of individual scheme members from being identified.

interest cover Profit before interest and tax divided by interest payable, calculates the number of times the interest payable is covered by profits available for such payments. It is particularly important for lenders to determine the vulnerability of interest payments to a drop in profit.

internal audit The UK Institute of Internal auditors defines internal audit as an independent appraisal function established within an organisation to examine and evaluate its activities as a service to the organisation. The objective of internal auditing is to assist members of the organisation in the effective discharge of their responsibilities. To this end, internal auditing furnishes them with analyses, appraisals, recommendations, counsel and information concerning the activities reviewed.

internal control As defined in the Cadbury Report, it is the whole system of controls, financial or otherwise, established in order to provide reasonable assurance of:

- effective and efficient operation
- internal financial control
- compliance with laws and regulations.

International Accounting Standards (IASs) The international financial reporting standards issued by the IASC, which are very similar to the UK's SSAPs and FRSs.

International Accounting Standards Board (IASB) The IASB is the body that is responsible for setting and publishing International Financial Reporting Standards (IFRSs). It was formed on 1 April 2001 and succeeded the International Accounting Standards Committee (IASC) which had been formed in 1973. The parent body of the IASB is the International Accounting Standards Committee Foundation, which was incorporated in the USA in March 2001, and was also responsible for issuing International Accounting Standards (IASs).

International Financial Reporting Standards (IFRSs) The international financial reporting standards issued by the IASB, which incorporate the IASs, issued by the IASC. IASs are very similar to the UK's SSAPs and FRSs.

inventories Inventories, according to IAS 2, comprise:

- assets held for sale in the ordinary course of business (finished goods)
- assets in the production process for sale in the ordinary course of business (work in progress) and
- materials and supplies that are consumed in production (raw materials).

inventories days Inventories value divided by average daily cost of sales, which measures the number of days' inventories at the current usage rate.

leave of the court This is where the court will make a decision after hearing all the relevant information.

liabilities An entity's obligations to transfer economic benefits as a result of past transactions or events (IAS 37).

limited company (Ltd) A Ltd company is one in which the liability of members for the company's debts is limited to the amount paid and, if any, unpaid on the shares taken up by them.

loan capital Also called debt, relates to debentures and other long-term loans to a business.

management accounting The application of the principles of accounting and financial management to create, protect, preserve and increase value so as to deliver that value to the stakeholders of profit and not-for-profit enterprises, both public and private. Management accounting is an integral part of management, requiring the identification, generation, presentation, interpretation and use of information relevant to:

- formulating business strategy
- planning and controlling activities
- decision-making
- efficient resource usage
- performance improvement and value enhancement
- safeguarding tangible and intangible assets
- corporate governance and internal control.

market risk See systematic risk.

market value added (MVA) The difference between the market value of the company and the adjusted book values of its assets.

materiality Information is material if its omission or misstatement could influence the economic decisions of users taken on the basis of financial information. Materiality depends on the size of the item or error judged in the particular circumstances of its omission or misstatement.

materiality concept Information is material if its omission or misstatement could influence the economic decisions of users taken on the basis of the financial statements. Materiality depends on the size of the item or error judged in the particular circumstances of its omission or misstatement. Thus, materiality provides a threshold or cut-off point rather than being a primary qualitative characteristic that information must have if it is to be useful.

money measurement concept Most quantifiable data are capable of being converted, using a common denominator of money, into monetary terms. The money measurement concept holds that accounting deals only with those items capable of being translated into monetary terms, which imposes a limit on the scope of accounting reporting to such items.

net assets The excess of the book value of assets over liabilities, including loan capital. This is equivalent to net worth, which is used to describe the paid-up share capital and reserves.

net present value (NPV) The difference between the sums of the projected discounted cash inflows and outflows attributable to a capital investment or other long-term project.

net realisable value The amount for which an asset could be disposed, less any direct selling costs (IAS2).

non-current assets Or fixed assets, are any assets, tangible or intangible, acquired for retention by an entity for the purpose of providing a service to the business, and not held for resale in the normal course of trading. These include, for example, equipment, machinery, furniture, fittings, computers, software and motor vehicles that the company has purchased to enable it to meet its strategic objectives; such items are not renewed within the operating cycle.

non-current liabilities Liabilities which fall due for payment after one year. They include that part of long-term loans due for repayment after one year.

non-executive director A director who does not have a specific functional role within the company's management. The usual involvement of non-executive directors is to attend board meetings and chair corporate governance committees.

non-related company A company in which a business has a long-term investment, but over which it has no control or influence. If control exists then the company is deemed to be a subsidiary.

off balance sheet financing The funding of operations in such a way that the relevant assets and liabilities are not disclosed in the balance sheet of the company concerned.

operating cycle The operating cycle, or working capital cycle, is calculated by deducting payables days from inventory days plus receivables collection days. It represents the period of time which elapses between the point at which cash begins to be expended on the production of a product or service and the collection of cash from the customer.

operating lease A lease is a contract between a lessor and a lessee for the hire of a specific asset. The lessor retains ownership of the asset but gives the right to the use of the asset to the lessee for an agreed period in return for the payment of specified rentals (IAS 17). An operating lease is a lease other than a finance lease, where the lessor retains most of the risks and rewards of ownership.

operating profit Operating profit is calculated from gross profit plus or minus all operating revenues and costs, excluding interest and taxation. It is the profit of an entity regardless of its financial structure.

ordinary shares Shares which entitle the holders to the remaining divisible profits (and, in a liquidation, the assets) after prior interests, for example payables and prior charge capital, have been satisfied.

payables days Average trade payables divided by average daily purchases on credit. It indicates the average time taken, in calendar days, to pay for supplies received on credit.

periodicity concept The requirement to produce financial statements at set time intervals. With regard to companies, this requirement is embodied in the Companies Act 2006.

post balance sheet events Favourable and unfavourable events that occur between the balance sheet date and the date on which the financial statements are approved by the board of directors.

preference shares Shares carrying a fixed rate of dividend, the holders of which, subject to the conditions of issue, have a prior claim to any company profits available for distribution. Preference shares may also have a prior claim to the repayment of capital in the event of a winding-up.

prepayments Prepayments include prepaid expenses for services not yet used, for example rent in advance or electricity charges in advance, and also accrued income. Accrued income relates to sales of goods or services that have occurred and have been included in the profit and loss account for the trading period but have not yet been invoiced to the customer.

present value The cash equivalent now of a sum receivable or payable at a future date.

price earnings ratio (P/E) The market price per ordinary share divided by earnings per share shows the number of years it would take to recoup an equity investment from its share of the attributable equity profit.

profit The residual amount that remains after all expenses and costs needed to sustain the business, including depreciation, impairment, finance costs and taxes, have been deducted from revenue.

profit and loss account The profit and loss account is the section of the general ledger that records all revenue and expense transactions. See also income statement, which is a report that summarises the profit and loss account transactions.

profit before tax (PBT) Operating profit plus or minus net interest.

profit for the year Or profit after tax (PAT), is profit before tax (PBT) minus corporation tax.

provision An amount charged against profit to provide for an expected liability or loss even though the amount or date of the liability or loss is uncertain (IAS 37).

prudence concept The principle that revenue and profits are not anticipated, but are included in the income statement only when realised in the form of either cash or other assets, or the ultimate cash realisation can be assessed with reasonable certainty; provision is made for all known liabilities (expenses and losses) whether the amount of these is known with certainty or is a best estimate in the light of information available.

public limited company (plc) A plc is a company limited by shares or by guarantee, with a share capital, whose memorandum states that it is public and that it has complied with the registration procedures for such a company. A public company is distinguished from a private company in the following ways: a minimum issued share capital of £50,000; public limited company, or plc, at the end of the name; public company clause in the memorandum; freedom to offer securities to the public.

purchase invoice A document received from a supplier by an entity showing the description, quantity, prices and values of goods or services received.

purchase invoice daybook A list of supplier invoices recording their dates, gross values, values net of VAT, the dates of receipt of the invoices, the names of suppliers, and the general ledger allocation and coding.

purchase ledger See accounts payable.

qualified accountant A member of the accountancy profession, and in the UK a member of one of the six professional accountancy bodies: CIMA; ICAEW; ICAS; ICAI; ACCA; CIPFA.

quick ratio (or **acid test ratio**) Quick assets (current assets excluding inventories) divided by current liabilities, measures the ability of the business to pay accounts payable in the short term.

realisation concept The principle that increases in value should only be recognised on realisation of assets by arm's-length sale to an independent purchaser.

receiver A person appointed by secured creditors or by the court to take control of company property, usually following the failure of the company to pay principal sums or interest due to debenture holders whose debt is secured by fixed or floating charges over the assets of the company. The receiver takes control of the charged assets and may operate the company's business with a view to selling it as a going concern. In practice receivership is closely followed by liquidation.

Registrar of Companies (in some countries the Chamber of Commerce) Government official agency that is responsible for initial registration of new companies and for collecting and arranging public access to the annual reports of all limited companies.

repayable on demand This refers to the definition of cash where there is a loss of interest if cash is withdrawn within 24 hours.

reporting entity A public or private limited company required to file its annual report and accounts with the Registrar of Companies.

reserves Retained profits or surpluses. In a not-for-profit entity these are described as accumulated funds. Reserves may be distributable or non-distributable.

residual income (RI) Profit before tax less an imputed interest charge for invested capital, which may be used to assess the performance of a division or a branch of a business.

retained earnings (or retained profit) Profits that have not been paid out as dividends to shareholders, but retained for future investment by the company, and reported on a cumulative basis within the equity section of the balance sheet.

return on assets (ROA) Return on assets compares operational profit with the total assets used to generate that profit. Profit is calculated before net finance costs and corporation tax.

return on capital employed (ROCE) ROCE, or return on investment (ROI), is the profit before interest and tax divided by average capital employed. It indicates the profit-generating capacity of capital employed.

return on equity (ROE) A form of return on capital employed which measures the return to the shareholders on their investment in a company. The return is measured as the residual profit after all charges and appropriations other than to ordinary shareholders have been made, and the equity is ordinary share capital plus reserves.

return on investment (ROI) See return on capital employed (ROCE).

return on sales (ROS) Return on sales compares profit for the year as a percentage of sales revenue for the year.

revenue (or sales, or sales revenue) is the gross inflow of economic benefits (cash, receivables, other assets) arising from the ordinary operating activities of an entity, such as sales of goods, sales of services, interest, royalties and dividends (IAS 18).

revenue expenditure Expenditure on the manufacture of goods, or the provision of services, or on the general conduct of the entity, which is charged to the profit and loss account in the accounting period of sale. This includes repairs and depreciation of non-current assets as distinct from the provision of these assets.

rights issue The raising of new capital by giving existing shareholders the right to subscribe to new shares or debentures in proportion to their current holdings. These shares are usually issued at a discount to the market price. A shareholder not wishing to take up a rights issue may sell the rights.

risk management The process of understanding and managing the risks that the organisation is inevitably subject to in attempting to achieve its corporate objectives. For management purposes, risks are usually divided into categories such as: operational; financial; legal compliance; information; personnel.

sales invoice A document prepared by an entity showing the description, quantity, prices and values of goods delivered or services rendered to a customer.

sales invoice daybook A list of customer invoices recording their dates, gross values, values net of VAT, the names of customers, and the general ledger allocation and coding.

sales ledger See accounts receivable.

scrip issue (or **bonus issue**) The capitalisation of the reserves of a company by the issue of additional shares to existing shareholders, in proportion to their holdings. Such shares are normally fully paid-up with no cash called for from the shareholders.

segmental reporting The inclusion in a company's report and accounts of analysis of turnover, profits and net assets by class of business and by geographical segments (IFRS 8).

separate valuation concept In determining the aggregate amount of any asset or liability, the amount of each individual asset or liability making up the aggregate must be determined separately (IAS 16).

share A fixed identifiable unit of capital which has a fixed nominal or face value, which may be quite different from the market value of the share.

share capital The book value of share capital, reported in the equity section of the balance sheet, is the number of shares issued by the company multiplied by the nominal value of the shares.

share premium account The difference in price between the original nominal value of shares and the price new investors will have to pay for shares issued by the company.

small to medium-sized enterprises (SMEs) SMEs are currently defined, by the European Union, as enterprises which have fewer than 250 employees and which have either an annual sales revenue not exceeding 50 million euro, or an annual balance sheet total not exceeding 43 million euro. In the UK, the thresholds are less than 250 employees, annual sales revenue not exceeding £25.9m and a balance sheet total not exceeding £12.9m (Companies Act 2006).

spreadsheet A spreadsheet is a type of computer software package developed in the late 1970s and used in a variety of business operations. The spreadsheet is named after the accountant's manual spreadsheet in which text or numbers or formulae are displayed in rows and columns. Spreadsheet programs enable information to be introduced that automatically and speedily affects entries across the entire spreadsheet. Complex spreadsheet programs exist that enable the transfer of spreadsheet information through word processing techniques, and there are also three-dimensional spreadsheets for multi-department, multi-division and multi-company budgeting, planning and modelling.

statement of affairs Details submitted to the Official Receiver during the winding-up of a company identifying the assets and liabilities of the company. The details are prepared by the company directors, or other persons specified by the Official Receiver, and must be submitted within 14 days of the winding-up order or the appointment of a provisional liquidator.

statement of cash flows (or **cash flow statement**) A statement that summarises the inflows and outflows of cash for a period, classified under the following standard headings (IAS 7):

- operating activities
- investing activities

– financing activities.

The statement of cash flows is one of the three key financial statements.

Statement of Principles (SOP) The UK conceptual framework of accounting issued by the Accounting Standards Board in 1999.

Statements of Standard Accounting Practice (SSAPs) The accounting standards of practice published by the Accounting Standards Committee up to 1 August 1990.

subsidiary companies A subsidiary company, defined by IAS 27, is a company for which another company (the parent company) owns more than half the voting shares or has power:

– over more than one half of the voting rights by virtue of an agreement with other investors
or
– to govern the financial and operating policies of the entity under a statute or an agreement
or
– to appoint or remove the majority of the members of the board of directors
or
– to cast the majority of votes at a meeting of the board of directors.

substance over form concept Where a conflict exists, the structuring of reports should give precedence to the representation of financial reality over strict adherence to the requirements of the legal reporting structure.

systematic risk (or **market risk**) Some investments are by their very nature more risky than others. This is nothing to do with chance variations in actual compared with expected returns; it is inherent risk that cannot be diversified away.

tax shield A reduction in corporation tax payable due to the use of tax-allowable deductions against taxable income, for example the corporation tax relief on debt interest that should be recognised in calculating the cost of debt capital to calculate an after-tax cost of debt.

trade payables An amount reported in the balance sheet in respect of money owed by suppliers, persons or entities, as a consequence of the receipt of goods or services in advance of payment.

trade receivables An amount reported in the balance sheet in respect of money owed to customers, persons or entities, as a consequence of goods or services provided on credit.

treasury management The corporate handling of all financial matters, the generation of external and internal funds for business, the management of currencies and cash flows, and the complex strategies, policies and procedures of corporate finance.

trial balance The list of account balances in a double-entry accounting system. If the records have been correctly maintained, the sum of the debit balances will equal the sum of the credit balances, although certain errors such as the omission of a transaction or erroneous entries will not be disclosed by a trial balance.

true and fair view The requirement for financial statements prepared in compliance with the Companies Act to 'give a true and fair view' overrides any other requirements. Although not precisely defined in the Companies Act this is generally accepted to mean that accounts show a true and fair view if they are unlikely to mislead a user of financial information in giving a false impression of the company.

UK Corporate Governance Code The corporate governance code applicable to listed companies, issued by the Financial Reporting Council (FRC) in June 2010, and described as a 'guide only in general terms to principles, structure and processes'.

unsystematic risk Risk that can be diversified away.

value added statement An alternative presentation of the traditional income statement that measures the wealth created by a company through its activities, through value added by the business rather than the profit earned by the business. It shows how value added is distributed among the relevant parties: employees; lenders; shareholders; Government; and the amount to provide maintenance and expansion of the business.

value added tax (VAT) A tax charged on most goods and services that VAT-registered businesses provide in the UK and other countries. VAT is charged when a VAT-registered business sells to either another business or to a non-business customer. In the UK, there are three rates of VAT, depending on the goods or services the business provides. The current rates are: standard (20%); reduced (5%); zero (0%).

vendor-managed inventory (VMI) The management of inventories on behalf of a customer by the supplier, the supplier taking responsibility for the management of inventories within a framework that is mutually agreed by both parties. Examples are seen in separate supermarket racks maintained and stocked by merchandising groups for such items as spices, and car parts distributors topping up the shelves of dealers/garages, where the management of inventories, racking and shelves is carried out by the merchandising group or distributor.

vertical analysis An analysis of the income statement (or balance sheet) in which each item is expressed as a percentage of the total. The vertical analysis provides evidence of structural changes in the business such as increased profitability through more efficient production.

voluntary winding-up A voluntary winding-up of a company occurs where the company passes a resolution that it shall liquidate and the court is not involved in the process. A voluntary winding-up may be made by the members (the shareholders) of the company or by its creditors, if the company has failed to declare its solvency.

weighted average cost of capital (WACC) The average cost of the company's finance (equity, debentures, bank loans) weighted according to the proportion each element bears to the total pool of capital. Weighting is usually based on market valuations, current yields and costs after tax.

window dressing A creative accounting practice in which changes in short-term funding have the effect of disguising or improving the reported liquidity position of the reporting organisation.

working capital Also called net current assets, is the capital available for conducting day-to-day operations of an organisation; normally the excess of current assets over current liabilities.

working capital requirement Inventories plus receivables plus prepayments less payables less accruals. This investment in the operating cycle represents the financial resources specifically required for the company to purchase and create inventories while it waits for payments from its customers.

work in progress (WIP) Products or services in intermediate stages of completion.

wrongful trading Wrongful trading occurs where a director knows or ought to have known before the commencement of winding-up that there was no reasonable prospect of the company avoiding insolvency and he/she does not take every step to minimise loss to creditors. If the court is satisfied of this it may (i) order the director to contribute to the assets of the business, and (ii) disqualify him/her from further involvement in corporate management for a specified period (Insolvency Act 1986).

Index

Highlighted terms are defined in the Glossary.
Companies and firms mentioned in the book are shown in **bold** type.